Patrimoine en mouvement

Collection sous la direction de Laurier Turgeon

La collection « Patrimoine en mouvement » veut décentrer la notion de patrimoine en mettant l'accent sur le mouvement, les mutations et les mélanges.

Le patrimoine est, aujourd'hui encore, trop souvent exclusivement centré sur l'idée de pérennité, d'authenticité et d'identités originaires enracinées dans des lieux et des temps immuables. Généralement représenté comme moyen de transmission et de conservation pour lutter contre la dégradation ou la destruction, il est associé à ce qui disparaît plus qu'à ce qui apparaît. Et si l'on traite souvent de son désir de récupération et de restauration, son aspect créatif est rarement mis en exergue. Les biens à transmettre sont sélectionnés, un statut leur est accordé, mais on explique peu comment le patrimoine se construit, se transforme et s'actualise.

Or, loin d'être fixe et figé, le patrimoine est sans cesse fait, défait et refait au fil des déplacements, des contacts, des interactions et des échanges entre individus et groupes différents. Il est une continuelle réinterprétation du passé, une recréation anachronique des traces que les acteurs sociaux tentent souvent de stabiliser, voire d'« essentialiser ». Mais les différentes stratégies de cette « essentialisation » révèlent elles-mêmes des appropriations et des transformations. Les modes de transmission du patrimoine varient dans le temps et dans l'espace et entraînent des usages divers, voire concurrents, qui répondent à une société en perpétuel devenir. Le patrimoine est aussi mouvement, s'inscrivant autant dans les contextes régionaux que nationaux et internationaux, s'exprimant tant dans le matériel que dans l'immatériel et s'imposant, dans la société contemporaine, comme un enjeu à la fois économique, politique et social.

Une liste des ouvrages parus est disponible à la fin du volume.

THE SPIRIT OF PLACE
Between Tangible and Intangible Heritage

L'ESPRIT DU LIEU
entre le patrimoine matériel et immatériel

THE SPIRIT OF PLACE
Between Tangible and Intangible Heritage

L'ESPRIT DU LIEU
entre le patrimoine matériel et immatériel

Edited by /
Sous la direction de
Laurier Turgeon

LES PRESSES DE L'UNIVERSITÉ LAVAL

2009

Les Presses de l'Université Laval reçoivent chaque année de la Société de développement des entreprises culturelles du Québec une aide financière pour l'ensemble de leur programme de publication.

Nous reconnaissons l'aide financière du gouvernement du Canada par l'entremise du Programme d'aide au développement de l'industrie de l'édition pour nos activités d'édition.

Coordination : Marie-Claude Rocher
Revision linguistique : Anne-Hélène Kerbiriou, Mac Wigfield et Catherine Briand
Traduction : Mac Wigfield, Timothy Mellin et Anne-Hélène Kerbiriou
Graphisme de la couverture : Hélène Saillant
Illustration de la couverture : Michel Corboz
Mise en pages : **Santö** *graph*

ISBN 978-2-7637-8894-4

Les Presses de l'Université Laval
Pavillon Maurice-Pollack
2305, de l'Université, bureau 3103
Québec (Québec) G1V 0A6

www.pulaval.com

Table of Contents / Table des matières

II
Memory as Spirit of Place / La mémoire comme esprit du lieu

III
Involving Communities / Impliquer les communautés

IV
Developing Sustainable Tourism / Développer le tourisme durable

Preface

Gustavo F. Araoz
President
**International Council of Monuments
and Sites (ICOMOS)**

For four days in October 2008, the eyes of the world's heritage community were fixed on Québec, where three years of arduous work on the part of the members of the Canadian National Committee blossomed into the spectacular 16th General Assembly and International Symposium.

Never before had an ICOMOS General Assembly been conceived and flawlessly staged with such broad professional and scholarly ambitions. For the first time in the history of ICOMOS, the importance of the coming generation was recognized with a Youth Forum for young professionals from all corners of the world. It was the perfect way to usher in and capture those who in a few years will be taking over the reins of our organization.

To underline our multi-disciplinary membership, ample room was made for every one of the 28 International Scientific Committees of ICOMOS to meet, deliberate and plan their work for the following triennium. Workshops on key issues, such as World Heritage, Historic Urban Landscapes and Global Climate Change were held after hours, satisfying the intellectual needs of members and attendees.

Among all the achievements, the most lasting contribution of the General Assembly was the International Symposium, which addressed one of the most pressing and timely issues facing the cultural heritage community: how to recognize, identify, characterize and safeguard the spirit of place in heritage sites.

Because the concept of *genius loci* has always been at the core of our work, at first glance the topic may have seemed superficial or banal to some. However, for those who labor day to day on preserving the world's heritage, this forum could not have come at a more ideal moment.

Over the past two decades, the dream of the founders of ICOMOS that heritage conservation become mainstream came to fruition, and along with that success have emerged a number of foreseen as well as unexpected issues that in some cases are challenging the way we conceive heritage and the way we protect it.

Heritage democratization has ushered in the participation of communities and stakeholder groups that in the past had to content themselves with the judgments and decisions of experts. The ICOMOS Symposium demonstrated that these formerly marginalized groups are central to the conservation process because the spirit of the place actually resides in the communal memories of those who live in heritage places or care deeply for them. They are the ones who assign values to a place that have the power to resonate across space and time.

The symposium also recognized the growing convergence between tangible and intangible heritage that may be most emblematic in the adoption of the UNESCO Convention on Intangible Heritage. Once almost exclusively focused on the conservation of material culture, ICOMOS members everywhere have realized that values go much beyond merely residing on the physical and spatial aspects of a place. Our days in Québec reaffirmed the rapidly spreading recognition for the role that heritage places can play in strengthening cultural identity, providing coherent continuity to society, setting the stage for traditional communal rituals. It also drew attention to the many intangible attributes that like a breeze or an aroma can fill and permeate the space of heritage places in ways that can induce us to introspection, joy or tears. Such is the power of the spirit of heritage.

This timely publication must be seen as a continuation of the commitment on the part the Canadian Committee of ICOMOS, with the support from Laval University, to disseminate in a broader and more permanent manner the knowledge generated in the crucible of the 16th General Assembly. In these pages the reader will find some of the fresh ideas and new instruments that emerged from the Symposium and that are now ready to be added to the conservationist's expanded toolkit.

While the select papers contained herein can never replace the totality of the October experience in Québec, together they are a canvas on which all the principal ideas, concerns and discussion are well represented. In a very real way, this publication can be said to capture the Spirit of the Place that ICOMOS members shared fraternally in Québec.

Préface

Gustavo F. Araoz
**Président du Conseil international
des monuments et sites (ICOMOS)
États-Unis**

Durant quatre jours, en octobre 2008, toute la communauté dédiée au patrimoine mondial avait le regard tourné vers le Québec, où le travail acharné des membres du Comité national canadien s'est, au bout de trois ans, épanoui sous la forme spectaculaire de la 16ᵉ Assemblée générale et du Symposium international.

Jamais auparavant une Assemblée générale de l'ICOMOS n'avait été conçue avec de si grandes ambitions professionnelles et universitaires, et ne s'était déroulée aussi impeccablement. Pour la première fois dans l'histoire de l'ICOMOS, l'importance de la génération à venir était reconnue sous la forme d'un Forum réservé aux jeunes professionnels provenant du monde entier. C'était la meilleure manière de présenter et de retenir ceux qui, dans quelques années, reprendront les rênes de notre organisation.

Afin de valoriser la multidisciplinarité de nos membres, un grand espace avait été réservé afin que chacun des participants aux Vingt-huitièmes Comités scientifiques internationaux de l'ICOMOS puissent se rencontrer, discuter et planifier leurs travaux en vue du prochain triennat. Des ateliers portant sur des questions essentielles telles que le Patrimoine mondial, les Paysages urbains historiques et le Changement climatique se prolongeaient au-delà des horaires qui leur étaient impartis, à la grande satisfaction intellectuelle de ceux qui y assistaient.

Parmi toutes ses réussites, la contribution la plus durable de l'Assemblée générale fut le Symposium international, qui exposait les problèmes les plus pressants et les plus aigus auxquels est confrontée la communauté du patrimoine mondial : comment reconnaître, identifier, caractériser et préserver l'esprit du lieu dans les sites patrimoniaux.

Le concept de *genius loci* a toujours été au cœur de nos travaux, quoique ce sujet, à première vue, puisse paraître à certains superficiel ou banal. Cependant, pour ceux qui travaillent de jour en jour à sauvegarder le patrimoine mondial, ce forum tombait au moment le plus opportun.

Au cours des deux dernières décennies, le rêve des fondateurs de l'ICOMOS, que la conservation du patrimoine parvienne au premier plan, s'est réalisé, et, de pair avec ce succès, un certain nombre de problèmes, certains prévus, d'autres inattendus, sont apparus, lesquels parfois mettent au défi la manière dont nous concevons le patrimoine et la manière dont nous le préservons.

La démocratisation du patrimoine a introduit la participation active des communautés et des parties prenantes qui, par le passé, devaient simplement se contenter des jugements et des décisions de nos experts. Le Symposium de l'ICOMOS a démontré que ces groupes auparavant marginalisés sont essentiels aux processus de conservation, parce que l'esprit du lieu, en réalité, réside dans les mémoires communes de ceux qui vivent dans ces lieux patrimoniaux ou qui s'en soucient fortement. Ce sont eux qui assignent une valeur à ces lieux qui détiennent un pouvoir de résonance à travers le temps et l'espace.

Le Symposium a également reconnu la convergence grandissante entre le patrimoine matériel et immatériel, fait qui s'incarne le plus emblématiquement dans l'adoption par l'UNESCO de la Convention sur le patrimoine immatériel. Auparavant exclusivement préoccupés de la conservation de la culture matérielle, les membres de l'ICOMOS, partout dans le monde, ont pris conscience que les valeurs se prolongent bien au-delà de leur simple présence dans les aspects physiques et spatiaux d'un lieu. Ces journées passées à Québec nous ont donné l'assurance de cette reconnaissance, qui se diffuse rapidement, du rôle que les lieux patrimoniaux sont susceptibles de jouer dans le renforcement de l'identité culturelle, dans le fait de procurer cohérence et continuité à la société, dans la mise en scène physique des rituels communautaires traditionnels. Elles nous ont également permis d'attirer l'attention sur les nombreux attributs immatériels qui, à l'instar d'une brise ou d'un arôme, imprègnent l'espace des lieux patrimoniaux de manière à nous plonger dans l'introspection, la joie ou les larmes. Tel est le pouvoir de l'esprit du patrimoine.

Cette publication, si opportune, doit être considérée comme le prolongement de l'implication du Comité canadien de l'ICOMOS, avec le soutien de l'Université Laval, dans la diffusion des connaissances générées dans le creuset de la Seizième Assemblée générale, sous une forme plus accessible et plus durable. Au fil de ces pages, le lecteur découvrira quelques-unes des idées nouvelles et des nouveaux outils qui sont apparus au cours du Symposium et qu'il est à présent opportun d'ajouter à l'outillage plus performant des conservateurs.

Bien que les articles sélectionnés ici ne puissent remplacer l'intégralité de cette expérience du mois d'octobre à Québec, leur rassemblement constitue la toile sur laquelle les idées maîtresses, les préoccupations et les discussions sont bien représentées. De manière très concrète, on pourrait dire que cette publication a capturé l'esprit du lieu que les membres de l'ICOMOS ont fraternellement partagé à Québec.

Foreword

The Organizing Committee of the 16th ICOMOS General Assembly and ICOMOS Canada, its host, are pleased to present this collection of forty of the best articles presented during this Scientific Symposium. Each in its own way explores the theme *Finding the Spirit of Place*.

We suggested the spirit of place as a topic of debate for the ICOMOS conference because we firmly believe that the spirit inhabiting historic sites is central to the preservation process. We wanted to encourage top-level researchers, professionals and managers from all disciplines to reflect upon and discuss the spirit residing in monuments. The invitation was also extended to those interested in preserving materials, such as the stone, wood and clay of peasant dwellings, but also objects, such as ancient stained-glassed windows, prehistoric mural paintings, shipwrecks, fortresses, and sites, such as historic cities and cultural landscapes, itineraries and routes like the Silk Road and the Road of St. Jacques de Compostelle. The interest of some delegates lay in the policies and laws that protect – or attempt to protect – our heritage, while others focused on ensuring succession in the field. Finally, some of the articles featured in this collection pertain to the theoretical and philosophical aspects that frame the study and practice of cultural preservation.

The goal of the event was to ensure that the intangible value behind every site and every monument is not overlooked as we attempt to preserve our heritage, but rather that it becomes the driving force behind our efforts. We needed to focus the debate on the fundamentals and sought to create symbiosis, or at least bridge the gap between the tangible and intangible elements of cultural heritage.

We were, in fact, inviting ICOMOS members to temporarily set aside their restoration activities to reflect on what makes a place significant, on what gives it a soul, and sometimes a heart, on the states of mind and of consciousness that emanate from the monuments and sites and finally on the myths and legends that inhabit them, giving each culture its distinctive character.

Native Peoples from Canada and abroad came to share their concerns about the occupation of their ancestral land and the safeguarding of the traditions that shape their lives. These territories, which for the most part were taken from them during colonization wars, are inhabited by the spirit of their Ancestors. Native Peoples claim the right to renew with these sites and ask that their sacred character be respected. This calls upon the sacralization of sites, which reflect their collective memory. Could it be that the spirituality of nations, and perhaps even that of individuals, stems from a bond with the spirits that inhabit the sites that surround us and bear our memory?

Quebec ICOMOS 2008 also served as an opportunity to look ahead and ponder the future of our heritage and how to preserve it in these times of great change. Thirty-two resolutions on as many topics of interest were adopted at the General Assembly. This included a resolution recommending the renewal of the *International Forum of Young Researchers and Professionals of Cultural Heritage,* held for the first time in the history of ICOMOS in Quebec City.

The Forum was the brainchild of the General Assembly's Organizing Committee, which wanted to encourage youth to participate in ICOMOS activities by asking them to provide their unique input on the Symposium's topic, *Finding the Spirit of Place.* More than 130 young people from all over the world answered the call.

I would like to extend special thanks to the team, which under the leadership of the Institut du patrimoine culturel de l'Université Laval (IPAC), designed a compelling program and demonstrated that young people are willing and able to take up the torch and continue the preservation work of our tangible and intangible cultural heritage. I would also like to thank architect Marie-Josée Deschênes and ethnologist Dr. Célia Forget for their commitment and dedication to organizing the Forum and ensuring its success. The best articles to come out of the Forum were published by IPAC under the title, *Penser et pratiquer l'esprit du lieu,* as well as in the *Patrimoine en mouvement* collection.

In conclusion, I would like to acknowledge Dr, Laurier Turgeon, Director of IPAC, and his assistant Dr. Marie-Claude Rocher, for the energy and effort they put forward in producing this collection. Selecting 40 texts from some 250 submitted by the delegates was by no means an easy task! Dr. Turgeon was especially involved in preparing the scientific content of the meeting. We also owe him a debt of gratitude for coordinating the drafting of the *Quebec Declaration on the Preservation of the Spirit of Place,* the final version of which was adopted at the 16th General Assembly and translated into four languages. It can be found in this work and on the ICOMOS Website.

The present collection of texts will certainly be of interest to all those wishing to learn how the preservation of our tangible and intangible cultural heritage is practised every day by professionals working in the field. I hope you will enjoy discovering it.

Michel Bonnette
President
Quebec ICOMOS 2008

Avant-propos

C'est avec un immense plaisir que le Comité organisateur de la 16ᵉ Assemblée générale de l'ICOMOS ainsi qu'ICOMOS Canada, hôte de l'événement, vous offrent aujourd'hui l'occasion de lire et d'apprécier une quarantaine des meilleurs textes qui ont été présentés dans le cadre de ce Symposium scientifique. Chacun à sa façon en explore le thème : *Où se cache l'esprit du lieu?*

Nous avons proposé aux membres de l'ICOMOS d'interroger *l'esprit du lieu* parce que nous avions la conviction que l'esprit qui habite le lieu historique est au cœur de la démarche de conservation. Nous voulions inciter ces chercheurs, professionnels, gestionnaires, toutes disciplines confondues, qui ont en commun de pratiquer la conservation du patrimoine au plus haut niveau, à entamer une réflexion et un dialogue avec l'esprit qui habite le monument. La convocation s'étendait plus largement à tous ceux et celles qui s'intéressent à la conservation des matériaux comme la pierre, le bois, l'argile des maisons paysannes, mais aussi à celle des objets tels que les vitraux anciens, les peintures murales préhistoriques, les épaves et les forteresses ; ou encore à celle des sites, notamment les villes historiques, les paysages culturels, les itinéraires et les routes culturels, comme la route de la Soie et la route de Saint-Jacques-de-Compostelle par exemple. D'autres s'intéressent aux politiques et aux lois qui protègent, bien ou mal, beaucoup ou peu, notre patrimoine, d'autres à la formation de la relève, d'autres enfin à l'examen de la théorie et de la philosophie qui sont nécessaires à l'encadrement de l'étude et de la pratique de la conservation du patrimoine.

La rencontre de Québec avait pour but d'assurer que les valeurs immatérielles que recèle chaque site, chaque monument, ne soient pas oubliées dans le projet de conservation, mais qu'au contraire, elles en soient le moteur. Il était nécessaire de recentrer le débat sur l'essentiel et de tenter une symbiose, sinon un rapprochement, entre le patrimoine matériel et le patrimoine immatériel.

Nous avons en effet proposé aux membres de l'ICOMOS de mettre de côté pour un instant leurs activités de restaurateurs de patrimoine pour réfléchir à ce qui rend les sites et les monuments sur lesquels ils interviennent non seulement distinctifs mais aussi significatifs, à ce qui leur donne une âme, parfois même un cœur, à ces états d'esprit et de conscience qui émanent des monuments et des sites, enfin aux mythes et légendes qui habitent le patrimoine bâti de chaque peuple et qui donnent à chaque culture un contour unique.

Les nations autochtones du Canada et d'ailleurs sont venues partager leurs préoccupations quant à l'occupation de leurs territoires ancestraux et à la sauvegarde des traditions qui donnent un sens à leur vie. Ces territoires qui, pour une bonne part, leur ont été enlevés lors des guerres de colonisation, sont habités par l'esprit de leurs Ancêtres. Ils réclament le droit de pouvoir renouer avec ces lieux et exigent que leur caractère sacré soit respecté. Voilà qu'ils appellent à la sacralisation des lieux qui font partie de leur mémoire collective. Serait-ce que la spiritualité des collectivités et peut-être celle de chacun d'entre nous se fonde sur une complicité avec les esprits qui habitent les lieux que nous fréquentons et qui sont porteurs de notre mémoire ?

Cette rencontre fut également l'occasion de faire porter le regard vers l'horizon pour interroger l'avenir de nos patrimoines et imaginer comment il faudra les préserver en ces temps de grands bouleversements. Trente-deux résolutions touchant autant de sujets d'intérêt furent adoptées par l'Assemblée générale, dont celle réclamant que soit assurée la pérennité du *Forum international des jeunes chercheurs et professionnels en patrimoine culturel* qui s'est tenu à Québec, pour la première fois dans l'histoire de l'ICOMOS.

Ce Forum fut une initiative du Comité organisateur de l'Assemblée générale qui souhaitait par ce biais encourager la participation des jeunes aux activités de l'ICOMOS en les amenant à réfléchir à leur manière à la question soulevée lors du Symposium : *Où se cache l'esprit du lieu ?* Plus de cent trente jeunes venus de toutes les régions du monde y ont participé.

Je tiens à remercier tout particulièrement l'équipe qui, sous la gouverne de l'Institut du patrimoine culturel de l'Université Laval (IPAC), a su bâtir un programme attrayant et démontrer que les jeunes sont en mesure d'assurer la pérennité de l'œuvre de conservation de notre patrimoine culturel, matériel et immatériel. Je veux remercier en particulier mesdames Marie-Josée Deschênes, architecte, et Célia Forget, Ph.D., ethnologue, pour leur engagement et leur dévouement à coordonner l'organisation de ce Forum et à lui assurer le succès qu'il a connu. Les meilleurs textes de ce Forum ont été publiés par l'IPAC sous le titre *Penser et pratiquer l'esprit du lieu*, et également dans la collection *Patrimoine en mouvement*.

En terminant, je tiens à transmettre mes remerciements les plus sincères au professeur Laurier Turgeon, Ph. D., directeur de l'IPAC et à son adjointe Marie-Claude Rocher, Ph. D., pour l'énergie et les efforts qu'ils ont mis à produire le présent ouvrage. La tâche n'a sans doute pas été facile de choisir parmi les deux cent cinquante textes qui ont été soumis par les participants du Symposium! Laurier Turgeon, en particulier, fut un précieux complice dans la préparation du contenu scientifique de la rencontre. On lui doit aussi la coordination de la rédaction de la *Déclaration de Québec sur l'esprit du lieu* dont la version finale, adoptée par la 16ᵉ Assemblée générale, et traduite dans quatre langues, est reproduite dans cet ouvrage ainsi que sur le site Internet d'ICOMOS.

Cet ouvrage devrait intéresser tous ceux et celles qui sont curieux de savoir comment, au quotidien de la pratique professionnelle, se conjuguent conservation du patrimoine immatériel et conservation du patrimoine matériel.

Je souhaite à chacune et à chacun de belles découvertes et d'agréables lectures.

Michel Bonnette
Président
Québec ICOMOS 2008

Her Excellency the Right Honourable Michaëlle Jean
Speech on the Occasion of the International Council on Monuments and Sites General Assembly and Scientific Symposium
City of Québec, Tuesday, September 30, 2008

I am so pleased to welcome such ardent champions of heritage to this city steeped in history, rather appropriately known as the Gibraltar of North America, particularly as we celebrate this year the 400th anniversary of its founding by explorer Samuel de Champlain.

We are here in the heart of the Historic District of Québec, at Place d'Youville, in a building built on the foundations of an old market.

This public market, once one of the busiest in the region, was converted into a concert and performance hall that became very popular with artists.

It is said that the acoustics in this room are perfect, as though, like a musical instrument, the sound had mellowed over time.

To understand the spirit of this place, you almost need to close your eyes and listen.

Listen for the sound of merchants and farmers calling out the price of their wares.

Listen for the sound of lively conversations between shoppers moving from stall to stall.

Listen for the sound of the strings of Les Violons du Roy, of the warm, deep voice of Félix Leclerc, the great Édith Piaf, the mythical B. B. King, resonating within these walls.

Listen and imagine.

Imagine the hustle and bustle outside, in the square, long before cars filled the streets once travelled by horses.

Imagine the traditions, the cultural and religious practices, the currents of thought passed from generation to generation, in this very place.

The visible traces of our time here on Earth are little more than the material representation of the values, beliefs, myths, and customs that shape who we are and influence our vision of the world and how we live in it.

They are the privileged witnesses to all of those intangible things embedded in the deepest recesses of our collective memory that define the essence of each civilization.

It is through these traces and witnesses that the soul of a people is revealed, and it is in that revelation that we find meaning.

The meaning of history.

The meaning of life.

We all share a profound belief that this intangible heritage must exist beyond the reach of time, archived and conserved, safe from every threat, just as we do with the most extraordinary building projects and important archaeological sites.

Failure to do so would be to betray or undermine the meaning – the spirit – of those places that we have inherited and that enrich our present.

In some parts of the world, and this is true of the Americas, preserving intangible heritage has reached a critical point.

When the Europeans arrived on these shores, they saw the Americas as a new world.

Because of this, they made a clean sweep of a world that was very real, that had been the cradle of ancient civilizations.

The people that had been living here for thousands of years and their descendants were dispossessed of themselves, of their languages, of their cultures.

As an example, barely two hundred years ago, an entire people, the Beothuk, who roamed across the island of Newfoundland in search of food, was decimated.

Thankfully, an explorer and philanthropist, William Cormack, took into his care the last of the Beothuk. Her name will not be forgotten: Shawnadithit.

For six years, Shawnadithit taught Cormack the rudiments of her language and the customs of her people. Through drawings, she illustrated the tools used by the Beothuk, their dwellings, their way of life.

The result is that the history, culture, legends, myths – in other words, the intangible heritage of that semi-nomadic people – are remembered to this day.

Without Shawnadithit and Cormack, the Beothuk would not only have disappeared; the very essence of their spirit would have been snuffed out, and they would have fallen into oblivion.

Likewise, it has taken a great deal of historiographical work to restore entire chapters of the history of the Americas that had been wiped from memory, whose meaning had been twisted or simply tucked away into shadow.

Work that is by no means finished.

In Canada, nothing is cause for greater concern than the decline of Aboriginal languages.

According to a study by the Assembly of First Nations, of approximately 53 Aboriginal languages in Canada, 50 are on the verge of extinction.

In the case of many languages, only the elders speak them regularly; the young know the languages but use them less often.

Which is why nothing is as moving, why nothing makes me happier, than to see and hear young Aboriginal artists reconnect with their first language and use it with pride.

I recently heard Samian and Shauit, two young Montagnais singers who rap in Algonquin and in Innu. They are part of that music scene so rich in possibilities. Others are doing the same in Cree, Inuktitut and Mohawk.

In their own way, these young artists are protecting our heritage and keeping it alive. It is a responsibility they take on with determination, and one that we must encourage.

Without language, the principal vehicle for passing on cultural values and traditions no longer exists.

An entire way of life and a wisdom dating back thousands of years risk disappearing if we are not careful.

And being careful means looking beyond the straight line of the present in which we are all too often mired in this era of instant access and seeing things in a broader perspective.

I think Chesterton said it best when he said, "all the men in history who have really done anything with the future have had their eyes fixed upon the past."

This is why it is so important for us to refocus our concerns on history, to give history its rightful place in the public space and to promote heritage, particularly among our youth.

To do this – and I know that you understand this, for you are holding a youth forum as part of this symposium – we must include youth in our reflections on the preservation of heritage.

I have made youth my priority because I love that almost organic and vital way they have of turning cultural expression into essential and incredibly effective tools for social change and handing down values.

Young people will keep us moving forward. They define themselves in relation to the past. The future is already their present.

We must never forget about them, and we must remember that the history of peoples and civilizations exists beyond the time of our own lives and forms the memory of the places we live.

That memory is what we leave behind and what you are helping to perpetuate through your work and commitment.

In all of those places around the world, where the past is alive and can be seen, touched and felt, every fragment whispers with the voices of a civilization, revealing the essence of those who came before us.

These places speak to us, if we know how to listen. Of places near and far, of yesterday and today, of those around us and those who have not yet crossed our path.

This is how the spirit of these places guides us to look to the past to find roots that dig deep; how it compels us to strive constantly and forever to improve the fate of humanity.

Thank you for undertaking this very important work, and may you find the spirit of this magnificent place, where Europe and the Americas meet.

Thank you.

Son Excellence la très honorable Michaëlle Jean
Discours à l'occasion de l'assemblée générale et symposium scientifique
du Conseil international des monuments et sites
Québec, le mardi 30 septembre 2008

Quelle joie d'accueillir de fervents défenseurs du patrimoine dans cette ville chargée d'histoire, que l'on surnomme à juste titre la Gibraltar de l'Amérique du Nord, et en cette année où nous célébrons son 400e anniversaire de fondation par l'explorateur Samuel de Champlain.

Nous sommes ici au cœur de l'arrondissement historique de Québec, sur la place d'Youville, dans un édifice construit sur les fondations d'une ancienne halle.

Ce marché public, autrefois l'un des plus fréquentés de la région, a été converti en une salle de concert et de spectacle prisée des artistes.

On dit de cette salle que son acoustique est parfaite. Comme si, à la manière d'un instrument de musique, sa sonorité avait acquis une profondeur avec le temps.

Pour capter l'esprit de ce lieu, il faut presque fermer les yeux et écouter.

Écouter pour entendre commerçants et cultivateurs crier à la volée le prix de leur marchandise.

Écouter pour entendre les conversations animées des passants entre les étales.

Écouter pour entendre résonner entre ces murs les cordes des Violons du Roy, la voix chaude et grave de Félix Leclerc, la grande Édith Piaf, le mythique B. B. King.

Écouter pour imaginer aussi.

Imaginer l'activité au dehors, sur la place, alors que les voitures n'avaient pas encore remplacé les chevaux.

Imaginer les traditions, les pratiques culturelles et religieuses, les courants de pensée qui ont traversé les générations et qui ont traversé ce lieu.

Les traces visibles de notre passage dans le monde ne sont jamais que la représentation matérielle des valeurs, des croyances, des mythes, des coutumes qui nous façonnent et qui marquent notre vision du monde et notre façon d'être au monde.

Ce sont les témoins privilégiés de toutes ces choses intangibles inscrites dans les profondeurs de notre mémoire collective et qui constituent la richesse des civilisations.

L'âme des peuples est par ces traces et ces témoignages révélée, et c'est dans cette révélation que nous est donné le sens.

Le sens de l'histoire.

Le sens de la vie.

Nous toutes et tous ici partageons la conviction que ce patrimoine immatériel doit être mis « hors du temps », archivé et conservé, à l'abri des périls qui le guettent, au même titre que les plus beaux ouvrages de construction et que les grands sites archéologiques.

Ne pas le faire, ce serait trahir ou subvertir, justement, le sens, l'esprit de ces lieux dont nous avons hérité pour notre enrichissement collectif.

En certaines régions du globe, et c'est le cas dans les Amériques, la préservation du patrimoine immatériel est un enjeu devenu une urgence.

Lorsque les Européens sont arrivés ici, ils ont vu dans les Amériques un nouveau monde.

Du coup, on a fait table rase d'un monde pourtant bien réel qui a été le berceau d'anciennes civilisations.

Les peuples qui vivaient ici depuis des millénaires et leurs descendants ont été dépossédés d'eux-mêmes, de leurs langues, de leurs cultures.

Par exemple, il y a à peine deux siècles, un peuple entier, les Béothuks, qui parcourait l'île de Terre-Neuve à la recherche de nourriture, a été décimé.

Fort heureusement, un explorateur et philanthrope du nom de William Cormack, a accueilli auprès de lui la dernière des Béothuks. Son nom nous est resté : elle s'appelait Shawnadithit.

Pendant six ans, Shawnadithit a enseigné à Cormack les rudiments de sa langue et les coutumes de son peuple. À l'aide de croquis, elle a illustré les outils utilisés par les Béothuks, leur type d'habitation, leur mode de vie.

Si bien que l'histoire, la culture, les légendes, les mythes, en somme le patrimoine immatériel de ce peuple semi-nomade, ont traversé les âges et sont parvenus jusqu'à nous.

Sans Shawnadithit et Cormack, les Béothuks n'auraient pas seulement disparu; le souffle de leur esprit se serait éteint, et ils seraient tombés dans l'oubli.

De même, il a fallu tout un travail d'historiographie pour restituer des pans entiers de l'histoire des Amériques qui avaient été effacé des mémoires, qui avaient été détournés de leur sens ou tout simplement occultés.

Et ce travail est loin d'être terminé.

Au Canada, rien ne sonne l'alarme avec plus de force que le déclin des langues autochtones.

Selon une enquête menée par l'Assemblée des Premières nations, sur environ cinquante-trois langues autochtones au Canada, cinquante d'entre elles sont en voie d'extinction.

Dans le cas de nombreuses langues, les seules personnes qui les parlent couramment sont les aînés, les jeunes étant ceux qui les connaissent et les utilisent le moins.

Par conséquent, rien ne m'émeut et ne me réjouit davantage que de voir et d'entendre de jeunes artistes autochtones renouer avec leur langue d'origine et l'exprimer avec fierté.

J'ai entendu récemment Samian et Shauit, deux jeunes chanteurs montagnais qui rappent en algonquin et en innu. Ils s'inscrivent dans cette mouvance riche de possibilités. D'autres le font en cri, en inuktituk et en mohawk.

À leur façon, ces jeunes artistes sont des protecteurs de notre patrimoine et le maintiennent vivant. C'est une responsabilité qu'ils assument avec détermination et qu'il nous revient d'encourager.

Sans la langue, le principal moyen de transmission des valeurs et des traditions culturelles n'existe plus.

C'est tout un art de vivre et une sagesse qui remonte à des milliers d'années qui risquent de disparaître si l'on n'y prend garde.

Et prendre garde veut dire ici se sortir de l'horizon étroit du présent dans lequel nous sommes trop souvent confinés en cette ère de l'instantané et voir plus loin.

Pour reprendre la formule choc de Chesterton, « les hommes qui, dans l'histoire, ont eu une action réelle sur l'avenir avaient les yeux rivés sur le passé ».

D'où la nécessité de remettre l'histoire au centre de nos préoccupations et de l'espace public et de revaloriser le patrimoine, plus particulièrement auprès des jeunes.

Pour cela, et vous l'avez compris puisque vous tenez un forum jeunesse en marge de ce symposium, nous devons inclure les jeunes dans la réflexion actuelle sur la préservation du patrimoine.

J'ai fait de la jeunesse ma priorité parce que j'aime leur façon presque organique et vitale de faire de l'expression culturelle des outils essentiels et des plus efficaces de transformation sociale et de transmission de valeurs.

Les jeunes poursuivent la marche du monde. Ils se définissent par rapport au passé. L'avenir est déjà leur présent.

Ne les oublions pas, et rappelons-nous que l'histoire des peuples et des civilisations existe par-delà le temps de nos vies pour constituer la mémoire du lieu de nos ancrages.

Cette mémoire est ce qui reste de nous et que vous contribuez à perpétuer par votre travail et votre engagement.

Dans tous ces lieux sur la planète où le passé s'offre au regard, au toucher et aux sens, chaque fragment restitue les murmures et les traits d'une civilisation.

Ces lieux nous parlent, si nous savons les écouter, de l'ici et de l'ailleurs, d'hier et d'aujourd'hui, de proximités et de rencontres.

C'est ainsi que l'esprit de ces lieux nous guide pour trouver dans le passé des racines profondes et il fournit la sève qu'il faut pour améliorer sans cesse et toujours le sort de l'humanité.

Merci de votre travail si essentiel, et puissiez-vous trouver l'esprit qui se cache dans cette ville magnifique, lieu de métissage au confluent de l'Europe et des Amériques.

Je vous remercie.

Introduction

Spirit of Place:
Evolving Heritage Concepts and Practices[1]

Laurier Turgeon
Canada Research Chair in Cultural Heritage
Director of the Institute of Cultural Heritage
Laval University
Canada

The bridge gathers the earth as landscape around the river [...]
The location is not already there before the bridge is.
Before the bridge stands, there are of course many spots
along the river that can be occupied by something.
One of them proves to be a location, and does so because of the bridge.
Thus the bridge does not first come to a location to stand in it;
rather, a location comes into existence only by virtue of the bridge.

Martin Heidegger, "Building, Dwelling, Thinking" (1954).

Rethinking Spirit of Place

In this book, we make the supposition that the concept of spirit of place can play a useful heuristic role in enhancing the way in which we practice and think about heritage. More importantly, it can shed light on the various

---

1. This book presents a selection of 35 of the 100 or so papers presented at the Scientific Symposium of the 16th ICOMOS General Assembly held in Quebec City (Canada) on October 1-2, 2008. The Scientific Committee received more than 600 proposals from some 80 different countries. To encourage the participation of young scholars and professionals, the Committee created a two-day Youth Forum – the first in the history of ICOMOS – and invited the participants to actively participate in the drafting of the *Quebec Declaration*, which summarizes the conclusions of the Symposium.

heritage "how-to's, whether dealing with heritage motifs, the modes of its construction, the effects of experiencing it, or the *heritagization* process itself. Even if some consider the expression "spirit of place" to be an outmoded concept, preferring more contemporary terminology such as "memory of place" or "significance of place," it remains a fundamental heritage concept. Often referred to, but rarely defined, this notion is founded on the belief – whether true or false – that heritage landscapes, sites and monuments transcend the realm of the ordinary, so as to touch a superior dimension, a higher, more sacred order. Because of their ancientness, singularity and the profound symbolic values with which they have been invested, they are considered as inhabited by a guiding supernatural force that gives them a life of their own and protects them. At the beginning of the 20th century, the great art historian, Aloïs Riegl, did not hesitate to define such admiration for the inherent value of the ancientness of historical monuments as a "modern cult" that tended to become a substitute for traditional religious practices. He remarked that the ancientness of monuments spontaneously aroused "a pious awe" in the breast of every man (Riegl 1903: 47).

Beyond its role in the practice of contemporary heritage conservation, the concept of the spirit of place has existed, in one form or another, in every civilization throughout time. This universal character makes it particularly relevant and fundamental for an organization such as ICOMOS, whose mission is to provide heritage management worldwide. According to Western tradition, the spirit of place has its origins in Ancient Rome, when it was known as *genius loci* [local divinity]. The *genii* of Roman mythology were immanent beings, which not only inhabited places, but also people. (Grimal 1976, referenced under the article "*génie*"). They represented the spiritual existence of human beings and material objects and had the essential role of preserving them or keeping them alive (Lucier and Petzet, this publication). Due to its specific nature, the *genius* would watch over a location, conferring its characteristic identity on the place while imbuing it with a vital principle. Humankind could negotiate with it by offering it gifts in order to obtain favors, and thereby, on occasion, initiate contact with the gods. The idea that there are places instilled with a vital, spiritual force is not unique to the West, for in Asian civilizations also, such locations are described as places of "life" or "enjoyable life" or even "ideal life" (Han, Kim, Sugio, Yano, this publication[2]). Such concepts are in keeping with Confucianism and Taoism, which advocate a harmonious relationship between man and nature, as well as the uniqueness and completeness of nature. In Islam, important heritage sites are often designated as *Waqf,* an abstract concept, which refers to an

---

2.   Whenever the publication date is not present, this type of reference indicates that one of the book's authors is being cited.

inalienable religious legacy (Pirbabaei). Because the location is the abode of the spirit of the benefactor, the inhabitants of the place can communicate with him and carry out his will so as to ensure the well-being of all. The concept of spirit of place is likewise widely prevalent in African societies. Powerful supernatural beings lay claim to a locality by binding themselves to mountains, lakes, rivers or even trees. They are, however less frequently associated with the uncultivated areas in forest clearings (Pecquet 2004). Not only do they have the power to revitalize the place and those who frequent it, but also to strike them with an evil spell or even to destroy them. Humankind can negotiate with the *genius*, redeeming itself from a transgression through sacrifice, thereby transforming hostility into benevolence. In Africa, the *genii* disrupt group ceremonies and manifest themselves in possession rituals, which are intended to instigate soul-searching and the renewal of a social entity (Bondaz). In North America, the notion of spirit of place is also known to exist among most Amerindian peoples. For example, among the cultural traditions of the Algonquins, the concept appears under various appellations and can take on various meanings, depending on the tribe and the historical period. Among the Cree it is *Memquash*, with the Ojibwa it is *Maymaygwayshi* and the Inuit called it *Memekueshuat*, which is to say "the rock *genii* which are in the water" (Désveaux 1998: 265; Flannery 1931: 2). They are often described as small, flat-faced immanent beings that hide in cracks of boulders. Moreover, the rock formations that they inhabit are considered sacred and are marked with pictograms (Arsenault 1998: 29). Even if the appearance and roles of these supernatural beings vary from one culture to another, the concept of spirit of place is widely prevalent in the mythologies of a large number of world civilizations.

Far from referring to a unique, unchanging concept, spirit of place has not ceased to evolve and adapt itself to the requirements of each era. If the concept of *Waqf* has succeeded in surviving practically every Islamic government and legal system over the course of its long history, it is because it has been able to adapt to even the most radical cultural, social and economic metamorphoses (Pirbabaei). Similarly, the Asian traditions that define "true life" have not only been able to meet the needs of new groups of people, but the spirituality of these requirements have been relocated to new sites (Sugio). As far as the Western tradition of spirit of place is concerned, the custom has also evolved considerably, for although, in Ancient Rome, *genius loci* referred to supernatural beings and occult powers, during the Renaissance and the Modern Era, it underwent secularization and was altered by humanist influence. Since the 16th century, it has found expression in the gardens, parks and fountains created by man. Today the *genius* is no longer a deity that inhabits a locality, but rather, it is humanity itself, whose innovative and creative spirit is able to design and construct enchanting surroundings. We now describe a person who is particularly talented and gifted, such as a city planner, architect, artist or landscape architect, as a genius – one of the new creators and transformers of the landscape (Nitzsche 1975: 131-136). During the 17th and 18th centuries, the *genius loci* was used to represent the harmony between very diverse elements – which were sometimes geographical, historical, social, but particularly aesthetic – so as to achieve the ideal in urban planning that would be on a human scale (Pevsner 1978: 1; Grenet 2004: 113-115). Moreover, this conceptual transformation has been accompanied by a lexical change: the expression *genius loci* [local divinity] was progressively replaced by "spirit of place" which refers to the characteristic ambiance that man wanted to confer on the place (Murray 1989: 6-11). In the 19th century, it is the ancientness of the historical monument itself that, as Aloïs Riegl would point out in 1903, had become the object of worship in modern times (Choay 1999: 124-127; Poulot 2006: 166-171). This concept of ancientness combined simultaneously with modernity would continue to amply and fuel the heritage conservation movement's reason for existence throughout the 20th century. In fact, the *heritagization* of culture has become an instrumental part of the process of modernization and a characteristic emblem of modernity, to the point that, any nation-state today that is without monuments and museums is considered to be underdeveloped (Kirshenblatt-Gimblett 2006: 180-183; Turgeon 2005: 19-32).

Even more important than spirit of place's rich history as a concept, is its promising future as a key component in 21st century world heritage conservation. The Norwegian architectural theorist, Christian Norberg-Schulz describes the *genius loci* as an "existential space," which he defines as the "fundamental relationship between man and his environment" (Norberg-Schulz 1980: 5). With this view he breaks away from functionalism, structuralism, urban morphology architecture and the other forms of geographical determinism, which maintain that the spirit of place has its origins in the locality itself and that location determines the very spirit of a human settlement, as well as its physical structure (Alexander 2004; Richot 1999). More than just arbitrarily separating spirit from place, these approaches tended to *essentialize* place – to reduce it to an essential quality, an object of singularity that is permanent and static. Norberg-Schulz puts emphasis on the psychic rather than the physical aspects of a place, on the *habitus* rather than the structure, so as to restore man's fundamental role of agent in the process of creating the spaces that define his existence. Existential spaces are not just shaped by those who build them, but also by those who inhabit them. In the end, it is the inhabitants that give a place its character and meaning by giving it an identity and a spiritual quality. Man is an integral part of his surroundings; disregard for this fact will only serve to alienate him from his environment and lead to its destruction (Norberg-Schulz 1980: 23). Norberg-Schulz's theory of existential space is founded on the central concept of "inhabiting" a place, which is inspired from Martin Heidegger's phenomenology that defines inhabiting as the building of a relationship between man and a living space. In order to better understand this relationship, Heidegger makes use of the visual concept of a bridge, which represents a passage uniting the two banks of a river, and by extension, the adjacent hinterlands and regions. The connection with a place or a location "comes into existence only by virtue of the bridge" (Heidegger 1975: 154). The very choice of a bridge's location creates a place, which in turn, determines the layout of the routes and how inhabitants will occupy the area. Michel de Certeau enables us to understand even better this relationship man has with a place. For him, a space becomes meaningful from the moment when human beings "occupy" it (de Certeau 1990: 155-158, 173). Such occupations might be in the form of a physical transformation of the landscape, an organized ritual or festival enacted on the site, or even just a simple pacing off the grounds or the reciting of a poem, a tale or a legend that "speaks" of the place. It is via the actual experiences, which are sustained by meanings and associations, that individuals or groups begin to interact with a site and gradually work out their relationship with the locality, thereby constructing their identity, as well as that of the place (Bédard 2002: 234-236; Tuan 1977: 8-18).

The term, "spirit of place," constitutes not only a dynamic relationship, but also a process involving living human beings. It is an expression that articulates, in and of itself, the two fundamental components of this relationship: "spirit", which refers to thought, to human beings and to the intangible; and "place", which evokes a geographical location, a physical environment and all the tangible elements. Both are inextricably joined in close interaction, each component constructing and being constructed in a relationship of complimentary synergy: the spirit builds the place and, at the same time, the place gives structure to the spirit. Thus, the relationship between thought and the material world is not unilateral but two-way, for it is ever evolving and continually exchanging in a dynamic of mutual give and take. Following a fresh analysis of the works of Roland Barthes (1970) and Pierre Bourdieu (1980), anthropologists Daniel Miller (1987, 1998) and Christopher Tilley (1994, 2006) came up with the concept of "objectification," referring to the process by which an idea espoused by an individual or a group of individuals becomes material. The authors did not hesitate to challenge Descartes' rationalism, according to which the spirit always dominates matter, the form of the latter being predefined in a mental model before it is ever produced in the real world.

For they believed that rather than the idea preceding the material form, it is being constructed at the same time as its material counterpart, in a perpetual two-way exchange between the abstract conceptualization of thought and the physical reality of the place or the object. One nourishes the other and each makes itself an integral component of the other. For example, in his study of basket weaving, Tim Ingold (2000) observes that the basket maker doesn't have a precise mental model of the object he wants to create, but rather the skills and practical knowledge which guide his interaction with the material. The size, the type and the quality of the wicker are also variables whose involvement will contribute to the final form of the product. The basket maker works with the material, fashioning it in concordance with the natural limits he encounters. Each step of the fabrication process restricts the possibilities governing the subsequent steps. The shape emerges from this engagement, from the basket making process itself, rather than from the mental model of the artisan alone. This phenomenological approach, which emphasizes empirical observation of real-life situations, also sheds light on the sculptor's art, as well as that of the architect. That is because architects have to deal with time restrictions, budgetary constraints, inherent material limitations (and characteristics), the surrounding buildings and the needs of the population at large – all factors that contribute to the form of the resulting building. This two-way dialectical exchange between the conceptualization and construction of a place is not only limited to the building process, for it continues on, as the structure is put to various uses, social or otherwise (Miller 1987). And so visitors and consumers of objects, monuments and sites come up with a particular idea, which they make their own by adjusting it in accordance with their values, whether economic, social, aesthetic or historic (Poulot 1997: 32-34). It is particularly during the appropriation process that these values are defined and even the site itself is modified, in order to remove the traces of certain values and bring others to life. Possession is taken not only of the site itself, but also of those to whom it once belonged, in order to have dominion over them. The history of Colonial America abounds in eloquent examples of this phenomenon (Friedman).

Therefore the purpose of this book is to reflect upon the role of various socially involved individuals (the creators, as well as the visitors of heritage sites) and to define the concept of place using elements, which include the tangible components (sites, buildings and associated objects) as much as the intangible (orally recited stories, values, rites and festivals) that contribute to its overall significance. The tangible aspects of place make it possible to evoke the enduring qualities and the layers of memory corresponding to the various levels of occupation of the site. The intangible aspects, or the spirit of those who once inhabited a site, make it possible to renew the original significance of the place or even invest it with a variety of meanings, in order to satisfy the competing claims of the groups of people co-inhabiting the location. When considered in all its interrelated dynamism, spirit of place is, just as is the case of all relationships, unstable and undergoing constant transformation, and therefore a process that changes over time and effects change in the lives of those who it involves. And so, just like heritage itself (Smith 2006: 44), it assumes a dialectical and multi-faceted nature, can be associated with multiple meanings and can be shared by various groups of people. This perspective seems particularly well adapted to a world undergoing globalization that is characterized by more and more transnational migrations, relocated populations, intercultural exchanges and manifold attachments and allegiances (Appadurai 1996).

The *Spirit of Place* and Current World Heritage Issues

The concept of spirit of place, as we have defined it, enables heritage practitioners to face new challenges encountered by the world heritage movement, particularly that of integrating the intangible aspects of cultural heritage, as well as involving communities in heritage site, monument and cultural landscape conservation. In this collection of essays, Christina Cameron, the current president of the World Heritage Committee, emphasizes that the committee's ideology and methods have evolved considerably since it was inaugurated 30 years ago, moving away from a largely materialist approach, towards giving more attention to the intangible values associated with heritage conservation. And although, originally the sites on the World Heritage List were essentially isolated monuments, they have progressively expanded to clusters of buildings and vast areas of cultural landscape that embrace numerous intangible elements. According to the former World Heritage Committee president and the UNESCO's current Director-General, Koïchiro Matsuura, this is due to the growing number of sites requesting to be registered on the World Heritage List on the basis of their intangible cultural qualities. It is because of the difficulty of recognizing such sites according to the 1972 *Convention Concerning the Protection of World Cultural and Natural Heritage*, that he supported the creation of the *Convention for the Safeguarding of the Intangible Cultural Heritage*, which was adopted by UNESCO in 2003 (Matsuura 2004). This convention, which has already been ratified by more than 110 countries, is a tool for international standardization, that is intended to protect, preserve and, most particularly, to promote the intangible cultural elements. In order to ensure effective, coordinated interpretation and application of the two conventions, the 2004 *Yamato Declaration* was written to encourage participating countries to make provision for applying an integrated approach for safeguarding tangible and intangible cultural heritage, with the active participation of the concerned communities.[3]

ICOMOS has reacted promptly to these developments, for it dedicated its Scientific Symposium of the 14th General Assembly, held in 2003 in Victoria Falls, Zimbabwe, to the theme of preserving the intangible qualities of monuments and sites (ICOMOS 2003). Upon signing the *Kimberley Declaration*

---

3.   The *Yamato Declaration*: http://portal.unesco.org/culture/en/files/ 23863/10988742599Yamato_Declaration.pdf/Yamato_Declaration.pdf.

of 2003, ICOMOS committed itself to better integrating the intangible heritage components and the local communities concerned into the management and conservation of the monuments and sites regulated by the 1972 *Convention Concerning the Protection of World Cultural and Natural Heritage.* The International Committee on Intangible Cultural Heritage (ICICH) was also created, and it has just written up a document whose objective is to establish a set of ethical guidelines for the management of the intangible cultural heritage associated with cultural spaces. The 2005 *Xi'an Declaration* also stresses the importance of the intangible context, when recognizing and protecting world heritage sites. Held in 2008, the Scientific Symposium of the 16th General Assembly in Quebec City, which dealt with the spirit of place, was in keeping with this desire to better take into consideration and to integrate the intangible elements of communities and groups associated with tangible heritage.

The authors of the articles included in this collection of essays offer up-to-date analyses and original answers to current world heritage issues, of which five are dealt with in this volume. The first topic is concerned with determining the significance of spirit of place. The question is raised as to whether the significance originates from the place itself or from the common spirit sustained by those who occupy or frequent the site. Thus, in order to preserve and assure the continuity of the spirit of place, is it simply necessary to preserve the place or is it rather a matter of maintaining the spirit of those who built and inhabited it? Although some authors may have emphasized the role of place (Lucier, Petzet) or the singularity of its design or aesthetic properties, and others, the thought and practical knowledge of humankind (Harrington and Sullivan), all recognize that both elements (the tangible and the intangible) interact and work together to provide the meaning – or at least a major part of it. As we have already emphasized, significance springs from the way in which people experience a site. The guided tours, artistic skills, the festivals and the rituals are all elements that enable the visitor to interact with the site more intensely and to increase the significance and the emotional and even spiritual potency of the experience (Bondaz, Pirbabaei, Sugio, Yano). Places in and of themselves do not have significance. Important battlefields (Ogle) or the sites of shipwrecks (Maarleveld – whose existence is not due to choice, but rather to the simple fated meeting of navies or to the gales of a storm – bring us to realize to what degree the spirit of these places is fabricated by human beings afterwards, in order to celebrate or mourn an important event in the past. These chance, circumstantially designated spaces become gathering places where relationships are formed and new identities are worked out (Harrington and Sullivan).

Social memory is the second major issue to be dealt with in this book. Nowadays, it is often confused with spirit of place, because it is the concept that most strongly expresses the connection people have with a particular place or material object (Harrison *et al.* 2008: 2-3). The works of Pierre Nora (1984, 1987, 1992) and Daniel Fabre (2000) shed light on the ways in which places are used to sustain memories and how they actively contribute to developing and structuring them. The layout and buildings of sites make such memories more of a tangible reality, prolonging the memory of those who occupied them, as well as serving as mnemonic devices (Turgeon 2007: 13-36). Nevertheless, such physical elements are today thought to be insufficient to completely convey the living memory of a place, particularly to tourists who have an ever-growing appetite for cultural and social history. Social memory is also thought to be "essential" to the political, social and economic life of local communities (Assi). It is for this reason that the initial occupants determine the orientation of future site uses and often leave noticeable traces of their presence – whether real or symbolic – upon later occupants (Friedman, Binan and Binan). Social memory is transmitted by oral or even written tradition, particularly by prose or poetry (Bernal), which is a sure sign of a deep emotional attachment. In China, poetry is an important means of constructing social memory and the spirit of place. Lake Hangzhou, one of the most lauded sites in China, has been the subject of no less than 20,000 poems (Han). Although it is very powerful, social memory is also very fragile, because it is carried in human vessels, which means it can disappear with them – almost unnoticed. The ruin of buildings is heralded by a gradual deterioration that can often occur over long periods of time, whereas social memory is practically invisible, and therefore it can fade or be deliberately erased without anyone taking any notice (Binan and Binan, Albuquerque Lapa and Almeida de Melo). The dissipating of social memory is often irreversible, particularly when it is conveyed orally (Turgeon and St-Pierre). There are, however various ways to record these memories, such as interviewing inhabitants of sites in order to collect oral data, collecting samples from historical and literary texts, carrying out archaeological digs, as well as observing festivals and rituals, which sometimes subtly, through constant repetition, transmit the memory of an event. Preserving and promoting the value of social memories enables heritage organizations to offer a much richer, life-like interpretation of sites and monuments (Friedman).

The best means of preserving and promoting the value of social memory, as well as the other intangible elements of a site (stories, festivals, rituals, practical knowledge and skill and cuisine) is to involve the communities that inhabit and frequent a site. Site and monument restoration and promotion projects are still too often the exclusive responsibility of experts who are motivated by a desire to fully develop the "architectural" potential of the site, but who tend to exclude the communities involved. This often enables the project to preserve the place, but not necessarily its spirit. It is in this line of thinking that Francis Engelmann, UNESCO representative and resident of Laos' Luang Prabang describes the conservation of the site's monastery as follows: "We have saved the buildings of Luang Prabang, but we have lost its soul" (Engelmann 1998, Suntikul). On the other hand, the projects that have favored the active participation of the local population have generally been very successful (Mackay and Sullivan, Prieto, Ritch and Becerril, Bell and Johnston, Burgess *et al.*). Involving the communities associated with the sites offers numerous advantages: it favors the conservation of the site's intangible elements, allows them to participate in site management and interpretation, thereby increasing their employment opportunities and sense of belonging, as well as contributing to the sustainable development of the project (Corsane *et al.*). Cutting-edge site reconstitution projects of aboriginal communities carried out in Australia and New-Zealand were very conclusive; not only did letting Aboriginals take charge of project management result in interpretation enrichment and touristic development, but also in economic and social renewal of native communities, as well as the environmental restoration of the sites (Bell and Johnston, Burgess *et al.*). Partnerships with the various groups of professionals and the local communities lead to profitable exchanges and the development of new models for collaborating between project and community (Mackay and Sullivan). However, planning the implementation of such partnerships is sometimes impossible, because the rivalry between local peoples competing for the same location is so intense (Amit-Cohen). Nevertheless, these very selfsame sites, where violent conflicts and even atrocities occur, can become places of such effective mediation and reconciliation, that previously quarrelsome individuals commit themselves to make peace on the very same location where the confrontations took place (Ogle). Ratified in Quebec City in 2008, the new *Charter on the Interpretation and Presentation of Cultural Heritage Sites*, more commonly known as the *Ename Charter*, provides ICOMOS with an invaluable normative instrument for resolving conflicts and reconciling groups of contested sites.[4]

Developing sustainable tourism is an issue that represents another major challenge. The World Tourism Organization estimates that tourism will continue to increase exponentially over the next few decades. The organization has affirmed that cultural tourism is the sector that is currently experiencing the most rapid growth. This raises the question of how to protect such sites from the threat of a burgeoning tourist industry. As tourism has become an essential area of economic activity (Abdulac, Messeri, Suntikul), or at least a sector on which economies rely heavily for potential development (Jean Julien), it does not seem feasible to conceive of putting measures in place intended to prohibit or even seriously limit access to sites. Therefore, how can the seemingly conflicting issues of site preservation and increased visitor

---

4.   *ICOMOS Ename Charter*: http://www.enamecharter.org/.

activity be reconciled? Even though the physical protection of the sites has long been a priority, there is now a desire to facilitate human interaction, particularly to link the communities that inhabit or frequent the sites with the tourists, so as to improve their interpretative experience, as well as to increase their awareness of the need to protect the place and its spirit. According to the *International Cultural Tourism Charter*,[5] ratified in 1999, it is a matter of bringing tourists to contribute to the conservation of heritage sites. Instead of considering tourists to be a threat, the charter suggests conversely that they should be seen as partners in heritage conservation and sustainable development (Brooks, Egloff and Comer). For example, having the Aborigines themselves manage native sites allows them to make a profit from tourism and assures the continued development of their communities, all the while offering the tourists an authentic experience of a living culture (Ketz and Ketz). Furthermore, more and more tourists will only visit sustainable tourist locations, as it has become one of their travel planning criteria.[6]

The latest information technology offers almost unlimited possibilities for the conservation and communication of the spirit of place. For many, direct physical and visual contact with a place was considered to be the best means of experiencing a place and its spirit. With the arrival of the Internet and its rise in popularity, it was feared that the potent "virtual effect" of the Web would lead to the "destabilization of identity" (Choay 1999: 183-184). But in reality, it had the opposite effect, for the Internet made increased exposure possible, with improved publicity, which resulted in greater visitor volume, better interpretation and decreased site management expenses. A Web presence has practically become a prerequisite for the routine operation of tourist sites – for about 75% of tourists (at least in North America), who have an Internet connection, plan their trips following a visit to the Web (Steinbrink 2008). Wikipedia, YouTube, Facebook and Flickr are much more efficient than traditional methods of compiling and circulating the intangible elements of heritage sites (Burke). Digital modeling offers the possibility of reconstituting entire sites at various eras of history and of transmitting historical reconstructions using animated interactive media (El-Khoury *et al.*). Site inhabitants have the possibility of recording their oral traditions and uploading them onto bit stream or torrent stations that make the site's social memory directly accessible to Internet users (Wolfe). With digital multimedia databases, it is possible to take things even a step further, by presenting, in images and full sound, the day-to-day routine of

---

5.   *The International Cultural Tourism Charter*: http://www.icomos.org/tourism/charter.html.
6.   For example, see: Rachel Dodds, "Assessing the demand for sustainable tourism," in *Réseau de veille en tourisme* (Website: http://tourismintelligence.ca/2008/04/04/assessing-the-demand-for-sustainable-tourism).

the location's inhabitants, their traditional skills, knowledge and activities (Turgeon and St-Pierre). All of these innovations are means by which it is possible to substantially increase a heritage site's capacity for communicating its living culture, involving its communities of inhabitants, interacting with visitors, as well as democratizing heritage.

To conclude this collection of essays, the *Quebec Declaration* is presented at the end of the book. It contains ten recommendations that summarize the rich and varied ideas exchanged at the Scientific Symposium and the Youth Forum. The proposed measures are intended to rise to the new challenge of creating a more inclusive, interactive world heritage movement that is consequently more dynamic and sustainable.

Acknowledgements

I would like to express my heartfelt thanks to the some 40 anonymous evaluators and members of the Scientific Committee for the time spent evaluating the proposed papers, particularly Dinu Bumbaru (Canada), Andrew Hall (South Africa), Neil Silberman (Belgium), Boguslaw Szmygin (Poland), and Marilyn Truscott (Australia). I am very grateful to Michel Bonnette, President of the 16th ICOMOS General Assembly's Organizing Committee, for the confidence he placed in me by offering me the title of President of the Scientific Committee. I would also like to express my profound gratitude to Célia Forget and Marie-Josée Deschênes for taking responsibility for the Youth Forum and organizing it brilliantly. My sincere thanks go to Bruno Bégin, François LeBlanc, Louise Mercier, William Moss, and Marie-Claude Rocher, for their tireless support during the entire symposium organization process. I would moreover like to thank, from the depths of my heart, all those who worked on the preparation of the manuscript of this book: Catherine Briand (editions), Marie-Claude Rocher (project coordination), Chantal Santerre (formatting), Anne-Hélène Kerbiriou (French translation and edition) and Mac Wigfield and Timothy Mellin (English translation and revision). My final thanks to Neil Silberman for reading and commenting on the final draft of the introduction.

References

Alexander, Christopher. 2004, *The Nature of Order*. Vol. 1: *The Phenomenon of Life*. Berkeley: Center for Environmental Structure.

Appadurai, Arjun. 1996. *Modernity at Large. Cultural Dimensions of Globalization*. Minneapolis: University of Minnesota Press.

Arsenault, Daniel. 1998. "Esquisse du paysage sacré algonquien". *Recherches amérindiennes au Québec* (28) 2: 19-39.

Barthes, Roland. 1970. *L'empire des signes*. Genève: Skira.

Bédard, Mario. 2002. "De l'être-ensemble à l'être-au-monde: Le rôle du haut-lieu." *Ethnologies* (24) 2: 229-241.

Bourdieu, Pierre, 1980, *Le sens pratique*. Paris: Minuit.

Cameron, Christina. 2000. "The Spirit of Place: The Physical Memory of Canada." *Journal of Canadian Studies* (35) 1: 77-94.

Choay, Françoise. 1999. *L'allégorie du patrimoine*. Paris: Le Seuil.

De Certeau, Michel. 1990. *L'invention du quotidien. Les arts de faire*. Paris: Gallimard.

Désveaux, Émmanuel. 1988. *Sous le signe de l'ours. Mythes et temporalités chez les Ojibwa septentrionaux*. Paris: Éditions de la Maison des sciences de l'homme.

Engelmann, Francis. 1998. *Luang Prabang*. Paris: ASA Éditions.

Fabre, Daniel. 2000. *Domestiquer l'histoire: ethnologie des monuments historiques*. Paris: Éditions de la Maison des sciences de l'homme.

Flannery, Regina. 1931. A Study of the Distribution and the Development of the Memegwecio Concept in Algonquin Folklore. M.A. thesis, Catholic University of America, Washington, D.C.

Grenet, Sylvie. 2004. Le génie du lieu dans l'aquarelle anglaise (1750-1850). Ph.D. thesis, Université de Paris IV.

Grimal, Pierre. 1976. *Dictionnaire de la mythologie grecque et romaine*. Paris: Presses universitaires de France.

Harrison, Rodney, Graham Fairclough, John H. Jameson Jnr. and John Schofield. 2008. " Heritage, Memory and Modernity ." *The Heritage Reader*, eds. Graham Fairclough, Rodney Harrison, John H. Jameson Jnr. and John Schofield: 1-12. London and New York: Routledge.

Heidegger, Martin. 1975 (1954). "Building, Dwelling, Thinking", *Poetry, Language, Thought*. Translated from German to English by Albert Hofstadter. New York: Harper & Row.

ICOMOS. 2003. *Proceedings of the 14th General Assembly and Scientific Symposium*, " Place, Memory, Meaning: Preserving Intangible Values in Monuments and Sites." Victoria Falls, Zimbabwe (site Web: http://www.international.icomos.org/victoriafalls2003/papers.htm).

Ingold, Tim. 2000. *The Perception of the Environment: Essays in Livelihood, Dwelling and Skill*. London and New York: Routledge.

Kirshenblatt-Gimblett, Barbara. 2006. "World Heritage and Cultural Economics." *Museum Frictions: Public Cultures / Global Transformations*, eds. Ivan Karp *et al.*: 161-202. Durham and London: Duke University Press.

Matsuura, Koïchiro. 2004. "Préface." *Museum International*, 221-222: 4-5.

Miller, Daniel. 1987. *Material Culture and Mass Consumption*. Oxford: Basil Blackwell.

—. 1998. "Why Some Things Matter." *Material Cultures: Why Some Things Matter*, ed. Daniel Miller: 3-21. Chicago: University of Chicago Press.

Murray, Penelope. 1989. *Genius: The History of an Idea*. Oxford: Basil Blackwell.

Nitzsche, Jane Chance. 1975. *The Genius Figure in Antiquity and the Middle Ages*. New York and London: Columbia University Press.

Nora, Pierre (ed.). 1984-1992. *Les Lieux de mémoire*. Paris: Gallimard. 3 volumes: vol. 1 *La République* (1984), vol. 2, *La Nation* (1987), vol. 3, *Les France* (1992).

Norberg-Schulz, Christian. 1980. *Genius Loci, Towards a Phenomenology of Architecture*. New York: Rizzoli.

Pecquet, Luc. 2004. "The Mason and the Banco, or Raw Material as a Power for Building a Lyela Home (Burkina Faso)." *Paideuma* 50: 151-171.

Pevsner, Nikolaus. 1978. *The Englishness of English Art*. New York: Penguin Books.

Poulot, Dominique. 2006. *Une histoire du patrimoine en Occident*. Paris: Presses universitaires de France.

—. 1997. "Introduction générale." *L'esprit des lieux: le patrimoine et la cité*, eds. Daniel J. Grange and Dominique Poulot, 15-34. Grenoble, Presses universitaires de Grenoble.

Prats Michèle and Jean-Pierre Thibault. 2003. "Qu'est-ce que l'esprit des lieux?" *Proceedings of the ICOMOS 14th General Assembly and Scientific Symposium*. "Place, Memory, Meaning: Preserving Intangible Values in Monuments and Sites." Victoria Falls, Zimbabwe (site: www.international.icomos.org/victoriafalls2003/papers).

Richot, Gilles. 1999. *Québec, forme d'établissement. Étude de géographie régionale structurale*. Paris, L'Harmattan.

Riegl, Aloïs. 1984 (1903). Translation into French by Daniel Wieczorek, *Le culte moderne des monuments*. Paris: Le Seuil.

Smith, Laurajane. 2006. *The Uses of Heritage*. London and New York: Routledge.

Steinbrink, Susan. 2008. "The PhoCusWright Consumer Travel Trends Survey Tenth Edition." *PhoCusWright (site: http://www.phocuswright. com/)*.

Tilley, Chris. 1994. *A Phenomenology of Landscape: Paths, Places and Monuments*. Oxford: Berg.

—. 2006. "Objectification." *Handbook of Material Culture*, eds. Chris Tilley, Webb Keane, Susanne Küchler, Mike Rowlands and Patricia Spyer, 60-73. London: Sage.

Tuan, Yi-Fu. 1977. *Space and Place: The Perspective of Experience*, Minneapolis: University of Minnesota Press.

Turgeon, Laurier. 2005. "Introduction." *Le patrimoine religieux du Québec: entre le cultuel et le culturel*, ed. Laurier Turgeon: 17-39. Quebec City: Les Presses de l'Université Laval.

—. 2007. "La mémoire de la culture matérielle et la culture matérielle de la mémoire." *Objets & mémoires*, eds. Octave Debary and Laurier Turgeon: 13-36. Paris and Quebec City: Éditions de la Maison des sciences de l'homme and Les Presses de l'Université Laval.

Introduction

L'esprit du lieu : pour mieux penser et pratiquer le patrimoine culturel[1]

Laurier Turgeon
Chaire de recherche du Canada en patrimoine
Directeur de l'Institut du patrimoine culturel
Université Laval, Québec
Canada

Le pont rassemble autour du fleuve la terre comme région.[...]
Le lieu n'existe pas avant le pont. Sans doute, avant que le pont soit là
y a-t-il le long du fleuve beaucoup d'endroits qui peuvent être occupés
par une chose ou une autre. Finalement l'un d'entre eux devient un lieu
et cela grâce au pont.

Martin Heidegger, « Bâtir, Habiter, Penser » (1954).

(Re)penser l'esprit du lieu

Dans ce livre, nous faisons le pari que la notion d'esprit du lieu possède une valeur heuristique qui permet de mieux penser et pratiquer le patrimoine. Plus encore, elle éclaire les différentes façons de « faire » du patrimoine, les

---

1. Ce livre regroupe 35 des quelque 100 communications présentées au Symposium scientifique de la 16ᵉ Assemblée générale d'ICOMOS tenu à Québec (Canada) les 1 et 2 octobre 2008. Le Comité scientifique a reçu plus de 600 propositions de communication provenant de quelque 80 pays. Pour inciter la participation des jeunes, il a créé un Forum des jeunes de deux jours qui a eu lieu dans le cadre du Symposium scientifique – une première dans l'histoire d'ICOMOS – et invité les jeunes à participer activement à la rédaction de la *Déclaration de Québec* qui reprend les principales conclusions du Symposium.

motifs et les modalités de ses constructions, les effets de ses usages, soit les processus de patrimonialisation. Même si l'esprit du lieu est considéré par certains comme suranné, lui préférant des locutions plus actuelles et à la mode, telles «la mémoire du lieu» ou «le sens du lieu», il demeure un concept fondateur du patrimoine. Souvent utilisé, mais rarement défini, il repose sur la croyance – vraie ou fausse – que les monuments, les sites et les paysages patrimoniaux transcendent l'ordre de la réalité ordinaire pour atteindre un au-delà, un ordre supérieur, voire sacré. En raison de leur ancienneté, de leur singularité et de leur fort investissement symbolique, ces lieux sont considérés comme étant habités par une force tutélaire ou surnaturelle qui les anime et les protège. Le grand historien de l'art autrichien, Aloïs Riegl n'hésitait pas, au début du 20e siècle, à qualifier cette admiration de la valeur d'ancienneté du monument historique de «culte moderne», qui tendait d'ailleurs à se substituer aux pratiques religieuses traditionnelles. Il remarquait que l'ancienneté du monument suscitait spontanément à tout un chacun «une pieuse attention» (Riegl 1903 : 47).

Au-delà de son inscription dans la pratique moderne du patrimoine, l'esprit du lieu existe sous une forme ou une autre dans toutes les civilisations et il traverse tous les temps. Son caractère quasi universel le rend d'autant plus pertinent et opératoire pour un organisme tel qu'ICOMOS, dont la mission est d'assurer la gestion du patrimoine à l'échelle mondiale. Dans la tradition occidentale, l'esprit ou le génie du lieu remonte à l'Antiquité romaine, connu alors sous le nom de *Genius Loci*. Les *Genii* de la mythologie romaine sont des êtres immanents qui habitent non seulement les lieux, mais aussi les individus (Grimal 1976, entrée «génie»). Ils symbolisent l'être spirituel des choses et des personnes, et ils ont pour fonction essentielle de les conserver en vie (Lucier et Petzet dans ce livre). Le génie, par sa nature unique, veille au lieu et lui donne son identité propre, tout en l'animant d'un principe vital. Les humains peuvent négocier avec lui, lui apporter des cadeaux pour obtenir des faveurs et, à l'occasion, entrer ainsi en contact avec lesdieux. L'idée qu'il existe des lieux investis de forces vitales et spirituelles n'est pas propre à l'Occident seulement. Dans les civilisations asiatiques, ces espaces sont qualifiés de lieux de la «vie» ou de la «bonne vie», ou encore de la «vraie vie» (Han, Kim et Sugio dans ce livre[2]). Ces notions s'inscrivent dans le confucianisme et le taoïsme qui prônent des rapports harmonieux entre l'homme et la nature, ainsi que l'unicité et la totalité de la nature. En Islam, les hauts lieux patrimoniaux sont souvent désignés par la notion abstraite de *Waqf* qui renvoie à un legs religieux inaliénable (Pirbabaei). Le lieu porte l'esprit du donateur et permet aux habitants de communiquer avec lui et

---

2.   Lorsque le date de publication n'est pas indiquée dans la référence, celle-ci renvoie au texte d'un auteur du présent livre.

d'accomplir ses volontés pour le bien-être de tous. La notion de l'esprit du lieu est très répandue dans les sociétés africaines. Des êtres surnaturels puissants marquent des lieux en se fixant à des montagnes, des lacs, des rivières ou encore à des arbres; mais, ils se trouvent moins souvent sur les terres incultes des clairières (Pecquet 2004). Ils ont non seulement le pouvoir de vitaliser les lieux et les personnes qui les fréquentent, mais aussi de les frapper d'un mauvais sort ou même de les détruire. Les humains peuvent négocier avec les génies, racheter une faute par le sacrifice et transformer leur hostilité en bienveillance. En Afrique, les génies font parfois irruption lors de cérémonies collectives et se manifestent par des «cultes de possession» destinés à remettre en question et refaire le corps social (Bondaz). L'esprit du lieu existe aussi chez la plupart des peuples amérindiens de l'Amérique du Nord. Dans la tradition culturelle algonquienne, par exemple, il prend différents noms et sens, selon les groupes et les périodes historiques : *Memequash* chez les Cris, *Maymaygwayshi* chez les Ojibwas et *Memekueshuat* chez les Innus qui veut dire «génies des roches qui sont en l'eau» (Désveaux 1988 : 265; Flannery 1931 : 2). Ils sont souvent décrits comme de petits êtres immanents à visage plat qui se réfugient dans les fissures des rochers. D'ailleurs, les rochers dans lesquels ils demeurent sont considérés sacrés et souvent marqués de pictogrammes (Arsenault 1998 : 29). Même si les formes et les fonctions de ces êtres surnaturels varient d'une culture à une autre, la notion de l'esprit du lieu est répandue dans les mythologies d'un grand nombre de civilisations du monde.

Loin de renvoyer à une notion unique et figée, l'esprit du lieu n'a cessé de se transformer et de s'adapter aux besoins de son temps. Si le *Waqf* a réussi à survivre à presque tous les régimes politiques et juridiques islamiques au cours de sa longue histoire, c'est parce qu'il a su s'adapter aux transformations économiques, sociales et culturelles les plus radicales (Pirbabaei). De même, dans la tradition asiatique, les lieux qui renferment la «vraie vie» peuvent non seulement répondre aux demandes de nouveaux groupes, mais leur spiritualité peut aussi être transplantée sur de nouveaux sites (Sugio). La pratique de l'esprit du lieu a aussi beaucoup évolué dans la tradition occidentale. Si dans l'Antiquité romaine, le génie du lieu renvoie à des êtres surnaturels et à des forces occultes, il tend à se laïciser et à s'humaniser à la Renaissance et à l'époque moderne. À partir du 16ᵉ siècle, il s'incarne dans les jardins, les parcs et les fontaines aménagés par l'homme. Désormais, le génie n'est plus un dieu qui habite un lieu, mais l'homme lui-même qui, grâce à son esprit créateur et inventif, sait aménager des sites enchanteurs. On qualifie de génie un homme particulièrement doué et talentueux : urbaniste, architecte, artiste, paysagiste, soit les nouveaux créateurs du paysage (Nitzsche 1975 : 131-136). Aux 17ᵉ et 18 siècles, le génie du lieu sert à désigner l'harmonie entre des éléments très divers – géographiques, historiques, sociaux et surtout esthétiques – pour parvenir à un bon aménagement urbain, qui soit à l'échelle de l'homme

(Pevsner 1978 : 1; Grenet 2004 : 113-115). D'ailleurs, ce changement de sens est accompagné d'une mutation lexicale. L'expression «génie du lieu» tend à être remplacée par «esprit du lieu» qui désigne le «caractère» que les hommes ont voulu donner au lieu (Murray 1989 : 6-11). Au 19e siècle, c'est l'ancienneté du monument historique elle-même qui devient objet de culte, qualifié par Aloïs Riegl, en 1903, de moderne (Choay 1999 : 124-127; Poulot 2006 : 166-171). Cette notion d'ancienneté, couplée en même temps à celle de modernité, continuera à nourrir largement la raison patrimoniale pendant tout le 20e siècle. En effet, la mise en patrimoine de la culture est devenue un instrument de modernisation et une marque de modernité, au point où les états aujourd'hui sans monuments et sans musées sont considérés sous-développés (Kirshenblatt- Gimblett 2006 : 180-183; Turgeon 2005 : 19-32).

Plus important encore que sa riche histoire, l'esprit du lieu est une notion prometteuse d'avenir pour le patrimoine mondial du 21e siècle. Le théoricien de l'architecture, Christian Norberg-Schulz qualifie le *genius loci* d'«espace existentiel», défini comme «les relations fondamentales qui existe entre l'homme et le milieu» (Norberg-Schulz 1981 : 5). Il vise ainsi à rompre avec le fonctionnalisme, le structuralisme, le morphologisme et les autres déterminismes géographiques, qui soutiennent que l'esprit du lieu vient du lieu lui-même, que le lieu détermine la forme et l'esprit de l'établissement humain (Alexander 2004; Richot 1999). En plus de séparer arbitrairement l'esprit du lieu, ces approches tendaient à essentialiser la notion du lieu, à le réduire à une essence, à une chose singulière, permanente et statique. Norberg-Schulz met l'accent sur les aspects psychiques plutôt que physiques, sur l'habitat plutôt que sur le bâtiment, afin de redonner à l'homme son rôle fondamental d'agent dans la constitution des espaces de son existence. Les espaces existentiels ne sont pas uniquement fabriqués par ceux qui les construisent, mais aussi par ceux qui les habitent. Ce sont les habitants d'un lieu qui finissent par lui donner son «caractère» et son sens, par lui donner une identité et un esprit. L'homme fait partie intégrante du milieu; ne pas en tenir compte conduit à l'aliénation de l'homme et à la destruction du lieu (Norberg-Schulz 1981 : 23). Sa théorie de l'espace existentiel repose sur la notion centrale d'«habiter», inspirée de la phénoménologie de Martin Heidegger, pour qui habiter signifie construire une relation entre l'homme et l'espace. Pour mieux penser cette relation, Heidegger recourt à l'image du pont. C'est le passage que représente le pont qui unit les deux rives du fleuve et leurs arrière-pays en une région. Le lieu, précise-t-il, «n'existe pas avant le pont» (Heidegger 1980 : 182). Par le choix de son emplacement, le pont crée le lieu qui, à son tour, détermine les places et les chemins par lesquels un espace est aménagé. Michel de Certeau permet d'approfondir encore davantage la relation au lieu. Pour lui, un espace prend sens dès lors qu'il est «pratiqué» par des humains (de Certeau 1990 : 155-158, 173). Ces pratiques peuvent prendre la forme d'un aménagement physique, ou s'exprimer par l'organisation d'un rituel ou d'un festival sur le site, ou encore par la simple marche ou par la récitation d'un poème, d'un conte ou d'une légende qui vont « dire » le lieu. C'est donc par des expériences concrètes, portées surtout par les sens et les affects, que les individus ou les groupes établissent une interaction avec des sites, négocient leur relation au lieu et construisent leur identité ainsi que celle du lieu (Bédard 2002 : 234-236; Tuan 1977 : 8-18).

L'esprit du lieu constitue une relation dynamique et un processus humain vivant. L'expression « esprit du lieu » énonce elle-même les deux éléments fondamentaux de cette relation, l'esprit qui renvoie à la pensée, aux humains et aux éléments immatériels, et le lieu qui évoque un site géographique, un environnement physique, soit les éléments matériels. Les deux sont unis dans une étroite interaction, l'un se construisant par rapport à l'autre. L'esprit construit le lieu et, en même temps, le lieu investit et structure l'esprit. La relation entre la pensée et le monde matériel n'est donc pas univoque mais dialectique, plurielle et évolutive. Reprenant les travaux de Roland Barthes (1970) et de Pierre Bourdieu (1980), les anthropologues Daniel Miller (1987, 1998) et Christopher Tilley (1994, 2006) ont développé la notion de « l'objectification », c'est-à-dire le processus par lequel l'idée d'un individu ou d'un groupe d'individus se concrétise dans une forme matérielle. Ils n'ont pas hésité à remettre en question le rationalisme de Descartes selon lequel l'esprit domine toujours la matière et la forme matérielle est prédéfinie dans un schéma mental avant d'être réalisée concrètement.

Plutôt que de précéder la forme, l'idée se construit en même temps qu'elle, dans un va-et-vient perpétuel entre l'abstraction de la pensée et la matérialité du lieu ou de l'objet. L'une nourrit l'autre et se fait donc constitutive de l'autre. Par exemple, dans son étude de la fabrication de paniers, Tim Ingold (2000) observe que le vannier n'a pas une représentation mentale précise de l'objet qu'il veut fabriquer, mais plutôt des habiletés et savoir-faire qui orientent son engagement avec la matière. La taille, la nature et la qualité de l'osier participeront aussi à la détermination de la forme. Le vannier compose avec la matière, travaille les matériaux en fonction des contraintes rencontrées. Chaque étape de la fabrication détermine les étapes successives. La forme émerge de cet engagement, du processus même de fabrication plutôt que de la seule pensée de l'artisan. Cette approche phénoménologique, qui met l'accent sur l'expérience concrète, éclaire aussi l'art de la sculpture ou l'œuvre archi-tecturale. Les architectes doivent composer avec des contraintes de temps, des limitations budgétaires, la nature des matériaux de construction, la présence d'autres bâtiments, et les besoins de la population, qui participent tous à la forme que prendra le bâtiment. Ce processus dialectique entre cognition et construction du lieu n'est pas limité uniquement au moment de création; il se poursuit à travers les différents usages que l'on en fait (Miller 1987). Les visiteurs se l'approprient selon les valeurs qu'il renferme; économiques, sociales, esthétiques ou mémorielles (Poulot 1997 : 32-34). C'est surtout lors de l'expérience de l'appropriation que ces valeurs se précisent, que le site est lui-même souvent modifié pour faire oublier certaines valeurs et en ressusciter d'autres. Ce n'est pas seulement le site proprement dit qui est approprié, mais aussi ceux à qui il a appartenu, pour exercer une domination sur eux. Le contexte colonial américain offre des exemples éloquents de ce phénomène (Friedman).

Ce livre vise donc à ouvrir la réflexion au rôle des différents acteurs sociaux, tant les concepteurs que les utilisateurs des lieux patrimoniaux, et à définir ce «lieu» autant par ses composantes matérielles (sites aménagés, bâtiments, objets matériels) qu'immatérielles (récits oraux, valeurs, rites, fêtes) qui participent à la construction de son sens. La matérialité du lieu permet d'évoquer la pérennité de certaines valeurs, voire de différents groupes qui l'ont occupé. L'immatérialité, c'est-à-dire l'esprit des groupes qui l'habitent, donne la possibilité de renouveler le sens du lieu ou même de lui attribuer plusieurs sens en fonction des besoins du «vivre ensemble» du ou des groupes. Envisagé dans sa dynamique relationnelle, l'esprit du lieu est, comme toutes les relations, instable, en constante transformation, il est donc un processus qui change avec le temps et qui change aussi celles et ceux qui le pratiquent. Il prend ainsi, comme le patrimoine lui-même (Smith 2006 : 44), un caractère pluriel et polyvalent, il peut posséder différentes significations et être partagé par plusieurs groupes. Cette perspective nous semble mieux adaptée à un monde globalisé, caractérisé de plus en plus par les migrations transnationales, les populations délocalisées, les échanges interculturels et les appartenances multiples (Appadurai 1996).

L'esprit du lieu et les enjeux actuels du patrimoine mondial

La notion de l'esprit du lieu, telle que nous l'avons définie, permet de répondre aux nouveaux défis du patrimoine mondial, notamment l'intégration du patrimoine culturel immatériel et la participation des communautés dans la sauvegarde des sites, des monuments et des paysages culturels. Comme le souligne dans ce recueil l'actuelle Présidente du Comité du patrimoine mondial, Christina Cameron, les pratiques du comité ont considérablement évolué au cours des trente ans de son existence, passant d'une approche assez lourdement matérialiste à une attention plus marquée aux valeurs immatérielles. Si les sites classés sur la Liste du patrimoine mondial étaient à l'origine essentiellement des monuments isolés, ils se sont progressivement étendus à des groupes de bâtiments et à de vastes paysages culturels qui embrassent de nombreux éléments immatériels. D'après l'ancien Président du Comité du patrimoine mondial et l'actuel Directeur général de l'UNESCO, Koïchiro Matsuura, c'est en réponse à la demande croissante d'inscription de sites sur la Liste du patrimoine mondial pour leurs valeurs culturelles immatérielles et aux difficultés de les faire reconnaître selon la *Convention pour la protection du patrimoine mondial, culturel et naturel* de 1972, qu'il a soutenu l'élaboration de la *Convention pour la sauvegarde du patrimoine culturel immatériel*, adoptée par l'UNESCO en 2003 (Matsuura 2004). Cette convention, déjà ratifiée par plus de 110 pays, représente un instrument normatif international destiné à protéger, conserver, et promouvoir tout spécialement les éléments immatériels de la culture. Afin d'assurer une bonne coordination entre les deux conventions, la *Déclaration de Yamato* de 2004 encourage les états signataires à envisager la mise en œuvre d'approches intégrées pour la sauvegarde du patrimoine culturel matériel et immatériel, avec la participation active des communautés et des groupes concernés[3].

ICOMOS n'a pas tardé à réagir à ces développements, en consacrant sa 14ᵉ Assemblée générale et son Symposium scientifique de 2003 à Victoria Falls, au Zimbabwe, au thème de la conservation des valeurs immatérielles de monuments et de sites (ICOMOS 2003). Par la *Déclaration de Kimberley* de 2003, ICOMOS s'est engagé à mieux intégrer les composantes immatérielles et les communautés locales qui les portent dans la gestion et la conservation des monuments et sites régis par la *Convention pour la protection du patrimoine mondial, culturel et naturel* de 1972. Un Comité scientifique international sur le patrimoine culturel immatériel (ICICH) a également été créé et celui-ci vient de préparer un document qui vise à établir un code de pratiques éthiques dans la gestion du patrimoine culturel immatériel lié aux espaces culturels. La *Déclaration de Xi'an* de 2005 rappelle aussi l'importance du contexte immatériel dans la reconnaissance et la protection des sites du patrimoine mondial. Le Symposium scientifique, tenu lors de la 16ᵉ Assemblée générale d'ICOMOS à Québec en 2008 sur l'esprit du lieu, s'inscrit dans cette volonté de mieux valoriser et intégrer les éléments immatériels des communautés et des groupes au patrimoine matériel.

Les auteurs des articles de ce recueil offrent des analyses et des réponses originales aux enjeux actuels du patrimoine mondial. Nous en avons identifié cinq; chacun est traité individuellement dans une partie de ce livre. Le premier enjeu porte sur les sens à donner à l'esprit du lieu. Le sens émane-t-il du lieu lui-même ou de l'esprit porté par les personnes qui l'occupent ? Pour conserver et transmettre l'esprit du lieu, faut-il simplement conserver le lieu ou plutôt l'esprit de ceux qui l'ont construit? Bien que certains auteurs aient mis l'accent sur le rôle du lieu (Lucier, Petzet), sur la singularité de sa forme ou de son esthétisme, et d'autres sur la pensée et le savoir-faire des humains (Harrington et Sullivan), tous reconnaissent que les deux interagissent et produisent ensemble le sens ou, du moins, une part importante du sens. Comme nous l'avons souligné précédemment, le sens découle de l'expérience du site. Les visites guidées, les pratiques artistiques, les festivals et les rituels

---

3.   *Déclaration de Yamato*: http://unesdoc.unesco.org/images/0013/001376/137634f.pdf.

permettent d'intensifier cette expérience avec le site et d'accroître sa signification et sa charge émotive, voire spirituelle (Bondaz, Pirbabaei, Sugio, Yano).
Les lieux seuls ne signifient pas. Les sites de batailles importantes (Ogle) ou
de naufrages de navires (Maarleveld), non pas choisis mais désignés par le
simple hasard de rencontres militaires ou de tempêtes, nous font réaliser à
quel point l'esprit de ces lieux est construit *a posteriori* par les humains pour
célébrer ou faire le deuil d'un événement important de leur passé. Ces espaces marqués fortuitement par les circonstances du moment deviennent des
lieux de rassemblement où des relations sociales se tissent et où de nouvelles
identités se négocient (Harrington et Sullivan).

La mémoire sociale représente un deuxième enjeu majeur. Elle tend
aujourd'hui à se confondre avec l'esprit du lieu car c'est elle qui exprime le
plus fortement le lien avec le lieu ou l'objet matériel (Harrison *et al.* 2008 :
2-3). Les travaux de Pierre Nora (1984, 1987, 1992) et de Daniel Fabre (2000)
nous ont éclairé sur les manières dont les lieux servent à soutenir la mémoire
et participer activement à sa construction et à sa structuration. Les aménagements et les bâtiments concrétisent et prolongent dans le temps la mémoire de
l'occupation et servent d'outils mnémoniques (Turgeon 2007 : 13-36). Mais
ils sont jugés insuffisants aujourd'hui pour révéler pleinement cette mémoire
vivante du lieu, notamment par des touristes de plus en plus friands d'histoire
sociale et culturelle. Cette mémoire est jugée tout aussi «essentielle» pour
la vie économique, sociale et politique des populations locales (Assi). C'est
pour cette raison que les premiers occupants orientent les usages ultérieurs
du site et conservent souvent une présence – réelle ou symbolique – dans les
occupations subséquentes (Friedman, Binan et Binan). La mémoire sociale est
transmise par voie orale ou encore par l'écrit, notamment par la poésie ou la
prose (Bernal), signe d'un fort investissement affectif. En Chine, la poésie est
un instrument important de la construction de la mémoire et de l'esprit du
lieu. Le Lac Hangzhou, l'un des sites les plus valorisés de Chine, a fait l'objet
de non moins de 20 000 poèmes (Han). Puissante, la mémoire sociale est
aussi très fragile. Portée par des personnes, elle peut disparaître avec eux et de
manière inaperçue. Les bâtiments annoncent leur abîme par une dégradation
qui s'étale généralement sur des périodes longues alors que la mémoire, elle,
pratiquement invisible, peut s'éclipser ou encore être volontairement enrayée
sans que personne ne s'en rende compte (Binan et Binan; Albuquerque Lapa et
Almeida de Melo). Et sa disparition est souvent irréversible, surtout lorsqu'elle
est orale (Turgeon et St-Pierre). Il y a différentes manières de la recueillir : par
des enquêtes orales auprès des habitants des sites, par des recherches dans les
textes historiques et littéraires, par des fouilles archéologiques et par l'observation de festivals et de rituels qui transportent parfois de manière discrète cette
mémoire. La conserver et la mettre en valeur permet d'offrir une interprétation
beaucoup plus riche et vivante du patrimoine (Friedman).

Le meilleur moyen de préserver et valoriser la mémoire et les autres éléments immatériels du lieu (récits, fêtes, rituels, savoir-faire, cuisine) est d'impliquer les populations qui habitent et utilisent le site. Les projets de restauration et de mise en valeur des sites et des monuments sont encore trop souvent pris en charge par des experts animés par un désir de grandeur architecturale qui tend à exclure les communautés directement concernées, ce qui permet de conserver le lieu, mais pas nécessairement son esprit. C'est ainsi que Francis Engelmann, représentant de l'UNESCO et résident de Luang Prabang, au Laos, décrit le projet de sauvegarde du complexe monastique de cet endroit : « Nous avons sauvé les bâtiments de Luang Prabang, mais nous avons perdu son âme » (Engelmann 1997, Suntikul). En revanche, les projets qui favorisent une forte implication des populations locales sont généralement couronnés de succès (Mackay et Sullivan, Prieto, Ritch et Becerril, Bell et Johnston, Burgess *et al.*). L'association des communautés concernées offre de nombreux avantages : elle favorise la sauvegarde des éléments immatériels du site, permet d'intégrer les membres de ces communautés à la gestion et à l'interprétation, accroît leur possibilité d'emploi et leur sentiment de d'appartenance, et contribue au développement durable (Corsane *et al.*). Des projets avant-gardistes de restitution de sites à des populations aborigènes, menés en Australie et en Nouvelle-Zélande, se sont avérés très concluants. La prise en charge de la gestion par les Aborigènes a non seulement conduit à enrichir l'interprétation et à développer le tourisme, mais aussi à la revitalisation économique et sociale des communautés autochtones et à la restauration écologique des sites (Bell et Johnston, Burgess *et al.*). Les partenariats entre différents groupes de professionnels et les communautés du milieu conduisent à des échanges et à l'élaboration de nouveaux modèles de collaboration (Mackay et Sullivan). Mais ces partenariats sont parfois impossibles à envisager tellement les luttes entre groupes rivaux pour un même lieu sont exacerbées (Amit-Cohen). Il n'en demeure pas moins que ces sites de conflits violents, voire même d'atrocités, peuvent devenir des lieux de médiation et de réconciliation, d'autant plus efficaces qu'ils amènent les belligérants à s'engager à faire la paix sur les lieux mêmes des affrontements (Ogle). La nouvelle *Charte sur l'interprétation et la présentation des sites du patrimoine culturel*, mieux connue sous le nom de *Charte d'Ename*, ratifiée à Québec en 2008, fournit à ICOMOS un outil normatif qui sera d'un précieux secours pour la résolution de conflits et la réconciliation sur des sites contestés[4].

Le développement d'un tourisme durable représente un autre enjeu de taille. L'Organisation mondiale du tourisme prévoit que le tourisme continuera à croître de manière exponentielle au cours des prochaines décennies. Elle constate que le tourisme culturel est le secteur qui connaît actuellement

---

4.   *Charte d'Ename* : http://www.enamecharter.org/.

la plus forte augmentation. Dans un tel contexte, il est urgent de réfléchir aux moyens de protection des sites face aux menaces du tourisme. Il semble difficile d'envisager des mesures destinées à interdire l'accès aux sites dans la mesure où le tourisme est devenu une activité économique essentielle (Abdulac, Messeri, Suntikul), ou en laquelle on met beaucoup d'espoir pour assurer le développement (Jean Julien). Comment alors concilier l'augmentation de la fréquentation des sites et leur préservation ? Si pendant longtemps la priorité était donnée à la protection physique des sites, il y a maintenant une volonté de favoriser l'interaction humaine, soit d'associer les communautés qui habitent ou utilisent le site à l'interprétation et à la sensibilisation des touristes à la protection du lieu et de son esprit. Il s'agit de mettre le touriste à contribution de la conservation du site, comme le veut d'ailleurs la *Charte internationale sur le tourisme culturel* de 1999[5]. Au lieu d'envisager le touriste comme une menace, la Charte propose d'inverser la perspective et de le considérer comme un agent de préservation du patrimoine et du développement durable (Brooks). Par exemple, la gestion des sites autochtones par les Aborigènes eux-mêmes leur permet de profiter des revenus du tourisme et d'assurer ainsi le développement de leurs communautés, tout en offrant aux touristes une expérience authentique de cultures vivantes (Ketz et Ketz). D'ailleurs, de plus en plus de touristes choisissent leur destination expressément en fonction de la possibilité de pratiquer un tourisme durable[6].

Enfin, les nouvelles technologies de l'information offrent des possibilités quasi illimitées de conservation et de communication de l'esprit du lieu. Pendant longtemps, le contact visuel et physique direct était considéré comme le meilleur moyen de faire l'expérience authentique du lieu et de son esprit. Avec l'avènement d'Internet, on craignait que «la puissance déréalisante» du Web conduise à une «déstabilisation identitaire» (Choay 1999 : 183-184). En fait, c'est tout le contraire qui s'est produit. Internet a permis d'accroître la publicité et la fréquentation des sites, de mieux les interpréter et de les gérer à des coûts moindres. La présence sur le Web est presque devenue une condition *sine qua non* de l'exploitation touristique des sites dans la mesure où les trois quarts des touristes connectés au Web, du moins en Amérique du Nord, planifient leurs voyages à la suite d'une navigation sur Internet (Steinbrink 2008). Des sites comme Wikipedia, YouTube, Facebook et Flickr contribuent à capter et à diffuser plus efficacement les éléments immatériels et l'esprit des lieux (Burke). La modélisation numérique donne la possibilité de reconstituer les sites à différentes époques de leur vie et de visualiser ces reconstitutions à l'aide d'animations interactives (El-Khoury *et al.*).

---

5.   *Charte internationale sur le tourisme culturel* : http://www.icomos.org/tourism/charter.html.
6.   Voir, par exemple : Rachel Dodds, «Évaluation de la demande en matière de tourisme durable», dans *Réseau de veille en tourisme* (site Web : http://veille-tourisme.ca/2008/04/04).

Les habitants des sites peuvent enregistrer leurs récits oraux et rendre la mémoire des lieux directement accessible sur place, grâce à l'installation de postes d'écoute (Wolfe). Les bases de données numériques multimédias permettent d'aller encore plus loin, en montrant, par le son et l'image, le déroulement de la vie des personnes qui y habitent, leurs savoir-faire et leurs pratiques (Turgeon et St-Pierre). Tous ces nouveaux moyens augmentent considérablement les capacités de diffusion de la culture vivante des sites, de participation des communautés, d'interaction avec les visiteurs et de démocratisation du patrimoine.

La *Déclaration de Québec* est présentée à la fin du livre en guise de conclusion. Ses dix recommandations résument les échanges riches et variés du Symposium scientifique et du Forum des jeunes. Les mesures proposées visent à faire face aux nouveaux défis et à construire un patrimoine mondial plus inclusif, participatif, donc dynamique et durable.

Remerciements

Je tiens ici à remercier chaleureusement les quelque 40 évaluateurs anonymes et les membres du Comité scientifique pour le temps consacré à l'évaluation des propositions de communication, notamment Dinu Bumbaru (Canada), Andrew Hall (Afrique du Sud), Neil Silberman (Belgique), Boguslaw Szmygin (Pologne) et Marilyn Truscott (Australie). Ma gratitude est très grande envers Michel Bonnette, Président du Comité d'organisation de la 16e Assemblée générale d'ICOMOS, pour la confiance qu'il a bien voulu m'accorder à titre de Président du Comité scientifique. Que Célia Forget et Marie-Josée Deschênes, qui ont assumé avec brio l'organisation du Forum des jeunes, trouvent ici l'expression de ma profonde reconnaissance. Mes remerciements s'adressent aussi à Bruno Bégin, François LeBlanc, Louise Mercier, William Moss, Marie-Claude Rocher pour leur soutien indéfectible tout au long du processus d'organisation du Symposium. Je voudrais égale-ment remercier du fond du cœur toutes celles et tous ceux qui ont travaillé à la préparation du manuscrit du livre : Catherine Briand (révision linguisti-que), Marie-Claude Rocher (coordination), Chantal Santerre (mise en page), Anne-Hélène Kerbiriou (traduction française et révision linguistique) et Mac Wigfield et Timothy Mellin (traduction anglaise et révision linguistique). Je tiens enfin à remercier Neil Silbermann pour sa relecture de l'introduction.

Références

Alexander, Christopher. 2004. *The Nature of Order. Vol. 1 : The Phenomenon of Life*. Berkeley : Center for Environmental Structure.

Appadurai, Arjun. 1996. *Modernity at Large. Cultural Dimensions of Globalization*. Minneapolis : University of Minnesota Press.

Arsenault, Daniel. 1998. « Esquisse du paysage sacré algonquien ». *Recherches amérindiennes au Québec* (28) 2 : 19-39.

Barthes, Roland. 1970. *L'empire des signes.* Genève : Skira.

Bédard, Mario. 2002. « De l'être-ensemble à l'être-au-monde : Le rôle du haut-lieu ». *Ethnologies* (24) 2 : 229-241.

Bourdieu, Pierre. 1980. *Le sens pratique.* Paris : Minuit.

Cameron, Christina. 2000. « The Spirit of Place : The Physical Memory of Canada ». *Journal of Canadian Studies* (35) 1 : 77-94.

Choay, Françoise. 1999. *L'allégorie du patrimoine.* Paris : Le Seuil.

De Certeau, Michel. 1990. *L'invention du quotidien. Les arts de faire.* Paris : Gallimard.

Désveaux, Émmanuel. 1988. *Sous le signe de l'ours. Mythes et temporalités chez les Ojibwa septentrionaux.* Paris : Éditions de la Maison des sciences de l'homme.

Engelmann, Francis. 1997. *Luang Prabang.* Paris : Asa Editions.

Fabre, Daniel. 2000. *Domestiquer l'histoire : ethnologie des monuments historiques.* Paris : Éditions de la Maison des sciences de l'homme.

Flannery, Regina. 1931. A Study of the Distribution and the Development of the Memegwecio Concept in Algonquin Folklore. Mémoire de maîtrise, Catholic University of America, Washington, D.C.

Grenet, Sylvie. 2004. Le génie du lieu dans l'aquarelle anglaise (1750-1850). Thèse de doctorat, Université de Paris IV.

Grimal, Pierre. 1976. *Dictionnaire de la mythologie grecque et romaine.* Paris : Presses universitaires de France.

Harrison, Rodney, Graham Fairclough, John H. Jameson Jnr. et John Scho-field. 2008. « Heritage, Memory and Modernity ». *The Heritage Reader* (dir.) Graham Fairclough, Rodney Harrison, John H. Jameson Jnr. et John Schofield : 1-12. Londres et New York : Routledge.

Heidegger, Martin. 1980 (1954). *Essais et conférences.* Traduit de l'allemand par André Préau. Paris : Gallimard.

ICOMOS. 2003. Proceedings of the 14th General Assembly and Scientific Symposium, « Place, Memory, Meaning : Preserving Intangible Values in Monuments and Sites ». Victoria Falls, Zimbabwe (site Web : http://www.international.icomos.org/victoriafalls2003/papers.htm).

Ingold, Tim. 2000. *The Perception of the Environment : Essays in Livelihood, Dwelling and Skill.* Londres et New York : Routledge.

Kirshenblatt-Gimblett, Barbara. 2006. « World Heritage and Cultural Economics ». *Museum Frictions : Public Cultures / Global Transformations* (dir.) Ivan Karp *et al.* : 161-202. Durham et Londres : Duke University Press.

Matsuura, Koïchiro. 2004. « Préface ». *Museum International*, 221-222 : 4-5.

Miller, Daniel. 1987. *Material Culture and Mass Consumption*. Oxford : Basil Blackwell.

—. 1998. « Why Some Things Matter ». *Material Cultures: Why Some Things Matter* (dir.) Daniel Miller : 3-21. Chicago : University of Chicago Press.

Murray, Penelope. 1989. *Genius: The History of an Idea*. Oxford : Basil Blackwell.

Nitzsche, Jane Chance. 1975. *The Genius Figure in Antiquity and the Middle Ages*. New York et Londres : Columbia University Press.

Nora, Pierre (dir.). 1984-1992. *Les Lieux de mémoire*. Paris : Gallimard, 3 tomes : t. 1 *La République* (1 vol., 1984), t. 2 *La Nation* (3 vol., 1987), t. 3 *Les France* (3 vol., 1992).

Norberg-Schulz, Christian. 1981. *Genius loci : paysage, ambiance, architecture*. Traduit par Odile Seyler. Bruxelles : Pierre Mardaga éditeur.

Pecquet, Luc. 2004. « The Mason and the Banco, or Raw Material as a Power for Building a Lyela Home (Burkina Faso) ». *Paideuma* 50 : 151-171.

Pevsner, Nikolaus. 1978. *The Englishness of English Art*. New York : Penguin Books.

Poulot, Dominique. 2006. *Une histoire du patrimoine en Occident*. Paris : Presses universitaires de France.

—. 1997. « Introduction générale ». *L'esprit des lieux : le patrimoine et la cité* (dir.) Daniel J. Grange et Dominique Poulot : 15-34. Grenoble : Presses universitaires de Grenoble.

Prats Michèle et Jean-Pierre Thibault. 2003. « Qu'est-ce que l'esprit des lieux ? ». Proceedings of the ICOMOS 14th General Assembly and Scientific Symposium. « Place, Memory, Meaning : Preserving Intangible Values in Monuments and Sites ». Victoria Falls, Zimbabwe (site : www.international.icomos.org/victoriafalls2003/papers).

Richot, Gilles. 1999. *Québec, forme d'établissement. Étude de géographie régionale structurale*. Paris : L'Harmattan.

Riegl, Aloïs. 1984 (1903). *Le culte moderne des monuments*. Traduction française par Daniel Wieczorek. Paris : Le Seuil.

Smith, Laurajane. 2006. *The Uses of Heritage*. Londres et New York : Routledge.

Steinbrink, Susan. 2008. « The PhoCusWright Consumer Travel Trends Survey Tenth Edition ». PhoCusWright (site : http://www.phocuswright.com/).

Tilley, Christopher. 1994. *A Phenomenology of Landscape: Paths, Places and Monuments*. Oxford: Berg.

—.   2006. «Objectification». *Handbook of Material Culture* (dir.) Chris Tilley, Webb Keane, Susanne Küchler, Mike Rowlands, Patricia Spyer, 60-73. Londres: Sage.

Tuan, Yi-Fu. 1977. *Space and Place: The Perspective of Experience*, Minneapolis: University of Minnesota Press.

Turgeon, Laurier. 2005. «Introduction». *Le patrimoine religieux du Québec: entre le cultuel et le culturel* (dir.) Laurier Turgeon: 17-39. Québec, Les Presses de l'Université Laval.

—.   2007. «La mémoire de la culture matérielle et la culture matérielle de la mémoire». *Objets et mémoires* (dir.) Octave Debary et Laurier Turgeon: 13-36. Paris et Québec: Éditions de la Maison des sciences de l'homme et Les Presses de l'Université Laval.

I

THE MEANINGS OF SPIRIT OF PLACE

LES SENS DE L'ESPRIT DU LIEU

Port Arthur: Heritage, Home, Haven or Horror?

Jane Harrington
Sharon Sullivan
Port Arthur Historic Site Management Authority
Australia

ABSTRACT

This paper explores the way in which places and senses mutually create/ recreate each other. Emphasis is placed on how places are experienced, but are also created through conceptualisation and imagining: place is not only the physicality of being "here", but also imagined through layers of memories, often of other places, and sometimes grounded in the memory of others. Specific reference is made to the Port Arthur Historic Site, which is conceptualised variously as convict heritage place (World Heritage nominated), community place, tragedy place and tourism place. The paper applies theoretical approaches combining philosophical and anthropological understandings of space and place, which explicate the multi-vocality of landscapes that enmesh people, place and time. It is shown that spirit and place become embedded in a flow of power and negotiation of social relations that are rendered in the physicality of tangible elements and the embodiment of imagination, memories and symbolic attributions.

RÉSUMÉ

Cet article explore la manière dont les lieux et les sentiments se créent et se recréent mutuellement. L'emphase est mise sur la manière dont les lieux sont ressentis, mais aussi créés à travers la conceptualisation et la mise en images : faire l'expérience du lieu ne consiste pas seulement physiquement à « être là », mais aussi à l'imaginer à travers différents niveaux de mémoires, d'autres lieux souvent, parfois ancrés dans la mémoire des autres. Cet article porte plus spécifiquement sur le Site historique de Port Arthur, qui est diversement conceptualisé : en tant que site patrimonial lié au bagne (mention sur la liste du Patrimoine mondial), en tant que lieu communautaire, en tant que lieu tragique et en tant que lieu touristique. Cet article applique des approches théoriques combinant des compréhensions philosophiques et anthropologiques de l'espace et du lieu, qui expliquent le caractère multivoque des paysages qui entremêlent les personnes, le lieu et le temps. Ceci dans l'intention de démontrer que l'esprit et le lieu finissent par s'inscrire dans un flux de pouvoir et de négociations de relations sociales qui se concrétisent dans des éléments matériels et s'incarnent dans l'imagination, les mémoires et les attributions symboliques.

1. Introduction

As this symposium is appositely addressing, heritage is not just the material "things" around us, but is inclusive of aspects that are intangible, such as language, myth, ritual, custom, oral traditions, practices, knowledge and stories. It incorporates the symbolic manifestations of culture that are passed on (and changed) over time in a process that transmits ideas, beliefs, values and emotions. Intangible heritage is interlinked with the things we do and with what we experience. The process is one which links places, people and senses, which act to mutually create and re-create each other. It is through practices and experiences that people, memory, identity and place interact. An understanding of practices also reveals the ways that life is learned and passed on through processes of socialisation. The processes involved are integral to the creation and maintenance of identity and belonging, and of "being in place", all of which reinforce how people engage with the "spirit of place".

An analysis of these engagements can valuably rely on a number of theoretical platforms, including the experiential understandings that can be gained through a phenomenological approach. The role of perception, both as constituted and constitutive, is integral to the way in which place, meaning, senses and action continuously interact in a process of creation and recreation. Individual lives and experiences are enmeshed in a web of social interactions and meanings that reach out from the immediate community and locale to engage with broader national and global influences. By complementing this approach with the understanding of life as a series of transformations, it is possible to understand the way in which material and social relations are situational and influenced by processes of change. Place, memory, community and identity are all mutable. Because all are reliant on social processes, they are also inseparable from power relations and the inevitable negotiations that accompany hegemonic encounters (Harrington 2004, 326).

2. Port Arthur

The Port Arthur Historic Site in Australia provides an exemplary location to consider the relationship between the landscape, people, history, heritage, the intangible, and the Spirit of Place. The site has national heritage significance that recognises the role of convictism in the symbolic construction of Australian nationhood. It is Tasmania's most visited tourism destination, with the majority of visitor awareness acknowledging the site's convict heritage. It is a significant place for the local community as part of their lived, experienced and remembered landscape. In 1996 Port Arthur was the place of a horrific shooting by a lone gunman that resulted in the loss of 35 lives and injury of another 19 people. This tragic event imposed another layer of pain and suffering on Port Arthur and touched the lives of many.

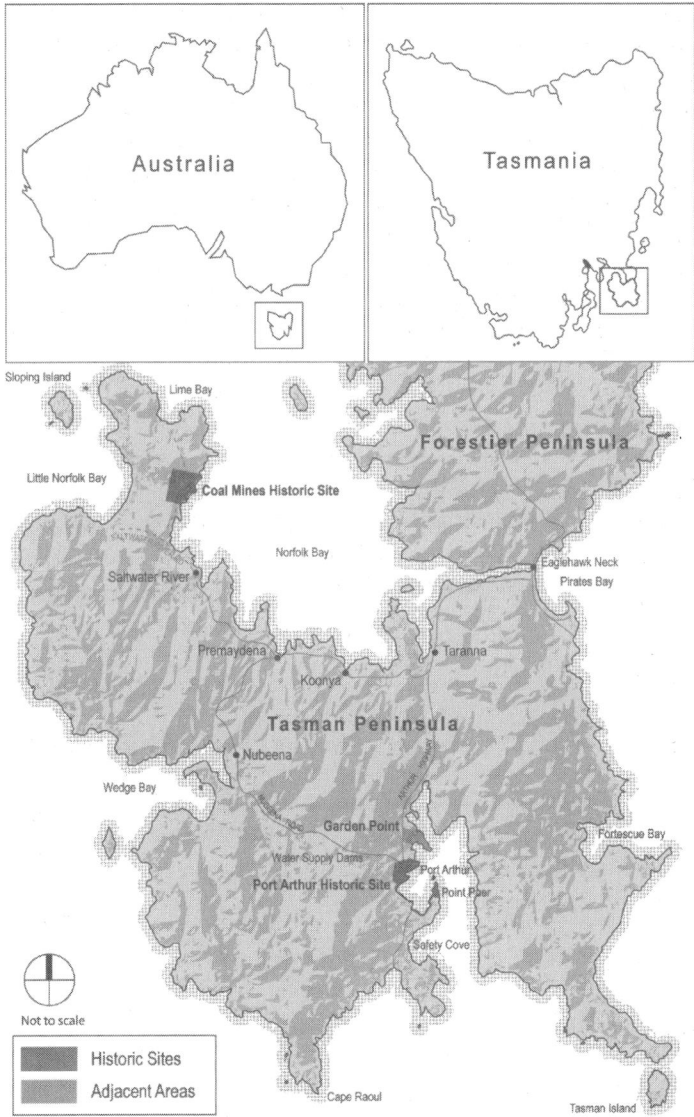

Figure 1. Location and context of the Port Arthur Historic Site.

2.1. History

The site comprises 98.1 hectares on the Tasman Peninsula in the southeast of the island state of Tasmania (Fig. 1). Archaeological evidence suggests that the Peninsula has an Aboriginal history at least 5400 years old, but it is probable that it was occupied much earlier. The penal station of Port Arthur had its origins as a convict timber camp in 1830. In 1833 Port Arthur became the focus of the secondary punishment system in Van Diemen's Land (as Tasmania was originally named). The convict settlement saw various stages of expansion over the next 40 or so years until the establishment was closed for convict purposes in 1877.

Following this, the land was parcelled up for private sale and a township grew among the ruins of the penal settlement. A burgeoning tourist trade saw the area devoted to a combination of tourism, agriculture and timber-getting. Visitors were initially mainly Tasmanians, keen to see first-hand the "horrors" of a penal station, but soon the site was attracting increasing numbers from the mainland and overseas. Ironically this attraction was aided by the quintessential Australian phenomenon – bushfire – which in multiple destructive events served to create a landscape of ruins and to impose an "instant" picturesque Gothic quality (Young 1996, 37).

Recognition of the site's importance prompted the Tasmanian Government to create the Scenery Preservation Board in 1915, which took the management of parts of Port Arthur out of local hands. By 1948 most of the township was reserved as a historic site. The National Parks and Wildlife Service took over management in 1971, by which time the entirety of the site was government owned. In 1986 management passed to the Port Arthur Historic Site Management Authority.

On Sunday 28 April, 1996, a lone gunman shot and killed 35 people and wounded 19 others in and around Port Arthur. In the years following the event, a memorial garden was established, which includes the partially demolished ruins of the Broad Arrow Café, where many of the victims lost their lives. As a result of this event, national gun laws were introduced, which included a general ban on the private ownership of automatic and semi-automatic firearms (PAHSMA 2007, 21-33).

2.2. Port Arthur Today

The Historic Site retains evidence of all its phases of use and occupation from Aboriginal occupation, penal settlement, township and its gradual transformation into an internationally recognised historic site and tourism destination. It is included on the National List and the Tasmanian Heritage List and is one of 11 sites in the Australian Convict Sites World Heritage nomination. The site receives some 300,000 visitors a year. The Authority is today the major employer on the Peninsula, reinforcing the site's traditional role as a centre of economic activity. The site retains strong links with the community, not only as a place of employment, but through powerful and enduring associations and meanings as a landmark and as a symbolic centre.

A number of families have long-term connections with Port Arthur, dating to the township period. In some cases, these families lived in houses now within the Port Arthur Historic Site, which were subsequently restored or demolished. For many members of today's community, the site was once the place they called home, worked in, went to school, farmed, had children and simply lived. Their ongoing involvement is one that involves a sense of attachment and "ownership" (PAHSMA 2007, 41–42).

Figure 2. Port Arthur Penitentiary Building. A Tasmanian icon.

3. The Spirit of Port Arthur
3.1. Heritage as Enduring Practice

Port Arthur typifies that what and who we are is entangled with the place we occupy, whether this is for a brief moment or a longer period of time. But it does not preclude that our engagement with places can also be one of memory and imagination. The co-existence of the material and the imagined of place together act to articulate identity at various levels. For a place such as Port Arthur, this arises through multiple and overlapping experiences: a place of memory, of home and belonging, of work, of nation building, of punishment and rehabilitation, of pain and suffering, of sadness, of history, of learning and fun, a place of tourism. At Port Arthur, the past and the present are variously engaged, re-engaged and re-presented, formally through heritage interpretation programs and more informally through the memories and stories that create multi-vocal landscapes.

One of the historical layers of Port Arthur lies in its early establishment as a historic reserve and as a tourism destination. The conferring of heritage values and the evolution of Port Arthur as a tourism destination have been established by punctuated but persistent processes since the penal settlement closed in 1877. Both have served to reinforce the wider cultural appreciation of the Port Arthur landscape as encompassing both paradox and mystery (PAHSMA 2003, 19). This "history of heritage" has implicated the site in the evolution of heritage discourse and practice in the Australian context and more broadly. One result has been a relationship with several generations of heritage practitioners, for many as a professional "rite of passage". Through various modes of heritage interpretation and practice, the Port Arthur landscape has accrued another set of layers, providing an anticipated, experienced and multivalent landscape that links a "practised" heritage in a meaningful way with people in the present. In this sense, the practice of heritage – and the people involved with that practice – has become part of the field of social relations that link identity, place and the social practices that make place.

3.2. Heritage as Memory

In 2007 a contemporary art exhibition (the Port Arthur Project) was installed at the site. The intent was to engage with the history and culture of Port Arthur using a collection of site-specific artworks. Artists were encouraged to uncover under-recognised elements of the landscape, or to reinvestigate conventional readings of history. One installation was based on the poignant notion of memory and representations of death, loss and mourning. The artist's work consisted of a series of photographic prints of various headstones on the Isle of the Dead, the small island used as the cemetery during the time of the penal settlement. The installation highlighted that even here at "the end of the earth" people tried to inscribe an eternal memory of the dead. The work illustrated the poignancy and futility of such actions in the face of nature and time. Of the 90 gravestones, 68 have the word *memory* inscribed upon them. However, "rather than perpetuate the life they honoured, the slow disintegration of the gravestones creates a *momento mori* or premonition of death and decay… reflect[ing] the fading away of these exquisitely rendered headstones" (Frankham & Clark 2007, 10).

This astute artistic rendering of a major conservation problem exemplifies one of the goals of any conservation program: to work to ensure that the multiple memories, stories, attachments and meanings – and the ways of reading them – are not allowed to disappear from the landscape. Complementing efforts to protect the fabric of the cemetery, the continuation of memory is enhanced through an ongoing association by many who identify themselves as descendents of those buried there, both convicts and free persons.

One of the more poignant places within the landscape of the Historic Site is the Memorial Garden, created following the tragic 1996 shooting. Its installation involved an intensive project of community consultation. The feelings of the community varied (and continue to vary), and include strong polarised opinions arising from the highly emotional nature of the tragedy. The Broad Arrow Café and Memorial Garden have become a symbol and focus of remembrance for those who died in, were injured by or assisted during the tragedy and is a place of memory, remembrance and mourning for many visitors, survivors and relatives of those who were lost (Lennon 1998). It is a particular place of remembrance for the people of Tasman Peninsula, a number of whom were working at the site on the day, and some of whom are still involved with the site.

It has been argued that memory is not simply a process of recalling the past. Instead, it remains a complex process of "selection, negotiation and struggle over what will be remembered and what will be forgotten. [It] involves remembering and forgetting, changing and restructuring one's perception of the past so that it both supports the needs of the present and projects a logical future" (Natzmer 2002, 164). Memories also act to create interpretive frameworks to help make experience comprehensible and can become deeply implicated in contemporary matters. These include the truth of memory, history and culture, who owns them and their roles in identity, hegemonic relationships and nation building. They can tear a community apart, but they can also bring a community together (Cattell & Climo 2002, 4-5). The Memorial Garden has become a place of remembrance for many and a place of healing and recovery for others. For some it remains a place of mourning and one that is kept separate from their embodied experience: it is a sad place for its horror and sorrow. It is also a place of significant interest to visitors who are curious as to how the 1996 tragedy has been remembered. Over time, a challenge will develop in ensuring that the event and the memories are not subsumed in a process of objectification and artefact making – that is, that the tangible remains at the site of the Broad Arrow Café do not take on a greater significance than the memories of the event itself and the meaning of the memorial as a symbol of resilience and remembering.

Figure 3. Memorial Pond and Garden.

3.3. Community Heritage

One of the strongly expressed sentiments of the Port Arthur community is that the Historic Site is not "Port Arthur", and that Port Arthur is a larger township within which the site is located. This fact is one that confounds many visitors – and compounds the need for local assertions of ownership. Port Arthur is a small town in its own right, with some 200 permanent inhabitants, many of whom have a multi-generational connection to the area.

The site clearly cannot be, and will not be, separated from the voices of the local people: it remains a focal point in their areas of interest. Many of these relate to ongoing practices associated with the environment: fishing, farming, gardening, relationships, all of which incorporate processes of learning that are both practical and social. These are the things that tell us who we are, what we need to do, how to do it, and where we belong. In a rural environment they include place specific environmental information, are related to ways of using the land, of climate, agricultural practices, the best places to fish and the right times to do so. They also include an awareness of dangers, which are particularly relevant in a sea-based environment. These practices and processes are significant components of the way a community creates and reinforces meanings and relationships. The transfer of knowledge between generations is also one that reinforces belonging and notions of stewardship in contexts that are simultaneously practical, spiritual and emotional (Crumley 2002, 41). For today's Port Arthur community, many of these practices were learned during the period of earlier occupation of the township, before the land was taken over by the government or have been passed on through memories of that time. A number of community activities are still part of practices and engagement with the site. Local fishermen continue to access a jetty within the site and a small fishing fleet is moored close by. One of the enduring local traditions and an integral part of the heritage of the Port Arthur community is the Boxing Day wood chops, held in the site grounds. The chops, an event which sees competitors pitted against each other in various timber cutting activities, are the remaining event of the Port Arthur sports day, which commenced in 1863 and is believed to be the longest running sporting event in Australia. Held annually, it attracts competitors and spectators from across Tasmania.

Figure 4. Boxing Day Wood chops.

The ongoing tradition of such practices at Port Arthur is a reminder that the meanings, experiences and local stories of the community are reinforced in places of meeting, interaction and exchange. The wood chops as a modern-day practice also provide an unbroken connection with the origins of Port Arthur as a timber getting camp. Cultural and social activities – whether organised events or just day-to-day recreational experiences – enhance community identity and reinforce the closely intertwined relationship with the broader environment, both natural and constructed, and with historical connections. For many communities their cultural and social values are inseparable from their knowledge, experience and understanding of place, and of the broader landscape within which community and home are conceptualised and understood.

4. Conclusion

The multiplicity of places, spaces and meanings and their resonance in the concept of landscapes have attracted substantial philosophical debate. For Heidegger (1993, 349), we inhabit the earth in a way that reinforces the habitual nature of experience. De Certeau suggests that sociocultural production and socioeconomic order act to (re)appropriate space through the practices of "everyday life". We use places through activities such as frequenting or dwelling in a place, and to provide "the many ways of establishing a kind of reliability with the situations imposed on an individual, that is, of making it possible to live in them by reintroducing... the plural mobility of goals and desires" (de Certeau 1984, xxii). Bourdieu (1977, 72) relies on the concept of *habitus* as a set of principles that ground and explain practices in both specific and general sociocultural contexts. Experiences, including the processes of heritage, can hence be seen to merge into habitus – or social norms – for those who engage with them as a set of professional principles, as a way of knowing and as a way of being known. They can also be seen to act on the way people reinforce identities and imbue with attachments and meanings the landscapes and places that are complicit in this reinforcement.

A place is contextually constituted by differing human experiences, attachments and involvements. It is what people do – through a process of social participation – that serves as a form of mortar, bonding the features of a landscape together. These bonds act to provide a model for the multiple systems of social relationships and governance (Olwig 1995, 317). The material remains of the past can be considered as an imprint of the normal, the banal, habitual but nonetheless socially and culturally specific environment in and through which people negotiate their lives.

The Port Arthur landscape is complex, intricate and worked upon; for many it is an experienced, remembered and lived-in place. If, as Bender (1998, 7) reminds us, "we continue to try to create, not *the* past, but *our* past" through landscape interpretation and conceptualisation, it becomes clear that there are multiple created, interpreted and conceptualised pasts in the Port Arthur landscape. All landscapes have the conceptual capacity to contain, hold and preserve experiences and memories and to represent that which is "the familiar, the small, the 'in place,' the dense with meaning, sensation and memory" (Bender 2003). This is not to deny the relevance of material "things" in place, but to acknowledge their capacity to draw memory and place together in a significant way. This can also be people who have lived, experienced, played and worked together, all of whom construct a consciousness of their social world out of their engagement with and conceptualisation of lived experience and their relationship with others.

Landscapes do not have "voices" as such, nor are memories written across them. These belong to the people who interpret them, creating a complex relationship between the object and the narrator/interpreter (Bender 1995, 15). Values arise out of the interrelationship of places, the interpretation of landscapes or the attachments that impart a "spirit of place". The shared experiences of those who have worked, lived, visited or imagined Port Arthur act as a component of the bricolage from which communities variously define and identify themselves.

There is ongoing discussion of the way in which landscapes, buildings and places have lost, or are in the process of losing, their meaning and significance – particularly in Western and capitalist society. A landscape that is stripped of sedimented human meanings can be considered to be irrelevant, and becomes "set apart from people, myth and history, something to be controlled and used" (Tilley 1994, 21). It loses its spirit of place. To varying degrees a combination of heritage approaches, tourism and development are influencing the lives of many communities, and the community at Port Arthur is not divorced from these same global processes. One particular challenge is reconciling the broader stories and spirit of Port Arthur with the overwhelming identification of Port Arthur as a penal settlement by most visitors to the Historic Site. The necessity is to avoid the marginalisation of contemporary community meanings, particularly those that arise through practice and experience, and to ensure that the multiple attachments and engagements that together create and reinforce the spirit of place are not compromised.

References

Bender, B. 1995. Introduction. In *Landscape: Politics and Perspective*, ed. B. Bender: 1-18. Providence: Berg.

Bender, B. 1998. *Stonehenge: Making Space*. Oxford: Berg.

Bender, B. 2003. Landscapes-on-the-Move. Unpublished seminar paper delivered to the School of Anthropology, Archaeology and Sociology, JCU.

Bourdieu, P. 1977. *Outline of a Theory of Practice*. Cambridge: Cambridge University Press.

Cattell, M. & J Climo eds. 2002. *Social Memory and History*. Walnut Creek: Altamira Press.

Crumley, C. 2002. Exploring Venues of Social Memory. In *Social Memory and History*, eds M Cattell, & J. Climo: 39-52. Walnut Creek: Altamira Press.

de Certeau, M. 1984. *The Practice of Everyday Life*. Berkeley: University of California Press.

Frankham, N & J Clark, eds. 2007. *Port Arthur Project*. Hobart: UTas.

Harrington, J. 2004. *"Being Here': Heritage, Belonging and Place Making*. PhD diss., School of Anthropology, Archaeology and Sociology, James Cook University, Townsville.

Heidegger, M. 1993. Building Dwelling Thinking. In *Martin Heidegger: Basic Writings*, ed. D Krell: 343–364. San Francisco: Harper Collins.

Lennon, J. 1998. Broad Arrow Café Conservation Study.

Natzmer, C. 2002. Remembering and Forgetting. In *Social Memory and History*, eds M Cattell & J Climo: 161-180. Walnut Creek: Altamira Press.

Olwig, K. 1995. Sexual cosmology: nation and landscape at the conceptual interstices of nature and culture. In *Landscape: Politics and Perspective*, ed. B Bender: 307-344. Providence: Berg.

PAHSMA. 2003. PAHS Archaeology Plan. Port Arthur: Port Arthur Historic Site Management Authority.

PAHSMA. 2007. Port Arthur Historic Sites Draft Management Plan. Port Arthur: Port Arthur Historic Site Management Authority.

Tilley, C. 1994. *A Phenomenology of Landscape: Places, Paths and Monuments*. Oxford: Berg.

Young, D. 1996. *Making Crime Pay*. Hobart: THRA.

Finding the Spirit of Place: A World Heritage Perspective

Christina Cameron
Canada Research Chair on Built Heritage
School of Architecture, Faculté de l'aménagement
University of Montreal

ABSTRACT

This paper examines the theme of finding the spirit of place from two points of view. It begins with observations on the presentations of the keynote speakers at the opening session of the Scientific Symposium. It then traces the degree to which spiritual and intangible values have been duly recognized in the implementation of UNESCO's World Heritage Convention of 1972. It concludes with questions that challenge traditional conservation approaches for heritage properties.

RÉSUMÉ

Cet article examine le thème de la découverte de l'esprit du lieu à partir de deux points de vue. Il commence par des observations relatives aux communications des intervenants lors de la session inaugurale du Symposium scientifique. Il définit ensuite jusqu'à quel degré les valeurs spirituelles et immatérielles ont été dûment reconnues par la mise en œuvre de la Convention de 1972 de l'Unesco sur le Patrimoine mondial. Il se conclut par des interrogations qui remettent en question les approches traditionnelles de conservation des biens patrimoniaux.

World Heritage Convention of 1972

From the outset, spirit of place has been part of the 1972 UNESCO Convention concerning the Protection of the Cultural and Natural Heritage, known as the World Heritage Convention. Despite some views to the contrary, the World Heritage Committee has considered associative and intangible values of properties from the earliest years of its deliberations. The keynote speakers' remarks are particularly pertinent to the challenges of determining which sites merit inscription on the World Heritage List. As for the post-inscription challenges of conserving World Heritage Sites, the speakers' reflections are useful in envisaging innovative approaches to monitoring the state of World Heritage Sites and determining appropriate means of intervening to ensure the transmission of their values to future generations.

Since its first session in 1977, the World Heritage Committee has wrestled with the relationship between the material qualities of historic places and their associated intangible values. Early proposals from States Parties for sites to be inscribed on the World Heritage List brought the issue of associative values into clear focus. These proposals included the slave holding centre at the island of Gorée, Senegal (Figure 1), the remains of the concentration camp at Auschwitz-Birkenau Nazi Concentration Camp, Poland, and the reconstructed historic centre of Warsaw, Poland (Figure 2).

Figure 1. Slave quarters at the Island of Gorée, Senegal, World Heritage Site. Photo Wikipedia.

Figure 2. Reconstructed Historic Centre of Warsaw, Poland, World Heritage Site. Photo SuperStock.

The Committee asked for an analysis from Michel Parent, at that time Inspecteur général des monuments historiques in France and Rapporteur for the 1979 Committee meeting – and later President of ICOMOS International. His 1979 report, entitled "A Comparative Study of Nominations and Criteria for World Cultural Heritage," provided a basis for Committee discussion and fundamental choices about the future implementation of the World Heritage Convention. Referring to his report, Michel Parent said: "Its purpose was to identify the dilemmas which face us today – today, while the weight of precedent is not too heavy to be overturned, forcing us into irremediable anomalies" (Parent 1979).

While insisting that the text of the World Heritage Convention "pointed to an emphasis on concrete properties whose historical importance depends on tangible features of self-evident quality", Parent went on to state that the concept of listing an "idea" which haunts a historic place is also consistent with the letter of the Convention. He did caution however that such sites should stand as unique symbols for whole groups of similar sites, specifically making reference to the Auschwitz concentration camp – a restriction that he did not see the need to apply to other more tangible types of properties (Parent 1979).

The criterion used to assess intangible associative values is cultural criterion (vi). The original wording for this criterion states that a property should "be most importantly associated with ideas or beliefs, with events or with persons, of outstanding historical importance or significance" (OG 1977). In responding to Parent's report, the World Heritage Committee directed that particular attention be paid to criterion (vi):

> ... so that the net result would not be a reduction in the value of the List, due to the large potential number of nominations as well as to political difficulties. Nominations concerning, in particular, historical events or famous people could be strongly influenced by nationalism or other particularisms in contradiction with the objectives of the World Heritage Convention (WHC Report 1979).

The Committee changed the wording of criterion (vi) to shift the balance towards material values by adding that "the Committee considered that this criterion should justify inclusion in the List only in exceptional circumstances or in conjunction with other criteria" (OG 1980). Over the ensuing thirty years of implementation, the World Heritage Committee has been ambivalent about the application of criterion (vi) to determine the associative values of properties. Sometimes it has opted for using the criterion by itself, without any other criteria that would take into account the more physical and tangible evidence. For instance, the Viking site at L'Anse-aux-Meadows in Newfoundland is a Canadian site (Figure 3) that was listed in 1978 under criterion (vi) alone because it provides evidence of the first European presence in North America. But most of the time, the Committee has insisted that other criteria be used in addition to criterion (vi).

Figure 3. L'Anse-aux-Meadows, Canada, World Heritage Site. Photo Christina Cameron.

The debate over criterion (vi) notwithstanding, the implementation of the World Heritage Convention can be characterized as evolving from a more materials-based approach towards a greater emphasis on intangible values. One of the contributing is the changing definition of what constitutes heritage. The definition has gradually expanded beyond free-standing monuments to include groups of buildings and latterly vast cultural landscapes. Indeed the current consideration of the term "historic urban landscape" expands the definition even more. The adoption of a landscape approach necessarily puts greater emphasis on the spirit of place.

There are well-known benchmarks that mark this evolution in World Heritage thinking. The 1994 international meeting at Nara on the concept of authenticity as it relates to historic places, known as the Nara Conference on Authenticity, has been instrumental in opening up consideration of intangible and associative values. The Nara Declaration on Authenticity (Larsen 1995) has led to a better understanding of cultural and heritage diversity, the relativity of values and the relevance of non-written sources in documenting historic places. The World Heritage Committee's *Global Strategy* for a representative, balanced and credible World Heritage List (GS 1994) provides a thematic framework which moves away from monumental manifestations of heritage and encourages consideration of properties high in associative value. The subsequent 2003 UNESCO Convention for the Protection of Intangible Cultural Heritage, while not specifically aimed at historic places, serves to reinforce the relationship between cultural spaces and intangible cultural expression.

In some recent examples of World Heritage listings, the Committee has determined that their Outstanding Universal Values are almost entirely spiritual. Robben Island, South Africa, stands as a symbol to the resilience of the human spirit and the desire for freedom; the sacred forest of Osun-Osogbo, Nigeria (Figure 4), continues to be used for spiritual ceremonies; and the reconstructed bridge at Mostar in Bosnia-Herzegovina (Figure 5) was listed for its "restoration of intangible dimensions", giving it "an overall authenticity" (Cameron 2008).

Figure 4. Sacred Forest of Osun-Osogbo, Nigeria, World Heritage Site. Photo Wikipedia.

Figure 5. Reconstructed bridge at Mostar, Bosnia-Herzegovina, World Heritage Site. Photo Sinisa Sesum, UNESCO WHC.

Conclusion

One can conclude that the World Heritage system has been involved in recognizing spiritual values in the inscription process since the signing of the Convention in 1972. What is less clear is how spiritual values are factored into the subsequent treatment of properties following inscription. There are many questions to be asked. How best can associative values be conserved at World Heritage Sites? How can their meaning be transmitted to present and future generations? How important is it to conserve the physical fabric of the property? Is it more important to conserve the totem poles at the Canadian Haida site of Sgang Gwaay, or is transmission of the art of carving these wooden figures sufficient? How important are the existing relationships among buildings and their landscapes? How should new insertions within such properties be assessed? Who has the right to interpret and present a property? Whose heritage is it?

These are challenges for ICOMOS members. It is therefore entirely appropriate that the 16ᵗʰ General Assembly in Quebec explored the four themes related to associative values: rethinking the spirit of place; the threats to the spirit of place; safeguarding the spirit of place; and transmitting the spirit of place. The ICOMOS discussions are important and will contribute to a better understanding of how to conserve the spiritual values of heritage properties.

References

Cameron, Christina. From Warsaw to Mostar: the World Heritage Committee and Authenticity. *APT Bulletin*, Vol. 39, Nos. 2-3 (2008), p. 19-24.

Expert meeting on the Global Strategy and thematic studies for a representative World Heritage List. *Report of the Rapporteur on the eighteenth session of the World Heritage Committee in Phuket, 12-17 December 1994* (Paris, 13 October 1994): WHC-94/CONF.003/INF. 6, p. 7. Available from http://whc.unesco.org/archive/repcom94.htm; accessed 9 March 2009.

Larsen, Knut Einar, ed. Nara Document on Authenticity. *Nara Conference on Authenticity* (Paris: UNESCO 1995), p. xxi-xxiii.

Operational Guidelines for the Implementation of the World Heritage Convention. *Report of the Rapporteur on the first session of the Intergovernmental Committee for the Protection of the World Cultural and Natural Heritage in Paris, 27 June-1 July 1977* (Paris, 20 October 1977): CC-77/CONF.001/8 Rev. Available from http://whc.unesco.org/archive/opguide77a.pdf; accessed 6 March 2009.

Operational Guidelines for the Implementation of the World Heritage Convention," WHC/2 Revised (October 1980). Available from http://whc.unesco.org/archive/opguide80.pdf; accessed 9 March 2009.

Parent, Michel. Comparative Study of Nominations and Criteria for World Cultural Heritage. *Report of the Rapporteur on the third session of the World Heritage Committee in Cairo and Luxor, 22-26 October 1979* (Paris, 30 November 1979): CC-79/CONF.003/11 Annex. Available from http://whc.unesco.org/archive/repcom79.htm; accessed 6 March 2009.

Report of the Rapporteur on the third session of the World Heritage Committee in Cairo and Luxor, 22-26 October 1979 (Paris, 30 November 1979): CC-79/CONF.003/13, p. 9. Available from http://whc.unesco.org/archive/repcom79.htm; accessed 6 March 2009.

Le génie du lieu
La *fusion des patrimoines matériels et immatériels* au Musée national du Niger

Julien Bondaz
Université Lumière Lyon 2
Centre de Recherches et
d'Études anthropologiques
France

ABSTRACT

Drawing on the case of a spectator's entery into trance during a Niger National Museum parade, on May 1[rst] 2007, this presentation seeks to examine the complex history and the ambiguous status of traditional clothing exhibited by the museum and held in its collections. Several of these costumes are in fact considered as that of «genius'» and, as such, play an essential role in possesion rituals. Hence they are extremely useful to study of both the «spirit of object» and the «spirit of place». They offer the opportunity to show how the fusion of the visible and invisible worlds – such as occurs during a possession crisis – reveals the specific relationship between material and immaterial heritage within the National Museum.

RÉSUMÉ

Cette contribution a pour objectif, à partir de l'entrée en transe d'une spectatrice lors du défilé syndical du Musée national du Niger, le 1er mai 2007, de questionner l'histoire complexe et le statut ambigu des tenues traditionnelles exposées dans le pavillon des costumes ou conservées dans les réserves du musée. Certaines d'entre elles sont en fait des vêtements de génies et jouent un rôle essentiel dans les cultes de possession. À ce titre, elles constituent un objet privilégié pour interroger à la fois le génie de l'objet et l'esprit du lieu. Il s'agit en effet de montrer comment la fusion des mondes visibles et invisibles que constitue la crise de possession se traduit par des relations spécifiques entre patrimoine matériel et patrimoine immatériel au sein du Musée national.

Le 1er mai 2007, à 7 heures du matin, les agents du Musée national du Niger, à Niamey, s'étaient donnés rendez-vous pour un défilé syndical préparé des semaines à l'avance. Il avait fallu choisir quels animaux allaient participer au défilé – puisque le Musée national du Niger est aussi un zoo (pour plus de détails sur le musée, voir entre autres Toucet 1963, 1972 ; Gado 2000 ; Chaibou 2001) ; et surtout, pour Habsatou, la responsable du service des collections, il avait fallu sélectionner les tenues traditionnelles devant être portées par les jeunes femmes du centre éducatif du musée. Peu après 8 heures, ayant rejoint la place de la grande mosquée de Niamey, le cortège se met en bon ordre, les jeunes femmes en tenue traditionnelle derrière la banderole du musée, puis les soigneurs et les gardiens en uniforme kaki, suivis par les trois animaux sélectionnés (un mulet, un lion en cage à l'arrière d'une Peugeot et un crocodile naturalisé fixé sur le toit du même véhicule) ; enfin, clôturant le cortège, un camion sert de présentoir ambulant aux différentes formations proposées par le centre éducatif. Presque trois heures plus tard, juste avant d'arriver au stade où attendent les officiels, à un carrefour, une femme, vite délestée de son bébé par un spectateur, se jette dans le cortège et s'accroche de toutes ses forces à l'un des agents du musée en hurlant : « c'est mon mari, c'est mon mari ». Quatre autres agents parviennent à lui faire lâcher prise et la confient à un policier en faction au carrefour. Mais, de nouveau, elle se jette dans le cortège, cette fois dans la banderole puis contre le capot de la Peugeot. On m'explique que c'est une folle. Puis j'entends une autre explication : « C'est le *bori* : elle est possédée par un génie. C'est la vue d'une tenue traditionnelle qui a déclenché la crise de possession ».

Dans ces aléas du regard, tout semble donc s'être passé comme si la vue d'un « objet sur le corps » (la tenue traditionnelle portée par une jeune femme) avait convoqué un « sujet dans le corps » (le génie incorporé par la spectatrice). À propos de cette intrusion d'une entité invisible dans ou à travers l'acte de voir, on pourrait parler de « confusion visuelle », à l'origine d'un phénomène de « condensation rituelle » (Houseman et Severi 1994 : 205) : la tenue traditionnelle exhibée comme objet muséal, comme élément du patrimoine national, devient l'attribut d'un génie et le signe d'une alliance immédiatement réactivable sous la forme d'une crise de possession. Le regard instaure un rapport entre le fait qu'une personne puisse être en même temps un génie (possession) et le fait qu'une tenue traditionnelle puisse être en même temps un vêtement de génie (« confusion visuelle »). « Ne pas se contenter d'être ce que l'on est » ne serait donc pas seulement le privilège de la personne, comme le proposait Michel Leiris au sujet de la possession (1980), mais aussi celui de certains objets.

Envisager les tenues traditionnelles du musée comme des objets privilégiés revient à les questionner à la fois en tant qu'objets rituels formant « la transition matérielle entre le visible et l'invisible » (Rouch 1945 : 50) et en tant qu'objets muséaux analysables en termes de «points de contact» (Feldman 2006), dans la mesure où ils ne mettent plus en jeu le corps des participants aux cultes de possession, mais celui des visiteurs d'une exposition (ou des spectateurs d'un défilé). Dans une perspective muséale, cela revient à poser la question des génies comme patrimoine immatériel, la relation entre l'objet et son génie ayant pour continuité la relation entre le lieu et son esprit. La «fusion des mondes visibles et invisibles» que provoque la possession (Stoller 1989) semble en effet avoir pour pendant muséographique la fusion des patrimoines matériels et immatériels.

Habiller les génies : le vêtement comme point de contact entre le monde visible et le monde invisible

Je voudrais présenter, pour commencer, le traitement et l'usage des tenues traditionnelles dans le cadre des cultes de possession, situation dans laquelle elles ne sont plus seulement des tenues traditionnelles, mais des vêtements de génies, où elles constituent ce que Jean Rouch appelle la «garde-robe compliquée d'un théâtre surnaturel» (1945 : 53). Le vêtement de génie s'inscrit dans un processus ambigu, entre objectification et personnification d'une entité invisible. Plus généralement, il s'inscrit dans le cadre de transactions d'objets, de médiations sociales et de transmissions mémorielles, comme l'a très bien montré Adeline Masquelier à propos du *bori* hausa (Masquelier 1996, 1997).

Il faut préciser tout d'abord que les cultes de possession à Niamey sont des pratiques minoritaires, la population étant majoritairement musulmane (Vidal 1990 : 62-65). Il conviendrait de mentionner la complexité des relations entre les cultes de possession et l'islam (Masquelier 1994) ; mais, pour résumer, les minorités qui pratiquent les cultes de possession, composées essentiellement de femmes, appartiennent à deux ethnies différentes, parlent deux langues différentes, et nomment leurs pratiques différemment : *holley* pour les Songhay-Zerma (sur le vocabulaire songhay-zerma, voir Olivier de Sardan 1982) et *bori* pour les Hausa (Monfouga-Nicolas 1972 et Masquelier 2001).

Dans ces deux ethnies, la plupart des génies sont communs, le déroulement des cérémonies est globalement identique et, pour ce qui nous concerne, les vêtements des génies y jouent le même rôle et subissent le même traitement rituel. Il est clair cependant que la question de leur origine peut faire l'objet d'une réappropriation ethnique : ainsi, les tenues utilisées dans le cadre du *holley* sont réputées provenir de la région de Tillabéri, et seraient donc confectionnées par des tisserands songhays ou zermas, alors que celles qui sont utilisées dans le cadre du *bori* viendraient de la région de Doutchi, une région hausa. Mais les cultes de possession paraissent au contraire posséder également une dimension syncrétique (Olivier de Sardan 1986). La majorité des ethnies du Niger sont représentées par au moins un génie, auquel est associée la tenue traditionnelle de cette ethnie, complétée le plus souvent par un attribut (une épée pour le génie touareg ou une calebasse de lait pour le génie peul, par exemple) ; dans le cadre des cultes de possession apparaît donc un processus de représentation ethnique au moyen des tenues traditionnelles. Mais cela, en réalité, dépasse le cadre de la nation (qui est celui qui motive le discours muséographique du Musée national du Niger), par exemple avec les génies *Hauka*, génies occidentaux ayant intégré le panthéon du *holley* et du *bori* au moment du colonialisme (Rouch 1956 ; Stoller 1995).

D'autre part, les éléments associés à un génie ne se résument bien sûr pas seulement à un vêtement (entendons désormais par ce mot une tenue traditionnelle plus, le cas échéant, un attribut spécifique). Chaque génie ou catégorie de génies est également associé à une musique, à une danse, à un parfum et à une couleur (pour une liste détaillée, voir Rouch 1989 : 145-187). Ces deux derniers éléments, en particulier, ont une conséquence directe et essentielle sur le vêtement du génie : il doit être de la couleur du génie (noir, rouge, blanc ou rayé) et, avant chaque utilisation, il faut qu'il soit parfumé avec le parfum du génie. Les différents parfums sont conservés dans des boîtes subissant un traitement rituel spécifique et placées à proximité des tenues. Notons que ces parfums ne sont pas conservés au Musée national du Niger.

Par ailleurs, la propriété, la conservation et l'entretien des vêtements de génie dans le cadre des cultes de possession dépendent de différents cas de figures.

1. Les génies concernés sont des génies personnels ou familiaux : leurs vêtements sont conservés dans une malle ou dans la pièce la plus intime de la concession ou de la maison.

2. Les génies concernés sont convoqués dans le cadre de pratiques individuelles de guérison ou de divination : leurs vêtements sont accrochés au mur de la pièce où a lieu la consultation (une pièce spécialement aménagée ou la chambre du guérisseur).

3. Les génies concernés sont convoqués dans le cadre de cérémonies collectives : leurs vêtements sont accrochés au mur d'une pièce spécialement aménagée à proximité du lieu où sont organisées les cérémonies, dans la concession d'un responsable du culte. Lors de l'entrée en transe, soit la personne possédée est menée dans cette pièce pour être revêtue du vêtement du génie qui la possède, soit le vêtement du génie est sorti de la pièce et la personne possédée habillée en public. Quoi qu'il en soit, les vêtements ne sortent en public qu'après la venue du génie dont ils sont l'indice.

Dans tous les cas de figure, on voit ainsi qu'un traitement particulier et un lieu spécifique sont attribués aux vêtements de génies. Dans tous les cas également, c'est la personne possédée ou le responsable du culte qui est le propriétaire des vêtements de génies et, à ce titre, responsable de leur entretien et de leur remplacement en cas d'accrocs ou de déchirures. De même, si cette personne est possédée par un nouveau génie, elle doit se procurer la tenue correspondante. C'est sur le marché que l'on peut acheter ces tenues traditionnelles, qui sont en fait, pour la plupart, importées du Nigeria. On les trouve plus particulièrement dans les boutiques du petit marché, à proximité du Musée national. Trois types de clientèle sont en effet visés par les commerçants : les personnes qui pratiquent le *holley* ou le *bori* (appelés « féticheurs » par les vendeurs), certaines personnes qui, en période de fête, souhaitent porter une tenue traditionnelle (critères esthétiques et distinction sociale), et enfin les touristes (souvenir).

Le « musée-transe » : conserver le génie du lieu

Ces différentes relations à l'objet nous ramènent ainsi au Musée national, où coexistent trois traitements distincts des tenues traditionnelles.

1. Certaines tenues traditionnelles sont exposées en tant que symboles de l'unité nationale, en tant qu'objets construisant la mémoire collective (Turgeon 2007 : 26-30). Le pavillon des costumes, qui porte le nom du premier directeur du musée, Pablo Toucet, a en effet pour objectif de présenter les tenues traditionnelles de chaque ethnie, aussi bien pour les touristes que pour les Nigériens. L'un des agents du musée explique ainsi :

   Quand il y a des troubles, on montre le musée. C'est la synthèse de la diversité dans une seule institution. Si on est hausa, on voit dans le pavillon des vêtements que la tenue traditionnelle hausa est à côté de la tenue traditionnelle zerma, de la tenue toubou, de la tenue touarègue. Comme ça, on sait que s'il y a des troubles, c'est seulement pour gouverner (11 mai 2007).

   Les tenues exposées sont en fait des tenues d'apparat, ce qui a valu à cette section le surnom de « pavillon des jeunes mariés ». C'est pour cette raison d'ailleurs qu'il est le pavillon préféré des visiteurs nigériens et qu'il est l'enjeu de revendications de la part de certains visiteurs gourmantché (il manque encore en effet une tenue traditionnelle gourmantché).

2. D'autres tenues traditionnelles sont conservées dans la réserve principale du musée, au niveau du service des collections. Ce ne sont pas des tenues luxueuses. Ce sont celles qui étaient portées par les jeunes femmes du défilé et qui ont déclenché la crise de possession.

3. Les dernières tenues traditionnelles ont une histoire plus complexe. Ce sont des vêtements de génie, utilisés dans le cadre du *holley* (et non du *bori* : se joue ici une distinction entre cultes de possession songhay-zerma et hausa). C'est en fait sous l'impulsion de Jean Rouch que des génies ont été installés au musée. Peu après son inauguration en 1959, un autel (*tooru*) leur est consacré dans l'une des cases de l'habitat traditionnel songhay reconstituée en plein centre du musée. Dès lors, chaque année à la fin de la saison chaude,

le *yenendi*, cérémonie à base de possessions visant à demander la pluie, est organisé au musée. C'est cet événement qui a permis à Jean Rouch de tourner *Hampi*, en 1960. Cette fusion entre le musée et la transe orchestrée par Rouch, inventeur du «ciné-transe», invite alors à parler d'un «musée-transe» pour qualifier l'intrusion des génies de possession dans l'espace muséal.

	le lieu	l'esprit
l'objet	1. confusion visuelle	
	tenue traditionnelle	vêtement de génie
la personne	2. possession	
	corps	génie
le musée	3. fusion	
	patrimoine matériel	patrimoine immatériel

Figure 1. Les trois modes de fusion du monde visible et du monde invisible, du lieu et de l'esprit.

Le culte rendu aux génies du musée fut suspendu en 1974, avec l'arrivée d'un nouveau directeur. Cependant, différents événements inhabituels étant survenus, celui-ci fut convaincu de la nécessité de reprendre l'organisation du culte, et en particulier des sacrifices annuels. Mais le culte fut finalement à nouveau abandonné suite à une série de mystérieux incendies attribués aux génies, et en raison des tensions qui s'étaient ravivées entre les responsables du culte et certains musulmans, qui s'accusaient mutuellement.

Ces incendies avaient causé la destruction de plusieurs habitats traditionnels. Le dernier, mais aussi le plus dévastateur, en 1992, détruisit le hangar des artisans, ainsi que les cases où étaient exposés les vêtements des génies. Une partie de ces cases n'a toujours pas été reconstituée, non plus que l'autel consacré aux génies. Les termites sont également désignés comme les responsables de la destruction de certaines tenues traditionnelles. De nouveaux vêtements de génies ont été offerts par les *zima*, les responsables du culte, et sont exposés dans l'une des cases de l'habitat traditionnel; ils ont également figuré dans une exposition temporaire organisée par l'ambassade de France en 2004 et intitulée «Les cent plus beaux objets du Musée national». Durant toute la durée de leur exposition au niveau de l'habitat traditionnel, il est arrivé assez fréquemment que leur vue provoque une crise de possession chez certaines visiteuses.

Depuis bientôt trois ans, ces vêtements de génies ont été retirés des cases, pour des raisons variées (risques de vol, problèmes d'infiltration lors de la saison des pluies). Ils n'ont cependant pas rejoint les autres tenues traditionnelles dans la réserve du musée, mais ont été placés dans une ancienne réserve qui sert de magasin pour certains produits d'entretien. Ils sont désormais pliés dans une armoire métallique et n'ont pas figuré dans le défilé du 1er mai. Selon Zakou, technicien au niveau du service des collections et qui travaille au musée depuis 1972 : « les tenues traditionnelles, on ne peut pas les sortir pour défiler, c'est délicat. Les gens qui les portent seront mal à l'aise. Par contre, on peut les exposer, mais il n'y a pas de mannequins à disposition » (3 mai 2007). Il n'y a cependant pas de différence visible entre les tenues traditionnelles dont parle Zakou, qui se trouvent dans la petite réserve et ne peuvent pas sortir pour défiler, et celles de la grande réserve qui ont été portées lors du défilé du 1er mai. Cependant, contrairement aux secondes, les premières sont réputées avoir servi, du moins pour la plupart, dans le cadre des cultes de possession. C'est donc la « biographie » (Appadurai 1986 ; Bonnot 2002 ; Grognet 2005) des tenues traditionnelles qui justifie une différence de traitement. Leur séparation technique (grande réserve/petite réserve) est donc aussi une séparation mnémotechnique (tenues traditionnelles/vêtements de génies). Elle met en jeu à la fois la relation à l'objet et sa mise en espace.

L'histoire du Musée national apparaît ainsi comme l'histoire d'une rencontre entre la mise en scène de la Nation (Gaugue 1997) et la patrimonialisation des génies. Cette rencontre n'est cependant plus à l'ordre du jour : les vêtements de génies ne sont plus exposés. En réserve cependant, la distinction entre tenues traditionnelles et vêtements de génies continue d'être entretenue. Comme dans le cadre des cultes de possession, une place à part (un lieu sûr ?) leur est, au sens littéral, *réservée*. Mais, contrairement aux vêtements de génies du *bori* et du *holley* ou aux tenues traditionnelles de la grande réserve, ils ne peuvent pas sortir pour être portés. Tout se passe comme si le musée ne pouvait ou ne voulait pas prendre le risque d'une fusion entre objet muséal et objet rituel, le risque d'une « confusion visuelle » susceptible de convoquer, de nouveau, les génies. Tout se passe comme si, en définitive, la conservation de vêtements de génies au Musée national du Niger reposait désormais à la fois sur l'oubli du génie de l'objet et sur l'occultation de l'esprit du lieu.

Remerciements

Les données présentées dans cette contribution résultent d'un travail de recherche en anthropologie effectué au Musée national du Niger au printemps et à l'automne 2007. Je tiens à remercier vivement le directeur du musée, Kélessi Mahamadou, et son adjoint (et récent successeur), Mamane Ibrahim, ainsi que l'ensemble du personnel, pour avoir permis que mes recherches se déroulent dans les meilleures conditions. L'éclairage historique apporté par Albert Ferral, ancien directeur du musée, a également été largement bénéfique pour ma réflexion. Enfin, je remercie Michèle Cros (ma directrice de thèse), Julien Bonhomme, Carlo Severi et Thomas Fillitz pour les remarques qu'ils ont bien voulu faire sur ce texte.

Références

Appadurai, Arjun (dir.). 1986. *The Social Life of Things. Commodities in Cultural Perspectives*. Cambridge: Cambridge University Press.

Bonnot, Thierry. 2002. *La vie des objets*. Paris: éditions de la Maison des sciences de l'Homme.

Chaibou, Neino. 2001. Le Musée National du Niger: un exemple symbiotique entre la culture et l'environnement. In *Le patrimoine culturel africain*, dir. Caroline Gaultier-Kurhan. Paris: Maisonneuve et Larose 41-66.

Feldman, Jeffrey David. 2006. Contacts Points: Museums and the Lost Body Problem. In *Sensible Objects. Colonialism, Museums and Material Culture*. Elizabeth Edwards, Chris Gosden and Ruth B. Phillips: 245-267. Oxford: Berg.

Gado, Boubé. 2000. Niger. Museums & history. In *Museums & History in West Africa*, ed. Claude Daniel Ardouin et Emmanuel Arinze: 75-77. Washington-Oxford: Smithsonian Institution Press et James Currey.

Gaugue, Anne. 1997. *Les Etats africains et leurs musées. La mise en scène de la Nation*. Paris: l'Harmattan.

Grognet, Fabrice. 2005. Objets de musée, n'avez-vous qu'une vie? *Gradhiva*, 2 (n.s.): 49-63.

Houseman, Michael, et Carlo Severi. 1994. *Naven ou le donner à voir. Essai d'interprétation de l'action rituelle*. Paris: CNRS-éditions de la Maison des Sciences de l'Homme.

Leiris, Michel. 1980. «Ne pas se contenter d'être ce que l'on est...». Préface de Gilbert Rouget *La Musique et la transe*. Paris: Gallimard.

Masquelier, Adeline. 1994. "Lightning, Death and the Aventing Spirit: «Bori» Values in a Muslim World". *Journal of Religion in Africa*, 24, 1: 2-51.

Masquelier, Adeline. 1996. "Mediating Threads: Clothing and the texture of spirit/medium relations in Bori, Niger". *Clothing and Difference: EmbodiedIidenties in Colonial and Post-colonial Africa*, ed. Anne A. Hendrickson: 66-93. Raleigh Durham NC: Duke University Press.

Masquelier, Adeline. 1997. "Vectors of Witchcraft: Objects Transactions and the Materialization of Memory in Niger". *Anthropological Quarterly*, 70, 4: 187-198.

Masquelier, Adeline. 2001. *Prayer has Spoiled Everything: Possession, Power, and Identity in an Islamic Town of Niger*. Raleigh Durham NC: Duke University Press.

Monfouga-Nicolas, Jacqueline. 1972. *Ambivalence et culte de possession. Contribution à l'étude du Bori Hausa*. Paris: Anthropos.

Olivier de Sardan, Jean-Pierre. 1982. *Concepts et conceptions songhay-zarma. Histoire, culture, société*. Paris : Nubia.

Olivier de Sardan, Jean-Pierre. 1986. Des Cultes de possession comme phénomènes syncrétiques. In *Afrique plurielle, Afrique actuelle, Hommage à Georges Balandier*, 233-239. Paris : Karthala.

Rouch, Jean. 1954. *Les Maîtres fous*. 36 min. Les films de la pléiade. 16 mm.

Rouch, Jean. 1965. *Hampi*. 25 min, 16 mm.

Rouch, Jean. 1989. *La religion et la magie Songhay*. Deuxième édition revue et augmentée. Bruxelles : éditions de l'Université de Bruxelles.

Rouch, Jean. 1997. Culte des génies chez les Sonray. In *Les Hommes et les dieux du fleuve. Essai ethnographique sur les populations songhay du moyen Niger. 1941-1983*. Paris : éditions Artcom' : 37-62.

Stoller, Paul. 1989. *Fusion of the Worlds*. Chicago : University of Pennsylvania Press.

Stoller, Paul. 1995. *Embodying Colonial Memories. Spirit possession, Power, and the Hauka in West Africa*. New York and London: Routledge.

Toucet, Pablo. 1963. Le Musée national de la République du Niger, Niamey. *Museum*, 16 (3): 192-196.

Toucet, Pablo. 1972. Le musée de Niamey et son environnement. *Museum*, 24 (4) : 204-207.

Turgeon, Laurier. 2007. « La mémoire de la culture matérielle et la culture matérielle de la mémoire » in *Objets & Mémoires*, dir. Octave Debary et Laurier Turgeon: 16-36. Paris-Québec : Éditions de la Maison des sciences de l'Homme et Les Presses de l'Université Laval.

Vidal, Laurent. 1990. *Rituels de possession dans le Sahel. Exemples peul et zarma du Niger*. Paris : L'Harmattan.

L'esprit du lieu
et le désenchantement du monde

Pierre Lucier
Chaire Fernand-Dumont sur la culture
Institut national de la recherche scientifique
Centre Urbanisation Culture Société
Canada

ABSTRACT

Does the notion of a *spirit of place* hidden within belong to an "enchanted world," which is currently being deconstructed? Is it not the case that essentially "material" sites, objects, lines, shapes, colours and scents produce non-material effects in that they represent and project a meaning that is still relevant? Some sites seem to be less "inspiring" because they are "inhabited" and because they "represent" something else here and now. Following the Oracle at Delphi mentioned by Heraclitus (fragment 93), a site "neither speaks nor conceals, but indicates." Beyond all mystical, romantic or voluntarist approaches, deciphering signs and the power of their meaning might well constitute the key to effectively locating, preserving and passing on *spirit of place*. Because in the long term, we only retain what is truly significant.

RÉSUMÉ

L'idée d'un *esprit du lieu* qui se cacherait quelque part appartiendrait-elle à un « monde enchanté » en voie de déconstruction ? N'y a-t-il pas, en effet, que des lieux, des objets, des lignes, des formes, des couleurs, des parfums, « matériels » pour l'essentiel, qui produisent leur effet « immatériel » en cela même qu'ils signifient et qu'ils projettent un sens toujours opérant ? Il y a des lieux qui « inspirent », moins parce qu'ils seraient « habités » que parce qu'ils « veulent dire » quelque chose ici et maintenant. À l'instar de l'oracle de Delphes qu'évoque Héraclite (fragment 93), un lieu « ne dit pas, ne cache pas, mais signifie ». Par-delà toutes les approches de type magique, romantique ou volontariste, le déchiffrement des signes et de leur pouvoir de signification pourrait bien dès lors constituer la clef des stratégies efficaces de repérage, de conservation et de transmission de l'*esprit du lieu*. À long terme, on ne tient vraiment qu'à ce qui est signifiant.

Devant une assemblée qui entend réfléchir systématiquement à l'*esprit du lieu*, il convient évidemment d'identifier d'entrée de jeu le lieu d'où l'on s'adresse à elle. Disons-le d'emblée, ce n'est pas ici celui de ce qu'on pourrait appeler un spécialiste du patrimoine ou des lieux de mémoire. C'est plutôt celui d'un philosophe de la culture et d'un historien des idées, essentiellement préoccupé par le déchiffrement des signes dans lesquels se dit l'expérience humaine à travers les âges, les lieux et les cultures.

Le présent propos porte sur la question thème de ce symposium scientifique de Québec : où se cache l'*esprit du lieu* ? Dans une première partie, seront rappelés quelques traits majeurs du concept *d'esprit du* lieu et des conditions particulières de son émergence. La deuxième partie s'emploiera à expliciter certaines ambivalences qui entourent ce concept dans le contexte – d'abord occidental, il est vrai – de sociétés qui tiennent à proclamer leur rationalité et leur « sortie de la religion ». En troisième lieu, si l'on peut dire ici, et en guise de contribution à la construction de la réflexion commune, on entend suggérer comment une approche centrée sur le pouvoir des signes, leur déchiffrement et leur réappropriation, pourrait permettre d'œuvrer au service de l'*esprit du lieu* sans devoir réendosser des perspectives que nous ne voudrions ou ne pourrions plus promouvoir.

Un concept né dans un monde « enchanté »

L'histoire du concept romain de « génie du lieu », qui est l'ancêtre de celui d'*esprit du lieu*, est tout à fait passionnante (Murray 1989 ; Nitzsche 1975 ; Zilsel 1993). Elle montre à l'évidence qu'il s'agit d'un concept que nous qualifierions volontiers d'« animiste », voire de « magique ». La pensée antique était convaincue que les lieux sont habités par des êtres mystérieux, insaisissables mais individualisés, chargés de veiller sur eux, voire de les défendre ou d'en éloigner les intrus hostiles et les profanateurs, parfois même d'autres « génies » aux intentions malveillantes. On a progressivement humanisé ce « génie » et considéré les gens talentueux comme porteurs d'un génie, voire comme des génies eux-mêmes. Mais il y a toujours, en arrière-plan, un monde « habité » par des forces vivantes qui, d'une manière ou d'une autre, interviennent dans le cours des événements et de l'existence des humains, et d'abord de ceux qui fréquentent leurs lieux. Des sites émergent ainsi comme plus forts, plus « habités », plus « inspirés » et « inspirants ».

Sans justifier nécessairement l'appellation de « religieuse », cette trame de fond évolue d'emblée dans un monde où toutes les forces et toutes les présences ne sont pas de l'ordre du visible et du mesurable. Les humains doivent y traiter avec les « génies » des lieux, dans des échanges dont il est d'ailleurs possible de ne pas sortir indemne, comme Jacob après sa lutte nocturne avec l'Ange. Il faut négocier avec eux, leur offrir des présents, parfois des sacrifices coûteux, les honorer – en tout cas, respecter leur demeure, leur silence ou leur musique. S'instaure ainsi un réseau complexe de relations avec ceux qui habitent, invisiblement mais efficacement, les lieux naturels et les lieux érigés par les humains. La littérature ancienne foisonne de cette reconnaissance d'un monde qui ne se réduit pas à ce qui est visible et cernable. C'est largement en référence à cette vision des choses que l'on a parlé d'un monde « enchanté », « magifié » en quelque sorte, dans lequel les humains sont en interaction avec les esprits et les dieux et essaient de composer avec ce qui pourrait compromettre leur « salut », c'est-à-dire l'heureuse issue, ici et maintenant, de l'aventure humaine.

Il s'agit là d'un faisceau sémantique extrêmement complexe, qu'il n'est pas question de réduire ou de reléguer au pays des merveilles d'Alice ou au génie sortant de la lampe d'Aladin. Il faut plutôt en percevoir la prégnance pour la compréhension de la dynamique qui, dans la fréquentation des lieux naturels ou humains, relie la matérialité à quelque chose que l'on veut bien qualifier d'« immatériel », c'est-à-dire qui ne se limite pas à l'immédiatement perçu et mesurable. C'est un peu cela, « l'esprit » : une présence qui inspire et aspire, à la manière d'un souffle dont de grandes traditions religieuses ont reconnu l'importance primordiale pour le pouvoir créateur lui-même : « l'esprit de Dieu planait sur les eaux », raconte le premier verset de la Genèse. Comme si l'*esprit* précédait l'émergence du *lieu* lui-même, comme si l'*esprit* construisait son *lieu*.

Point n'est besoin de céder ici au lyrisme pour apprécier la richesse sémantique et anthropologique du concept d'*esprit du lieu*. Ce qu'il faut voir, cependant, c'est que ces perspectives, qui exercent toujours un certain pouvoir de séduction, appartiennent tout de même à des visions du monde de type sacral, animiste selon les uns, religieux selon d'autres, magique selon d'autres encore. Selon les visions de ce type, les lieux sont, à des degrés divers, habités par des êtres invisibles qui ont réalité substantielle et capacité d'agir et d'imposer les règles et le décorum de leur fréquentation, voire leurs rituels d'échange. On ne durcira pas indûment les choses au point de devenir nous-mêmes plus « naïfs » que les Anciens, mais nous ne devons pas occulter ces liens du concept d'*esprit du lieu* avec un monde essentiellement « enchanté ».

Un monde en voie de « désenchantement »

Qu'en est-il de ce monde enchanté dans des sociétés dont plusieurs annoncent haut et fort qu'elles s'en sont affranchies à jamais ? La réponse à cette question est plus complexe qu'il n'y paraît. C'est que, à sa face même et jusque dans « l'épistémè » dont elles s'abreuvent, les civilisations dominantes ont bel et bien rompu avec le monde sacral (Gauchet 1985, 1998). Il le fallait, d'ailleurs, dans la mesure où la connaissance scientifique et la percée technologique, sinon l'organisation sociale elle-même, n'auraient pas été possibles sans une entrée résolue dans la rationalité, celle-là même dont l'histoire a montré qu'elle s'est formée en émergeant progressivement de la domination d'un « arrière-monde ». Max Weber a finement décrit cette sortie du monde magique comme un « désenchantement », un *Entzauberung* au sens premier d'une sortie de la magie et du sortilège (Weber 1964, 1995, 1996).

En s'imposant comme univers de perception et d'action, le *Logos* a permis le développement d'un mode d'intervention sur la réalité auquel s'identifie l'idée actuelle de développement. Des sociétés sont ainsi considérées comme développées ou en voie de développement selon qu'elles ont plus ou moins réalisé leur « désenchantement », quitte à laisser l'enchantement au vestiaire du folklore et de la vie privée, et selon qu'elles seraient entrées dans la rationalité. Le cadre de fonctionnement dominant, celui de la science, de la technologie, de l'ingénierie sociale, est un cadre de rationalité à cent lieues de toutes les références magiques ou sacrales. Nous évoluons dans un monde réticent à se soucier de quelque génie pouvant habiter les lieux naturels ou humains, voire ces « non-lieux » (Augé 1992) que nos quêtes de sens nous amènent à découper dans nos espaces. Mais cela ne signifie pas que les individus et les sociétés elles-mêmes aient délaissé toute expérience poétique. Il y aurait même bien des motifs d'estimer que, par d'autres voies et sous d'autres figures, surgissent des mouvements de « ré-enchantement » (Berger 2001), comme si le sacré se déplaçait en d'autres lieux et en d'autres expériences, à l'extérieur du temple ou des expériences religieuses dûment brevetées (Bailey 2006). Nos sociétés seraient ainsi traversées par un accueil inédit de l'irrationnel. Protestation contre l'envahissement d'une rationalité dont on verrait bien qu'elle n'est ni neutre ni froidement logique, mais imprégnée de valeurs et d'intentions, à commencer par celle de vouloir dominer ? Besoin irrépressible inhérent à la condition humaine, sans cesse en quête de références significatives ? Penchant fâcheux de parieurs impénitents suspendus à toutes les loteries de salut ?

L'analyse même élémentaire nous oblige ici à d'infinies nuances, comme toujours lorsqu'on s'intéresse à ce qui ne se mesure ni ne se compte tout bêtement. Retenons-en à tout le moins deux enseignements, contradictoires en apparence seulement. D'une part, reconnaissons que, dans les cultures dominantes et dans ce qu'on pourrait appeler la culture internationale – ce qui inclut celle de l'Unesco, par exemple –, il n'est guère possible de pratiquer des approches magiques ou religieuses de l'*esprit du lieu*. Certains s'étonnent d'ailleurs de nos engouements pour un concept et un univers épistémique qui ne résistent manifestement pas au mouvement tectonique de « désenchantement » du monde. Par ailleurs, et c'est le second enseignement dont il faut prendre acte, il doit bien y avoir moyen de donner droit de cité aux visées qui sous-tendent le discours sur l'*esprit du lieu* et selon laquelle des lieux peuvent renvoyer à autre chose qu'à leur seule matérialité. En tout cas, on peut penser que, même dans un monde désenchanté, des voies sont possibles pour déchiffrer ce potentiel symbolique énorme. À travers sa vision résolument intégratrice, la *Déclaration de Québec* traduit sûrement une volonté de surmonter ce clivage entre deux visions du monde et deux ordres du pensable radicalement différents. Elle invite aussi à explorer par quelles voies on peut penser et pratiquer une promotion de la réalité de l'*esprit du lieu* qui ne nous ramène pas à la pensée magique. C'est dans ces voies que la troisième partie de cet exposé propose de s'engager.

L'esprit du lieu et le pouvoir des signes

Nous avons besoin d'approches de la conception, de l'interprétation et de la transmission de l'*esprit du lieu* qui nous renvoient, bien sûr, aux humains qui «donnent» un sens aux lieux et qui peuvent donc en changer. Mais ces approches doivent reconnaître d'emblée qu'un lieu «impose» aussi son sens et qu'il n'est ni possible ni légitime de lui faire signifier n'importe quoi – «tous esprits confondus», pourrait-on dire. En d'autres mots, les configurations et les arrangements d'éléments matériels – les seuls qui soient vraiment observables et mesurables, d'ailleurs – commandent des lignes de signification qui ne peuvent pas être laissées au seul bon plaisir du prochain occupant et qui ne tiennent pas davantage dans la seule émotion que peut en tirer un observateur ou un pèlerin. Et ce n'est pas le contenu d'une affiche explicative ou d'un audio-guide qui peut créer l'*esprit du lieu*, pas davantage une politique volontariste de conservation, encore moins quelque intuition aléatoire de qui y passe.

Il doit bien y avoir, dans les éléments matériels d'un lieu, dans leur forme, leur disposition et leur environnement, «quelque chose» qui parle et impose respect par ce qu'il est en lui-même et en cela même qu'il projette une signification. Les penseurs médiévaux enseignaient couramment que le mode de causalité des symboles rituels réside dans leur pouvoir de signification : *significando causant*, ils causent en signifiant, c'est-à-dire en cela même qu'ils signifient.

Telle est bien la dynamique de l'ensemble du monde des symboles. À la base, il y a toujours une réalité observable, palpable, qui a son sens en elle-même et qui, ancrée dans cette signification première, est susceptible de déployer d'autres couches concentriques de signification. Par exemple, si l'eau n'avait pas, d'elle-même, le pouvoir de faire surgir et de donner la vie, de désaltérer, de rafraîchir, de détruire aussi, il n'y aurait aucun sens à en faire un symbole de renaissance spirituelle, de salut ou un instrument de déluge. Si le feu n'avait pas, de lui-même, le pouvoir de réchauffer, d'embraser, de fondre, de cautériser, de «marquer», il n'y aurait aucun sens à en faire un symbole de réconfort, d'énergie, de passion dévorante, de purification, de conflagration, de destruction ou de quelque Pentecôte. Et on ne pourrait pas faire du pèlerinage un cheminement intérieur et une reprise de contact avec les sources du moi et du monde, s'il n'était pas, par nature, une marche sur des routes réelles, un contact physique avec la terre et les pierres d'un pays, une victoire sur un espace-temps.

L'*esprit du lieu*, n'est-ce pas le pouvoir de signification de ce lieu, l'ensemble des couches de sens que ses éléments matériels et leur configuration particulière projettent et offrent au déchiffrage de celles et ceux qui y viennent ? Ces couches de sens interpellent notre capacité de saisir et de comprendre, c'est-à-dire notre capacité de saisir les significations à travers les éléments mesurables et explicables. «Comprendre» est une activité cognitive qui dépasse la seule émotion romantique de communion ou la seule empathie de type fusionnel. C'est une opération de décodage. C'est ainsi que, même après l'oubli des rites ou des faits entourant l'histoire d'un site, le pouvoir de signification de ce site peut demeurer puissamment opérant. Pourquoi ? Parce qu'il a toujours en lui-même les ingrédients de son pouvoir de suggestion et de rêverie qui ont déjà pu le faire considérer comme un lieu habité par un esprit, un lieu enchanté, voire sacré. Homme du Nord et du froid, je peux ainsi percevoir quelque chose de l'*esprit du lieu* de cette oasis du grand désert de sable ou de cette vallée de la forêt tropicale. Homme de la mer, je peux saisir quelque chose de l'*esprit* de ces lieux de montagnes du Toit du monde. Homme de la postmodernité, je peux comprendre quelque chose d'un temple maya, d'un masque africain, d'un grenier du sud marocain, d'un temple shintoïste ou d'un cirque romain.

Il y a bien telle chose que l'inscription du sens dans les éléments matériels eux-mêmes. Telle chose aussi qu'un sens qui n'en finit plus d'émerger et de se déployer en cercles concentriques. Certains de ces cercles sont plus accessibles à certaines personnes qu'à d'autres, ou opèrent à certains moments, en certaines circonstances ou à certains âges plutôt qu'à d'autres. Mais jamais on ne peut «faire» du sens à partir de ce qui n'en porterait pas. On peut améliorer et affiner ses capacités de voir, d'entendre ou de lire, mais cela ne crée pas les chefs-d'œuvre, cela ne donne pas un *esprit* à un lieu qui n'aurait pas en lui-même la capacité d'en faire habiter. Nos capacités de saisie et de récollection du sens ne peuvent jamais suppléer à la pauvreté et à la minceur d'un signe. C'est sans doute pour cela qu'il arrive que des sites et des œuvres périssent, et sans qu'on puisse toujours accuser les humains d'avoir été des vandales sans scrupules. Dans la culture aussi, il y a des mécanismes liés à la survie du plus apte. Heureusement, d'ailleurs, sinon nous serions condamnés à tout conserver en l'état et nous perdrions jusqu'à la possibilité de repérer les vrais immortels.

Nos stratégies de repérage, de conservation et de transmission du patrimoine matériel et immatériel ne peuvent pas faire l'économie d'approches ainsi axées sur la signification des lieux et des sites eux-mêmes. Nous avons dès lors besoin d'outils de déchiffrement des signes pour déployer la signification culturelle des lieux et des sites, pour décoder et nous approprier cela même que l'*esprit du lieu* semble avoir voulu exprimer dans des épistémès en voie de disparition dans plusieurs de nos sociétés, mais qui n'a pas perdu pour autant tout pouvoir de signification et toute capacité de s'offrir à de nouvelles traductions.

Traduction, disons-nous. Traduction des signes et donc tradition du sens. C'est bien là que conduit inévitablement l'attention à *l'esprit du* lieu. Tradition : « to trade », c'est-à-dire livrer, échanger – Hermès, à la fois dieu des échanges et du commerce et messager du sens, n'est-ce pas ? Redire, interpréter – interpréter, au double sens du mot, l'interprète désignant autant le traducteur que l'artiste qui joue Sophocle ou Mozart. Réactualiser, dire en d'autres signes, dans un geste qui est à la fois déchiffrage et recréation, décodage et recodage. C'est qu'il n'y a pas de moment où le sens subsisterait ou flotterait entre deux signes. Il y a plutôt et seulement cette fissure insaisissable, cette « rupture instauratrice » que Michel de Certeau suggérait d'appeler « l'inter-dit » (Certeau 1971), ce moment où, dans la confiance ou dans la foi, un sens se transmet à même la mise en place d'autres signes et où un lieu est recréé en une sorte de « non-lieu ». Entre l'épistémè d'un monde sacral, voire magique, et celle de la rationalité qui est largement la nôtre, un pont peut ainsi être jeté, par-delà l'inter-dit, là où campe et opère *l'esprit du lieu*. Notre volonté de repérer, de conserver et de transmettre *l'esprit du lieu* découpe d'elle-même, on le voit, des tâches de lecture et d'interprétation qui – oui, toujours Hermès – nous plongent dans le cercle herméneutique, là où un sens émerge à condition qu'on l'accueille, là où un sens est reçu à condition qu'on le donne ou le redonne.

Il ne se cache donc pas, *l'esprit du lieu*. Il ne cache pas non plus. Il signifie plutôt, selon ce qu'évoquait Héraclite, ce grand maître de la pensée antique, à la fois si près du monde de l'enchantement et si attaché à la rationalité du *Logos*. Dans un texte qui a été classé sous l'austère titre de « fragment 93 » (Kirk et Raven 1966), Héraclite dit de l'oracle de Delphes qu'il « ne dit pas (οὔτε λέγει), ne cache pas (οὔτε κρύπτει), mais signifie (ἀλλὰ σημαίνει) ». Tel est le pouvoir d'une parole riche et d'un symbole : ne pas dire trivialement, encore moins dissimuler, mais bien signifier, c'est-à-dire offrir un sens au déchiffrement de qui veut et peut l'accueillir. Telle est la puissance d'un sens qui se dit et s'offre à la lecture interprétante et, dès lors, à la transmission. Tel est *l'esprit du lieu*, qui n'est ni à découvert, ni caché, mais qui se projette dans des signes et s'offre ainsi à saisir et à traduire.

« Où se cache *l'esprit du lieu* ? », demandons-nous. En fait, il ne se cache pas. Il est dans les signes, pour autant et aussi longtemps que les signes signifient, pour autant et aussi longtemps qu'il y a quelqu'un – des individus, des communautés – pour le repérer, l'interpréter, le traduire, le conserver et le transmettre. Et, pour cela, point n'est besoin de ressusciter quelque vision animiste du monde. Point n'est besoin d'abuser du sacré.

Ce symposium s'est tenu à Québec. Ce fut là une belle occasion, à travers la façon qu'ont les gens d'ici d'habiter l'espace et d'y faire leur *lieu,* de saisir *l'esprit* qui fonde et nourrit leur volonté quadricentenaire d'y vivre, de le conserver et de le transmettre.

Références

Augé, Marc. 1992. *Non-lieux. Introduction à une anthropologie de la surmo-dernité.* Paris: Seuil.

Bailey, Edward I. 2006. *La religion implicite. Une introduction.* Traduction, présentation et notes de Guy Ménard. Montréal: Liber. (Titre original: Implicite Religion: An Introduction. 1998. Middlesex University Press).

Berger, Peter L. (dir.). 2001. *Le réenchantement du monde.* Paris: Bayard. (Titre original: The Desecularisation of the World. Resurgent Religion and World Politics. 1999. Grand Radpids: William B. Eerdmans Publ. Co.).

De Certeau, Michel. 1971. La rupture instauratrice ou le Christianisme dans la culture contemporaine. *Esprit* (juin): 1177-1214.

Gauchet, Marcel. 1985. *Le désenchantement du monde. Une histoire politique de la religion.* Paris: Gallimard.

Gauchet, Marcel. 1998. *La religion dans la démocratie. Parcours de la laïcité.* Paris: Gallimard.

Kirk, G.S., and J.E. Raven. 1957. *The Presocratic Philosophers. A Critical History with a Selection of texts.* Cambridge University Press.

Murray, Penelope. ed. 1989. *Genius: The History of an Idea.* Oxford: Basil Blackwell.

Nitzsche, Jane Chance. 1972. *The Genius Figure in Antiquity and the Middle Ages.* New York and London: Columbia University Press.

Weber, Max. 1995. *Économie et société (1911-1920),* 2 vol. Paris: Plon, 1995.

Weber, Max. 1964. *L'éthique protestante et l'esprit du capitalisme (1920),* Paris: Plon.

Zilsel, Edgar. 1993. *Le Génie. Histoire d'une notion de l'antiquité à la re-naissance.* Paris: Minuit. (Titre original: Die Entstehung des Ge-niebegriffes. Ein Beitrag zur Ideengeschichte der Antike und des Frühkapitalismus. 1926. Tübingen: J.C.B. Mohr).

Genius Loci
The Spirit of Monuments and Sites

Michael Petzet
President
16th General Assembly of ICOMOS

ABSTRACT

The expression « Spirit of place » is inspired from the Roman tradition. Towns and villages, mountains, valleys and fields, city squares and temples, homes, doors and windows, each private space or public place was inhabited its own *genius loci*, a spirit who protected the site and defined it. Similarly, the idea of a spiritual entity inherent to a place is fundamental to most ancient traditions, cultures or spiritual representations. Today, the *genius loci* is understood as a secularized "spirit" which helps to identify the "places of significance" and warrants the recognition of their authenticity – or rather, their authenticities. It stands as an important guideline in the current practices of conservation, rehabilitation and enhancement of monuments, based on the Nara Document on Authenticity (1994). By its complex nature, however, the *genius loci* raises many problems, particularly if material and immaterial heritage are considered in a antithetical perspective. Various components of the *Zeitgeist* will then oppose one another, as will the successive layers of historical change in places as well as in communities. Each of these bears a witness and claims its right to anamnesis. The idea of the *genius loci* as guarantor of a certain diversity and continuity in a globalized world could perhaps help us better understand and manage heritage in these difficult times dominated by rather profane spirits of radical change.

RÉSUMÉ

C'est de la tradition romaine que vient l'expression « l'esprit du lieu ». Villes, villages, montagnes, vallées, champs, places, temples, résidences,

portes et fenêtres : ces lieux, tant publics que privés, étaient habités chacun par un *genius loci*, génie protecteur et définisseur de l'endroit et de
sa fonction. Loin d'être exclusive au monde gréco-romain, cette notion
d'un génie propre au lieu se retrouve sous diverses formes dans la plupart
des récits anciens et des représentations culturelles voire, spirituelles.
Aujourd'hui, le *genius loci*, désormais laïcisé, sert à définir les « lieux si-
gnifiants » et à en reconnaître l'authenticité – ou plutôt, les authenticités.
Il fait partie intégrante des lignes directrices des pratiques actuelles de
sauvegarde, de conservation et de valorisation des monuments et des
sites, fondées entre autres sur le Document de Nara (1994). Complexe,
le *genius loci* soulève cependant de nombreuses problématiques, particulièrement si le matériel et l'immatériel sont envisagés dans une perspective
dialectique. S'opposent alors non seulement les diverses constituantes
du *Zeitgeist*, mais aussi les superpositions des traces du temps, des usages
et des appartenances, chacune témoignant d'une mémoire et réclamant
l'anamnèse. L'idée d'un *genius loci* garant de diversité et de continuité
dans un monde globalisé pourrait peut-être nous aider dans ces temps
difficiles dominés par l'esprit sacrilège d'un changement radical.

It is an honour for me to address delegates to this symposium *The Spirit
of Place / between the Intangible and Tangible* to evoke the authentic genius loci
connected with the work of ICOMOS since its foundation more than four
decades ago. For of course, behind the theme of the 16th General Assembly –
Spirit of Place / Esprit du Lieu – is nothing less than a literal translation from
the Latin of the time-honoured *genius loci*, which sometimes resists rational
explanations, but nonetheless has to be taken seriously as a spirit inherent in all
monuments and sites. This is the reason behind the somewhat old-fashioned
title of my speech *genius loci – the Spirit of Monuments and Sites*, – even if, in
the call for papers for this conference, neither this kind of guardian angel of
the conservationists is mentioned nor the word "monument," a term some
colleagues seem to shun as the devil flees holy water. However, during my
attempts to better grasp the *genius loci* connected with millions of monuments
and sites ("où se cache l'esprit du lieu?"), I discovered that this is still – or
once again – a phenomenon of topical interest. Even the Internet offers us,
apart from a link to a music band by the name of *genius loci*, an abundance
of serious and not-so-serious literature, including popular esotericism.

Originally, our *genius loci* was a Roman invention. As is well known, in
Roman antiquity it was not only man that had his genius, a sort of guardian
angel that accompanied him through life and determined his fate, but also
certain places, be it the location of a temple or an entire city, had their *genius
loci*. In the Forum Romanum stood a statue of the genius of the Roman
people and in connection with the imperial cult Augustus gave orders that
in the chapels of the districts of Rome his own genius be placed between
the LARES (other protecting spirits, which I won't deal with further). Aside

from the popular genii related to a certain person (the word is derived from gignere, which means to engender or man's power to engender) there were also countless genies related to a place. According to our understanding as conservationists and especially in their function as guardian spirits, these are of particular importance, together with the LARES who were also to be found on the family altar. Aurelius Prudentius writes in late antiquity: "You also tend to give genii to the gates, to the houses, the thermae, the stables, and one has to assume that there are many thousands of genii for each place and all parts of a town so that no angle has to be without its own spirit." Not only villages, towns and communities had their *genius loci* (*genius vici, oppidi, municipi, genius urbis Romae,* etc.); also the places of natural landscape were attributed to a genius, that is, the genius of the valley, the spring, the river, the mountain (*genius valli, fontis, fluminis, montis*) or of a certain part of a mountain (*genius huius loci montis*). The genius was represented as a sacrificing man or personified as a snake, – in Roman houses also living snakes were kept, and their death was considered a bad omen.

The Greek *daimon*, which to some extent is also related to the *genius loci*, was also depicted as a snake. Some of its attributes could be transferred to the Roman genius. Without wanting to go any further into the relationship between the Roman *genius loci* and the *daimones,* more closely linked to the underworld, or into the later connection between the genii and the Christian guardian angels shown as winged beings, I would only like to emphasise that in many regions of the world and in different periods, there have been ideas comparable to these genii. This starts with animistic or totemistic phenomena – for example, in connection with the mythical place of origin of a clan or the holy places of the ghost-ancestors of the Aborigines; sites marked by totem poles in our host country, Canada; or places in Iceland inhabited by elves and trolls, which sometimes obstruct road constructions. Under these circumstances it is not surprising that even in our globalised world the term *genius loci*, normally only used metaphorically, plays a not so unimportant role, namely in the various scientific fields: in the study of religions, geography and in a kind of eco-psychology in combination with the auratic experience of certain ecological and also aesthetic and synaesthetic qualities of certain places. It also plays a role in modern architectural theory with regard to investigating the possibilities of landscape design and the influence of the individual landscape on architecture ("architecture compatible with landscape"), or of architecture on landscape (see the publication by the Norwegian architectural historian Christian Norberg-Schulz, *Genius Loci. Towards a Phenomenology of Architecture*, New York 1980). And finally, after our symposium in Quebec, might there perhaps also be an increasing influence on theory and practice in conservation?

Even in the metaphorical sense, the term *genius loci* is used today, namely as a secularised "spirit" responsible for so-called "places of significance." It can help not only for future challenges, but also for the occasionally necessary return to the key tasks of ICOMOS, "the international organisation concerned with furthering the conservation, protection, rehabilitation and enhancement of monuments, groups of buildings (ensembles) and sites on the international level" (ICOMOS Statutes, art. 4). If in our principles and guidelines little was said about spirit of place, this has to do with the fact that the message of the *genius loci* has always been a phenomenon accepted as a matter of course. Already in the preamble of the foundation paper of ICOMOS, the Venice Charter, this message finds expression: "*Chargées d'un message spirituel du passée, les oeuvres monumentales des peuples demeurent dans la vie présente le témoignage vivant de leurs traditions séculaires.*" ("Imbued with a [spiritual] message from the past, the historic monuments of generations of people remain to the present day as living witnesses of their age-old traditions"). As is well known, behind these words is a very broad concept of monuments: monuments as an archive of authentic sources for cultural history, social history, industrial history, etc. are evidence created by man that, according to the definition in a late classical commentary on Cicero, "should evoke remembrance of something" (*omnia monumenta sunt, quae faciunt alicuius rei recordationem*). The material from which the monument as an object of remembrance is made can thus be just as variable as the degree of "materialization" of the spiritual message that the monument represents – from the traces of a prehistoric settlement, detectable now only in the dark-colored negative form of potholes, to the immense stone blocks of an "immortal" pyramid created, as it were, for eternity. As an idea that took on shape, the monument is, in any case, more than an "object" consisting of a certain material. There are even monuments whose materials are so ephemeral that they are in need of renewal again and again; indeed even the mere replica of a monument that no longer exists materially could still "evoke remembrance of something."

Our most important guideline for the topic of genius loci/spirit of place is certainly not the so-called Yamato Declaration of 2004, as one would perhaps assume from the subheading of our symposium: "Between the Intangible and the Tangible." Instead, it is the, in many respects, fundamental Nara Document on Authenticity of 1994, which contains statements on authentic spirit and authentic location. Here for the first time spirit and place are explicitly included in the reform of the old test of authenticity. Particularly important is article 13: « *Dépendant de la nature du monument ou du site et de son contexte culturel, le jugement sur l'authenticité est lié à une variété de sources d'information. Les dernières comprennent conception et forme, matériaux et substance, usage et fonction, tradition et techniques, situation et emplacement, esprit et expression, état original et devenir historique. Les sources sont internes à l'œuvre ou elles lui sont externes...* » (*"Depending on the nature of the cultural heritage, its cultural context and its evolution through time authenticity judgments may be linked to the worth of a great variety of sources of information. Aspects of these sources may include form and design, materials and substance, use and function, traditions and techniques, location and setting, and spirit and feeling, and other internal and external factors."*) An example which could illustrate the various authenticities of the Nara Document is one of the first references to the term "monument" in the Bible: Jacob's dream is also a wonderful example for the birth of a *genius loci* connecting heaven and earth. After his dream of the ladder to heaven, Jacob marks the place where the vision occurred with an enduring sign made of stone: "*Then Jacob rose early in the morning, and took the stone that he had put at his head, set it up as a pillar and poured oil on top of it. And he called the name of that place Bethel*" (Genesis 28:10 ff.). The authentic place here is "locus sacer," a holy place that refers to something supra-human. Jacob's stone, the authentic material, obtained from Jacob an intentional authentic form to differentiate it from other ordinary stones in that it was erected with the help of a particular (in this case rather simple, but anyway authentic) technique in order to make clear its authentic function. The function of this monument was for the stone to be a reminder of his dream, an authentic "matière à mémoire," by miracle later identified with the "Stone of Destiny" in Westminster Abbey, which subsequently has been returned to Edinburgh. In connection with the word "monument" the Bible also mentions individual burial places, burial tombs being a wide field closely linked to local spirits, from the Roman tombs in the Via Appia to the cemeteries of the 19th and 20th centuries, where the ghosts of the dead and their genii also appear in person in countless statues.

Different examples of spiritual places could be taken from all over the world and from very different cultures, including "intended monuments" in the sense of the intentional creation of a monument from the very beginning, but above all a wealth of objects whose monument quality as an "object of remembrance" has first evolved over the course of centuries. With these monuments there would also be distinctions to be made between various authentic historical layers from the original up to the present state. Consider, for instance, a historic town that has evolved over centuries as a testimony to history, or an old house in this town, whose spiritual message encompasses not only its architectural history but also the history and the traces of many generations who have lived there. A perfect example for the spirit of place in connection with monuments and sites would, of course, be houses connected with the genius of certain people. Here only two examples from Europe: in Goethe's house in Weimar, the rooms are still as he had them arranged, including the large plaster head of Juno Ludovisi that had been transported from Italy to Weimar, the books that he collected and used, etc. – reminders of a great poet whose genius seems present in the objects he left behind, tangible traces of his life concentrated here into an "aura" marked by his unique personality. The same is true, by the way, of the Goethe House in Frankfurt, destroyed in the war, rebuilt in situ over the old foundations and exhibiting the old inventory. Some of my colleagues, still obsessed with a blind fetishism for historic fabric, maintain that the house never should have been rebuilt – although in the meantime thousands of school children and other visitors have been able to experience the *genius loci* that survived there despite war and destruction.

In any case, for a differentiated evaluation of the chances and possibilities of a strong *genius loci*, indicated here so far with these few examples, the Nara Document on Authenticity and our traditional monument values are a sound basis. For instance, the historic, aesthetic and scientific values in the World Heritage Convention of 1972 (values that occasionally have dropped from view during attempts to define "OUV"). There is also the still useful system of commemorative and present-day values developed a century ago in Alois Riegl's *Modern Cult of Monuments* (1903) going far beyond the question of material/immaterial or tangible/intangible. But does the subheading of our symposium imply that we really want to launch once again into the debate "between the intangible and the tangible" that was already successfully held at our General Assembly in Victoria Falls? A decade after the Nara Paper on Authenticity came the *Yamato Declaration on Integrated Approaches for Safeguarding Tangible and Intangible Heritage* (2004), drawn up at another conference in Nara. This declaration tries to interpret the new *UNESCO Convention for the Safeguarding of the Intangible Cultural Heritage* (2003), but in fact leads to misunderstandings, because in this paper focusing on "folk art," traditional culture and folklore, different areas overlap. The urgent concerns of the Convention of 2003, such as the conservation of languages threatened with extinction or the protection of traditional craftsmanship, particularly important for our work as conservationists and disappearing fast worldwide, are included in an "integrated approach" and, to a certain degree, also comprise the wide field of conservation. However, not everything belongs to this – our – field of "heritage;" instead, according to the definition of the Convention of 1972 "heritage" is clearly defined as "monuments, ensembles (groups of buildings) and sites," including the "work of man and nature (cultural landscapes)." And in this field tangible and intangible values are not separate; they are rather – according to a very helpful definition by Mounir Bouchenaki – "two sides of one coin." Quite likely, thanks to the appropriate *genius loci*, they are a natural unity. This field of heritage immediately affecting ICOMOS is in many respects also integrated in the objectives of the Convention of 2002 that understand heritage as a general source of cultural identity, creativity and diversity. This comprises "customs and oral traditions, music, languages, poetry, dance, festivities, religious ceremonies as well as systems of healing, traditional knowledge systems and skills connected with the material aspects of culture, such as tools and the habitat." All these elements, music and dance, and especially the mastering and passing on of handicraft skills were already presented at the International Colloquium organised by Suzanna Sampaio and our South American colleagues in Salvador de Bahia back in 2002. Nonetheless, despite our enthusiasm for music and folklore, for storytellers and snake charmers in the Jemaa-el-Fnâ market square in Marrakech, we are aware that in accordance with the Yamato Declaration, there are "countless examples of intangible cultural heritage that do not depend for their existence or expression on specific places or objects" We would, however not agree with the following phrase "that the values associated with monuments and sites are not considered intangible cultural heritage ... when they belong to the past and not to the living heritage of present-day communities" (Yamato Declaration, art. 10). Such unclear phrases have unfortunately led to a situation where "living" intangible heritage is being played off against "dead" tangible heritage – a real insult to the very much alive *genius loci* of our monuments and sites. In addition, the distinction occasionally made between a "more tangible monumental heritage" as in Europe and a "more intangible" and therefore "non-monumental" heritage, for instance in Africa, is absurd and comes from a misconceived understanding of what a monument is. Incidentally, we should stop acting as if, in the 21st century, we have finally discovered the "intangible" side of our work. After all, the spiritual and immaterial sides of the phenomena we as conservationists have been dealing with for decades have always been a self-evident axiom. Without going into the wide philosophical field of phenomenology, which of course also includes the phenomenon of *genius loci*, I would like to point out, however, in anticipation of the usual tangible/intangible debates that the classification of the world into "tangible" and "intangible" phenomena should, in accordance with our Nara Document of 1994, be replaced by much more differentiated reflections. The sometimes rather banal differentiation between tangible as "capable of being touched" and intangible as "something that cannot be touched or grasped" – I am quoting from my Oxford Dictionary – is simply not enough.

In the following, I will therefore try to look into certain phenomena of the spirit of place (*genius loci*) from the viewpoint of conservation theory and practice, hopefully without falling into the gap of our subheading *"between the Intangible and the Tangible."* For that reason, I would here like to refer, or better, defer to all the dialectic processes of so-called "objectivation" developed since the early works of Roland Barthes. Under these circumstances, I'm afraid I can hardly follow the main thread of our call for papers concerning the general topic "Spirit of Place" if it simply equates "spirit" with "intangible" and "place" with "tangible" ("we suggest examining the relationship between spirit and place, between the intangible and the tangible..." etc.). For apart from the fact that place can also be an ideal or unreal, at any rate an intangible place – for example, Parsifal's awe-inspiring, "unapproachable" Castle of the Holy Grail – for the time being, I would like to equate place with what is called *locus* in Latin or *topos* in Greek; a certain place in the sense of location or emplacement, if you like, even definable by the corresponding GPS number. Such a place may be characterised by traces of human activity and by "objects of remembrance" in accordance with the Roman monument definition quoted earlier; it is a built-up place, possibly changed time and again in the course of the centuries. And not without reservation, particularly as far as our *genius loci* is concerned, I would like to connect such a place, to which, of course, a certain environment and "setting" belong, with the definition of "place" in article 1 of the Burra Charter: *"site, area, land, landscape, building or other work, contexts, spaces and views"* etc. This Australian definition may not be wrong, but nonetheless it is very general. It refers to anything and everything, and in our context I wish to regard place – in the sense of the Nara Document – as an authentic location and setting of authentic monuments and sites.

But before we talk about monuments and sites, let us think of nature untouched by man, where according to Roman perception, rivers and mountains, trees and forests, caves and grottoes had their *genius loci*; a friendly, sometimes also dangerous *numen* (divine being), which obviously had to do with the aura and the atmosphere (not only in the meteorological sense) of a place. Naturally, to this also belong the breathtaking "wonders of nature," whose special *genius loci* have again and again been discovered and rediscovered by man and which, due to their specific form (nature as "architect"), have evoked comparable sensations and associations. Part of this context is, for example, holy trees and holy mountains and much that was already characterised as "monument of nature" in the conservation theory of around 1900, after the famous explorer Alexander von Humboldt had already coined the term "monument of nature" around 1800. But for the time being, I shall refrain from going any further into this topic, which has only been given serious consideration once again since our conference in Manaus organised in connection with the International Day for Monuments and Sites 2007: "Cultural Landscapes and Monuments of Nature." I would only like to mention that the individual "atmosphere" can also play an important role for built-up places and monuments and sites in the creation of a corresponding *genius loci*. An action by Marcel Duchamps, one of the most important artists of the 20th century, may be interpreted accordingly: in 1919, he brought his collector Arensberg in New York the Paris atmosphere in a small apothecary's phial – Duchamps' ready-made "Air de Paris" transfers the *genius loci* of a metropolis in a slightly ironic form. Besides, for obvious reasons the *genius loci* will on principle refuse to be transferred. Although transferral is a practice also occasionally applied in conservation, at best it can only be justified by special circumstances, for example, the imminent inundation of monuments in the area of a dam. Otherwise it contradicts our principle of preserving buildings and objects "in situ."

Among the strongest appearances of the *genius loci* is its obvious presence at holy places. These exist also in the open country, where celestial beings, for instance, in connection with holy mountains or holy trees, have enough space to reveal themselves. In any case, the term of the "atmosphere" noticeable only "in situ," at the authentic location, is by all means useful for the characterisation of a *genius loci*. It can also be easily combined with the term "aura" defined by Walter Benjamin in his essay *The Work of Art in the Age of Mechanical Reproduction* (1936). This aura linked to a place and embedded in history does not only characterise works of art but also monuments and sites, even when the monument is hardly comprehensible as "historic fabric" or is already badly damaged. For example, the empty niches of the Bamiyan Buddhas as *locus sacer* possess – despite their destruction – the aura of an incredibly strong *genius loci*. This may also apply to many *genius loci* of archaeological sites which may have existed unnoticed for centuries, below ground or under water, or overgrown by the jungle, like many Maya sites or the Khmer temples in Cambodia, probably not exactly waiting to be disturbed by any excavations. Actually, the ghosts of the dead don't want to be excavated either, and also the skeletons of the castle ghosts prefer to be left in peace. An example is the ghost of Canterville, which according to the story by Oscar Wilde (1887) desperately tried to renew the blood spot in the library that had several times been removed by the family of the American ambassador. The family had reacted completely insensitively to the atmosphere of the castle. At any rate, the phrase "the spirit of place is transmitted by living people in their everyday experience and therefore depends entirely on them for its survival" (see call for papers) is only valid to a certain extent. Such is true, for instance, with regard to the so-called "present-day global villages...characterised by major trans-national population movements, increased inter-cultural contacts and the emergence of pluralistic societies" (see call for papers), – places that would be an ordeal to every true *genius loci*. By the way, it is to be hoped we as conservationists agree that there are monuments and sites which should remain "inapproachable" or "intangible" in the original sense of the word. Among these are historic traces that should not be renewed, but rather preserved in their age-old value; archaeological sites that should not be excavated, because to a certain degree the subterranean historic archive would be destroyed. The secret of the *genius loci* is definitely better preserved if not everything is "accessible" and overly managed.

Such reflections also apply to the world of indigenous people mortally threatened in the course of globalisation. With their spirits and places, these indigenous people justly play an important role in our symposium. In this regard I want to refer to the roundtable on *Development with Culture and Identity in light of the UN Declaration on the Rights of Indigenous People*, organised by UNESCO a few days ago (see also the Secretary General's message of 9 September, 2008). However, if we talk about "spirit of place" the holy places – churches and monasteries, mosques, temples, synagogues, chapels representing the majority of conservation tasks in most countries – should play a key role, even if "Religious Heritage and Sacred Places" were not the topic of the International Day for Monuments and Sites 2008. Although in the concept of our symposium "beliefs, rituals and festivals" are mentioned in passing as "intangible things," the major relevance of religion, of all world religions, in connection with a differently defined spirit of place, should not be ignored in view of the so-called "dialectics between spirit and place, the intangible and tangible." First and foremost, it is a matter of belief, adoration and worship of the holy place, *locus sacer* as the house of God. If we look, for instance, at such an exemplary spiritual space as the interior of one of the famous French cathedrals still in authentic use, alone able to preserve the authentic spirit, for some colleagues who think mainly in materialistic categories, it might be a classic example of "tangible heritage." – In reality, it is a holy place created as an image of heaven, a place of worship used for centuries, as well as being a place of important historical events. And to this day the *genius loci* of such a monument speaks to everyone, not only to the believer, but even to the tourist who, during his sort of pilgrimage, feels the breath of history and the spirit of craftsmen and artists who created this work.

Under these circumstances, the aura of a place or an object embodied by the *genius loci* is also an important criterion as far as the questions are concerned of how to conserve, restore, renovate or, under certain conditions, to reconstruct. We have to ask: can our planned measure and our conservation concept do justice to the individual *genius loci*? Are we preserving the spiritual message of a monument which, compared with a long history, has only been entrusted to us for a short time? Such questions need to be raised by all who are involved in a restoration measure, starting with the engineer who is in charge of the structural consolidation concept and moving on to the restorer who takes care of the conservation of artistically important surfaces, individual furnishings or works of art. The first aim will always have to be to interfere as little as possible with the existing "matière à mémoire" and to do only what is necessary for the conservation of the historic structure. For despite the impressive wealth of possible investigations and documentations and the whole range of consolidation techniques, as well as conservation and restoration methods which are available today, even a thoroughly prepared conservation measure can lead to a dead end. This happens if the spirit of the monument and the corresponding monument values are not understood, or, using the conservationist's jargon so readily borrowed from the field of medicine, if the profound "diagnosis" and "anamnesis" concentrate, as it were, on the tangible material substance lying on the dissecting table, while the soul is being ignored.

Once again I would like to go back to the authentic spirit of monuments and sites determined by the *genius loci* and to the emotional basis of our work (the authentic "feeling" in the sense of art. 13 of the Nara Document). As an old-fashioned conservationist, in this context I will stick to the above-quoted Roman definition of monument as "matière à mémoire," an object "that should evoke remembrance of something." Added to this of course is time as a historical dimension: time that has passed at this place, a process that has left many traces since the creation of an object, which has perhaps become an object of remembrance only in the course of centuries, a monument in the sense of the Roman definition quoted above; time that is also present in the form of the "Zeitgeist" that the monument embodies, a hard-to-translate German word suggesting the spirit of the times in which the way of life and the "style" of a particular period or epoch are reflected. Space and time can even become one in the spiritual message of the monument – the apparently paradoxical but quite tangible presence of the past. Thanks to the *genius loci* in the still extant "matière à mémoire," for example, the decaying remnants of a castle ruin evoke generations of knights that lived and fought there, or the stones on the floor of a cloister, worn down over the centuries from footsteps, recall the monument's function as a place of prayer by monks. Finally, the spirit of monuments and sites that is conceivable in space and time, and as evidence of the "Zeitgeist," is considerably determined by another essential factor, the already mentioned authentic use. The function that in some circumstances may have continued in its original or modified form into the present also has a special social dimension; for example, the old house that is still occupied, in which generations of inhabitants have already left their traces. These traces contribute not only to the historic value but also to the "feeling value."

Therefore, finally, a brief comment on the emotional basis of conservation practice or, if you like, "monument feeling," an aspect that is hardly ever taken into account in our professional discussions but which should not be underrated in our context of "spirit of place," since this emotional basis can often help achieve a lot in public disputes over the fate of certain monuments. An example was my rather successful struggle to prevent the building of a large hotel near Neuschwanstein Castle. To show the harm that would be done to one of the most beautiful cultural landscapes in Bavaria, I did not confine myself to the usual arguments but instead evoked the spirit of dream king Ludwig II as *genius loci* looking down on to the hotel project and being particularly worried about his sleigh rides at night, which would have ended forever at the golf course planned together with the hotel. Not only in this case can the emotional values be of great importance for our conservation policy. For these values have not only to do with the aesthetic dimension, in the sense of enthusiasm for a work of art; with the historical dimension of a monument (the "breath of history"), but also with a monument's spirit, its "trace," "aura" and "atmosphere." Monument feeling finds expression in the love of a monument, for example, an old house that makes one "feel at home," or in the emotion generated by a historic site that serves as a memorial. Georg Dehio, a famous German conservationist from around 1900, emphasized national feeling above all as a motive for preservation, whereas the Austrian art historian Alois Riegl refers to a general human awareness of life, "an irresistibly compelling feeling, not an avocation for aesthetics and history, that drives us to the cult of monuments." In his "modern cult of monuments," he links this monument feeling to the central concept of age-value expressed in traces of transience. If Riegl's age-value is connected with a certain longing for death – the idea of the fin de siècle of "letting things pass away in beauty" – in contrast, at the beginning of the 21st century, a kind of longing for survival can be presumed as an essential motive in view of the general environment catastrophe. It is an attempt to preserve memory in a world that is changing as never before, and thus to ensure a continuity, for which our *genius loci* could be considered its guardian angel.

If indeed we take the spirit of monuments and sites seriously, the idea of a *genius loci* as a guarantor of a certain diversity and continuity in a globalised world could perhaps help us in these difficult times dominated by rather profane spirits of total change.

Occasionally, in reports of major international conferences, a good *genius loci* is mentioned whose atmosphere contributed considerably to the success of the negotiations. I am sure the special atmosphere of the City of Quebec celebrating its 400th anniversary will contribute to the success of our General Assembly.

Life as Spirit of Place
The Case of a Traditional Korean Village

Sungwoo Kim
Yonsei University
Korea

ABSTRACT

This paper is to identify the way "spirit of life" is represented in a traditional village of Korea, and the meaning of "life" as the spirit of place in modern times. A traditional Korean village called "Yang Dong", located in southeastern part of Korea, will be discussed as an example of a case study.

RÉSUMÉ

Cet article se donne pour intention d'identifier la manière par laquelle «l'esprit de la vie» est représenté dans un village traditionnel de Corée, et la signification de la «vie» en tant qu'esprit du lieu dans les temps modernes. Cet article discutera d'un village traditionnel du nom de Yang Dong, situé au sud-est de la Corée, en tant qu'étude de cas.

Life-oriented worldview (Introduction)

Man develops his places to live based on his own worldview – the point of view he sees the world through – and the view forms the root of a spirit of place. Every culture has its own worldview and it brings a distinct spirit of place. East Asian culture that includes Korea, Japan and China has had a worldview of its own and accordingly, architecture in this area was shaped by the same view. East Asian architecture reflects its own spirit of place, which is completely different from that of Western society.

I would represent the spirit of Eastern architecture as the term of "life". It implies that the traditional East Asian worldview is analogous to a life-oriented worldview. Therefore, creating places through architecture was based on the spirit of a life-oriented worldview. Compared with Western culture, this stems from the uniqueness of cultural features of East Asia that sees the world as an organic whole and perceives it as a phenomenon of mutual functions of certain life energies. Two kinds of place spirit –"mechanical place spirit" and "life – oriented place spirit" – have existed in human life, and we need to find a new balance of the two for a future architecture and city.

This article centers on how the life-oriented worldview of East Asia has become a reality in a village of Korea and its implication and distinctive features. The village is called "Yang-dong village", which consists of a multitude of houses. In this article, I am particularly focusing on the observation of how a spatial plan of the village and a life-oriented place spirit have been connected. In other words, I would like to discuss how a life-oriented view has been reflected in architectural places in everyday life and what the results mean to us living in the present time.

Yang-dong village is one of the hundreds of traditional villages that exist in Korea. They were formed following the life-oriented place spirit, but each of them has its own way of representation. Yang- dong village is one of the representative traditional villages that have been preserved for more than 500 years since 1500. It is located in Wol-sung, North Kyung-sang Province, near the historical City of Kyung-joo.

2. Life-oriented Place Spirit in Yang-dong Village
2.1. Sky and Earth

In the East Asian worldview, any existence of life including man has originated from an encounter of sky and earth. The encounter does not portray a physical connection of sky in the upper and earth in the lower one. Rather, it should be appreciated that every life phenomenon including that of man could exist with the dynamic and mutual "life-oriented relation" of sky and earth. In other words, every aspect of human life such as architecture needs to be approached with an understanding of the "life-oriented relation of sky and earth". Eating earth and breathing sky implies that elements of sky and earth function mutually forming a life- oriented relation; they do not just physically co-exist. Life could be sustained only by a continuous fusion of the elements of sky and earth with an aim of producing energy inside the body.

This also applies to architecture. The hard components of architecture are the continuum of earth and inner space is the expansion of sky. This is somewhat parallel to how the human body functions. Therefore, architecture is how sky and earth forms a life-oriented relation. And the quality and quantity of the life-oriented connection between architecture and man determine the value of architecture. The life-oriented connection is inseparable from an entire frame of connection of sky and earth. For this reason, the explanation of architecture begins with an appreciation of sky and earth and this idea should be also applied to the arrangement of the village.

The purpose of architecture is to create an artificial encounter of sky and earth and integrate a life-oriented reaction of the two in architecture. Sky and earth were regarded as an energy resource in human life and architecture, and architectural sites were designed with a purpose of maximizing their mutual function of a life-oriented reaction. In this respect, both the purpose and motivation of architecture should be appreciated from the standpoint of the life-oriented mutualism of sky and earth. Yang-dong village should be observed with a perspective that explains how this village integrated a life-oriented relation of sky and earth with its space.

2.2. Location

Location is a matter of deciding where to build the houses of the village. It presents what is to be considered first when selecting the location of a village. Two factors are considered here: the condition of sky and earth. To meet the condition of sky, the wind needs to blow modestly so that the flow of air should not be too fast. This is the most pertinent condition for man to live, and it is only possible when the earth serves as a form of basin with a stable flow of air and in an appropriate direction. Valleys and mountain tops are not suitable for residential areas because they hinder a stable flow of air. All the Korean villages, including Yang-dong village, are not sited in valleys or on the tops of hills. The primary concern of selecting locations of villages and houses is to find a spot where energies flowing under the ground are most vigorous. Revealing the flow of energy inside it, features of the land are used to read energy conditions underneath. The high-density area of good energy is the most prized as residential areas for a village.

Believing that good places have a great influence on human life, people have put much effort into finding them. A high mountain behind, and a wide field and a low mountain in front a house are regarded as good conditions for the house. Ranges high mountains behind a house, encompassing the left and right sides of it, are also counted as a good point for the house. These features are believed to possess the concentrated energy of earth as well as to stabilize the wind, and a residential area meeting these conditions is valued as the most desirable place for living since it contributes to a life-oriented village. These are not the fixed conditions; however, they represent a basic concept. The actual features of earth are varied in different situations, and accordingly, each village should be arranged by its unique energy conditions.

Yang-dong village is located at the end of mountain ranges stretching from the Taebaek Mountains of the eastern part of Korea. An extensive field is sited at the southwest area of the village and water flows from north to south. The end of ranges is significant because energy is concentrated there, not merely passing by. The location of Yang- dong village is very different from that of other Korean traditionalvillages. As the mountains of Yang-dong village do not form a basin-like space, the site for the village is not a single flat field. Sited along small ranges of mountain formed inside the village, houses are arranged with the shape of a Chinese character "_". In this respect, it can be viewed as an exceptional case; however, it still has in common with the others the fact that it seeks to maximize the life-oriented conditions of its natural environment.

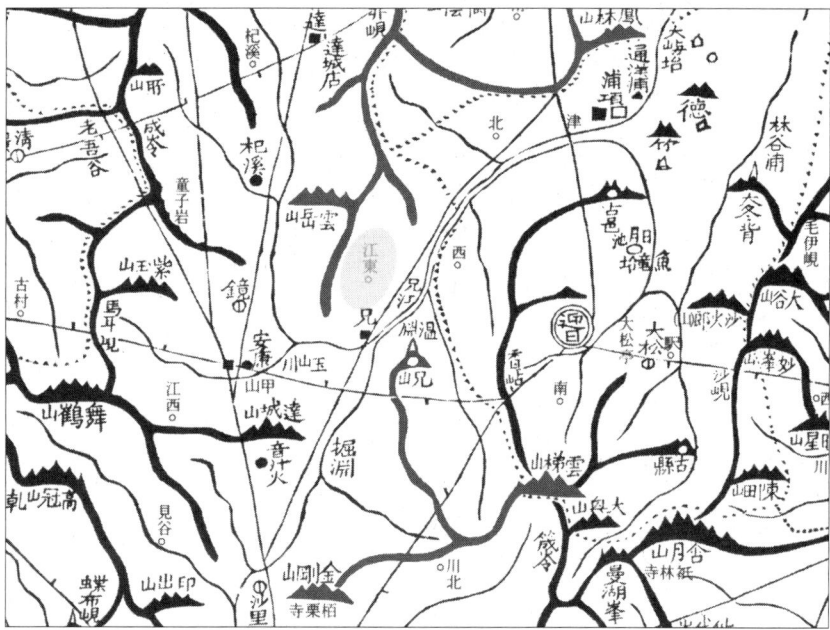

Figure 1. Location of Yang-dong Village.

2.3. Site Arrangement

Once the location of a village is selected, the arrangement of the site plan follows. A village is laid out by an arrangement of houses and adjacent roads. In Yang-dong village, each house makes use of its own earth condition. Every house is sited following life-oriented principles while making full use of features of the ground where it is located. A few paths branch into several ways and houses are sited around the paths. Located on the south-facing slopes of mountains, most houses are aligned with the axis of Ansan (mountains behind and in front of the house). Houses are favored to be built facing south, southeast or southwest. However, varied features of the ground create unique directions for houses. Favoring the south comes from a plan to manage sunlight more efficiently in all four seasons because the management of sunlight is directly related to life.

The structure of the access also plays a critical role since each house should be reached through alleys. The majority of accesses have a branch-shaped hierarchical structure, but irregular rather than geometrical. The alleys of Yang-dong village are also formed as a branch shape, following the features of the ground. Consequently, the features of the ground and architecture seem to be attached together as one, giving a sense of impossibility to follow geometrical rules. Houses are arranged irregularly, just as the features of natural ground are irregular. The arrangement plan shows an attitude that an artificial creature respects natural environments as they are and human architecture is willing to accommodate itself to the features of natural ground. The arrangement plan of Yang-dong village should be approached with an understanding of how the features of ground and village adapt to each other. What may be considered as an integral peculiarity of this village could be the fact that self-regulating diversity and uniformity as a whole can co-exist at the same time.

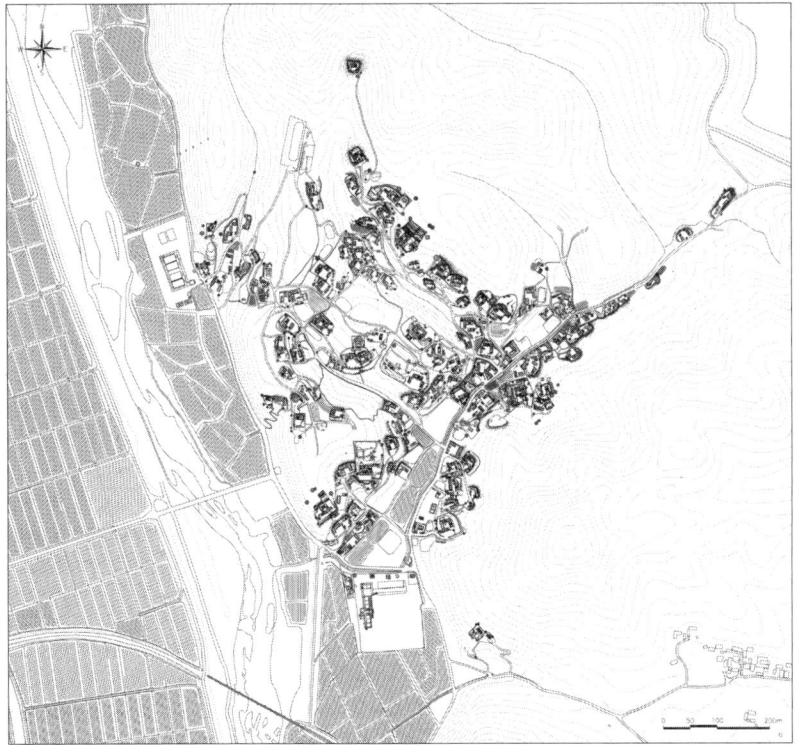

Figure 2. Arrangement of Yang-dong Village.

2.4. Architecture

The next step following the previous ones – sky and earth, location and arrangement – is the architecture of houses. Individual houses of Yang-dong village have their own styles of scale, arrangement and spatial composition. Here, observation is needed of life-oriented features in a spatial composition shared by the houses. With buildings and walls connected together, most houses take the shape of a horizontal structure, and are not separated individually. At the heart of the structure is an empty Madang (courtyard). Buildings are not sited at the center of a house , but rather encircle the empty Madang, which makes the structure that man naturally faces the Madang while in buildings. If a man stands in the Madang, he becomes the center of the empty outdoor space. While quarters for servants, women and men serve distinct functions and have different residents, yet they are linked to one another, centering on the Madang. The relation between the Madang and buildings and the way a man stands in the Madang demonstrate a desirable spatial condition of life-oriented forces.

Madang is where sky and earth meet, holding air in it and reaching into the sky at the same time. Therefore, man enters a house from outside through Daemoon (gate), reaching the Madang first and the Daechong (main living room) through the Teotmaru (wooden verandah), and finally The Anbang (main room). The unique access of a house in Yang-dong village reduces the distinction of inside and outside even to the point that man cannot distinguish the two, with repeated sensation that inside becomes outside and vice versa. As this process is repeated, man is led to a more private and stable space. Spaces are distinguished by the process of approach and the way of connection, and are not divided by their functions. In terms of the approach process, the movement of man brings the changes of inside and outside, a feature which eventually unites the spaces. What is an important element in a Korean traditional house is the way that spatial units are connected and the movement of man. Spatial connection and the movement of man construct a life-oriented structure of air flow and a spatial experience for man.

The connection between man and air and the management of flow are significant since they allow the life-oriented connection of elements and eventually unify them as an organic whole. It is hard to verify this in a scientific way, but it is obvious that everything, including anunderstanding of the energy of sky and earth, location, arrangement and every part of architecture, is governed by consistent life-oriented thinking at whose core stands a purpose of rich life-oriented connection.

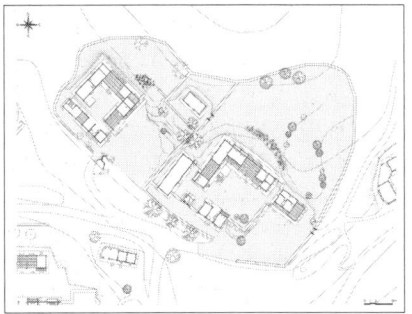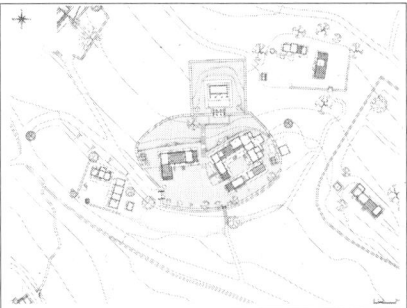

Figure 3. Sangchungotaek (Left) & Mucheomdang (Right).

3. Meaning of the life-oriented place spirit
3.1. Dualistic Balance

A habit that categorizes things into two contrary groups such as "good and evil", "beauty and ugliness", "heaven and hell", and "god and devil" justifies our action that takes one and denies the other. This dualistic distinction is grounded in a premise that one would be chosen and the other would be refused. However, a dualistic distinction such as "yin and yang", "sky and earth" and "son and daughter" means dualism that considers harmony of the two without an intention to refuse one of them. If we see the first as "selective dualism" and the latter as "balanced dualism", we could find that the difference comes from distinct ways of thinking deeply rooted in Eastern and Western cultures. Yet, it is obvious that each continent has its own cultural tendency or way of thinking and these have a great impact on it. What is important is the fact that the life-oriented view requires balance between two elements more than choice between the two. While it is possible to refuse ugliness and take beauty, in some cases, ugliness could be needed for beauty. It is of importance that the life phenomenon is based on the dynamic relation between two contrary elements for survival. This way of thinking directly affects architecture. In houses of Yang-dong village, we could see an effort to realize balanced dualism in architecture in a floor system which is composed of Ondol (stone) and Maru (wood), the distinction of men's and ladies' quarters, as well as the roof and walls of a building. This is not only due to such Yin-Yang theory, but to a life-oriented worldview that sees the mutual relation of two contrary components as essential. In the flow of modernization, we are getting more accustomed to selective dualism, and this also wields an influence on architecture. For a more life-sensitive future, we need to focus on the meaning of balanced dualism or dualistic balance.

3.2. Interactive Relation

Our modern architecture is more concerned with existence than relation. Visible being is more valued than invisible and individuality is more important than mutuality. However, life is sustained by the interactive relation of individuals, not by their physical existence. Individuals have no value if they become beings without mutual relation. It is synonymous with a human body where the esophagus or small intestine is meaningless without the stomach or large intestine respectively. This issue may have already reached a serious level in modern architecture or city. Yang-dong village demonstrates how individual beings are closely linked, forming an organic relation among houses or the inner spaces of a house, as well as a house and sky and earth. Compared to our modern architecture, the architecture of Yang-dong village should be called an "architecture of mutual relation". A house where a family resides is divided into quarters for men and women, but they are closely related, and the house is deeply connected with air and terrain. The house is also related to an adjacent one, and these houses are organized as a village. Structure of the relation is interconnected with a life-oriented network, rather than being a functional organization.

3.3. Autonomous Order

We think that architecture is what is to be created by man. This implies that man as a subject should give an order, distinguishing himself from objects which are given the order. Modern architectural design, too, is based on this idea and no one casts doubt on it. Architecture becomes an object that receives order given by man outside the architecture. Modern architecture that features the rational and reasonable is justified in this way. However, life is autonomous and gives an order by itself, rather than only receiving it. A question might be proposed at this point: How can architecture have autonomous order?

The essence of this question is what attitude man takes toward the orders that already exist in nature. It also asks whether man is willing to ask nature or architectural materials about an order he is about to give so that he would respect the order of nature and the features of materials. Taking a step forward, this deals with an issue where man could be humble in his attitude towards nature and life so that he could be humble in his architecture. It asks if he could respect life-oriented orders, abandoning his position as a self-centered and omnipotent creator. Before man gives an order to nature, there were already existing life-oriented orders in nature and the same order still exists. Man was also created by the same order and can survive only when he follows it. The order is autonomous and the autonomous order should be respected in architecture. The action of going against the order brings about damages that will directly harm man. Yang-dong village and its houses are a good example of an architecture that follows the autonomous order of nature.

3.4. Unity as a Whole

Unity and wholeness are matters to be discussed here. Separation from autonomous order and weakened mutual relation make it impossible for a whole body to be united. It is very natural that individuals could not be united as a whole in a situation where individuals are not related and a controlling order of the relation of individuals is not respected. The natural world is already united, and man is the only one who is accustomed to being in a disunited state.

Consequently, only man would ask about the necessity of unifying individuals as a whole. The human body, however, is an example of a united body. Nature, earth and even the universe are united. Being united is an indispensable, not optional, element to all living beings. Only self- centered and individual-focused man feels it difficult to be united. Architecture reflects this difficulty. Every city and architecture in history might be judged from the perspective of to what degree it is united or divided individually. Such judgment also enables us to measure the degree of its life-oriented possibility. What we could learn from cases such as Yang-dong village is that numerous houses form a united village while each house possesses its own autonomous solution. The unity encompasses sky and earth, trees, wind and the moon as well as buildings. The disability to be united might be considered as a weakness of man, but it is not acceptable in a life-oriented world. Only man is not familiar with being united.

4. Machine and life (conclusion)

With the passing of more than 100 years to bring about Western modernization in our society, the 21st century began a few years ago. In the meantime, our cities and architecture have already taken on a mechanical look. The main theme of this international conference is "spirit of place". Focusing on "life" in a discussion of the place spirit in a traditional village of Korea is important as well as natural because we who live in a city and architecture based on mechanical thinking discuss an issue of "life" that has originated from a completely different worldview.

Yang-dong village demonstrates how a village could be formed with a life-oriented view. What is most significant to us living in the present time is the fact that the worldview that created the village is based on life-oriented values. We must learn the life-oriented spirit from howthe village has accepted sky and earth, how the village selected its location and how architecture and arrangement was managed with a life-oriented view. We must learn the spirit of life from an empty space of Madang, the choice of putting a rock in the back yard, and the way of imposing a view of the rising moon on the wall. We should observe these in Yang-dong village and learn from it.

However, it is hard to actualize the methods conducted in Yang- dong village in future architecture and houses since the system and concept of architecture are different from those of Yang-dong village. It would be advisable to find values to be pursued in an environment of a life-oriented view as evidenced in Yang-dong village and realize the values in modern architecture. Those spiritual values may be summarized as follows:

Shift the way of thinking from taking only one while refusing the other between two contrary elements in order to make a dynamic balance by recognizing and sharing values of the two with the purpose of realizing life;

Emphasize the mutual relation of individuals and life through the relation, not just focusing on individual beings and their visible features;

Change the behaviors of man from giving an order as a subject to objects to respecting existing orders, following their autonomous features and cooperating with them;

Unite and connect all individuals to make a whole through a network structure with an understanding that a physical collection of individuals and parts is not desirable.

These four lessons are essential for the survival of life. This applies to man in the same way. "Life" is not restricted to the spirit of place of a Korean village. Man should anchor his hope in "life" for his own survival.

References

Jantsch, Erich. 1980. *The Self-Organizing Universe*. Oxford and New York: Pergamon Press.

Relph, Edward. 1976. *Place and Placelessness*. London: Pion. Translated by D. Kim, Nonhyung Publishing.

Kim, Ji Ha. *Life and Autonomy*. Sol Publishing, 1996.

Kim, Sungwoo. 2005. "Space and Sky-Earth". *Journal of Architectural History in Korea* vol. 14 no. 4: 7-28.

Kim, Sungwoo. 2005. "Proportion and Vitality". *Journal of Architectural History in Korea*, vol. 14 no. 2: 103-142.

Kim, Sungwoo. 2000. "View of Architecture and the View of the world in the East and the West". *Architecture and Environment*, no. 185-196.

Lee, Donggeol. 1987. *Oksan School and Yangdong Village*. Korea: Woori Publishing.

Shimizu, Hiroshi. 1994. *Life and Place*. Translated by Sungwon Lim. Jeonpa Publishing, 1994.

Mang, Injae *et al.* 1972. *Yangdong Village*. Korea: Bureau of Cultural Assets.

Mang, Injae. 1978. *Yangdong, and Hahoye Village*. Korea: Bureau of Cultural Assets.

Needham, Joseph. 1956. "The Fundamental Ideas of Chinese Science". *Science and Civilization in China*, vol. 2, 13, Cambridge, 1956.

Samsung Architectural Design. 1979. *Research Report of Yang Dong Village*. Korea: Northern Province of Kyungsang.

Examples and Significance of Culture that is Created through Transmission of the Spirituality of Space

Kunie Sugio
ICOMOS CIIC member
PREC Institute Inc.
Japan

ABSTRACT

The spirit or spirituality of place or space (hereinafter "the spirit of place") can exist in a fixed or static fashion at the place; on the other hand, as part of people's inspiration, memory, or impression, it can move with the people who are inspired by, keep memory of, or are impressed by the place.

It can even transcend time and space, by being transplanted and transmitted by people, resulting in a new culture (tangible or intangible) in another space. When established, the chain of transmission of the spirit of place continues further over time and space.

In other words, the spirit of place can be said to be a mother to cultural heritage or a creator of diverse culture over time and space.

This paper introduces several examples to explain the above with the aim of demonstrating the concept and diverse values of the spirit of place or space.

RÉSUMÉ

L'esprit ou la spiritualité du lieu ou de l'espace (désigné sous l'expression de «l'esprit du lieu») peut avoir une existence sur un mode fixe ou statique dans le lieu lui-même ; d'un autre côté, en tant que partie de l'inspiration, de la mémoire ou des impressions des gens, il peut se déplacer avec les gens qu'il inspire, qui en gardent la mémoire, ou qu'il a sensibilisés. Il peut même transcender le temps et l'espace, en étant transplanté et transmis par les gens, ce qui peut résulter en une nouvelle culture (matérielle ou immatérielle) dans un autre lieu. Lorsqu'elle est instaurée, la courroie de transmission de l'esprit du lieu se prolonge au-delà du temps et de l'espace. En d'autres termes, on peut dire de l'esprit du lieu qu'il fait naître le patrimoine culturel ou qu'il est le créateur de différentes cultures à travers le temps et l'espace. Cet article présente plusieurs exemples pour expliciter ce phénomène, dans le but de démontrer le concept et les différentes valeurs de l'esprit du lieu ou de l'espace.

1. Introduction

The role of the spirituality of space is most outstandingly evident in its role as the abundant source of culture that produces various forms of culture. People have various feelings and inspirations from space such as respect, awe, fear, relaxation, excitement, dream, expectation, trust, salvation, etc. Broadly speaking, space can be understood as tantamount to the concept of the environment. In addition, the environment is construed as the sum of complex and diverse forms of space. The environment is something that people can physically feel and experience or something that appeals to the physical perceptions of people. The source of what makes such an appeal is, it can be said, nothing other than the spirituality of space.

Space that spiritually moves people so powerfully is often sacred places that are revered as the object of worship or faith, places of scenic beauty, and/or environmental places that have strong interaction with people and therefore have great importance to people. The most outstanding example of this spirituality is the space conceived as sacred sites.

2. Spirituality of Space

When we think about the spirituality of space, sacred areas are the proper entrance to understanding the various characteristics revolving around the concept of the spirituality of space. Therefore, I give my thought firstly to sacred sites as a motif.

- Sacred sites in folk religions are viewed as follows:
- Space of a certain extension where a certain sacred statue, icon, grave, a site or a monument associated with a saint, etc. is worshipped;
- Rough and difficult site deep in the mountain that forbids or defies human access;
- Place where a certain special power exists: natural features such as mountain, forest, river, tree, rock, stone, waterfall, cave, and animals that inhabit the area are conceived as being gifted with a certain special power;
- Sacred sites that are associated with especially important persons or divinities such as saints, martyrs, and heroes; and
- Space as a chaotic and integral combination of the above-mentioned.

Characteristics of the genes of cultural spirituality of space

Space assumes cultural characteristics and transmits the spirituality of cultural value as its genes. The cultural genes of space can be dynamically transformed through human interactions – without being changed at the core – into a space that moves people by different modes of "appearance", "transmission", and "reproduction", depending upon how "time", "place", and "occasion" are intertwined.

Such spiritually exhibited by space can transport and transmit freely to anywhere, and reproduce its cultural genes that lie at the core of the generation of spirituality. It is one of the outstandingly distinctive characteristics of Japanese culture that it has a system in which the spirituality of space and its cultural genes make dynamic appearances anywhere.

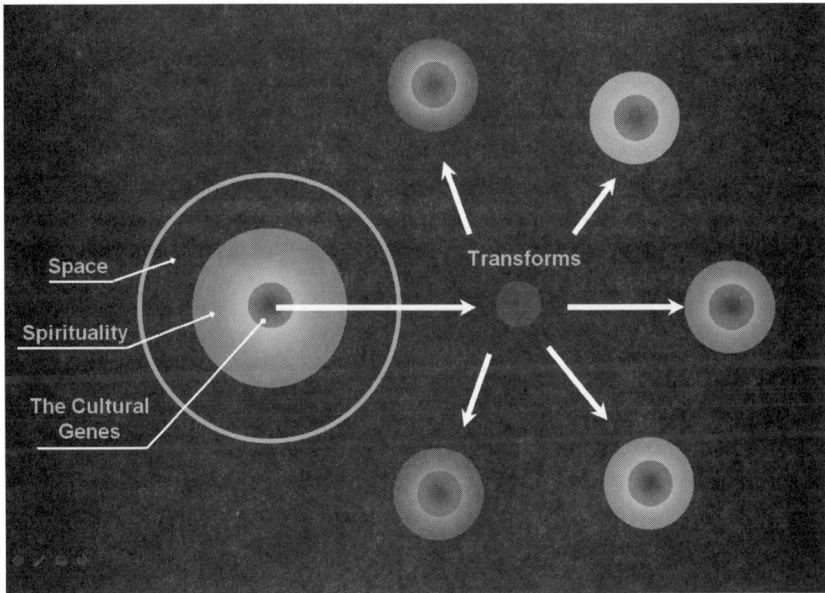

Figure 1. Spread of cultural genes (concept diagram).

3. Culture that is Formed by the Transmission of Cultural Spirituality of Space

The core of the spirituality of space becomes cultural genes and spreads from the place of origin to new places, where it takes root and reproduces the space akin to the original spirituality. Traditional gardens of Japan show many such examples; these can also be seen in how styles as well as unique forms and garden techniques of Japanese gardens have been produced.

3.1. Reproduction

Outstanding examples of this phenomenon are given below.

3.1.1. "Fujizuka" (Mt Fuji Mound) as the Reproduction of the Sacred Mountain, Mt Fuji

Mt Fuji, the sacred mountain symbolic of Japan, has traditionally been the object of worship in Japan since ancient times; it attracts the worship of many Japanese people even today. During the Edo Period, earth mounds in the shape of Mt Fuji were built in many places throughout Edo as a substitute object of worship for elderly people and women for whom climbing Mt Fuji by way of worship was too tough and arduous. These earth mounds are called "Fujizuka" (Mt Fuji mound) and spread through the citizens of Edo (present Tokyo), who worshipped Mt Fuji.

Mt Fuji mounds were built in many places where the real Mt Fuji was visible at that time. The part of Mt Fuji that was visible from Edo was the mountain body higher than the 5th stage (10th stage corresponds to the summit area) and the direction ranged from southwest (from Edo) to northwest (from Edo).

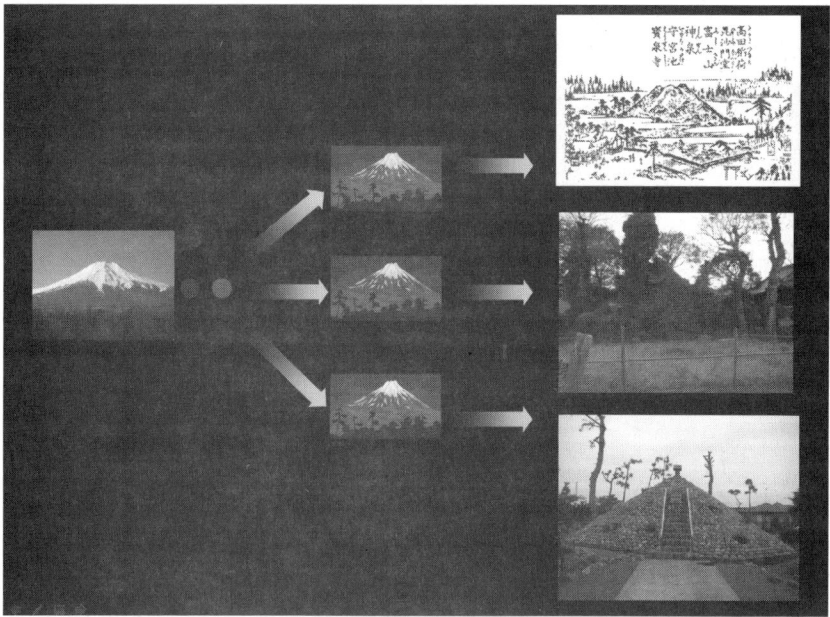

Figure 2. Concept diagram of "reproduction".

The part of Mt Fuji higher than the 5th stage was considered to be the celestial area where gods and divinities dwelled and it was distinguished from the secular world. In particular, the phenomenon known as "divine appearance" on the summit of Mt Fuji was most revered and worshipped. "Divine appearance", also known as "divine light of sunrise", was likened to the appearance of the triad Bodhisattvas of Amida, Avalokiteshvara, and Mahasthamaprapta in the sunlight.

Mt Fuji is the space or place that produces the spirituality in the form of worship in the minds of those who perceive the Pure Land of Utmost Bliss. The distant view of Mt Fuji was the spiritual center of the citizens of Edo during the Edo Period and was considered to be the symbol of Edo. A large number of Mt Fuji mounds, which copied Mt Fuji in miniature, were built throughout Edo, of which as many as 80 exist today.

Mt Fuji-shaped mounds are approximately 10 m in height and covered with lava stone from Mt Fuji or similar-looking stone; at the top of Mt Fuji mounds, the soil taken from Mt Fuji was buried. They were built for the purpose of creating Pure Land in miniature where men and women of all ages could experience the climbing of Mt Fuji even if they were unable to climb the real Mt Fuji in their real life.

In other words, this is an example in which the spirit of place, or the worship of Mt Fuji in this case, transmitted its cultural genes to other places that are located far away from the original and reproduced as a pseudo-Mt Fuji.

3.2. Substitution of scenes

This is a method of bringing "extraordinary scenes" into the daily and ordinary space of people's life. Original landscapes are shrunken and "imitated" into Japanese gardens. This is one of the garden-making methods for Japanese gardens, known as "shrunken scenery".

Beautiful landscapes representing Japan such as the view of Mt Fuji are transferred and copied on a reduced scale into Japanese gardens; this garden-making technique transports the spirituality from the original places of scenic beauty to other places.

Examples of this are given below.

3.2.1.Miniature Scenes of Mt Fuji

Mt Fuji is a classical example of a famous Japanese scene, and Fuji-style volcanic-shaped) mounds constitute an integral part of many gardens. The best example is found in the Suizen-ji temple, a garden in Kumamoto Prefecture, where clipped grass swells up in the shape of a large, pointed mound.

Figure 3. A method of bringing "extraordinary scenes" into the daily and ordinary space of people's life.

3.2.2. Miniature Scenes of Japan's Representative Place of Scenic Beauty, "Ama no Hashidate" (Bridge to Heaven)

"Ama no Hashidate" (Bridge to Heaven), which is situated on the coast of the Sea of Japan is reproduced with a spit of land in the foreground of Katsura Detached Palace, Kyoto.

Figure 4. Miniature scenes of Japan's representative place of scenic beauty.

3.2.2. Spatial Substitution

The space that divides the divine space and the human world is called "kekkai" (literally, boundary) in Japan; it is a special type of space that is sequestered for the purpose of religious practice or training. This type of space is set up often to prohibit the entry of people who would disturb the religious training of Buddhist monks (as is practiced, for instance, on sacred mountains such as Koyasan, Hieizan, Nantaisan, and Ominesan). While the "kekkai" area is closed to women, special worship areas for women were created outside the mountain area to substitute for the "kekkai" area.

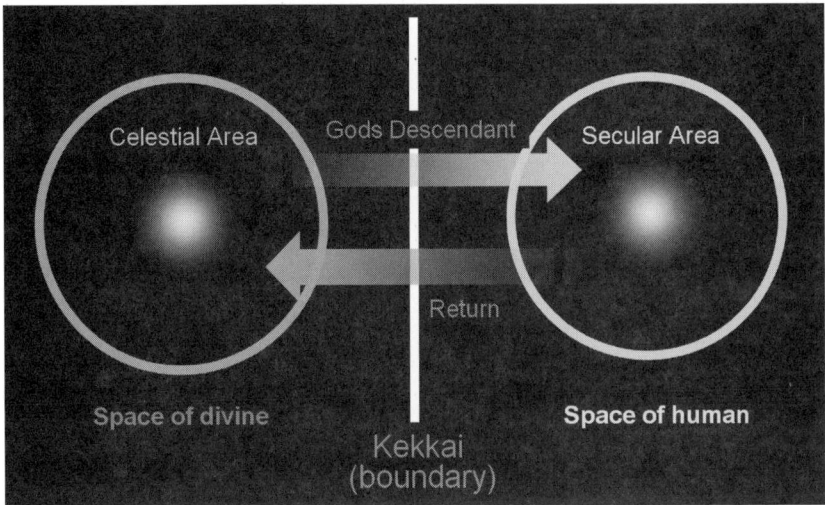

Figure 5. Descent of gods (concept diagram).

The spirituality of the worship for mountains, forests, rivers, waterfalls, etc. produced the space where gods descended from their dwelling to the places of people's daily life and where gods and people communicated with each other through rituals, traditional arts, festivals, and other intangible aspects of culture.

On the other hand, there were cases where space itself was revered as sacred; water in waterfalls and trees in forests were brought back to the places of people's daily life as holy water or sacred trees that contained and maintained the spirituality of the sacred place.

"Amagoi", the Japanese ritual to call for rain, is a tradition that mediates between gods and people and is considered to be an interesting example showing how people can feel the unique spirit of space as real and alive.

These examples lead to the understanding that the spirit of space is the source of various historical and cultural properties; it is therefore important to conserve and transmit the space that exhibits special spirituality to future generations.

3.3. Spirituality and Genius of Space

3.3.1. Animism

Even before animism, recognition of spirituality in all entities (including space), existed, there had been a pre-animism, primitive belief known as "manaism". This type of belief had existed in the West, too, since olden times. In relation to this, legend says: "the sword of *mana* enabled its holder to beat as many enemies as it wished. Therefore, people fought each other for the sword".

"Tamaism" of Japan is based upon the "sun worship" at its root; houses and tombs are made in circular shapes with an open space at the center.

Stone circles were "observatories of the sun", "ritual stages for the sun", "sacred sites to receive the round gem of the sun", and also the playing grounds where people communicated with gods. Particularly in the case of the sun worship of the Japanese people, it is characteristically easy to see the signs of the energy of the sun; geological and natural conditions of Japan made the existence of the sun easily recognizable and it was the origin of people's life.

3.3.2. Festivals of Shinto Shrines

This is an example in which gods inhabiting a certain space (e.g. *genius loci*, spiritual gods) show up before people.

The "mikage" festival of the Shimogamo-jinja Shinto shrine (a.k.a. Kamomioya-jinja), Kyoto, is a sacred ritual in which a "god" descends from Mt Mikage, 4 km away in the northeast, to the Mikage-jinja Shinto shrine and then down to the Shimogamo-jinja Shinto shrine, where the god settles on a stone seat called "iwakura" and performs a festival. There exist archeological remains of the "iwakura" stone seats, consisting of fist-size stones being packed in holes of 25 to 80 cm in diameter and 10 to 50 cm in depth.

Figure 6. "Iwakura".

Today, it is believed that the god settles on the "iwakura" situated in the garden in front of the main hall of the shrine. On the occasion of a ritual, people dance enthusiastically, waving arms in the air and stamping the ground heavily; the shrine compounds become a playing ground where people become intoxicated with the joy of receiving the god.

3.3.3. "Asobinaa" and "Utaki" of Okinawa, Japan

The ancient settlements of Okinawa, Japan have sacred mountains or forests called "utaki" (sacred mountain) and sacred spaces called "kamina" (gods' garden). While "utaki" was a place where prayer was given to gods, the place where rituals and festivals were conducted was called "asobinaa". "Sefa Utaki" (literally meaning a sacred site of high spiritual power) was the most sacred site in the Kingdom of Ryukyu and is characterized by space surrounded by gigantic rock and sacred trees, a sacred place of prayer-giving in a hollow on a rock hill, and the extraordinary triangular cave-like space that is formed by two gigantic pieces of rock leaning upon each other. The mysterious and fantastic scene of the sunbeam shining through from the opposite side of the prayer-giving place is strong enough for those who see it to feel instinctively that this is a sacred site. This sacred site does not have any single artificial object but a series of awe-inspiring natural landmarks such as gigantic rock, picturesque rock, stalactites, caves, lavish forests, and trees. Nature sometimes dies and confronts humans harshly but at other times gently embraces humans with grace. The sacredness that springs out of this nature or the spirituality, inspiration, and moving sensations of the natural environment become the object of worship.

3.3.4. Water Boundary to the Sacred Area

At the entrance to sacred space, objects that symbolically indicate the boundary to separate the sacred space from the secular world are put up. Torii gates standing on the Ujibashi Bridge that spans the Isuzugawa River, leading to the Isejingu Shinto Shrine, signify the "gateway" to the sacred area and symbolize the division between the sacred and the secular. Just before the sacred area begins, there is a water spot for purification. The rite of purifying one's body with water is of religious significance and reminds people of the ideal of humans – pure and clean both physically and spiritually.

Without touching water or going through water, no entry to the sacred area will be granted. The "purification" through nature is an essential process, although it took different forms ranging from "mitaraigawa" (a stream running near Shinto shrines where worshippers wash their mouth, etc. for purification), "shinchi" (sacred pond) to "tsukubai" (water basin).

The moats surrounding ancient tumuli have the function of water boundaries; islands or river isles are perceived as river gods, as is still evident in traditionally-observed festivals in which people go around an island in a boat.

The spirituality of the space that has acquired a common purpose is transmitted to anywhere and reproduced to serve the same purpose shared by people there in harmony with local climate and characteristics.

4. Spirituality of Space in the West

Now the author turns his attention from Japan to the West.

In the West, "[e]very clearing was called a *lucus*, in the sense of an eye, as even today we call eyes the opening through which light enters houses" (qtd. in Harrison 1993). The Roman Empire, in its effort to conquer the world, conquered forests. In ancient Europe, forests existed more dominantly, e.g. in Italy, Gallia, Spain, and the Mediterranean coast of the United Kingdom.

Since forests of ancient times were foreboding to the entry of people, forests functioned as walls to protect cultural uniqueness as well as sovereignty and diversity of tribal states. They provided "hides " for unique languages, customs, divinities, traditions, styles, and so forth. Forests nurtured the diversity of culture. Forests defied the moves toward standardization. Because of this buffer provided by forests, settlements maintained independence and nurtured endemic spiritualities. Each forest had its own fairies, divinities, or pans, which differed from forest to forest.

The Roman forces cleared and conquered these forests not by rampage or destruction but through the construction of a long-distance communication network consisting of roads and infrastructure facilities. Their rule promoted standardization. Consequently, unique cultures that had been maintained by the existence of forest-separated lands were eliminated. As a result, the space became more homogeneous and the spirituality became less diverse. The more homogeneous the space is, the less necessary it is for the spirituality of space to spread its genes.

Therefore, examples of "culture that is created through transmission of the spirituality of space" are to be seen more often in the East, including Japan, and characteristic of the formation of Occidental or Japanese culture.

References

Harrison, Robert Pogue. 1993. *Forests: The Shadow of Civilization*. Chicago: University of Chicago Press.

Kawai, Yasuyo. 2003. *Seichi "Fujisan"* [Sacred Site, "Mt Fuji"]. Tokyo: Kokinshoin.

Matsui, Keisuke. 2003. *Minshu Shukyo ni-miru Seichi no Fukei* [Scenes of Sacred Sites in Folk Religions]. Tokyo: Kokinshoin.

Ueda, Atsushi. 2008. *Niwa to Nihonjin* [Gardens and Japanese People]. Tokyo: Shinchosha.

Sacred Mountains Where the being of *Kami* is found

Kazuyuki Yano
Secretary General, Japan ICOMOS National Committee
CEO, Japan Cultural Heritage Consultancy
Japan

ABSTRACT

From primeval days to date, the Japanese have regarded certain mountains as objects of worship believing that mountains are places where multitudinous gods reside. This belief in mountains as sacred places still lives on and is practiced in the Japanese traditional religion, Shinto, which is based on animism and ancestor worship. Today, this notion of sacredness is generally accepted and understood together with concepts from Chinese philosophies, such as Confucianism and Taoism, and Buddhism, which have evolved over a long time. In Japan, volcanoes or high, well-formed mountains, as well as smaller hills standing close to human settlements, were believed to be sacred places. This paper explores how temples and shrines have been intentionally situated in relation to such mountains in order to create the sacred place as a whole area.

RÉSUMÉ

Depuis les jours de leurs origines jusqu'à l'époque actuelle, les Japonais ont considéré certaines montagnes comme des objets de vénération, du fait de la croyance que les montagnes sont les lieux où résident d'innombrables dieux. Cette croyance en ces lieux sacrés que sont les montagnes se perpétue et est toujours mise en pratique dans la religion japonaise traditionnelle, le shinto, qui se fonde sur l'animisme et le culte des ancêtres. Aujourd'hui, cette notion du sacré est généralement acceptée et comprise de pair avec des concepts provenant de philosophies chinoises telles que le confucianisme, le taoïsme et le bouddhisme, qui ont évolué au cours d'une longue période. Au Japon, les volcans ou les hautes formations montagneuses, ainsi que des collines plus petites et plus proches des établissements humains, étaient considérés comme des lieux sacrés. Cet article explore la manière dont les temples et les autels ont été intentionnellement placés en relation avec de telles montagnes, dans le but de sacraliser le lieu en son entier.

1. Introduction

The intimate connection between Japanese culture and reverence for mountains has been widely observed, but the reasons behind it and its source are much less clearly understood. The *sangaku shinko,* or Japanese mountain creed, is not based on any one particular religious belief or folklore myth. In fact, mountains are venerated not only in Japan, but also in many other parts of the world within different faiths: for example, Mount Sinai is revered in Judaism, Mount Kaliash in Hinduism, and Mount Ararat in Christianity. One mountain may even become an object of worship for multiple creeds. What makes Japanese *sangaku shinko* unusual is how all Japanese, in harmony, unquestioningly, naturally look upon mountains with awe.

There has been almost no religious conflict throughout Japanese history, apart from the historic 6th Century conflict between the Soga and Mononobe clans.[1] Eventually, the Buddhist Soga clan prevailed over the anti-Buddhist Mononobe. The Soga deliberately used Buddhism politically, on a nationwide scale, but did not damage existing shrines, massacre innocent followers, or attempt to destroy the indigenous nature religions.

Thus, even though mountains embody different beliefs for different groups, they are generally held to be the abode of various *kami* (gods) and, as such, are not to be disturbed. Various forms of god-inhabited mountains are found everywhere in Japan. Nor are mountains the only object of worship; sometimes a huge rock or a tree can serve the same purpose. In addition, it is believed that all natural things co-exist with the gods, as channels of communication. People can sense messages from the gods through natural signs. If they purify themselves, they can approach closer to where the *kami* reside and receive the messages more easily.

This idea, never clearly written down in doctrinal form, nevertheless lives on in the public mind. There is no clear distinction between man and nature, or between deity and nature. *Kami* live in all forms of nature, from rivers to trees, rocks to flowers, fish to animals. Thus Japanese believe all natural things are living, even rocks. Moreover, Japanese totally accept the fundamental idea that nothing is absolute, but rather protean – flexible and ever changing. People handle parallel sets of values in the same way as they accept that different laws of nature rule different plants in different seasons.

---

1.   The Tokugawa regime banned Christianity from 1612 until 1868. However, this was a political decision to limit external influence on Japan, rather than a reflection of internal conflict between religious groups.

This paper attempts to characterize Japanese sacred mountains both by their appearance and the beliefs they embody. It looks at how to identify and differentiate Japanese sacred mountains, specific examples being the cities of Obama and Hiraizumi.

2. Historical Background: the Amalgamation of Buddhism and Shinto in Japan

To understand the architectural manifestations of mountain veneration in Japan, we must first touch on Japanese religion and its historical background. H. Byron Earhart, an American scholar specializing in *sangaku shinko*, describes Japanese religion as a "variegated tapestry created by the interweaving of at least five major strands: Shinto, Buddhism, Taoism, Confucianism, and folk religion." (Earhart 2004:2) This excellent metaphor encapsulates the idea of the various religious strands interwoven together to make one intricate tapestry that gives the whole picture. No strand makes sense independently; nor can anyone make out the whole picture by peering at it too closely.

This tapestry of beliefs was formed mainly between the 6th and 8th Centuries A.D. However, while Buddhism became the official national religion in the 6th Century, the word *shinto,* to describe the amalgam of indigenous religious ideas pre-dating Buddhism, did not appear in classical literature until the 8th Century. Traditional, somewhat vague shared moral values gradually developed through animism and ancestor veneration, until ultimately consolidated into the main body of Shinto belief. New waves of ideas – Buddhist culture, art, knowledge, and technology – followed one after another; however, the rituals and moral values of Shinto culture were never completely replaced. Instead, by the 10th Century, the syncretization of Shinto and Buddhism led to the emergence of a formal doctrine called *honji suijaku*: Buddhist deities, *honjibutsu,* manifest themselves as *suijaku* in order to save sentient beings. These manifested deities are what are referred to as *kami*. This philosophy is most clearly expressed on the Hie-sannno Mandala scroll.

Over time, Buddhist/Shinto syncretism developed and was assimilated throughout Japan. The word "temple" is used to describe Buddhist places of worship, while "shrine" is used for Shinto places. However, people began to build *jinguji,* official Buddhist temples, on Shinto shrine ground, for example, Kashima Jinguji in Ibaraki, Kamo Jinguji in Kyoto, and Kasugataisha Jinguji in Nara. The word *jinguji* is a composite of the words *jingu* and *ji. Jingu* means a shrine and *ji* means a temple. Therefore the word itself expresses the assimilation of Buddhism and Shinto. Conversely, shrines were often built for the guardian deity of a particular temple. Kofukuji and Kasuga Taisha, two of the eight significant World Heritage Historic Monuments of Ancient Nara, are of this nature. Such guardian deity shrines were often located in esoteric temples deep in the mountains.

However, in 1867, after 1200 years of religious assimilation, Japan decided for political reasons to reinstate Shinto over Buddhism. Government policy compelled Buddhism to be separated from Shinto. Many temple grounds were expropriated and some were forced to abolish temple activities. Unexpectedly, quantities of Buddhist art disappeared abroad at this time. Ironically, this unfortunate loss finally led to the establishment of legal protections to safeguard Japanese historic and cultural property.

Following World War II, Japan entered a new era of political and philosophical democracy, including freedom of religion as officially stipulated by the new postwar constitution. Thus Shinto and Buddhism were placed on equal grounds with other religions such as Christianity and Islam. However, how ordinary people practice religion now is perhaps not so different from centuries ago. People still have vague feelings of reverence and appreciation towards nature, regardless of their individual intellectual theological beliefs. This differs significantly from a monotheistic religion based on solid mutually held doctrine. According to Japanese statistics on religion in 2005,[2] the total number of people registered with some kind of religious organization was about 211 million, while the total population was just under 128 million. Although these figures hardly reflect reality, they do show that Japanese unwittingly register themselves with multiple religious organizations. Doing the right thing to maintain harmony in the community, and not upsetting the laws of nature, are basic expectations placed on all members of Japanese society, that take precedence over individual intellectual choices. However, social and economic change in recent years, together with globalization, is markedly affecting the Japanese and their feelings about religion.

3. Visual definition of sacred mountains in Japan

The theological definition of a sacred mountain is a widely discussed thesis topic in itself. This paper will concentrate on the visual conditions for nomination as sacred. Japanese sacred mountains vary considerably, which begs the question as to whether there are certain rules or a specific set of characteristics that define them as sacred. If so, it is interesting to discover what they might be.

Archaeological studies have often been instrumental in understanding the kind of ancient rituals, practiced on mountains. In Yamanashi prefecture, at the southern foot of Mount Yatsugatake, Kinsei ruins, dating back to 2500 B.C, underwent extensive archaeological study in the 1980s. The study confirmed that the community living there considered Mount Yatsugatake as their sacred mountain. According to legend,

---

2.   2005 Survey: http://www.mext.go.jp/b_menu/toukei/001/index39.htm.

Mount Yatsugatake was competing in height with Mount Fuji. Is height then an essential element for sacredness? It does not seem so. Some sacred mountains, such as Mount Fuji and Mount Aso, are volcanoes, while others are high snow-crowned mountains, such as Mount Hakusan. There are also numbers of rather small sacred mountains protruding singly in the middle or at the edges of plains. In China, the ragged character of the rocks can be an essential element, but in Japan, this does not seem to be a key factor.

Figure 1. Kinsei Ruin with *Yatsugatake* in the background.

There appear to be three major visual characteristics of Japanese sacred mountains: volcanic, snow crowned and *kannabi*. The first two characteristics are fairly self-explanatory, universal concepts. The third, *kannabi*, the main focus of this paper, is more specifically Japanese, and will be defined at more length.

3.1. Volcanic mountains

Active volcanoes are viewed as transcendental beings that possess awesome power to cause catastrophe by eruption. Japan, sitting right on top of the Pacific Ring of Fire, has many volcanoes that have been revered as objects of worship. Mount Fuji, the most prominent mountain in Japan, is also a volcano, which last erupted about 300 years ago. In particular, the stratovolcano's beautiful regular shape often leads to its being revered as sacred. Many archaeological finds have been unearthed from locations from which one can view such mountains. Mount Fuji is surrounded by *sengen jinja*[3], shrines dedicated to it, and has its own religious followers, the Fuji-ko. Mount Aso in Kumamoto, while not a stratovolcano, is nevertheless venerated. An active volcano with a huge inhabited caldera (from the edge of which the volcano vent can be viewed), it has many dedicated shrines in its vicinity. Other examples of this category are Mounts Asama in Nagano and Miharayama in Oshima, Tokyo.

Figure 2. A stratovolcano, Mount Fuji.

3.2. Snow-crowned mountains

Taller mountains, such as Mount Fuji, with snow-covered peaks, which stand out in stark contrast to their surroundings, are revered without exception. This is true worldwide: Chomolungma in Tibet/China and Tongariro in New Zealand are two examples among many. In Japan, Mounts Hakusan, Chokaisan, Gassan, Kurikomayama, Tateyama, Myoko, Mitake and Daisen all belong to this category. Throughout Japan, such mountains have attracted shrines and esoteric temples, since the mountainous setting suits ascetic training. It was natural for reverence for such mountains to emerge among people heavily dependent on agriculture. High snow-capped mountains made people aware of the source of abundant pure water. It was also believed that the mountain deities could call clouds to collect rain when needed.

---

3.   *Sengen jinja* is a common name for shrines revering Mount Fuji. More than 1300 *sengen jinjas* are in Japan.

Figure 3. Mount Kurikomayama.

3.3. Kannabi mountains

   Kannabi mountains, the main focus of this paper, are the most significant manifestation of Japanese beliefs towards the highest being. The word "*kannabi*" is not a commonly used term, but is used here to refer to a revered natural phenomenon such as a sacred forest or mountain.[4] It appears to originate from a term meaning "abode of divinity". The height of a *kannabi* mountain can be relatively low: no more than a hill with a vertical drop of several hundred meters. To be recognized as a *kannabi*, a mountain must be: a) beautiful and of regular proportions (close to a circular cone); b) located within a reasonable distance of a settlement on a nearby plain; c) covered with dense green forest. It should also have: d) a river running nearby so that divine seclusion is possible; and e) a big tree or gigantic stone in the vicinity. The last item is a desirable but not necessary condition. In China, the presence of an odd-shaped rock is evidence of the presence of a special spirit, but in Japan this is not the case.

---

4.   "*Kannabi*" can be used in the name of a specific location or mountain (e.g. *Kannabi*yama or *Kannabi* Mountain). However, these are by no means the only *kannabi*.

In East Asia, where Chinese Feng Shui principles have been used to select desirable city locations, major settlements may be located south of one or more mountains. A desirable mountain located to the north of a settlement is a valued concept. The cities of Fujiwara-kyo (7th Century), Heijo-kyo (8th Century) and Heian-kyo (9th Century) were all based on this planning philosophy. *Kannabi*, however, must be looked at separately from this philosophy, even though cardinal directions are also very important.

The most classic example of *kannabi* is Miwayama (Miwa Mountain), in the Yamato basin in Nara. The design of the shrine in Miwayama shows the ancient Shinto style of worship: the mountain itself serves as the main sanctuary building of the shrine. With Shinto shrine architecture, the natural phenomenon is frequently the actual sanctuary; shrine buildings are often merely a substitute for the natural phenomenon. To apply this to a church setting involves a paradigm shift. It would probably seem quite bizarre to most Christians to have a gateway and entrance hall leading only to a natural site, with no main building. In contrast, *kannnabi* often complete the architectural complex, in the same way as the body of a church provides the focus and location for Christian worship.

Figure 4. *Kannabi mountains: (left)Miwayama* and its *Torii* gate *(right)* Tambaizumosha (ca.1234) (Kageyama1971: frontispiece).

A typical example of *kannabi* embodying the assimilation of Shinto and Buddhism is Hie-sannosha (Hiyoshi Sannosha) and the related *kannabi*, Hie-Sanno, nearby. When the monk Saicho returned from China, he brought with him the idea of Chinese deities protecting Mount Tientai (Tendai in Japanese). In 788, Saicho opened an esoteric Buddhist Tendai school at Enryakuji temple on Mount Hiei, northeast of Kyoto, then capital of Japan. The Chinese idea of a deity protecting a natural phenomenon developed along with Japanese ideas to become ultimately a Japanese tradition. A mandala depicts this relationship between Enryakuji temple and Mount Hiei; Hie-sannnosha shrine is clearly depicted in the scroll to the east at the foot of Mount Hie-sanno, the *kannabi* for the shrine.

Other variations on *kannabi* mountains for fishermen can be found along the coast. The concept, however, also embraces other natural phenomena. Isolated islands in bays are also venerated: for example, the island shrines of Itsukushima in Hiroshima, Okinoshima in Fukuoka, Kamishima in Mie, and Chikubushima in Lake Biwa, Shiga.

Figure 5. *Sannomiya Mandarazu*, depicting both temple and shrine complex and *kannabi*: *Sannomiya Mandarazu*, Hietaisha shrine.

4. Key examples of *kannabi*: Obama and Hiraizumi

4.1. Obama City: a dense concentration of shrines and sacred mountains

Obama City in the Wakasa region has an incredible concentration of temples, shrines and *kannabi*. Obama is directly north of the ancient cities of Nara and Kyoto, facing the Sea of Japan, and was once active in trade with Korea and China. The deeply indented coastline of Obama yields spectacular views, with a series of capes jutting into the ocean. Situated behind the port and plain is the handsome Mount Tadagatake, formerly used as a navigation landmark, since its peak can be instantly recognized from the sea.

While some town houses in the port town of Obama date back as far as the early modern era, the old city blocks date back even further to the medieval era. Obama has a rich, diverse concentration of cultural assets, including Buddhist sculpture and paintings, historic buildings and districts, traditional landscapes and historic landmarks such as castle ruins. A large number of shrines and esoteric temples dating from the Nara and Heian periods (7th to 12th Centuries) are spread widely across an area centering on Mount Tadagatake. This clear manifestation of religious assimilation in Japan includes several classic examples of Buddhist halls of the 13th to 15th Centuries.

The entire landscape, created around a concentration of temples and shrines of this magnitude, is quite unusual, even in Japan. Small *kannabi*, called *shirayama*, are coupled with each temple in Obama to complete temple complexes. One theory states that the word "shirayama" originates from the word "Silla" (the Silla Dynasty in Korea), and reflects the connection between the Obama region and the external world.

Mount Tadagatake is also the *kannabi* of Tada shrine; Jinguji's *kannabi* is Mount Nagao. In these cases, buildings and mountains are located directly opposite one another, the main gate facing the mountain. In the cases of Wakasa Jinguji, Myoutsuji, Myourakuji, and Hagadera, one prays to the mountains from distant main pavilions. The step canopy of Jinguji main pavilion has a Shinto ceremonial rope and in the sanctuary, a Buddhist statue and a *kami* stand side by side. When these temples were at their height, each complex was much larger in scale, the many subordinate buildings creating an area of much more grandeur than now. People today, however, hardly recognize these *kannabi* and their significance. (See Fig. 6 on the following page.)

4.2. HIRAIZUMI: SAIHOJODO (WESTERLY PURE LAND) AND KANNABI MOUNTAINS

The "Pure Land" is the concept of ultimate bliss in Buddhism. It is imagined as a calm conflict-free utopia, with abundant greenery, surrounded by pure air and water, with water lilies in full bloom. Grass, trees, birds, animals, fish, insects, and all kinds of sentient beings live in harmony in the Pure Land.

In 12th Century northern Japan, the warrior leader, Kiyohira Fujiwara, attempted to actualize this concept, with the bold decision to build a city based on Buddhist Pure Land philosophy. Numerous cities along the Silk Road (the path of Buddhism from India, through China and various other countries, ultimately to Japan) were built with Buddhist concepts in mind. However, Hiraizumi is the most eastern of these ancient cities. Although there are no giant golden Buddha statues as in Bamiyan, there is a breathtaking Golden Pavilion.

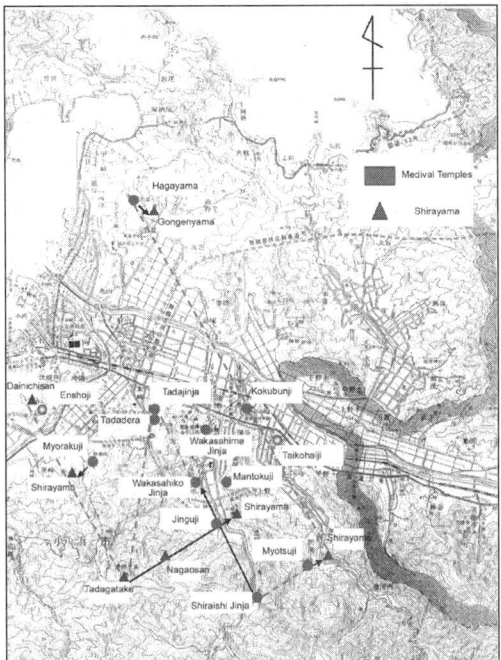

Figure 6. Distribution of temples, shrines and kannabi in Wakasa section of Obama.

The third generation Hidehira Fujiwara built Muryoko-in temple, following the same philosophy. *Muryoko* is Japanese for the Sanskrit *Amithaba* (Buddha of Infinite Light). Hidehira chose the location carefully so that the sacred mountain or *kannabi*, Mount Kinkei, can be viewed directly to the west, while a large pond lies east of the Golden Pavilion. The Pure Land is thought to be located in an imaginary realm, somewhere further west of where the Sun sets. At the summer solstice, viewed from Muryoko-in, the sun sets directly behind Mount Kinkei.

Inside Muryoko-in, there is a statue of *Amida-nyorai* (the Buddha who leads dead souls to the Pure Land). For Hidehira, it was important to reconcile both Shinto and Buddhist ideas of the after life harmoniously: according to Shinto, the souls of the dead should return to the mountains, signifying nature, while, according to Buddhist ideas, the enlightened among them would be taken to the Pure Land. Thus from Muryoko-in, souls would first pass through Mount Kinkei, where the *kami* would bless them; and then be led on to the westerly Pure Land. Further proof of the integration of Buddhism and Shinto beliefs exists in the Buddhist scrolls found buried at the peaks of surrounding mountains to delineate the boundaries of existing Pure Land. Hiraizumi is therefore quite a sophisticated example of the syncretistic role played by *kannabi*.

Figure 7. The Sun sets behind Mount Kinkei.

5. Conclusion

Regardless of formal education, the average Japanese person is brought up to sense the *kami* in all their various forms while, at the same time, seeing the light of Buddhism. The Japanese traditional belief in multitudinous gods (expressed literally as "eight million gods') results in a feeling that numerous gods and spirits surround us in every aspect of life. Many folklore traditions, based on the idea that both animate and inanimate things are sentient, still continue today, practiced even by Japanese who follow non-Shinto religions. Each season, people offer sake to the gods for permission to cut down trees; and before commencing new buildings, ground-calming ceremonies are held, even for high-tech buildings, to placate the earth spirits and ask their blessing. People take used needles and scissors to a shrine, before discarding them, to thank them for their hard work in the service of humans. People may also bring children's stuffed animals to shrines to be thanked and blessed before being discarded or burned at the shrine.

Figure 8. Harikuyo: People are placing their used needles into Tofu to rest.

In the world of Japanese philosophy, there is no dichotomy between men and nature, gods and men, or gods and nature. Even right and wrong can exist simultaneously and somehow be reconciled. This multitudinous existential philosophy, embracing spirituality, is strongly expressed in the works of both Hayao Miyazaki, the Academy Award winning animator of the film, Princess Mononoke, and the late Osamu Tezuka, the renowned Japanese forerunner of modern *manga* artists. As this paper has shown, the principles are also reflected in Japan's architecture and cultural heritage. In a sense, this is the Japanese traditional way to bring about peace and harmony. I believe that disseminating and explaining this idea to the world, as it is expressed through our cultural heritage, is a valuable Japanese contribution to world thought.

References

Earhart, H. Byron. 1965. *A religious study of the Mount Haguro Sect of Shugendo: an example of Japanese mountain religion.* Chicago: University of Chicago Press.

Earhart, H. Byron. 2004. *Japanese religion: unity and diversity,* 4th ed., Belmont: Wadsworth/Thomson Learning.

Harada, Toshiaki. 1970. *Nihon Kodai Shukyo.* Tokyo: Chuokoronsha.

Kalland, Arne and Pamela J. Asquith. *1997. Japanese Perceptions of Nature., Surrey, England: Curzon Press,*.

Kageyama, Haruki. 1971. *Shintaisan*. Tokyo: Gakuseisha.

Kyburtz, Josef A. 1997. *Magical Thought at the Interface of Nature and Culture*. Surrey, England: Curzon Press.

Oba, Iwao. 1977. *Genshi Bunkaronko*. Tokyo: Yuzankaku.

Takase, Shigeo. 1969. *Kodai sangaku shinko no shiteki kousatsu (Historical Consideration of Mountain Worship in Ancient Times)*. Tokyo: Kadokawa shoten.

Phenomenology of *Waqf* in Material Forming of Islamic Cities

Mohammad Taghi Pirbabaei
Tabriz Islamic Art University
Iran

Abstract

Waqf as an abstract idea is a legal, social, and economic institution of fundamental importance in Islamic societies. Its decisive role in influencing, material forming, and developing urban space and structure has been formulated within the framework of Islamic urban studies. In this paper, through a material culture theory and practical findings of studies in the historic Iranian City of Tabriz, we discuss that *Waqf* as a social practice contributes to the construction and reconstruction of places and their spirits. This survey shows that in this city *Waqf* as a popular institution in social use was continuously modified and adapted according to the needs, wishes and ideas of the people involved with it.

Résumé

Le *Waqf*, en tant qu'idée abstraite, est une institution juridique, sociale et économique d'importance fondamentale dans les sociétés islamiques. Son rôle décisif en ce qu'il a influencé, constitué matériellement et développée les structures et les espaces urbains a été formulé dans le cadre des études urbaines dans le monde musulman. Cet article, à travers une théorie de la culture matérielle et des découvertes concrètes effectuées dans la ville historique iranienne de Tabriz, montre que le *Waqf*, en tant que pratique sociale, contribue à la construction et à la reconstruction des lieux et de leur esprit. Cette étude montre que dans cette ville, le *Waqf*, en tant qu'institution populaire dans les usages sociaux fut continuellement modifié et adapté selon les besoins, les désirs et les idées des gens qui le mettaient en pratique.

The city is a cultural mould from which the personality of urban residents and their mode of social relations have arisen. The city or urban structure is the creator of values, attitudes and specific behaviors or, in other words, a mode of life, or a special cultural form. This special mode of life can include the nature of experiences and human awareness and behavior, or new forms of social organization (Flanagan, 1999: 342).

Rapoport remarks that most Moslem cities had quarters within which people lived together, bound by ties of language, religion, occupation, family, or common origin (Rapoport, 1980: 21)

The concepts of urban spaces – The square, street and so on – in the Middle East are quite different from those in the west. Kostof (1992) mentions that the *maidan* (square) is not the equivalent of the Roman Forum or the Campo in Sienna. There was no distinct civic arena in an Islamic city, because there was no municipality as such with its own character of privileges and responsibilities (Kostof, 1992: 127).

Stefano Bianca (2000), an architectural historian, explains some basic principles of Islam and their social implications in the historic Arab Islamic city. He says that "Perhaps the most significant social implication of Islam was the fact that the strength of its ritualized living patterns dispensed with the need for many formal institutions. A large number of administrative structures which are normally identified with cities – at least in Europe – did not develop, simply because society had internalized its structuring constraints, thus minimizing the need for external controls. Hence, the Muslim *res publica* was not the result of civil rights wrested from oppressive authorities but the outcome of the shared desire to follow certain religiously prescribed patterns of life... (Bianca 2000:169)."

The studies in the formation of Islamic cities reveal that the approaches, theories and methods of the discipline focus on one aspect of dwelling, i.e., on people's attitudes and value or on buildings, urban forms and urban structures. Heidegger (1971) argues that dwelling is no mere extension of existential space or place, rather it becomes itself the fundamental human activity, in the light of which both place and space find their first clarification. He interprets dwelling, the built environment, as crucial because it supports and reflects a person and group's way of being-in-the-world (Heidegger, 1971: 154).

Phenomenology and Material Culture

Pivcevic maintains that the aim of phenomenology is the study of experiences with the "aim of bringing out their essences, their underlying reason" (Pivcevic 1970: 11). Phenomenology is also described as a school of philosophy that studies the phenomena or the appearance of human experience while attempting to suspend all consideration of their subjective association or objective reality. Phenomenology is therefore neither a science of objects nor a science of subject, it is instead a science of experience (Thevenaz 1962). It does not focus on the objectivity or subjectivity of experience, but rather concentrates on the "point of contact where being and consciousness meet" (Thevenaz 1962: 19).

The foundations or roots of knowledge were to be found in the "things", in the phenomena to which all concepts referred. Phenomenology is thus the scientific study of the experience of things or phenomena just as they are seen by us and appear to us in consciousness. Phenomenology may be defined as the study of how phenomena appear. However, this is not limited to the visual domain. "Phenomenology demands receptivity to the full ontological potential of human experience. It therefore calls for a heightened receptivity of all senses and offers a depth model for understanding human existence." (Leach 1997: 83).

Space needs to be perceived with all its phenomenological associations. The cultural anthropologist Hall explicitly integrated the material environment as an "extension of the body". In "Hidden Dimensions", he dealt with details regarding the role of architecture, of furniture, and of the automobile, and above all, the aspect of proxemics and the perception of space (Hall, 1966, p. 51-63, 174-177). One cannot ignore the fact that values, attitudes, and norms are made "visible" only through their manifestations in artifacts and in their use, and that it is a vital ability of humans to draw conclusions from the visible objects to the invisible attitudes, values, thoughts, and feelings of their producers, owners or users. The material environment gained an ever growing importance for the everyday life and for the self-definition of people in industrialized societies which increasingly defined themselves through their material consumption. Also the objects by themselves are transferred or "communicated" across cultural boundaries. Probably the most important aspects, however, are the various relationships between humans and objects, particularly the cultural-specific usage of things and their symbolic aspects. Finally, it is a very important precondition for the understanding of, and the adequate behavior in, foreign cultures to be able to "read" the material environment adequately. The knowledge about things, their "proper" usage and the "proper" attitude towards them is culturally transmitted (Roth 2001).

It is not only the use of things and the attitudes towards them that are transmitted through everyday communication. The discursive exchange in a group or society also constructs ethnic, regional or national value attributions and the charging of objects with symbolic or identifying meaning (Roth 2001). These discourses can be intercultural and lead to the formation of identities

The physical nature of the artifacts is the key to understanding their power and significance in cultural construction. This physicality acts as a bridge between the mental and physical worlds, between consciousness and

the unconscious (Miller 1987). The material environment is not only produced and shaped by humans but as a quasi-natural environment it directly
affects their lives. In every culture, it constitutes a specific context and reality
which strongly determines the experience and the everyday life of the individual. In an often forceful way, it can influence, paralyze or stimulate the
individual and generate positive or negative feelings.

Everyday knowledge (which is self-evident for the native) comprises the
typical functions, uses, and behaviors. Material orders are thus indicators
of concepts of social order and values. Everyday knowledge finally extends
to the ideological, religious, social, and cultural norms and values, also the
attitudes and basic assumptions with which the objects are imbued. They
can differ greatly between cultures (Roth 2001).

The material environment and the way it is used are indicators of social
and aesthetic norms, values, attitudes, basic assumptions, ideologies, and
myths of a society.

Waqf as a Material Culture

Waqf is a legal, social and economic institution of fundamental importance
in Islamic societies. Its decisive role in influencing, shaping and developing
urban space and structures has been formulated within the framework of
Islamic urban studies, and it adds religious endowment as a major characteristic
to the definition of an "Islamic City" (Gaube 1984). A *waqf* is an inalienable
religious endowment in Islam, typically devoting a building or plot of land
for Muslim religious or charitable purposes. It is conceptually similar to the
common law trust. In common law legal systems, a trust is an arrangement
whereby property (including real, tangible and intangible) is managed by one
person (or persons, or organizations) for the benefit of another.

The *waqf* in Islamic law, developed in the medieval Islamic world from
the 7th to 9th centuries, bears a notable resemblance to the English trust law.
The trust law developed in England at the time of the Crusades, during the
12th and 13th centuries. The trust was introduced by Crusaders who may
have been influenced by the *waqf* institutions they came across in the Middle
East (Gaudiosi 1988). Every *waqf* was required to have a *waqif* (founder),
mutawillis (trustee), *qadi* (judge) and beneficiaries (Gaudiosi 1988: 1237).
Under both a *waqf* and a trust, "property is reserved, and its usufruct appropriated, for the benefit of specific individuals, or for a general charitable
purpose; the corpus becomes inalienable; estates for life in favor of successive
beneficiaries can be created" and "without regard to the law of inheritance or
the rights of the heirs; and continuity is secured by the successive appointment
of trustees or *mutawillis*" (Gaudiosi 1988: 1247).

More recently, the significance of *waqf* for an economic and social history that incorporates the "normal population", as well as for a history of

mentalities has been conceived and developed (Leeuwen 1999). Still, there is much to be inquired about concerning the changing role of *waqf* as a legal and social institution. Like all aspects of Islamic law in practice, it was much more subject to change and transformation than hitherto assumed. Lambton (1997) argues that, *waqf* as a popular institution in "use" was continuously modified and adapted according to the needs, wishes and ideas of the people involved with it. In its general objectives and purposes as well as in the minute stipulations concerning its administration and the disbursement of its revenues, the institution of *Waqf* reflects changes in the economic sphere along with more subtle transformations in value and belief systems. Moreover, through an analysis of the persons participating in its implementation, whether as founders, administrators, beneficiaries, or jurists, one can attain a view of the society as a whole. In this regard, the importance of *Waqf* as an indicator and mirror of social change cannot be overestimated (Werner 2000: 97).

Waqf in Material Forming of Tabriz

Tabriz, a city in northwest Iran and the centre of the historical Province of Azerbaijan is one of the most important cities of Iran with a long historical tradition and culture of its own. It was a major urban center located on the Great Silk Road, an ancient trade route between China and the Mediterranean. Tabriz was in its heyday 700 years ago, the capital of the Mongol dynasty in Iran and a regional intellectual and cultural hub under Il-Khan Mahmud Ghazan (1295-1304). Ghazan Khan's wazir, or Lord Chancellor, Khajeh Rashid al-Din Fazlollah Hamadani, founded an academic complex known as the *Rab' i-Rashidi*, or suburb of Rashid as a *waqf*, on the outskirts of Tabriz. This contained a paper mill, library, teaching hospital, orphanage, caravanserai, textile factory, teachers' training college and seminary and attracted students and thinkers from as far away as China. The purpose of this endowment, or *waqf*, was to ensure that as many of the scientific treatises authored by Rashid al-Din, or which fell into his possession, could be copied as protection against destruction. The manuscript with 382 pages of the Deed of Endowment was submitted to the Memory of the World Register and inscribed in 2007. Due to the vast scope of the endowed properties and the high value of them as well as the high status of the *Rab' i-Rashidi*, this manuscript is of universal significance. Moreover the institution of the *waqf*, or endowment, is a central pillar of Islamic society, and this Deed therefore provides an important record of political and economic administration in Central Asia at a time of great dynamism and change (Memory of the World Register 2007).

The list of such *Waqfs* (endowments) in the history of Tabriz is impressive and considerable in the material forming of the city: the endowments by Abu al-Nasr Hasan Beg, a prominent Aq Quyunlu *amir* in the 15th century, that was known as the *mauqufa-i Nasriya* or the complex of Hasan Padishah, the endowments of Sadiqiya, founded by Mirza Mohammad Sadiq in the 18th century, a bazaar alley in the main bazaar which is known as the *Bazar-i Sadiqiya*, a set of endowments known commonly as the *mauqufat-i Qaim-Maqami*, or the Qaim-Maqam endowments, which includes six independent *Waqf*-deeds in the 19th century, and so many other examples.

Another endowment known as *Zahiriya* represents an example of a large *Waqf*-complex in the Safavid era in the 17th century in Tabriz. It was placed around the important tomb of Sayyid Hamza, incorporated a mosque, a *madrasa*, and additional buildings like a pharmacy, and was endowed with huge properties (Karang 1995: 361). These endowments were made by Mirza Mohammad Ibrahim Zahir al-Din, who was the *vazir* of Azerbaijan under the Safavid Shah Sulaiman. He completed the buildings in 1680 and made the endowments in the same year (Werner 2000: 99). This pious foundation is remarkable and is still in existence. It survived the fall of the Safavid dynasty, the Ottoman occupation of Azerbaijan, as well as the numerous local wars daunting Azerbaijan and Iran. Nevertheless the character of these endowments did not remain the same and they continued to undergo significant changes and alterations in our period, particularly concerning their size and their management.

Examining this continuity and these transformations helps to answer the question of who actually controlled the *waqf*, and how the *waqf's* properties were defended against usurpation.

Waqf endowments belonged to society but not as a public realm as in modern cities. It was not only a tangible but also an intangible heritage of the city. This paper, through a material culture theory and phenomenological approach to urban spaces, reveals that *Waqf* as a popular institution in social use contributed to the construction and reconstruction of places and their sprites in the City of Tabriz and has an important role in making sense of place in this historic city. The values and meanings assigned to these *Waqfs*, as material cultures, indicate the people's connection to the city, Tabriz.

References

Bianca, Stefano. 2000. *Urban Form in the Arab World: Past and Present*. London and New York: Thames and Hudson.

Flanagan, William G. 1999. *Urban Sociology: Images and Structure*. Boston: Mass, London: Allayn and Bacon.

Gaube, Heinz. 1984. Die grosen Stiftungen (*Waqf*). *Aleppo*. ed. H. Gaube and E. Wirth. Wiesbaden (TAVO, B 58): 126-139. Quoted in Werner, Christoph. 2000. *An Iranian Town in Transition: A Social and Economic History of the Elites of Tabriz, 1747-1848.* Wiesbaden: Harrassowitz Verlag.

Gaudiosi, Monica M. 1988. The Influence of the Islamic Law of *Waqf* on the Development of the Trust in England: The Case of Merton College. *University of Pennsylvania Law Review* 136 (April): 1231-1261.

Hall, E.T. 1966. *The Hidden Dimension.* Garden City, NY: Doubleday. Quoted in Roth, Klaus. 2001. Material culture and international communication. *International Journal of Intercultural Relations* 25: 563-580.

Hayashi, Kayoko. 1992. The Vakif Institution in 16th Century Istanbul: An analysis of the Vakif Survey register of 1546. *The Memories of the Toyo Bunko,* 50, 93-113.

Heidegger, Martin. 1971. *Poetry, Language, Thought.* New York: Harper and Row.

Karang, Abdal Ali. 1995 (1374). *Asar-i bastani-i Azerbaijan: Asar va abniye-i tarikhi-i shahristan-i Tabriz.* Tehran: Rasti Nou Press.

Kostof, Spiro. 1992. *The City Assembled.* London: Thames and Hudson Ltd.

Lambton, Ann K. S. 1997. Awqaf in Persia: 6th to 8th /12th-14th Centuries. *Islamic Law and Society* 4, 298-318.

Leach, Neil. 1997. *Rethinking Architecture: A Reader in Cultural Theory.* London: Routledge.

Leeuwen, Richard Van. 1999. *Waqfs and Urban Structures: The Case of Ottoman Damascus.* Leiden: E.J. Brill.

Memory of the World Register. 2007. *The Deed for Endowment: Rab'I-Rashidi 13th Century Manuscript.* Internet. Available from http://portal.unesco.org/ci/en/ev.php-URL_ID=22372&URL_DO=DO_TOPIC&URL_SECTION=201.html; accessed 20 June 2008.

Miller, Daniel. 1987. *Material Culture and Mass consumption.* Oxford: Blackwell.

Pivcevic, Edo. 1970. *Husserl and Phenomenology.* London: Hutchinson University Library.

Rapoport, Amos. 1980. *Human Aspects of Urban Form.* Oxford: Pergamon Press Ltd.

Roth, Klaus. 2001. Material culture and international communication. *International Journal of Intercultural Relations* 25: 563-580.

Thevenaz, Pierre. 1962. *What is Phenomenology? And Other Essays.* Edited and Translated by Edie, James M. Chicago: Quadrangle Books.

Werner, Christoph. 2000. *An Iranian Town in Transition: A Social and Economic History of the Elites of Tabriz, 1747-1848.* Wiesbaden: Harrassowitz Verlag.

Drama, Place and Verifiable Link
Underwater Cultural Heritage, Present Experience and Contention

Thijs J. Maarleveld
International Committee on the
Underwater Cultural Heritage (ICOMOS / ICUCH)
Maritime Archaeology Programme
Syddansk Universitet
Denmark

ABSTRACT

If heritage is defined by the way it is experienced, then underwater cultural heritage is in a very specific position indeed. Is it defined by adventure and diving? Is it the realm of meticulous scientists engaging in detailed analysis? Or is it the exclusive domain of "in situ" protectionists who take draconic measures and spoil every experience of the spirit of place? All positions can be taken. Contemporary thinking on being in the landscape, embodiment and the experience of place are an inspiration for heritage management. However, such thinking does not provide practical answers for those places which are beyond the horizon, outside the common field of vision. Imagination and dramatic mystery compensate for the absence of direct experience, but are hardly helpful as a basis for well-considered decisions. The drama of shipwreck is just one aspect. Submerged lands- capes extending beyond national borders raise similar concerns. Like wreck sites they reflect the connection of places, besides being a place in themselves. Underwater cultural heritage is central to global interaction and development. It is central to the concentration of population and power. However, it is never centrally located. Does that affect its signifi- cance? Such questions are explored in view of practical implementation of protective policies such as the 2001 UNESCO Convention promotes, putting forward such concepts as that of "verifiable link". Significance is never equivocal, but may be much larger in a global perspective, than in relationship to one specific place, whatever its spirit.

Résumé

Si le patrimoine se définit par la manière dont il est ressenti, alors le patrimoine culturel sous-marin se trouve de fait dans une situation très particulière. Peut-on le définir par l'aventure et la plongée sous-marine ? Est-ce le royaume des scientifiques méticuleux engagés dans des analyses détaillées ? Ou n'est-il que le domaine exclusif de protectionnistes « in situ » qui prennent des mesures draconiennes et gâchent toute expérience de l'esprit du lieu ? Toutes les prises de position sont possibles. La pensée contemporaine portant sur le fait d'être dans le paysage, sur l'incarnation et l'expérience du lieu, constitue une source d'inspiration pour la gestion patrimoniale. Cependant, une telle pensée ne fournit pas de réponses pratiques pour ces lieux qui se trouvent au-delà de l'horizon, hors du champ de vision habituel. L'imagination et le mystère spectaculaire viennent compenser l'absence d'expérience directe, mais n'apportent aucune contribution aux décisions réfléchies. Le drame des naufrages n'en constitue qu'un aspect. Les paysages sous-marins qui s'étendent au-delà des limites territoriales nationales soulèvent des problèmes similaires. Comme les sites de naufrages, ils reflètent la connexion entre les lieux, en plus d'être des lieux en eux-mêmes. Le patrimoine culturel sous-marin est essentiel à l'interaction globale et au développement. Cela affecte-t-il sa signification ? De telles questions sont explorées dans la perspective d'une mise en œuvre concrète des politiques de protection telles que celle recommandée par la Convention de l'Unesco de 2001, qui met de l'avant des concepts tels que le « lien vérifiable ». La signification n'est jamais équivoque, mais peut se révéler plus étendue dans une perspective globale que dans la relation avec un lieu particulier, quel que soit son esprit.

1. Rethinking the Spirit of Place

The spirit of place is an inspirational topic. Rethinking it binds the entire spectrum of heritage, of heritage efforts (or their absence) and of heritage experience through the intangible dimension. Rethinking the spirit of place leads us along many stations. The romantic sir Walter Scott's for instance, in whose Antiquary's study "…midst of this wreck of ancient books and utensils, with a gravity equal to Marius among the ruins of Carthage, sat a large black cat, which, to a superstitious eye might have presented the genius loci, the tutelar dæmon of the apartment…" (Scott 1821, 22). Another important station is the dense, long denied (and for good political reasons) but lately much revitalized and cherished thinking of the philosopher Martin Heidegger on dwelling and "being in the world" (Heidegger 1927; Thomas 1996). And finally, we should not forget the basic, down-to-earth thinking that informs the profitable cash-machine of the experience economy (Bærenholdt 2004).

Wonderful! What a concept! And nevertheless I have a problem with it. Not so much personally, perhaps. I am a human and a consumer too. I like to live in an attractive place I can connect to, and I like to visit interesting places. And it is not beyond me to wonder why I experience the one place as moving, wonderful, impressive, eerie or depressive, whereas in other places I just switch off and have no use for my surroundings. So far so good, but professionally, I have a problem. Or worse, the more I think about it the more problems I have. What profession is that? My field is maritime and underwater heritage and indeed, you are right: if I would just change profession I would not have a problem or bring it forward. But I stay put and I even think that the issues are not just interesting in their own right, but have wider implications as well.

The issues arising from the developing field of maritime heritage management stretch our approaches to heritage in such a way that perhaps we should reconsider some of the implicit assumptions that underlie archaeology and heritage management in a national and a terrestrial setting. Rethinking the spirit of place is a case in point. The problems I see refer to or interfere with the setting of priorities, with national administration and international coordination. As such their continuation or resolution has wide and vigorous implications for our approaches to heritage, to shared heritage worldwide. What better platform than ICOMOS to discuss them at the conceptual as well as at the operational level.

2. A Place at Sea

In architecture and especially monumental architecture, place by definition is a matter of choice. In maritime heritage this is evidently less so, but that does not necessarily diminish the dramatic meaning of the events to which such heritage refers. They have become a theme in art and literature since art or literature was created. Shakespeare's Tempest' (2001) and the remains of the "Sea Venture" on Bermuda (Wingood 1986; Adams 2003), the remains of the event that inspired the play, are intricately related. Besides that – but that is not the point now – shipbuilding has evidently produced architecture of outstanding universal value of great significance to the development of humankind at regular intervals at least as far back as the Middle Paleolithic (Maarleveld 1994; Renfrew 2007, 139). And this architecture – ship architecture – has always been more likely to end up somewhere else than where it was created. Are we talking "displaced" heritage by the virtue of that simple fact? Perhaps, but that does not deprive the place where it ended up of drama or of a "spirit of place" (Figure 1).

Figure 1. The wreck of the SS American Star on the coast of Fuerteventura, Canary Islands, as photographed by Thomas Wollex on July 2, 2004. The ship, on which construction began in 1936 was launched in 1939 and baptized as SS America by first lady Eleanor Roosevelt. After a long and partly eventful career, for instance as troop carrier USS West Point during World War II and as liner and charter under a variety of names, she was to be turned into a luxury hotel at Phuket in Thailand under the name SS American Star, but ran aground at the beginning of January 1994 and was wrecked.

Not every wreck site, however, looks as dramatic as this one. Let us dwell on the site in Figure 2. It is an important site, for myself and for my discipline, especially in Holland. After a dramatic struggle on what should prevail, private interest of the finder or public interest of preservation, it was the first wreck site in Dutch waters that was listed as a protected monument, and it was the first such monument to be physically protected in situ (Maarleveld 1988; Manders 2006). Moreover, quite intrinsically it is an important site as well. It is the best preserved example of a western European Eastindiaman of the early 17th century that we know of, reflecting contacts that have structurally influenced cultures and societies in very different parts of the world. It was so on discovery in 1986. It lost that status shortly when two shipwrecks, the "Nassau" and the "Middelburg", were discovered in the Straits of Malacca. But a quick salvage operation put an end to that (Bound 1998). Porcelain was recovered, site and ship architecture were quickly annihilated in both cases and that adds to the rarity, the exclusiveness of this particular site. It is also an illustration of the fragility and the finality of the resource, by the way.

So the importance of the site, *Burgzand Noord III* stands out. But what of drama, what of "spirit of place"? Well, plenty of that at the time of sinking, but 350 years later, some ten years ago, I took my then incoming director, Henriette van der Linden, to the place: she was not very impressed at all. And no one looking at Figure 2 will be very impressed either.

Figure 2. Burgzand Noord III, a dramatic place? Below, under 6 metres of murky water, fine-grained tidal deposits, protective netting and no less than 6000 sandbags lies the best preserved example of a seventeenth century European Eastindiaman that we presently know of. By the tacit extension of ancient monuments legislation, archaeological remains in Dutch waters are under blanket protection. Moreover, this site was listed as a national monument in 1988. But what of the "Spirit of the place"? Photo RACM.

That had been different with the Director General, Jan Riezenkamp, who had preceded her in visiting the place when it had just been consolidated in 1988. But then, the day that suited his calendar was windy and this is at sea and he was dramatically seasick all day. The "tutelar demon", the evil spirit of the place certainly impressed him and he will never forget.

3. Experiencing the Past and a Problem or Two

Nevertheless, the question whether a wreck site, an underwater site can be subject to the same sort of experience of spirit of place as any other site is not really at issue. It can, and that is true both for wreck sites and sites resulting from submerged settlements. Of course there are limitations to access. But on the one hand some sites are accessible to ever larger groups who learn to dive as a hobby, and on the other hand there are additional ways of visualization and recreation of experience (Grenier 2006; Leino et al. 2004; Manders 2004). More techniques and alternatives will be developed. Virtual access through Internet or GPS and phone messages is certain to develop (Thomsen 2007). These alternatives may never replace authenticity, but will evoke a real experience all the same, realistically or not. It is quite clear that heritage management, researchers and stakeholders in the experience economy face many challenges in that respect, but these are only different in degree from the challenges faced in similar efforts, recreations, re-enactments of other parts of the heritage spectrum.

What then is my problem if it is not the concept of spirit of place as such? Well, actually it is two problems, but if we do not heed, they may reinforce each other. One is the link of spirit of place to the concept of landscape and the other is the link of spirit of place to the concept of community. Both are based in lucid and influential thinking. Tuan, Olwig, Ingold, these are all names I have heard during this conference. Their work can and should be explored with a view to include the fallout (dramatic or less dramatic) of maritime activities, maritime society and maritime history. But the way in which the link of spirit of place to the concept of landscape and the link of spirit of place to the concept of community are presently explored may actually block that, if we are not aware of some of the pitfalls.

4. Being in Landscape and its Distractions

The thinking on landscape, on physical being in the landscape, on physically experiencing the landscape, embodiment of the environment and experiencing the past in the landscape is thoroughly influencing both archaeology, anthropology and human geography (Lemaire 1997; Ingold 2000; Olwig 2002; Tuan 2007). Heritage perception follows suit. Nothing wrong with that. For the acute problems facing an individual site it is not necessarily helpful. But is that problematic? Only if a whole category is systematically left out. Within each category, after all, there is lots of compensation through those examples that get more attention. But what of the sea? Although there are some inspiring studies on the maritime cultural landscape (Westerdahl 1987-1989, 1992; McErlean, McConkey & Forsythe 2002), even these tend to focus on coastal zones rather than maritime space. Moreover, the rising fascination with landscape concepts, monumental landscapes, urban landscapes, ritual landscapes etc. inevitably puts a stronger focus on inland tracts and inland travelling than on maritime contacts. In other words, the fascination inadvertently denies the fact that maritime contacts have been at least as intensive and significant as movements through the landscape. Likewise, it inadvertently denies that such contacts have equally left their traces, their heritage in the real present-day world, albeit that some of the most significant monuments and assemblages are covered by water, loads of water in many cases. By sheer preoccupation with other interesting topics, such maritime heritage is more or less automatically left out of the equation. For all practical purposes the landscape canvas is delimited in such a way as to exclude it. That unconsciously feeds back into what is considered significant and what is not. In other words this otherwise interesting conceptual development risks leading away from the recognition of very significant heritage indeed. Lack of scientific consideration may be the result. But that is just one side of a double effect. The other side is more serious, more potentially destructive socially and more awkward for the credibility of traditional heritage protection policies. Leading away from the consideration of underwater sites as significant heritage gives a free ticket for antiquarianism and object- oriented approaches. And obviously there is an over-greedy antiquities market at the extreme end.

5. Being in the Community and its Consequences

The second issue, the link between the spirit of place and community, is perhaps even more problematic. No, actually it is not. In principle it is not. But it needs to come a long way and that is why I highlight it here. An implicit assumption of studies addressing the issues is that there is a community – a present-day community, however diverse, however multi-cultural, however self-defined – with a range of interests, vested or not, in the heritage concerned. The approach underscores that heritage is not the prerogative of heritage professionals as an accessory of the nation state and quite rightly so (Cleere 1988; Merriman 2004; Holtorf 2007; Tully 2007). There is a corollary, however, and that is the tacit assumption that at least part of that community is "local". Mostly, that assumption is real enough, but at sea? Not really!

The problem here again is not so much that there is a flaw in the line of thinking. As a matter of fact there is no reason to doubt that the assumption of a community relating to heritage in maritime zones may be applicable. However, the major pitfall is that this heritage is not physically located in the space of a community. In other words, whereas we tend to accept that "significance and spirit of place relate to the experience of a local community and the way in which that experience gives meaning to the heritage," that is just a completely wrong assumption. That is odd, as in itself such a tenet is reasonable and acceptable enough. But the pitfall is that in the absence of a local community, the significance of heritage would then be less. The pitfall is very serious in the real world. Logically, after all – and this perhaps is the logic of the local politician listening to his or her local constituency – the consequence is that heritage at sea is not significant. And although that may be sound logic, I do not want to accept it. I do not want to accept that heritage that has no local basis for debate is intrinsically less important than heritage that has a local community identifying with it. There must be better ways to think through the link between place and landscape and the link between spirit of place and community.

6. Communinity, Place and Constituency

Heritage at sea has a constituent community as well. But even more so than with heritage on land, this community is spread far and wide. There are several reasons for this. The dramatic event of shipwreck can impact a large area. It can even have structural effects in its aftermath that affect communities not involved in the first place. "Torrey Canyon" (1967) "Amoco Cadiz" (1978), "Exxon Valdez" (1989) and "Prestige" (2002) are more or less contemporary disasters that stress the point at a huge contemporary scale. More localized and with more positive effects is the example of cranberry cultivation on the Dutch coastal island of Terschelling. The cranberry (*Oxus macrocarpus*) is North American and not indigenous to Europe. Its spread on Terschelling is the direct result of a barrel washed ashore on the island's coast in 1840 (de Feyfer-Teutelink 1976).

Moreover, it is as good as a rule that the ship itself, the goods it carries and its complement have very varied and widespread cultural backgrounds. It is not a contemporary development or an exception that a Danish owned ship, registered in Panama, with a German captain, a White Russian second officer, a South African engineer and a mixed crew from the Philippines and Cape Verde transports Asian goods to Canada. As a result, an archaeological wreck site, encapsulated in the local environment, can invariably be linked to a range of different areas, communities and – in a very revealing manner – to their contacts and exchange. A major part of their significance lies in that simple fact.

In a very Dutch ship, sunken in very Dutch waters in the late 16th century, that we excavated with an international team in the 1990s we found connections ranging from Poland and Germany to Portugal and Italy (Daalder et al. 1998). No wonder! After all, it was a ship! In the Bronze Age site of Ulu Burun in Turkey, the entire Middle East is represented, together with the Eastern Mediterranean and further afield (Yalçin, Pulak & Slotta 2005). The consequences in terms of community or community empowerment have hardly been explored. On the one hand it is clear that in one way or another more and more people around the world come to relate to this heritage in general or to a specific wreck site in particular. But on the other hand it is equally clear that such wider identification only comes about if and when the existence of that heritage gets to be known – through publications, exhibitions and other forms of exposure. Generally, that only happens many years after first discovery, many years after the time when the first assessment of significance has to be made. It is therefore inconceivable that such a constituent community can contribute in the decision making that leads to protection, exposure or annihilation. Conversely, it is purely imaginary to make decision making dependent on the strength of such a constituent community. But in the everyday reality of civil society, where decisions depend to a large extent on the strength of their proponents, that is nevertheless exactly what happens, not necessarily with satisfactory results.

For younger periods occasional studies have been carried through that look into the community relating to a heritage site that originated in shipwreck. An emotive example that comes to mind is Gribble's research into the meaning of the proud Steam Ship ss. Mendi (Wessex Archaeology 2007, 2008). It was a South African ship used as a troop carrier in the First World War. It sank in the cold waters of the British Channel in February 1917 and 33 crew, 22 white officers and 805 black privates of the fifth Batallion of the South African Native Labour Contingent that would have been destined for the battlefields of the Somme, fatefully went down before they could face that other fate. Other tentative examples relate to the remains of slave ships, transport ships of contract and conscripted labor, immigrants and pilgrims, not a minor subject in the history of today's intercultural and international relations (Gesner 1991; Nutley 1995; Webster 2008). But in general terms, the relationship between a place originating from maritime displacement and a community that is dispersed far and wide, remains unexplored.

7. Verifiable Link as a Concept in Management

In purely practical terms of protection and management, the UNESCO Convention on the Protection of the Underwater Cultural Heritage of 2001 introduces the concept of "verifiable link". The Convention entered into force on January 2, 2009, but has started to influence policy and practice since its conclusion in 2001 (Dromgoole 2006). The concept of "verifiable link" is introduced in order to cater for the involvement of others – particularly states with strong feelings of identification – in management under the coordination of the most appropriate, most nearby coastal state. It thereby tries to resolve the potential and all too real contention between claimants of exclusive rights and public responsibilities that should be shared among states. It is in the spirit of this concept that English Heritage and the South African Heritage Resources Agency (SAHRA) jointly commissioned the survey of ss Mendi's wreck site in the Channel. It is in the spirit of this concept also that the widely varied thinking on exclusive ownership and sovereign immunity can be reconciled with shared public responsibility for heritage values. At present many discoveries are veiled in confusion and unnecessary contention Let us hope that States indeed will adopt these principles in practicse, so that they can assert their perceived historical rights without compromising heritage protection (Maarleveld 2008).

The network of links encapsulated in a site, however, is so complex, and may be so extremely extensive, that it risks diluting into "everyone responsible, no one taking responsibility". And although in principle and in many practical ways that may be preferable to many kinds of exclusive appropriation that we have seen in the past, it still poses a problem. It needs some wisdom on behalf of decision makers involved. Coastal states need to take the lead. They will only do so, if our thinking on significance and landscape, spirit of place and community empowerment does not lead them away from the universal value of dramatic places with such widespread communities and so many verifiable links; if our thinking does not dilute the issues. I challenge you to incorporate those challenging aspects in general thinking on heritage and to explore a solution for the tension between Drama, Place and Verifiable link.

Acknowledgements

This essay which was presented in the Scientific Symposium in Québec on the theme "Rethinking the spirit of place" profited strongly from the feedback of my colleagues in ICOMOS-ICUCH as well as the dialectic confrontations that archaeology and underwater heritage management continue to have with those who appropriate underwater cultural heritage to feed the antiquities market. Confrontations with those who condone and "legitimize" such a line of action have perhaps been even more influential. Moreover, I would like to thank all participants and discussants at the Ph.d. seminar "At opleve (på) stedet" (Experience Place) that we held at the Esbjerg Campus of SDU in Oktober 2007, especially Jørgen Ole Bærenholdt and Kenneth Olwig, as well as Carina Ren and Beate Knuth Federspiel, who, besides taking the load of organization, defined the discussion topics and put me to work.

References

Adams, Jonathan. 2003. *Ships, Innovation and Social Change*. Stockholm: Stockholm University.

Bound, Mensun, Ong S. Hin, & Nigel Pickford. 1998. The Excavation of the Nassau. *Excavating Ships of War*, ed. Mensun Bound, 84-105. Oswestry: Anthony Nelson.

Bærenholdt, Jørgen Ole. 2004. *Performing tourist places*. Aldershot: Ashgate Publishing.

Cleere, Henry, 1988. Whose archaeology is it anyway? *Extracting Meaning from the Past* ed. John Bintliff, 37-43. Oxford: Oxbow.

Daalder, Remmelt, Els van Eyck van Heslinga, J. Thomas Lindblad, Peter Rogaar & Peter Schonewille. 1998. *Goud uit Graan, Nederland en het Oostzeegebied 1600-1850*. Zwolle: Waanders.

Dromgoole, Sarah (ed.). 2006. *The Protection of the Underwater Cultural Heritage. National Perspectives in Light of the UNESCO Convention 2001*. Leiden: Martinus Nijhoff.

de Feyfer-Teutelink, F.E. 1976. *De cranberry van Terschelling: geschiedenis, teelt, verspreiding en beschrijving van de plant: enige bereidingswijzen van cranberry-gerechten.* Midsland: Stichting VVV-Terschelling.

Gesner, Peter. 1991. A maritime archaeological approach to the Queensland labour trade. *Bulletin of the Australian Institute for Maritime Archaeology*, 15.2, 15-20.

Heidegger, Martin. 1927. *Sein und Zeit.* Halle a.d. Saale: Niemeyer.

Holtorf, Cornelius. 2007. *Archaeology is a brand: the meaning of archaeology in contemporary popular culture.* Walnut Creek: Left Coast Press.

Ingold, Tim 2000. *The perception of the environment: essays on livelihood, dwelling and skill.* London: Routledge.

Leino, Minna, Hauke Jöns, Stefan Wessman & Carl Olof Cederlund. 2004. Visualizing Underwater Cultural Heritage in the MoSS-project. *Monitoring, Safeguarding and Visualizing North-European Shipwreck Sites: Final Report*, ed. Carl Olof Cederlund, 49-51. Helsinki: The National Board of Antiquities.

Lemaire, Ton. 1997. Archaeology between the invention and the destruction of the landscape. *Archaeological Dialogues*, 4 /1 (May), 5-38.

Maarleveld, Thijs. 1988. Texel – Burgzand III: een scheepswrak met bewapening. *Archeologie in Nederland. De rijkdom van het bodemarchief*, ed. W.A. van Es, H. Sarfatij and P.J. Woltering, 189-191. Amsterdam: Meulenhoff.

Maarleveld, Thijs. 1994. Het ruime sop of wanneer de mens ging varen. *Spiegel Historiael* 29 (7/8): 277-282.

Maarleveld, Thijs. 2008. Why and How will Underwater Cultural Heritage Benefit from the 2001 Convention? *Museum International* No. 240, 60/4, 57-69.

Manders, Martijn. 2004. Combining "Monitoring, Safeguarding and Visualizing" to Protect our Maritime Heritage. *Monitoring, Safeguarding and Visualizing North-European Shipwreck Sites: Final Report*, ed. Carl Olof Cederlund, 74-75. Helsinki: The National Board of Antiquities.

Manders, Martijn. 2006. The In Situ Protection of a 17th-Century Trading Vessel in the Netherlands. *Underwater Cultural Heritage at Risk: Managing Natural and Human Impacts*, ed. Robert Grenier, David Nutley, Ian Cochran, 70-72. Paris: ICOMOS.

McErlean, Thomas, Rosemary McConkey & Wes Forsythe. 2002. Strangford Lough: an archaeological survey of the maritime cultural landscape. Belfast: Blackstaff Press.

Merriman, Nick. 2004. *Public archaeology.* London: Routledge.

Nutley, David. 1995. More than a shipwreck: the convict ship Hive – Aboriginal and European contact site. Bulletin of the Australian Institute for Maritime Archaeology 19/2, 17-26.

Olwig, Kenneth Robert. 2002. *Landscape, nature, and the body politic: from Britain's renaissance to America's new world.* Madison: University of Wisconsin Press.

Renfrew, Colin. 2008. *Prehistory: The Making of the Human.* London: Weidenfeld & Nicolson.

Scott, Walter. 1821. *The Antiquary. A Romance.* Boston: Samuel H. Parker.

Shakespeare , William. 2001. *The tempest*, ed. Virginia Mason Vaughan and Alden T. Vaughan. London: Arden.

Thomas, Julian. 1996. *Time, Culture and Identity: An Interpretive Archaeology,* London: Routledge.

Thomsen, Mikkel. 2007. Worlds Beneath: multimedia information about underwater sites and monuments on a mobile terminal Available from http://vikingeskibsmuseet.dk/index.php?id=1271&L=1; accessed 5 February 2009.

Tuan, Yi-fu. 2007. *Space and place: the perspective of experience.* Reprint 1st. edition 1977. Minneapolis: University of Minnesota Press.

Tully, Gemma. 2007. Community archaeology: general methods and standards of practice. *Public Archaeology, 6/3*, 155-187.

Webster, Jane. 2008. Slave Ships and Maritime Archaeology: An Overview *International Journal of Historical Archaeology* 12, 6-19.

Wessex Archaeology. 2007. SS Mendi Archaeological Desk-Based Assessment. Ref: 64441.01. Available from http://splash.wessexarch.co.uk/author/john-gribble/; accessed 5 February 2009.

Wessex Archaeology. 2008. SS Mendi Geophysical Survey:

Data Processing and Assessment. Ref: 64442.02. Available from http://splash.wessexarch.co.uk/author/john-gribble/; accessed 5 February 2009.

Westerdahl, Christer. 1987-89. *Norrlandsleden: The Norrland sailing route.* Härnösand: Länsmuseet-Murberget.

Westerdahl, Christer. 1992. The maritime cultural landscape. *International Journal of Nautical Archaeology* 21.1, 5-14.

Wingood, Allan J., Peggy Wingood & Jonathan Adams.1986. *Sea Venture: the Tempest Wreck.* Bermuda: Island Press.

Yalçin, Ünsal, Cemal Pulak & Rainer Slotta (eds.). 2005. *Das Schiff von Uluburun. Welthandel vor 3000 Jahren.* Bochum: Deutsches Bergbau-Museum.

II

MEMORY AS SPIRIT OF PLACE

LA MÉMOIRE COMME ESPRIT DU LIEU

The Making of Place:
Myth and Memory at the Site
of Tiwanaku, Bolivia

Leslie A. Friedman
Conservator
City of Los Angeles
USA

ABSTRACT

The archaeological site of Tiwanaku, Bolivia, has, for almost 3,000 years, been appropriated by various groups, including the Inca, the Spanish, the Bolivian State, European travelers, spiritualists, and the indigenous Aymara people who claim the World Heritage site as their ancestral home. Investing the site with meanings, myths, and memories, each group has created – or re-created – the site of Tiwanaku. Today Tiwanaku continues to be a vortex of competing claims and a location for performance, such as Aymara cultural ceremonies and modern music videos; a newly created solstice festival that is held yearly at the site; and, arguably, the rituals of archaeology and world heritage. This paper traces the development of place-making at Tiwanaku; how, from its inception through today, multiple histories and collective memories have physically altered the site, impacting its excavation, conservation, and presentation.

RÉSUMÉ

Le site archéologique de Tiwanaku, en Bolivie, fut pendant près de 3000 ans approprié par des groupes variés, y compris les Incas, les Espagnols, l'État bolivien, les voyageurs européens, les spiritualistes et le peuple autochtone des Aymara, qui revendique, en tant que son foyer ancestral, ce site du Patrimoine mondial. Ayant investi ce site de sens, de mythes et de mémoires, chaque groupe a créé – ou recréé –Tiwanaku. Aujourd'hui, Tiwanaku demeure un vortex de revendications rivales et un lieu de représentations scéniques, telles que les cérémonies culturelles aymara et les vidéos musicales modernes, un festival annuel du solstice (de création récente) et, on peut l'ajouter, les rituels de l'archéologie et du patrimoine mondial. Cet article retrace les développements de la fabrication du lieu à Tiwanaku, et la manière dont, depuis ses débuts jusqu'à aujourd'hui, de multiples histoires et des mémoires collectives ont physiquement altéré le site, ce qui entraîne des conséquences sur les fouilles, la conservation et la présentation du lieu.

The World Heritage site of Tiwanaku, located near the border between Bolivia and Peru, dominated the Central Andes between 500 C.E. and 1000 C.E., its political and cultural influence spreading far into what is present day Peru, Chile and Argentina. Tiwanaku exemplifies the concept of "place-making", as it has been continually created and re-created for thousands of years. Utilized first by the Inca in the 15th century and appropriated to justify their own powerful empire, the site was dismantled by the conquering Spanish in the 16th century who sought to destroy its power in the myths and historic memory associated with it. Centuries later, the rediscovery of the ruins inspired travelers' and explorers' accounts which were eventually adopted to help form the state of Bolivia's founding narrative; and more recently, the symbolic locus of indigenous identity. Tiwanaku continues today to be a site of contention and multiple visions – claimed by the local Aymara people who believe it to be their ancestral home; considered a place of national pride and importance to the nation of Bolivia (indeed, almost every schoolchild visits the site); visited by thousands of foreign tourists a year, many of whom come to experience a newly created version of a traditional solstice festival; and highly valued by archaeologists hoping to decipher the Tiwanaku civilization.

Among the different cultural, political and research groups invested in the site, the most vocal has been Bolivia's Aymara speakers, who perform sacrifices and religious rituals at the site. In 2001, Tiwanaku was taken over by the Aymara in a violent struggle with the government as part of the Aymara demand for recognition of their autonomous territory and the Aymara Nation. The belief that the site of Tiwanaku is the Aymara ancestral homeland is strongly embraced among the Aymara people. As anthropologists Denise Arnold and Juan de Dios Yapita observe, "Even young urban musicians of Aymara descent like to flaunt themselves in front of Tiwanaku's 'Gateway of the Sun' in their digital videos" (2005:146). The incorporation of this nationally significant monument by young Aymara artists, in such a contemporary medium, illustrates the competing uses of the site of Tiwanaku and exemplifies the fluctuating relationship between the tangible and intangible values that occurs at this site.

This paper will examine how the history of use, appropriation, excavation, reconstruction, presentation, and interpretation has altered the physicality of the site of Tiwanaku through time; and how the site that is presented to us today is a confluence of tangible and intangible forces. These multiple heritages, set within a context of competing claims, ideologies, and interests, must be taken into account when addressing the issues of conservation and management that face the site of Tiwanaku. An understanding of how the site of Tiwanaku was and continues to be made is crucial if any management plan is to succeed.

The Making of a Place 500 C.E. – 1400 C.E.: the Tiwanaku

The first true city-state of the south-central Andes, the site of Tiwanaku was designed to impress its visitors. Beginning as a small settlement around 1200 B.C. and located on a flat Altiplano about 20 km from the south shore of Lake Titicaca, the site of Tiwanaku rapidly expanded into a small town. Raised-field agriculture supported increased food production, encouraged population growth and the development of organized labor, leading to the development of large settlements, social stratification, and craft specialization (Binford *et al.* 1997). State-sponsored religious ceremonies and practices transformed the site of Tiwanaku into a vast ceremonial center that materialized into a distinct artistic style, expressed in architecture, sculpture, textiles, metalwork, and ceramics. Recent investigations support the interpretation of the site of Tiwanaku as a major planned city with a large urban and regional population (Stanish 2002). The site of Tiwanaku is largely defined by and revered for its remote location. Despite the harsh environment, some researchers believe Tiwanaku's location is deliberately due to the site's orientation to four major geographical features, as well as its arrangement among countless other peaks, that contribute to the dramatic vistas (Vranich 2006b).

When the Tiwanaku Empire declined around 1000 C.E., many of the site's monuments and ritual complexes were intentionally dismantled and destroyed, including important religious symbols, gateways, and sculpture, possibly by the departing inhabitants themselves to promote forgetting (Janusek 2005:191-92).

The Making of Multiple Places 1400-1950: Reappropriation

The site of Tiwanaku had been abandoned for several centuries when the Inca arrived in the middle of the 15th century. Using the architectural remains of the site to justify their claims for divinity and initial creation, the Inca redefined the site of Tiwanaku, in essence, as the place of their birth. Creating a mythic story, the Inca believed the sculptures of human forms found at the site were the first Andean people created by the Inca deity Viracocha, who made the first Incans out of clay. Appropriated by the Inca people, the region around Lake Titicaca became an important center for Incan power. In fact, the Inca built a palace among the ruins of Tiwanaku in order to associate themselves with the status of the Tiwanaku Empire (Kolata 2003).

When the Spanish colonists arrived in 1525, they were amazed at the scale and apparent age of the monumental architecture at Tiwanaku and mined the site for valuable stone to build their own church, among other structures, in the modern-day town of Tiahuanaco (Janusek 2005). Additionally, intentional destruction of the site's monuments and destruction of the elaborately carved sculptures was a way for the Spanish to ideologically and spiritually dominate the area's population by dismantling the memory and mythology of Tiwanaku and other competing indigenous cultures such as the Inca.

Over the next few centuries, numerous European travelers visited the site. Scientific investigation, including the first archaeological research, began in the mid-to-late 19th century, fueled by growing European interests in natural history and ancient cultures (Young-Sanchez 2004). Archaeological studies of Tiwanaku began with Ephraim George Squier's survey of the site in the 1860s. Squier's interpretation of the site as a sparsely populated ceremonial center dominated Tiwanaku studies until the middle of the 20th century (Kolata 1993).

The German researchers Max Uhle and Alphonse Stübel published a more scientific and detailed account of the site of Tiwanaku in 1892. Uhle, distressed at the looting and state of conservation of the site, wrote a letter to the Bolivian government in which he discussed seeing stonework from Tiwanaku used for the church, private houses, and other buildings in town, and requested permission to bring stonework back to Berlin for safekeeping. Even more shocking to Uhle, however, was witnessing the Bolivian army using the "best figure" at the site of Tiwanaku as a mark for target practice (Loza, unpublished). Uhle's letter, however, was also possibly written for other motives: museums in both Europe and the United States sought to acquire sculpture and monuments from the site of Tiwanaku and Uhle hoped to bring some of the carved monoliths back to Berlin.

Until the 1940s, a number of researchers dramatically shaped the site through excavation and impacted its interpretation. In 1903, Arthur Posnansky, a German-born Bolivian citizen, began extensive study of the site and introduced the theory that American civilization originated from Tiwanaku, then disseminated throughout South, Central and Northern America (Kolata 1993). During the 1930s, the excavator Wendell Bennett uncovered a massive stele which became the subject of an enduring political struggle between the Aymara and the Bolivian government. The government moved the stele to downtown La Paz against Aymara wishes, where it was severely damaged by air pollution, traffic, and bullet marks, a victim of numerous uprisings and wars. Heavily damaged, the monument was eventually installed in 2002 at the new site museum.

The Making of a Place 1950-2000: Nationalism and Beyond

Bolivian supervision and involvement in archaeological research at the site of Tiwanaku did not occur until the 1950s. As a direct response to the National Revolutionary Movement (MNR), which gained control of the Bolivian government in 1952, the excavations, led by party member and archaeologist Carlos Ponce Sangines, focused on creating a national emblem for Bolivia (Isbell and Vranich 2004). The ultimate goal of the excavations was documentation and exposition of the structures in order to promote tourism. Propelled by governmental request as well as his own staunch nationalistic ideology, Ponce Sangines reconstructed architectural elements and discarded any architectural features that were not considered sufficiently monumental (Isbell and Vranich 2004). A new interpretation of the site arose from these excavations which declared the site of Tiwanaku a major pre-Incan urban center by calculating the total area of occupation and the estimated population density, discarding the previous perception of the site as only a religious center (Isbell and Vranich 2004). Ponce Sangines, overall, wanted to present the site of Tiwanaku as a monumental apogee of Bolivian civilization and history – a site that could compare with Peru's Machu Picchu.

In 1978, Alan Kolata began a project sponsored by the Bolivian National Institute of Archaeology (INAR) to explore Tiwanaku's hinterland. This multidisciplinary study investigated technology and agricultural production through the excavations of smaller hamlets, subsidiary sites, and raised fields in the Tiwanaku area (Kolata 1993). Reflecting larger trends in archaeological research abroad concerning the archaeology of landscape, this project expanded the boundaries of the site beyond its monumental core, enlarging the region of interest to the larger Tiwanaku area and its landscape.

While the site of Tiwanaku has been studied, excavated, and reconstructed for over one hundred years, very little attention has been directed towards the conservation of the site or its monuments. In 1987, the Getty Conservation Institute (GCI) offered a course at the site of Tiwanaku in the field conservation of objects and buildings. Reflecting broader interests in the management of archaeological sites, this workshop included a proposal for the conservation of one of the complexes, an analysis of the current tourist flow and its impact on the site, and recommendations for improving the visitor experience (DINAR 1989). Recently, archaeologists from the University of Pennsylvania excavations are applying some of these recommendations, including temporarily supporting exposed excavation trench walls and filling in gaps of the architecture with adobe so that visitors and researchers can observe the difference between ancient and modern construction and material (Vranich 2006a).

Despite these efforts, an ICOMOS statement of September 2000 declared that "little, if any, conservation has taken place." (ICOMOS 2000) 'Conservation work' has been focused on the confiscation of specific artifacts deemed important works of art and the reconstruction of certain monuments. The Kalasasaya Platform was reconstructed by Ponce Sangines in the 1950s and 1960s as a direct response to the Bolivian nationalist movement to create a national site that would attract tourism. Some scholars, however, question the accuracy of this reconstruction (Vranich 2006a). Likewise, the monumental Gateway of the Sun, the most emblematic structure of the site, had been partially restored by the Ponce Sangines team in the 1950s, and the authenticity of its present location is in question.

In the year 2000, Tiwanaku was listed by UNESCO as a World Heritage Site. This listing has brought worldwide attention to the site, as well as contributing to the national pride felt by Bolivians about their site and perhaps increased interest by the Aymara.

Through the years, Tiwanaku's origins became fodder for the strange. The creation of the site has been attributed to such causes as aliens and a moon crashing, among other theories. Additionally, thousands of visitors come to the site every year, many for the summer solstice to watch the sun rise over the monuments at Tiwanaku. This mass influx of visitors directly impacts the monuments and the conservation of the site, affecting visitor experience and site conditions. To provide easier access to tourists, two highways were built across a portion of the site, destroying remains and detracting further from the monumental setting.

Tiwanaku Today

The appearance of the site of Tiwanaku today is the result of a millennium of growth and construction, including several building campaigns, centuries of abandonment, intentional destruction and looting of stone for building materials, reconstructions, and excavations. During the early 20th century, a railroad was built through the site of Tiwanaku, further denigrating the site and increasing the rate of pillage (Isbell and Vranich 2004). A combination of severe destruction through looting, uncontrolled and unmanaged local development surrounding the site, limited management and irresponsible excavations and reconstructions have resulted in a site with serious problems of erosion, illegibility, and poor conservation.

Today's visitors to Tiwanaku encounter a rather empty expanse of partially reconstructed temples and fields of large stones. Composed mainly of a monumental core, Tiwanaku contains architectural remains that, while certainly impressive, do not necessarily inspire great awe, as they once did. Recent research hypothesizes that the role of the architecture was not to inspire visitors on its own; rather the role of the monuments was to harmonize with the landscape and the magnificent views of the mountains and the then nearby lake (Vranich 2006b). Uncontrolled development of the modern town of Tiahuanaco, however, is threatening the view sheds from the pre-Columbian site which may relate to astronomical phenomena and the night sky. Additionally, questionable reconstructions, ongoing excavation, and poorly planned visitor accoutrements, such as modern staircases, barbed wire fences, and cement platforms, not only create an unattractive site, but an inauthentic one as well.

In recent years, there have been more concerted efforts to protect the site and collaborate internationally. This has included cooperation with other Andean states and the adoption of international cultural charters established by ICOMOS and UNESCO. However, authority turnover makes the effective implementation of these resolutions a difficult task. Additionally, rapid agency re-organization complicates the situation even further. Overall responsibility for the management of the archaeological remains at Tiwanaku has generally been the responsibility of the government's department of archaeology(DINAR), while other areas of the UNESCO World Heritage nominated area are still managed by the Roman Catholic Church as well as private individuals (ICOMOS 2000). However, in 2001, after years of disagreement with the national government, the Aymara people took over the site of Tiwanaku and the Municipality of Tiwanaku now makes all management decisions regarding the site (Vranich 2006a).

The importance of the site of Tiwanaku to the Aymara may be further illuminated by two events. The Bennett Stele was moved into downtown La Paz on July 3, 1932 despite outrage by the local Aymara (Arnold and Yapita 2005). After years of conflict and protest, the Bennett Stele was returned to Tiwanaku in March 2002 in an elaborate processional culminating in a traditional ceremony at the site. And in January 2006, Evo Morales became president of Bolivia. The first Bolivian president of Aymara descent, Morales held his inauguration ceremony at the site of Tiwanaku, dressed in traditional ceremonial robes, and standing in front of Tiwanaku's emblematic monuments.

Despite the competing claims over Tiwanaku, recognition exists by the Aymara of the benefits offered by other interest groups. Although the Aymara attempt to defend their political and cultural interests in the site of Tiwanaku against competing nationalist and World Heritage claims, the Aymara acknowledge that "if it were not for the vigilance of international organizations that have claimed the site [Tiwanaku] as World Patrimony, 'it would have been dismantled already'" (Aymara Today 2001).

Conclusion

Tiwanaku began as a vast ceremonial city-state, dominating much of the central Andes until AD 1000, when its carefully constructed buildings and elaborately carved stone monuments were desecrated, possibly by the Tiwanaku themselves. Both the Inca and the Spanish used Tiwanaku to support their own claims to power, the Inca by building within the existing site and the Spanish by destroying it. Visitors and foreign archaeologists have studied, excavated and interpreted the site to suit their own intentions, and subsequently strong Bolivian nationalism re-formulated the monuments to fit a nationalist identity. The formalized rituals of archaeology and cultural heritage have contributed to the myth of Tiwanaku by calling it a World Heritage Site in 2000, and in the process increased pressure by both the Bolivian government and the Aymara people to call it their own. The Aymara people, who claimed the site in an extremely tangible way – through violent uprising in 2001 – maintain the strongest modern collective memory to the site, as the direct descendents of the Tiwanaku people.

Archaeological sites are formed and transformed over time, by countless forces. Thus, understanding the agents that have shaped the site of Tiwanaku in the past, and which forces continue to do so, is integral to the present day presentation and interpretation of the site as well as for making recommendations regarding its future conservation and management. The culmination of the creation and re-creation of these multiple heritages is how the site comes to us today and how these changes are interpreted. Any plan for the presentation of the site must include the palimpsest of history represented by the entire site of Tiwanaku, through time, both by its creators and its users.

Tiwanaku and its monuments are at great risk. A lack of interest in the site's longue durée coupled with a general lack of conservation, inconsistent and short-sighted management decisions, irresponsible excavations and reconstructions, and lack of cooperation between invested parties, has resulted in a site that has been called "disappointing." Tiwanaku is one of the most important archaeological sites in South America. Cooperation, on the local, national, and international levels, is direly needed in order to ensure the long-term preservation of the site of Tiwanaku. Archaeologists, researchers, the world heritage community, the national Bolivian government, and the local Aymara population need to work together to ensure the appropriate stewardship of Tiwanaku, a site that means so much to so many.

Acknowledgements

The author would like to thank Frank Matero for his efforts on many levels; and Gionata Rizzi and Alexei Vranich for their help and enthusiasm.

References

Aymara Today. 2001. "Pieza religiosa aymara sufre aggression en La Paz." *Aymara Today* No. 07, December 2001. Quoted in Arnold and Yapita. Strands of Indigenism in the Bolivian Andes, 148. *Public Archaeology*, 2005.

Arnold, D.Y., and J.D. Yapita. 2005. Strands of Indigenism in the Bolivian Andes: Competing juridical claims for the ownership and management of indigenous heritage sites in an emerging context of legal pluralism. In *Public Archaeology* 4: 141-149.

Binford, Michael W., Alan Kolata, Mark Brenner, John Janusek, Mark Seddon, M. Abbott, and J. Curtis. 1997. Climate Variation and the Rise and Fall of an Andean Civilization. In *Quaternary Research* 47: 235-248.

DINAR. 1989. *Workshop of Archaeological Conservation*, the Getty Conservation Institute. Report prepared by Leocadio Tuclla Coloque for Oswaldo Rivera S., Director of DINAR.

ICOMOS. 2000. Advisory Board Evaluation Tiwanaku (Bolivia). No 567rev.

Isbell, Willem and Alexei Vranich. 2004. Experiencing the Cities of Wari and Tiwanaku. In *Andean Archaeology*, ed. H. Silverman: 167-182. New York: Blackwell.

Janusek, John. 2005. Collapse as Cultural Revolution: Power and Identity in the Tiwanaku to Pacajes Transition. In *Archaeological Papers of the American Anthropological Association* 14: 175-209.

Kolata, Alan. 1993. *The Tiwanaku: Portraits of an Andean Civilization.* Cambridge: Blackwell.

Kolata, Alan L. 2003. Tiwanaku Ceremonial Architecture and Urban Organization. In *Tiwanaku and Its Hinterland: Archaeology and Paleoecology of an Andean Civilization*, ed. A. L. Kolata: 175-201. Washington, D.C.: Smithsonian Institution Press.

Loza, C. B. *Max Uhle in the Bolivian Highlands.* Unpublished.

Stanish, Charles. 2002. Tiwanaku Political Economy. In *Andean Archaeology I: Variations in Socio-Political Organization*, ed. W. Isbell and H. Silverman: 169-198. Kluwer Academic, New York.

Vranich, Alexei. 2006a. Personal Communication. University of Pennsylvania, Philadelphia, PA.

Vranich, Alexei. 2006b. National Science Foundation Grant Application.

Young-Sanchez, M. 2004. *Tiwanaku: Ancestors of the Inca.* Denver Museum of Art. Denver: University of Nebraska Press.

Memory and Place

Eman Assi
Architectural Heritage Department
Dubai Municipality
Dubai

ABSTRACT

The landscape of the environment we live in is an image of our common humanity. The sense of place individuals and people as a whole have is both a biological response to the surrounding physical environment and a cultural creation. People get attached to places that are critical to their well-being or cause them distress.

This paper sketches the story of *Sahet Alqaryoun*, a public open space in a residential neighborhood in the historic City of Nablus, West Bank. The question of how *Sahet Alqaryoun* as an open public space is appropriated by the various segments of the population, and how this has been changing over time is addressed here through investigating various stakeholders and users of this place, starting from individuals to the families living in this neighborhood or even the municipality and professionals who are responsible for any future intervention proposed for *Sahet Alqaryoun*. This paper will attempt to explore the structure of such a shared place, how it is related to social meaning and also its cultural connotation as a place of collective use that is perceived through representation and images produced by its residents. It will also study the physical evolution and different factors that shaped *Sahet Alqaryoun* and demonstrate the sustainability of this historic place through time, re-identifying it and re-establishing it as an essential part of the social, socio-economic and political fabric of the city.

This paper argues that urban spaces do present a public history. Our responsibility as professionals in preserving our historic spaces is to try to understand all factors that have played a role in shaping this space and to try to recognize and respect the long social and cultural history as successive stages of the city's evolution.

RÉSUMÉ

Le paysage de l'environnement dans lequel nous vivons est à l'image de notre humanité commune. Le sentiment du lieu qu'éprouvent les individus et les populations dans leur ensemble est à la fois une réponse biologique à l'environnement physique et une création culturelle. Cet article esquisse l'histoire de *Sahet Alqaryoun*, un espace public dans un quartier résidentiel de la ville historique de Naplouse, sur la rive ouest.

Comment les divers segments de la population s'approprient-ils le *Sahet Alqaryoun*, en tant qu'espace public, comment ce phénomène s'est-il modifié au fil du temps? La question est examinée ici en interrogeant diverses parties prenantes et divers usagers du lieu, en commençant par des membres des familles vivant dans le quartier, voire par des élus de la municipalité et des professionnels responsables des interventions futures proposées pour *Sahet Alqaryoun*. Cet article tentera d'explorer la structure d'un tel lieu partagé, la manière dont il s'articule à une signification sociale, ainsi que sa connotation culturelle en tant que lieu d'usage collectif qui est perçu à travers les représentations et les images qu'en produisent les résidents. Il étudiera également l'évolution physique et les différents facteurs qui donnent forme à *Sahet Alqaryoun* et en démontrent la stabilité historique à travers le temps, en le ré-identifiant et en le réinstaurant comme partie essentielle du tissu social, socioéconomique et politique de la ville.

Cet article avance que les espaces urbains présentent une histoire publique. Notre responsabilité, en tant que professionnels chargés de préserver nos espaces historiques, est d'essayer de reconnaître et de respecter la longue histoire sociale et culturelle dans les étapes successives de l'évolution de la ville.

1. Introduction

Sahet Alqaryoun (Alqaryoun Square) is located on the southwestern edge of the Ottoman part of the City of Nablus in *harat* (or quarter) Alqaryoun, one of the city's seven old residential quarters. Historically, it used to be one of the main open public spaces and had some commercial importance, soap factories and the cotton industry being located there. *Sahet Alqaryoun* was also a significant popular neighborhood in the old city, being the largest un-built space, surrounded by Ottoman architectural façades. It is now an almost empty, deserted area, frequented only by males and in particular by teenagers who interact there during the day; children also use the space to meet and play. The place contains a few small shops, which are often just extensions of the houses and as such, act as magnets that strengthen the social fabric of the neighborhood.

Sahet Alqaryoun has been subjected to many changes during the last century. One of them was the 1927 earthquake which destroyed many historic buildings in the city and resulted in changing the physical and spatial experience of this space. Seventy years later, in 1987, the first efforts to rehabilitate the historic square took place: the Municipality of Nablus, with funding from the French Government, initiated a project to enhance the aesthetic quality of the square by placing in it artwork by Fleur-Marie Fuentes, a French artist. She worked closely with the community to create a painting on one of the walls overlooking the *Sahet*. In 2002, after the Israeli invasion of the city, the square was severely affected by the consequences of this military action: the total destruction of the Alshubi family's *hosh* that constituted one of the sides of this open place.

The question of how Sahet Alqaryoun, as an open public space, is appropriated by the various segments of the population, and how it has changed over time, is addressed through investigating the various stakeholders and users from individuals to families living in this neighborhood. A short theoretical introduction on the meaning of "place" and how it is perceived by its users, will lead to an understanding of the dynamics of this square. This will be followed by presenting all the issues, which influenced and affected the physical transformation of the *Sahet*.

2. The Concept of Place

The concept of place can be traced back to the ancient philosophical writings of Aristotle. Place or *topos*, in his view, was the "where" dimension in people's relationship to the physical environment, conjuring up a feeling of "belonging". The Romans, centuries later, used the term *genius loci*, the "spirit of a place", a "genius spirit" of a physical location. Recent years have seen a revival of the concept of place in many disciplines. In his writings, Venturi (1966) encouraged to not only consider the semiotic meaning of the external façade of buildings, but also the meaning of the spaces behind the walls. He claimed that architecture occurs at the meeting of interior and exterior forces of uses and "space". On the other hand, Canter (1977) in his book *The Psychology of Place*, stated that "place" is a combination of actions, conceptions and the physical environment. Canter's visualization of *placeness* formed when actions, conceptions and physical attributes were interrelated. The concept proved helpful in establishing linkages with planning practice. His "conceptions", which are similar to Relph's "meaning", were expanded to include the mythical aspects of human experience to bring into the designers" consciousness the need to attune to the "essential core of the culture". Saarinen (1982) describes a "sense of place" as a "unifying concept bringing together a number of separate strands of geographic research in the general environment-behavior "design field"". Essentially, the term "place", by definition, extends the focus of attention beyond geographic space to the experience people have of being in a particular landscape environment. The value of the term "sense of place" is in highlighting the "sense of identity" of particular environments. This definition of "place" is also mentioned by Proshansky (1983), who argued that the role of places and spaces in a person's development has been neglected in psychology. He introduced the concept of "place-identity" as a physical environmental referent for a better-known and widely used term: "self-identity". As he suggested, "Humanistic geographers have argued that through personal attachment to geographically locatable places, a person acquires a sense of belonging and purpose which give meaning to his or her life."

So the primary function of "place", as Proshansky believed, is to gather a sense of belonging and identity. Place attachment is strongest in relation to a person's own home. Individuals may strive to project their self-concept into the design of an environment (Assi 2000). Thus the term "place", as opposed to "space", implies strong, long-lasting emotional ties, between a person and a particular physical location. Sime (1986) refers to the "place" ascribed to a physical location, which engenders a positive, satisfactory experience. Creating places, according to this author, refers to "places" which the architect and/ or potential users of the "space" actually like. The Norwegian architect and phenomenologist Christian Norberg-Schulz is a key theorist in elucidating the concept of *genius loci*, which he explores in several works spanning three decades. Norberg-Schulz claims that the *genius loci* of a particular place is important for our sense of identity, which may be bound up with a particular place; we may refer to this, for example, by the expression "I am a Parisian". The location itself marks the position of the place, but place itself consists of the totality of the natural and man-made things, assembled in a unique way and may well include the history and associations attached to the place by the people who identify with it. While all places have a character, this in itself is not adequate to induce *genius loci*. It is the uniqueness which makes it special and with which we can readily associate.

On the other hand, the original intention of Schulz in his thesis (Schulz 1963), was to investigate the psychology of architecture. Based on the same *gestalt* psychological theory used by Kevin Lynch, Schulz (1980) explores the character of places on the ground and their meanings for people, while Lynch (1960) ignored meanings and focused on structure and identity. Norberg-Schulz uses a concept of townscape (although not in the same way as defined by Cullen) to denote skyline or image. He sees the skyline of the town and the horizontally expanded silhouette of the urban buildings as keys to the image of a place. He promotes the traditional form of towns and buildings, which he sees as the basis for bringing about a deeper symbolic understanding of places (Schulz 1985). The culmination of Schulz's examination of the *genius loci* concept is found in *Genius Loci: Towards a Phenomenology of Architecture*. It is described as representing the sense people have of a place, understood as the sum of all physical as well as symbolic values in both nature and the human environment.

When Jackson writes of "atmosphere" he indicates that *genius loci* has also became allied to the concept of the "character" of a place. Many writers on urban form and design have discussed the issue of "character", some implicitly, others explicitly, using terms such as *spirit of place* or *genius loci* (see for example Conzen (1966) and Steele (1981). In this way, "character" and *genius loci* become further enmeshed. This fusion of ideas is most clearly seen in discussions of "the past" and conservation. Lowenthal (1979)·has suggested that "the past" exists as both an individual and a collective construct, with shared values and experiences being important within cultural groups. Group identity is thus closely linked with the form and history of place, creating a sense of place or *genius loci*.

In the course of time the landscape, whether that of a large region like a country or of a small locality like a market town, acquires its specific *genius loci*, its culture- and history-conditioned character which commonly reflects not only the work and aspirations of the society in occupancy at present but also that of its precursors in the same area. Conzen regarded changes to urban form in relation to a cyclic building development by repletion, transformation, clearance and even urban fallow. Yet it has been suggested here that it is group identity, the people as a society that is closely linked with the form and history of place, creating a sense of place.

More recently, the French historian Pierre Nora (1996) in his book: *Rethinking the French Past: Realm and Memory, lieux de mémoire* outlines a concept developed in order to help explain the construction of a nation or a community; it offers a useful tool for architectural historians by emphasizing the importance of physical and conceptual sites. A *lieu de mémoire* is any significant entity, whether material or non-material in nature, which, by dint of human will or work, in time, has become a symbolic difference between history and memory. Nora claims that "memory is life" whereas "history is the reconstruction of what is no longer". "Memory" is subject to remembering and forgetting; it is vulnerable to appropriation and manipulation. The *lieux de mémoire*, material, symbolic, and functional sites, are the products of the interaction between memory and history. They embody a will to remember (memory) and to record (history). They also display the exciting quality of being able to change, that is, to resurrect old meanings and generate new ones, along the sites of memory (Celik 1997, 2002).

Nora's concept pertains to all societies. The concept can be extended to the Palestinian struggle and show how the *lieux de mémoire* expresses the endurance of identity in the context of an armed conflict. Symbolic sites, which reflected the Palestinians' struggle during the *Intifada* and their capacity to change and acquire new meanings allowed them to also act as places of memory. Nora notes,

Acceleration of history: the metaphor needs to be unpacked. Things tumble with increasing rapidity into irreversible past. They vanish from sight, or so it is generally believed. The equilibrium between the present and the past is disrupted. What was left of experience, still lived in the warmth of tradition, in the silence of custom, in the repetition of the ancestral, has been swept away by a surge of deeply historical sensibility. Our consciousness is shaped by a sense that everything is over and done with, that something long since begun is now complete. Memory is constantly on our lips because it no longer exists.

Our curiosity about the places in which memory is crystallized, in which it finds refuge, as Nora claims, is associated with this specific moment in history, a turning point in which a sense of rapture with the past is inextricably bound up with a sense that a rift has occurred in memory. When it comes to social meaning, Maurice Halbwachs stipulated that human beings require a social framework in order to remember. He thereby tried to dismiss psychological definitions of memory that emphasized the individual encoding, storing and retrieving of data (Halbwachs 1992). Therefore it is possible to compare Halbwachs' treatise on memory with a more contemporary definition of culture. Clifford Greetz described culture as a web of meaning within which each individual is suspended (Greetz 1973:5). In other words, culture/memory sets up shared rules and understandings that allow persons to think, speak, relate or remain in solitude. By this definition there is an implicit bias towards memory as a cognitive knowledge (Volok 2001, 2005). The privileged concern for "knowledge memory" was sharply criticized by Paul Connerton (2003), who argued that bodily memories are profoundly social. The component of memories as knowledge of how to do something has public and ritual aspects that engage every single person during the course of a day, as each individual performs and takes part in shared behaviors (Koselleck 2002).

One could argue that the practice of commemoration becomes a counter-strategy, or even an act of resistance, a trend of modernity (Davis 2005). Going back to the past symbols, rituals and practices or behaviors, even if they are out of time and place in our modern days, or even if the process of retrieval changes the "authentic" aspects of memory, is still an act that has enormous symbolic power within the larger structure of our capitalist world system.

Connerton's critique of modernity finds its eloquent parallel and elaboration in Nora's works (Nora 1998), who famously argues that modern post-industrial societies have lost their sense of real memory (*milieu de mémoire)*, and have reverted to the weak substitute of "history" (*lieux de mémoire)*, the former being defined as integrated memory, all-powerful, sweeping, unselfconscious, and inherently present-minded, whereas the second is "the reconstruction, always problematic and incomplete, of what is no longer" (Nora

1996). He goes on to declare that modernity has eradicated the practice of shared traditions of village life where everyone participated in celebrating birth, death, harvest, etc.

In addition to the question above, Nora's writings raise another important concern, namely the re-appropriation of traditional sites of memory as agents of modernity. Not only are sites of memories lost, falling into despair or disrepair, but they are also reclaimed and redone. In this case, we are faced with the continuation of actual sites, but with loss of what used to generate shared experience and social ties.

Referring to the historic centre of the old City of Nablus, it is part of one of the most significant traditional Arab cities in Palestine, whose history goes back hundreds of years; its Ottoman urban fabric still exists. A brief analysis of the traditional Arab urban form will help understand the structure of the city and how public spaces (such as Sahet Alqaryoun) have been created and transformed.

3. Public Open Spaces in Traditional Arab Cities

Looking at earlier research on public spaces in the traditional Arab city, one finds that space by itself is an important physical element that is typical in most Muslim cities. Islamic cities had no space equivalent to the Greek *agora* or the Roman *forum*. The open courtyard of the mosque in most Muslim cities provides the space needed for public gatherings for the political and social processes. Public squares, when they existed, acted only as visual nodes. With their semi-public space, they relate to the residential quarters, which in traditional Islamic terms are private spaces for the residents. Few collective social activities take place in these spaces: they retain most of the time the role as nodes of intersection or can be used by the male population to interact.

The main patterns of land use of the historic Arab-Muslim city are usually focused on a multifunctional core structure enveloping or at least partially surrounding the central mosque by different layers of interconnected *suqs*. As a rule, these are interspersed with a number of *hammams*, *madrasas*, and caravanserais, which constitute the support for the mosque and retail shops. In such urban structures everything seems to be "under one roof" and thus the city can be compared to a spacious but coherent single mansion. By analogy, the mosque would be the main living room, the *madrasas* and caravanserais would correspond to the teaching, guest and utility rooms, and the *suqs*, equipped with long rows of cupboards, would represent the connecting internal corridors. The residential district provides the private quarter of this collective urban "house" and is structured along similar principles as the public places but with greater emphasis on the articulation and intermediate passages (Bianka 2000).

The *intra muros* residential quarter, analyzed by Stefano Bianka in *Urban Form in the Arab World: Past and Present*, grew in the space left between the edges of the multi-functional core complex and the main pedestrian spines. The structure of residential quarters was generated and sustained by strong micro-communities, often sharing the same tribal origins. These neighborhoods were largely self-reliant in the sense that each one formed a virtually autonomous social unit, embracing a representative cross-section of society and establishing, controlling and maintaining the basic shared facilities, such as the local mosques, one or several small *hammams* and public ovens and a number of street fountains. By mediating in a subtle manner between the "inner" and the "outer" world, it enabled the self-contained units of individual houses to merge and to become components of a coherent residential cluster, which in turn was entrenched within a larger multi-cluster unit representing a complete neighborhood. At each respective hierarchical level, each residential unit of the urban structure had its own inbuilt circulation system, the individual section and ramifications being separated and connected by interior gates that preserved the territorial integrity of the various sub-communities.

The issue of privacy remains the main question in Islamic urban environment, whether be it a street, a house or a public square. It is very important in Islamic teaching to keep a clear separation between private and public life and it is considered the most significant social characteristic of Islamic culture (Mortada 2003). Similarly, in an attempt to reflect the great value of privacy and distinction between private and public life, the Prophet Mohammed did not recommend using roads for public meetings but laid down specific conditions for doing so. Thus the issue of privacy, particularly that of women, is a major concern of Islamic beliefs and principles. For Islam, it is the right and duty of the family to live enclosed in its house. Hisham Mortada (2003) claims that keeping a clear separation between private and public life is the most significant social characteristic of Islamic culture. Considering privacy as a religious principle, Mortada stated that the privacy of the individual and his family should be maintained in both houses and neighborhoods alike. This was successfully achieved in the traditional environment, whose outdoor spaces and streets were in a hierarchical but integrated form of order.

The outdoor spatial order of the traditional Arab Islamic cities prevented any urban space from being ambiguous in terms of function, use and ownership. Likewise S. Bianka acclaims the socio-religious quality of this hierarchy as it gives priority to the privacy of neighborhood and houses. He states,

> The complex of movement patterns which are designed in such a way as to avoid crossing enclosed spaces and to establish transition zones between public, semi-public, and semiprivate domains, and the articulation of gateway for stressing the penetration of successive levels of public and private life. These and other

features together form a whole coinage of three dimensional signs and symbols, which intimately related to the Islamic way of life.

This language, according to Bianka, not only established appropriate differentiations between the individual components of the city, but also acted as the cohesive factor, which integrated the single elements into a comprehensive and meaningful urban fabric. The density of the traditional Islamic fabric is hence not just a matter of spatial compression, but also the expression of a tightly woven social network.

4. The Story of Sahet Alqaryoun

The analysis of the traditional urban form of Arab cities can be applied, to a great extent, to the historic City of Nablus and to Sahet Alqaryoun. The latter has a dual function, being a semipublic open space for a residential quarter that hosts several commercial and industrial activities. Usually public squares, when they exist, act only as visual nodes, as we mentioned earlier. With their semipublic space, these nodes usually relate to the residential quarters, private spaces for the residents where a certain amount of interaction is possible. This is not the case with Sahet Alqaryoun, which used to be the centre of the local cotton industry and soap production during the eighteenth and nineteenth centuries (Nimir 1961-1975). Its location at the edge of the old city made it very convenient for trade and the moving of goods to and from buildings in this area; it was thus the commercial hub for light industry and had the largest concentration of soap factories and cotton warehouses. Because of its relatively large dimensions, at least when compared with *Sahet* An-Nasir, the main public square in the historic City of Nablus, *Sahet Alqaryoun* hosted several cultural and social activities not only for the residents of the *harat* itself, but also for the nearby residential quarters.

Sahet Alqaryoun has been subjected to many changes during the 20th century. On 27th July 1927, a powerful earthquake shook the City of Nablus, killing fifty people and destroying around six hundred houses. The earthquake became a watershed in the city's collective memory, as the destructions in the old city were enormous, and traces of its effects are still visible to this day. As a result of the earthquake, people were frightened to stay in the historic city, and they left their houses to live outside. The earthquake had both physical and social consequences on the *Sahet*: it had a major effect on transforming both its physical image and unique local character. Physically, the destruction of many historical houses negatively influenced the coherent compact urban tissue and the spatial experience of the place. Also, gradual changes in the social structure started at that time. Most of the abandoned houses, many of them luxurious, were divided into small units and inhabited by low-income families. Later, with the crisis of the soap economy and the cotton industry, the *Sahet* further declined. By 1947, many soap factories were closed (Sharif

1999) and *Sahet Alqaryoun* entered another phase and became a neglected and deserted residential place that served only its residents.

In 1997, in its first effort to rehabilitate the historic city, the Municipality of Nablus, with funding from the French Government, initiated a project to enhance the aesthetic quality of the square by placing in it artwork by Fleur-Marie Fuentes, a French artist. She worked closely with the community to create a work on one of the walls overlooking the *Sahet*. *Sahet Alqaryoun* was selected among different sites proposed by the Municipality. The French artist, in her proposal, strived to identify expectations of the municipal representatives. She said:

> I wanted to work in an inhabited, lively and protected space, and get the feeling of being accepted there as an individual and as an artist designing a new place. I wanted to find common ground for a project based on hope and exchanges. These places – such as the wall of the Abdel Majid soap factory and the old garden bordering the square, which was destroyed during the Intifada – I found them at Alqaryoun, a popular neighborhood to the south of the Old City. This empty area with its dull and forgotten façades, where the children had no other space than the rare cracks left empty by the parked cars, was nonetheless the greatest un-built space in the Old City. This spot seemed interesting to me because of its light, its potential harmony, its houses peopled with large families and its craft shops, its Ottoman architecture and its available space.

Fuentes tried to understand the context with all the historical and cultural implications of the local community. She felt the need to adapt to a new dimension. For that she was keen on working closely with residents: she held several workshops with the children in order to identify some of the key elements and symbols that could be adopted in her artwork. She added,

> Completely immerged into the cultural, economic, political and sociological reality of the inhabitants of the Old City of Nablus, I felt the need to adapt to the dimensions of the site, to understand the architectural and urban fabric of the "Qasbah". I started by interpreting the symbols and observing the places of memory. With the children, teenagers and adults, I had to find actions that would enable them to restore the national heritage as well as to prepare them to the reception of the contemporary work. Through my experiences as a plastician, I had to develop a kind of pedagogy of Urban Art – an abstract notion, and even an unknown one, because of long years of Israeli occupation.

The implantation of the project was funded by the Municipality of Nablus, who paid for the cleaning and plastering of the exterior façades surrounding the *sahet*, and for the painting of the entrance gates of its shops. The budget was around US$ 7,000 included the installing of light fixtures. The project in itself can be considered as a starting point towards thinking seriously about the idea of rehabilitation and beautification of the old city. It was a collective effort by the city council, the professionals and the community. Everyone felt that this project was his. The French artist said in her report,

> …*Nice constructive dynamics were set up. Hundreds of people – craftsmen, industrials, bankers, workmen, engineers, architects, neighbors and families from the square, overseas development students and artists – gave a hand and this something "extra" enabled the project to take on all its dimensions and to exceed our expectations.*

On April 3, 2002, Nablus was hit by another earthquake, lasting not just a few seconds but seven long days. It also left in its wake the destruction of many historic buildings. It was launched from the skies above as Israeli fighter planes and helicopters bombarded the Qasbah of the city. The Israeli tanks and bulldozers razed to the ground the 17th century *Wakaleh Al-Farroukhiyyeh* caravanserai as well as the 18th century Kanaan and Al-Nabulsi soap factories.

During the attack on the city, *Sahet Alqaryoun* was severely hit by military action, causing the total destruction of the Alshubi *hosh*, which formed one of the sides of the square. The *hosh* is located on the southern edge of the Old Town, where nine low-income families used to live in an area of 300 m². Traditionally, one family used the *hosh*, but it was divided into different units housing several families, each unit consisting of one or two rooms used by one family. As the *hosh* lay on the boundary of the Old Town, the Israeli army used heavy bulldozers to pull it down in order to access that part of the city. Its demolition was carried out at night while residents were still inside. Eight people were killed – 3 children, 3 women and 2 men – while two old people, a man and a woman, were rescued one week after the incident.

This *hosh* is typical of traditional houses built during the Ottoman era. Part of the urban fabric of the Old Town, it enclosed one of the rare public open spaces while contributing to its spatial quality. The destruction of the house endangered the adjacent buildings and affected the structural stability of the whole block.

Today *Sahet Alqaryoun* has become a memorial place for the Palestinians who were killed by the Israelis during the second *Intifada*, and the place has become a symbol of resistance and patriotism. Around the square were built six martyr memorials. All of them, in marble or stone, offer pictures of the heroes, together with a text from the Quran. Some of the memorials recount the story of the martyrs and their death. *Sahet Alqaryoun* once again was loaded with memory which has added even more to its collective identity.

5. Discussion

Sahet Alqaryoun is a physical node of semipublic space that has been used by its local community. It is also a social space used by its residents, specially teenagers and children; they gather during the day and interact with each other or use the space as a playground. Today the place contains few small shops, just extensions of the houses, that act as magnets strengthening the neighborhood's social fabric by providing for local needs.

The many physical transformations did not erase the past, and the old historic fabric of the place has survived in the inhabitants' memories and has passed from generation to generation. Fleur-Marie Fuentes's action added memory to the place and its stimulating quality enhanced the preservation of Palestinian memory. The appropriation of this public space hence embraced a new symbolism, without radically transforming its physical character, namely its boundaries and surrounding buildings. This can be confirmed if one refers to de Certeau's analysis of everyday spatial texts, alternative experiences split into clear texts of planned and readable cities.

Zaher Mostafa, a resident of this area for about fifty years who owned a small grocery shop which used to be the mukhtar's place (the community representative) said,

> I remember Sahet Alqaryoun since my childhood: it used to be a very beautiful green open space. I remember many shops of the textile industry. There used to be a round elevated open area with beautiful carved stone seats where the English and Jordanian soldiers sat to discuss administrative matters related to the community with Al-Haj Sulieman Jeryes who used to be the mukhtar at that time.

Like many people, Um Imad, a housewife living in this area for quite a long time, liked *Sahet Alqaryoun* in the old times, and she still likes it today. The transformation of *Sahet Alqaryoun* was accepted by the residents, as all the changes were a response to community needs at that time. She said,

> We were happy with the French artist's intervention, and the beautification carried out by the municipality in 1998. became better, we had trees in the main space and kids were happy with it and with the paintings, they used to enjoy gathering and playing, but sadly after the Intifada and because of neglect, the trees were uprooted and the place was not maintained with many garbage bags seen thrown here and there. Sahet Alqaryoun is not anymore like it was in the old days.

Names of public spaces coalesce into text and define the city on a socio-logical level. They tell the history of a city and act as "a system of representation through which the collective identity defines itself, to itself and to the world beyond". Many people in the old times used to call *Sahet Alqaryoun* "*Sahet Altouteh*". Alqaryoun referred to the name of the main spring in this neighborhood and it has all the memory of women going to it for their daily needs. *Altouteh* referred to the big mulberry tree that used to be in the middle of the square. Many people still remember this place and how it used to be green with two large mulberry trees and the water spring that women used to frequent. This is what Um Imad said:

I love my neighborhood. We used to go to the spring and carry our water to our house. The place was very active. We used to have many celebrations and social activities in the square.

The "urban text" (the nomination of public spaces) is thus not fixed, but changes in a continual process of interpreting and accommodating social transformations. The physical transformation of the urban tissue of the square was associated with changes of the social structure. Low-income families were displaying middle-class values to well-known families who used to own the soap factories. Zaher Mustafa, living in this area, noted:

In the old days many large well-known families used to live here but not anymore: the Al-Nimir, Touqan and An-Nabulsi families used to live here but they left the neighborhood and their houses were rented to low-income families.

6. Conclusion

Public spaces are like humans beings. They have ups and downs; sometimes they are vivid, live and active, and sometimes they are dull, empty and dark. Also, public open spaces influenced and were influenced by the world around them. With their impeded memories, loaded symbols and codes, people can identify with them. At the same time, these spaces embrace particular events that have collective social, historical and political associations; projections of these events influence the physical transformations, which can each be re-identified through time.

The various segments of the population appropriated *Sahet Alqaryoun* as an open public space, and this has been continually changing over time. This paper argues that urban spaces present a public history. The value of such historic places resides in the complexity of their structures, which are impregnated with the record of life and human thoughts and activities: the whole is much greater than the sum of its parts. Indeed, the meaning of an urban entity draws on the interaction between monuments, houses, meeting places and places of work, movement pattern, social habits and ritual commemorations. Through subtle transformation over time, the urban matrix incorporates and perpetuates the memory of the past generations of users. It thus reflects the *genius loci*, as conditioned by the given site factors and by the imprint of respective communities who collectively shaped their living space and were, in turn, molded by their environment.

Undoubtedly a heritage site as old as *Sahet Alqaryoun*, which has undergone so many historic transformations, is a challenging site for analysis. It is important to pay attention to the human efforts in labor, money, and staging of commemorations that go into the historical site in order to analyze the role of memory practice in contemporary society.

Each historic site that becomes the focus of conservation and restoration efforts needs its own analysis in order to ascertain which meanings, emotions, knowledge and behaviors are created through the contemporary memory work. It might be useful to begin a new classification system whereby we begin to distinguish between different kinds of *lieux de mémoire*, so that we can assess more concisely what kind of memory and history determine the content of memories put on public display. But it is important to note that the memory agents working within the confines of existing social processes of creating instances of recurrence and repetition need more scrutiny, as cultures and communities continue to envision themselves in this forward-looking, fast-paced environment.

The continuity – one can say the tradition – of this rhythmical "give and take" accounts for the essential quality of historic cities, which must be carefully managed in order for it to remain alive for the coming generations.

References

Al Sayyad N. 1986. "Notes on the Islamic city: Aspects of Urban Structure and Physical form". *Proceedings of the Seventeenth Annual Conference of the Environmental Design Research Association*. EDRA. USA.

Assi E. 2000. "Searching for the Concept of Authenticity: Implementation Guidelines". *Journal of Architectural Conservation*, 6 (2).

Assi E., Amad E., Dabeek J. 2003. "Post-Disaster Damage Assessment for The City of Nablus". Municipality of Nablus. www.Nablus.org. May 2002.

Bianka S. 2000. *Urban From in the Arab World: Past and Present*. London: Thames and Hudson Ltd.

Canter D. 1977. *The Psychology of Place*. London: Architectural Press.

Celik Z. 1997. *Urban Forms and Colonial Confrontations: Algiers under French Rule*. Berkeley. University of California Press.

Celik Z. 2002. "Colonial/Post Colonial Intersections: Lieux de Mémoire in Algiers". *Historical Reflections*, vol. 28, n° 2.

Connerton P. 2003. *How Societies Remember*. Cambridge: Cambridge University Press.

Conzen M.R.G. 1966. "Historical Townscapes in Britain: A Problem in Applied Geography", in J.W. House (Ed.) *Northern Geographical Essays in Honour of G.H.J. Daysh*. Newcastle upon Tyne: Oriel Press.

Davis E. 2005. *Memories of the State: Politics, History, and Collective Identity in Modern Iraq*. Berkeley: University of California Press.

Greetz C. 1973. "Thick description: Toward and Interpretive Theory of Culture" in *The Interpretation of Cultures*. New York: Basic Books, p. 2-32.

Halbwachs M. 1992. *On Collective Memory*. L.A. Coser transl. Chicago: The University of Chicago Press.

Hyden D. 1995. *The Power of Place: Urban Landscape and Public History*. Library of Congress. USA.

Lowenthal D. 1979. "Environmental Perception: Preserving the Past". *Progress in Human Geography*, 3 (4).

Lynch K. 1960. *The Image of the City*. Cambridge, Mass. MIT Press.

Mortada H. 2003. *Traditional Islamic Principles*. New York: Routledge Curzon.

Nimir I. 1961-1975. *Tarikh Jabal Nablus wa al Balqa*. Nablus, West Bank (Arabic).

Norberg-Schulz C. 1963. *Intentions in Architecture*. Oslo: Universitetsforlaget.

Norberg-Schulz C. 1980. *Genius Loci: Towards a Phenomenology of Architecture*. New York: Rizzoli.

Norberg-Schulz C. 1985. *The Concept of Dwelling: On the Way to Figurative Architecture*. New York: Electa/Rizzoli.

Nora P. 1996. *Rethinking the French Past: Realm of Memory*, Vol. 1, Conflict and divisions, under the direction of Pierre Nora, translated by Arthur Gold hammer (1996). New York: Columbia University Press.

Proshansky H.M., Fabian A.K. & Kaminff R. 1983. "Place-identity: Physical World Socialization of the Self". *Journal of Environmental Psychology*, 3, p. 57-83.

Koselleck R. 2002. *The Practice of Conceptual History: Timing History, Spacing Concepts*, translated by Todd Samuel Presner and others. Palo Alto: Stanford University press.

Relph E. 1976. *Place and Placelessness*. London: Pion.

Saarinen T., Stell J.A. 1982. "Environmental Perception: International Developments". *Progress in Human Geography*, 6, p. 515-546.

Sharif H. 1999. *Senaet Alsaboun Anabulsi*. Municipality of Nablus. 1999 (Arabic).

Steele F. 1981. *The Sense of Place*. Boston, MA. CBI.

Venturi R. 1966. *Complexity and Contradiction in Architecture*. New York. New York Museum of Art.

Volk L. 2001. *Missing the Nation: Lebanon's Post-War Generation in the Midst of Reconstruction*. PhD. Dissertation. Harvard University.

Volk L. 2005. "Lebanese heritage at Nahr al Kalb: From a Wall of Shame to a Wall of fame". Paper submitted to the Seventh Mediterranean Social and Political Research meeting. Florence, Italy. Shuman Center for Advanced Studies at the European University.

L'esprit du lieu à Bergama (Pergame) Identification et analyse des menaces

Can Sakir Binan
Université Technique de Yildiz
Turquie

Demet Binan
Université Beaux-Arts Mimar Sinan
Turquie

ABSTRACT

Located in Western Anatolia, the ancient city of Pergamon was founded during the Hellenistic period and lived through the Roman, Byzantine, pre-Ottoman and Ottoman ages. Today, it stands as a vibrant historic city called Bergama. Normally, in such ancient cities, the superimposition of history covers most of the material and immaterial layers that lay beneath. This is not so for Bergama, where the "spirit of place" still bears the marks of its rich past. This "place" is a living, vibrant organism, whose constant evolution takes on a universal character. It is hard to suitably analyze, and even harder to identify, the threats that weigh upon it as a result of this evolutionary process of transformation. But that is exactly what we will attempt to do in the case of Bergama.

RÉSUMÉ

L'antique ville de Pergame, située en Anatolie occidentale, fondée à l'époque hellénistique, et ayant traversé les époques romaine, byzantine, pré-ottomane et ottomane, est une ville historique vivante aujourd'hui, Bergama. Dans les villes anciennes de ce type, les strates historiques superposées masquent la plupart des couches matérielles et immatérielles inférieures. Mais dans le cas de Bergama, nous constatons une grande profondeur historique du point de vue de «l'esprit du lieu». Le «lieu» est un organisme vivant et dynamique, dont l'évolution continuelle est un caractère universel. Il est difficile de l'analyser efficacement, et encore plus difficile d'identifier les menaces qui pèsent sur lui, dans cette dynamique de transformation et d'évolution, ce que nous tenterons de faire pour le cas de Bergama.

Le nom de la ville turque actuelle de Bergama dérive de celui de la ville antique de Pergame, signifiant «forteresse» dans une langue ancienne du bassin méditerranéen. Plusieurs légendes relatent la fondation de la ville (Bayatlı 1949 : 18-19 ; Radt 2001 : 21-23). L'*Anabase* de Xenophon, relatant le périple des *Dix Mille*, nous apprend qu'elle faisait partie de l'empire perse aux Ve et IVe siècles av. J.C. Conquise par Alexandre, elle entre dans l'empire macédonien, puis après la mort de ce dernier, elle devient une ville de science et d'administration. Sa bibliothèque était l'une des plus importantes du bassin méditerranéen. L'un des grands centres de la culture hellénistique, son acropole et son environnement bâti remontent à cette époque. À l'époque romaine, et jusqu'en 395 ap. J.C., elle était un important centre d'administration de la province d'Asie mineure ; à partir du IIe siècle, et tout au long de l'époque byzantine, le christianisme y prend de l'importance ; elle devient un évêché (résidence du métropolite). Conquise en 1302, Pergame devint le centre de l'émirat de Karesi, puis après 1341, passa sous la domination de l'émirat ottoman, devenu par la suite l'empire ottoman (Uzunçarşılı 1984 : 99 ; Zachariadou 1997 : 247).

Figure 1. Bergama (Pergame) en Turquie.

Sur la colline de l'Acropole, d'une hauteur de 330 m, appelée montagne de Kale ou Kent, les fouilles archéologiques ont montré que Pergame n'était pas qu'une citadelle sur une colline, mais une ville fortifiée (Radt 2001 : 51). Celle-ci, qui recouvrait une superficie relativement restreinte de la colline au IIIe siècle av. J.C. est devenue une grande ville, s'étendant jusqu'aux berges de la rivière Bakırçay. Le sanctuaire d'Asclépios, centre médical de grande renommée, remonte à cette époque, ainsi que des édifices tels que le grand autel de Zeus, le temple d'Athéna, la Bibliothèque, le Grand Palais et le théâtre, qui témoignent de son antique splendeur. Au IIe siècle av. J.C., hors de son enceinte, la ville a pris le plan quadrillé typique de l'époque romaine, où s'élevèrent des édifices remarquables tels que le théâtre romain, l'amphithéâtre, le stade, et un extraordinaire temple de 100 m sur 270 m dédié à Sérapis, dieu égyptien (Radt 2001 : 57, 198).

À l'époque ottomane, puis sous la république turque, la ville poursuit son extension en direction de la vallée. Actuellement, Bergama est une sous-préfecture de la province d'Izmir.

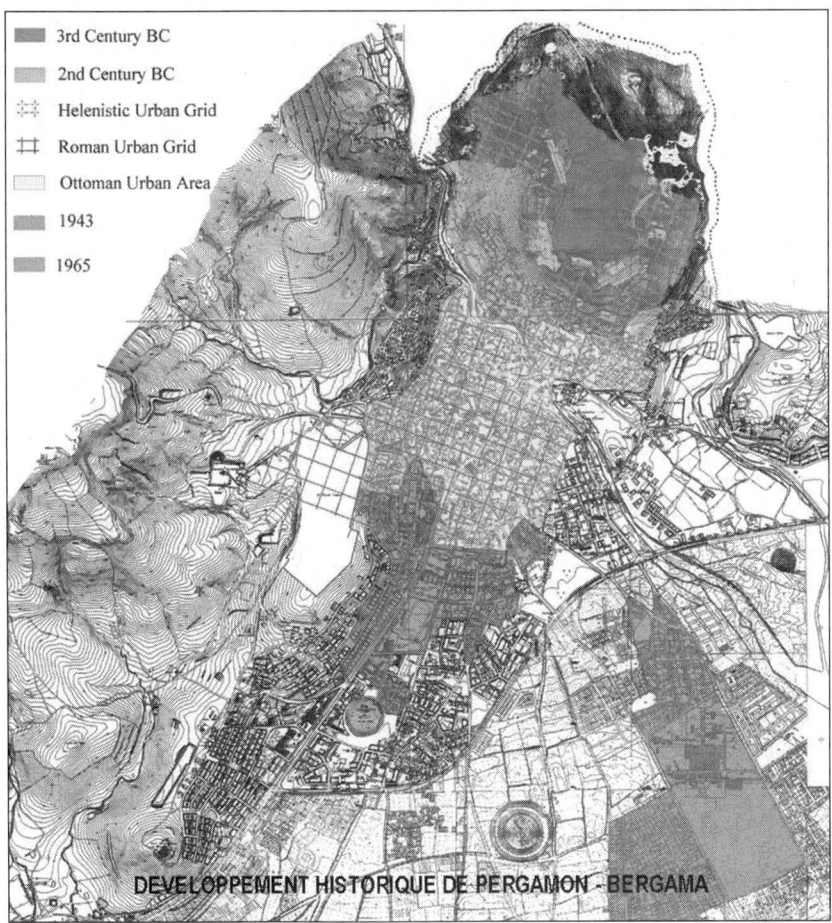

Figure 2.1 Développement historique.

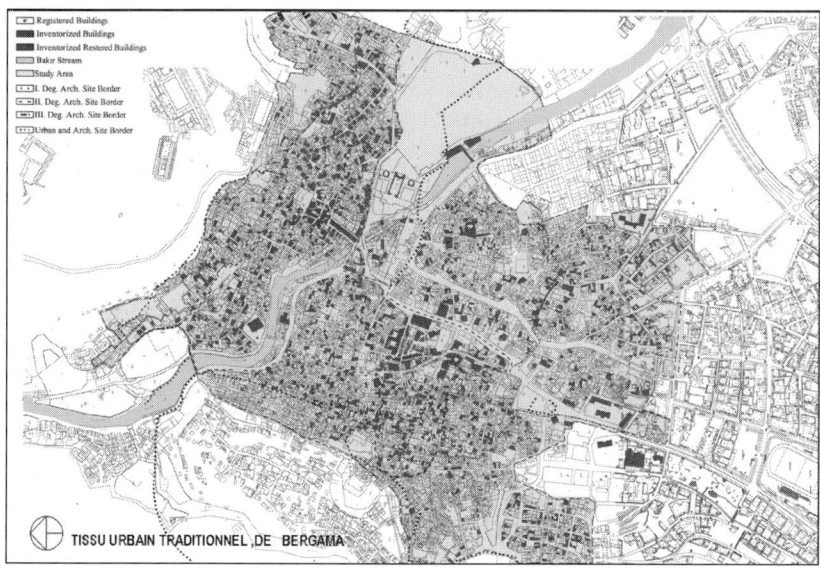

Figure 2.2 Tissu urbain traditionnel.

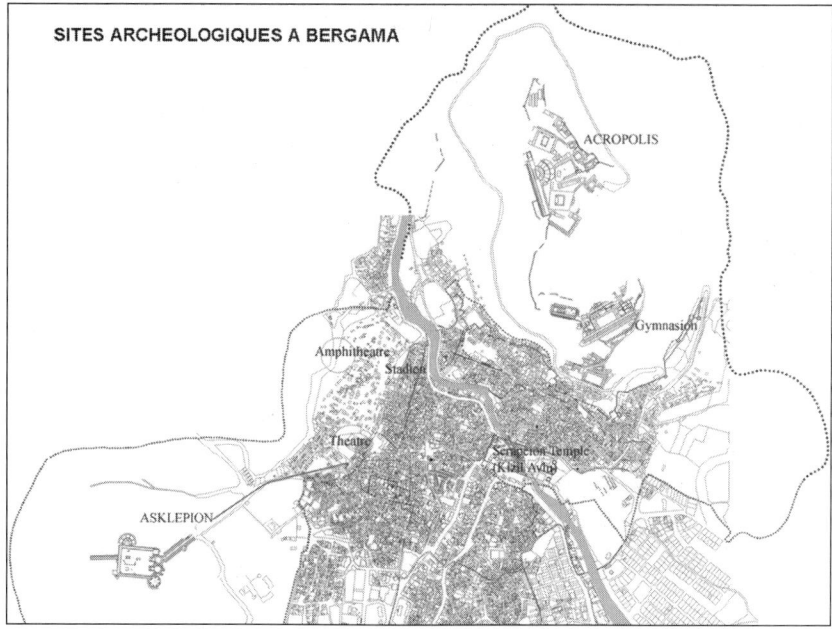

Figure 2.3 Répartition des sites archéologiques.

Éléments constitutifs de l'esprit du lieu à Bergama-Pergame

Dans le cadre de cette analyse, nous pouvons rassembler les éléments qui forment l'esprit du lieu à Bergama en trois groupes : les éléments de l'environnement naturel, les éléments socioculturels et les éléments de l'environnement bâti.

Éléments de l'environnement naturel

Pour ce qui est de la topographie, Bergama se situe à 63 m d'altitude, au nord-ouest d'Izmir (l'antique Smyrne), un peu en retrait de la mer Égée (Isıtman 1939 : 9). La ville ancienne était implantée au sud du mont Madra et orientée vers la vallée de la rivière Bakırçay. La rivière Bergama Çay (nommée Selinos dans l'antiquité) traverse la ville, située au flanc de deux collines, celle de l'Acropole et de la ville antique au nord-est, et une autre au nord-ouest. Trois autres collines sont en vue au sud et au sud-ouest, mais il s'agit en réalité de tumuli, appelés Maltepe, Yığmatepe et Tavşantepe (Isıtman 1939 : 14), qui, pour les habitants de Bergama, sont si anciens qu'ils les considèrent comme des collines naturelles. Ces différents points de vue sur la ville, avec les tumuli et les autres éléments naturels, constituent une partie importante de l'esprit des lieux à Bergama. Pour ce qui est du climat, la ville appartient à la zone climatique méditerranéenne. L'agriculture se base sur la production du tabac, du coton, de la betterave, des pistaches, du raisin et des olives (Peker 1992 : 9).

Éléments socioculturels

Au début du XXᵉ siècle, la population de Bergama se composait de Turcs, de Grecs, de Juifs arméniens et de Tziganes (Emecen 1992 : 493 ; Eriş 2003 : 125, 133). Après les guerres balkaniques et la Première Guerre mondiale, la population de Bergama a augmenté avec l'afflux des immigrants provenant des anciens territoires balkaniques de l'Empire ottoman. Après la signature du traité de Lausanne en 1923 eut lieu la *Mübadele*, ou échange de population, entre la Grèce et la Turquie. La composition démographique de la ville changea une fois de plus. Après la fondation d'Israël en 1948, une partie importante des Juifs de la ville émigrèrent. Après cette période, les Juifs et les Arméniens restants partirent pour les grandes villes comme Izmir et Istanbul. La population actuelle est de 52 162 habitants. Elle est constituée d'autochtones, d'immigrants en provenance des villages des alentours et d'autres régions de Turquie. La ville de Bergama a connu un fort apport d'immigrants pendant la période de la République turque.

Actuellement, l'islam est l'unique religion pratiquée dans la ville, où se trouvent 19 mosquées, dont la plupart datent des XVᵉ et XVIᵉ siècles. L'une d'elle, la mosquée Ulu Cami, convertie au XVᵉ siècle, était auparavant l'église Sainte-Sophie. La ville compte encore les ruines de deux synagogues, ainsi que les vestiges d'anciens cimetières, dont un cimetière juif.

Les anciens lieux de culte, convertis, sont toujours en activité. Par exemple, la « Cour rouge », ou Kızıl Avlu, fait partie du temple de Sérapis, construit au IIᵉ siècle ap. J.C., qui est évoquée dans les *Révélations* de saint Jean, où elle est qualifiée de « trône de Satan » (Radt 2001 : 12 ; Eriş 2003 : 75) ; ce lieu fut converti en église Saint-Jean au IVᵉ siècle, et une partie de cet édifice mystérieux, auquel toutes les croyances attribuaient un caractère sacré, fut convertie en mosquée en 1950, la mosquée Kurtuluş, encore en activité aujourd'hui.

Traditions et coutumes ont beaucoup d'importance dans l'esprit du lieu à Bergama, l'environnement construit s'unissant aux traditions.

Figure 3.1 Kızıl Avlu. Archives de la Mairie de Bergama.

Figure 3.2 Temple de Sérapis. Archives de la Mairie de Bergama.

Figure 3.3 Messe chrétienne. Archives de la Mairie de Bergama.

Figure 3.4 Prière musulmane dans le même édifice. Archives de la Mairie de Bergama.

Figure 4.1 Bergama Ulucamii, ancienne église convertie au XIVe siècle.

Figure 4.2 Bergama Ulucamii, ancienne église convertie au XIVe siècle, offre des repas après la prière.

Les traditions de la vie quotidienne sont fortement liées à la maison et à son environnement. Certaines de ces coutumes préservent l'authenticité des bâtiments traditionnels, ces derniers constituant un exemple particulièrement visible de la culture locale. Les cafés et les cours des mosquées sont des lieux traditionnels de rencontre et de réunion, «aller au café» tous les soirs étant une coutume très ancrée dans la population masculine turque. La plupart de ces traditions constituant l'environnement socioculturel sont directement liées à l'environnement bâti et naturel.

L'environnement bâti

Il s'agit de l'élément le plus important de l'esprit du lieu, avec les maisons traditionnelles et les quartiers anciens, les esplanades et les places, les cafés, les vestiges archéologiques de la ville, les cimetières et les édifices funéraires, les lieux de commerce traditionnels (Pazar, Arasta, Çarşı), les hammams, les ponts, les fontaines, les thermes et le grand canal…

L'esprit du lieu se constitue par la superposition de l'environnement naturel et des éléments socioculturels de l'environnement construit; il se cache dans les édifices, les coutumes, les modes de vie, de commerce, la production agricole, la vie quotidienne, etc. Les exemples présentés ci-dessous nous montrent plusieurs aspects de l'esprit du lieu dans la Bergama contemporaine.

Figure 5. Çukurhan. (XVIᵉ siècle) Caravansérail dans le centre commercial. On trouve un café au rez-de-chaussée mais les étages supérieurs n'ont pas d'affectation.

Figure 6. Deux ponts sur la rivière de Bergama (sur laquelle se situent des tanneries), pont de Tabaklar (pont des tanneurs) et pont de Üç Kemer.

Les menaces potentielles sur l'esprit des lieux

En commençant par les causes « naturelles », on peut aisément prédire que l'assèchement de la rivière Bergama, en raison de la construction de barrages, constitue une importante menace pour plusieurs valeurs. D'autre part, la disparition des matières premières provenant directement de l'environnement naturel, pour diverses raisons, aura des répercussions jusque sur la production artisanale traditionnelle. De nouveaux projets affectant l'aspect et la topographie de la ville constituent également une menace.

L'intensité du bouleversement démographique a une influence directe sur la structure culturelle de la ville de Bergama. L'apport de cultures de différentes régions de la Turquie contemporaine, dont les différences, mêmes mineures, suscitent certes un enrichissement culturel, provoque aussi des pertes dans les traditions et les coutumes de la vie et de l'usage des espaces traditionnels de la ville où réside l'esprit du lieu.

L'autre facteur essentiel de l'esprit du lieu à Bergama est la continuité de l'usage des lieux de culte anciens par la population contemporaine. Cette continuité est indispensable à l'esprit du lieu, tout comme le fait de servir un repas composé de riz, de *nohut* et de *lokma* les jours de fête. La mémoire collective de la ville tient aussi aux noms des rues, des places et des quartiers. Par exemple, la place appelée « Karadut Dibi » (Mur noir), était autrefois un jardin public où les habitants de Bergama allaient boire le thé. La place et l'arbre ont été détruits par un incendie à la fin du XIXe siècle, des bâtiments les ont remplacés, mais le nom persiste (Bayatlı 1997 : 128). Parmi les autres éléments constitutifs de l'esprit du lieu à Bergama, il y avait aussi une coutume remontant à 1937, une kermesse organisée à l'époque pour faire connaître la ville au monde. Cet événement est devenu une tradition des temps modernes. L'importation excessive de produits industriels marquera la fin de cet événement traditionnel dont le but était de faire connaître à l'extérieur les productions de Bergama.

La production des matières premières est indispensable à la fabrication des produits traditionnels vendus dans le centre commercial historique de la ville. Une baisse dans la production de ces matériaux entraîne la fermeture d'un certain nombre de magasins dans le marché traditionnel. Par exemple, au marché, la zone appelée Arasta était auparavant l'emplacement traditionnel des magasins et des ateliers de maroquinerie, cordonniers, bottiers et selliers (Peker 1992 : 81-87). Au cours des dix dernières années, trente magasins vendant des productions artisanales à Arasta ont fermé. Arasta est une enclave historique, faisant organiquement partie du tissu urbain avec ses magasins anciens, mais sans les artisans, ce n'est plus qu'une coquille vide, sans esprit !

Figure 7. Ancienne Arasta (marché) et l'un des derniers artisans chausseurs.

Figure 8.1 Ancienne Tannerie avec l'acropole en arrière-plan.

Figure 8.2 Kızıl Avlu, Temple de Serapion.

La disparition des ateliers de cuir et des tanneries est d'autant plus déplorable que cette activité à Pergame remontait à l'antiquité. C'est à Pergame qu'avait été inventé le parchemin (mot venant de *pergamena*, « peau de Pergame »). La petite rivière traversant la ville est parfois surnommée « rivière des tanneurs », et l'un des anciens ponts, « pont des tanneurs ». La production de parchemin n'existe plus, mais la production d'autres produits du cuir se prolongeait.

Les places de marché (Pazar) sont également importantes dans la vie économique et quotidienne de Bergama. Certaines existent depuis le XVe siècle (Domuz Alanı, la place des porcs, par exemple). Un nouveau projet d'urbanisme prévoit que ces lieux seront déplacés à l'extérieur de la ville.

Figure 9. Minaret seldjoukide, mosquée Şadırvanlı, cafés et fontaine.

Figure 10. Place du Café aux Platanes (mosquée Hacı Hekim, café aux Platanes, ancienne Halle.).

La vie quotidienne dans les quartiers d'habitation traditionnels représente un autre aspect de l'esprit du lieu à Bergama. Les maisons à l'architecture vernaculaire risquent de perdre leur âme si elles perdent leurs habitants et leur mode de vie traditionnel. Les enfants jouant dans les rues et les impasses, les femmes faisant le ménage le matin et bavardant l'après-midi, les vieillards installés près des barrières des jardins pour regarder les passants, et à la fin de la journée, tout le monde se faisant la conversation dans la rue… À notre époque, il est très difficile de faire coexister les bâtiments traditionnels avec les nouveaux modes de vie. Mais il est pourtant clair que l'esprit du lieu dépend de cette combinaison.

En 1968, l'ensemble de la ville de Bergama a été décrété zone archéologique, en raison des strates antiques existant sous la ville. Cela ne s'accompagna d'aucun plan d'aménagement. Depuis cette date, personne n'a pu obtenir de permis de construire, ne serait-ce que pour restaurer les maisons traditionnelles. Les habitants autochtones ont délaissé le tissu urbain vernaculaire pour s'installer dans les nouveaux quartiers d'habitation construits dans la vallée. Les maisons traditionnelles désertées ont été réoccupées par des immigrants aux faibles revenus et dont les modes de vie sont tout à fait différents de la culture ayant donné naissance à ce tissu vernaculaire.

Figure 11. Maisons vernaculaires et vie à Bergama.

Figure 12. Coexistence des vestiges archéologiques et de l'habitation vernaculaire.

Le canal antique qui passe sous le temple de Sérapis (Kızıl Avlu) est un élément très important pour l'identité, et la nécessité de sa conservation est indiscutable, de même que pour tous les autres vestiges archéologiques existant dans le tissu urbain. Le tissu traditionnel ancien s'est superposé aux vestiges antiques, notamment le quartier «ne yerde ne gökte» (Eriş 1979: 189-190). L'esprit du lieu à Bergama-Pergame est indissociable de cette coexistence des vestiges archéologiques et de la vie quotidienne dans la ville traditionnelle. Il est impossible de choisir entre les deux sans rompre cet équilibre, ce qui serait catastrophique pour l'esprit du lieu contemporain, qui est fragile. Ajoutons ici que l'antique Pergame et le temple d'Asclépios sont de grands centres archéologiques auxquels les brochures, les guides, les orientations des agences de tourisme et du Ministère de la Culture et du Tourisme attribuent plus d'importance qu'à la ville traditionnelle. Mais, puisqu'elle est un organisme vivant, l'esprit de la ville de Bergama réside aussi dans ses traditions, ses coutumes, ses modes de vie, ses légendes anciennes toujours vivantes, autant que dans son tissu urbain superposé à la ville ancienne. La population contemporaine accepte comme un lieu sacré un tombeau dit «de la Sainte», exemple de continuité des lieux sacrés.

Autre tradition liée à l'environnement bâti traditionnel, le Taşhan, caravansérail du XVᵉ siècle. Le mur sud de cet édifice, situé sur la rue İncirli mescid, a servi d'étalon pour les mesures de terrain (40 mètres, ou 60 pas), depuis le XVᵉ siècle jusqu'aux temps modernes (Bayatlı 1943: 32), cette mesure étant «l'acre de Karaosman» ou «acre de Taşhan». Ce mur étant fait de grands blocs de pierre, comme les édifices de l'antique Pergame, il est probable que son existence (et cette mesure) remonte à la Pergame de l'antiquité. Actuellement, le Taşhan, ainsi que le Çukurhan, l'autre caravansérail, font partie des édifices désertés du marché, et représentent des «vides» dans l'identité du centre commercial traditionnel.

Figure 13. Caravansérail Taşhan (XVᵉ siècle) et mur servant d'étalon aux mesures de terrain.

Une partie des bâtiments datant de l'époque de la République sont actuellement désaffectés. La ville est soumise aux menaces d'aménagements de modernisation envisagés par les gouvernements, aménagements destinés à résoudre les problèmes quotidiens mais dépourvus d'une approche prenant en compte l'identité et l'esprit du lieu de la ville. De nouvelles voies sont ouvertes, qui déchirent le tissu urbain traditionnel, causent la perte d'édifices vernaculaires et provoquent un bouleversement immédiat des alentours.

Enfin, Bergama-Pergame est une ville historique dont les strates profondes peuvent se percevoir au moyen d'indices diachroniques et synchroniques. Une partie de la ville est une zone archéologique, mais l'autre partie est vivante. Les valeurs tangibles de toute la ville sont si fortes qu'elles peuvent laisser inaperçues les valeurs intangibles de la ville vivante. Pour percevoir ces dernières, il faut regarder avec d'autres yeux et y vivre pendant un certain temps. L'esprit du lieu à Bergama-Pergame est une valeur intangible, difficile à analyser, voire à comprendre, même par ses habitants. L'environnement bâti peut se comprendre, se mesurer et se dessiner ; mais l'esprit du lieu ne peut se mesurer ni se dessiner. Il faut une approche sensible pour l'appréhender. Il est tellement volatile et insaisissable que si on ne veut pas le voir… il disparaîtra. C'est la plus grande menace !

Références

Bayatli, Osman. 1943. *Bergama'da Yakın Tarihten Olaylar,* İstanbul. Vakıt Matbaası.

Bayatli, Osman. 1949. *Bergama Tarihinde İlk çağ ve Bakırçay Havzası, Arkhaik-Klasik Kültürler,* Fasikül 1, İstanbul : Saka Matbaası.

Bayatli, Osman. 1997. *Bergama'da Yakın Tarih Olayları 18. ve 19. Yüzyıl,* Bergama Belediyesi Kültür Yay., n° 53, İzmir : Bergama Belediyesi.

Emecen, Feridun. 1992. Bergama, *Türkiye Diyanet Vakfı İslam Ansiklopedisi,* C. 5, 492-495. İstanbul : *Türkiye Diyanet Vakfı.*

Eriş, Eyüp. 2003. *Bergama Tarihinde İnanç Coğrafyası,* Bergama Belleten 12, Bergama. :BERKSAV Yayını.

Eriş, Eyüp. 1979. *Bergama Uygarlık Tarihi,* İzmir.

Peker, Filiz. 1992. *Cumhuriyetin İlk Yıllarında Bergama Kazasının Sosyal ve Kültürel Durumu,* Bergama Belediyesi Kültür Yay., No :8.

Radt, Wolfgang. 2002. Pergamon Antik Bir Kentin Tarihi ve Yapıları, İstanbul :Yapı Kredi Yayınları 1619.

The River Duero in Soria or the Literary Construction of a Heritage Landscape

Begoña Bernal
Universidad de Burgos
España

ABSTRACT

"Where the Duero River twists to form its crossbow curve along Soria" (Spain), there is a landscape shaped by cultural heritage sites from diverse ages, similar in typology and contradictory in their heritage making process. Today, from the viewing point of Cuatro Vientos and the viewing point of Soria Castle we may relish a landscape rich in heroic memories, literary evocation and legends. Added to the memory of this heroism (Numancia) or of artistic expressions is the transformational gaze of writers that were transcendental in Spanish culture. Bécquer, Machado and Gerardo Diego gave literary wording to their nostalgia and experience. Thus, at the same location, the heritage value springs from human activity in the past and also from the cultural projection of feelings onto the surrounding reality. The strength of the poetic word, recited and commented on in the classroom, has transformed the River Duero into a heritage landscape.

RÉSUMÉ

« Là où la rivière Duero s'incurve pour former un arc autour de Soria » (Espagne), il existe un paysage constitué de sites culturels patrimoniaux de diverses époques, similaires sur le plan de la typologie, mais contradictoires dans les processus qui les constituent en patrimoine. Aujourd'hui, depuis les hauteurs de Cuatro Vientos, et du point de vue du château de Soria, nous pouvons admirer un paysage riche de mémoires historiques, d'évocations littéraires et de légendes. À la mémoire de son héroïsme (Numance) ou de ses expressions artistiques, s'ajoute le regard d'écrivains ayant profondément imprégné la culture hispanique, ce regard exerçant un pouvoir de transformation. Bécquer, Machado et Gerardo Diego ont donné une dimension littéraire à leur nostalgie et à leur expérience. Dans le même lieu donc, les valeurs patrimoniales prennent leur source à la fois dans l'activité des êtres humains du passé et dans la projection culturelle de sentiments dans la réalité environnante. La force de la poésie, récitée et commentée à l'école, a transformé la rivière Duero en paysage patrimonial.

Introduction

In the City of Soria, on the river Duero, a series of projects have been proposed for the economic development of the area, such as the unfortunately named *Ciudad del Medio Ambiente* [Environmental City] or the SORIA II Industrial Polygon, which are an affront to the natural and cultural landscape. The irrationality of both projects implies the destruction of the cultural landscape of Soria threatening an irremediable loss of authenticity for the heritage sites of the City of Soria.

The proposals for the Environmental City, as well as the industrialization of a part of the landscape around Soria of great heritage value, have provoked immense concern in the international scientific community, because it is an attack on culture, and the cultural landscape, and because those promoting it are precisely the very local and regional public authorities that are entrusted with the responsibility and the powers to conserve our heritage.

Today, the public has accepted the concepts of landscape, environment and setting, which are already well defined in different disciplines, amongst which geography. The same is true for the categories of natural heritage and cultural heritage or landscape heritage, defined by UNESCO in order to catalogue the heritage listed in the World Heritage List. There are legal texts, charters, conventions and directives of international scope that define the landscape, that recognise its leading role as a key component of the territory and a watermark of the natural and cultural heritage of a place, and that set out ways of promoting and securing satisfactory protection. So, now that the regulatory dimension on the environment, on landscape protection and on heritage conservation is very clear, political and economic authorities are acting as if the law did not exist, stressing indeterminate or contingent features of these regulations.

A controversial project plan backed by the public authorities in a unique area of the City of Soria has focused our attention on the design plans to build the SORIA II Industrial Polygon. We have seen how this polemical issue referred to as "the new siege of Numancia", has in turn led the scientific community, at first alarmed by the disastrous consequences for the archaeological site, to set its sights on the existing elements that make up that space, to recognize the heritage values that constitute that space, and to delve into the causes and the consequences of heritage making in a geographic area which come together in the creation and identification of a cultural landscape.

We have also noted that any real protection of the landscape in Spain is immensely fragile. The blurred confusion of the public authorities, as it is a matter of a landscape, provokes exasperation among intellectuals that express concern for heritage. The pathological behaviour of the authorities leads them to affirm that the SORIA II Industrial Polygon planned for El Cabezo will affect neither the archaeological site of Numancia nor the City of Soria.

They deliberately forget that "Where the Duero River twists to form its crossbow curve along Soria" a landscape stretches out that is shaped by cultural heritage sites of various ages, of a similar typology and contradictory in their heritage-making process. Added to the memory of this heroism (Numancia) and artistic expression (San Juan de Duero) is the transformational gaze of literary evocation and legend, of transcendental writers in the Spanish culture: Bécquer, Machado and Gerardo Diego. Thus, at the same location, the heritage value springs from human activity in the past and also from the cultural projection of sentiment onto the surrounding reality. The strength of the poetic word has turned the River Duero into a heritage landscape.

The public company Gesturcal S.A. (belonging to the Regional Government of Castile and Leon, the *Junta de Castilla y León*), in collaboration with Soria town council intends to develop an industrial polygon, called SORIA II, in a zone situated at beauty spots such as El Cabezo, La Colorada and Los Pajarejos, to the south-east of Numancia and to the north-east of the City of Soria, on the right bank of the River Duero. The chosen space is an extension of common agricultural land, on which clumps of holm oak combine with uncultivated fields and scrub land, limestone outcrops, crooked shaped cereal fields, slopes with bushy vegetation and low hills, plantations of pine trees, in brief, a landscape in harmony with the image that the area around the City of Soria has traditionally transmitted, a landscape that has served as a necessary and acceptable channel through which the most celebrated and well-known of Spain's poets have expressed their feelings and emotions in verse read thousands of times, recited and studied in the classroom:

> Aquellos diminutos pegujales / de tierra dura y fría, / donde apuntan centenos y
> trigales / que el pan moreno nos darán un día! [...] Y otra vez roca y roca, pedregales
> / desnudos y pelados serrijones, / la tierra de las águilas caudales, / malezas y jarales,
> / hierbas monteses, zarzas y cambrones. [...] Entre cerros de plomo y de ceniza /
> manchados de roídos encinares, / y entre calvas roquedas de caliza, / iba a embestir
> los ocho tajamares / del puente el padre río, / que surca de Castilla el yermo frío
> (ANTONIO MACHADO).

The land chosen to develop the Industrial Polygon SORIA II is in contact with, surrounded by and related to various Assets of Cultural Interest and other architectural monuments singled out for special protection. That space, that stretches undulating between the plain and the escarpments on the left bank of the River Duero (between the mound of Numancia and the remains of the encircling Roman encampments, to the north, and the Monte de las Ánimas, San Juan de Duero and the river, to the south) constitute a natural and cultural landscape of exceptional value. Hence, the planned urban development of SORIA II, in the opinion of many people, presents very alarming aspects for the conservation of heritage that is highly infused with cultural and natural value, which make it, on the one hand, irreplaceable and, on the other, highly fragile. It demonstrates the ambiguity of the public authorities in their concern for the integrity of a group of heritage assets (natural and cultural) that might be affected by the project.

The Resolution of the General Secretariat of the Environmental Department of the Regional Government of Castile and Leon (2007) denies that the planned Industrial Polygon will impact on the surrounding Assets of Cultural Interest, despite including a statement that, inexplicably, bears no consequences for the possible impact on the "environment" or setting in which the plots of land are situated: "The visual fragility [of the project area] may be considered high due to the proximity of the capital Soria, as there is high ground in the surrounding area from which the zone is discernable (Numancia, Ermita del Mirón, Cerro del Castillo, Monte de las Ánimas)".

This sentence reflects a pathological paradox as, without wishing to, it is referring to the landscape of Soria, given that it is talking about a landscape (that of Soria) that bestows meaning on the viewing points at *Los Cuatro Vientos* next to the *Ermita del Mirón* and on the *Cerro del Castillo*. And it is Numancia that looks over to Soria across that country landscape that they intend to turn into an industrial one. This is a good example of the deterioration affecting the premises and foundations upon which our knowledge of the concepts of landscape, environment and setting is based, because the Regional Government departs from all logic when it speaks of visual fragility and fails to conclude that there is a need to preserve "the views" from such attractive high ground.

Art. 42 of the *Ley de Patrimonio Cultural de Castilla y León* (2002) states that: "the conservation of historic complexes entails the maintenance of the urban and architectural structure and of the silhouette of the landscape, as well as the general characteristics of its environment". The construction of an industrial polygon on the agricultural land situated between Numancia and the Roman siege forts of Garray, the left bank of the River Duero and the historic city centre of Soria would seriously alter the silhouette of the landscape and the general characteristics of the very environment of such Assets of Cultural Interest, because, in reality, it is the same silhouette of the landscape that stands before us, the same landscape, whatever the legal status accorded to each of its important constituent parts. Because the whole is much more than the sum of the parts; what defines the whole is the interactions between the parts.

2. Meaning of "landscape", "environment" and "setting" in international and national doctrine.

The European Landscape Convention (Florence 2000*)*, ratified by Spain on 6th November 2007 affirms that "the landscape has an important public interest role in the cultural, ecological, environmental and social fields, and constitutes a resource favourable to economic activity and whose protection, management and planning can contribute to job creation".

It also acknowledges that "the landscape is an important part of the quality of life for people everywhere: in urban areas and in the countryside, in degraded areas as well as in areas of high quality, in areas recognised as being of outstanding beauty as well as everyday areas".

The landscape is "an area, as perceived by people, whose character is the result of the action and interaction of natural and/or human factors".

It is defined in the same way in (art. 3.26) of *la Ley del Patrimonio Natural y de la Biodiversidad* (2007). This Law points to "the predominance of environmental protection over urban and territorial planning" (art. 2. f).

Many years ago now, ICOMOS grappled with the relations between historic urban areas in the *International Charter for the conservation of Historic Towns and Urban Areas* "This charter concerns historic urban areas, large and small, including cities, towns and historic centres or quarters, together with their natural and man-made environments. (Charter of Washington 1987)**.**

As an objective, it points to the values to be conserved, "the historic character of the town or urban area and all those material and spiritual elements that express this character, especially: [...] relationships between buildings and green and open spaces; [...] the relationship between the town or urban area and its surrounding setting, both natural and manmade; [...] Any threat to these qualities would compromise the authenticity of the historic town or urban area."

> As for the landscape that surrounds the City of Soria –"*¡Colinas plateadas, / grises alcores, cárdenas roquedas! / por donde traza el Duero / su curva de ballesta/ en torno a Soria, oscuros encinares, / ariscos pedregales, calvas sierras, / caminos blancos y álamos del río...*" (Antonio Machado) – with the development of the Industrial Polygon SORIA II, its image will undergo a serious alteration, a loss for the historic City of Soria and an irreparable loss of authenticity.

In the Declaration of Xi'an (2005), on the conservation of the setting of heritage structures, sites and areas, ICOMOS acknowledged the contribution of the setting to the meaning of heritage monuments, sites and areas. "Beyond the physical and visual aspects, the setting includes interaction with the natural environment; past or present social or spiritual practices, customs, traditional knowledge, use or activities and other forms of intangible cultural heritage aspects that created and form the space as well as the current and dynamic cultural, social and economic context." (point 1). Further on it says: "Heritage structures, sites or areas of various scales, including individual buildings or designed spaces, historic cities or urban landscapes, landscapes, seascapes, cultural routes and archaeological sites, derive their significance and distinctive character from their perceived social and spiritual, historic, artistic, aesthetic, natural, scientific or other cultural values. They also derive their significance and distinctive character from their meaningful relationships with their physical, visual, spiritual and other cultural context and settings. These relationships can be the result of a conscious and planned creative act, spiritual belief, historical events, use or a cumulative and organic process over time through cultural traditions." (point 2).

In other words, the heritage value not only arises from the prior "objective" characteristics of the asset, but of the transmission and perception of that asset by the public. An act of cultural communication is established between the "reality" of the people that know, use and feel that reality. Furthermore, in that communication between the generations, the shining examples of history, the magical and the mythical, and the aesthetics of thought and feeling expressed in words are no longer the setting of a site, the invisible shroud of a site, but become integrated within it so as to turn it into a ("one single") heritage asset. There are numerous examples of literary creation that combine historic references and symbolic values:

> *Numancia del silencio y de la ruina, / alma de libertad, trono del viento...* (GERARDO DIEGO), *¡Gentes del alto llano numantino / que a Dios guardáis como cristianas viejas, / que el sol de España os llene/ de alegría, de luz y de riqueza!* (ANTONIO MACHADO); or within history, the suggestive images and feelings woven into the landscape: *¡Oh, en el azul, vosotras, viajeras golondrinas / que vais al joven Duero, zagales y merinos, / con rumbo hacia las altas praderas numantinas, / por las cañadas hondas y al sol de los caminos;/ hayedos y pinares que cruza el ágil ciervo;/ montañas, serrijones, lomazos, parameras [...] ¡Adiós, tierra de Soria; adiós el alto llano/ cercado de colinas y crestas militares,/ alcores y roquedas del yermo castellano,/ fantasmas de robledos y sombras de encinares!* (ANTONIO MACHADO).

This is why the so-called setting assumes capital importance in the evaluation, protection and transmission of a heritage asset, and if the setting is destroyed, so too is the asset. In consequence, if the landscape to the north-east of the City of Soria is destroyed when constructing the Industrial Polygon SORIA II, the meaning and the distinctive character of the historic City of Soria are destroyed.

"The definition of setting requires an understanding of the history, evolution and character of the surroundings of the heritage resource. Defining the setting is a process of considering multiple factors to include the character of the arrival experience and the heritage resource itself." (Declaration of Xi'an, point 3). It is a process that must take into account multiple factors that have to include the experience of approaching the site and the heritage asset itself.

Given that the setting constitutes a multi-faceted entity, is composed of very similar elements in their quality and from very diverse ages, then:

> Understanding the setting in an inclusive way requires a multi-disciplinary approach and the use of diverse information sources. Sources include formal records and archives, artistic and scientific descriptions, oral history and traditional knowledge, the perspectives of local and associated communities as well as the analysis of views and vistas. Cultural traditions, rituals, spiritual practices and concepts as well as history, topography, natural environment values, use and other factors contribute to create the full range of a setting's tangible and intangible values and dimensions. The definition of settings should carefully articulate the character and values of the setting and its relationship to the heritage resource. (Declaration of Xi'an, point 4).

Thus, in studies on the possible impacts of an urban project on a heritage asset, reports from various disciplines should necessarily be included, and should not be limited solely to an archaeological report. Perhaps there is a need for interventions with multidisciplinary teams in Spain that contribute geographic and interpretive knowledge without which the legal protection of the cultural landscape is left without protection.

3. Soria on the banks of the River Duero offers a natural and cultural landscape that is both tangible and intangible, archaeological and literary.

The old city centre of Soria is an historic complex of relevant heritage value that stands in the Duero Valley and is reflected in the waters of a river that runs towards the sea of "Castilla". But, where the Duero River twists to form its crossbow curve, an irreplaceable and repeated landscape reveals itself in which are scattered close by to each other, various patrimonial assets. The Ruins of Numancia and San Juan de Duero are the memory of an ancient and exemplary heroism and are an exceptional artistic statement from the past.

To this backdrop of heritage from the north and the east of the River Duero, we may add the ongoing transformational gaze of writers of unquestionable transcendence in Spanish literature and culture. Bécquer, Machado and Gerardo Diego gave literary wording to their experiences and nostalgia gazing over and feeling the landscape of Soria around the Duero. Thus, not so long ago, in 2006, the force of the poetic word, oft repeated and commented on in the classroom, has turned the left bank of the River Duero into an Asset of Cultural Interest, classified as an Historic Complex and composed of natural values, environmental values, intangible cultural values (literary) and of historic cultural and artistic values.

In addition, the view that extends from the Sierra de Santa Ana, with San Polo and San Saturio reflected in the river, going on to San Juan de Duero at the foot of the Monte de las Ánimas, and on up to the heroic plains of

Numancia, must necessarily pass over without losing continuity and following the colours, the contours and the natural elements, across the hilltops and riverbeds that constitute El Cabezo, La Colorada and Los Pajarejos, the chosen countryside upon which to violently and inappropriately "graft" the Industrial Polygon SORIA II. It is evident that this project will break up the continuum of the landscape – all of which is of a patrimonial nature – which is seen from Soria when looking out to the north and to the east.

This landscape – "part of the territory whose character is the result of the action and interaction of natural and human factors as perceived by the population" (*Ley del Patrimonio Natural y de la Biodiversidad*, art. 3.26) – has been perceived in a positive way for many years by the population of Soria and others not from Soria. This explains the indispensable and perennial contemplation of this area from el Mirón and from the Castle.

If these two viewing points have any sense, not only is it because looking out from them, Antonio Machado suffered alongside Leonor and her illness and because the views, in his memory, caused him intense and painful days, but also because these viewing points in the City of Soria lend coherence to a landscape rich in heroic memory, natural elements and literary evocation and legend. Thus, in the same north-eastern sector of the area of Soria, the heritage value arises many times from the physical realities of human activity in the past, but in others, from the cultural projection of certain feelings onto the surrounding reality, which has given birth to a landscape with a strong feeling of heritage. That is why the landscape, so pregnant with cultural and natural value, so full of archaeological remains and literary associations, overflowing with values that are cherished and transmitted from generation to generation in Soria, will be irremediably altered and destroyed by the installation on that coherent horizon of an industrial polygon.

The Cultural Heritage of Soria is, among many other things, its landscape, seen from the city and seen from its surrounding area. It is a landscape because nature and history have decided as much and it is a landscape of the soul, of feeling and of intelligence, because illustrious and celebrated poets wished it to be so and inhabitants of Soria and its visitors have perceived it so: "Soria, citadel of past events, the land written over with the pens of Bécquer, Machado, Gerardo Diego and Unamuno, authors on a literary map that words and people travel across on a multifarious route. Thus poetic heritage becomes the landscape here. The space made lyrical memory, reveals the traveller born to rhymes and legends. It is the reiterated verse, unique and diverse, written without respite on the skin of this province, overlapping in its universe new itineraries on which to add to the reading of its prodigious poetry." This text is taken from the official Website of Soria Town Council on the "La Ciudad" page, which reminds us once again of a sort of bipolar disorder of the public authorities. There appears to be a clear awareness and consciousness faced with the cultural values that infuse the landscape of the City of Soria and which confer a greater sense of heritage upon it. The Town Council of Soria acknowledged as much in March 2006, when it approved the *Plan General de Ordenación Urbana* [General Plan for Urban Planning], whose primary objective is "the defence of cultural heritage and the natural environment and landscape of the City". However, the projects that it has set in motion demonstrate quite the opposite.

The cultural landscape of the Duero constitutes the image that Soria presents to the world and that is recognised by visitors and scholars and is an unquestionable asset to be protected, above and beyond utopian or "gilt" industrial dreams in an age of unmerciful delocalization without scruples. An intelligent city should be aware of the singular and exceptional nature of its cultural patrimony, combined with natural, historical, magical and literary elements and should accept it as one of the principal riches of the City of Soria.

References

Ayuntamiento de Soria. Available from http://www.ayto-soria.org/html/laciudad/index.htm; last accessed 15 July 08.

Boletín Oficial de Castilla y León. 2002. *Ley 12/2002, de 11 de julio, de Patrimonio Cultural de Castilla y León.* 19 de julio de 2002.

Boletín Oficial de Castilla y León. 2007. *Resolución de 18 de abril de 2007, de la Secretaría General de la Consejería de Medio Ambiente, por la que se hace pública la no necesidad de evaluación ambiental de la modificación puntual nº 1 del PGOU Polígono Industrial Soria II, promovido por el Ayuntamiento de Soria.* 27 de abril de 2007.

Boletín Oficial del Estado. 2007. *Ley 42/2007, de 13 de diciembre, del Patrimonio Natural y de la Biodiversidad.* 14 de diciembre de 2007.

Diego, Gerardo. 1986. *Alondra de Verdad; Ángeles de Compostela.* Edited by Francisco Javier Días de Revenga. Madrid: Castalia.

ICOMOS, 1987. *Charter for the conservation of historic towns and urban areas (Washington Charter – 1987).* Available at http://www.international.icomos.org/charters/towns_sp.htm; last accessed 15 July 08)

ICOMOS, 2005. *Xi'an Declaration on the conservation of the setting of heritage structures, sites and areas.* Available from http://www.international.icomos.org/charters/xian-declaration.pdf; last accessed 15 July 08.

Machado, Antonio. 2006. *Campos de Castilla.* Edited by Geoffrey Ribbans.15ª ed. Madrid: Ediciones Cátedra.

The West Lake of Hangzhou
A National Cultural Icon of China
and the Spirit of Place

Feng Han
Department of Landscape Studies
College of Architecture and Urban Planning (CAUP)
Tongji University
China

ABSTRACT

The ancient city Hangzhou with the essence of the West Lake is known as "Heaven on Earth." Today having successfully inherited its grand historic fame and respect, the West Lake is a national cultural icon and representative of a living cultural landscape of true life undergirded by Chinese philosophy and aesthetics on the relationship between human beings and nature. This paper illustrates the evolution of the West Lake from a natural lagoon to a symbolic landscape and examines the physical and spiritual interaction between the society and the lake. It will be argued that the spirit of the West Lake is socially and culturally constructed through history. The lessons and debates of inheriting and re-thinking the spirit of the West Lake as evolving and continuing landscape will also be in focus.

RÉSUMÉ

L'ancienne ville de Hangzhou, imprégnée de l'atmosphère du lac de l'Ouest, est surnommée «le paradis sur terre». Aujourd'hui, le lac de l'Ouest, ayant hérité d'une immense gloire historique qui impose le respect, est une icône culturelle nationale et le représentant d'un paysage culturel véritablement vivant, étayé par la philosophie et l'esthétique chinoises de la relation entre les êtres humains et la nature. Cet article illustre par quel processus le lac de l'Ouest est passé de l'état de lagune naturelle à celui de paysage symbolique et examine les interactions physiques et spirituelles entre la société et le lac. Cet article soutient que l'esprit du lac de l'Ouest fut socialement et culturellement construit à travers l'histoire. Les leçons et les discussions portant sur la transmission et la réévaluation de l'esprit du lac de l'Ouest en tant que paysage en évolution dans la continuité feront également l'objet de cet article.

Introduction

West Lake （西湖）, the essence of the ancient city Hangzhou （杭州） with a history of 2,100 years, has been known by the Chinese as "Heaven on Earth" for a thousand years because of its sophisticated culture, exquisite beauty of landscape, romantic and enjoyable life. This heaven is also known to many foreigners through *The Travels of Marco Polo* where Hangzhou was described as the City of Quinsai or Quinsay, the most enchanting city in the world. Through two thousand years the Chinese have been devoting enormous energy and emotion to continually constructing this cultural landscape from structure to forms until every detail is extremely fine and is in perfect harmony for an ideal life with nature. As a national cultural icon through history, the lake and its surroundings carry the Chinese subtle, romantic and elegant ideas of nature. It is the most distinguished living cultural landscape in China which perfectly represents the Chinese philosophy of "oneness with nature." Cultural identities and the sense of the place have been successfully enhanced by passing on its traditional spirit through history to the point where the West Lake has become an exemplary living cultural landscape in China.

The evolving history of the West Lake from a natural seashore bay to a lagoon then to a symbolic landscape presents a unique spiritual and physical interaction between Chinese society and the lake. This process demonstrates that the West Lake is a representative cultural landscape which is socially and culturally constructed through history. Also the history of identifying the heritage values of the West Lake and its conservation regarding its submission to the World Heritage Tentative List manifests the significant contribution of World Heritage Cultural Landscapes and its holistic methodology of conservation. However, the evolving nature of the West Lake cultural landscape also challenges the frontier of the conservation of cultural landscapes, such as the management and evaluation of authenticity and integrity. The lessons and experiences from the conservation of the West Lake are inspiring in terms of keeping the spirit of a heritage site.

Physical function of the West Lake as water source for the City of Hangzhou

Today's West Lake covers 59.04 square kilometers, of which the area of the water body is 6.5 square kilometers. It was originally a shallow sea inlet near Quantang River （钱塘江） at the mouth of Hangzhou Bay (杭州湾) and the east was connected with the sea in the middle of China's eastern coastal line. Normally for a lagoon, siltation is an inevitable process and will eventually form cultivated land. However, unlike the other lagoons in China, the West Lake has always been a lake of green water ever since its formation as a lake because the process of siltation has been artificially constrained. Although human settlements in this area can be traced back to four thousand years ago, the first human interference with this water body occurred 2000 years ago when a seawall was built in the Guang Wu Period of the Eastern Han Dynasty (东汉光武帝时期, 6-57 BCE) making this lake a source of fresh water for the growing Qiantang County (钱塘县) and the later City of Hangzhou. In the Sui Dynasty (隋朝, 581-618 CE), located in the fertile south of the Yangzi River (长江) and at the end of the Grand Canal (大运河) connecting the central capital cities, Hangzhou was growing rapidly into a commercial city near the coast. At the end of the Xian Chun Period of the Southern Song Dynasty (南宋咸淳年间, 1265-1274 CE, a bit earlier than Marco Polo's travel), the population of Hangzhou had reached more than one million as a prosperous capital city. Located in the west of the city, the West Lake had been the only fresh water source for the city so that the work of dredging the overgrown weeds and piling up the mud from the lake had been continuing dynasty after dynasty. Meanwhile, much construction had been done during that time to supply water to the city for domestic use and also for irrigating the surrounding farmland. This was the initial imperative of the society and therefore, a response to the environmental conditions of the time, determining the original layout of the landscape. Thus, a lake and a city became interwoven over 2000 years.

From the natural towards the cultural: undergirded by Chinese philosophies

Without manpower the West Lake would have become farmland as in many other places in China. However, with only manpower and without Chinese culture, the West Lake would be no more than a reservoir. The West Lake became key to the present cultural landscape because of its enchanting encounters with the most famous ancient Chinese scholars, encounters which are recognized as the most romantic between the Chinese culture and nature.

Philosophical and Cultural Foundations of the Chinese Landscapes

However, these encounters were not coincidences. They were predestined because they were deeply grounded in the Chinese philosophical views of nature which were the origin of Chinese landscape cultures. Centered on the relationship between nature and humans, humanity and "oneness with nature" is the essential spirit of traditional Chinese philosophies (Zhang 1986; Wang 1990; Xu 1996). The discovery of the values of the West Lake was strongly driven by this spirit of philosophies.

In Chinese traditional philosophies, Confucianism (儒家) and Daoism (道家) are the two most important schools. Orthodox Confucianism supplemented by Daoism, is one of the most distinguishing characteristics of Chinese culture. While Confucianism took responsibility for politics and ethics for the country, because of its social involvement, positive and morally cultivated attitudes, Daoism prevailed due to its negative outlook on human society and its romantic retreat in nature. It is important to note that the humanistic pursuit to be "harmonious with nature" and to be in "oneness with nature" is their common principle.

From the perspective of Confucianism, "The wise man delights in water, the good man delights in mountains" (仁者乐山，智者乐水) (The Analects, Book Six, 21). Represented by water and mountains, nature was greatly valued for its humanized moral qualities. Humans, earth and heaven are in oneness. Daoism, from a thorough scepticism of human , chooses an escape from the society and a return to nature. Associated with the recluse, retirement to the mountain, the worship of rural life, the pursuit of spiritual freedom and the romantic personality, and the banishment of all worldly cares and worries, we derive the most characteristic charm of Chinese culture, the rural ideal of life, art and literature. Nature was an independent aesthetic object for Daoism. It is of note that what Daoism escapes is human society, not life itself. Both of them are philosophies about life; belief in the earth is the only heaven.

However, no one could truly escape from society. The Chinese applied the Doctrine of the Golden Mean (中庸之道) (half and half, moderate) of Confucianism to harmoniously reconcile this conflict. We are all born half Confucianist and half Daoist. Confucianism is the working mood of the Chinese, as Daoism is their playing mood. Confucianism is urban and Daoism is rural. "Every Chinese is Confucianist when successful and Daoist when a failure. The romantic spirit of Daoism relieves the pain of practical society. "It provides a safe retreat for the Chinese human heart and the balm to their wounded soul" (Lin 2002, 55). "When a Chinese scholar is in office he moralises, and when he is out of office he versifies, and usually it is good Daoistic poetry." This was the standard for a perfect Chinese scholar.

Here we see, from these fountain springs of thought, harmonizing them into a whole, and using the abstract outlines of their wisdom, had been created the art of living in the flesh, the visible, palpable and understandable world by the common man. It is the philosophy of the Chinese art of living, "a wise disenchantment and a hearty enjoyment of life, the most constant, most characteristic and most persistent refrain of Chinese thought" (p15). The highest ideal of the Chinese then is to create a worldly paradise for artistic and human life, enjoyment, being with nature forever. They were looking for a place between Confucianism and Daoism which carried all the moral and aesthetic expectations in and out of worldly society,. The West Lake became such a heavenly place on earth.

Enchanting Encounters of the Chinese Culture and the West Lake

Traditional Chinese culture was represented and centered by the unique social class of the scholar. This class created splendid traditional Chinese cultural artifacts including Chinese landscapes. Generally, official positions could only be obtained through selection and examination according to personal qualities and knowledge instead of family blood. These opportunities were offered to every scholar. It was this class that communicated to the upper class and the lower class and moved between success and failure. This class represented the oneness of Confucianism and Daoism. Two of the representatives of this class, Bai Juyi (白居易) and Sushi (苏轼) happened to be the governors of Hangzhou in two great dynasties: the Tang Dynasty (618-907 CE) and the Song Dynasty (960-1279 CE).

In Chinese landscape cultures, landscape poems emerged first, landscape paintings followed and then landscape gardens. The celebrated poet Bai Juyi came to be the governor of Hangzhou in the middle of the Tang Dynasty (822 CE) when landscape poems reached their great importance. At that time, composing poems was a must for every scholar and there was no poem without landscape description. Nature was sensed subjectively and aesthetically. Emotions were expressed freely and skillfully in landscape poems: they were in perfect harmony with scenery. In his twenty-month stay in Hangzhou, his contribution was not only water management to serve his people and country but also his aesthetic discoveries and constructions of the West Lake. The artistic construction of a dyke with a dam to control the flow of water had eventually turned the West Lake from a natural to an artificial lake and from an irrigation lake to a spiritual aesthetic lake (Chen 2007). A causeway constructed to connect isolated landscapes was later named Bai Di (白堤) in his honor. Peach trees and willows symbolizing spring and charm were planted along the causeway, making it a beautiful landmark of the West Lake. As an accomplished poet, he left more than two hundred landscape poems of the West Lake which were widely circulated and popularly recited in ancient China. Bai Juyi laid the aesthetic and literary foundation for the West Lake and was recognized as the first one who discovered its beauty.

Two hundred years later, the West Lake encountered another soul mate in Su Shi (苏轼), a versatile genius: writer, poet, painter, calligrapher, pharmacologist and statesman. The Song Dynasty was a period of great maturity for Chinese culture and art, especially for landscape painting and calligraphy (Wang 1990). Nature could be painted with high proficiency from any point of view and from any time, in its entirety or in detail. Paintings could maturely express all emotions of poems. Gardens, as examples of subjectively ideal staged nature, were rapidly prevailing. It was the initial time for landscape poems, paintings and gardens to be integrated into one, to make something with the material landscape that was between "real" and "unreal", "heaven and earth". Symbolic and metaphorical meanings of traditional Chinese philosophies and cultures were attached to the material landscapes.

With this blueprint in his heart and as an artist of living, Su Shi had endless enthusiasm to explore the poetic charm and shape the beauty of the West Lake. While managing the water, he composed nearly 500 enchanting poems to the West Lake during his five years in Hangzhou (he had twice been an officer of Hangzhou). To explore the lake in depth, he constructed across it the most artistic causeway which still bears his name: Su Di (苏堤); and he created the most poetic scenery on the lake to reflect the moon. In his most famous poem he likened the West Lake to Xi Zi (hei), the most beautiful woman in ancient China, because of its allure. After that, Xi Zi Lake became the favorite name of the Chinese for the lake. The symbolic meaning of humanized softness, female beauty and elegance had been attached to the West Lake.

The fame of the West Lake has been spread widely and can be accredited to these two influential scholars. Since then, numerous West Lakes emerged in China, but the best was always the one in Hangzhou. The West Lake became an attraction for all scholars, including the emperors. In the Southern Song Dynasty, Hangzhou was selected as a capital city from 1138-1276 CE. This pushed Hangzhou towards becoming a cultural, commercial and political center. Numerous scholars were gathering here and left more than 20,000 poems recorded. Mature culture, luxurious and elegant life, artistic beauty and ideal life with nature had made Hangzhou the most enchanting city in the world, as Marco Polo later wrote. A heaven on earth was born.

A Product of Culture and a National Cultural Icon: the Spirit of the West Lake

Cultivated by the Chinese culture for more than one thousand years, the West Lake has become a classical masterpiece and a national cultural icon. It presents the Chinese philosophy of the art of living: "In art, aim at being exquisite, and in life at being reasonable ." ( ) It has achieved the most romantic and aesthetic objective of the Chinese: to create a worldly heaven for their life, for harmony, enjoyment, to be with nature forever.

The West Lake was an open garden where emperors, scholars, citizens, officials, the successful, the failures and the religious gathered. It had fundamental characteristics of high culture but its language was shared by all Chinese. It was a collective work by multiple social groups. It was this tolerance and openness of the West Lake that created such unlimited values in poetry, novels, paintings, legends, operas, gardens and architecture that influenced the whole country. While local people were celebrating worldly weddings, the Buddhist temples were hidden in quiet rolling mountains.

When Su Shi was serving his country and people were enjoying the natural beauty, the failures came here to rest in the soft beauty to heal their wounded hearts. The most important characteristic of the West Lake was that every school of thought found its own space here and made it a place of its own while sharing the poetic beauty of the West Lake without escaping human life. It was such a diverse place that all people encountered each other but lived in a most harmonious way. It was a homeland and a paradise for everyone in the real world. Worldly social life and retreat in nature could be artistically and enjoyably interchanged when the City of Hangzhou had the West Lake.

Essentially, the West Lake is a human-made landscape which has influential aesthetic achievement in Chinese landscape gardens. Hills embrace the lake on three sides; the city proper lies to the east. The West Lake appears natural with cultural construction harmoniously decorated around it. However, this intoxicating "natural" landscape is not natural; rather, it is culturally constructed according to the Chinese philosophical and landscape aesthetic principles. The islands in the lake are composed according to the Chinese traditional model for the landscape – "one lake, three islands" (一池三山). The essential elements of Chinese landscape, mountain and water are sophisticatedly organized and orientated. The water body is not large but seems endless by dividing it into connected spaces. Mountains are not strikingly high but modest, rolling and waving. These principles reflect the Chinese moderate philosophical attitude and the wise use of open space, which later became the model principles of Chinese gardens. Also, the vegetation around the lake in the mountains was carefully selected for its aesthetic and moral personality and was almost all replanted through history. The humanity spirit infiltrates every corner of the mountains and waters and all natural elements have been symbolically humanized through historical construction.

The spirit of the West Lake can be characterized as romantic, elegant, exquisite and enjoyable. Walking along the West Lake, sophisticated culture is everywhere. The West Lake is a proud heritage of all Chinese, especially for those people living in this heaven. The spirit of tradition, of loving nature and life has been deeply understood by the locals and the spirit of the heritage has been perfectly inherited. Today, although Hangzhou is one of the most developed cities in China, it refuses to hurry its pace of life. The locals consciously slow down their daily rhythm and enjoy their leisure life along the lake just like their ancestors. They deeply understand that "culture is essentially a product of leisure".

The heritage spirit is amazingly maintained and inherited in the West Lake. The story of this heaven is continuing and is known by almost all Chinese. In ancient times, it was a heaven that "one dreamed of for thousands of years" and where "one should travel to to grow old." Today travelling to the West Lake in Hangzhou is still something that one must do in his life as a Chinese person. To sense the West Lake is to sense the quintessence of Chinese culture.

The conservation and sustainable development of the West Lake: Contributions to World Heritage Cultural Landscapes

After being silent for ten years in the 1990s, recently the West Lake has become a new star of sustainable heritage conservation in China. However, it has experienced a very painful period in conservation. It encountered two most difficult issues in conservation. One was the methodology and another was the attitude to history.

During the conservation history of the West Lake, it was firstly listed under the protection of the State Council of the People's Republic of China in 1982. It was always under consideration for nomination to World Heritage. But interestingly, it was hard for the government to decide in which category it should be nominated. On the UNESCO World Heritage tentative list, we could find the West Lake first submitted as a natural heritage site in 1996. Obviously, this category was inappropriate for the West Lake and misled conservation efforts for the West Lake. Further, the West Lake was considered as a static heritage of the past instead of a dynamic evolving landscape. Natural settings, historic cultural relics were separately preserved from human beings and become the opposite of people. Locals were removed from the site. Landscapes became discrete and opposed each other. Social conflicts occurred. The most difficult thing of heritage conservation was "fighting with people". In the 1990s, while the other cities in China were experiencing great changes in development, Hangzhou and the West Lake were very quiet and stagnated.

It was not until 2001 that it was proposed that the values of West Lake be considered as a cultural landscape (Chen 2007). In 2008 it was formally submitted and changed as a cultural heritage on the tentative list. Since then the cultural landscape has provided a holistic conservation methodology for the West Lake. As a cultural landscape, the interactions of nature and culture become one. Today local people are embraced in the West Lake and become a powerful partnership of conservation. The government provides master planning to guide the development and conservation for this area. The landscapes once again begin to evolve with vibrancy. This was a milestone for the conservation of the West Lake.

The spirit of the site links today and yesterday and is guiding the path of tomorrow. With intensive understanding of nature as the Chinese spiritual homeland, the Lake has come to the public in a non-commercial way. Maximum opportunity is provided for the public to access the lake and its surroundings. Construction is continuing and new scenic spots are being added. But the golden principles of harmonious relationship between nature and human beings have been applied in new construction work. The characteristics and the sense of the place are being intensively enhanced. Even the newly constructed Western "Starbucks Coffee" is poetically located in beautiful tree shadows and shows a special elegance. The West Lake is attaching heritage Chinese cultural spirit to contemporary life and creating future heritage.

The successful conservation of the West Lake as a living cultural landscape has greatly demonstrated the importance of the holistic conservation methodology of cultural landscapes provided by World Heritage. Its excellent achievement of sustainable conservation is also a great example of heritage community-based management and a great contribution to World Heritage.

Conclusion

The symbolic meaning of the West Lake can only be decoded through historic contexts of Chinese philosophies and culture. The evolving procedure of the West Lake from a lagoon to China's national cultural icon presents the physical and spiritual interaction between Chinese society and the lake. The spirit of the West Lake is socially and culturally constructed through history. To identify and safeguard this spirit is the essential task of heritage conservation. World Heritage Cultural Landscapes provide a new methodology for heritage conservation according to its holistic and dynamic perspective, an integration of nature and culture, and an interaction between tangible and intangible features. The West Lake is an exemplary case of living cultural landscape conservation.

References

Chen, Wenjin. 2007. *The Discovery of the West Lake: on World Heritage Values.* Hangzhou: Zhejiang Ancient Books Publishing House.

Lin, Yutang. 1998. *My Country and My People.* Beijing: Foreign Language Teaching and Research Press.

Wang, Yi. 1990. *Gardens and Chinese Culture.* Shanghai: Shanghai People's Press.

Xu, Fuguan. 1996. *Elaboration and Promotion of Traditional Chinese Humanity.* Beijing: China Broadcast And TV Publish.

Zhang, Jiaji. 1986. *History of Chinese Garden.* Haerbin: Heilongjiang People's Publisher.

Le développement économique, menace voilée sur la conservation de l'esprit des lieux

Tomás de Albuquerque Lapa
Université Fédérale de Pernambuco
Brésil

Raphael Ferraz Almeida de Melo
Université Fédérale de Pernambuco
Brésil

ABSTRACT

If the city is a living entity undergoing constant change, it can then be said that integrated urban conservation involves accounting for the new elements introduced into the existing urban fabric. That being said, the spirit of place will always be threatened by a city's ongoing building and rebuilding activities. Of all the contemporary practices, which is the most serious threat to preserving the spirit of place? In developing countries, civilian construction activities are presented as issues of job creation and tax revenue generation. In parallel with the promotion of historic sites as tourist attractions, we must also pay special attention to civilian construction activity, as it may represent a veiled threat to the preservation of spirit of place, based on arguments of economic development.

RÉSUMÉ

Si la ville est une entité vivante en permanente transformation, on pourrait dire que la conservation urbaine intégrée signifie que les éléments nouveaux introduits dans le tissu urbain existant seront compatibles avec ce dernier. Ceci dit, l'esprit des lieux sera toujours menacé par l'action continue de bâtir et rebâtir la ville. Parmi les pratiques contemporaines, laquelle représente le plus sérieux danger pour la conservation de l'esprit des lieux? Dans les pays en voie de développement, l'activité de la construction civile est présentée comme un moyen de créer des emplois et de percevoir des impôts. Parallèlement à la promotion touristique des sites historiques, il faut être vigilant quant à l'activité de la construction civile, car elle paraît menacer la conservation de l'esprit des lieux, sous prétexte de développement économique.

1. De la reconnaisance à la conservation de l'esprit des lieux

Après la Charte d'Athènes de 1931 qui mentionnait des monuments isolés, la Charte de Venise de 1964 mit en relief l'importance de la préservation de l'encadrement urbain où se situe le monument. Quelques années plus tard, la Déclaration d'Amsterdam de 1975 a posé la question de la valeur patrimoniale des bâtisses modestes, mais dont la signification se rattache à une époque et à un contexte historique. La Déclaration d'Amsterdam a pris en considération le tissu urbain des alentours des monuments dans toute sa complexité et sa charge symbolique. On a compris que la ville est une entité vivante, en permanente transformation, et que les monuments ne peuvent pas être isolés de leur contexte urbain. Dès lors, le concept de la conservation intégrée a pris corps et se place à la base de toutes les interventions contemporaines impliquant des transformations urbaines.

La Recommandation de Nairobi de 1976 ne fait pas explicitement allusion à l'esprit des lieux, mais la référence à la préservation de l'ambiance et du caractère des ensembles historiques nous renvoie à la question qui nous préoccupe à présent. Le document de Nairobi anticipe les menaces de l'urbanisation moderne et montre qu'au risque d'une destruction directe des ensembles historiques s'associe le danger réel des nouveaux bâtiments, qui peuvent détruire indirectement l'ambiance et le caractère environnants.

En ce qui concerne la conservation des sites d'intérêt patrimonial, la préoccupation exprimée dans les documents directifs internationaux ne fait que s'accroître. Les recommandations formulées dans ces documents considèrent l'importance, non seulement de la conservation des constructions et du maintien des habitants dans leurs lieux d'origine, mais aussi de la conservation du rapport entre eux, c'est-à-dire des significations culturelles, des pratiques quotidiennes, des croyances et des mythes.

Le Mémorandum de Vienne (2005) parle de paysage urbain historique, par rapport aux éléments qui définissent son caractère, parmi lesquels figurent les usages urbains et les tendances, l'organisation spatiale, les aspects visuels, le relief et la nature des sols, la végétation et tous les éléments de l'infrastructure technique, y compris les petits objets et détails architecturaux tels que les corniches, les différents types de pavés, les gouttières et l'éclairage.

Le Mémorandum met en relief l'impact du développement contemporain sur l'ensemble du paysage urbain doté de signification patrimoniale. Dans le document, la notion de paysage historique urbain s'étend au-delà du sens traditionnel de termes tels que «centre historique», «ensembles» et «alentours». Par ailleurs, on prend en compte le lien émotionnel entre les êtres humains et leur environnement, qui génère le sens de lieu, pour assurer la qualité de vie dans le milieu urbain, de façon à contribuer à la réussite économique et à la vitalité sociale et culturelle de la ville.

2. La conservation de l'esprit des lieux face à la transformation des structures urbaines

Quelques théoriciens considèrent que, dans la ville, comme dans tout organisme vivant, ce qui ne change pas n'a pas de chance de se développer. Serait-ce donc une fatalité que l'esprit des lieux soit condamné à disparaître ou à se transformer en permanence?

Il ne faut pas oublier que la ville n'est pas constituée d'un tissu uniforme, ni du point de vue de la morphologie, ni du point de vue des périodes qui ont donné naissance aux différents lieux. L'effort pour la conservation de l'esprit des lieux sous-entend le respect des pratiques et des savoir-faire des communautés locales et le maintien de ces mêmes communautés. À la suite de Bernardo Secchi (2006), nous pourrions dire que l'ambiance de la ville naît de l'accumulation de traits culturels et de faits évoquant différentes périodes, avec leurs styles et leurs manières de penser, ainsi que de la construction du quotidien. La question qui se pose est: serait-il possible de conserver l'esprit d'une ville toute entière?

Bien que le concept de développement durable soit au cœur des controverses entre ceux qui tiennent pour la conservation des structures urbaines et ceux qui sont partisans de leur transformation, cette manière de penser peut contribuer à la permanence des valeurs patrimoniales urbaines et au *modus vivendi* des populations locales. Mais la sauvegarde des structures urbaines existantes, qui ne sont en réalité qu'un support matériel à l'existence de ces valeurs et de ce *modus vivendi*, peut-elle assurer la survie de l'esprit des lieux? Parfois, même un champ de ruines conserve un certain esprit des lieux, du moins dans l'imaginaire de quelques-uns. C'est ce que cet article essaie d'approfondir dans les sections suivantes.

3. Le paradoxe du caractère à la fois concret et imaginaire de l'esprit des lieux

Il est vrai que l'action continue de bâtir et rebâtir la ville contient déjà en germe une transformation des espaces urbains. Étant donné que la référence à l'esprit des lieux ne se fait que par rapport à un support matériel, il ne serait pas hors de propos de signaler les principes qui conduisent à des limites acceptables dans le contexte de ces transformations. D'après Yi-Fu Tuan (1975), le lieu est un centre de significations construites, fondées sur l'expérience.

La genèse du lieu s'effectue à partir de la signification attribuée à certaines structures spatiales par un groupe de personnes directement en rapport avec elles, et qui y établit son cadre de vie. Au-delà de l'attribution de signification, l'exercice des pratiques et des interventions humaines contribue à façonner le territoire, à l'image d'un plasma qui vient s'ajouter à l'ambiance et duquel émane l'esprit des lieux. À la limite, ce processus permet même à un étranger de percevoir l'esprit des lieux.

D'autre part, après l'interpénétration des cultures au niveau de la planète, les personnes, y compris les populations locales, revendiquent de plus en plus les commodités et conforts de la vie moderne, ce qui suppose l'introduction de nouvelles structures, de matériaux et d'équipements conçus dans un esprit qui n'est plus celui qui imprégnait les lieux à l'origine. Compte tenu des exigences de la vie contemporaine, devons-nous nous contenter d'une perte relative et progressive de l'esprit des lieux? Que deviendra l'esprit des lieux et quel sera son temps de survie? Est-ce que l'esprit des lieux, comme toute autre valeur contemporaine, sera de plus en plus marqué par le caractère éphémère?

Reprenons le paradoxe selon lequel l'esprit des lieux présente à la fois un caractère concret et imaginaire. C'est par rapport aux attributs physiques de la forme architecturale et urbaine qu'il est possible de faire référence à l'aspect concret de l'esprit des lieux. Les principaux attributs physiques susceptibles d'altérations se trouvent au niveau de l'échelle urbaine, vue comme une conséquence de la somme des différentes réalisations architecturales.

En ce qui concerne l'aspect imaginaire, plusieurs éléments peuvent menacer l'esprit des lieux. Parmi ceux-là, les données fournies par l'industrie de la construction civile, concernant les taux de la croissance économique, l'adaptation des sites historiques aux intérêts du tourisme et la transformation des pratiques et rites en marchandises constituent des menaces voilées sur la conservation de l'esprit des lieux.

4. Conséquences de l'introduction d'éléments nouveaux dans le tissu urbain existant

Dans l'histoire de la conservation du patrimoine historique bâti, certains cas sont devenus emblématiques, notamment ceux des villes européennes bombardées pendant la Deuxième Guerre mondiale. D'après De Gracia (1996), les interventions dans le milieu urbain bâti peuvent adopter différentes «attitudes en fonction du contexte». Dans l'Europe de l'après-guerre, compte tenu de l'étendue des destructions, les villes endommagées ont adopté différentes positions en ce qui concerne la conservation de leur patrimoine historique.

Le cas de Varsovie a constitué une situation dramatique, en raison de l'étendue des destructions dans le centre historique urbain et du sentiment de perte ressenti par la population. La décision de reconstruire tout le vieux centre historique a été soutenue par l'UNESCO, en se basant sur des documents et sur l'iconographie existante, afin de combler le vide laissé par la destruction d'un des symboles nationaux. Pour les Polonais, il s'agissait de racheter l'esprit des lieux qui subsistait dans leur imaginaire.

Dans le centre historique de Londres, en dépit des dégâts produits par les bombardements, on décida d'insérer des bâtiments modernes dans le tissu urbain et de faire cohabiter le nouveau et l'ancien. Dans ce cas, il ne serait juste de parler de la conservation de l'esprit des lieux que dans des zones circonscrites. Après les grands travaux de reconstruction de la ville, à l'esprit des lieux d'avant, d'autres significations sont forcément venues s'ajouter à l'ensemble du patrimoine bâti historique.

Figure 1. Centre historique de Londres (www.wikipedia.org).

Le château d'eau d'Olinda

La ville d'Olinda, située dans le Nord-Est du Brésil, a été déclarée Patrimoine Mondial de l'Humanité en 1982. Dans les années 1930, la ville avait été dotée d'un système d'approvisionnement en eau. À cette occasion, on a considéré que le point le plus élevé et le plus indiqué du point de vue technique pour l'installation d'un château d'eau se trouvait au sommet de la colline qui marque la fondation de la ville, au XVIᵉ siècle. La forme choisie fut celle d'un volume correspondant à un prisme de base rectangulaire, monté sur pilotis, selon les tendances modernistes de l'époque. Le bâtiment abritant le château d'eau fut placé entre l'église et l'ancien palais épiscopal, tous les deux datant de la période coloniale.

Au moment de la construction du château d'eau, le site n'était pas officiellement classé, d'autant plus que le service de protection du patrimoine historique et artistique brésilien ne fut institué qu'en 1937 (Iphan 1937). Cependant, le site d'Olinda a toujours occupé une place importante dans le contexte historique et symbolique du Brésil, étant donné le rôle de la ville au temps de la colonisation, sur les plans économique, politique et culturel. La ville n'a jamais cessé de présenter un cadre de vie authentique, y compris dans le site historique, occupé par une population de résidents.

Pendant longtemps, et pour une grande partie de la population, le château d'eau fut perçu comme un corps étranger dans le site historique. D'une part, la prise de conscience de l'importance du mouvement moderniste au Brésil a contribué à ce que la population comprenne la signification de ce bâtiment moderne aux côtés de deux autres de l'époque coloniale. D'autre part, peu à peu, la population a appris à respecter le château d'eau pour son caractère pionnier, conçu selon des lignes sobres, monté sur une structure en béton armé et faisant usage d'éléments architecturaux locaux.

On peut s'interroger sur l'unité formelle de l'ensemble architectural, mais, depuis une soixantaine d'années, le château d'eau d'Olinda fait partie du paysage historique urbain local.

Figure 2. Le château d'eau et l'église de la Sé, à Olinda.[1]

Le musée Rodin à Salvador de Bahia

Installé dans un petit palais de style éclectique datant du début du XXᵉ siècle, à Salvador de Bahia, le musée Rodin constitue un exemple de cohabitation du nouveau et de l'ancien. Derrière le bâtiment ancien, on a construit un bâtiment moderne respectant les proportions primitives et les masses constructives. Reliant les deux bâtiments, une rampe de béton armé, faisant office de passerelle en plein air, marque la différence d'époque et de style entre les deux bâtiments.

Pour les architectes chargés de l'intervention, l'enjeu était d'introduire un ascenseur pour répondre aux normes d'accès pour les handicapés. La touche d'audace fut de substituer à un bastion anciennement rajouté dans un angle du volume principal du bâtiment, la caisse de l'ascenseur, montée sur une structure en béton armé et translucide sur un côté.

---

1.   *The Architectural Review*, mars 1944, photo Kidder Smith, www.vitruvius. com.br/arquitextos/arq072/arq072_02.asp.

Figure 3. Musée Rodin. Photo Nelson Kon, Portal Vitruvius 2006.

Figure 4. Musée Rodin. Photo Nelson Kon, Portal Vitruvius 2006.

Les immeubles « d'intérêt spécial » (IEP)

En 1997, la ville de Recife a créé un dispositif légal permettant aux propriétaires d'immeubles classés « d'intérêt spécial »[2] d'appliquer, dans les limites de la parcelle sur laquelle s'élève l'immeuble, un coefficient d'utilisation du sol suffisamment élevé pour compenser les restrictions de modifications imposées par le classement IEP. Après la promulgation de ce dispositif permissif, les cas de construction de tours d'appartements, partageant le même lot de terrain qu'un IEP, se sont multipliés, à l'image de l'exemple illustré ci-dessous.

Figure 5. L'Immeuble « Costa Azevedo » à Recife, s'élevant sur la même parcelle que le petit palais. Photo Lapa et Melo 2007.

---

2.   Les IEP ne sont pas des monuments historiques, mais simplement des exemples importants de l'architecture d'une certaine époque que l'on considère devoir être préservés (Loi nº 16.284/97 sur les Immeubles d'intérêt spécial).

Cette décision a satisfait les promoteurs immobiliers, mais le résultat pratique se traduit par la destruction de l'esprit des lieux précédent et par l'implantation d'un paysage mixte confus.

5. La menace voilée

Parmi les pratiques contemporaines, quelques-unes présentent des risques pour la conservation de l'esprit des lieux, d'autant plus qu'elles sont présentées au titre du développement économique. Dans les sociétés en voie de développement notamment, où souvent les taux de croissance sont assez élevés, cette manière de penser représente une menace voilée. Les gestionnaires publics se servent de l'argument du développement économique pour justifier un accord tacite établi entre les pouvoirs publics et le secteur immobilier. Ce même argument sert à assouplir les exigences dictées par l'expectative du progrès matériel.

Dans les sites historiques, le principal enjeu est celui de la remise en valeur des lieux par l'introduction de nouveaux usages urbains. Il est important d'insérer les bâtiments anciens dans une logique productive contemporaine en leur attribuant de nouveaux usages et fonctions. Néanmoins, dans ces situations, l'adaptation des sites historiques aux intérêts du développement économique, et en particulier du tourisme, mène souvent au remplacement des populations locales, à travers le processus de la *gentrification*. Le projet de remise en valeur de la zone du Pelourinho, à Salvador de Bahia, à la fin des années 1980, en constitue un cas typique. Ce projet avait été conçu dans les cabinets gouvernementaux, en excluant la participation populaire. L'opération avait été soutenue par des lignes de financement extérieures et avait également compté sur l'appui politique et financier du gouvernement local de l'État de Bahia.

L'une des raisons expliquant le maintien des pratiques et des rites de la communauté afro-brésilienne qui y vivait était les faibles revenus de cette population. L'incapacité de la population locale à faire des investissements visant la mise en valeur de la zone du Pelourinho et la simplicité de leurs habitudes constituaient un frein à l'activité touristique. Le projet fut donc marqué par le volontarisme des institutions gouvernementales, qui ne prévoyaient pas le maintien de la population. Actuellement, le site véhicule l'esprit artificiel et spectaculaire d'un parc à thème (Magnavita 1996).

Figure 6. La zone du Pelourinho, à Salvador de Bahia. Photo James Johnson, www. pbase.com/paddchas/image/51049232.

6. L'illusion du développement fondé sur la substitution de l'ancien par le nouveau

Les travaux entrepris dans les années 1960 à Bologne et à Ferrare furent exemplaires d'une remise en valeur de sites historiques respectant les valeurs patrimoniales et l'esprit des lieux.

Dans les pays en voie de développement, le manque d'information et d'éducation patrimoniale laisse croire que les bâtiments et les ensembles architecturaux anciens ne sont que des obstacles au progrès. L'activité de la construction civile est présentée comme un moyen de créer des emplois et de percevoir des impôts.

Pour beaucoup de gestionnaires publics, il n'est pas évident que le patrimoine culturel représente un actif économique. Pourtant, en assurant la permanence des valeurs culturelles et environnementales, la conservation urbaine renforce l'identité de la population et crée les conditions pour le développement durable social, politique et économique ; de plus, elle contribue au rayonnement d'une image attirante, où la tradition et la nouveauté cohabitent harmonieusement. Dans ce sens, le résultat des opérations qui s'appuient sur le concept de la conservation urbaine intégrée bénéficie à toute la société, y compris au secteur du tourisme.

7. Le danger de la promotion touristique dans les sites historiques

L'UNESCO ayant déclaré Olinda Patrimoine Culturel de l'Humanité, en 1982, cette ville a attiré des artistes et des intellectuels, qui sont venus s'y installer. Au début, les anciens résidents considéraient ces nouveaux habitants avec réticence, mais progressivement, les nouveaux venus, mieux informés sur les risques que représentait l'introduction de nouveaux usages et pratiques, ont contribué à l'élaboration des statuts et des attitudes urbaines en faveur de la préservation de l'esprit des lieux.

Ceci dit, les anciens et les nouveaux résidents se sont donnés la main dans une lutte qui avait pour but d'empêcher la prolifération de bars, de restaurants et de commerces qui ne correspondaient en rien aux besoins des habitants. D'autre part, les véhicules lourds, les gros autocars et les camions d'approvisionnement menaçaient de détruire certaines des infrastructures (Barreto 2008).

La population d'Olinda a compris qu'au lieu « d'apporter des bénéfices à la communauté et de procurer les moyens nécessaires au maintien du patrimoine et des traditions vivantes » (ICOMOS 1999), le tourisme altérait leurs habitudes et attirait des foules, surtout pendant le Carnaval. Les habitants ont créé l'Association pour la Protection de la Cité Ancienne (SODECA), qui a entrepris des batailles importantes, dont quelques-unes visant certaines mesures prises par les institutions de protection du patrimoine. L'exemple d'Olinda a eu une répercussion favorable dans le contexte brésilien, bien que, vingt ans après les premières revendications, les mêmes problèmes persistent.

Autre exemple intéressant, celui de la capitale cubaine. À propos du processus de revitalisation de La Havane, Rodríguez Alomá (2001) affirme que la vie réelle doit être montrée au visiteur telle qu'elle est. D'après l'auteur, les valeurs de *La Habana Vieja* ne se trouvent pas que dans ses bâtiments. Ce sont ses habitants qui lui confèrent son caractère singulier et, sans eux, les lieux manqueraient d'esprit. Le paysage urbain est indissolublement lié au paysage humain.

8. Considérations finales

La conservation intégrée cherche à respecter la diversité du patrimoine matériel et immatériel présent dans le milieu urbain. Nonobstant cette diversité, un sens commun, composé d'aspects captés par la perception humaine, est présent dans les attributs physiques de l'environnement et du milieu urbain, dans les pratiques sociales des habitants et dans leurs croyances et rituels.

Ce sens commun, qui est partout, mais qui peut aussi être circonscrit à des espaces délimités, risque d'être altéré ou de disparaître. Certaines interventions, provoquées par l'action humaine ou par des forces de la nature, sont identifiables et, à l'aide de méthodes scientifiques, il est possible de réparer les dégâts qui en découlent. Pourtant, dans des sociétés où le patrimoine n'est pas considéré comme un témoin de la mémoire et de l'identité collectives, l'idéologie du développement économique peut constituer une menace sur la conservation de l'esprit des lieux.

Références

Barreto, Juliana. 2008. *De Montmartre nordestina a mercado persa de luxo : o Sítio Histórico de Olinda e a participação dos moradores na salvaguarda do Patrimônio Cultural.* Mémoire de maîtrise, Universidade Federal de Pernambuco.

De Gracia. Francisco. 1996, *Construir en lo construido : la arquitectura como modificación.* Madrid: Nerea.

Icomos. 1999. *Charte internationale du tourisme culturel.* En ligne, http://www.international.icomos.org/charters/tourism_f.ht.

Iphan. 1937. *Decreto n° 25/1937.*

Lapa, Tomás. 2008. « Requalificação Urbana : aporte de melhorias à qualidade de vida ou arranjo político-institucional para acomodação dos atores em novos papéis? ». *Arquimemória 3*: 1-13.

Lapa, Tomás et Raphael Melo. 2007. « Interpreting charters and defining the limits of healthy co-habitation between the new and the ancient ». *5ᵗʰ International Seminar on Urban Conservation*, Recife, Centro de Estudos da Conservação Intergrata (CECI) : 1-9.

Lei n° 16.284/97 dos Imóveis Especiais de Preservação, 1997, Recife, Prefeitura da Cidade do Recife.

Magnavita, P.R. 1996. « Quando a história vira espetáculo do poder : a condição pós-moderna na preservação ». *Seminário Internacional de Estratégias de Intervenção em Áreas Históricas*, Recife, Anais do Seminário, MDU/UFPE, vol. 1: 149-156.

Portal Vitruvius. 2006. en ligne, http://www.vitruvius.com.br/institucional/inst149/inst149.asp

Rodríguez Alomá, Patricia. 2001. « El centro histórico de La Habana : un modelo de gestión pública ». Dans Fernando Carrión (dir.). *Centros históricos de América Latina y el Caribe.* Quito : FLACSO.

Secchi, Bernardo. 2006. *Primeira Lição de Urbanismo.* São Paulo : Perspectiva.

Tuan, Yi-Fu. 1975. « Place : an Experiential Perspective ». *Geographical Review* 65 (2) : 151-165.

UNESCO. 2005. *Vienna Memorandum.* En ligne, http://www.koh.hu/vilagorokseg/pdf/whc05-15ga-inf7e.pdf.

III

INVOLVING COMMUNITIES

IMPLIQUER LES COMMUNAUTÉS

Ecomuseology:
A Holistic and Integrated Model for Safeguarding Spirit of Place in the North East of England

Gerard E. Corsane
Peter S. Davis
Stéphanie K. Hawke
Michelle L. Stefano
**International Centre for Cultural
and Heritage Studies
University of Newcastle upon Tyne
U.K.**

Abstract

This article explores whether or not ecomuseology can provide a model for safeguarding "spirit of place" in the North East of England. The philosophy of ecomuseums is briefly explained, paying particular attention to the relationship between places, communities and their heritage to explore the idea of how intangible and tangible heritage resources contribute to "spirit of place". Expressions of intangible heritage from which senses of belonging, pride and place stem, along with various community-based heritage projects in the rural area of the North Pennines, are described and analysed to examine community-heritage interaction. The limitations of the more "traditional" approaches to heritage management and museum work are compared to those embedded in ecomuseum processes.

Résumé

Cet article cherche à définir si l'écomuséologie peut proposer un modèle de sauvegarde de «l'esprit du lieu» dans le Nord-Est de l'Angleterre. Nous exposons brièvement la philosophie des écomusées, en portant une attention particulière à la relation entre les lieux, les communautés et leurs patrimoines, afin d'explorer la manière dont les ressources patrimoniales matérielles et immatérielles contribuent à «l'esprit du lieu». Certaines expressions de patrimoine immatériel, desquelles émergent un sentiment d'appartenance, de fierté et de lieu, de pair avec différents projets patrimoniaux à base communautaire, dans la région rurale du nord des Alpes Pennines, sont décrits et analysés afin d'examiner les interactions dans le domaine du patrimoine communautaire. Nous comparons les limites des approches plus « traditionnelles » de la gestion patrimoniale et du travail des musées à celles inhérentes aux procédés des écomusées.

1. Introduction

In response to the challenges of globalisation, people have become increasingly interested in the notions of "local distinctiveness" and "spirit of place". These are important for many people as they are closely associated with the construction of identities and feelings of belonging. As people have become increasingly interested in these notions, they have also become more and more concerned with the promotion and safeguarding of the range of intangible and tangible heritage resources that form the very essence and fabric of local distinctiveness and "spirit of place". The North East of England is rich with these types of heritage resources and there are community-led projects and groups that are working to ensure that they are not lost. Many of these projects and groups are using principles and practices that are in line with the "ecomuseum" ideal, which break from the more traditional approaches to heritage management and museum work. The aim of this article is to highlight the synergies between ecomuseum philosophy and practice and the promotion, safeguarding and conservation of heritage resources associated with some representative regional case studies, even though none of the latter directly use the term "ecomuseology" to describe their work. In order to do this, the article will begin with an introductory discussion on the links between communities, defining place and the significance of heritage resources. This will be followed by an overview of ecomuseum philosophy, which will lay the platform for considering two selected intangible cultural heritage expressions unique to the region, and case studies of community-based heritage projects being facilitated by the North Pennines Area of Outstanding Natural Beauty (AONB) Partnership.

1.1. Defining your Place – Heritage and Local Distinctiveness

What do small local communities value most about their environment, the features of their natural and cultural landscape for which they share communal ownership and responsibility? What is it about our local environment that provides a feeling of belonging, a sense of place, the knowledge that we inhabit somewhere with distinct characteristics? Meinig's (1979:45) view of landscape is consistent with the "holistic" paradigm for museology proposed by Corsane and Holleman (1993:121). It also provides a strong indication of the importance of place, not simply for the tangible elements within it, but also for its intangible features. It is how these elements relate to one another and the meanings attached to them that provide a sense of continuity and identity, a "spirit of place".

However, the idea of place needs to be treated with care, as it embodies much more than physical components and for each individual it is a unique experience. For example, Buttimer (1980:178) suggests that "it is the style of life associated with place which is still far more important for me than its external form". Relph (1976:29) quotes Donat's warning that "places occur at all levels of identity, my place, your place, street, community, town, county, region, country and continent, but places never conform to tidy hierarchies of classification. They all overlap and interpenetrate one another and are wide open to a variety of interpretations". Davis (1999:18) when exploring place within the context of ecomuseum philosophy, concluded that "...place is a chameleon concept, changing colour through individual perception, and changing pattern through time". However, despite these complexities, there is no doubt that the elements of place – tangible and intangible – are vital in helping people to understand their own and other places in the world. These elements provide us with the resources to construct cultural identities.

The need to recognise and appreciate the richness of individual places has been promoted in the UK by the organisation Common Ground. They stress that it is important to value the detail and the commonplace in the landscape, the characteristics that give "local distinctiveness", defined by Clifford and King (1993:7) as "that elusive particularity, so often valued as "background noise" ... the richness we take for granted". To Common Ground (1996)

> (...) local distinctiveness is about everywhere, not just beautiful places; it is about details, patina and meaning, the things which create identity. Importantly it focuses on locality, not on the region – small-scale approaches are essential. It is about accumulation and assemblages ... accommodation and change ...it includes the invisible as well as the physical; dialect, festivals, myths, may be as important as hedgerows, hills and houses.

Traditionally the preservation, conservation and documentation of the cultural and natural landscape have been carried out by designated (often governmental) organisations. "Experts" who attach their own meanings to sites or objects have largely carried out these processes but have not empowered the people who experience them. It might be argued that the complexity of place and what it represents to individuals and communities makes it evident that the traditional approaches can never capture their elusive qualities. The essence of place lies in the environment itself and is defined by the individuals and the communities that live there.

If communities are going to play a major role in conserving places, in protecting their environment and "spirit of place" then a new approach is required, one that demands community empowerment. From the 1970s, ecomuseum practitioners have attempted to use their new philosophy to try to reach these goals, having at their core the need to represent their place, their past and the cultural identity of their inhabitants.

1.2. Ecomuseum Principles

The ecomuseum paradigm, its origins, development and diversity have been most fully described by Davis (1999). The ecomuseum was originally defined by comparing it to a traditional museum, with Rivard (1984, 43-53; 1988, 123-4; and also see Boylan 1992; Corsane 2006:404) stating that the:

- *Traditional Museum = building + collections + expert staff + public visitors;* and,

- *Ecomuseum = territory + heritage + memory + population.*

More recently the European Network of Ecomuseums (2004) provided a concise definition, namely that: "An ecomuseum is a dynamic way in which communities preserve, interpret, and manage their heritage for sustainable development. An ecomuseum is based on a community agreement". This definition has been further modified by Davis (2007:199) who regards the ecomuseum as "a community-driven museum or heritage project that aids sustainable development". Ecomuseums demonstrate remarkable diversity, yet, despite these variations, Davis (1999:228) suggested that the following list of attributes can be applied to most of them:

- The adoption of a territory that is not necessarily defined by conventional boundaries.

- The adoption of a "fragmented site" policy that is linked to in-situ conservation and interpretation.

- Conventional views of site ownership are abandoned; conservation and interpretation of sites is carried out via liaison, co-operation and the development of partnerships.

- The empowerment of local communities; the involvement of local people in ecomuseum activities and in the creation of their cultural identity.

- The potential for interdiscipliniarity and for holistic interpretation is usually seized.

This list, along with the ecomuseum characteristics identified by Corsane and Holleman (1993), have been further developed as a set of indicators that have been utilised to assess how far ecomuseums reach the tenets of the philosophy (Corsane 2006: 405 and Corsane *et. al.* 2007:105). It would seem that the guiding principles for ecomuseums should enable them to conserve local heritage resources in a democratic manner and effectively capture local distinctiveness. Ecomuseum principles have now been deployed in many countries throughout the world, and in a variety of ways, responding to local physical, economic, social, cultural and political environments in order to manage the full range of environmental and heritage resources through processes that encourage public participation. Where these ecomuseum principles are utilized there is often an emphasis on: self-representation; full community participation in, and ownership of, heritage resources and the management processes; rural or urban regeneration; sustainable development; and responsible tourism. So how might these processes aid the formation of "spirit of place"? The following sections explore examples of community-based intangible and tangible heritage projects and phenomena found in the North East of England, to see if there are parallels with ecomuseum processes and whether there is scope for these to be more widely applied.

2. Expressing "Spirit of Place" Through Intangible Cultural Heritage in the North East

Just as history and culture form foundations for experiences of place, so can they shape the meanings of a "spirit of place" that is held by inhabitants of a particular region (Rodman 2003:208). Crang (1998:108) notes that creative cultural expressions can be vehicles for conveying a certain "spirit of place" for various groups of individuals by writing:

> (…) people experience something beyond the physical or sensory properties of places and can feel an attachment to a "spirit of place". If the meaning itself extends beyond the visible, beyond the evident into realms of emotion and feeling then one answer may be turning to literature or the arts as being ways people can express these meanings.

Coupling artistic practices with the communication of meanings brings to mind the very nature of intangible cultural heritage or, as Smith (2006:56) argues, all heritage. She states, "Whether we are dealing with traditional definitions of "tangible" or "intangible" representations of heritage, we are actually engaging with a set of values and meanings, including such elements as emotion, memory and cultural knowledge and experiences" (ibid). Nonetheless, it can be said that a certain "spirit of place" – and all the values, meanings and emotions within which are living – can be manifested in both physicality as well as the immateriality fundamental to intangible cultural heritage. Interestingly, this notion of expressing "spirit of place" through intangible cultural heritage lacks recognition within the heritage sector at present. This section aims to highlight the resonance between an attachment to place and the senses of belonging and pride that are embedded within particular intangible cultural practices found within the North East of England.

Intangible cultural heritage finds many unique examples within the culturally rich counties of Northumberland, Durham and Tyne and Wear. Particular occupational skills, culinary techniques, dances, music and dialects, among others, have both their roots and evolutionary paths in the countryside and urban areas of this region. This section will focus upon a sword dance and the folk music, two intangible cultural expressions of the performing arts that are centuries old and still thriving today. Through an examination of senses of belonging and pride expressed by the devotees, or communities, of these living traditions, a strong existence of "spirit of place" is demonstrated.

The following subsection will provide a brief introduction of these two expressions, as well as an account of their current states. The second subsection, entitled *Senses of Belonging and Senses of Pride*, will present data collected in an ongoing study of over forty dancers and musicians on the significance and values embedded within these living traditions, which began in September, 2007. The last subsection is an analysis of "spirit of place" based on the interconnectedness of heritage, community and place articulated by the above mentioned community members when talking about motivations and the importance attributed to their intangible cultural practices.

2.1. Two Intangible Cultural Expressions of the North East

The first intangible cultural expression of this study is a sword dance, the Rapper dance, which originated around the 18th century coal mines of the North East (Lawrenson 2007). The dance consists of five men (or women in recent history) continually stepping in and out of configurations whilst holding each other's swords, otherwise known as rappers. The records of Cecil Sharp, the founder of the English Folk Song and Dance Society, who travelled around Northern England and wrote about several sword dances in the early 20th century, have documented an otherwise orally transmitted tradition. However, there are accounts dating back to the mid 18th century as various historians and writers made reference to the sword dances they encountered in childhood, or by travelling (Sharp 1913:v.1:69). In general, the Rapper dance was performed on special holidays, as well as in pubs throughout the region for making extra money for beer. The second expression consists of the folk music traditions of both the countryside and the City of Newcastle using a range of instruments from the fiddle to the flute. These musical traditions developed over centuries with their largest divergence occurring in the late 19th century. At that time, Newcastle was becoming more cosmopolitan and, in turn, music halls were opening at a rapid pace. Thus, musicians moved from the countryside to the city and developed new styles that blended with the popular music of the time, which was not as prevalent in the countryside (Harker in Allan 1972:xiii; Murphy 2007). Within these traditions lies the music specifically written for a bagpipe, the Northumbrian Smallpipe, unique to this region. The earliest known Northumbrian Smallpipes date from the late 17th century, although bagpipes throughout the United Kingdom have existed for hundreds of years as seen in medieval manuscripts and images (Say 2003).

These two living traditions have remained in the care of community-based societies and networks even if the people and settings have changed. Folk musicians are still out in pubs and other cultural venues playing tunes that are centuries old, or recently written, in a style particular to the region. The Rapper dance is no longer performed around the coal mines of the North East; the venue has shifted solely to pubs and festivals due to the decline in the mining industry. During the 20th century, the dance shifted hands from the miners to a more general community of devotees (as well as descendents of miners) with differing occupations and interests. However, it is this devotion and the relationships embedded within these expressions that give them their vitality. The significance and values attributed to them by these devotees are part of the reason why these expressions continue to exist. Investigating such significance and values not only provides insight into the survival of such expressions, but highlights both senses of belonging and pride that, as examined in the following subsection, constitute a certain "spirit of place".

2.2. Senses of Belonging and Pride

As examined elsewhere (Stefano & Corsane 2008), strong linkages between heritage, community and place have emerged from fieldwork (primarily interview) data. When asked about why they partake in these living traditions, as well as about what feelings stem from this participation, a majority of respondents (over two-thirds) expressed senses of belonging to the history and heritage of the particular practice, the region within which it has evolved, as well as to the groups of participants who had come before and practice today. Respondents often cited all three entities when expressing their motivations for involvement, although degrees of specificity varied, as presented below. In addition, when asked why they consider these living traditions as important, this same interconnectedness between the history and heritage of the expression, the surrounding environment and their own community of fellow dancers and musicians emerges (again, within over a two-thirds majority). In order to keep this discussion to a manageable length, key respondent quotes have been selected to highlight these multi-layered senses of belonging and pride.

Throughout the responses, it was found that the history and heritage of the region went hand in hand with the history and heritage of the particular living tradition. Oftentimes, within the same train of thought, a respondent would express a sense of belonging to both the tradition and the region as if one implied the other. For example, one Rapper dancer noted, "I do get a definite feeling of belonging because I do this dance, but it's actually most enhanced when you're not in the North East... so, it's when you're somewhere else, you can talk about coming from the North East... talk about being a part of this tradition".. Moreover, a bagpiper who is explaining why he plays the Northumbrian

Smallpipes states that, "it's a skill which is embedded in the county, itself… the tunes which are played, the actual instrument itself". Another bagpiper poetically notes, "when they played the music and you walked around that countryside, it was almost as though it was just expressing the whole location… you could picture scenes… matching every note to a blade of grass… it was so close to that part of the country and that's where I was living".

Attaching the notion of belonging to a community,, the environment and the heritage of the music traditions, another piper recalled that, "as soon as I started, I became a member of the society… so, you're sort of becoming a member of the tradition and keeping the tradition going, I suppose… so, being able to play these tunes on this local instrument is a sense of belonging". A fiddler also a noted that, "it gives people who get involved in it a way of expressing themselves that relates to their locality". Here, it is expressed that the first step into this world of belonging to the heritage of the North East and these traditions is through a belonging to a community, an established network of people with common goals. A dancer succinctly phrases this by saying, "I mean, we don't just all meet to dance every Wednesday night… we were all at [another dancer's] house at the weekend for her birthday… or we'll go down to somebody else's house just for fun and a barbeque… if there are enough drinks around, we may actually start dancing… and if we don't have swords, we'll use tea towels!" Although these communities have long histories of musicians and dancers who had come before, senses of belonging have also been felt upon joining these groups with warm support. A bagpiper mentions that, "they took me in and let me feel very welcome and part of this whole scene… so, it's really a sense of belonging… a sense of expressing the land through the music; it's amazing".

Sources of the expressed senses of pride were also rooted in an interconnected relationship between the heritage of the tradition, the community and the region. One Rapper dancer has said that she is "proud of the origins of it and proud of the fact that it is something specific to the North East of England". Further explaining the source of her pride, she notes, "back two hundred years ago during the mining industries, it was only in the North East of England that you would ever see this dancing". In addition to the pride felt for the region, the traditions, the communities and their heritages, half of the respondents mentioned their pride of creating interest among new audiences. When asked overall feelings in participating, another dancer comments:

> I feel quite proud, actually… when people see the dance and they've never heard of it before and you're explaining it all to them and how it's so old as well… it dates back at least two hundred years… and they've never heard of it and you go through the whole thing with them… they just love it and I love explaining it to them".

On the whole, the senses of belonging and pride that were expressed again related to a deeply layered relationship between heritage, community and place. Nonetheless, what has been reflected both in the above quotes and throughout the study is this encompassing theme of preservation of all three entities as well. A strong source of pride came from participating on both personal and communal levels in these safeguarding efforts. This is most exemplified by half the respondents who specifically cited a pride in bringing these traditions to new audiences. In the words of one musician, "I've become more interested recently in where I'm from… Northumberland and Newcastle… the North East traditions… and I'm interested in keeping those things alive, especially in young children". The following discussion will examine how this data can be interpreted as evidence for a certain "spirit of place" amongst this network of people.

2.3. "Spirit of Place"

"Spirit of place" for these musicians and dancers has its roots within their senses of belonging and pride to the heritage of the region, the communities and the traditions themselves. Moreover, belonging and pride were expressed in relation to the present – to their fellow community members, the living traditions themselves and the connection to place at this current time. Moreover, the pride of being involved, both on personal and communal levels, in the safeguarding of these intangible expressions, bringing them to new audiences and sparking interest, resonates strongly with the "spirit" of "spirit of place". Every respondent stated that these expressions are important and that they personally are involved with their preservation. They detailed, in varying degrees, the reasons of this importance and demonstrated that certain values and meanings are truly present at rehearsals, performances and even birthday parties. By highlighting the components of both senses of belonging and pride expressed by the respondents, a certain "spirit of place" has emerged. It can be argued that this spirit is for the multi-layered relationships between the heritage and land of the North East, the heritage of the expressions and all the people who had come before and with whom they currently share these ongoing experiences. In the words of one folk musician, "you don't have to be born here, you just have to have the knowledge of the place and the music and it's accessible to anybody… and then that wholeness just comes to anybody who wants to find it".

3. Communities, Heritage and "Spirit of Place" in the North Pennines Area of Outstanding Natural Beauty

Contemporary pressures on rural England pose threats to cultural landscapes (or "spirit of place') that have been shaped and valued by traditional residents. The North Pennines region, situated at the top of the Pennine mountain chain described as the "spine" of England, exemplifies these difficulties. Whilst threats to the physical appearance of the landscape are understood, the cultural landscape, as sustained by local communities, also finds itself under increasing pressure. Agricultural employment opportunities for young people are limited, a situation compounded by rising house prices caused by the desirability of rural housing for urban commuters. This changing profile of rural residency can, in worst-case scenarios, lead to a loss of key local services with severe ramifications for the sustainability of traditional communities and the particular "spirit of place" that their culture creates. This section briefly investigates how "spirit of place" is appreciated by local people through oral reminiscence and traditional music. Then a description is given of a protected landscape organisation's efforts to sustain two important elements of local distinctiveness, namely species-rich hay meadows and dry stone walls.

3.1. Community Guided Phenomena

A visit to the North Pennines in 2003 by a group of Swedish traditional musicians inspired the development of *SNAP*, an international musical exchange project. Musicians aged between 14 and 23 years were able to explore and share their musical heritage and pride in their local traditions, resulting in 2005 with a three-way musical and cultural partnership between Sweden, France and England. Funded by LEADER +, a European Union and Department for Environment, Food and Rural Affairs sustainable development grant programme, the success of the project is characteristic of a wider community interest in safeguarding intangible cultural heritage. In particular, individuals in the North Pennines are recording cultural heritage through oral reminiscences. When pressed to explain their motivations, such individuals talk of a realisation of the mortality of older generations, of an interest in cultural heritage and desire to somehow preserve it for the appreciation of the young. The *SNAP* project addresses such concerns and has proved that it is possible for young people to be enthused by cultural heritage. Now in its fourth year, *SNAP* continues to engage the young, safeguarding this particular "spirit of place" in a way that is entirely community driven.

3.2. North Pennines Area of Outstanding Natural Beauty Partnership

The North Pennines is one of 40 AONBs in England and Wales and was designated in June 1988 for its distinctive features. Management of the area is aided by the North Pennines Area of Outstanding Natural Beauty (AONB) Partnership, a protected landscape organisation that is made up of 22 statutory agencies, local authorities and voluntary/community organisations which all have an interest in, and help care for, the North Pennines AONB and UNESCO European & Global Geopark. The AONB Partnership aspires to conserve and enhance natural beauty and the cultural landscape through grant aiding and developing projects related to social and economic sustainability and the celebration of place. It has developed a project to support the passion for "spirit of place" that is exercising people in the North Pennines, embarking on the *Living North Pennines* project, one aspect of which, *Our Pennine Stories,* seeks to involve people in interpreting their heritage. Popular interest in the recording of oral reminiscences has been supported by delivering free training sessions. In this way the North Pennines AONB Partnership has begun to explore, acknowledge and support the local appreciation of "spirit of place" with some parallels to the ecomuseum model. The AONB Partnership has also identified threats to the cultural landscape, including a loss of traditional craft and agricultural skills and the associated loss of the traditional patterns of dry stone walls and characteristic hay meadows (North Pennines AONB Partnership 2004: 25). Specific action has been taken to address these issues through the *Hay Time* and *Dry Stone Walling Apprenticeships* projects.

3.2.1. Hay Time

The AONB Partnership has been working with farmers to restore and enhance "spirit of place" in the form of locally distinctive hay meadows through the *Hay Time* project. The North Pennines is home to some 40% of the UK's upland hay meadows, one of rarest grassland types in the country. In recent decades, intensive farming practices have threatened the quality of these species-rich hay meadow habitats, stifling wild flower growth through the production of heavier crops of grass. Farmers have been offered advice on a return to more traditional, sustainable farming methods and volunteers have supported mechanical methods of harvesting seed. Twenty-five local volunteers collected seed by hand, creating "plug plants" to aid restoration, whilst twelve amateur botanists volunteered to help survey the meadows. *Hay Time* finds itself increasingly concerned with cultural heritage: the role of farming families in the creation of hay meadows is vital as each hay meadow is a result of the idiosyncrasies of each individual farm. Retired farmers were consulted about their practices (North Pennines AONB Partnership 2008), leading to a partnership with a local museum to record oral history and create a touring exhibition. Opportunities have been provided for people to enjoy hay meadows, an in-situ approach to interpretation that resonates with ecomuseology. Walks and a plant identification guide have been published and this summer saw a Hay Time History event that invited people to come and learn about hay making though talks, handling of tools, oral histories and photographs. An element of "spirit of place" is thus preserved by local farmers, attracting visitors whilst sustaining traditional practices. Upland hay meadows however, are not the only element of "spirit of place" in jeopardy and the AONB Partnership has also turned its attention to dry stone walls.

3.2.2. Dry Stone Walling Apprenticeships

The North Pennines is characterised by thousands of miles of dry stone walls, in varying states of repair, a serious maintenance issue being the dearth of professional dry stone wallers in the region which the AONB Partnership has sought to address through an apprenticeship scheme (North Pennines AONB Partnership 2008a:8). The historic walls are a visual link to the past, contributing to "spirit of place" and also serve to provide barriers for stock, nesting sites for birds and habitats for small mammals and reptiles (North Pennines AONB Partnership 2008b:6). Seeking to address the skills shortage, the AONB Partnership teamed up with the British Trust for Conservation Volunteers and developed ten apprenticeships in dry stone walling which were delivered in 2007. In providing employment, the scheme has addressed issues of joblessness affecting sustainable communities. Furthermore, by making the built heritage of the walls and the associated intangible heritage of traditional walling techniques more sustainable, the apprenticeship scheme has sought to further safeguard elements of "spirit of place" through a practical initiative delivered by local people.

3.3. A North Pennines Ecomuseum?

Activities currently being undertaken to safeguard and interpret cultural heritage indicate some similarity to the ecomuseum ideal. Revisiting the list of ecomuseum attributes described above (Davis 1999:228) some parallels can be drawn. Physically the AONB, like an ecomuseum, sits outside of conventional boundaries, cutting through three county boundary lines and encompassing several local authorities. The AONB Partnership through projects such as *Hay Time*, *Dry Stone Walling Apprenticeships* and *Our Pennine Stories* evidence an approach to conservation and interpretation which is carried out via liaison, co-operation and the development of partnerships. Local communities are empowered to decide how the region should be interpreted and visitors are encouraged, through published guides, to engage with the cultural landscape by travelling from site to site within the AONB. In developing the skills to record oral histories and accessing financial support to deliver folk music projects for example, local communities are empowered to create their own cultural heritage. Research is now underway to investigate through in-depth interviews, the motivations of members of these projects and others to find out what involvement in such heritage related activities can reveal about "spirit of place" in the North Pennines and its ecomuseum potential.

4. Conclusion

With the brief overview of the ecomuseum principles and the discussion of the selected case studies, it can be noted that people have followed approaches very similar to those of ecomuseology in the North East of England. These approaches are aimed to promote and safeguard a number of intangible and tangible heritage resources that are crucial in terms of defining local distinctiveness and which help to provide the essence and fabric associated with the "spirit of place", linked to specific places within the region. Because the approaches used are more democratic, they give people the opportunity to participate in heritage management processes that bring together heritage resources (both intangible and tangible), place, identity construction, self-representation, affirmation, local pride and feelings of belonging. With the apparent synergies between ecomuseology and the approaches taken in the case studies, the authors would like to suggest that people interested in "sense of place" and "spirit of place" acquaint themselves with the literature on ecomuseums that has been produced by academics and practitioners. Due to their understanding of what is meant by the terms "eco" and "museum", some English speakers sometimes find the name ecomuseum difficult to concep-tualise. However, it is the principles and practices of ecomuseology that are of use when researching, or working with, heritage resources associated with "spirit of place". Unlike traditional heritage management and museum work, the principles of ecomuseology ensure that people have fuller access, control and sense of ownership of the heritage resources that are retained in their original contexts thereby giving colour and texture to "spirit of place".

References

Allan, T. 1972. *Allan's Illustrated Edition of Tyneside Songs*. 7th ed. Newcastle upon Tyne: Frank Graham.

Boylan P. 1992. Ecomuseums and the new museology – some definitions. *Museums Journal*, 92 (4), 29.

Buttimer, A. 1980. Home, reach and the sense of place. In *The Human Experience of Space and Place* eds. Buttimer A. and Seamon, D. 166-187. London: Croom Helm.

Clifford, S. and King, A. 1993. Losing your place. In *Local Distinctiveness: place, particularity and identity*, eds. Clifford, S. and King, A. London: Common Ground.

Common Ground 1996. *Promotional Leaflet; Common Ground*. London: Common Ground.

Corsane, G. 2006. Using ecomuseum indicators to evaluate the Robben Island Museum and World Heritage Site. *Landscape Research*, 31(4), 399-418.

Corsane, G., Davis, P., Elliot, S., Maggi, M., Murtas, D. and Rogers, S. 2007. Ecomuseum evaluation: experiences in Piemonte and Liguria, Italy. *International Journal of Heritage Studies*, 13(2), 101-116.

Corsane, G. and Holleman, W. 1993. Ecomuseums: a brief evaluation. In *Museums and the Environment* ed. De Jong, R. 111-125. Pretoria: Southern Africa Museums Association.

Crang, M. 1998. *Cultural Geography*. Routledge, London and New York.

Davis, P. 1999. *Ecomuseums: a sense of place*. Continuum, London and New York.

Davis, P. 2007. Ecomuseums and sustainability in Italy, Japan and China: adaptation through implementation. In *Museum Revolutions: How Museums Change and are Changed*, eds. Knell, S.J., MacLeod, S. and Watson, S.E.R. 198-214. London and New York: Routledge.

European Network of Ecomuseums 2004. *Declaration of Intent of the Long Net Workshop*. May 2004. Trento (Italy). Available from http://www.localworlds.eu/PAPERS/intents.pdf;accessed 14 July, 2008.

Lawrenson, T. 2007. *Lecture: History of Rapper Dancing*. 17 September, 2007. Newcastle on Tyne.

Meinig, D.W. 1979. The beholding eye: ten versions of the same scene. In *The Interpretation of Ordinary Landscapes*. ed. Meinig, D.W. 33-50. New York and Oxford: Oxford University Press.

Murphy, J. 2007. Northumbrian Music from the Smallpipes to Alex Glasgow. In *Northumbria History and Identity 547 – 2000*. ed. Robert Colls. Chichester: Phillimore.

North Pennines AONB Partnership 2004. North Pennines Area of Outstanding Natural Beauty Management Plan 2004 – 09.

North Pennines AONB Partnership. 2007. North Pennines Area of Outstanding Natural Beauty Partnership Annual Report 2006/2007.

North Pennines AONB Partnership. 2008. Apprenticeship Success. *North Pennines News*. Autumn & Winter 2007/2008: 6.

North Pennines AONB Partnership. 2008. Spotlight on... the History of Hay Time. *North Pennines News*. Autumn & Winter 2007/08: 8.

Relph, E.E. 1976. *Place and placelessness*. Pion, London.

Rivard, R. 1984. *Opening up the museum*. Quebec City. [Typescript at the Documentation Centre, Direction des Musées de France, Paris].

Rivard, R. 1988. Museums and ecomuseums – questions and answers. In *Okomuseumsboka – identitet, okologi, deltakelse*. Eds. Gjestrum, J.A. and Maure, M. 123-128 Tromso, Norway: ICOM.

Rodman, M. 2003. Empowering Place: Multilocality and Multivocality. In *The Anthropology of Space and Place: Locating Culture*, eds. Low, S.M. and Lawrence-Zúñiga, D. 204-224. Oxford: Blackwell.

Say, B. 2003. Northumbrian Pipers' Society [online]. Available from http://www.northumbrianpipers.org.uk/history.htm; accessed 3 November, 2006.

Sharp, Cecil J. (1913) *The Sword Dances of Northern England.* London: Novello and Company.

Smith, L. 2006. *Uses of Heritage.* Oxon: Routledge.

Stefano, M. & Corsane, G. 2008. The applicability of the ecomuseum ideal in safeguarding intangible cultural heritage in North East England. In *World Heritage and Sustainable Development,* eds. Amoêda, R., Lira, S., Pinheiro, C., Pinheiro, F., & Pinheiro, J. Barcelos: Green Lines Institute.

Living with Heritage at Angkor

Richard Mackay
**La Trobe University,
Godden Mackay Logan Pty Ltd
Getty Conservation Institute
Australia**

Sharon Sullivan
**Sullivan Blazejowski
"Redbank"
Australia**

ABSTRACT

The World-Heritage citation for Angkor celebrates its artistic and technical achievement as testament to a "past" civilization; yet contemporary Cambodians see Angkor as a continuing, integral part of their culture.

Recent work by the Cambodian APSARA Authority, Sydney University and other partners recognises Angkor as home to hundreds of thousands of Khmer, who through cultural and religious practises are part of the spirit of the place.

The Living With Heritage project is using a consultative, participatory approach to identify heritage values and the threats to them in the Angkor region. The traditional role of the "expert" has thereby evolved to include stakeholder consultation and facilitation.

Through close collaboration with key stakeholders and an inclusive participatory approach, the Living With Heritage project is endeavouring to build capacity for Cambodian heritage managers to address the interrelated nature of tangible and intangible values of the Angkor cultural landscape through values-based management.

RÉSUMÉ

Le Patrimoine mondial, en qualifiant Angkor, fait l'éloge des accomplissements artistiques et techniques de ce site en tant que testament d'une civilisation « passée ». Cependant, les Cambodgiens d'aujourd'hui conçoivent Angkor comme une partie intégrante et toujours vivante de leur culture.

Des travaux récents effectués sous l'Autorité APSARA du Cambodge, l'Université de Sidney et d'autres partenaires reconnaissent qu'Angkor est le foyer de centaines de milliers de Khmers qui, à travers des pratiques culturelles et religieuses, font partie de l'esprit du lieu.

Le projet *Living with Heritage* (Vivre avec le patrimoine) utilise une approche consultative et participative pour identifier les valeurs patrimoniales et les menaces auxquelles celles-ci sont exposées dans la région d'Angkor. Le rôle traditionnel de « l'expert », par conséquent, a évolué, pour prendre en compte, en la facilitant, la consultation des parties prenantes.

Au moyen d'une étroite collaboration avec les personnes concernées et une approche participative inclusive, le projet *Living with Heritage* s'efforce de construire, pour les gestionnaires du patrimoine cambodgien, une capacité de répondre à la nature entremêlée des valeurs matérielles et immatérielles du paysage culturel d'Angkor, au moyen d'une gestion fondée sur les valeurs.

Context

The great Khmer city of Angkor in Cambodia has breathtaking artistic, design and planning values, and is justifiably described in the World Heritage List citation using terms such as "unique artistic realisation" and "chef d'oeuvre of the human mind." The citation also indicates that Angkor gives unique testimony on a past civilisation. (UNESCO 2008).

By stark contrast, contemporary Cambodians see a prime value of Angkor as a continuing symbol of Khmer culture; their beliefs, cultural practices and traditions are therefore an integral part of the ongoing spirit of the place.

The Challenge of Multiple Values

For 200 years the focus at Angkor has been on research, including archaeology and documentation, restoration and physical conservation of spectacular temple monuments. (Ang et al 1998). The outstanding aesthetic values of these monuments certainly appear to be behind the 1992 World Heritage listing. The ongoing traditional and religious connections between the local population and remains of Khmer civilization, however, do not form part of the reasons for World Heritage listing. These connections have been all but ignored. In the popular imagination they are subservient to images, recently reinforced by blockbuster movies, of mysterious jungle-covered ruins of unknown origin.

Until recently, the local people at Angkor have been excluded from management decisions, have laboured as workmen under the direction of foreign "experts" and their longstanding rights to farm and utilise the area for religious practice have been increasingly restricted in the interests of conservation of World Heritage values and the perceived amenity of tourists who are arriving in dramatically increasing numbers (Miura 2004, Winter 2007).

A major challenge for heritage management at Angkor is to provide an appropriate response to all of the heritage values of this place – world, national and local values, including significant attributes that may not yet be formally recognised – even when these may be in conflict with other management objectives. A values-based approach, founded on active involvement of interested people, offers a framework for the establishment of effective management and monitoring regimes. Values-based planning is increasingly becoming a benchmark of best practice heritage management for cultural places (Australia ICOMOS 1999, de la Torres 2005).

Since the western world "discovered" Angkor in the eighteenth century, it has been at once fascinated by its romance and beauty and confused about its real nature and extent (Chandler 1996). What has been interpreted in the past as a "site" or the "remains of a lost civilization" is now understood as a complex and different place: not just one site, but a great many interrelated sites, together comprising a layered cultural landscape of World Heritage significance; not the ruins of a former society, but the hub of a still thriving culture and religion.

The Greater Angkor Project

Research work by the University of Sydney, the Ecole Française d'Extrême-Orient and APSARA (the Cambodian "Authority for the Preservation and Safeguarding of Angkor and Surrounding Areas") in a collaboration generally known as the "Greater Angkor Project" (or "GAP"), has been contributing to the reappraisal of Angkor through archaeological survey, excavation and related techniques, generating a vast body of data that is being synthesised and analysed through advanced Geographical Information System ("GIS") programs. It is now known that the current archaeological park at Angkor was the cultural centre of a massive low density metropolis extending over more than 1,000 square kilometres – the largest known city in the pre-industrial world; herein referred to as "the great city of Angkor" (Evans et al 2007, Fletcher et al 2003, Pottier 1999).

Community Impacts

Ironically, the exciting results of the GAP project also highlight the potential for direct conflict between the protection of a thousand square kilometres of archaeological site and the ongoing life and livelihood of the people living there. The impacts on local communities occur in three broad areas:

Firstly, the population of approximately 100,000 Khmer who live within the Angkor Heritage Park need to manage their day-to-day activities so as not to cause physical damage to significant features, including the extensive archaeology beneath their homes and fields. The use of mechanised equipment for agricultural purposes, for example, may be problematic in areas with underlying earthen archaeological features from the Angkorian period; yet such advances are worthy initiatives in such a poor nation whose people rely on local farming for their very subsistence.

Secondly, in an attempt to preserve, present and display traditional Khmer culture, local communities are experiencing some enforced restrictions on their traditional cultural practices and lifeways in the name of tourism. Some of these, such as obligations to build village houses using traditional techniques (rather than embracing modern materials and technologies), have the effect of retarding moves towards what developed nations see as "modern living".

Thirdly, the sheer numbers of visitors and their often uncontrolled visitation patterns can inadvertently prevent, displace or modify ceremonies and social activities that would otherwise form part of important ongoing traditions – traditions which are all the more important in the context of the people's recovery from decades of war and the Khmer Rouge regime. The affected practices range from important rites of passage rituals – such as the cutting of adolescent topknots, to the day-to-day lifeways – such as Khmer family picnics on the grass beside the moat at Angkor Wat (Ang et al 2007, Sokrithy 2007).

Living With Heritage

Some of the GAP researchers have stepped outside their traditional archaeology-focused role and responded to these emerging issues with a new project, known as "Living With Heritage" which is being run under the auspices of APSARA (University of Sydney 2008). Living With Heritage has a multi-national and multi-disciplinary project team funded by the Australian Research Council and involves cross-sector collaboration between the academic, government and private sectors.

The overall aims of the APSARA Living With Heritage project are to adopt spatial analysis and mapping approaches along with other sources of information to identify:

• key elements of cultural significance of the great city of Angkor;

• issues and threats which will affect their conservation; and

• policies and tools, including specific databases, required to ensure the ongoing conservation of the identified heritage values.

This process can potentially facilitate effective ongoing management of all the heritage values of Angkor, thereby maximising its value to the entire Cambodian community. While it is not the intention of the Living With Heritage project to prepare a new World Heritage nomination, the identification of these new values of universal significance and the increasing need to manage and protect them makes the re-nomination of Angkor to the World Heritage List (encompassing an enlarged conception of the great city of Angkor) a course of action to be seriously considered.

Values-based Participatory Planning

APSARA has demonstrated strong commitment to conservation, developing a range of projects which seek to protect Angkor's heritage while considering issues of contemporary sustainability. In its approach to management, APSARA has adopted a framework that includes consideration of social, economic and environmental issues. This approach draws from a broad range of elements which make up the Angkor World Heritage site and the people who live and work in it, including those involved in tourism, trade, traditional culture, urban development, heritage management, landscape change and archaeology (Khun-Neay Khuon 2006).

Living With Heritage relies on and extends this issues-based, consultative approach to the identification of all heritage values and the threats to those values in the Greater Angkor region. This methodology has necessitated a change in the traditional role of the "expert," who must now give up some of the power inherent in this expertise, no longer prescribing the cultural values of the place in elite isolation, but functioning as a stakeholder, consultant and facilitator to ensure that all the ways in which the place has cultural value to different groups are revealed and taken into account in the way the place is managed (Sullivan 2002).

The project methodology is simple. Using available data and consultation with local people, those places within the Greater Angkor area that may have importance for aesthetic, historical, scientific or social reasons are being identified. Consultation occurs through discussions with key groups and individuals in facilitated workshops. Particular emphasis is placed on the reasons why the great city of Angkor or individual sites are important to the community or particular stakeholders as well as to researchers. Maps are being produced showing important places and their values.

This process is iterative – commencing with a Steering Committee of senior APSARA and other government and community representatives, then through a Technical Committee, whose members are being trained in heritage management processes (while at the same time contributing information) to the local community and from there back to the Steering Committee. The required tasks are therefore time consuming, challenging across three languages and at times distracted into discussions about other matters of concern to the officials and communities who are involved in the process. However, the results are rewarding and extremely informative for the project team members (who are constantly gathering new information about individual places and their attributes) but also for participants (who are broadening their own views of what constitutes their heritage).

By engaging stakeholders across a full spectrum – from senior government officials to community members – the Living With Heritage methodology extends the concept of holistic values assessment into actual place management, taking many of the concerns expressed by commentators such as Miura (Miura 2004) and providing a mechanism to address them in a management context.

The project is gaining momentum and significant progress has been made. Australian heritage managers and project researchers – functioning as facilitators – are working closely with APSARA and with the community on the identification of all the values of the place and the major threats and issues to these values. These issues relate to archaeological conservation, but also to day-to-day needs of residents, tourism pressures and visitor expectations.

2008 is year four of a five-year program. Future phases will involve further work with the community and local authorities to produce tools that will assist in conserving all of the heritage values of Angkor – those in the World Heritage citation and those of the local people – while beginning to address issues and problems that have been identified through the consultative process. The program also involves development of monitoring tools, including computer-based maps showing places of heritage value and areas under possible threat, as a basis for priority setting and ongoing monitoring programs.

Conclusion

In a complex, multi-layered cultural place like Angkor, effective conservation cannot occur in isolation. To conserve the heritage values of the place – either those in the current World Heritage citation or those which may emerge from the project itself – other values must also be acknowledged and managed. An open, respectful collaboration between heritage managers and local stakeholders serves not only to identify all of the values of the place, but also to establish a well-founded sustainable model for their ongoing conservation.

Through close collaboration with APSARA and UNESCO and through application of the values-based principles and processes of the Burra Charter of Australia ICOMOS, the Living With Heritage project is endeavouring to build capacity for Cambodian agencies and managers to recognise all of the values of the cultural landscape of the great city of Angkor and to use GIS as a mechanism for sharing information and values-based management.

There have been many exciting discoveries in the process of moving from the values expressed in the original World Heritage citation to a much wider set of values expressive of Angkor in its contemporary setting. Strong cultural continuity and traditional links are apparent, which demonstrate Angkor to be not only an architectural and engineering masterpiece from the past, but a living cultural and sacred landscape. In turn, formal recognition of these values by all parties should have a profound effect on conservation, management and tourism at Angkor and should strengthen the hand of managers and community in preventing inappropriate development and activities.

The Living With Heritage project recognises that, as well as being a major World Heritage place and burgeoning tourist destination, Angkor is the continuing home to hundreds of thousands of Khmer who not only make an invaluable contribution to the area's sustainable management, but through cultural and religious practices actually enhance the heritage significance of Greater Angkor and are an important part of the spirit of the place.

Acknowledgements

This paper draws heavily on the Greater Angkor Project undertaken over a number of years by the University of Sydney, the Ecole Française d'Extreme-Orient and APSARA Authority. We acknowledge particularly the work of Eleanor Bruce, Damian Evans, Roland Fletcher, Bess Moylan, Christophe Pottier and Tim Winter. We also acknowledge the major contribution of the Living With Heritage Project Partners: the APSARA Authority, the University of Sydney, UNESCO (UNESCO Phnom Penh Office), Ecole Française d'Extrême-Orient (EFEO) Angkor, Horizon Geoscience Consulting Pty Ltd, the Australian Department of the Environment, Water, Heritage and the Arts, Godden Mackay Logan Pty Ltd, ESRI Australia, Leica Geosystems and the Finnish Environmental Institute.

The project would not have been possible without assistance and support from the APSARA Authority through the Living With Heritage Steering Committee, chaired by the APSARA Director General, His Excellency Bun Narith and including His Excellency Sou Phirin, the Governor of Siem Reap, as well as nominees from community monasteries, villages and the tourism industry, together with APSARA colleagues Khuon Khun-Neay, Mao Vibol and Im Sokrithy. Many other APSARA personnel have also contributed.

Funding for both the Greater Angkor Project and Living With Heritage has been provided by the Australian Research Council under the Linkage Grants Program.

References

Ang Choulean, Choulean Preap, and Choulean Sun. 2007. Cause of Khmer lifetime through the Rite of Passage. In Khmer. Phnom Penh: Hanuman Tourism.

Ang, Choulean, Ashley Thompson, and Eric Prenowitz. 1998. *Angkor: A Manual for the Past, Present and Future*. Phnom Penh: APSARA/ UNESCO.

Australia ICOMOS. 1999. *The Burra Charter: The Australia ICOMOS Charter for Places of Cultural Significance*. Burwood: Australia ICOMOS.

Chandler, David. 1996. *A History of Cambodia*. Boulder: Westview Press.

de la Torre, Marta, ed. 2005. Heritage Values in Site Management – Four Case Studies. Los Angeles: Getty Conservation Institute.

Evans, Damian, Christophe Pottier, Roland Fletcher, Scott Hensley, Ian Tapley, Anthony Milne and Michael Barbetti. 2007. *A comprehensive archaeological map of the world's largest pre-industrial settlement complex at Angkor, Cambodia. Proceedings of the National Academy of Sciences of the United States of America*. 104 (36): 14277-14282.

Fletcher, Roland J., Michael Barbetti, Damian Evans, Heng Than, Im Sokrithy, Khieu Chan, Dan Penny, Christophe Pottier and Somaneath Tous. 2003. "Redefining Angkor: Structure and environment in the largest, low density urban complex of the pre-industrial world". *Udaya* 4: 107 – 121.

Khuon, Khun-Neay. 2006. "Angkor – Site Management and Local Communities". Unpublished paper delivered to the Angkor – Landscape, City and Temple Conference, University of Sydney.

Miura, Keiko. 2004. *Contested Heritage: People of Angkor*. Ph.D. dissertation, University of London.

Pottier, Christophe. 1999. *Carte archéologique de la région d'Angkor Zone Sud*. Ph.D., Université Paris III – Sorbonne Nouvelle.

Sokrithy, Im. 2007. *Social values and community content. Living with Heritage: Report of the Living With Heritage Technical Committee*. APSARA Authority.

Sullivan, Sharon. 2002. "The Expert and the Community". Unpublished paper delivered to the US ICOMOS Annual Conference.

UNESCO. 2008. *World Heritage List*. Internet. Available from http://whc. unesco.org/en/list; accessed 25 July, 2008.

University of Sydney. 2008. *Living With Heritage*. Internet. Available from http://acl.arts.usyd.edu.au/angkor/lwh; accessed 25 July, 2008.

Winter, Tim. 2007. *Post-Conflict heritage, postcolonial tourism, culture, politics and development at Angkor*. London: Routledge.

Budj Bim:
Caring for the Spirit and the People
Finding the Spirit of Place

Damien Bell
Lake Condah Sustainable Development Project
Australia

Chris Johnston
Context Pty Ltd
Australia

ABSTRACT

Budj Bim National Heritage Landscape represents the extraordinary triumph of the Gunditjmara people in having this place recognised as a place of the spirit, a place of human technology and ingenuity and as a place of resistance.

The Gunditjmara are the Indigenous people of this part of south-western Victoria, Australia. In this landscape, more than 30,000 years ago the Gunditjmara witnessed an important creation being reveal himself in the landscape.

Budj Bim (known today as Mount Eccles) is the source of an immense lava flow which transformed the landscape. The Gunditjmara people developed this landscape by digging channels, creating ponds and wetlands and shaping an extensive aquaculture system, providing an economic basis for the development of a settled society.

This paper will present the complex management planning that has gone into restoring the lake and re-establishing Gunditjmara management, reversing the tide of Australian history and enabling the spirit of this sacred place to again be cared for.

RÉSUMÉ

Le paysage patrimonial national de Budj Bim (*National Heritage Landscape*) représente l'extraordinaire triomphe du peuple Gunditjmara qui est parvenu à le faire reconnaître comme lieu spirituel, lieu d'ingéniosité technique et lieu de résistance. Les Gunditjamara sont les Autochtones de cette région située au sud-est de la province de Victoria, en Australie. Dans ce paysage, il y a plus de 30 000 ans, les Gunditjmara avaient été les témoins d'un important phénomène de la création, qui se révèle dans le paysage. Budj Bim (connu aujourd'hui sous le nom de mont Eccles) fut la source d'une immense coulée de lave qui a transformé le paysage. Les Gunditjmara ont développé ce dernier en creusant des canaux, en créant des retenues d'eau et des lieux humides et en élaborant un système extensif d'aquaculture qui a procuré une base économique au développement d'une société sédentaire. Cet article présente le projet de gestion complexe qui a entrepris de restaurer le lac et de réinstaurer l'activité des Gunditjmara, inversant ainsi le cours de l'histoire australienne et permettant à l'esprit de ce lieu sacré d'être à nouveau vénéré.

Introduction

The ancestral creation-being is revealed in the landscape of south-western Victoria (Australia) at Budj Bim (Mt Eccles). At Mount Eccles the top of his head is revealed, his teeth tung att are the scoria cones. His spirit is embedded deep in this place and in the people – Gunditjmara.

Listing of Budj Bim National Heritage Landscape on Australia's new national heritage list in 2004 was an extraordinary achievement for a remarkable people. Since, a native title claim has succeeded and more Gunditjmara traditional country has been handed back.

This paper tells the story of the courage and determination of Gunditjmara people in their fight for their country and looks forward with their vision of the future and plans to restore Lake Condah with permanent water.

Inspirited landscapes

For Aboriginal people, country is a "nourishing terrain" – a place that gives and receives life. Country is everything – people, plants, animals, earth, water, Dreaming, air, sky – and every Aboriginal person has a country to which they belong (Rose 1996, 7-8).

Each country has its sacred origins, its Dreamings written in the land and known through traditions and cultural practices. Spiritual associations to country through the activities of creation beings at particular places are characteristic of Aboriginal societies throughout Australia. Through story and totems, the land, the people and other species are connected together in a complex web of meanings, responsibilities and reciprocities.

Dreaming or creation time refers to the time in which the land was formed and shaped, and living things created. Ancestral beings were the creators of all things. The Dreaming is ever-present. It is not a past time or a past event that has concluded.

Country is a really important word too. In Aboriginal English it means more than just land.

People talk about country in the same way that they would talk about a person: they speak to country, sing to country, visit country, worry about country, feel sorry for country. People say that country knows, hears, smells, takes notice, takes care, is sorry or happy… Country is a living entity with a yesterday, today and tomorrow, with a consciousness and a will toward life. Because of this richness, country is home and peace; nourishment for the body, mind and spirit; heart's ease (Rose 1996, 7).

For Gunditjmara people, the whole of their country in western Victoria on the edge of the southern ocean is inspirited – filled with the spirit of creation and rich with significance and stories of the ancestral past.

The "high head" of Budj Bim is ever present in the landscape, not as a large feature that dominates visually, but as a presence that is felt as much as seen. The massive flows of lava that accompanied the revelation of Budj Bim completely reshaped the land, flowing through and filling valleys and tributaries of Darlot Creek, covering the land. This flow, the Tyrendarra lava flow, extended to the south for nearly 50 kilometres. Today, after the sea-level rise following the last global ice age, the lava flow extends 14 kilometres into the sea off the southern coast of Australia.

The revelation of Budj Bim and the lava flow is spiritually connected to Deen Maar, a small island 5 kilometres off the coast. As part of Gunditjmara tradition, Deen Maar is the last stepping stone for the spirit before it departs this world. The belief that spirits go to an island of the dead or cross some water after death is widespread throughout Australia. One tradition describes how the island was formed when the dead body of a giant was thrown into the sea. There are accounts that the rotting body gives the sea in the area a strange smell (DEWHA Lady Julia Percy Island) Opposite the island, on the mainland, is an important cave – Tarn wirring or the "road of the spirits" – which formed part of the passage between the mainland and the island. (Clark 1990, 65).

These are just a few of the many stories and spiritual meanings that are alive in Gunditjmara country.

Restoring connections to this spiritual landscape is a significant challenge. Loss of land and traditions are just two of the many impacts of colonisation on Gunditjmara people. Through years of fighting for land justice, Gunditjmara are seeking to reverse these impacts. Recent achievements – National Heritage listing, native title and community initiatives at Lake Condah – are starting to bear fruit.

Budj Bim National Heritage Landscape

Three places heralded the launch of the National Heritage List in July 2004 – one of the three was Budj Bim National Heritage Landscape, listed Budj Bim was listed under four of the nine criteria. It was the first place listed under the new criterion (criterion [i]) designed to recognise places of outstanding significance as part of Indigenous tradition.

The National Heritage List includes places of outstanding importance to the nation as a whole. The Minister for the Environment and Heritage describes the National Heritage List as containing:

(…) the nation's most outstanding natural, cultural and Indigenous places and stories that make the country distinctively Australian. It will be something which will make us all feel proud of this amazing country the highest recognition the nation could offer (Minister for the Environment and Heritage 2004).

Budj Bim National Heritage Landscape is of outstanding national significance to Australia because the landscape demonstrates the "process through which ancestral beings reveal themselves in the landscape" (NHL listing).

This process of the revelation of ancestral beings is known from across Australia where it involves Aboriginal people recognising (or having revealed to them) the form of an ancestral being in a feature of the landscape. In Queensland's Atherton Tablelands, Aboriginal creation stories about volcanism are cast within the framework of transgressions and reprisals by ancestral beings (DEWHA 2004a). In the younger volcanics in Victoria, which includes Mount Eccles, the stories are of a creation being Budj Bim (Clark 1990a; 1990b; Builth 2003).

The other values of the Budj Bim National Heritage Landscape are also outstanding nationally, and potentially internationally. These include:

- the remarkable and extensive aquaculture systems that enable Gunditjmara society to develop and be strengthened
- the sustained and organised Gunditjmara resistance to Europeans in a conflict that has become known as the Eumeralla Wars
- the continuity of connection by Gunditjmara people with their country, and their passionate fight to retain and return culture and land.

The Budj Bim National Heritage Landscape covers two large areas, together 14,000 hectares (or 140 square kilometres).

The Lake Condah – Mt Eccles section stretches from Mt Eccles (Budj Bim) in the east to Darlot Creek in the west, a landscape of rugged stony rises (lava flows) covered with eucalypt woodland. As the lava filled the prior streams, lakes and swamps, a new landscape was created. Lake Condah formed about 8,000 years ago, and is one of a series of large wetlands on the edge of the lava flows.

The Tyrendarra section comprises an area of the lava flow to the south of Lake Condah containing the remains of extensive and "complex systems of natural and artificially created wetlands, channels, the stone bases of weirs and stone fish traps that were used by Gunditjmara people to grow and harvest eels and fish. The remains on Tyrendarra are part of the same system as the remains in the Mt Eccles/Lake Condah area, and are hundreds and probably thousands of years old" (DEWHA 2004b).

Fighting for country

The extent of Aboriginal dispossession and disadvantage since the arrival of Europeans in Australia is difficult to imagine and painful to describe. In southern and eastern Australia the impacts are especially severe, and many Aboriginal people have been disconnected from country, tradition, language, knowledge and family.

Gunditjmara people retained connections to their traditional country, with two missions being established on country, one right next to Lake Condah. The mission period lasted from the 1860s through to 1918. But even after the official closure of the Lake Condah Mission, Gunditjmara people kept living there and continued their connection to Lake Condah and the stony rises.

The fight for land justice – the return of their traditional country – was long and hard and there were many "battles". In the mid 1980s, following legal action against aluminium producer Alcoa by Sandra Onus and Christina Saunders, the Victorian State Government commenced negotiations with the traditional owners of Lake Condah. As a result the mission site and cemetery were returned to Aboriginal ownership, and the State government commenced a program of land purchase with the intention of returning this land to the Aboriginal community. The Commonwealth Government passed legislation to enable the return of the mission and other land, using for the only time the power granted to it in the 1967 referendum to pass special laws in relation to Aboriginal people. The significance of the unique legal processes by which the land was returned to the community is also recognised in the National Heritage List (Winda Mara 2008, 25).

Gunditjmara continued their fight for country under the Native Title Act 1993, achieving success in 2007. In the decision, Justice North notes that the determination is just one more step in a long history of the fight for recognition, seeing it as part of a continuum which includes the Eumeralla War, legal proceedings against the Alcoa Aluminium smelter and the fight to protect the Convincing Ground. The significance of this finding against the context of previous Victorian native title claims (most significantly that of the Yorta Yorta people) cannot be underestimated.

The latest initiative – the Lake Condah Sustainable Development Project – is another step in the Gunditjmara's long connection with Lake Condah. The next section of this paper explains how the return of water to the lake will protect its spiritual and other values and describes some of the policies that have been created to achieve this outcome.

Restoring Lake Condah

Standing on the edge of the lava flow, looking across the dry bed of Lake Condah to Mount Eccles on the horizon, the landscape is vast. But there is something missing.

From the 1870s until the 1950s, drains were cut through the deep sediments of the lake, draining its waters into an artificial channel and then into Darlot Creek.

A description of the lake in the Portland Mercury (a local newspaper) in the summer of 1843 demonstrates its natural abundance:

> a splendid freshwater lake (…) about a mile and a half long and three quarters of a mile wide, and contains almost every variety of fish in abundance, with swans, ducks &c. It is of considerable depth, and receives a river about 50 yards broad; one side is bold and rocky and contains a number of small coves into one of which a beautiful stream empties itself, and the other side is a gently sloping shore surrounded by a fine tract of country (Portland Mercury, 11 January 1843).

As the lake was drained, farmers gained control over the land for the grazing of stock.

But the lake was more than just a natural body of water. It was – and is – a cultural creation. Through a weir lower down on Darlot Creek, Gunditjmara managed the water flows through a system of wetlands from Condah Swamp, Whittlebury Swamp and Lake Condah; together these wetlands cover 500 hectares (5 square kilometres). Within Lake Condah and in other wetland areas towards the coast, Gunditjmara created extensive aquaculture systems to harvest eels and fish.

In Lake Condah itself, these stone and earth structures – weirs, races, canals, walls – enabled active management of water flows and effective trapping using woven nets. Use of deeper pools suggests that eels and fish were held over extended periods, enabling extended use of this resource.

Recent investigation of weirs on Darlot Creek has added to Gunditjmara knowledge of the extent of the landscape management practised in the past.

> What would happen, these low-lying areas here, the eels would come in here to feed, and then they would come swimming up these areas, the low areas, and then come to these channels. They would then be forced into these channels and moved down through here into places where the holding pens are.
>
> This is part of a farming system. We actually managed the eel. We just didn't come out here and hunt and fish. We actually came out here to collect and manoeuvre

and farm and move these eels into places where we wanted them to go so then we could pick them up when we wanted to pick them up (Daryl Rose, Gunditjmara Elder, Radio National 2007).

Back in the early 1990s, Gunditjmara determined to return water to Lake Condah, bringing it to life again. A management plan was prepared in 1993 and has guided actions since.

The *Lake Condah Sustainable Development Project* is currently the most significant strategic planning initiative for Lake Condah and establishes the framework for all current activities. The project is an Indigenous initiative that came out of an economic development plan for Winda-Mara Aboriginal Corporation and was launched in February 2002 with a visit from the Hon. Philip Ruddock, the federal Minister for Aboriginal Affairs.

The key elements of the project are:
1. To gain national and world heritage listing.
2. To restore and re-flood Lake Condah wetland.
3. To rebuild the old mission church.
4. To develop land management plans.
5. To develop an international learning centre.
6. To develop employment centred on tourism, accommodation, aquaculture and bush tucker, etc.
7. To build a strong partnership of active members supporting the project.

A key part of the project is the return of water to Lake Condah and extensive hydrological studies have been undertaken to determine how this will occur.

In parallel, a conservation management plan (CMP) has been developed to ensure that the heritage values of Lake Condah are fully understood and that effective Gunditjmara management policies and practices are established.

The CMP is founded on an empowering Gunditjmara vision – or *Yarkeem*:

Gunditjmara will conserve Lake Condah. It is an important Gunditjmara place and we have fought hard over many generations to see it returned to us so that we can heal this land. Gunditjmara acknowledge the ancestral Kerrup Jmara and the Kerrup Jmara today.

Gunditjmara will restore the natural abundance of the lake. Water will again flow into the lake and remain there year round, enabling native plants and animals to return and be nurtured by the life-giving waters of the lake.

Lake Condah will again be central to Gunditjmara life and culture. Gunditjmara people will experience the landscape, engage in eel and fish harvesting using the stone trap systems and apply traditional knowledge and practices in land and water management. As the water returns into this landscape, we will learn more about the ways in which previous generations cared for and used the land, and we will pass what we learn on to the next generation so that traditions and knowledge are never lost again.

We will welcome guests to Gunditjmara traditional lands and they will experience the landscape with us as we care for the land. This will enable us to share aspects of Gunditjmara history, culture and knowledge that may be shared.

Gunditjmara welcome the support and contributions of many other people and organisations to this restoration project.

Restoring Lake Condah will help us achieve our cultural, economic and social aspirations. Lake Condah will become one of the foremost Indigenous cultural destinations, consistent with the aspirations of the local Aboriginal people.

The healing of Lake Condah within a generation is our vision for the future. It is a legacy from us today to future generations whom we are asking to carry forward this important work.

From this powerful *Yarkeem* six principles have been defined to guide the plan:

1. The significance of Lake Condah is paramount.
2. Lake Condah is a dynamic living place.
3. Lake Condah sustains Gunditjmara culture and people.
4. Lake Condah is a place of learning.
5. Connections with Lake Condah are strengthened.
6. All uses and users of Lake Condah respect its significance.

Lake Condah is a significant place for Gunditjmara people. It has sustained generations of Gunditjmara. At Lake Condah, important aspects of Gunditjmara culture and history are evident; it is a place that has been strongly defended and a place where culture and traditions are being reasserted and renewed. Passing on of knowledge, traditions and connections to the next generation requires that Gunditjmara people have control over access and use.

The Lake Condah landscape is a dynamic place, shaped by nature and people over millennia. The reintroduction of a more natural water regime and the return of the land to Gunditjmara to manage will create an opportunity to manage the progressive restoration of this landscape, responding and adapting management techniques as the landscape changes.

As the landscape is restored, perceptions of the landscape, its history and its story will change. In fact, the proposal to return water to the lake demonstrates that this change in perceptions is already underway.

A restored Lake Condah will be even more significant. Reintroducing water into the lake will help unlock new understandings of its significance as a Gunditjmara place. And symbolically the return of water represents a significant healing process, and this is likely to heighten the appreciation of the heritage values of Lake Condah and the wider landscape.

For Gunditjmara, Lake Condah will again be an important learning and teaching place: a place where culture and traditions are passed on and where guests will be invited to learn about Gunditjmara culture.

Adaptive management

One of the fundamental approaches built into the CMP is the idea of adaptive management – a learning approach to management. The reintroduction of water to the lake will return a more natural ecological system and seasonal cycles to the lake, enhancing its cultural values. Management practices will need to be responsive to this changing environment.

Adaptive management will use Gunditjmara knowledge and traditions as the basis for an Indigenous approach to land and water management. There are five steps in the adaptive management approach: planning, action, monitoring, learning and adaptation.

Some of this learning will be formalised, for example, by documenting the eel trap systems and observing water flows and eel movements so as to add to an understanding of the whole aquaculture system. These systems have not operated to full capacity in living memory.

Because the aquaculture systems were created by past generations of Gunditjmara and because this place is of outstanding heritage value to Australia, great care will be taken before changes are made to the aquaculture structures.

Returning water to the lake could have both positive and negative impacts, and these issues have had to be considered in shaping policy. For example, a significant benefit is that returning water will probably offer the greatest insight into the complexity and operation of the system. On the other hand, it may result in changes to the stone structures that comprise the system, although this has been assessed as an unlikely outcome.

And once water is returned to the lake, the aquaculture systems at Lake Condah will be able to be used again, introducing the requirement for maintenance and reconstruction. Decisions will therefore need to be made about how components of the aquaculture systems are to be replaced or reconstructed, who will undertake this work and how "new" work will be distinguished. The ephemeral components of the system – nets, bags and weirs – will need to be made. Limited availability of local materials may require new solutions to be developed.

To address this range of issues and based on the proposed learning and adaptive management approach the CMP proposes a two-year learning period in which Gunditjmara will monitor the reintroduction of water in relation to the aquaculture system – especially the stone structures that form the traps and races. Gunditjmara will monitor water flows and associated natural cycles, assess the current condition and functionality of the structures and document any impacts. At the same time, through Gunditjmara collaboration with researchers, universities and other organisations, any important research questions about the aquaculture system will be defined.

All this information will then inform a Gunditjmara decision about which traps should be re-activated for aquaculture and which should be left as historical evidence of the activities of the Gunditjmara ancestors.

Connection to Country

At Lake Condah, Gunditjmara connections that go back millennia will be able to be sustained into the future. These long-term connections are a vital part of Gunditjmara culture and community well-being:

Connection to country is not simply a reflection of history. Lake Condah is a living Gunditjmara place and offers spiritual nourishment to Gunditjmara.

Lake Condah is the heart of Gunditjmara country ... we have always been with the lake and it has always looked after us ... if the lake is good then we are good ... we have been different since the lake was drained by authorities but with water soon to return, we will achieve an important healing for the country and for ourselves. (Ken Saunders, Gunditjmara Elder).

Gunditjmara connections to country reflect a substantial body of knowledge (or intellectual property) handed down from one generation to the next and containing information about the nature or use of objects, sites and knowledge (including as well natural systems, ecological knowledge, flora and fauna, medicinal uses etc).

The experience of the occupation of Gunditjmara country, however, has impacted on these connections and on the holding and passing on of traditional knowledge about the management of the environment and the operation of the aquaculture systems.

Aboriginal knowledge and intellectual property often goes unrecognised at best, and at worst is exploited. The CMP encourages Gunditjmara to document their knowledge and traditions and to take full control over this information. Likewise Gunditjmara intellectual property associated with land, water, natural and cultural resources is to be recognised and protected, to ensure any economic benefits arising from its use accrue to Gunditjmara.

Gunditjmara welcome what western science can bring to an understanding of their traditional country and to processes of repairing the land. Traditional knowledge and science may reveal more than either can do alone

Other community connections

Lake Condah is also a place of strong connection for people other than Gunditjmara: for those who live locally and who have experienced the lake over many years; for those who have worked out on the lake documenting its natural and cultural riches; for those who have visited and taken tours with Gunditjmara people.

Lake Condah will be conserved as a place that has and continues to allow many community connections to be made with this place, primarily for the Gunditjmara community and those that they invite to visit as guests, but also for the local community. Opportunities to strengthen these connections will be supported.

Looking to the future

The challenges to be faced are still many until Gunditjmara country is healed. But the native title decision, the return of land to traditional owners and the return of water to the lake are all important steps in a long struggle for survival.

Country is more than land. The spirit of the land guides Gunditjmara always. And as the land is healed, the Gunditjmara story will reveal itself to us again.

Reflooding the lake's very symbolic in lots of ways. I think that what it's about is that it's about accepting Aboriginal culture and history and heritage as important, and I think the symbolism involved in it is going to be so important because this is one of the most important places, we believe, in Australia in cultural heritage issues. So, therefore, to put water back into a lake will be fantastic. We will be able to regenerate our fish traps, be able to show it to the world. (Daryl Rose, Gunditjmara Elder, Radio National 2007).

References

Aboriginal Affairs Victoria and Kerrup Jmara Aboriginal Corporation. 1993. *Lake Condah: Heritage Management Plan and Strategy*. Report prepared by Context Pty Ltd. Melbourne: Aboriginal Affairs Victoria.

Builth, Heather 2002. *The Archaeology and Socio-Economy of the Gunditj-mara: a Landscape Approach.* Ph.D. dissertation, Adelaide: Flinders University.

Builth, Heather 2003. "Tyrendarra Property: Plan of Management." Unpublished Report to Winda-Mara Aboriginal Corporation and Environment Australia.

Clark, Ian D. 1990a. "The People of the Lake, Lake Condah, Victoria, Australia: an Information Manual." Unpublished Report by Koorie Tourism Unit, Victorian Tourism Commission.

Clark, Ian D. 1990b. *Aboriginal Languages and Clans: An Historical Atlas of Western and Central Victoria.* Monash Publications in Geography, 37.

Coutts, Peter, Frank, Richard and Hughes, Phillip 1978. *Aboriginal Engineers of Western Victoria.* Records of the Victorian Archaeological Survey, 7.

Department of the Environment, Water, Heritage and the Arts (DEWHA). *Lady Julia Percy Island – Tyrendarra Area, Yambuk, VIC, Australia (Id. 105679).* National Heritage List nomination. Internet. Available from http://www.heritage.gov.au/ahp; accessed 10 July 2008.

Department of the Environment, Water, Heritage and the Arts (DEWHA). 2004a. *Budj Bim National Heritage Landscape – Mt Eccles Lake Condah Area, Mt Eccles Rd, Macarthur, VIC, Australia (Id. 105673).* National Heritage List. Internet. Available from http://www.heritage. gov.au/ahp; accessed 10 July 2008.

Department of the Environment, Water, Heritage and the Arts (DEWHA). 2004b. *Budj Bim National Heritage Landscape – Tyrendarra Area, Tyrendarra, VIC, Australia (Id. 105673).* National Heritage List. Internet. Available from http://www.heritage.gov.au/ahp; accessed 10 July 2008.

Minister for the Environment and Heritage, 2004. *"What's next for the National Heritage List?"* Media Release 16 July 2004.

North, Justice. *Consent determination. Lovett (on behalf of the Gunditjmara People) v State of Victoria [2007] FCA 474 (30 March 2007).* Internet. Available from http://www.atns.net.au/agreement.as; accessed 10 July 2008.

Rose, Deborah Bird. 1996. *Nourishing terrains: Australian Aboriginal views of landscape and wilderness.* Australian Heritage Commission, Canberra.

Rose, Daryl. 2007. *Native Title.* Australia Wide, ABC Radio National, Broadcast 16 April 2007.

Winda Mara Aboriginal Corporation. 2008. *Lake Condah Restoration Project Conservation Management Plan.* Report prepared by Context Pty Ltd. for Winda Mara Aboriginal Corporation, Heywood.

Wai Ō Puka/Fyffe Historic Area
Transmitting the Spirit of Place

Robyn L. Burgess
New Zealand Historic Places Trust Pouhere Taonga
New Zealand

Alan G. Jolliffe
University of Canterbury
New Zealand

Raewyn J. Solomon and John W. Wilson
Te Rūnanga o Kaikōura
New Zealand

ABSTRACT

Wai ō Puka/Fyffe Historic Area in Kaikōura, New Zealand, has had over eight
centuries of human habitation. Its powerful landscape and unique marine
environment have enabled the establishment of a succession of settlements by
enterprising and innovative people. With the objective of ascertaining how
spirit is transmitted, consultation and an analysis of visitor surveys identify
differing levels of response to both place and transmission tools. Structural
and archaeological remains, printed and electronic material, guides and oral
histories all tell stories. These especially revolve around notable Māori settlement
phases and later European whaling and farming. Recently a contemporary pole
carving was erected, emphasising both the place's Wāhi Tapu status and the
guardianship role that local Māori, Ngāti Kuri, have in actively managing the
cultural landscape. It is concluded that the environmental an cultural landscape
is an integral part of the spirit of this place and its communities safeguard and
revitalize that spirit.

RÉSUMÉ

En Nouvelle-Zélande, le site de Wai ō Puka, ou Région historique de
Fyffe, a connu des habitations humaines pendant plus de huit siècles.
Son paysage impressionnant et son environnement maritime unique ont
permis l'établissement d'une succession d'habitats de gens entreprenants

et novateurs. Dans le but de définir la manière dont se transmet l'esprit du lieu, une consultation et une analyse de sondages effectués auprès des visiteurs identifient différents niveaux de réponses, à la fois au lieu et aux outils de transmission. Les vestiges structurels et archéologiques, le matériel imprimé ou électronique, les guides et les narrations orales, tous racontent des histoires. Ces dernières, en particulier, tournent autour des phases d'occupation maori les plus importantes, et plus tard des installations d'Européens venus chasser la baleine et cultiver la terre. Récemment fut érigé un poteau sculpté contemporain, soulignant à la fois le statut *wahi tapu* (sacré pour le peuple Maori) du lieu, et le rôle de gardiens qu'ont les Maoris locaux, la tribu des Ngati Kuri, dans la gestion active du paysage culturel. L'article conclut que le paysage environnemental et culturel fait partie intégrante de l'esprit de ce lieu et que ses communautés préservent et revitalisent cet esprit.

The purpose of this study is to identify those aspects of Wai ō Puka/Fyffe Historic Area that contribute to Spirit of Place and investigate reasons and methods for transmitting the layers of spirit to current and future generations. A number of different approaches were taken.

The Māori *hapū* (sub-tribe) Ngāti Kuri holds a special *kaitiakitanga* (guardianship) role for the area. A key component of the investigation has been to look at how they interpret the concept of Spirit of Place and see its transmission occurring.

In addition, observations made by curator-guides at Fyffe House have been examined. Such guides provide personalised visitor interaction and report anecdotally the interests, experiences and comments by visitors. Data from regular visitor surveys carried out at Fyffe House over three years has also been considered to identify methods visitors thought best in transmitting messages about the place.

The authors too have had the opportunity to observe community and visitor behaviour and reactions to identify both new and old ways of transmission.

From a variety of sources the authors are able to draw some conclusions about the transmittal of Spirit of Place that stretch well beyond the defined site of Fyffe Historic Area alone.

Identifying Spirit of Place

The ICOMOS New Zealand Charter for the Conservation of Places of Cultural Heritage Value (1993) recognises that New Zealand retains a unique assemblage of places of cultural heritage value relating to its indigenous (Māori) and its more recent peoples.

Loh (2007) suggests that Spirit of Place in historic sites encompasses the meanings of the place accrued through time and through its past and present uses, and that these intangible values are expressed through tangible built heritage. However, if only *built* heritage is considered as a conduit for giving character to intangible values, it excludes heritage sites where *natural* heritage embodies the intangibles. The geography and location of New Zealand with its awesome natural landscapes is a strong part of the cultural identity of the nation.

In particular, Māori do not distinguish built heritage from the natural environment as places of cultural heritage significance. This is because the natural landscape equates to cultural landscape which in turn relates to *tīpuna* or ancestral landscape. Physical place is an expression of *whakapapa* (genealogy). It includes indigenous perspectives about the relationships between people and the environment and is also the story of the individual elements of that environment. This concept of the indivisible nature of Māori culture with the environment, and culturally appropriate ways to interpret this, is increasingly being explored (Keelan 1993). The Tongariro National Park, a series of three volcanoes in New Zealand's central North Island, is noted as being the first place inscribed on the World Heritage List for its associative cultural values linked to the natural environment, the mountains being ancestral entities to Māori of that region (Fraser 2007).

The interweaving of cultural, archaeological, built and natural heritage is integral to Wai ō Puka/Fyffe Historic Area. Set on the Kaikōura Peninsula looking out to both the sea and nearby mountains, the area represents a microcosm of the history of New Zealand. It contains an inter-related group of historic places that provide evidence of successive occupation and use of the area since the earliest times of settlement in what is the youngest country in the world to have been discovered and occupied by humans. The sea beside Kaikōura is astonishingly deep, with an ocean trench reaching depths of 870 metres only a kilometre offshore, and more than 1600 metres in canyons further out. The trench is a source of rich nutrients and home to a wide variety of sea life, including whales.

Ngāti Kuri see this area as an integral part of a much larger cultural landscape that is part of their cultural identity:

The origin of Te Wai ō Puka lies within the history of how the canoe of Aoraki was wrecked upon a reef in the ocean waters. The eastern or lower side of the canoe was splintered and scattered. Tu te Raki Whanoa sent his son Marokura to re-assemble the fragments in order to make that side of the canoe welcoming to humans (the new creation of Tane).

Marokura gathered the broken thwarts and decorations of the canoe and arranged them in such a way that they became the home for sea life and which also caught the warmth of the sun which would in turn enhance the growth of plants.

The eastern side of the South Island has many peninsulas which trace their origin to the work of Marokura. One of the major peninsulas is Kaikōura. The shaping task of Marokura is remembered in the name Te Tai o Marokura, which is applied to the sea along the Kaikōura coastline.

The coming of Maui is also recalled in this area through the story of his discovery of the North Island from the viewpoint of the peninsula hills. The spirit of his discovery is embedded in the story of how he stood in his canoe, braced his foot against the thwart and with the great weight of the sacred fish on his line, broke out the timber thwart. Henceforth the name for the Kaikōura Peninsula became Te Taumanu o te Waka a Maui (the thwart of the canoe of Maui). The baiting of the hook which he used to catch the fish is remembered in the nearby Marae – Te Whaka Takahanga a Maui.

Each successive ancestral canoe is remembered in the place names which surround Wai ō Puka/Fyffe Historic Area.

The sheltering range of mountains is known as the "standing food stores of Rakihouia", the cliffs of the peninsula as the "food store of Rakihouia".

Kaikōura itself, as a town and district, receives its name from the visit of Tama ki te Rangi, who fished the crayfish (kōura) resources of the rocky coast. Te Ahi Kai Kōura a Tama ki te Rangi being the correct form of the common, modern name of Kaikōura.

Beyond the coastal waters of Te Tai o Marokura is the vast ocean, the dwelling of Tangaroa. Ngāti Kuri have direct whakapapa links with Tangaroa and have accepted the Kaitiakitanga of the seashore and open waters complete with its myriad of living creatures. This acceptance and whakapapa relationship has been asserted by the erection of the carved post "Tangaroa" in the early years of this century.

These creation and ancestral stories have been passed on from generation to generation with meticulous attention to detail. Māori were without the written word until the arrival of Europeans in New Zealand from the late 18th century, and today oral history continues to be an important way of passing on knowledge.

The earliest occupants of Wai ō Puka/Fyffe Historic Area were hunter-gatherer Māori who camped some 800-900 years ago at what was then a sandy bay on the peninsula (Trotter & McCulloch 1989). Archaeological investigation shows that, from this site, early Māori hunted large flightless birds known as moa, now extinct, and other native birds, and they caught fish and seals (ibid). The place was also used for burial, as evidenced by an accidental discovery in 1857 of a grave from the moa-hunter period. Widely documented at the time of discovery in the mid 19th century, this significant grave contained the crouching skeleton of a male holding a deliberately perforated moa egg along with one or more adze heads (Trotter & McCulloch 1993).

Archaeology and oral histories record that the area was later visited by descendants of these earliest people from time to time. Later, about 300-400 years ago, the site was used by Māori for cultivation and other activities such as fowling and fishing (Trotter & McCulloch 1989).

From about AD 1500, a number of pā (fortified settlement areas) were built in the wider area of the Kaikōura Peninsula (Jones 2007). Takahanga itself was a pā and is now the site of Ngāti Kuri's modern *marae* (main meeting place) of the same name.

The first European settlement in the area was in 1842 with the establishment of Robert Fyfe's shore whaling station, the Wai ō Puka Fishery. By 1849 with the decline in the number of whales from over-hunting, Fyfe had turned to farming, making him the first pastoralist in the Kaikōura region. Graves and material relating to both whaling and sheep farming activities have been found in the area (Harris 1994).

Fyffe House is a significant survivor from this period of early European settlement. The eastern wing comprises the whaling station's cooper's cottage from the mid 1840s, built on whale bone vertebrae foundations. It was later added to by Robert Fyfe's cousin George Fyffe, who had managed the whaling station after Robert died in 1854.[1] Today Fyffe House appears much the same as it was by 1863.

Other 19th century European activity in the area included a hotel, customs, fishing, wharfage businesses and the use of Kaikōura as a port. Not all of these activities lasted but tangible evidence of them remains in the area. Structural remains include whale bone fence posts, foundations of buildings, remains of the old sea wall, a stone fireplace from a bonded warehouse, part of the old wharf itself and historic fence lines.

In 1981 Fyffe House was gifted to the New Zealand Historic Places Trust Pouhere Taonga ("the Trust") and since then it has been open to the public, serving as both a house museum and a place for interpreting the layers of history and surrounding environment. It is registered by the Trust as a Category I historic place in recognition of its outstanding significance, and is encompassed within the Trust registered Fyffe Historic Area which includes not only the house but a wider range of structural and archaeological features, both Māori and European. In 2007, the general area was also registered by the Trust as a Wāhi Tapu in recognition of the sacredness of the site to Māori, especially Ngāti Kuri, who acknowledge both the past occupation and uses of the site by their ancestors such as Rapuwai, Waitaha and Ngāti Mamoe.

Transmitting Spirit of Place

A key method of transmission of Spirit of Place is through interpretation. This occurs at a range of levels.

---

1.   Although first cousins, Robert Fyfe and George Fyffe spelt their surname differently.

Visitors to Fyffe House are hosted by the guide who is able to provide a personalised introduction and answer questions about the house and historic area, including aspects of human endeavour associated with the area. Guides also provide an explanation of the region, its natural elements, values, points of interest and economic activities. Displays and documentation throughout the house, grounds and general area provide further self-guided interpretation, including records of conservation and restoration programmes.

The guides have adapted to a changing world of interactive, inquisitive, authenticity seeking, knowledgeable visitors with a desire to learn in such a way that they now provide more information of a contextual and conceptual nature to put the Spirit of Place in a wider context. For example, Wai ō Puka/ Fyffe Historic Area can tell the story of whaling as part of the history of the place – and visitors can smell whale oil, touch and smell blubber and handle baleen and whalebone – but it can also be an opportunity to consider why New Zealand now opposes whaling. This sort of engagement of visitors' minds and emotions through interpretation and facilitation may be considered "meaning making" (Ham 2002) and an opportunity to "ask questions that lead to new insights" (Dural and Dural 2007).

Visitor surveys asking both national and international visitors what they enjoyed most about their visit to Fyffe House consistently show that "History/Authenticity" of the place together with "Staff/Guides" provide the highest level of enjoyment (75-90%) whereas "Displays and other information" have tended to rate lower (around 35%) (Khatep-Bardsley & McIntosh 2005-2008).

The concept of authenticity is essential to conveying the Spirit of Place. McKercher and du Cros (2002) write that "intangible heritage management principles suggest that the integrity of the cultural place plays an important role in presenting an authentic experience." There is an increasing awareness that house museums, such as Fyffe House, have a responsibility to ensure that "authentic" stories are told, including those of tangible and intangible heritage of indigenous communities. It is recognised that Ng ti Kuri have the right to determine how their own stories are told and increasingly in recent times they have been involved in broadening the range of transmission tools used at Wai ō Puka/Fyffe Historic Area.

A special transmission tool that has revitalised the way Spirit of Place is conveyed is the recent erection of a contemporary *pou* (carved pole) within Wai ō Puka/Fyffe Historic Area. Representing *Tangaroa* and carved in a modern style by Kaikōura carver Makarini Solomon, the *pou* represents the area's dual heritage. The bottom carving of a whale is significant for three reasons. Firstly, it links to Ngāti Kuri *whakapapa* from *Paikea* who came to New Zealand on the back of a whale. Secondly, the area is associated with whaling and thirdly, the fortunes of the town in the present and future are tied with eco-tourism and whale watching. Above the whale is the moa egg for this is the site where a significant early grave was found with the world's largest known moa egg. Above the egg is a stylised moa, from which the egg came, and which also was the prey of the earliest people of Kaikōura. Carved above the moa is a human form but without a head for two reasons. His head contained the knowledge and this has been lost over time. Also, when the early burial was found, his head was reburied separate from his body. On either side of the body are a *taiaha* (Māori spear) and a whaling harpoon, representing the separate and combined history of the site. Above the body are scrolls of *kowhaiwahi*, the symbol of life where the past, present and future are all intertwined. The head of the carving is that of *Tangaroa* who stares out to *Te Tai o Marokura* (the sea in front of Kaikōura). The sea and its gifts have been an integral part of the lives of the local people for centuries. *Tangaroa* guards and protects this heritage.

Since the *Tangaroa pou* was completed in 2002, two other *pou* (representing *Maui*) have been installed at the entrance to a well used and interpreted walking track on the peninsula, and it is likely that others will be added in the future. All these *pou* are akin to markers as described by Leiper (1995) which act, in conjunction with the existing built and natural heritage, to provide a link between visitors and place. As well as contributing to interpretation, the *pou* reinforce the status and the guardianship role that Ngāti Kuri have in actively managing the cultural landscape.

Te Poha o Tohu Raumati is Te Rūnanga o Kaikōura's environmental resource management plan that documents Ngāti Kuri's approach to environmental and cultural resources. It identifies the significance of *taonga* (treasure) species of the land, sky and sea. For Ngāti Kuri, the concept of Spirit of Place is based on the *whakapapa* of all things existing there and linked to the place, including birds, plants and sea creatures, rocks and streams, the earth beneath and the air above. They are elements of the Spirit of Place.

Knowledge of the environment and appropriate use for sustainability is seen not only by Māori as a treasure passed on by the ancestors to the present generations but also something which all New Zealanders are increasingly trying to grasp. Therefore resource management methods such as ecological restoration, including *rahui* (a community initiative for a restrictive take in the coastal waters), have a role to play in safeguarding Spirit of Place.

Spirit of Place comes alive in the ways an area is used and valued by communities (Loh 2007) and serving the needs of the local community is usually a valuable and sustainable goal for historic sites (Vogt 2007). While Fyffe House itself is a visitor attraction, the house and general area is also special to the Kaikōura community. Locals are able to visit Fyffe House without charge, and the grounds are used for community events such as "Jazz on the Lawn," Sea Week and Conservation Week events, and celebrating the launch of the *rahui*.

For the Kaikōura community, there are varied needs and desires. However, in recent times there is an increased appreciation of the cultural and historic significance of Wai ō Puka/Fyffe Historic Area, and of Māori culture generally, of the peninsula and its environs and of its relevance to present and future generations.

These days the modern town of Kaikōura has a population of around 3,200 residents and it attracts around one million short-stay visitors each year, the majority of whom are drawn to the environment and its eco-tourism attractions especially those revolving around marine mammal watching. Whale Watch Kaikōura is a tribally owned, managed and executed tourism venture that, by its huge commercial success, has helped take local Māori values and visibility to new levels. It has helped raised the status of Māori people and Māori values and, in conjunction with Takahanga *marae*, has contributed to attitudinal changes in the community.

Today the Kaikōura District Council consults with, and is guided by, Te Rūnanga o Kaikōura before determining whether to grant resource consents. Very recently established is *Te Korowai o Te Tai o Marokura*, a committee which draws together all user groups and stakeholders interested in coastal and land environmental issues in the area.

Weaving the Layers

The Spirit of Wai ō Puka/Fyffe Historic Area includes the layers of genealogy that acknowledge not only all those that have gone before but the whole of the environment. Most of the layers relate to Māori history, the later layers being Māori and European history interwoven.

Fyffe House, itself a rare and significant building, provides a pivotal on-site point for exploring the history of the site. However, as well as the usual techniques of interpretation through guiding, documentation, static and interactive displays, additional transmission tools are effective with respect to Wai ō Puka/Fyffe Historic Area.

Simply *being there* in this place allows people to experience the awe and wonder of this distinct powerful landscape and marine environment and understand at least something of why people have been drawn to the area over many centuries.

Ngāti Kuri, as the traditional people and *kaitiaki*, determine how their stories are transmitted. This includes conveying history through people, the recognition and use of traditional place names and protocols as well as new approaches such the *Tangaroa pou* contemporary carving. The successful whale watching eco-tourism business is incredibly powerful in terms of Ngāti Kuri storytelling and transmitting Spirit of Place to others. Such transmission has contributed to positive effects on improving community relationships and cultural and environmental awareness.

Resource management tools for sustainability such as heritage place protection and conservation, retention of landmarks, land and marine resource management and protection, and ecological restoration all help safeguard the wider Spirit of Place. Community involvement in Wai ō Puka/Fyffe Historic Area and the general environment revitalizes the spirit and encourages community engagement and an appreciation of the adaptive use of this place and its physical, spiritual and cultural values.

Acknowledgements

The authors are grateful to the following people for their guidance and assistance in writing this paper: Tim Manawatu, Roger Fyfe, Ann McCaw, Helen Brown, Dean Whiting, Kevin Jones and David Reynolds.

References

Dural, J and A N Dural. 2007. A Golden Age for Historic Properties. *History News*. Summer: 7-16.

Fraser, Liann. 2007. Tongariro National Park A Myth-laden View of Nature. *World Heritage* 46 (June): 8-17.

Harris, Jan. 1994. *Tohorā, The Story of Fyffe House, Kai Kōura, New Zealand*. Wellington: Historic Places Trust Pouhere Taonga.

Ham, Sam H. 2002. *Making Meaning – The Premise and promise of Interpretation*. Scotland's First National Conference on Interpretation, Edinburgh: 4 April, 2002.

ICOMOS New Zealand. 1993. *ICOMOS New Zealand Charter for the Conservation of Places of Cultural Heritage Value*.

Jones, Kevin L. 2007. *The Penguin Field Guide to New Zealand Archaeology*. Auckland: Penguin Group Ltd.

Keelan, Ngawini. 1993. Māori Heritage: Visitor Management and Interpretation. In *Heritage Management in New Zealand and Australia*, ed. C Michael Hall and Simon McArthur: 95-102. Auckland: Oxford University Press.

Khatep-Bardsley, Medihah and Alison McIntosh. Fyffe House: Quarterly visitor survey results over the period 2005-2007 (unpublished), The University of Waikato Management School, for New Zealand Historic Places Trust Pouhere Taonga.

Leiper, N. 1995. *Tourism Management*. Melbourne: RMIT Publishing.

Loh, Laurence. 2007. Conveying the Spirit of Place. In *Asia Conserved: Lessons Learned from the UNESCO Asia-Pacific Heritage Awards for Culture Heritage Conservation (2000-2004)*, ed. Richard Engelhardt and Montira Horayangura Unakul: 9-12 (August). Bangkok: UNESCO.

McKercher, B and H Le Cros. 2002. *Cultural Tourism: The Partnership between Tourism and Cultural Heritage Management.* New York: The Howarth Hospitality Press.

Te Rūnanga o Kaikōura. 2005. *Te Poha o Tohu Raumati: Te Rūnanga o Kaikōura Environmental Management Plan.* Kaikōura: Te Rūnanga o Kaikōura, Takahanga Marae.

Todd, Barbara. 1999. *Whales &Dolphins, Kaikōura, New Zealand.* Wellington: Barbara Todd.

Trotter, Michael, and Beverley McCulloch. 1989. *Unearthing New Zealand.* Wellington: Government Printing Office.

Trotter, Michael, and Beverley McCulloch. 1993. Fyffe's Revisited. In *Records of the Canterbury Museum*, Vol 10, No 7:73-94.

Vogt, J D. 2007. The Kykuit II Summit: The sustainability of historic sites. *History News.* Autumn: 17-21.

Mexican Vernacular Architecture and the Spirit of Place Case Study of Tlacotalpan

Valeria Prieto
ICOMOS CIAV
Universidad Autónoma Metropolitana
México

Luis Guerrero
ICOMOS CIAV
Universidad Autónoma Metropolitana
México

Abstract

In 1998 the city of Tlacotalpan, Veracruz, was selected by UNESCO to become part of the World Heritage List. However, the spirit of place has been exposed to many threats, such as the destruction of some of the traditional buildings and changes in cultural behavior. We have been identifying the causes for the abandoning or deterioration of the heritage and proposed several measures to the local authorities to prevent more destruction and to recover the heritage as a whole with all its immaterial expressions. In this proposal we are seeks ways for people to recover their pride in their cultural expressions and built heritage.

Résumé

En 1998, la ville de Tlacotalpan, dans la région de Veracruz, fut sélection-née par l'Unesco pour être inscrite sur la Liste du Patrimoine mondial. Cependant, l'esprit du lieu a depuis été exposé à de nombreuses menaces, telles que la destruction de quelques-uns des bâtiments traditionnels et des changements dans le comportement culturel. Nous avons identifié les causes de l'abandon ou de la dégradation du patrimoine, et proposé aux autorités locales plusieurs mesures destinées à prévenir d'autres destructions et à recouvrer le patrimoine dans son ensemble, avec toutes ses expressions immatérielles. Nous recherchons des voies pour que les gens retrouvent la fierté de leurs expressions culturelles et de leur patrimoine bâti.

Tlacotalpan is on the bank of the Papaloapan River – the « river of butterflies » – on the plains on the lee side of Veracruz, where the sun runs its course from east to west, moving from the Ixtlán de Juárez mountain chain – where the river's majestic current is born – to its mouth on the Alvarado Bar, in the Gulf of Mexico.

Chronicles claim that many of the Spaniards that came to Mexico were originally from the Canaries. The cult of the Virgin of Candelaria can be traced back to those times; an old Spanish family that settled in the region donated it when the first Catholic Church curate was established in the church in Tlacotalpan. The cult of the Virgin of Candelaria subsisted syncretically with the pre-Hispanic rites to the indigenous Chalchiuhtlicue, goddess of the waters, venerated in a large part of Mesoamerica during the post-Classic period. (Aguirre 1972)

The life of Tlacotalpan's inhabitants has been secularly linked to the river, which have been both a means of subsistence for them and the source of their afflictions when its waters overflow. This is one of the reasons why we insist that it is where the spirit of the place lies: it is the link between all activities, traditions and customs developed by this society over centuries in its riverbed and it surrounding areas.

Figure 1. Traditional glazed tile.

The urban grid responds to Spanish norms established in the Laws of the Indies [*Leyes de Indias*]: there is a main square, or *Plaza de Armas* – now called Plaza Zaragoza –, where the Council Hall [*Casa Consistorial*] was built and which today holds the Municipal Palace; and the Casa Mata, where gunpowder was stored and which was later used as a municipal jail, and currently serves as a handicraft shop. Also next to the plaza, alongside the stately homes, the temple dedicated to the Virgin of Candelaria was built in the 18th century. On another corner of the Plaza, the Parish of San Cristóbal, patron saint of the city, was completed in 1851.

As well as the main square, the foundational grid includes the religious plaza, called Parque Hidalgo, which is delimited by the above mentioned sanctuary to the Virgin of Candelaria, as well as the relevant facades and their porticos of the city houses.

Figure 2. Virgin of Candelaria Church.

Tlacotalpan's architecture is distinctive; it derives from Caribbean forms and climate, and from the customs of this historic community related to the river's deep currents, which provided it with a livelihood and an origin. Arcades, roofs, eaves, balconies, corridors and narrow, grass-covered streets which follow the meandering river captivate the visitor that explores plazas and open spaces which subtly intertwine. The spontaneous use of contrasting colors that characterizes the city was perhaps the result of the intense tropical luminosity and the brilliant tones of the nature around it.

Figure 3. Local trader.

All these compositional elements of its architecture, urbanism and nature are an indissoluble part of the Tlacotalpan spirit of place; it emerges in the expressions that make up the old city's context, which in turn are the result of this society's interaction with its natural environment.

However, it is important to recognize that this interaction is based on an incredibly fragile balance in which any alteration of its components and relationships would surely have an impact on the whole. There is a delicate organic relation between each part of the city, its community, nature and the traditions that needs to be preserved so that the spirit of place remains.

Life in the early 21st century in our country is certainly different to the way it took place in 19th century Tlacotalpan. Although the city remained unaltered in the decades after its economic displacement, it couldn't escape the impact of urban growth in other towns in the state and the country as a whole, as well as the influence of the mass media.

These phenomena have been reflected in the loss of a substantial part of their urban cultural heritage: the grass streets, for example, have given way in many areas of the city to concrete paving, adocret or asphalt, losing not only their attractiveness but also their profound relationship to nature.

Figure 4. Adocrete paving.

Traditional architecture has been partly affected by the introduction of unrelated elements to the old mansions. The indiscriminate introduction of urban furniture in accordance with the personal tastes of different mayors and authorities has resulted in the loss of the simple unity provided by the old street lighting, the early 20th century brickwork benches in the parks and other elements associated to the history of the city. When the vernacular architecture of the surroundings and the general environment of the city are affected, the true spirit of place is endangered.

The following text includes a proposal for reintegrating cultural heritage with the close participation of the city and its authorities, for the recovery of the riverbank, and the description of some of the values that give a sense to the spirit of Tlacotalpan, all of these as the basis for its safeguard and transcendence to future generations.

Figure 5. Panoramic view from the river.

The City in Time and Space

The area has been populated since pre-Hispanic times, and slightly before the European conquest its people depended on the Mexica Empire. It is said that Emperor Moctezuma sent his right-hand men to rule the place and collect tributes. (Del Paso 1961: 4)

The mouth of the Papaloapan River was discovered by Juan de Grijalva in 1518; later, Pedro de Alvarado explored its waters in an attempt to find inland routes after a small community had been established in the preexisting native village. (Malpica 1974: XIV)

In the beginning the village was built predominantly by natives and black slaves brought by the Spaniards who fished for a living. It took Tlacotalpan many years to be populated by Spaniards: in 1544 there were only 12 of them; in 1667, 30 were registered; by 1727 the number had grown to 240, and in 1777 there were already 320. In terms of the indigenous and black populations, demographic data are scarce and even contradictory. (Blázquez, 1989, 21)

Figure 6. Some of the streets follow the river shape.

Tlacotalpan was an island surrounded by the Papaloapan and the Chiquito rivers. However, as the years went by, the Chiquito's sediment transformed Tlacotalpan into a peninsula. Since the beginning the urban structure was guided by a grid formed by three streets, parallel to the river, which were crossed by narrow, perpendicular streets in a way that adapted to the topography. (César 1973: 25-27)

In the early 19th century, its singular image began to take shape around one-storey houses, continuous arcades with semicircular arches, and tiled roofs. On different occasions the high attics, designed as livable spaces, served as shelter for their inhabitants when they needed to protect themselves from the sporadic floods produced by the river.

Tlacotalpan became the commercial center for the region due to its privileged location near the port of Veracruz, and was connected to the Gulf of Mexico by the wide and navigable Papaloapan River, which was the region's means of communication.

The 19th century represented a moment of splendor for the city due to economic development attained from its success in fishing and cattle, but above all because of its center for trade activities at a national and international level. Products were exchanged with Havana, Cadiz, Malaga, Flanders, Genoa and Granada; later their mercantile dealings included Caracas, Marseille, New Orleans and other ports in the United States.

Towards the mid-19th century, the development of sugar cane and its rapid industrialization had great effect on the construction of haciendas. Simultaneously, the local society's culture developed.

The construction of arcades belongs to this period, as well as the tile roofs and the balconies with iron or wood bars. Many public buildings and roads, as well as the park with its kiosk and large mansions, resulted from the economic growth of the area, and have a European influence.

In these times of early 20th-century bonanza the city had 300 oil street-lamps, eight offices, six public schools and four private ones, three hotels, nine factories, a parish, two churches, one hospital, one jail, 54 huts, 1201 one-storey houses, 25 two-storey ones and one 3-storey house. (Alafita 1989: 61)

Figure 7. The construction of arcades belongs to the XIXth Century.

As opposed to other populations that perceived the railroad's arrival as their source of progress, for Tlacotalpan it meant the beginning of its decline, since the transport of goods through the river became unnecessary with time. With the crisis of the sugar mills and the Revolution of 1910, the city slowly began to be slip into oblivion.

In the 1940s, the typical character of the village and the fact that its architectural features had persisted, its urban grid and grass-covered streets made it attractive to tourism, and Mexican film stars began to visit it. In 1968 the Mexican government declared it a Typical City, and in 1986 it became a Historic Monument Zone, considering among other things that the "formal features of the city's constructions, the relationship between spaces, the urban structure formed by its neighborhoods and its natural environment, just as they are preserved today, are an eloquent testimonial which is of exceptional value for the social, political and art history of Mexico". (Diario Oficial 1986)

However, it was not until a bridge over the Papaloapan was built in the seventies that Tlacotalpan began to be rediscovered by many visitors.

In 1998, because of its distinctive features and its outstanding universal values, Tlacotalpan was declared Heritage of Humanity by UNESCO.

Figure 8. World Heritage UNESCO memorial.

Tlacotalpan: The Spirit of its Vernacular Architecture

A distinctive symbol of local architecture is the presence of arcade facades that create semiprivate spaces that are an extension of the house onto the street. These spaces also provide shade and protection, and cool the air that goes inside the house.

Sometimes the sidewalk protrudes beyond the arcade and pedestrians walk on it. In the middle of the street – opening a space for vegetation – is a zone where cars can circulate. This model for the streets and the way they are used is an urban quality that has survived from the Colonial period to our days.

It is worthy of note that the values of greatest importance for the creation of the World Heritage dossier were precisely the singularity of Tlacotalpan's vernacular architecture and its striking degree of conservation.

This document considered that the heritage city "met the second, fourth and fifth criteria of the Convention's Operational Guidelines, due to its architectural and urban singularity, its link to Caribbean culture, its communion with the natural environment and the impact it has on a traditional culture's identity, which is threatened by the myth of modernity increasingly more. (…) The acknowledgement of Tlacotalpan as cultural heritage of humanity means the recognition of the exceptional universal value of anonymous architecture, the simplicity and economy of the construction, of vernacular urbanism, traditional 19th and 20th century buildings, cultural plurality and the popular character of its inhabitants." (Guerrero 2000: 49)

Figure 9. The Tlacotalpan built heritage it is linked to Caribbean culture.

Unfortunately, in our country not only does vernacular architecture have no legal protection whatsoever; it is also undervalued by its own creators and by its inhabitants, who consider it to be part of a past that is linked to economic backwardness.

Tlacotalpan has not escaped that national phenomenon and suffers its consequences. In addition to this sentiment there is the influence held nowadays by large urban areas in the country which have apparent economic success, and the successful publicity that is given to industrialized construction systems that are totally foreign to traditional locations.

The Tlacotalpan cultural heritage is threatened by alterations due to the presence of buildings that are not quite authentic, as well as the introduction of materials to their streets that do not belong to the original setting, which for esthetic, historic, functional and even ecological reasons have an impact on this valuable heritage that has been preserved for nearly three centuries.

Some of the urban spaces where the spirit of place is particularly present are the ancient streets, which are planted with grass from Tlacotalpan and provide tranquility and freshness in face of the city's hot sun. Other elements that speak of this spirit are the arcades and the balconies, the tiled roofing and the facades with battlements and mouldings.

Without a doubt the use of color that the people from Tlacotalpan have spontaneously employed for various centuries is perhaps the best example of the way in which the spirit of place is kept alive, despite the threats that contemporary changes have posed for the city.

That spirit is also present in the famous wood and wicker rocking chairs; in the fabric used for women's white dresses; in the typical drink, *toritos*, a mixture of sugarcane liquor, milk, tropical fruits and sugar; in the music, through its famous *sones* and *cantares jarochos*, during which the singer improvises one verse after another, alluding to the people present or to some noteworthy event. These *sones*, vibrant and very cheerful music, also inspire something in *Jarocha* dancers and their companions, who dance in the fandangos, the popular fiestas that they celebrate in the outside plazas, taking advantage of the evening's fresh air.

The city's major fiesta is the one celebrated in honor of the Virgin of Candelaria, in which not only does the entire village participate, but also thousands of people from the entire region. The main attraction is the Bull Run, where they chase people through the narrow streets, in the best Pamplona style.

The spirit of place is also present in Tlacotalpan through its entire intangible heritage: its legends, recipes, music, verses and, of course, in the framework that encloses it – tangible heritage and zones of natural beauty.

Figure 10. Candelaria "fiesta" day.

Research and Proposal for the Reintegration of Heritage

As a city that is included in the List of World Heritage, Tlacotalpan receives financial support from the Mexican government for the rehabilitation and conservation of its built heritage. For this reason the Social Development Secretariat, which is in charge of providing consulting and support to the municipal government, requested a study from us on the current state of built heritage and the necessary means for its reintegration and conservation.

In order to analyze the situation of built heritage to date in the city of Tlacotalpan, the study included both fieldwork and documentary office-work. During fieldwork, buildings were analyzed as well as the physical elements of the surroundings included in the area that forms the Historic Monument Zone (HMZ).

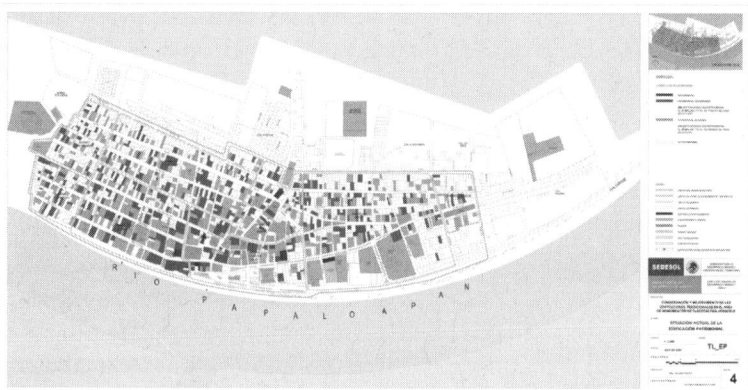

Figure 11. Tlacotalpan documentation urban chart.

In order to facilitate the analysis of buildings as well as the different interventions which over the years have taken place in the HMZ, a conventional classification was adopted in the buildings and land, which we quote here:

Monumental: heritage composed of buildings defined in the Federal Law on Archeological, Artistic and Historic Monuments and Zones as "buildings constructed from the 16th- to the 19th-century inclusive (…)". It also notes that it considers "artistic monuments to be those built in the 20th century with relevant esthetic value." The religious monuments are the Candelaria, San Cristóbal and San Miguel temples; the civil monuments are the Netzahualcóyotl theatre, the municipal market, the cultural center and the library.

Preserved Heritage: buildings that have been maintained without being altered, preserving their original characteristics.

Modified Heritage: heritage buildings that were later intervened and altered.

Contextual Non-Heritage: recent buildings that have attempted to maintain a harmonious relationship with the context.

Out-of-context: buildings that have not taken into account the architectural and urban characteristics of the heritage city.

Precarious Settlements: housing built with scarce resources.

Empty lots: lands without buildings of any sort.

An examination of the results indicates that more than 70% of the structures that make up the city can be considered to be heritage architecture, despite the fact that a part of this percentage refers to buildings that have been altered, but which can be feasibly recovered.

In terms of other aspects of the urban context, such as the street and sidewalk pavements, we indicate in the study that there are several materials that do not preserve the unity of the whole; the same happens with urban furnishings.

One of the most serious problems the current population faces in the city is the lack of jobs. For this reason many young people have migrated to other cities or countries. However, the city is appropriate for investments related to the tourist and agricultural industries, as well as small industries for restoration materials for the buildings.

In terms of the infrastructure, we saw that due to the floods experienced by the city when the river overflows, it is necessary to separate pluvial drainage from residual waters and build a treatment plant. On the other hand, in order to prevent trucks from circulating within the patrimonial city it is fundamental that a bypass be built from the access road.

It is a priority to consider the recovery of the river zone, which is of great natural beauty, and this demands an improvement in the services offered by the small fish and seafood restaurants as well as the restructuring of businesses. Also, fishermen that live in precarious houses by the riverside should be relocated; at the same time, this zone should be provided with a duly planned area for fishing and for selling fish.

We have been in contact with some of city dwellers who sound skeptical with regards to the advantages presented by their cultural heritage, composed as it is by the buildings and its urban context. Many people do not consider their quality of life to have improved at all as a result of the site being declared World Heritage.

It is necessary to promote the development of jobs so the population can to relate the conservation of the city to an increase in their well-being. Also, it is convenient to broadcast the concept of "heritage city" and its landscape attractions beyond the city's own borders, so that its inhabitants regain pride in their city, their customs and their exceptional traditions.

Figure 12. Cultural built heritage is threatened by alterations.

It is necessary to begin the rehabilitation, conservation and reintegration of buildings, as well as the progressive unification of pavements on all the roads and the adequate design of urban furnishings. The study also proposes a slow modification of pavements and the conservation of grass, typical of the traditional town.

A rehabilitation program was proposed in parallel for properties that require conservation (they are for the most part examples of vernacular architecture) and those that should be recovered to their original character.

The program must also include the simple transmission of knowledge about what needs to be done in each case and a stimulus that holds the interest of building owners. This process of reintegration should be fostered by granting one part of the work's cost as a stimulus to neighbors that decide to carry out these modifications. In terms of which architectural elements should be preserved and which should be eliminated, a simple graphic manual for conservation and reintegration of buildings was put together. Here we show some images of the manual, which will be published this year and distributed among the city's inhabitants.

In light of the fact that financial needs influence the deterioration and abandonment of architectural heritage, and in order to improve the general conditions of the population and create more jobs, a tourist development program has been proposed that includes some of the old mansions as hotels with few rooms and good service.

It is fundamental to include the city in tourist circuits that include other nearby sites, such as the archeological zones and other places of natural beauty, and ecological tourism. Also, boat tours can be offered on the river to eat baked fish in one of the many palm groves nearby.

Figure 13. One of the main tourist attractions is the Zaragoza plaza.

We have also suggested that advantage be taken of the magnificent 20th-century theatre to offer music and dance spectacles, as well as rehabilitating the small local museum established in an old, traditional house in the city, with the aim of attracting visitors.

But as well as tourism, other kinds of financial activities bring with them the preservation of the city, such as the development of a production workshop for baked clay tiles, which would not only generates jobs, but also produce materials for restoring roofs in the area and could then sell tiles throughout the entire region.

Finally, it is necessary to fortify the municipal technical areas responsible for Tlacotalpan's conservation by providing specialized training workshops and a larger number of technicians.

Conclusions

The city of Tlacotalpan is a unique example in Mexico of the presence of many cultural values associated to a particular site and a historic community that has maintained its presence and customs through time. It is evident that notable efforts have been made to safeguard it and to preserve its tangible and intangible heritage.

For this reason, Mexico cannot allow for the distinctive sprit of place to be lost, for it has been created over a long time and has been captured in all artistic and historic expressions of the city and its inhabitants.

It is necessary to continue with these efforts in order to keep on listening to Tlacotalpan music and enjoy *Jarocho* dances and tunes, to maintain the coolness of its arcades and corridors, to continue to contemplate the Papaloapan riverbank, to maintain the authentic festivities of Tlacotalpan's inhabitants and reintegrate to its authentic heritage all the architectural values that characterize it.

However, vernacular architecture is a type of heritage that is difficult to conserve, since among its main qualities are spontaneous manifestations and, above all, dynamism.

It is evidently not enough to merely identify the values of this urban whole to achieve its conservation. It is necessary, as it happens in many other cities in the country, to try to find a balance between uncontrolled growth and the abandoning of buildings, between real estate speculation and a lack of interest in the lands, between the artificiality generated by tourism and the isolation that has achieved its preservation to date, between development and stagnation.

Tlacotalpan as heritage, just like the other Mexican natural and cultural sites that are registered in the UNESCO's list, must have a much greater impact on a local and regional level than on an international one.

The first step in safeguarding the site depends on its own inhabitants. The authorities can establish guidelines for its balanced growth and even regulate actions that preserve the city just as it is today. But the value provided by the wealth of its popular vitality cannot be granted by decree. It is not enough for people to know their city; they have to *recognize* it, that is to say, to *value* it as heritage that makes them proud and they wish to bequeath to future generations in better conditions than those they received it in.

With these thoughts we have sought to show how, despite the danger that threatens this exceptional place, the effort that the city and its authorities are making to preserve their historic roots intact, its valuable tangible and intangible cultural heritage and its spirit of place will have to culminate in the integral revitalization and preservation of Tlacotalpan.

Figure 14. Urban spaces live thanks to the use of their inhabitants.

References

Aguirre, Humberto. 1972. *Tlacotalpan, compilación histórica preliminar de una localidad típica. Desde el año "chicueye calli" (8-casa:1461) hasta nuestros días.* México D.F.: Dirección General de Arte Popular, S.E.P.

Alafita M., Leopoldo et al. 1989. Tlacotalpan. Cuando puerto fue. In *Anuario VI,* Xalapa: Centro de Investigaciones Históricas, Instituto de Investigaciones Humanísticas, Universidad Veracruzana.

Blázquez D., Carmen. 1989. San Cristóbal de Tlacotalpan: postrimerías coloniales en una región sotaventina (1760-1800). In *Anuario VI,* Xalapa: Centro de Investigaciones Históricas, Instituto de Investigaciones Humanísticas, Universidad Veracruzana.

César, Juan N. 1973. *Tlacotálpam 1859.* México D.F.: Citlaltépetl.

Del Paso y Troncoso, Francisco. 1961. Relación de Tlacotalpan y su Partido. *Revista Jarocha,* México D.F. No. 12, abril: 4-5.

Diario Oficial de la Federación, Miércoles 10 de diciembre de 1986. México D.F.: Gobierno Federal.

Gaceta Oficial, 10 de noviembre de 1998, Órgano del Gobierno del Estado de Veracruz-Llave, Xalapa.

Guerrero, Luis. 1997. Descripciones de Tlacotalpan durante el siglo XIX. *Estudios Históricos, Arquitectura y Diseño Gráfico II.* México D.F.: U.A.M.-Azcapotzalco.

Guerrero, Luis. 2000. Tlacotalpan, patrimonio de la humanidad. *Revista Bitácora,* México D.F., No. 2. Invierno.

Guerrero, Luis. 2000. Documentación de los rasgos tipológicos de Tlacotalpan, Veracruz. *Diseño y Sociedad,* México. D.F., No. 11, Invierno: 70-85.

Iglesias, Andrés. 1961. Tlacotalpan en 1856. *Revista Jarocha,* México D.F. No. 12, abril: 10-14.

Malpica, José Ma. 1974. *Tlacotalpan 1842-1915,* México D.F., Citlaltépetl.

Prieto, Valeria. 1978. *La Vivienda Campesina en México.* México D.F.: Secretaría de Asentamientos Humanos y Obras Públicas.

Prieto, Valeria. 2006. La arquitectura vernácula y el caso Tlacotalpan. *La Gaceta del Instituto del Patrimonio Cultural.* Oaxaca. Enero-marzo: 18-28.

UNESCO–Word Heritage Centre. 1998. *Historic Monuments Zone of Tlacotalpan, Nomination file.* Internet. http://whc.unesco.org/en/list/862/documents/pdf .

The Sacred Itinerary of the Huichol: an Example of the Complexity of the Legal Protection of the Spirit of Place

James Ritch Grande Ampudia
Conservación Humana, A.C.
México

José Ernesto Becerril Miró
ICOMOS Mexico, A.C.
México

Abstract

The Huichol Route through Natural Sacred Sites to Huiricuta has been included in the Mexican Tentative List; it is an east-west corridor of 800 kilometers that stretches from the Pacific coast to the Chihuahan Desert. The route is sacred to the Huichol indigenous peoples, and has existed for millennia. It includes natural places (forests, rivers, rocks and landscapes) considered sacred sites. Following an ancient tradition, annually, the Huichol undertake a pilgrimage along the sacred route renewing its cultural and spiritual meaning. This route represents an excellent example of how the relation between the immaterial heritage and natural places creates transcendental meanings for the identity and religious life of a community. When we analyze the design of a strategy for the protection of this itinerary, it is evident that the legal treatment of the spirit of place represents a complex challenge for national cultural heritage legislation.

Résumé

La Route des Huichol menant à Huiricuta à travers les Sites naturels sacrés est inscrite sur la Liste indicative du Mexique ; il s'agit d'un corridor de 800 kilomètres de long, orienté est-ouest, qui s'étire depuis la côte du Pacifique jusqu'au désert de Chihuahua. Cette route, qui est sacrée pour les Huichol, peuple autochtone, existe depuis des millénaires. Elle comprend des lieux naturels (forêts, rivières, rochers et paysages) considérés comme des lieux sacrés. Suivant une ancienne tradition, tous les ans, les Huichol entreprennent un pèlerinage le long de cette route sacrée, renouvelant ainsi sa signification culturelle et spirituelle. Cette route représente un excellent exemple de la manière dont le patrimoine immatériel et les lieux naturels créent des significations transcendantales pour l'identité et la vie religieuse d'une communauté. Lorsque nous analysons la conception de la stratégie de protection de cet itinéraire, il apparaît que le traitement juridique de l'esprit du lieu représente un défi complexe, au niveau national, pour la législation du patrimoine culturel.

The Huichol

The Mesoamerican societies that are known today as the Huichol constitute one of the native cultures that have survived with more vitality in the American continent. The main driver of the survival and cultural reproduction of the Huichol is the collective tenacity to comply with ancestral traditions, as well as factors such as the topography of their territories, their de-centralized political organization and their capacity to adapt to the historical environment, including an active participation in the history of western Mexico.

Approximately 18,000 Huichol live in settlements dispersed in a territory of more than 400,000 square hectares located south of the Sierra Madre Occidental, where the states of Jalisco, Nayarit, Zacatecas and Durango converge. The Huichol or *Huixarica* language is one with no written expression. The political organization of the Huichol is complex since traditional hierarchies interact and are interwoven with modern forms of organization. In the first half of the 20th century, after the Mexican revolution and the Cristero war, the Mexican federal government recognized the Huichol as three large agrarian communities and various adjacent "ejidos", which encompass the five Huichol tribes or "governments", among which there are notable differences in dialect, ritual and dress.

The foundation of the social fabric of the Huichol is the ceremonial centres or *tuquipa*. There are more than 15 ceremonial centres in the Sierra Madre Occidental which vary in organization, prestige and importance, therefore creating a differential pattern of political power amongst the surrounding regions. The chairs of the elders or *cahuiteruxi*, the men who know all, and that embody the most ancient political hierarchy, are located in the *tuquipa*. At the ceremonial centres or *tuquipa*, each clan has at least one representative, who, among other duties, must guard the ceremonial gourd (*jicara*) of the clan, which is a small receptacle that symbolically contains the hope of life. Such representatives are generally known as *jicareros*.

Agro-ecological ceremonialism is a fundamental component of the religious life of the Huichol. In the Huichol religious life, ritual cycles are associated with activities such as how to ask for rain, to prepare the land, obtain a good harvest or hunt deer. The educational function of ritual cycles is fundamental for the historical future of the Huichol nation, because the ancestral heritage is recreated and transmitted through them, through chants, narratives and sophisticated rituals.

The Sacred Itinerary of the Huichol

The Huichol geography includes places so far distant between them as what is today the distance between Mexico City and the coasts of the State of Tamaulipas bordering with the United States of America. The most important sites, however, are located within an 800-kilometer corridor extending west-northeast from the Nayarita coast to Huiricuta, north of San Luis Potosi. The eastern route of the Huichol, towards Huiricuta, has special relevance due to its hierarchy in the ritual cycles, the frequency with which it is used and the number of users. The length of the route to Huiricuta is approximately 500 kilometers and runs east-northeast from the Huichol territory. It traverses the "fork" where the States of Jalisco and Zacatecas m, to then cross the latter transversally, going through its capital city. Once in the State of San Luis Potosi, the route goes towards the Sierra de Picachos de Tonalillo, to finally flow into the Natural and Cultural Reserve of Huiricuta.

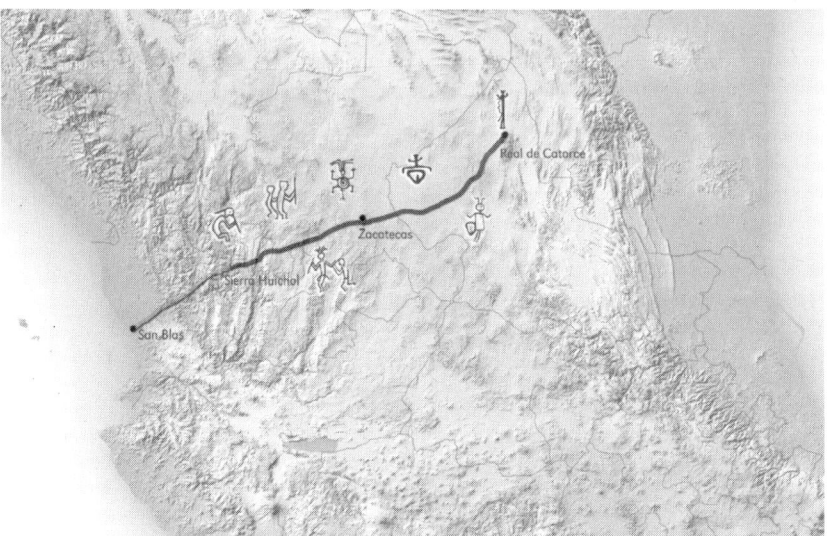

Figure 1. The route to Huiricuta.

The term "route to Huiricuta" actually refers to a "braid" of trails, dirt roads, and even asphalt roads that are walked on depending on several factors. It is important to emphasize that the route includes, in addition to ancestral Huichol trails, vestiges from colonial routes and cattle ways. The route to Huiricuta includes various Mexican states and municipalities with varying legal regimes on the ownership and use of land, in addition to the legal regime applicable at the Mexican federal level.

Members of the ceremonial centres have the obligation to make pilgrimages via the route to Huiricuta during winter, after the harvest. However, family groups or individuals also travel the route to Huiricuta year round. The Huichol consider that the route to Huiricuta is inhabited by deities and spirits of ancestors, the spirits of certain wild species (such as deer or wolf), and natural phenomena such as wind, rain or clouds or fertility of the earth. The Huichol also identify some of such elements as "elder brothers" or "teachers", the *tamatsi*, who anoint the pilgrims providing wisdom and spiritual guidance, or hardships and punishments.

The deities and spirits inhabit precisely the sacred sites, where, according to the Huichol, they "express their voices". The sacred sites are located in islets, wetlands, rivers, lagoons, water springs, forests, mountains, caves or rock formations. The "cahuis" are also natural rock formations that are, for the Huichol, tracks left by the *cacauyaris* who are demigods who became petrified and shaped the landscape when they failed to pass the tests of creation in primeval times.

The route to Huiricuta constitutes a perfect example of the "spirit of place": a constellation of natural places and phenomena with a profound and ancient spiritual meaning to the Huichol. When the Huichol see the landscape, they see an ancient mosaic of meaning which is nurtured constantly by the social rite of walking the route.

The fundamental purpose of the pilgrimage is to follow the steps of the ancestors to ask for rain and well-being. Another critical purpose of the pilgrimages is the educational and formative experience, its function as an itinerant university, where the neophytes learn the things related to the route, the tradition, the meaning of sacred sites and deities and the customs of the Huichol. Each sacred site contains tribal legacy which is remembered with the walking of the route, if accompanied by the proper guidance. Thus, the itinerary becomes the reading of a codex extended on the landscape. For these reasons, the preservation of the route is key to the survival of the Huichol.

Another well-known aspect of the pilgrimage is the ritual use of peyote since ancient times. Although the ritual use of peyote is permitted for indigenous peoples by international treaties to which Mexico is a party, the national and local regulation for ritual use and the enforcement thereof presents practical and legal challenges for the protection of an essential element of the pilgrimage by the Huichol of the route to Huiricuta.

In addition to being invaluable natural places to the Huichol, the sacred itineraries and landscapes are located in areas that have unique planetary environmental importance. The corridor traverses the southern portion of three eco-regions of planetary relevance due to their contribution to biodiversity: the Gulf of California, the Sierra Madre Occidental and the Chihuahuan Desert, all of which are prolific in endemisms and refuges of singular flora and fauna. The Chihuahuan Desert is one of the three wealthiest desert areas of the planet.

There are zones with a high degree of conservation along the territories traversed by this corridor through these eco-regions, unique habitats and endemic or relictual species, which in certain cases have deserved inclusion within some of the different categories of "priority areas for conservation" both by national organizations (CONABIO, SEMARNAT, CONANP), and international institutions (UNESCO, RAMSAR), such as the inclusion of the route in the national Tentative List for UNESCO's World Heritage Convention.

The route to Huiricuta and the other sacred Huichol itineraries also forms a part of a collection of colonial and ancient pre-hispanic routes of commercial and cultural interchange which need to be studied and which were fundamental for continental integration that occurred in multiple directions through the millennia.

Protection of the Sacred Itineraries of the Huichol

Despite a utilitarian environment, accelerated social changes and degradation, the Huichol ritual time, which seeks a profound identification with the natural phenomena, has managed to survive but the risks are enormous. Therefore, in order to secure its continuity, it is urgent to promote and design a special treatment for all the aspects involved in the safeguarding of the integrity and environment where these cultural itineraries flow. Many things have been done but the planetary significance of the itineraries and the increasing risks demand more vigorous action by all international, government and private participants.

Conservación Humana, A.C. (CHAC) is a private Mexican non-profit organization founded 13 years ago which is dedicated principally to the protection of the cultural landscapes of the Huichol. By means of an agreement with the traditional Huichol authorities, CHAC has developed an initiative to preserve the natural and cultural heritage linked to their routes and sanctuaries that will foster the sustainable development of the local inhabitants. To achieve this purpose, work has been done transversally during the last thirteen years with institutions of the three orders of government, international entities and other related groups of the organized civil society.

The strategy of the initiative is centred on promoting the application of the conservation and planning of land use tools, articulated with instruments of economic, social and cultural policy. The initiative promotes and is sustained by conceptual resources recently developed by the international community, including entities such as the World Bank, UNESCO, ICOMOS and the European Union.

Among other achievements, CHAC coordinated the formation of the Natural and Cultural Reserve of Huiricuta and promoted legislative changes in the state of San Luis Potosi designed to protect this outstanding cultural and natural legacy. For the first time, a unique legal precedent in Mexico was established both in the laws of culture and in the laws for the environment of such state. Another notable step was the inscription of the route in the Mexican Tentative List of UNESCO's World Heritage Convention. The next step is the finalization of the initiative to include the itineraries in the UNESCO World Heritage List.

As outlined in this document, the particular configuration of the cultural landscapes of the sacred itineraries of the Huichol and the many facets involved, exemplify the complexities raised by the legal protection of this unique cultural and natural asset of planetary importance.

Legal Challenges for the Protection of the Sacred Itineraries of the Huichol

Recently, CHAC and ICOMOS Mexico have begun to collaborate on the proposal of a legal strategy for the protection of the sacred itineraries of the Huichol.

The most important problem in the definition of a legal strategy for the conservation of the sacred itineraries is that "cultural itineraries" are not recognized as a protected category by Mexican legislation. For more than 10 years, ICOMOS Mexico has constantly proposed to the National Institute of Anthropology and History (INAH) the need to review and amend the Federal Law of Archaeological, Artistic and Historic Monuments and Zones (LFMZ) in order to recognize and protect cultural heritage categories like cultural landscapes and itineraries.

The definition of a legal strategy for the protection of the sacred itineraries of the Huichol would have to encompass tangible and immaterial assets, natural environment, the roles and responsibilities of the various governmental authorities involved and the design and implementation of the necessary legal instruments.

In the case of tangible assets, there are archaeological, historical and traditional constructions on the route. Archaeological monuments are protected by INAH in accordance with the LFMZ. The conservation of non-archaeological built elements would be the responsibility of state authorities by means of state cultural heritage legislation. In all cases, the legislation is limited to the regulation of construction activities in the monuments, control of archaeological research, supervision of activities and the imposition of penalties.

Natural environment represents a fundamental aspect of the protection of the itineraries. Environmental legislation and its planning, legal and technical instruments as well as their broad conceptualization of the joint conservation of natural and cultural values constitute an advantage as opposed to the limited vision of Mexican cultural legislation which is almost exclusively directed at the protection of buildings without taking into consideration the natural environment and the intangible cultural reality.

Federal and local environmental laws establish the authority of the corresponding agencies to declare National Protected Areas (ANP), at the federal level or Local Protected Areas (ALP), at the local level. In the case of the sacred itineraries of the Huichol, the declaration as ANP or ALP would be justified because it would achieve the creation, protection and promotion of traditional knowledge and practises, means of communication, the natural environment of monuments and sites as well as other important areas for the identity and culture of indigenous communities. However, as mentioned above, only the State of San Luis Potosi has declared the Natural and Cultural Reserve of Huiricuta as an ALP, which is a very important milestone.

In respect of the immaterial heritage that represents the spirit of place due to the close relationship between the Huichol nation and the natural sites, the LMFZ does not contemplate any protection of immaterial heritage. Some local cultural heritage laws do contain some regulation but it is very limited to the protection of inventory, investigation and promotion activities.

Article 2 of the Mexican Federal Constitution establishes that Mexico has a pluricultural conformation based on indigenous groups and recognizes their right to free determination and the preservation of their language, knowledge and all the elements that constitute their own culture and identity. Such constitutional provision has not been implemented by secondary legislation and therefore it remains merely declaratory.

The Mexican Federal Copyright Law establishes that the practises, uses and traditions without an identified author will be protected thereby. However, such a law is clearly not sufficient to protect the sacred itineraries of the Huichol which are complex cultural landscapes, as described herein.

As a conclusion, the limited vision of Mexican legislation of cultural heritage and the absence of legal mechanisms for the protection of immaterial heritage represent an important risk for the comprehensive conservation of the cultural and natural places with a relevant significance for a community or social group. In the case of the route to Huiricuta, and Huichol sacred itineraries in general, this situation is especially critical and highlights the complexity of the Mexican legal protection of cultural itineraries.

Cultural heritage is a concept in constant evolution and is constantly incorporating more complex categories. The development of cultural heritage sciences and international instruments recognizes the close relationship between built heritage, the natural environment and social life. It is urgent to make the necessary legal amendments to create protection mechanisms for new categories of our cultural heritage. Since cultural heritage represents a more complex social phenomenon and monuments, sites, routes and landscapes are subject to different social and private interests, it will be necessary to protect monuments and sites with a comprehensive approach in order to coordinate such interests to ensure effective protection.

Cultural heritage always has a human sense. Monuments and sites cannot be separated from the attributes granted thereto by society. Any conservation project will be incomplete if the values, symbols and meanings are not included in its design and execution. Cultural heritage and its meanings and values are a social property that has to be identified and protected. The route to Huiricuta, and the sacred itineraries of the Huichol in general, are excellent examples of this. The right of the Huichol to the conservation of their culture will not be achieved if governmental actions are limited to tangible assets. When managing spiritual, sacred or traditional assets, the opinion of the human culture in question is fundamental. The most powerful instruments for the protection of cultural heritage in the future will be education, planning and effective international and national legal mechanisms.

References

Becerril Miró, José Ernesto. 2003. *El Derecho del Patrimonio Histórico-Artístico en México.* Editorial Porrúa, S.A., México, D.F., México

Beltrán M., J. C. 2001. *La Explotación de la Costa del Pacífico en el Occidente de Mesoamérica y los Contactos con Sudamérica y con otras Regiones Culturales.* Universidad Autónoma de Nayarit, CONACULTA-INAH, Tepic, Nayarit.

Braniff C., B. (coord.). 2001. *La Gran Chichimeca. El Lugar de las Rocas Secas.* CONACULTA, México, Editorial Jaca Book Spa, Milán.

CIIC. 2006. Proyecto de carta internacional de itinerarios culturales. Acta de la reunión del Comité Científico Internacional de Itinerarios Culturales (CIIC) de ICOMOS. Xi'an (China). 18 y 19 Octubre, 2005. www.icomos-ciic.org.

Conservación Humana, A.C. 2001. *Plan de Manejo de la Reserva Natural y Cultural de Huiricuta.* Ciudad de México.

2007. Conservación Humana AC. *Ruta huixrárica y paisajes vinculados en Zacatecas, propuesta de área natural protegida.* México.

Fernández B., H. 1999. The Initative for the Conservation of Natural Sacred Sites and Traditional Pilgrimage Routes of the Huichol Indian People of Mexico. *Linking Nature and Culture.* (Report of the Global Strategy Natural and Cultural Heritage Expert Meeting, March 1998, Amsterdam, The Netherlands). UNESCO/Ministry for Foreign Affairs/Ministry for Education, Science and Culture. The Hague, The Netherlands.

——— 2003. La ruta Huichol por los sitios sagrados a Huiricuta. *Coloquio internacional. La representatividad de la Lista del Patrimonio Mundial.* Querétaro. INAH e ICOMOS.

J. G. Azcárate. 2005. El escenario de la ruta huichol a Huiricuta por los sitios sagrados naturales. *Hereditas 13*: 40-49. México, D.F.

ICOMOS. 2001. *El Patrimonio Intangible y otros aspectos relativos a los Itinerarios Culturales* (Congreso Internacional del Comité Internacional de Itinerarios Culturales de ICOMOS). Gobierno de Navarra, Departamento de Educación y Cultura, Pamplona.

INAH. 2004. *El Patrimonio de México y su Valor Universal. Lista Indicativa 2004.* CONACULTA-INAH, Dirección de Patrimonio Mundial. México, D.F.

Lilly, J. Junio 1986. La Nación Huichol: una ventana a nuestro pasado. *México Desconocido. No. 112.* Editorial Jilguero. México D.F, México.

Secretaría de Desarrollo Social y Conservación Humana AC. 2005. *El Camino del Abuelo Fuego, Tatehuarí Huajuyé.* México, D.F.

Von Droste, B., H. Plachter y M. Rössler (eds). 1995. *Cultural Landscapes of Universal Value – Components of a Global Strategy.* Gustav Fischer Verlag, Jena, Stuttgart, New York, in cooperation with UNESCO.

Weigand, P.C. (comp.). 2002. *Estudio Histórico y Cultural sobre los Huicholes.* Universidad de Guadalajara, Campus Universitario del Norte. Colotlán, Jalisco.

A. García. 2000. Huichol society before the arrival of the Spanish. *Journal of the Southwest, 42 (1)*: 12-36. Arizona.

Returning to Places of Wounded Memory
The Role of World Heritage Sites in Reconciliation

Rev. Canon Albert J. Ogle
Irish School of Ecumenics
Trinity College
Dublin

ABSTRACT

This paper explores the emerging role of cultural heritage in community reconciliation, particularly for identity-based conflicts. I utilize theories on the relationship between place, memory, identity and violence applied to interdisciplinary research on UNESCO World Heritage Sites (WHS) in Ohrid, Macedonia, and the Battle of the Boyne in Ireland. In both countries, heritage and religion have unique roles in identity-based conflicts. I conclude with recommendations as to how UNESCO and the International Council on Monuments and Sites (ICOMOS) might encourage the creation of a new body of mediation, reconciliation and community transformation specialists who would become partners in the utilization and preservation of tangible and intangible heritage.

RÉSUMÉ

Cet article explore le rôle émergent du patrimoine culturel dans la réconciliation communautaire, en particulier dans le cas des conflits basés sur l'identité. J'utilise les théories de la relation entre le lieu, la mémoire, l'identité et la violence appliquées à une recherche interdisciplinaire sur les Sites du Patrimoine mondial de l'Unesco à Ohrid, en Macédoine, et dans le cas de la bataille de la Boyne en Irlande. Dans les deux pays, le patrimoine et la religion ont un rôle unique dans les conflits basés sur l'identité. Je conclus par des recommandations quant à la manière dont l'Unesco et le Conseil international sur les monuments et sites (ICOMOS) pourraient inciter à la création d'un nouvel organisme de médiation, de réconciliation et de transformation communautaire, regroupant des spécialistes qui deviendraient des partenaires dans l'utilisation et la conservation du patrimoine matériel et immatériel.

1. Progression of ICOMOS – from Conservation to Community Reconciliation?

The first sentence of the Venice Charter (1964) contains the concept that historic monuments are "imbued with a message from the past" and are "living witnesses" to traditions. Andrzej Tomaszewski (Tomaszewski 2003) reminds us that in the history of the conservation movement, it was only a century ago that Alois Riegl wrote about the concept of a "memorial value". Fifty years later, Erwin Panofsky is concerned about the *interpretation* of material works. Accordingly, an architectural monument that is the backdrop of an event is a "silent witness" to that happening, and gains a new dimension of "memorial values", becoming a *"place of memory"*. Tomaszewski reminds us how a recent European theory of "German Places of Memory" emphasizes their *symbolic function* rather than their material objectification only.

Today, conservators are more open to experimentation with different forms of memorialization to help interpret the spiritual and intangible aspects of monuments. This has particular significance and challenges when there has been an atrocity committed on a site or a site is associated with an ongoing conflict between two identities. Shawn Landres and Oren Stier write, "control of sacred places is central to the articulation and revision of memory and through it the writing and rewriting of history. As such, both the physical excavation of place and the social excavation of memory are fraught with conflict....atrocities render places religiously charged, indigestible in their toxicity, while their commemoration creates of those sites sacred spaces, variously digestible in and through their memorialization and contestation" (Stier and Landres 2006). Within these interdisciplinary developments, UNESCO is being called upon to provide more resources resulting from its experience in reconciliation, mediation and healing, in some of the world's most troubled communities. UNESCO interprets key monuments as a "shared responsibility for all humanity." This role is consistent with Article 5 of the Venice Charter which calls for "making use of them (monuments) for some socially useful purpose". UNESCO, by earning the unique role of "an honest broker" in a recent evaluation by its Member States (*UNESCO Director General's Report* 2007) can perhaps offer previously untapped resources to conflicted communities where shared heritage might provide reconciliation and the healing of "wounded memory".

2. Good or Bad "Spirit of Place" – the Challenges of Multiple Interpretations of Sites

Slobodan Milosevic captured the "Spirit of Place" when he spoke in the Field of Black Birds, where, in 1389, Prince Lazar of Serbia was defeated by the Turks. Although the Serbs lost the battle, Milosevic used the field's symbolism to promise Serbians they would not be defeated again. He claimed, "They'll never do this to you again. Never again will anyone defeat you." (Kaplan 2005). An Ulster Protestant will see the site of the Battle of the Boyne (Figure 1), won by King William of Orange in 1690, as a symbol of Protestant domination in Ireland. An Irish Catholic will see the same battlefield as a place where dreams and aspirations were shattered, marking the beginning of the anti-Catholic Penal Laws, and the source of annual sectarian commemorative and paramilitary-style marches. Interpretation of history and sites is still controversial in both contexts. Distortions of history and "community memory" can feed sectarian hatred and fear to divide communities further. The Battle of the Boyne's annual commemoration and para-military style marches ensure these "wounded memories" never quite heal. For Protestants, the commemoration is primarily shaped by the need for social, political, and religious identity.

Figure 1. Oldbridge House at the site of the Battle of the Boyne, resides within the 5 mile buffer-zone of a Neolithic World Heritage Site, Bru Na Boinne.

In 2002, UNESCO focused on the theme of Reconciliation and Development. The international community had just experienced the destruction of two 1,500-year-old Buddha statues by the Afghanistan Taliban. That year, Mounir Bouchenaki spoke passionately at the UN Headquarters, "Cultural heritage has often been a military target or the flashpoint of political ethnic and religious conflicts. But when peace returns, the rehabilitation and enhancement of these highly symbolic sites, as well as that of cultural spaces or forms of cultural expression belonging to the intangible heritage, can sometimes help to strengthen the process of national reconciliation and revive economic activity" (Bouchenaki 2002).

UNESCO and the World Bank expressed their commitment by paying $15 million to rebuild the Mostar Bridge in Bosnia, a symbol of multiculturalism intentionally destroyed during the 1990s civil war. Croats and Bosnians worked together on its reconstruction. Another challenging example was Israel, where mixing cultural heritage with religion and politics has created ongoing difficulties and divisions. The Director General, Koichiro Matsuura, clarified some of the key principles at work between cultural heritage and reconciliation, by saying "Our task equally consists in supporting those groups and individuals committed to Israeli-Palestinian dialogue, so as to advance mutual understanding and respect as building blocks of peace" (Matsuura 2003). Globally, there are now 30 WHSs that continue on the Endangered Heritage List, including the historic city and walls of Jerusalem (Figure 2). Discussion on "Access to Holy Places" remains a taboo subject. UNESCO may be the only trusted and neutral organization to begin to design a process where these issues and dangers are resolved. Endangered "tangible heritage" is only one of many major concerns for UNESCO and ICOMOS. "Intangible heritage" (stories, rituals and community memories, language etc.) is also threatened. Proactively, UNESCO's commitment to equally protect intangible heritage could include the preservation of older forms of mediation and reconciliation that are present in older cultures, i.e. "Tree of Man" in Uganda or "Kanun" in Albania. These forms of mediation are associated with threatened cultural practices that modernism and democracy are replacing with other forms of justice and reconciliation.

Figure 2. The Dome of the Rock Mosque and Walls of Jerusalem remain one of the world's most endangered and controversial World Heritage Sites.

3. Resources for Shared Heritage from Academia –Research on Sectarianism

Drs. Joseph Liechty and Cecelia Clegg, in "*Moving Beyond Sectarianism*," spent 6 years researching at the Irish School of Ecumenics, Trinity College, Dublin, and identified complex core issues in the Irish identity-based conflict that may apply to other conflicts. They describe sectarianism as a hidden force within a society, where individuals are abrogated of full responsibility for attitudes and social consequences that a larger institutional "contract" can absorb or be blamed for. Individually, people may not have a sectarian bone in their bodies, yet they collectively maintain *systems* of sectarianism. It is within popular history, memory and myth, an efficient fuel that permeates millions of people who had no direct connection with particular past events, yet "live" in these events as they are interpreted by a small minority. The smallest event can cause thousands of intelligent and rational people to move into segregated areas almost overnight. Liechty and Clegg's definition of sectarianism is "A system of attitudes, actions, beliefs and structures at personal, communal and institutional levels which always involves religion, and typically involves a negative mixing of religion and politics which arises as a distorted expression of positive, human needs, especially for belonging, identity and the free expression of difference" (Liechty and Clegg 2001). They suggest a process whereby sectarianism is *transformed* rather than eradicated.

3.1. The Fusion of History, Place, Memory, Identity and Violence in an Irish Context

In 1990, the Irish government purchased 500 acres of parkland around Bru Na Boinne, a Neolithic UNESCO monument (O'Kelley 1995), that has the site of the Battle of the Boyne and an historic villa, Oldbridge House, within its five mile buffer zone. It was here on July 1, 1690, the battle was won by Protestant William of Orange, against his Catholic father-in-law, James II of England. The battle changed the course of religious and political history in Europe, and left a painful wound in Irish memory (Haddick Flynn 1999). The battlefield was left relatively untouched and unexplored for 300 years. The recent careful development of the site parallels the reconciliation and peace processes between the people of Northern Ireland, the Republic of Ireland and the United Kingdom. The motivation for the site's development is both cultural and political. The Irish government, as a result of the numerous Anglo-Irish agreements, is seeking to fulfill its obligation to protect the rights and heritage of the minority Protestant community. The development of the battle site (now with a new visitor's center) symbolizes this policy.

3.2. The FUSION of History, Place, Memory, Identity and Violence in a Balkan/Macedonian Context

Robert Kaplan describes a typical Balkan view of history, myth and culture as "History is not viewed as tracing a chronological progression, as it is in the West. Instead, history jumps around and moves in circles; and where history is perceived in such a way, myths take root. Evangelos Kofos, Greece's eminent scholar on Macedonia, has observed that these historical legacies... "sustained nations in their uphill drive towards state-building, national unification and, possibly, the reincarnation of long extinct empires" (Kaplan 2005).

Sectarianism, as defined above, is very much alive in the relations between Albanians and Macedonians living in Macedonia. They are peaceful but there are misunderstandings, fears and stereotypes in how they view each other. There is little contact (very little intermarriage) and trust is lacking. Kosovar Albanians in particular are viewed with distrust and suspicion about their negative influence in Macedonia, particularly their alleged involvement in organized crime. Schools in Macedonia are segregated with students sharing the same space in shifts (Macedonian children might attend a morning session and Albanian children would attend the same school in the afternoon). Albanians are mostly Muslims (25%) and Macedonians mostly Orthodox Christians (64%). A constant threat is the fear of the creation of a "Greater Albania" and partitioning part of Macedonia to Bulgaria (a long standing political aspiration). Macedonians feel their national identity and historic boundaries are being undermined. Heritage becomes an important weapon in this battle to maintain identity and authority.

Figure 3. Ohrid's newest Orthodox Church is rebuilt on the site of an Ottoman Mosque whose ruins were recently excavated and removed. An opportunity to demonstrate "shared heritage" was missed.

3.2.1. Sectarianism In Heritage – A Recent Example

Ohrid (a city of 50,000 people with over 100 historic churches) is a UNESCO WHS and is believed to be the cradle of history for many cultures, including the Macedonian/Slavic tradition that now dominates the religious and cultural heritage of the city. The history of Ohrid mirrors the larger history of Macedonia. When the ruins of an Ottoman mosque (built over the empty shrine of St. Clement in Ohrid), were recently removed to be replaced by an Orthodox shrine, costing the Macedonian government several million euros, the interpretation of the site became a wedge of contention between the two communities.

Behicuddin Shehapi, an art historian and President of the largest Muslim NGO in Macedonia, El Hilal, served on a variety of government cultural heritage projects and is familiar with the work of UNESCO. His book, "*Uncured Wounds*" (Shehapi 2003) documents the destruction of 50 mosques in Macedonia in the 20th century (including the mentioned ruins in Ohrid) through war, deliberate destruction and decay. There are clearly at least two sides to the story. The Christian Orthodox community would say the original church in Ohrid was destroyed by the Turks and a mosque built in its place. Church authorities, faced with desecration, moved the holy relics to another church. They have merely returned an important part of the region's heritage to its original place by re-interring St. Clement's relics. The new shrine that is now the most visited tourist venue in the country. What could have become an integrated shared heritage site and cultural center at Pantelejmon in Ohrid, became a missed opportunity for a deeply divided community. We might have seen a different utilization of a heritage site if the *Ename Charter* (a new ICOMOS document approved in 2008 that encourages states to offer multiple interpretations of sites and monuments) was available to the UNESCO and Ohrid advisors a decade ago. However, this proudly designated "UNESCO City" had some recent successes with the signing of the Ohrid Agreement in 2001 (protecting the rights of the minority community in Macedonia and commitment to democracy) and two international conferences on religious reconciliation. The symbolic nature of Ohrid as a place of reconciliation gives authority and credibility to agreements and conferences that are made and held there.

4. An Emerging Understanding of History, Place, Memory, Identity and Violence

In exploring the relationship between intangible heritage and how the "Spirit of Place" is invoked or re-*membered,* religion plays a central role. Religion, from an anthropological point of view, could be described as a cultural system that is heavily reliant on the use of symbols, remembering and retelling of stories and the association of physical places with supernatural people or events. These symbols, stories, and places reinforce a sense of identity and belonging for the people of the Earth. Many of our WHSs are places of "Eruption" where it is believed, the sacred breaks through the profane. The *axis mundi*, the *omphalos* – the axis or the navel of the world, gives human beings an orientation, often marked by buildings with brilliant mathematical and astronomical properties. These unique places are highly sought after, fought over and remain some of the most valuable properties on the Earth. Mircea Eliade (Eliade 1961, 1970 and 1985) would describe "history being compressed" in these places and our genealogies and thus our identities are realized in space and time. Rodger Freidland and Richard Hecht say:" Memory can "speak" in central places, holy places and sacred places" (Stier and Landres 2006). However, the international community's experience in Kosovo (OSCE Report 1999), Ireland and Macedonia has shown that history can be easily distorted, religion can fuel division, academia can become victim to revisionism, archaeology can be used to ensure one culture is devalued by another, and community memory cannot be fully trusted. Professional interdisciplinary collaboration may be the only way to keep everyone accountable and focused on the task of building a culture of shared heritage through healing and reconciliation.

4.1. Drawing from an Example of Christianity's Intangible Heritage – Forgiveness and Reconciliation

Miroslav Volf (A Christian theologian from Croatia) has written extensively on the subject of "remembering rightly". He describes a process where representatives of both sides of a story, victim and perpetrator, share in the process of gathering and challenging the fragments of memory, including the parts that have been sometimes conveniently forgotten, and creating a new shared future for each other in the process. In "remembering rightly", Volf further develops this process to include the transformation of wounds through "exemplary memory" where the community's pain is transformed by learning from past experiences at a particular site so it may be avoided in the future. "The past thus becomes a principle of action for the present" (Volf 2006). WHS's can offer important local and international opportunities for "exemplary memory" (See Figure 4).

Figure 4. Controversy surrounds a recent application to the World Heritage Program for a Rwandan genocide memorial site to be chosen as a national and international place of remembrance, to help ensure genocide will not happen again. Similar theory has been applied to Nazi death camps and other mass burial sites now part of the WHS program.

4.2. When Heritage, Religion, Politics and Reconciliation Rhyme

On May 9th 2007, following the first meeting of the new Northern Ireland Assembly (when Protestants and Catholics entered into a power-sharing government), there was a surprise visit to the Battle of the Boyne site by Rev. Ian Paisley and representatives of the Irish government. The site choice and the timing of the visit were historic, symbolic and particularly significant of the new "cross-border" relationship between Loyalist Protestants and Catholic Republicans. Dr. Paisley planted a tree, in what is to become a memorial garden in Oldbridge House and presented the Irish Prime Minister with a musket used at the battle.

Bru na Boinne and the Battle of the Boyne sites could become a model center of education, cultural preservation, and reconciliation where issues of "wounded memory" are addressed in a meaningful way. Northern Ireland could not have achieved its peace process without the international community's help. The growing body of expertise in Irish mediation and reconciliation is now responding to other identity-based conflicts in the Middle East, the Balkans, Sri Lanka and Africa. The Irish Government is creating a Conflict Resolution Unit (Department of Foreign Affairs 2008) to harness this expertise, apply to other international contexts where the Irish military serves as UN international peacekeepers, and combined with Ireland's ambitious Millennium Development Goals, is linking development issues with conflict reduction strategies. The Irish community is providing a model, where military, academic, heritage, civil society and government are all working together to be available to other conflicted communities. The development of an ICOMOS-like international network where Member States of UNESCO are encouraged to develop similar Conflict Resolution Units, would allow the noble principles of the Ename Charter to begin to take root.

Figure 5. Two former enemies meet: Dr. Ian Paisley, N. Ireland's First Minister and Bertie Ahern, the Irish Prime Minister, meet at the Battle of the Boyne site and exchange gifts.

5. Conclusions and Recommendations

5.1. A New Pro-active role for the UNESCO World Heritage Program

The role of "honest broker" in identity-based conflicts may become one of the most important roles UNESCO could play in the contemporary world. To meet this new challenge effectively, it would need a cadre of resources and expertise that the organization does not currently have. Mats Friberg describes the parallels between the Lebanese, Sri Lankan, Northern Irish, Cypriot and Israeli Palestinian conflicts as "conflicts over deep rooted social identities." He suggests the need for grass-roots decentralized and co-operative processes that would provide opportunities for safe spaces with a trusted "third party" facilitator (Kuzzmanic, and Truger,1992). UNESCO could provide this role in many of the current identity-based conflicts and use shared heritage as a symbolic tool for helping people to work together in new ways. A recent application from the historically divided Christian Churches in Galilee, Israel is one example of how the World Heritage Program can bring the owners and managers of valuable places of pilgrimage together that have previously been independently managed. If the Galilee Christian Sites owners can agree on a mutually beneficial future strategy, this may allow deeper and more creative discussions on access to and protection of all holy sites in Israel, including Jerusalem. The PUSH Project (www.pushproject.org) is another innovative program where Israeli, Jordanian and Palestinian heritage has come to significant agreements on shared heritage, interpretation and management of independent programs.

5.2. Member StateS Invited to SUPPORT the Ename Charter.

As the new Ename Charter is discussed by the international community, each Member State could agree on a common strategy by:

- Prioritizing how local and regional "intangible heritage" (specifically around conflict resolution and mediation), could be developed as a resource for local or international application. Special attention needs to be given to properties on the Endangered List and innovative strategies to use local resources.

- Supporting university-based research and community education models that encourage respect for different heritage, storytelling methods to heal past events, and community participation in shared memorial projects.

- Becoming familiar with models of good practice where WHS and other proactive peace-making museum programs (i.e. the Caen Memorial in Normandy).

- Developing their own reconciliation and mediation resources within their own community in partnership with other Member States. Integration of academic, military peacekeeping, development of civil society and interfaith dialogue is encouraged with strategies to meet their Millennium Development Goals.

• Reviewing the current use of historic and national sites for potentially divisive public expressions of memorialization, national identity or community solidarity at the cost of another (usually minority) community. Applying the principles of the Ename Charter, these events should be inclusive and be able to share creatively in the telling of multiple stories for interpretation and expression.

• Ecumenical and inter-faith conferences (i.e. the recent Ohrid conference on world religions held in October 2007) should be featured at WHSs on regular basis.

5.3. Establish a New International Organization of Reconcilers and Mediators Based on the ICOMOS Model by UNESCO

Member States who have invested significant resources in peace and reconciliation work, including the protection of indigenous intangible heritage are invited to form an international coalition to assist UNESCO with more challenging regions where identity-based conflict is prevalent. This emerging model could use the logistical experience of ICOMOS – how it was shaped by its dynamic mission and the development of polices and structures. This new entity might become a crucible of innovation for reconciliation through heritage. ICOMOS, as the parent organization of this new entity, with its 9,000 international members, could provide technical assistance, conference themes and cross-disciplinary publications of interest to these new partnerships. Most importantly, the Ename Charter (ICOMOS's latest contribution to reconciliation) would have the resources needed to build upon ICOMOS's 43 years of developing a culture of shared heritage and to have the personnel and expertise to shape the issues that still lie ahead.

References

Eliade, Mircea. 1970 [1949]. *Traité d'histoirie des religions*, 310-25; Paris: Payot.

Eliade, Mircea. 1961. *Images and Symbols; Studies in Religious Symbolism*, 27-56 Sheed and Ward: New York.

Eliade, Mircea. 1985. *Symbolism, the Sacred and the Arts*, ed. Diana Apostolos-Cappadona. New York: Crossroad, 105-42.

Freidland, Rodger and Richard Hecht. 2006. The Powers of Place in *Religion Violence Memory and Place*, 20. ed Steir and Landres. Bloomington: Indiana University Press.

Haddick Flynn, Kevin. 1999. *Orangeism*. Dublin: Wolfhound Press.

Kaplan, Robert D. 2005. *Balkan Ghosts*, New York: Picador, 35, 39.

Kuzzmanic, T., and A. Truger,1992. *Yugoslav War,* Peace Institution, Ljubljana, 133-34. Chapter by Mats Friberg, Mats. on, "The need for unofficial diplomacy in identity conflicts." in Kuzzmanic, T. and A. Truger,1992. *Yugoslav War.* Ljubljana: Peace Institution.

Liechty, Joseph, and Cecelia Clegg. 2001. *Moving Beyond Sectarianism.* Dublin: Columba Press, 102-3.

O'Kelley, Michael and Claire. 1995. *Newgrange, Archaeology, Art and Legend.* London: Thames and Hudson.

OSCE Report. 1999. *Kosovo as Seen and Told.* OSCE Office, Switzerland and *Cultural Heritage in Kosovo; Protection and Conservation of Multi-Ethnic Heritage in Danger* (2004) UNESCO Publications.

Steir, Orin B., and Landres, J. Shawn. 2006. *Religion, Violence, Memory and Place*, Bloomington: Indiana Press.

Shehapi, Behicuddin. 2003. *Uncured Wounds* (Ozel Yamim, private publisher) Skopje.

Toderov, Tzvetan. 1996. The Abuses of Memory in *Common Knowledge*, Edition 5 number 1, 14.

Volf, Miroslav. 2006. *The End of Memory. Remembering Rightly in a Violent World.* Michigan: Erdmans,. Quoting.

Electronic Documents

Bouchenaki, Mounir. 2002. *Address to the United Nations.* Internet. Available from www.unesco.org; accessed 14/06/07.

Ename Charter. 2008. Internet. Available from www.icomosinternational. org; accessed 12/07/2008.

Irish Government's Department of Foreign Affairs. 2008. 25/01/08. Internet. Available from www.foreignaffairs.gov.ie.; accessed 12/07/08.

Matsuura, Koichiro. 2007. *UNESCO Director General's Report.* Internet. Available from www.unesco.org.; accessed 14/08/07.

Matsuura, Koichiro. 2003. Address, "*Reconstruction and Reconciliation in the Middle East*". Internet. Available from www.unesdoc.unesco.org.; accessed 12/07/08.

The PUSH Project. Internet. Available from www.pushproject.org accessed 08/20/2008.

Tomaszewski, Andrzej. 2003. ICOMOS 14th General Assembly and Scientific Symposium "*Place Memory Meaning; Preserving Intangible Value in Monuments and Sites*". Internet. Available from www.icomosinternational.org. Documentation Center; accessed 6/6/07.

Contested Landscape and Spirit of Place
The Case of the Olive Trees and an Urban
Neighborhood in Israel

Irit Amit-Cohen
Bar-Ilan University
Israel

Abstract

Cultural Heritage and Cultural Landscape are a set of human products reflecting the needs, thoughts and memories of society. They represent and symbolize relationships of power and control – from which they emerged – and the human processes that transformed and continue to transform them. Such transformations create new cultural landscapes that often conceal the processes – political, social, cultural, ideological and economic – that have created them. The purpose of this paper is to analyze a contested geographical environment, where two cultures compete over the land and its cultural heritage and therefore each – the Jewish Zionist culture and the Arab Muslim culture – has its own interpretations. The aim is to define the landscape – its spirit and its representation – that emerges from these competitions and disputes, characterize it and analyze its symbols and its uses, primarily for the purpose of forming and constructing identities.

Résumé

Le patrimoine culturel et le paysage culturel sont un ensemble de productions humaines reflétant les besoins, les pensées et les mémoires de la société. Ils représentent et symbolisent des relations de pouvoir et de contrôle – desquelles ils sont le produit – et les processus humains qui les ont transformés et continuent de le faire. De telles transformations créent de nouveaux paysages culturels qui dissimulent souvent les processus – politiques, sociaux, culturels, idéologiques et économiques – qui les ont créés. L'intention de cet article est d'analyser un environnement géographique contesté, où deux cultures rivalisent pour le contrôle de la terre et de son patrimoine culturel et où donc, toutes deux – la culture juive sioniste et la culture musulmane arabe – formulent leurs propres interprétations. L'objectif est de définir le paysage – son esprit et sa représentation – qui émerge de ces rivalités et de ces contestations, de le caractériser et d'analyser sa symbolique et l'usage qui en est fait – dans le but premier de former et de construire des identités.

Introduction

Cultural landscapes developed in a geographical area for the needs of a specific community may undergo a change and become icons. In other words, they will not only reflect the customs, events and ideology of the community, but in their manifestations they will represent values and messages, to the in-group as well as to others. These values and messages will thus signify belonging to a group and testify to the ownership of the territory by the group. In the words of Jean Gottmann: "The abstract strength of an existing order is rooted in the spirit of the nation and its place or of the group of nations involved in their space [...]. What it signifies here is a psychological attitude resulting from a combination of actual events with beliefs deeply rooted in the peoples' mind. [...]These symbols are many and varied. A national iconography usually stops at a boundary; the frontier line is in grave danger when such is not the case" (1952). This quotation expresses the idea that observing the landscape is a matter of subjective reference. This reference stems from the emotional attitude that society develops towards landscapes, sites and places.

The emotional attitude to cultural landscapes and cultural heritage sites and monuments is shaped by historical events, influential figures, religious and national characteristics and fashionable effects and tendencies. Emotional attitudes to places and landscapes can be strengthened by education directed by the country leaders but also by interested bodies, and as Gottmann claims – the historical factor and local iconography combine to support the establishment of political authority over a certain area (*ibid.*).

A cultural landscape or heritage site that has become an icon will change its status to a symbolic landscape. As such it can be analyzed in different ways: as a text (Duncan and Duncan 1988; Duncan 1990), and according to Terkenli (2001) as a valuable text, or as an irreplaceable archive (Holdsworth 1997; Ewald 2001), which reflects the society and its mores at a specific time and place.

The role of landscapes and sites in helping to coagulate community values and reconstruct social identities and local pride for certain groups, while excluding or erasing others, was described by many researchers (Duncan 1973; Cosgrove 1984; Duncan & Duncan 1988; Daniels 1993; 2004; Lowental 1991; Rose 1995; Duncan & Lamber 2002; Amit-Cohen

2008). Another possibility is to view the cultural landscape and cultural heritage sites as a cultural product, a consumer product which like any other economic or industrial product, undergoes refinement and improvement. Rowntree and Conkey developed this approach and claimed in 1980 that the cultural-symbolic landscape and sites do not reflect a social structure but are an inseparable part of society, its landscapes and products (Rowntree & Conkey 1980).

Yet another way of examining the formation process of symbolic landscapes and sites would be to analyze the changes according to four criteria: heritage and memory – historical documentation and observation of the changes of the status of cultural heritage landscape and sites through time – scale; commemoration – the process that transforms the cultural landscape and sites into a symbolic landscape, involving classification and categorization of the landscapes and choosing the values and messages that the population and those representing it want to preserve; representation and modeling – the means chosen to represent memory and its messages; and purposes and functions.

These four components – history and memory, commemoration, representation and functions – occupy a significant place in the formation of society's identity as expressed and reflected in the symbolic landscape. Choosing the commemoration, the presentation, and how to "use" a symbolic landscape or a cultural heritage site almost always arouses broad public interest where opposing ideologies attempt to persuade each other. Perhaps more than any other cultural phenomenon, these attempts reflect the atmosphere of the era, its conflicts and sensitivities, as well as the political and national interests of the various groupings.

The purpose of this article is to present the four components comprising the cultural-symbolic landscape and examine their expression in a contested geographical environment. To do so, I have chosen two geographical localities in Israel containing cultural heritage sites and cultural landscapes that have became symbolic. Prominent in these environments is an encounter between two societies, Jewish and Arab, both with a culture of memory, heritage and myths encompassing four components: memory, commemoration, representation and function. The first such environment is an urban area, which encompasses two very dominant landscapes adjoining each other – a new commercial and business center alongside historical remnants – a mosque and an old building which became a historical museum. This area and the commercial project are known as "Manshiya," the name of the former Arab neighborhood. The second environment is an agricultural area planted with olive trees with a contested significance for the two societies.

History and Memory, commemoration and representation – theoretical background

Heritage and memory serve two primary functions: to supply continuity from the past to the present, to represent the culture and thus create self-identity (Schwartz 1982). At the same time, memory and heritage are not permanent; they assume different forms and are shaped according to the mood of the time. Each memory begins as an intimate historical story, amended due to constraints of time and space; then additional layers are added, "a mosaic of personal memories that are distinct from one another" (Ohana and Wistrich 1996: 27),; and so it finally becomes a collective memory, part of the identity of the social group, whether small or large. To preserve its memory, the group needs to resort to commemorative activity. Such activity is vital for consolidating a social-cultural identity. Commemoration combines social, cultural, political, ceremonial and artistic activities constituting various representative expressions. These can be an original cultural landscape, or a carefully designed artificial cultural landscape with ceremonial and textual components. The choice of the landscape and its representation, the filtering and the caution exercised in their selection, are designed to guarantee the survival of the ethos within local and national memory. The representative function chosen for these means and the cultural landscapes is what transforms them into intermediaries of memory. These intermediaries include tombstones, monuments, sculptures, ceremonies, memorial days and holidays, street names and signs, and symbols, historical structures slated for preservation, gardens, as well as natural or cultural landscapes. Historical events and figures are often connected to many of these "intermediary agents." Over time, they were sanctified, becoming a focal point of ritual (Lissovsky 2004).

Following this approach, research involves memory and heritage, commemoration and representation, can be divided into three discussion groups: 1. Sets of memory and the links between them which in turn form the basis for classifying subjects worthy of commemoration. 2. The form of their representation, which presents a choice of commemoration landscapes. 3. The cultural heritage landscapes, their purpose and function.

Symbolic landscapes – their purpose and function

Often the functions of the cultural-symbolic landscape expand and the landscape and site evolve into vicinity that meets contemporary needs. Such development stems from the social-cultural potential of the cultural heritage landscape and site with their historical subject and design providing added value, which in turn contributes to the economic development of the sites and their significance. Expansion of the functions of cultural sites sometimes leads to a situation where sites and landscapes adopted by the larger community change their status by being perceived in the community consciousness as active landscapes rather than just symbolic sites.

- The expanded designation of cultural heritage sites and symbolic cultural landscapes can be divided into three parts:
- The strengthening of communal identity, both on the local and the national levels (Kamen 1977; Troyansky 1994; Ashworth 1994).
- Economic development adjacent to the site that reinforces memory (vacation and leisure, assembly site, educational center) (Newcomb 1979; Ashworth & Larkham 1994).
- Advancing power and vested interests (Tudor 1972; Cohen 1989; Young1990; Zerubavel 1994).
- Since its war of independence in 1948, these three aspects have significantly affected the landscape of Israel.

A Contested Landscape in Israel: Authentic-Historical Remains in an Urban Area and a Landscape of Olive Trees in a Rural Area

Contested landscapes can be created in two ways:

- A common environment for both societies within which each group has its own separate cultural-symbolic landscape. Each group thus possesses the territory of its symbolic landscapes.
- An environment containing a joint cultural landscape for both societies, but to which each society ascribes different significance and purpose.

When an environment is contested, or when there is a struggle between two groups, with each group claiming ownership of the area, a struggle also ensues between the different icons of the groups. In the event of one group taking over the contested area, the result may well be a deletion of the symbols and icons of the group evicted from the disputed territory.

The geographical area called the Land of Israel by the Jews and officially named Palestine during the British Mandate (1918-1948), was populated by two principal religious-ethnic groups: Jews and Arabs. All residents of this territory – Jews as well as Arabs – were Palestinians, i.e., residents of Palestine under the rule of the British Mandate for Palestine. Each society developed its environs while shaping its unique symbols and iconography. Jewish society relied on symbols and icons about 3000 years old, some of these within the residential environment of the Arab population. Added to these were the icons of Zionist settlements, which began in the 1880s and were concentrated in the Jewish territory. The decision of the United Nations on November 29, 1947 to partition Palestine into two states – Jewish and Arab – was rejected by the Arabs who launched a war to thwart the partition. This war, which ended with ceasefire agreements signed in the summer of 1949, left some Jewish areas in the hands of the Arabs and some Arab areas in the hands of the Jews.

The Jewish areas taken over by the Arabs were emptied of all their Jewish residents. This happened to the residents of the Jewish Quarter in the Old City of Jerusalem, residents of the Gush Etzion settlements, the residents of Beit HaArava near the Dead Sea, as well as others. Arab rule erased almost every vestige of Jewish identity in its territory. All the old synagogues in the Old City of Jerusalem were destroyed, the tombstones in the old Jewish cemetery on Mount Olives were uprooted and Jewish settlements were razed to the ground.

In Arab areas taken over by the state of Israel in the same war, various processes transpired. Some areas were abandoned by their residents, with the encouragement of the Arab leaders in the unfulfilled hope of returning after the anticipated Arab victory; some fled or were chased out by the Israeli army, while some remained where they were under Israeli rule. Wherever Arabs remained under Israeli rule, their icons remained as well. Abandoned places usually lost their symbols, most of the villages were destroyed, although in some instances, the religious structures – the mosques – remained untouched, even if there were no worshippers.

Many studies devoted considerable attention to the deletion of Arab and Jewish icons, Arab and Jewish cultural heritage and cultural-symbolic landscapes. A good example is the research of Azaryahu and Golan (2001), Levine (2004), Yacobi (2003) and Shai (2002). The last analyzed an initiative adopted by the Israel Land Administration (ILA) to demolish uninhabited houses in abandoned villages in Israel in the years 1965-1967.

Since the summer of 1967, in the Jewish areas and Arab areas, their symbols and icons are not only in contact but they are under dispute and a reason for violent incidents.

Manshiya Neighborhood in Tel-Aviv – Jaffa: History, Tradition, Memory and Commemoration

History

Until the year 1948, the Arab neighborhood of Manshiya was situated between the old Arab City of Jaffa and the new Israeli City of Tel Aviv. The neighborhood was established in the 1870s following the razing of the old Jaffa city wall by the Turkish authorities and the development of new neighborhoods – for both Arabs and Jews – outside the old city. At the end of the 19th century, a number of Jewish families settled in Manshiya, some quite famous (such as the Amzalak family, entrepreneurs and public activists within the Jaffa Jewish community (see Glass and Kark 1991: 161-163). In 1916, the Ottoman rulers built a mosque at the northern end of Manshiya (Hasan Bek Mosque). On November 29, 1947, after the UN decision to partition Palestine into two states, the Arabs of Manshiya began to fire toward the southern Jewish neighborhoods of Tel Aviv. According to the partition plan,

Jaffa was to be part of the Arab state. In order to prevent this from happening, the "Irgun Tzvai Leumi – Etzel" a nationalistic military organization, with a paramilitary force that operated against both the British and Arabs to win Jewish sovereignty, decided to conquer Jaffa and the neighborhoods along the seashore, between Jaffa and Tel Aviv. On April 27, 1948, the neighborhood of Manshiya was taken, followed by the conquest of Jaffa.

On May 12, a delegation of Arab notables arrived at the Hagana (the Israel Defense Forces) headquarters, and following negotiations signed a surrender agreement. On May 13, 1948, the British left Jaffa and in 1950 Tel Aviv and Jaffa were joined into one city, renamed Tel-Aviv – Jaffa. The Arabs of Manshiya fled and Jewish immigrants were settled in the abandoned damaged houses. The neighborhood deteriorated and became part of the Tel-Aviv – Jaffa southern slums.

Commemoration, Representation and functions

In 1951, the city leaders planned to establish a memorial on the Manshiya site for soldiers who fell in the battle for Jaffa. The memorial site was meant to tell the story of the two cities – Tel Aviv and Jaffa – as it had transpired in the War of Independence (Azaryahu 1993) rather than the national story (a memorial relating the national story was planned for the City of Tel Aviv somewhere else). However, the memorial on the Jaffa Tel Aviv border was never erected.

Over the years, the houses of Manshiya were destroyed, and in the mid -1970s, the Tel-Aviv – Jaffa municipality evacuated from Manshiya Neighborhood 3,100 residents, mostly Jews who immigrated to Israel in the 1950s. Instead, the municipality built a park and planned a business center on 600 dunams (60 hectares). Only two authentic remains were left untouched – the village mosque and a house in whose ruins the Etzel Museum was built. The business center planned to be part of a large project and meant to represent the modern developing city in contrast to Old Jaffa. Ultimately, however, the large project was not approved by the regional planning authorities, although part of it was already built.

The museum and the exhibit in it do not represent the history of the neighborhood or that of Jaffa and Tel Aviv. It rather describes the activities of Etzel in the War of Independence from November 29, 1947 until it's dismantling on September 22, 1948. In September 1948, Etzel was incorporated into the Israel Defense Forces. A room in the Etzel Museum commemorates the history of the organization, which existed for 17 years, and honors the liberators of Jaffa. The exhibition includes historical documents, photographs, maps and movies which describe the Etzel organization and the battle to liberate Jaffa.

The Hasan Bek Mosque was left next to a parking lot and beside a small memorial park for . During the 1980s, the Tel-Aviv – Jaffa planning authorities planned to convert the Hasan Bek mosque into a tourist attraction as part of the new image of the business center. Public objections scotched the plan, but the adjoining tall modern buildings overshadow the mosque making it difficult to discern the old building from afar. In contrast, the museum remained an isolated island in the large park along the seashore; a park which is part of the open urban space of Tel-Aviv – Jaffa. The area where the two remnants are located remains the border where the new and modern Tel Aviv ends and the old and neglected Jaffa begins.

The Olive Tree

History, Heritage, Commemoration and Functions – Different rituals, messages and values of the two societies – Jewish and Arab – surround the olive tree, a symbolic feature in many cultures. An example can be seen in Thomas L. Friedman's book, *The Lexus and the Olive Tree* (2000). The tree plays an important role as an Arab-Jewish icon in that it is common to both cultures. However, over time, it has acquired different meanings. And in today's Israeli reality, it represents different and even opposing values in the two cultures.

The Israeli olive is a relatively short tree, up to six meters high, evergreen and long lived. The tree is distinguished by its thick gnarled trunk and silvery-green leaves and is very prominent in the Mediterranean flora. Its appearance arouses interest and easily explains its sacred status in the various communities. It is often planted – alone or in a grove – next to the grave of a righteous or a holy person. The tree has deep roots and can thus grow almost anywhere. It quickly takes root in the mountain slopes and rocky areas of Galilee. Frequently, when natural and manmade disasters injure or destroy orchards and forests, the olive tree remains standing.

A few olive trees in Israel, in Galilee, date from the Roman period, two thousand years ago, and there is testimony that olives were cultivated in the Land of Israel and Syria more than six thousand years ago. The old trees turn hollow inside as they age. These characteristics make the olive tree unique and also explain its values: its deep roots, hopes, aspiration for peace as well as providing security, light, beauty and health, a statement of control and victory and so on. Nations, states, cultures, religions – all have utilized the olive tree, its branches and leaves, to present their messages, creating many visual symbols which give expression to the tree, its branches and leaves.

The olive tree occupies an important place in Jewish tradition. It is one of the seven species that *Eretz Israel*, the Land of Israel, is blessed with – "a land of olive oil and honey" (Deuteronomy 8:8). We learn of the status and significance of the olive tree from many sources. One is the parable of Yotam

(Judges 9:8-10) "The trees went out to anoint a king over them; and they said to the olive tree, reign over us. But the olive tree said to them, Should I leave my fatness, with which by me they honor God and man, and go to hold sway over the trees?" The olive tree symbolizes fertility and rootedness: "Thy children like olive plants round about thy table" (Psalms 128:3) and its economic importance is emphasized in a harsh reproof: "Thou shalt have olive trees throughout all thy borders, but thou shalt not anoint thyself with the oil for thy olive shall cast its fruit" (Deuteronomy 28:40). The olive is a basic agricultural product (Babylonian Talmud, Brachot, 41, a). Many laws from the areas of agriculture and Jewish ritual are connected with the olive and its oil. Olive oil is the best of oils and is thus used for religious ritual.

The connection between the olive branch and the striving for peace originates in the story of Jonah and the olive leaf and the story of Noah and the ark (Genesis 8:11). The olive branch also had a great influence on Zionist renewal. The branch appears as the symbol of the State of Israel (Mishory 2000: 139-164) and in the symbols of the IDF (Israel Defence Force) and represents the striving for peace and security: in the IDF emblem the olive branch embraces the sword. The olive tree does not appear in national symbols only. It also appears in paintings, shields of local authorities, and in names of settlements. Its appearance in the local Jewish space, especially the Zionist space, symbolizes the hope for survival and the ability to cope with the difficulties of settlement.

The striving for peace and the relationship to the olive branches as symbols of peace are also expressed in international symbols. Among these symbols, the UN symbol stands out with its double motifs: the map of the world and the two olive branches next to it. The symbol expresses the UN's aspiration of spreading peace throughout the world.

In Christian tradition as well, the olive – the tree, its branches and fruit – has a symbolic meaning (for example, Christian tradition identifies the Garden of Oils on the Mount of Olives as the garden in which Jesus walked, surrounded by his students). The olive tree is also important in Muslim tradition. In the Koran, the olive is mentioned six times, as one of the fruits given by Allah. Olive oil is only mentioned once in the chapter which talks about the divine light which will shine in the hearts of believers.

The hollowness of the olive tree generated one of the legends in Islam: When the prophet Mohammad died, all the trees mourned for him and as a result of all the pain and suffering, their branches fell to the ground. Only the olive tree's branches remained green. The other trees asked the olive tree, "Why aren't you mourning the death of the prophet?" The olive tree answered, "I mourn him greatly, but you wither on the outside and my heart is burnt on the inside."

Despite the importance of the olive tree in both Jewish and Arab cultures, time brought with it many changes. To a great extent, Israeli-Jewish society underwent the processes of secularization, modernization and post-modernization. Today, this society is primarily urban, secular and post-modern. As such, it emphasizes the "Lexus" from the well-known title of Tom Friedman's book, i.e., the most up-to-date model of the prestigious car is more important than the symbolic old olive tree. The tree has lost its actual significance and only its symbolic significance remains.

In contrast, in Israeli-Arab society, the olive tree is not only a symbol but a central component in the life of the village and the community. In many villages the olive tree is an important part of the economic base and the olive harvest is the most important economic period of the year in village life. The family and its olive trees are deeply connected. The tree connects the villagers to their land and signifies their ownership of the land and its boundaries.

In the territorial competition between Jews and Arabs over spatial dominance, the olive tree serves as a first class instrument for expressing Arab ownership of the land. Planting the olive tree is a sign of a boundary, and its uprooting by Israeli groups – for security purposes – symbolizes an attempt to evict the Arabs from their land, to deny their territorial rights.

In recent years, the olive tree symbolizes the aspiration for shared life and coexistence in the same territory in the State of Israel. Every year an olive festival is held; alongside the olive picking are meetings and discussions. The event has twin goals: economic-touristic and social-cultural.

Interpretation of Landscape: Discussion and Conclusions

The landscape, like a written text, can be interpreted on two levels: appearance and image.

The historical museum on the Jaffa – Tel-Aviv border displays an architectural encounter of natural building materials from the environment with synthetic building materials – limestone at the base of the building and on the top, glass and metal. The modern-artificial materials grow out of the original natural materials. The building is a landscape relic in the area of contact between Tel Aviv and Jaffa. The foundation of the building is a remnant of a Jaffa neighborhood, Manshiya, which was erased from the landscape. On this foundation, a new addition takes over, adapted to the needs of a historical museum in a modern city.

The structure that serves the historical museum not only gives expression to the national Jewish-Arab encounter, it also expresses a process of urban renewal. In this process, old relics are ignored and new modern and post-modern structures are preferred, without the historical context and cultural tension.

The mosque, an authentic remnant of the Arab Manshiya neighborhood, is also outside its natural environmental context. Consequently it loses some of its urban and communal relevance and remains solely a monument. The encounter between Jaffa and Tel Aviv as it is described by the landscape remains, also raises a historical paradox. Until 1948, Tel Aviv functioned as the core of Zionist settlement in the Land of Israel. As such, it was not a frontier area. Jaffa was an Arab enclave that bordered the Jewish city. The area of contact between the two cities became the front line during the establishment of the State of Israel. The decision to build the historical museum atop a structure which remained from the Arab neighborhood, as well as the decision to leave the mosque as is, was intended to document this historical encounter. Over the course of time, alongside the historical encounter, a new urban encounter began to develop in the form of the business center. At the present stage, the historical encounter is already serving as decoration for the urban renewal.

The olive tree: branches and leaves of the olive tree are of universal status, symbolizing peace and hope. Contrasting with this universality, we can discern here the cultural differences between Jews and Arabs in respect to the olive tree. In a picture of a Zionist landscape, the olive tree will always appear in the background or adjoining other landscape symbols, such as a water tower, houses, orchards, etc. In a picture of an Arab village, the olive tree will always appear involved with a significant action – olive picking or planting – in order to display ownership of the territory.

An examination of the two landscapes indicates that, although the geographical environments are different, the struggle for cultural dominance between Arabs and Jews is the same struggle expressed by the different cultural landscapes. In some instances, the two landscapes may coexist in the same geographical area. In other instances, each community acquired different messages in respect to the same landscape. This approach shows that the cultural heritage and cultural landscape possess somewhat different and varied facets. Each community chooses for itself the components of the landscape that can be used for its cultural identity and the message it wishes to transmit and uses them to weave a tapestry of its unique cultural landscape. In this weaving process, it ignores and abandons the components that are foreign or do not belong. In this way, two cultures can exist side by side in the same area and relate to the same landscape with different interpretations. This shows that one interpretation of the landscape does not of necessity lead to the delegitimization of the other interpretation; it also shows that a definition of "Contested Landscape" can be used as added criteria to describe an outstanding value of cultural heritage sites or cultural landscapes. This definition might serve also as a solution for cultural landscape or cultural heritage sites which present disputes or uncertain national proprietorship. In other words, the very fact that the sites or the landscapes are contested, bestows upon them their uniqueness and singularity.

References

Amit-Cohen, I. 2008. Silicatescape – Preserving Building Materials in the Old Urban Center Landscape: The Case of Silicate Brick and Urban Planning in Tel Aviv. *Journal of Cultural Heritage* 9, p. 367-375.

Ashworth, G.J. and Larkham P.J. 1994. A Heritage for Europe: The Need, The Task, The Contribution. In *Building a New Heritage, Tourism, Culture and Identity in the New Europe*, edited by G.J. Ashworth, G.J. and Larkham, P.J., 1-9. London and New York: Routledge.

Ashworth, G.J. 1994. From History to Heritage: From Heritage to Identity: In Search of Concepts and Models. In *Building a New Heritage, Tourism, Culture and Identity in the New Europe*, edited by G.J. Ashworth, G.J. and Larkham, P.J., 13-30. London and New York: Routledge.

Azaryahu, M. 1993. A Tale of Two Cities: Commemorating the Israeli War of Independence in Tel Aviv and Haifa. *Cathedra* 68, 98-125 (Hebrew).

Azaryahu, M. and Golan, A. 2001. (Re)naming the Landscape: the Formation of the Hebrew Map of Israel 1949-1960. *Journal of Historical Geography*, 27 (2), 178-195.

Cohen, W. 1989. Symbols of Power: Statues in Nineteenth-Century Provincial France. *Comparative Studies in Society and History* 31, 491-513.

Cosgrove, D. 1984. *Social Formation and Symbolic Landscape Totowa*. New Jersey: Barnes and Noble.

Daniels, S. 1993. *Fields of Vision: Landscape Imagery and National Identity in England and in United States*. Princeton: Princeton University Press.

Duncan, J.S. 1973. Landscape taste as a symbol of group identity: A Westchester County village. *Geographical Review* 63, 334-355.

Duncan, J. 1990. *The City as Text: The Politics of Landscape Interpretation in the Kandayan Kingdom*. Cambridge: Cambridge University Press.

Duncan, J.S. and N. Duncan, 1988. (Re)reading the Landscape, *Environment and Planning D: Society and Space* 6, 117-126.

Duncan, J.S. and N. Duncan. 2004. *Landscapes of Privilege: The Politics of the Aesthetic in an American Suburb*. New York and London: Routledge, 2004.

Duncan, J.S. and D. Lamber. 2002. Landscape, Aesthetics, and Power. In *American Space/American Place: Geographies of the United States on the Threshold of a New Century*, edited by J. Agnew and J. Smith, 264-291. Edinburgh: Edinburgh University Press.

Ewald Klaus C. 2001. The Neglect of Aesthetics in Landscape Planning in Switzerland. *Landscape and Urban Planning* 54, 255-266.

Friedman, Thomas L. 2000. *The Lexus and the Olive Tree*, London and New York: Routledge.

Glass, J.B. and Kark. R. 1991. *Sepharadi entrepreneurs in Eretz Israel: The Amsalak Family 1816-1918*, 1991, Jerusalem: Magnes.

Gottmann, J. 1952. The Political Partitioning of our World: An Attempt at Analysis, *World Politics*, 4 (4), 512-519.

Holdsworth, D.W. 1997. Landscape and Archives as text. In: *Understanding Ordinary Landscapes*, edited by Groth, P. and T. W. Bressi, 44-55. New Haven and London: Yale University Press.

Kamen, C.S. 1977. Affirmation or Enjoyment? The Commemoration of Independence in Israel. *Jewish Journal of Sociology* 19, 5-20.

Levine, M. 2004. Planning to Conquer: Modernity and its Antinomies in the "New-Old Jaffa". In: H. Yacobi (ed.). *Constructing a Sense of Place: Architecture and the Zionist Discourse*. London: Ashgate, 192-224.

Lissovsky, N. 2004. Sacred Trees – Holy Land: Cultural, Natural and Visual Characteristics of the Sacred Geography of Eretz Israel. *Cathedra* 111, 41-74.

Lowental, D. 1991. British identity and the English landscape, *Rural History* 2, 205-230.

Mishory, A. 2000. *Lo and Behold: Zionist Icons and Visual Symbols in Israeli Culture*, Tel Aviv: Am Oved (Hebrew).

Newcomb, R.M. 1979. *Planning the Past, Historical Landscape – Resources and Recreation*, Hamden: Connecticut: Archon Books.

Ohana, D. and S. Wistrich. 1996. Jewish and Zionist Myth. In *Myth and Memory* , edited by Ohana, D., and S. Wistrich, 11-40. Tel Aviv: Am Oved (Hebrew).

Rose, G. 1995. Place and Identity: A Sense of Place. In *A Place in the World? Place, Cultures, and Globalization*, edited by D. Massey and P. Jess, 87-132. Oxford: Open University Press.

Rowntree, Lester B. and Margaret W. Conkey. 1980. Symbolism and the Cultural Landscape. *Annals of the Association of American Geographers* 70 (4). 459-483.

Shai A. 2002. The Fate of Abandoned Arab Villages in Israel on the Eve of the Six-Day War and its Immediate Aftermath. *Cathedra* 105, 151-170 (Hebrew).

Schwartz, B. 1982. The Social Context of Commemoration: A Study in Collective Memory. *Social Forces* 2 (61), 374-402.

Terkenli, Theano S. 2001. Towards a Theory of the Landscape: The Aegean Landscape as a Cultural Image. *Landscape and Urban Planning* 57, 183-196.

Troyansky, D. 1987. Monumental Politics: National History and Local Memory in French *Monuments aux Morts* in the Department of the Aisne since 1870. *French Historical Studies* 15(1), 3-11.

Tudor, H. 1972. *Political Myth*, London: Mcmillan.

Young, A.R. 1990. We Throw the Torch: Canadian Memorials of the Great War and the Mythology of Heroic Sacrifice. *Journal of Canadian Studies*, 24 (4), 12-21.

Yacobi, H. 2003. The Architecture of Ethnic Logic: Exploring the Meaning of the Built Environment in the "Mixed" City of Lod – Israel. *Geografiska Annaler*, 84 (B), 171-187.

Zreubavel. Y. 1994. *Recovered Roots: Collective Memory and the Making of Israeli National Tradition*, Chicago: Chicago University Press.

IV

DEVELOPING SUSTAINABLE TOURISM

DÉVELOPPER LE TOURISME DURABLE

Developing Guiding Principles and Policies for World Heritage and Sustainable Tourism – A Major UNESCO World Heritage Centre Initiative

Graham Brooks
President
ICOMOS International Cultural
Tourism Committee
Australia

ABSTRACT

This paper presents a mid-term progress report on a ground breaking project that is at the very heart of how ICOMOS protects and transmits the tangible and intangible values of heritage places and the communities who sustain them. The 18-month UNESCO World Heritage Centre project brings together the conservation and tourism sectors to generate shared and sustainable policies, guidelines and methods to ensure that tourism activities contribute to the protection and conservation of World Heritage sites. For the first time, a number of major international agencies including the UN World Tourism Organisation (UNWTO), ICOMOS, IUCN, ICCROM, The Nature Conservancy and the World Bank have joined UNESCO and representatives of the Tourism Private Sector to craft common tourism and visitor management principles. These will be used by all participants to improve the management of tourism at World Heritage sites. Such sites will become best practice exemplars for other heritage places throughout the world. This is a project of great importance for ICOMOS as it considers ways to protect and enhance the Spirit of Place from increasing tourism pressures at heritage places.

RÉSUMÉ

Cet article représente le rapport d'étape d'un projet novateur qui se trouve au cœur même de la manière dont ICOMOS protège et transmet les valeurs matérielles et immatérielles des lieux patrimoniaux et des communautés qui les font vivre. Le projet, d'une durée de dix-huit mois, du Centre du Patrimoine mondial de l'Unesco, rassemble des représentants des secteurs de la conservation et du tourisme pour générer des politiques valides et partagées, des lignes directrices et des méthodes pour assurer que les activités touristiques contribuent à la protection et à la conservation des sites du Patrimoine mondial. Pour la première fois, un certain nombre des plus grandes agences internationales, y compris l'Organisation mondiale du Tourisme des Nations Unies, l'ICOMOS, le Congrès mondial de la Nature, le Centre international d'études pour la conservation et la restauration des biens culturels (ICCROM), le Conservatoire de la nature et la Banque mondiale ont rejoint l'Unesco et des représentants du secteur privé du tourisme, pour concevoir des principes communs de gestion du tourisme et des visiteurs. Ces principes seront mis en pratique par tous les participants pour améliorer la gestion du tourisme sur les sites du Patrimoine mondial. De tels sites deviendront exemplaires des meilleures pratiques pour d'autres sites patrimoniaux à travers le monde. Il s'agit d'un projet auquel l'ICOMOS attache une grande importance car il envisage des moyens de protéger et de valoriser «l'esprit du lieu» devant la pression touristique croissante dans ces lieux patrimoniaux.

Introduction

One of the most significant developments in relation to the work of ICOMOS in conserving Cultural Heritage and enhancing the *Spirit of Place* is emerging through a project initiated by the UNESCO World Heritage Centre; *Developing Guiding Principles and Policies for World Heritage and Sustainable Tourism*. Although only at its midpoint, this project has a direct and powerful relationship to the main themes of the International Symposium held in Quebec as part of the ICOMOS General Assembly, particularly Sub Theme 3, which explores mechanisms for *Safeguarding and Transmitting the Spirit of Place*.

The theme of the ICOMOS Symposium, "Finding the Spirit of Place" opens a new chapter in the international work of ICOMOS with regard to the conservation of the world's cultural heritage. While there is a significant material component to the *Spirit of Place*, one that is inherent in the physical remains of monuments, historic places and cultural landscapes, another, equally powerful component must be considered – the human transaction that goes to the very heart of finding, understanding, appreciating, enjoying and ultimately sustaining that *Spirit of Place*. This human transaction is the core of the future challenge for ICOMOS as it strives to protect, sustain and conserve in a comprehensive manner the tangible and intangible characteristics that combine to create the *Spirit of Place*.

The human dimension of cultural heritage management was recognised by ICOMOS as part of the 1999 *ICOMOS International Cultural Tourism Charter*, "Cultural heritage is seen as a dynamic reference point for daily life, social growth and change. It is a major source of social capital and is an expression of diversity and community identity."

The *Charter* also recognised the important role of tourism and public engagement with cultural heritage as a key activity in communicating the *Spirit of Place* to people from the host community and elsewhere. "Domestic and international tourism is one of the foremost vehicles of cultural exchange, providing personal experience of that which has survived from the past as well as the contemporary life and society of others. Reasonable and well managed access to cultural development and cultural heritage is both a human right and a privilege. It brings with it a duty of respect on the part of the visitor. Interpretation or presentation, play an important role in making the cultural heritage accessible to people."

Finally, the *Charter* stressed the critical role played by the human transaction in working towards the ultimate goals of ICOMOS and the wider conservation community. "A major reason for undertaking the protection, conservation and management of heritage places, the intangible heritage and collections, is to make their significance physically and/or intellectually accessible to the host community and to visitors. Unless there is public awareness and public support for cultural heritage places, the whole conservation process will be marginalised and not gain the critical levels of funding or public and political support so necessary for its survival."

Domestic and international visitors to a heritage place have the potential to be its greatest champions for safeguarding its *Spirit of Place*. Visitors and local people who experience a place and absorb its *Spirit* often develop a strong interest that extends well beyond their actual visit. In his keynote address, *Enhancing Travel Experiences, Making a difference in the World, Your Travellers and Institutions*, to the Educational Travel Conference in Baltimore, Maryland, USA (February 22, 2007), Dr Sam H Ham quoted the eloquence of Mr Sven Lindblad, a successful operator of cruise ship travel in the Galapagos Islands, when he said; "Ultimately, it will be the insistence and passion of the traveller that will save the special places on earth".

Dr Ham continued, "These people represent an army of potential spokespersons, defenders and constituents of a sane and healthy planet. And sufficiently moved by their travel experiences to any given place, each of them is capable of acting in behalf of, or even in defence of, that place, whether its while they're there or long after they return home."

To fulfil its ultimate mission, ICOMOS has an inherent responsibility to contribute to the relationship between people and places that takes place through the mechanism of travel. The *UNESCO World Heritage and*

Sustainable Tourism project provides ICOMOS with an enormous opportunity to make a powerful contribution to this important mechanism.

Shared International Objectives

The UNESCO World Heritage Centre attaches overriding importance to the development of sound and sustainable tourism policies and practices to ensure that tourism activity contributes to the protection and conservation of heritage sites and the communities that sustain them. In developing the *World Heritage and Sustainable Tourism* Project the UNESCO World Heritage Centre and the UN World Tourism Organisation recognise that World Heritage sites cannot be successfully conserved without proactively responding to the challenges of increasing tourist visitation and the broader humanitarian context.

They have jointly identified a suite of initiatives to make tourism more sustainable within the context of the human transaction between visitors and the *Spirit of Place*.

These include:

- Raising World Heritage awareness to build community support for conservation
- Economic, educational and employment opportunities derived from tourism
- Empowering of local communities in decision making and conservation activities
- Poverty Alleviation, particularly in the communities that sustain heritage places
- Capturing diverse and innovative funding sources for site conservation
- Building the capacity of World Heritage Site management in tourism related issues
- Developing tools and techniques for tourism management at World Heritage sites.
- Integrating comprehensive tourism management with the Operational Guidelines of the World Heritage Convention.

This suite of initiatives clearly demonstrates the broader socio-economic and development context in which the relationship between heritage conservation and tourism is regarded at the international level. International development agencies such as the World Bank are deeply interested in the potential for heritage and tourism to contribute to their wider social and economic objectives.

For the first time, this UNESCO project brings together all of the major international leadership stakeholders in the relationship between tourism and

World Heritage Sites. Together they are moving to a new level of cooperation and a shared commitment to protect the *Spirit of Place*. The UNESCO World Heritage Centre is combining with its Advisory Bodies ICOMOS and the World Conservation Union (IUCN), with the UN World Tourism Organisation, The World Bank, ICCROM, The Nature Conservancy and with key representatives of the Tourism Private Sector to develop a common vision and a set of guiding principles and working tools to implement that vision. The relationship between tourism and conservation extends well beyond places inscribed on the World Heritage List. However for the purpose of the project, World Heritage sites are regarded as the exemplars of the issue, having the capacity to become beacons of best practice management.

Concurrently, and again for perhaps the first time in such a structured manner, the human transaction with the *Spirit of Place* of World Heritage listed natural heritage places, cultural heritage places, places of mixed values and cultural landscapes are being jointly considered by ICOMOS and IUCN. For too long these two major UNESCO advisory bodies have tended to confine themselves to their own fields of interest. A realisation of shared values and objectives is bringing ICOMOS and IUCN to the *UNESCO World Heritage and Sustainable Tourism* Project in a spirit of unity and mutual cooperation.

The *UNESCO World Heritage and Sustainable Tourism* Project is responding to one of the key lessons learned from past initiatives – the need for a deep engagement with the tourism sector, especially the tourism private sector. This engagement is required to find mutually applicable solutions to site management problems and to utilise the tourism sector to sensitise visitors and their own personnel on World Heritage issues and on low impact ways to visit fragile sites. Engagement is also important to help aid local tourism enterprises. Providing communities in and around World Heritage sites with enhanced livelihoods from tourism can reduce threats to heritage values and build local conservation constituencies.

The author, in his role as President of the ICOMOS International Cultural Tourism Committee, is the official ICOMOS representative on the Project.

Tourism: A Threat or Opportunity for Conserving the *Spirit of Place*?

Protecting and managing the *Spirit of Place* is no longer the exclusive domain of technically trained professional conservation practitioners and heritage focussed academics. The "democratisation" of heritage means that the tangible and intangible characteristics of heritage places are of considerable interest and value to the wider global community. The inscription of a place on the World Heritage List signifies that it "belongs" to both the host community within the particular State Party and to humanity at large. While protection and conservation are a fundamental responsibility within the World Heritage Convention, so too is the equivalent responsibility for the significance of the place to be transmitted to the visiting public and through other media to the wider community.

Tourism has become one of the world's biggest economic and social activities. In 2007 there were an estimated 900 million international arrivals and at least five times that number of domestic tourists, world wide, although a visit to many of the major heritage places in Europe or Asia indicates that at some sites domestic visitors can outnumber international travellers by ten, twenty or fifty times. The UN World Tourism Organisation expects that tourism will continue to grow exponentially, reinforcing the critical need to manage it in a responsible manner. Places of natural and cultural heritage, whether formally protected or not, and the lifestyles of traditional communities throughout the world are increasingly becoming the focus of visits by more than just those people who are classified as "cultural tourists". The great challenge for both the conservation and the tourism sectors is to harness this enormous energy for the conservation of the heritage resources that form the core experiences of so much travel activity.

The ultimate challenge for the conservation community is that the 858 World Heritage sites spread over 145 countries are some of the world's most seductive and most heavily marketed tourism attractions. The dynamic growth in tourism at World Heritage sites is generating important challenges on how to respond to the public's demand for access while protecting the Outstanding Universal Values for which they were inscribed. Some 25% of recent State of Conservation reports to the World Heritage Committee indicate that poor tourism management is a problem.

Tourism development brings a concentration of public use to places where this was never contemplated historically. The need to both protect and present sites generates major challenges for all parties in the complex and challenging balance of competing or overlapping goals and responsibilities. Carefully coordinated planning and cooperative decision making are required. Clear objectives for both conservation and tourism must be formulated between the parties and supported by all stakeholders in the process.

A Challenge for ICOMOS

An informal email survey within the ICOMOS community, undertaken in February 2008 by the author as preparation for the first Project Workshop, reinforced an overwhelming priority that the protection of heritage values far outweighed any obligation or opportunity to present and communicate heritage places to the visiting public, if by so doing the heritage values were degraded.

Many of those actively involved in the conservation of the physical cultural heritage have a background as architects, archaeologists, historians or as technical or scientific researchers. They have tended to regard cultural heritage within a framework of immoveable material space, which is rooted in the characteristics of a particular place and imbued with the spirit of past, often lost societies or social practices. The implementation of the World Heritage Convention reinforced and consolidated a focus on material culture, the physical expression of heritage values and on memorializing the achievements of past societies. There remains a widely held priority on the "traditional" with its inherent concern about the intrusion of the "modern" into those values.

Accordingly there has been a strong concentration in the conservation community to emphasise and prioritise physical protection over human interaction. In this context, the presence of visitors is widely regarded as a threat to the heritage values of the place. It is reasonable to assume that to a large extent those involved in the conservation of nature and natural heritage places also emphasise the protection of the physical characteristics and natural systems.

There needs to be a broader approach within the conservation community away from just managing heritage places primarily as self-contained physical space to one which includes the whole range of contemporary social, political, intellectual and economic forces that shape modern life – to a sort of social-cultural landscape, rather than just a physical-cultural landscape. These influences are inevitably not confined to a local level. There is a need to look beyond the site to the national and even global level to examine contemporary tourism as one of the key social, economic and political forces that converge on heritage landscapes.

The informal survey generated a strong call for a major paradigm shift in the relationship between the heritage conservation and tourism sectors. A great deal needs to be done before the tourism policymaking and planning bring lasting opportunities to safeguard heritage places and their *Spirit of Place*. The conservation community needs to do more to transmit the heritage as an essential repository of cultural diversity and knowledge for future generations. We have not yet sufficiently brought the lessons learned from heritage into the development discourse. Equally, we have yet to learn how to harness the energies of the tourism sector as a contributing force for heritage.

The conservation world must engage actively with the tourism sector to develop shared understanding and shared outcomes that can motivate the tourism private sector to regard heritage places as assets to be conserved as well as utilized.

A Challenge for the Tourism Private Sector

In the context of this project, it is important to distinguish between the Tourism Private Sector and the Visitor who actually comes to the heritage site. The tourism sector facilitates the choice of the destination and the journey to the heritage site. With the exception of on-site tour guides and transportation providers, it is typically the visitor, traveller or tourist who actually experiences the site.

The Tourism Private Sector is characterised by an interactive combination of small or local service providers and regional, national or international, transportation, accommodation and reservation organisations. The sector is service oriented, highly dynamic, competitive and typically profit driven. It is subject to the extremes and fluctuations of fashion, prejudice and curiosity, climactic conditions and natural forces, perceptions of security and public safety, and above all by competitive pricing. It is widely diversified across many sectors including transportation, hospitality and accommodation, food and beverage, merchandise retailing, entertainment and information, and property development. The broad Tourism Sector embraces all forms of public and private organisational structures, motivations and anticipated outcomes.

While the Tourism Private Sector is economically focussed and will naturally exploit available resources for its own outcomes, there is a growing awareness in the sector of the need to sustain natural and cultural heritage resources for its own long- term survival. However are the majority so focussed on the competitive pressures of the tourism supply chain that the final impact by the visitor on the heritage site is of little interest or concern? Does the property developer, hotel manager or bus driver in the nearby township really care about the same issues as the heritage site manager? There is of course no single answer. A far greater dialogue between the conservation and tourism sectors will determine among other things how tourism operators regard cultural or natural heritage values and the qualities that contribute to heritage sites.

Key Outcome: A Paradigm Shift in the Relationship between Tourism and Heritage

Something very special happened during the first Workshop, in March 2008, at the World Heritage listed Arc et Senans historic site in south-eastern France. Representatives from a range of professional, public sector and commercial organisations across the whole spectrum of heritage and tourism came together to create a shared commitment to advance common goals.

The four major outcomes of the first workshop can be summarised as follows:

1. There is now a shared agreement that both the tourism and conservation sectors regard heritage places and their multiple values as long-term assets that must be protected and conserved to ensure the sustainability of their respective objectives.

2. The concept that tourism simply exploits heritage sites was reversed to one where tourism should be an active contributor to the conservation of heritage places. This represents a change from the concept of "carrying capacity" to "caring capacity".

3. There was change from the mindset within the Tourism Private Sector away from creating public assets for private gain towards joint engagement of private enterprise and public policy to contribute to the provision of infrastructure that can enhance local community livelihoods, while serving tourism demand.

4. There was a realisation that heritage sites cannot be managed only within the confines of their legal boundaries. Site management needs to engage with such issues as protecting buffer zones and safeguarding the character of nearby Destinations. It should be aware of social, political and economic frameworks, of infrastructure, environmental management and cultural traditions, tourism activity and visitor expectations in the broader local or regional context. Site management must consider its relationship to the whole Tourism Supply Chain.

The first Workshop focussed on "Creating an Enabling Environment", hence the importance of the outcomes detailed above. In addition to developing a strong sense of mutual cooperation, the Workshop examined issues such as Site Planning, Site Financing and Licensing for Concessions.

A Key Role for ICOMOS in Tourism Management at World Heritage Sites

The *UNESCO World Heritage and Sustainable Tourism* Project provides a unique opportunity for ICOMOS to engage with a process that brings together all of the major stakeholders in the conservation and tourism sectors to develop a shared vision for the protection and transmission of the world's natural and cultural heritage. The ICOMOS International Cultural Tourism Committee has actively committed itself to the project and to contributing to the development of a new compact between stakeholders.

The emerging comprehensive approach is thus a key initiative for ICOMOS as it seeks to protect and enhance the *Spirit of Place*. There are many areas where ICOMOS can contribute to good tourism management at World Heritage sites.

Tourism at World Heritage sites cannot be managed in isolation. Tourism is characterised by a long supply chain, commencing when someone decides to visit a place and finishing when they eventually arrive. Tourism management for World Heritage sites needs to shift from self-contained site conservation to the sustainable use of heritage resources. It needs to regard the site as a component or end point of the Tourism Supply Chain. Site management needs to take an interest in the development of visitor expectations and in the quality of the experience as visitors move through the local destination and onto the site. It is essential for site management to consider and respond to issues and opportunities outside the boundaries of the site, to cooperate with local and regional agencies in the development of policies and programmes that are integrated with a broader context. Good destination planning and management is critical to ensure that the special features of the World Heritage site do not to stand in direct contrast with the degradation of urban, natural and scenic qualities in the surrounding cultural landscape.

The UNESCO Project continues for another year. The next workshop, to be held in Switzerland in late October 2008 , will concentrate on enhancing the visitor experience. The last, to be held in India in early 2009, will examine the issue of community benefit. The project will conclude with a major public event in the latter half of 2009.

This is a project for which ICOMOS should give its full-hearted support.

The Impact of Tourism on the Monks of Luang Prabang

Wantanee Suntikul
Institute for Tourism Studies
China

Abstract

The attractiveness of Luang Prabang's temples for both heritage and religious tourists reflects their profound embodiment of the spirit of the place, yet tourism can also be seen as a threat to this very spirit. Exposure to tourism and social contact with tourists is influencing the values and aspirations of the city's many monks, as evinced by trends such as monks eschewing the study of traditional skills in favour of foreign languages to help them enter the tourism industry. This paper explores the effects that contact with tourists has on the values and practices of the monks of Luang Prabang and, in turn, how these changes have affected the spirit of the place. It is based on on-site observation, surveys of monks and tourists, as well as elite interviews with religious leaders.

Résumé

L'attractivité qu'exercent les temples de Luang Prabang, tant sur le patrimoine que sur le tourisme religieux, reflète leur profonde incorporation à l'esprit du lieu ; cependant, le tourisme peut également être considéré comme une menace à cet esprit lui-même. L'exposition au tourisme et au contact social avec les touristes influence les valeurs et les aspirations des nombreux moines de la ville, comme le montrent des tendances telles que le fait que les moines délaissent l'étude des aptitudes traditionnelles au profit des langues étrangères, afin de pouvoir intégrer l'industrie du tourisme. Cet article explore les conséquences que le contact avec les touristes entraîne pour les valeurs et les pratiques des moines de Luang Prabang et, en retour, comment ces changements ont affecté l'esprit du lieu. Il se base sur des observations sur le site, sur des sondages effectués auprès des moines et des touristes, ainsi que sur des entretiens des élites avec des chefs religieux.

1. Introduction

Tourism is a cultural phenomenon in which two broad cultures, that of the host and that of the tourist, come into contact. Although both parties in this exchange are affected in some way, the "impact" of this contact is usually more pronounced on the host culture than on the tourists, because the practice of tourism takes place in the host's home territory. The potential for cultural impact and even conflict increases when tourism comes into contact with religious sites or practices, especially when the tourist and the host do not share a religious faith.

The northern Laotian City of Luang Prabang is famous for its well-preserved colonial atmosphere and especially its many UNESCO listed temples, which make it both an important center of Therevada Buddhism and a popular tourist destination, attracting visitors of both religious and non-religious natures. Increasing numbers of tourist arrivals in recent years have brought new challenges to Luang Prabang. Buddha images and even architectural elements are being plundered from temples to sell to tourists, many old families have sold or rented their properties to entrepreneurs who use them as guesthouses, restaurants or for other tourism-related uses, and religious practices such as the giving of alms have become components of commercial tour packages. The incidence of contact between monks and tourists has also increased, which can be seen as having both positive and negative influences on the monks' lifestyle. Through on-site interviews and surveys conducted with monks, supplemented with personal observation, desk research and interviews with tourists, the researcher aims to identify the current impacts of tourism on monks and to investigate the perceptions of the monks regarding tourists and tourism development.

2. Luang Prabang's spirit of place

The spirit of place of Luang Prabang is largely influenced by its rich cultural heritage, both tangible and intangible. With its concentration of religious culture, its many temples and monks, it is historically a place of high spiritual significance for Buddhists.

This paper addresses a group of inhabitants of Luang Prabang that are associated closely with the spirit of Luang Prabang in many senses: the many monks that live in the city's temples. They represent an important element of Luang Prabang's spirit for tourists and religious adherents alike, and are closely associated with the spiritual practices of the city. By gaining insights into the ways in which the changes brought to Luang Prabang by tourism are perceived through the eyes of monks, the author hopes to make a contribution to the understanding of the relationship between tourism and spirit of place in this particular context.

3. Religion, heritage and tourism in Luang Prabang

On the strength of its unique and well-preserved architectural heritage, including its many fine temples, Luang Prabang was declared a UNESCO World Heritage site in 1995. Luang Prabang town alone has 34 temples. The advent of tourism has led some in Luang Prabang to re-contextualise their understanding of their tangible religious heritage in terms of their value within the tourism industry, rather than within the local society. This has led to some negative side effects, such as the stealing of Buddha images and even architectural elements from temples to sell to tourists (UNESCO 2007). There have been uncoordinated attempts to beautify temples since Luang Prabang's listing, in part to attract more tourists to the smaller and less well-known of the city's many religious sites. Although they may be well-intentioned, these measures have compromised the integrity of some of these temples (UNESCO 2004: 45).

In 2006, Luang Prabang received 151,703 tourists compared to 51,207 in 2001: a 200 per cent increase within 5 years. For accommodation, in 1997, Luang Prabang had 29 establishments (UNESCO 2007: 61) and in 2006, the number of establishments had increased to 173 with 1,808 rooms (LNTA 2007). Twenty-eight per cent of international arrivals are Asian and 72 per cent are Western tourists. The majority of tourists are backpackers (Ashley 2006: 59). According to Travers, tourists are attracted to Luang Prabang mostly because of the relaxed lifestyle, friendly people, and peaceful and beautiful landscape (2008: 111). These statements match the findings of the survey of tourists conducted by the author.

Theravada Buddhism has a profound effect on the intangible heritage of the city as well, and has formed the anchor for the daily rhythms, systems of belief and social and cultural practices of the citizens. While the World Heritage listing has catalyzed efforts to preserve the tangible heritage of Luang Prabang, this does not necessarily translate into a preservation of intangible heritage. In some ways, the tourism industry that focuses on these heritage buildings poses a threat to traditional ways of life and traditional skills, as people leave traditional occupations to take jobs in the more lucrative tourism trade. This has a secondary side effect, as these jobs often keep people so busy that they do not have time to give alms (UNESCO 2007). Also, many old families have sold or rented their properties to entrepreneurs who use them as guesthouses, as restaurants or for other tourism-related uses (Mydans 2008). The new tenants are not in the habit of contributing alms to the temples, as the old families did, and as a result fewer monks can be supported (Gray 2008). The most evident aspect of a positive impact is income obtained from the tourism industry, strengthening the pride of local people, providing funds for the preservation and conservation of local heritage and the revitalization of traditional skills. According to Ashley, tourism in Luang Prabang proves to be alleviating poverty (2006).

As for the issue of commodification, some festivals and events are being scheduled to meet the needs of tourists rather than the cultural calendar, or repackaged as commercial endeavours by locals themselves, threatening the perceived relevance of these events in the lives of the local people. There was even an attempt to exclude girls not wearing Laotian traditional dress from participating in the *pimai* festival (UNESCO 2004: 45-72). Francis Engelmann, a former UNESCO expert and Luang Prabang resident, has been quoted as saying "we have saved Luang Prabang's buildings, but we have lost its soul", claiming that tourism is accelerating the dissolution of traditional ways. He cites the closure of one monastery due to diminishing income from alms, the intrusion of tourists into temple life to take snapshots uninvited, and the appearance of petty crime, drug use and sex among young novices, unheard of before their exposure to tourists (Gray 2008). As a Buddhist, the author had always believed that the temple was one of the safest places from petty crime or robbery. However, during this field study, this belief was proven wrong. While visiting the abbot of a temple, the researcher parked a bicycle unlocked in front of the *Khuti* (monk's quarters). One hour later, the bicycle had disappeared. Later, the author was told that temples are now good spots for robberies as there are always many tourists visiting them. The abbot jokingly told the researcher "this is also a finding for your research on the impacts of tourism".

Clashes between tourist and host cultures occur in most tourism destinations to some extent. A lack of knowledge or sensitivity to the local religion leads tourists in Luang Prabang to do things that are not intended as offensive and may seem normal to them in the context of their understanding of tourism, but which may be deeply offensive to the religious sensibilities of locals, such as consuming alcohol on Phousis mountain in Luang Prabang. For tourists it is a popular site for beautiful views of sunsets, but for locals it is the site of the sacred That Chom Si Temple (UNESCO 2004: 58).

4. Monks' Perception of the Effects of Tourism
4.1. Profile of Monks

About 87 out of the152 monks and novices surveyed are between 16 and 20 years old, representing a majority of the sampling. One hundred twelve come from Luang Prabang Province, the rest from provinces to the north of Luang Prabang. About 48 per cent of monks and novices have been at the temple for two to three years, 23 per cent for up to one year, and another 23 per cent for four to six years. In total, then, 94 per cent of all responding monks had been at the temple for six years or less, indicating that very few monks remain at the monastery into their middle age, leading to a large age gap between the young novices and the few elder monks who still remain.

As for the question of why they decided to become monks, "I always wanted to practise Buddhism" was chosen 122 times, followed by *"Thodtan Bounkhun"* (gratitude to parents) 95 times. The answer "I would like to study so I can get a job when I leave the temple" was chosen only 19 times. However, an elder abbot revealed that he believed that the primary reason for young men coming to temple was to obtain an education (interview 2008). This seems to be confirmed indirectly by monks' answers to another question. When asked why they had decided to become a monk in Luang Prabang, the most popular choice was "I can get a better education in Luang Prabang" which was chosen 95 times, followed in prevalence by "Luang Prabang is an exciting town with a lot going on", chosen 52 times. Very few (14) chose the reply "Luang Prabang has a lot of tourists".

4.2. Monks' Views on the Temple Life

As for the question "what are your favourite subjects studied at the temple?", the subject of Buddhism was selected 117 times and the second choice was English with 97 times. Conservation and preservation was mentioned 43 times. Traditional arts and crafts (chosen 12 times) were less popular than mathematics (22 times). Once more, the top answer seems to be what the monks felt obliged to say, rather than what they felt. This supposition seems to be supported by the answers to another question. When asked in what subject they would like to receive more education, English was the most often selected with 113 mentions, followed by Buddhism (89 times), Laotian culture (54), conservation and preservation (34), accounting skills (19) and business skills (18). Traditional arts and crafts, however, were chosen by only 7 respondents. One monk stated that he would like to learn more English so that he can spread Buddhism to tourists who visit Laos. A principal of a monk's school (Interview 2008) confirmed that students preferred learning English to learning the liturgical language *Pāli*, because English was seen as having more relevance in qualifying them for employment. The abbot told the author that *Dhamma* (teachings of the Buddha,) can be difficult for young monks to learn. The most obvious context for the use of English in Luang Prabang is in the tourism industry, and it is logical to correlate a high incidence of interest in learning English with a desire to work in the tourism industry after leaving the temple. The UNESCO report has already stated this fact (UNESCO 2004: 74). In informal discussions with shop and business owners in the town, the author learned that former monks are the preferred employees, because of their perceived higher sense of *vinai* (rules of discipline) and their good level of English proficiency.

For the question "what kind of skills learned at the temple do you think will be useful after you leave the temple?", English was selected 104 times, conservation and preservation skills 30 times. Only eight monks believed that traditional arts and crafts skills would be useful to them in their secular life. This shows a low awareness of the importance of these skills relative to English, likely in part because the teaching of these traditional skills is becoming increasingly rare in temples. To learn these skills, monks would have to attend a separate school outside the temple.

4.3. Monks' Relations with Tourists

Twenty-eight monks don't agree with the statement that tourists consider monks as objects or attractions. An almost equal number of 26 agreed with this statement, but the majority, 78 of them, said they don't know. The monks who agree with the statement were asked to explain why they think in that way. Examples of the explanations offered include: "Maybe in their countries, there aren't monks, and that's why they are interested and want to know more about Buddhism", "Buddhism, monks and temples are important and tourists want to see", "If there weren't monks, temples and local people, tourists wouldn't be interested to visit the town", "Some tourists might have never seen monks and want to see us" and "Because we are different in their eyes". The tone of these answers shows a level of acceptance of the differences between tourists" nature and the local cultural norms. Buddhism's great tolerance for non-Buddhists and other outsiders has also been mentioned by Hall (2006: 180).

Ninety-three of the respondents stated that they don't mind when tourists take their pictures. Twenty-four monks said that they feel annoyed, but cannot do anything about it. Only ten monks chose "I don't like it at all and I refuse tourists". About 20 monks wrote their opinions on this issue, indicating, for the most part, a shared opinion among the monks that tourists should ask them for permission first before taking pictures. A few monks told the author that sometimes tourists came when they were having a meal and took pictures of them eating food. Another recounted that tourists arrived when he was in his bedroom, which he shared with many other monks, and tried to take pictures. A younger novice recounted that a group of women ran towards him, as they wanted to take a picture with him, something inappropriate within the moral code of Buddhism.

However, despite some problems with tourists, the majority of the respondents would like to see more tourists in Luang Prabang. When asked about their impression of the effects brought by tourists visiting their temples, 43 per cent said they do not see any great effect. About 31 per cent agreed that tourists make life in the temple more interesting. However, 11 per cent shared the opinion that if tourists come during their prayers and ceremonies, they would feel disturbed.

As for the question "Do you think temples should do more to accommodate tourists?", about 65 per cent replied in the positive. When the author asked them to be more specific about what kind of measures could be undertaken to better accommodate tourists, educating tourists about Buddhism was the most often chosen (49 per cent), followed by giving more information for tourists about the temples and Buddhism (29 per cent). Only 12 per cent would suggest allowing tourists to participate in part of temple life.

Fifty-nine per cent of monks came to agree that communication with tourists is important. In terms of the reasons why they believe this is important, 46 per cent would like to give tourists a better appreciation of Laotian culture, traditions and Buddhist religion, 26 per cent see it as a way to practice their own language skills and 19 per cent would value this contact as a way to find out about other parts of the world. Only 11 per cent don't agree with the initial statement. Eighty-eight monks replied that they have talked to tourists. Forty-seven of those have exchanged emails with tourists. Of the 59 responding monks who have never talked to tourists, 37 would like to talk to tourists but cannot speak English. Nineteen would like to talk to tourists, but believe it is inappropriate.

4.4. Monks' Views on Tourism Development

A question regarding monks' opinions about tourism development in Luang Prabang proved to be difficult for the monks to answer. A large number of monks expressed their concerns such as "A lot of tourists see temples as places to visit, but do not see any importance and meaning in them", "If there are too many tourists in Luang Prabang, local people will be busy and won't give alms", "As many tourists stay in town and locals have to move outside the town, there will be fewer local people in Luang Prabang", "Tourists and we need to understand each other's cultures more", "Many tourists give alms without understanding the meaning of it. They need to dress properly and have good manners", "Tourists should help Luang Prabang preserve Lao culture and tradition for the younger generation, and dress properly. Even when they talk in a different language, tourists can still use the Laotian way of talking". The majority stated that they wanted tourists to learn more about the local culture and Buddhism.

A famous aspect of religious practice in Luang Prabang is *binthabat*, which refers to the practice of giving offerings of food to monks, who form a long procession through the city streets with their alms bowls early every morning to receive these offerings from donors kneeling at the side of the road. This is an important practice for local Buddhists, who thereby gain merit, but it has also become known as a spectacle and an activity among tourists, who rise early to photograph the event or to participate themselves in the giving of alms. An elder abbot told the researcher "Some tourists regard *binthabat* as an activity. They want to have their pictures taken while giving alms. Some tourists don't dress properly. They look like they just got out of bed. I don't like seeing that and I don't even feel like eating food. If they want to do it, they should follow our way of doing it" (Interview 2008). Another young novice said "We are actually happier when we see local people giving alms in the morning".

5. Tourists' Attitudes and Perceptions

5.1. Tourists' Views on Impacts

The surveyed tourists in general took a critical view of the cultural practice of tourism, and its effects on the host culture. When asked if they think that tourism is bringing negative impacts to Luang Prabang, 55 tourists said yes, 17 said no, and 12 tourists were not sure. The most prevalent negative impacts that tourists believe are being brought to the town by tourism are commodification (selected 34 times), loss of authenticity (28 times), and loss of spirit of place (20 times). As for the question whether they think that tourism might influence the monks' lifestyle, 44 tourists agreed, 23 didn't agree and 16 chose not to give any opinion on this issue. One tourist wrote that "Some people have requested me to give alms, or light incense when it is not my religion, thus it becomes commercialised". The term commercialisation was used repeatedly by other tourists as well. Another noted that "I don't like tourists go to the alms giving, like in a zoo".

In an article on Luang Prabang from The New York Times, dated 27 March 2008, Mydans wrote: "As the sky grows light along the Mekong River here, it is no longer the quiet footfalls of Buddhist monks that herald the day but the jostling and chattering of hundred of tourists who have come to watch them on their morning rounds… Here they come! Here they come!" a tour guide cries over his loudspeaker. "Hurry! Hurry!"

This writing clearly illustrates an almsgiving scene in Luang Prabang. A local compared this practice to a safari and said that tourists look at the monks the same as at monkeys or buffalo (Mydans 2008). This attitude was reflected on a travel blog the author came across, by a woman who participated in giving alms while in Luang Prabang. Under one picture of her waiting with food for monks to arrive, she wrote "This is me waiting to feed the monks".

The survey asked tourists to express their opinion about tourists taking pictures of monks. "I find it a bit irritating, but I do it myself" was selected by 18 respondents, and the same number of respondents chose "I don't like it at all and don't want to do that." "Nothing wrong with that, I do it myself" was selected by 14 tourists. Thirty tourists opted for writing statements on this topic. Most of the statements illustrated similar opinions about this issue. They noted that they find taking picture of monks is fine as long as you do it with respect, keep distance, and always ask for permission first. One tourist stated that "I definitely feel a bit wrong about it but I want to show my family back home." Another one said that "I did it with respect, but I would take a picture because I am in awe of them" Interestingly, most of statements appeared to be self-defensive in tone, "I took 3 pictures at morning almsgiving, from at least 60 meters away."

5.2. Tourists' Views on Contact with Monks and Buddhism

Forty tourists don't like to enter to temples while the monks are praying and mediating. Ten believed "Nothing wrong with that, I do it myself". Others replied "No opinion" (13), or "I find it a bit irritating, but I do it myself" (8). Twenty-two tourists chose to elaborate further on this concern. Again, most of the statements stated that if tourists do it with respect, it should be acceptable. One tourist said, "Try to sit in the corner and try not to disturb." However, it might be difficult to define a common understanding of "respect" from the point of view of the monks who are either mediating or praying and the tourists who are curious about the practices.

When queried about their level of curiosity about the Buddhist religion, the majority of the respondents replied that they are curious to know more about Buddhism. The author then asked further if they think temples should accommodate tourists more. Forty-nine per cent decided for "No". Only 29 per cent opted for "Yes" and 22 per cent of the tourists gave no opinion. It is interesting to see that even though the majority of the respondents are curious to know more about Buddhism, they do not think that temples should accommodate tourists more. Among the stated reasons for positive responses are: "It is good to show the lifestyle of the Buddhist", "Tourists need to be more educated, then they will have a better appreciation". The reasons given for "No" include that temples are places for worship, that tourism and religion do not belong together, and that temples are places to observe only. The main reasons can be summarised as reflecting an attitude among tourists that the only persons who should be accommodated by temples are local people, people who study Buddhism and tourists who practise Buddhism, with the implication that otherwise this activity will become commercialised. This reiterates the "hands-off" attitude of tourists to closer involvement in the temples.

6. Conclusion

The attitudes expressed by the majority of tourist respondents to the questionnaires indicate that they have a curiosity about the culture of the temples, but also a respect for propriety when dealing with religion in the host culture, and a concern for drawing the line between acceptable and unacceptable tourist behaviour.

In the responses to the questions asked of the monks and the tourists, there are indications that members of each group are making an effort to moderate their own statements through an attempt to empathize with the point of view of the other. Thus, tourists express curiosity about Buddhist life but are cautious about infringing on the territory of the temple. Monks may not be pleased with certain tourist practices, such as photography, but express an appreciation of the meaning and value of photographs for the tourists, on the basis of which they accept such practices. In general, monks' understanding of tourists seems to be more insightful and nuanced than tourists' more simple "hands-off" approach to showing respect to religion. The reasons for this may be explained partially by Maoz (2006: 229), who discussed the construction of the "gazes" of tourists and hosts, remarking that the gaze of the tourist is mostly constructed through their exposure to media images of the destination, before their actual travels. Locals, on the other hand, build a richer and more "real" image of tourists iteratively, through repeated contact with tourists over time.

Travers (2008: 111-113) has remarked that the success of Luang Prabang is due to its offering of a sanitized and increasingly Westernized heritage "experience" that is heavily influenced by attempts to create an atmosphere that corresponds to tourists' romantic images of the city's past. The high proportion of tourists who came to Luang Prabang with a pre-formed conception of the city attests to the wide dissemination of these media images, and the large percentage of these whose expectations were met or exceeded by their actual experience in the place lends credence to Travers' statement regarding the city's successfully engineered tourist product, of which the religious tangible heritage (including the monks themselves, seen as a spectacle) forms an important component. Ironically, though, the tourists surveyed were cognizant and concerned about Luang Prabang's perceived loss of authenticity due to the commercialization and other ills brought by tourism (although most of the respondents very likely never knew first hand the pre-tourism of Luang Prabang) and expressed a sense of guilt at their admissions that they see the monks as part of the tourism product to be seen and photographed. The complex relation between tourists' perception of a loss of authenticity in Luang Prabang, the realization that they themselves are participants in this loss of authenticity, and the nonetheless highly successful projection of an image of a sense of place is an interesting topic for further research.

Monks were far less likely to express that they felt a negative impact on their way of life from tourism. Nor, however, were they unreservedly enthusiastic about tourism. The general attitude seems to be one of acceptance of tourism, with an expectation that tourists also respect simple boundaries. Tourism certainly cannot be completely blamed for the difficulties being met by the temples in changing Laotian society, but it does introduce another contextual factor that makes monks think differently about their life after the temple, which can affect their choices while in the temple. For example, the most popular subject the respondents would like to learn more is English, and they also believe that English is the most useful skill when leaving temples. The majority of monk respondents would like to see more tourists and agreed that tourism does not bring great negative effects to their lives, but actually makes life in the temple more interesting. It can be said that, just as monks are a distinctive element of the image of Luang Prabang for tourists, tourists are also an important characteristic of the city's image from the point of view of the monks.

Tourists see the spirit of the place of Luang Prabang in terms of a consistent and nostalgic image, even before they arrive, and are sensitized to any threats that they see as diluting that image. For the monks, the city is the lived environment of their lives for a number of years. They also see changes, but do not necessarily see them as threatening. Contact between these two groups will only continue to intensify as tourism development in Luang Prabang continues, and their respective images of the city, by which the spirit of place of Luang Prabang is represented and understood, will continue to evolve.

References

Ashley, C. 2006. *Participation by the Poor in Luang Prabang Tourism Economy: Current Earnings and opportunities of Expansion*. ODI and SNV.

Condominas, G. 1998. *Le Bouddhisme au Village*. Vientiane: LNTA.

Engelmann, F. 1999. Luang Prabang: A Ghost Town Returns to Life. Available from http://www.unesco.org/courier/1999_08/uk/dossier/txt36.htm; accessed 7 July 2008.

Gray, A. 2008. Mass Tourism Swamps Asia's Once Unique, Remote Places. USA Today. Available from http://www.usatoday.com/travel/destinations/2008-03-27-disappearing-asia_N.htm; accessed 7 July 2008.

Guttman, C. 1999. Towards an Ethnic of Tourism. Internet. Available from http://www.unesco.org/courier/1999_08/uk/dossier/txt43.htm; accessed 7 July 2008.

Hall, M. 2006. Buddhism, Tourism and the Middle Way. In *Tourism, Religion and Spiritual Journey*, eds. Olsen A. and Timothy D: 172-185. Oxon: Routledge.

Ladwig, P. 2006. Applying Dhamma to Contemporary Society: Socially-Engaged Buddhism and Development Work in the Lao PDR. *Juth Pakai* 7:16-26.

LNTA (Lao National Tourism Administration). 2007. *2006 Statistical Report on Tourism in Laos*. Vientiane: LNTA.

Maoz, D. 2006. The Mutual Gaze. *Annals of Tourism Research* 33(1):221-239.

Mydans, S. 2008. Tourism Saves a Laotian City but Saps its Buddhist Spirit. Available fromhttp://www.nytimes.com/2008/04/15/world/asia/15laos.html; accessed 7 July 2008.

Robinson, M. 1999. Is Cultural Tourism on the Right Track? Internet. Available from http://www.unesco.org/courier/1999_08/uk/dossier/txt11.htm; accessed 7 July 2008.

Travers, R. 2008. Economic Corridors and Ecotourism: Whiter Tourism in Laos? In *Asian Tourism: Growth and Change*, ed. Cochrane, J.: 105-116. Oxford: Elsevier.

UNESCO. 2004. Impact: The Effects of Tourism and Culture and the Environment in Asia and the Pacific Tourism and Heritage Site Management in Luang Prabang, Lao PDR. UNESCO and School of Travel Industry Management University of Hawaii.

UNESCO. 2007. "UNESCO Cultural Survival and Revival in the Buddhist Sangha" Project Evaluation Workshop. Presentation. Mahachulalongkornrajavidyalaya Univeristy, Thailand.

Les restaurants de la vieille ville de Damas : invasion ou quête de l'esprit du lieu ?

Samir Abdulac
Architecte DPLG
France

Abstract

The spirit of place can be experienced differently within the same community. The example of the Old City of Damascus in Syria – a world heritage site – is significant in this regard. During the first half of the 20th century, there was a mass departure of well-off families followed by the arrival of rural immigrants.

In the early 1990s, developing tourism was considered a sound idea, both to preserve the built surroundings and to restore the value of the Old City in the eyes of its inhabitants. In only fifteen years, more than 100 ancestral homes with balconies were converted into restaurants, a completely new development. Many point to poor architectural adaptations. Customers, who are essentially from the modern districts, enjoy the illusion that they are re-experiencing the past for a few hours. The economic, social and cultural balance of historic cities is so fragile that a city's very soul will be threatened when a single component becomes excessive. The noise, traffic and environmental consequences of these changes are causing major problems for the traditional life of this district. An integrated preservation and development plan is currently under study and the restoration of existing residential dwellings has now become necessary.

Résumé

La vieille ville de Damas (Syrie), inscrite sur la liste du patrimoine mondial, est exemplaire de l'esprit du lieu qui se vit différemment au sein d'une même société. Les familles aisées l'ont massivement quitté au cours de la première moitié du XXe siècle pour être remplacées par des immigrants ruraux. Au début des années 1990, le développement du tourisme paraissait être une bonne solution pour sauvegarder le bâti et revaloriser la vieille ville aux yeux de la population. En une quinzaine d'années seulement, plus d'une centaine de restaurants ont ouvert dans les anciennes demeures à patio, parfois avec des adaptations architecturales maladroites, alors qu'il n'y en avait aucun auparavant. Leur clientèle, essentiellement originaire des quartiers modernes, aime se donner l'illusion de replonger quelques heures dans le passé. Mais l'équilibre économique, social et culturel des villes historiques est si fragile que l'âme de la cité est en danger quand le poids d'une seule de ses composantes devient excessif. Ainsi, les nuisances sonores, de circulation et environnementales représentent des inconvénients majeurs pour la vie traditionnelle du voisinage. Un plan intégré de conservation et de développement est à l'étude et des actions de réhabilitation de l'habitat résidentiel existant deviennent nécessaires.

La vieille ville de Damas

La ville de Damas en Syrie est l'une des plus anciennes capitales du monde. Elle est mentionnée dans les textes pharaoniques. Autrefois capitale de royaumes araméens, elle connut la splendeur avec l'établissement du califat des Omeyyades et elle demeura importante tout au long des époques ayyoubide, mamelouke et ottomane.

Damas est entouré par la plaine agricole de la Ghouta, bien irriguée par les bras et les canaux de la rivière Barada. L'un de ses bras borde le nord de la ville intra-muros. Le petit noyau araméen dut s'adapter à l'urbanisme hellénistique, avant que la composition et l'orthogonalité romaines ne s'imposent partout. Dans un rare esprit de continuité, la grande mosquée des Omeyyades succède, toujours au même emplacement, au temple de Haddad, à celui de Jupiter et enfin à la cathédrale byzantine de Saint-Jean Baptiste.

La ville était protégée de murailles qui furent particulièrement renforcées lors des croisades. Des faubourgs d'abord isolés se raccordèrent progressivement à la ville intra-muros à partir du XIIe, puis du XIVe siècle.

La vieille ville fut victime d'un bombardement de la puissance mandataire en 1925 et les faubourgs, de la spéculation immobilière qui se développa après l'indépendance. Comme dans quantité de situations similaires, les couches aisées quittèrent les vieux quartiers et furent dans une certaine mesure remplacées par une population rurale, avec un accroissement de la densité urbaine. Ces mouvements furent toutefois tempérés par le maintien d'une coloration communautaire confessionnelle dans différents quartiers.

Aujourd'hui, la ville intra-muros couvre 130 hectares et comprend une population de 30 000 personnes environ, après une diminution au cours des dernières années. Autour se développe une métropole de 4 millions d'habitants qui fait disparaître les champs cultivés de la Ghouta.

Le plan directeur de Michel Ecochard, en 1968, ne protégeait pas les anciens faubourgs et permettait encore des «curetages» et quelques élargissements de voirie dans la ville intra-muros. Une réglementation assez stricte imposait toutefois des reconstructions avec la même volumétrie (patio compris) et avec les mêmes matériaux.

Après avoir été classée en 1976, la vieille ville de Damas fut inscrite sur la liste du Patrimoine mondial en 1979. On doit toutefois déplorer vers 1987 des élargissements destinés à faciliter l'accès à la mosquée des Omeyyades pour les cortèges officiels, ainsi qu'à dégager l'espace autour d'elle. La restauration de la mosquée au début des années 1990 ne fut guère exemplaire non plus.

L'activité commerciale, toujours très dynamique dans les souks et les quartiers de la partie ouest, contribue à générer une circulation souvent difficile. Pendant longtemps, les habitants n'eurent guère les moyens de se doter de voitures. Le réseau d'adduction et d'évacuation de l'eau remonte parfois à l'époque romaine et a bien fonctionné jusqu'au XIXe siècle. Les fondations de quelques immeubles modernes, l'usure, le manque d'entretien, la perte de mémoire, ont condamné ce réseau. Les câbles électriques et téléphoniques courent par contre au-dessus des rues et sur les façades.

La Syrie est un pays touristique pour la population des pays de la région qui apprécient son climat, ses ambiances, sa cuisine et ses marchandises. Leur nombre annuel approcherait les deux millions en ville, d'après le ministère du Tourisme. Les touristes occidentaux sont essentiellement intéressés par son patrimoine culturel. Ils sont pourtant dissuadés par l'instabilité de la région environnante et leur nombre (quelques centaines de milliers dans le pays) a beaucoup baissé par rapport à la décennie précédente.

Figure 1. Un café traditionnel, *la Nofara*.

Ces deux catégories de touristes se rejoignent dans la visite des souks, de la mosquée des Omeyyades et même du Palais Azem (Musée des Arts et Traditions Populaire). Ce dernier accueille de 30 000 à 50 000 visiteurs occidentaux par an. Deux ou trois autres musées reçoivent une fréquentation plutôt confidentielle. Des maisons restaurées comme *Beit Sbaï* et *Beit Nizam* ne trouvent pas d'affectation.

Dans la présentation qui suit, en plus d'une série d'observations person-nelles, les informations utilisées ont été recueillies par l'auteur depuis une quinzaine d'années, au cours de missions effectuées pour différents organis-mes et programmes, notamment auprès de la commission du tourisme de la Direction de la vieille ville de Damas et dans le cadre du programme européen MAM de Modernisation de l'administration municipale.

L'apparition de nouveaux restaurants

Une poignée de cafés populaires (comme celui de la *Nofara*), de res-taurants en cave (*Qasr Umawi*) et d'hôtels bon marché (*Rabii, Haramein*) s'étaient maintenus jusqu'ici contre toute attente, appréciés par les habitants et les jeunes étrangers. Au début des années 1990, le ministère du Tourisme promulgua une nouvelle réglementation, faisant de toute transformation d'un bâtiment historique en hôtel un investissement touristique bénéficiant d'incitations fiscales.

Le premier nouveau restaurant de la ville ancienne ouvrit en 1992 dans le quartier chrétien de Bab Charki, peut-être pour pouvoir servir de l'alcool. Dans ce premier exemple (*Casa Blanca*), il s'agissait d'emblée de réutiliser l'ensemble d'une maison traditionnelle à patio. Architecturalement, l'adaptation n'était pas très heureuse. Le mouvement d'ouverture de restaurants se développa progressi-vement, avec des résultats architecturalement très variés, allant du maintien tel quel des maisons (*Elissar, Jabri*), à leur défiguration par des éléments exogènes (*Guitare*), en passant par la rénovation envahissante dans un style ancien fidèle (*Khaouali*) et même par l'introduction d'éléments structurels et stylistiques contemporains (*Al Dar*). Le nombre d'architectes restaurateurs s'accroît en ville, notamment grâce à l'antenne du Cours de Chaillot.

La plupart des maisons concernées disposent d'un patio avec bassin et végétation, entouré par des espaces intermédiaires (*iwan*, galerie) ou construits (*quaa*). La couverture du patio par un velum ou une verrière (parfois les deux) permet de s'adapter à certaines caractéristiques climatiques (soleil l'été et froid l'hiver). Pourtant les maisons traditionnelles étaient déjà climatiquement adaptées. Au pire, les clients s'installent dans des pièces fermées l'hiver. Si la situation et la saison le permettent, les terrasses sont mises à contribution avec une vue sur les monuments illuminés et les lumières de la ville (*Khaouali, Layla*). Même d'anciens ateliers de menuiserie ou une usine de brocart plus que centenaire sont transformés (*Narinj, Naassan*).

Figure 2. Une maison relativement peu touchée, *Beit Jabri.*

Figure 3. Une maison rénovée – *Al Khaouali.*

La fréquente utilisation d'une couleur ocre non traditionnelle permet de reconnaître plus facilement les restaurants de l'extérieur. Beaucoup de bâtiments n'étant pas encore ouverts, seule une enquête à grande échelle pourrait au fond permettre de juger du maintien ou non de l'intégrité et de l'authenticité des maisons transformées.

Plusieurs autres quartiers, et même les abords de la mosquée des Omeyyades, sont désormais touchés par l'ouverture de restaurants. Les clients se garent là où ils peuvent ou arrivent en taxi. Dans certains cas, le restaurant vient même les chercher avec un petit train.

Les premiers restaurants ne servaient qu'une nourriture occidentale, peut-être par snobisme, car la majorité de leurs clients sont du pays. Depuis, ceux où l'on sert de la cuisine orientale sont devenus majoritaires. La plupart des restaurants sont néanmoins d'un certain standing. Les damascènes ont l'habitude de sortir en couple et par groupes de couples. Ils pratiquent chez eux ou au restaurant une vie sociale assez intense. Il est bien sûr possible aussi de rencontrer dans les restaurants des touristes occidentaux ou arabes, mais ceux-ci restent minoritaires.

Figure 4. Une maison modernisée, *Al Dar.*

L'appellation de « restaurants touristiques » reste donc théorique, même si les restaurants apportent une contribution purement économique au développement local.

L'ampleur du phénomène

En quinze ans, les nouveaux restaurants de Damas ont, dans une bonne proportion, ouvert dans la vieille ville. Étant en charge de la direction de la vieille ville (dite *Maktab Anbar*), la municipalité a été saisie jusqu'en 2006 d'une centaine de demandes d'autorisations d'aménager des restaurants dans la vieille ville intra-muros. La transformation de locaux commerciaux ou industriels en restaurants ne nécessite pas d'autorisation et des aménagements de simples maisons sont parfois suspects d'autres intentions.

La proportion prise par les activités « touristiques » ne dépasse pas encore 2 % de la surface bâtie totale, mais son accroissement est spectaculaire et son impact environnemental, social et économique, considérable. Il ne serait pas surprenant que la vieille ville compte prochainement 200 restaurants.

Un tel phénomène mérite réflexion en raison de son ampleur et de sa rapidité. Pour une fois, ce n'est pas le tourisme qui est à mettre en cause, car son rôle n'est que marginal, qu'il soit régional ou occidental. Par ailleurs, malgré quelques tentatives ponctuelles, le mouvement de *gentrification* n'est pas encore significatif. S'il s'avérait que l'ouverture des restaurants ne corresponde qu'à un effet de mode, leur reconversion serait problématique. Et ces opérations n'auraient eu qu'une durabilité aléatoire.

Un psychosociologue parlerait peut être d'un large phénomène de retour dans la ville ancienne. Les clients, issus de la ville moderne, apprécient en effet l'ambiance et l'esprit d'autrefois qu'ils retrouvent non seulement au restaurant, mais aussi dans leur trajet nocturne pour s'y rendre. Mais les quartiers anciens sont investis uniquement le temps d'une soirée, sans jamais être réellement occupés. Cela ressemble à un acte manqué, peut-être à un désir incomplètement assumé. Le blocage psychologique envers une vie permanente dans les vieux quartiers semble être trop fort encore.

Figure 5. Transformation d'une maison en hôtel, *Beit Farhi*.

Par ailleurs, quatre nouveaux hôtels de luxe ont ouvert, dont le *Mamlouka* et le *Talisman* (maison *Chattahi*), qui ont essayé de rester fidèles à l'esprit traditionnel. La grande maison *Farhi* est également en cours de restauration avec un soin particulier (n'était la verrière centrale). Une quarantaine de demandes de permis auraient été déposés à la municipalité. La rencontre d'une nouvelle capacité d'investissement avec les goûts d'une clientèle locale est moins assurée dans le cas de l'hôtellerie. Certains hôtels iront-ils rejoindre le parc des restaurants?

Figure 6. Une maison transformée en hôtel de luxe, *le Talisman*.

Les restaurants génèrent différentes nuisances pour leur voisinage, comme le bruit nocturne, la perturbation d'un mode de vie traditionnel, la difficulté de stationner, la saturation des réseaux d'eau et d'égouts, les contraintes de ramassage des détritus. C'est pourquoi, suivant l'exigence de la municipalité, toute demande de permis doit s'accompagner de formulaires d'accord du voisinage ; mais ces enquêtes sont souvent bâclées. Le prix des propriétés immobilières a été multiplié par sept en cinq ans. Le coût moyen d'une maison à patio atteint actuellement l'équivalent d'un ou deux millions de dollars US. Les habitants qui avaient résisté jusqu'ici au départ se laissent tenter.

Vers de nouvelles orientations

Le ministère du Tourisme continue de demander que de grands axes soient choisis et consacrés aux activités touristiques dans la vieille ville. Il aurait pu être intéressant de discuter de cette question il y a une douzaine d'années, mais la multiplication et la dispersion qui se sont produites depuis la rendent aujourd'hui théorique. La municipalité a fini par imposer un moratoire sur l'attribution de nouveaux permis (concernant les restaurants) au début de l'année 2006. Des travaux d'infrastructure interminables, commencés à l'automne 2007 sur l'axe principal de la vieille ville (Souk *Medhat Pacha*), ont porté (provisoirement?) un coup sévère aux activités diurnes et nocturnes de la vieille ville.

Un récent plan d'aménagement stratégique aggrave plutôt le problème en permettant les installations « touristiques » sur beaucoup trop de parcelles. Il avait été élaboré au début de l'année 2006 et vient d'être adopté il y a quelques semaines.

Le programme européen de Modernisation de l'Administration Municipale (MAM) met au point pour l'automne 2008 un plan intégré de conservation et de développement de la vieille ville de Damas. Ce plan devrait enfin traiter à grande échelle le problème de la réhabilitation de l'habitat dans les quartiers anciens et permettre ainsi à la fois d'y habiter, d'y vivre et d'y travailler.

The Cherokee Cultural Tourism Program Seeking a Balance between Authenticity and Economic Development

Anne Ketz
David Ketz
The 106 Group Ltd.
Minnesota

ABSTRACT

The Cherokee Nation of Oklahoma is developing a cultural tourism program that is far reaching, both geographically and in its potential social, cultural, and economic impact. To inventory, restore, interpret, and protect significant historic and cultural places, the program is constantly seeking a balance between the inherent tensions of maintaining authenticity while developing marketing opportunities. An example of this challenge is the Trail of Tears, the most painful of memories in the community's history, yet the most identifiable and iconic when considering branding the program to attract tourists. This presentation will discuss the process for developing this ambitious program in a way that respects and promotes the identity of the Cherokee people through the active participation of the tradition bearers, such as elders, storytellers, and artists, while attracting national and international visitors to the Cherokee's home in present-day Oklahoma.

RÉSUMÉ

La nation des Cherokee en Oklahoma élabore en ce moment un programme de tourisme culturel de grande envergure, tant sur le plan géographique que sur celui du potentiel de ses impacts sociaux, économiques et culturels. Dans le processus d'inventaire, de restauration, d'interprétation et de protection des lieux significatifs sur le plan historique et culturel, ce programme cherche constamment à équilibrer les tensions inhérentes à la préservation de l'authenticité vis-à-vis du développement des opportunités commerciales. La Piste des larmes, la plus douloureuse des mémoires de l'histoire de cette communauté, mais celle qui est aussi la plus identifiable et la plus iconique quand on considère la place qu'elle peut prendre dans ce programme pour attirer les touristes, en constitue un exemple. Cette présentation discutera du processus consistant à élaborer cet ambitieux programme de manière à respecter et à promouvoir l'identité du peuple cherokee à travers la participation active des porteurs de tradition tels que les aînés, les conteurs et les artistes, tout en attirant des visiteurs nationaux et internationaux chez les Cherokee, dans l'Oklahoma d'aujourd'hui.

Vision

Chief Chad Smith of the Cherokee Nation of Oklahoma has a vision for his people that builds on the Cherokee people's past experience to achieve a sustainable future. Chief Smith's vision for his people is, "The Cherokee Nation shall achieve and maintain an enriching cultural identity, economic self-reliance, and a strong government." He aims to achieve this vision through the following mission statement:

> The mission of the Cherokee Nation is "ga du gi," working together as individuals, families, and communities for quality of life for this and future generations by promoting confidence, the tribal culture, and an effective sovereign government.

To implement this vision, the Cherokee Nation established a cultural tourism division to develop programs that communicate the cultural identity of the Nation and help sustain the economic self-reliance of its people. Before we explore this program, it is worthwhile to briefly revisit the history of how the Cherokee people came to be in Oklahoma and some of the broader challenges Native people have faced since Europeans set foot on North American soil.

Cherokee People in Oklahoma

Cherokee culture thrived for thousands of years in the southeastern United States before European contact in the 1500s. In the 1830s, gold was discovered in Georgia. The European settlers began to covet the Cherokee homelands, and a period of Indian removals began to make way for more white settlement. In 1838, thousands of Cherokee men, women, and children were rounded up and marched 1,000 miles to Indian Territory, known today as the State of Oklahoma. Thousands died along what became known as the Trail of Tears. In Indian Territory, the Cherokee soon rebuilt a democratic form of government, churches, schools, newspapers, and businesses, which continued up through Oklahoma statehood in 1907 (Figure 1).

Figure 1. 1870 Capitol Building of the Cherokee Nation.

The Cherokee Nation is the second largest, and some say the largest, American Indian tribe in the United States, with more than 200,000 tribal members. Almost 70,000 of these Cherokee reside in the 7,000-square-mile area of the Cherokee Nation, which is not a reservation but a jurisdictional service area that includes almost fourteen counties in northeastern Oklahoma.

Native Identity and Stereotypes

Before we look further at the cultural tourism program of the Cherokee Nation, I ask you to consider, for a moment, what immediately comes to mind when you hear the word "Indian" or "Native American." In many cases, the images and thoughts that materialize are bound within a EuroAmerican frame of reference, and, in turn, the negative and clichéd often supersede the positive and genuine. Common understandings of Native culture are often grounded in: history textbooks that present Native Americans as a defeated people; Hollywood's pop culture, from John Wayne to *Dances With Wolves;* and alcoholism, impoverishment, and casinos.

Conflict and struggle are often the central elements in these types of knowing. Yet what is largely missing is a depth of understanding. When most people think of the history of North America, they think of a relatively recent history. "Ancient" is a word associated with the pyramids of Egypt and the Paleolithic cave paintings of southern France, but ancient is rarely a term related to America. Yet, Native people and their ancestors are very much an ancient people. The temporal depth of their experience on the land is profound and thousands of years old. The stories and events of that past are not ancient history to Native people; they are as real and vivid as if they happened just yesterday. Therefore, this greatly affects and challenges the process of interpretation of Native stories and history by the descendants of the colonizers. Conflict and struggle are often the central elements in these types of knowing. This is one of the greatest challenges facing the creation of a Native American cultural tourism program, as there are inherent differences in expectations, perceptions, and realities from whichever perspective one looks.

Strategic Planning for Cultural Tourism

Cultural tourism is tourism that enhances or sustains the character of a place – its culture, heritage, environment, aesthetics, the well-being of its residents – and provides a meaningful visitor experience. Cultural tourism requires strategically addressing economic development needs, partnerships and community collaboration, interpretation and storytelling, resources management, site planning, and marketing.

- The Cherokee cultural tourism program is organized around these six components.
- Economic development: Economic development and financial analysis
- Community: Stakeholders, partners, and staff
- Interpretation: Identity, stories, education, exhibits, and programming
- Resources: Historical, archaeological, cultural, natural, and recreational
- Site planning: Aligning resources, programming, interpretation, and infrastructure
- Marketing: Analyzing and understanding market demographics, aligning programming with markets, branding, and advertising

However, none of these areas can be developed or implemented in isolation; the development of a successful program requires maintaining a delicate balance among all six components. When these components are developed in harmony with one another a synergy results that can transform the individual resources into a new and cohesive whole. Strategic planning and disciplined, thoughtful implementation are the keys to a successful program.

Successful, sustainable growth of the cultural tourism program requires a clear process – a strategic, staged process which provides an opportunity to evaluate progress and success, ensures systematic decision-making, provides accountability throughout the process, and allows for adjustments in decisions based on accumulating information. This cycle continually calls for revisiting the program's mission, vision, and principles ensuring that as the program develops it reinforces, rather than erodes, the foundation.

Trail of Tears

This framework for decision making can now be applied to one specific resource, a resource that has the capacity to revitalize the spirit of the people whose heritage and identity is so closely entwined with it.

The Trail of Tears is one of the most tragic and shameful episodes of United States history. The physical places associated with the trail confront us with making decisions about how something so shameful and painful from our past should be integrated into a tourism program that seeks economic development without diluting the story, or being at risk of exploiting heritage for economic gain.

To tell a painful story to people who pay a fee to hear that story is not exploitive. When my family visited Robben Island, South Africa last year, we never questioned paying a fee to enter the place, understanding that staff and properties have to be maintained. Where the risk lies in ensuring a balance between economic return and cultural identity is in altering or twisting stories to tell visitors what you think they may want to hear, or sanitizing or mythologizing a story by over-simplifying the circumstances and their meaning. We should not be afraid to make people feel uncomfortable, without preaching or talking down to them.

The Illinois Campground is one of three disbandment camps for the Trail of Tears located within the Cherokee Nation's jurisdictional area. It is currently farmland in private ownership. Even with power lines overhead and a sewage plant at the edge of the property, the place is powerful and compelling, some would say haunting. It probably contains remarkable archaeological resources, but I would argue that the true power of this place lies in its very existence as open space by the creek where the survivors of the long removal march stopped and realized this would be their new home in a strange land. Only a few people know of the significance of this place – hundreds drive by it daily completely unaware of what it represents and could reveal. The place is a metaphor of the recent history of indigenous people who have been made invisible on the American landscape. It is also iconic and therefore hugely powerful in how the Cherokee people choose to preserve, reclaim, and interpret this place and all it represents as their own. To ensure that the revitalization of this place will contribute to the revitalization of the spirit of the people, authenticity and economic development must work hand in hand – be in balance.

A preservation management plan for the Trail of Tears is proposed. The trail followed several routes, both on land and water, through the southeastern United States and all the way to the current Cherokee Nation. The development of a preservation and management plan for portions of the trail within the Cherokee Nation jurisdictional area will allow this complicated resource and its associated sites to be considered and overseen in a comprehensive manner that will enable the best possible stewardship of this important resource. Active participation by the Cherokee people should be key in the development, preservation, and interpretation of this significant resource as a tourism destination. The nature of the interpretation and the story that is told throughout the trail must be consistent with and true to the legacy of the Cherokee people.

The message or interpretation of the trail, as with any Cherokee site that will be developed as part of the cultural tourism program, will be part of a larger branding effort.

Branding

Successful branding is emotionally rewarding to consumers and financially rewarding for the business. For the Cherokee Nation, it was agreed that the brand should communicate truthful and distinct characteristics of Cherokee culture but make every effort to choose images that may be understood to a wide audience. The following criteria were proposed to guide brand development:

- The geographic location of significance is northeast Oklahoma;
- The time period of significance postdates the removal from the southeastern United States and places the Cherokee people very much in the present;
- Cherokee history is the story of cyclical renewal and rebirth; the Cherokee experience has been marked with periods of calm and success followed by conflict resulting in some form of resolution;
- Language of identity; the culturally distinct Cherokee language and syllabary reinforces cultural identity

Themes to avoid include:

- Imagery or messages associated with a location or tradition irrelevant to the Western Cherokee story;
- Imagery or messages that perpetuate stereotypes of Native Americans, e.g., a "red man," user of the tomahawk, frightening and warrior-like;
- Images of the Cherokee that are non-Cherokee but relate to other Native people, e.g. use of feathers.

Integrating Marketing and Economic Development

Good branding and marketing are key to developing a viable, sustainable cultural tourism program. Cultural tourism is a venue in which economic development takes place by attracting visitors to experience a community's unique culture and related resources. In order to attract visitors these resources need to be preserved, managed, and interpreted; this requires dedication, planning, good management practices, and financial commitment. Entrance fees and some related sales may generate minimal return, but the real economic benefit to the community manifests itself in new business growth, job creation, an expanded tax base, and a strengthened cultural pride and identity.

The program in itself is not meant to be economically profitable, but it is an effective tool for strengthening the economy. The first benefit takes the form of the economic opportunities that develop to support the needs of the visitor. These include lodging, food and drink, and other entertainment. Money from these services in turn provides jobs and opportunities for small businesses, and stimulates the economy by expanding the local tax base.

In contrast to efforts to attract firms from elsewhere using subsidies or other incentives, a small business network would initiate and cultivate business aspirations of Cherokee entrepreneurs. A small business network can support new and existing businesses with a range of tools, such as providing legal and technical assistance, and mentoring opportunities for young entrepreneurs.

The other significant benefit of a successful cultural tourism program comes in the form of heightened community and cultural pride based on strengthened cultural identity. If the visitor travels for an authentic experience of Cherokee culture, then the ground is fertile to develop Cherokee arts and crafts and to provide a venue for the next generation to tell the story of the Cherokee experience in new and dynamic ways.

Maintaining Authenticity While Developing Market Opportunities

To ensure that the necessary services are developed to support the needs of the visitor, it is important to understand how tourism businesses and infrastructure are developed, how they impact cultural resources, and how they are conceived and integrated into the local economy. This can be a crossroad for the success of the project. For if the associated businesses are not developed and marketed with sensitivity to the resource, it can minimize or even destroy the authenticity and actually weaken the cultural pride and identity that should be one of the key goals of any cultural tourism program.

The first, and most common, method of market development is an organic approach in which the primary funding and focus is on developing individual historic resources, but the participation of the surrounding community is loosely promoted subsequently through a series of meetings where people are encouraged to embrace the spirit of the resources and to respectfully integrate the interpretive themes and messages into their various services. However, there is no formal structure to control the entrepreneu-rial growth that would occur. Those who defined the original message of authenticity can only hope for the best as local entrepreneurs, chain hotels and restaurants, and other attractions take advantage of a developing market. Imagine again the haunting landscape of the disbandment camp at the Illinois Campground, only now with an enormous billboard just outside the limits of the property, advertising the world's largest water park.

The second method of development is a top-down approach as exem-plified with Disney and other types of large purpose-built resorts and tourist attractions. In this model, virtually all services and facilities are designed and controlled first from the drawing board and then from the boardroom. This method ensures a cohesive message, experience, and appropriate facilities, but usually lacks reality and therefore authenticity. More importantly, in order to have the control needed to maintain a consistent message and development, one needs to retain ownership, and ownership ultimately retains profits. The programs that have the most cohesive message and integrated facilities most often seem to lack authenticity, and view the local population as a workforce to manage rather than a community of partners.

This is the challenge. In order to maintain authenticity, there needs to be some level of strategic planning and control on development to ensure continuity and sensitivity in all of the individual messages and imagery of each service. However, in order to have true economic development that stays within the community, the services and infrastructure need to be owned and operated by local businesses.

To address this challenge, a third approach was proposed which strives to integrate the control and cohesion of the purpose-built developments but applies those key controls within a local free-market economy. This is accom-plished by expanding the planning process to include a clear overarching marketing and development strategy for the entire region. A storefront-style cultural tourism center would be established in the heart of the tourism district. Its primary role would be to provide an open door approach for interacting with local businesses, calming concerned citizens, and directing potential new business to the various community and economic resources available. The other key role such a business center would play is to encourage, educate, and award certification to small businesses that agree to market in a fashion that is sensitive to the resources and the vision and purpose of the overall cultural tourism program.

The six key components to safeguarding authenticity while providing market opportunities within a cultural tourism program are:

• Establishing a neutral authority to serve as a review agency, such as a Tribal Historic Preservation Officer, to ensure that all cultural resources are protected or treated in an appropriate manner

- Establishing a Main Street program to oversee the integrity and design of the community center
- Incorporating zoning laws that are in alignment with the goals and values of the cultural tourism plan
- Establishing a storefront cultural tourism office to serve as a meeting place, educator, and clearinghouse for all community redevelopment and business needs
- Establishing a small business network to educate, coordinate, and subsidize the marketing messages of local tourism-specific businesses though incentives and information
- Reviewing all new tourism-related businesses within the context of the missions, principles, and five-step review process outlined in the strategic plan

Program Success

Ultimately, the success of the program, or any cultural tourism program, is dependent upon four key factors:

- Always keeping sight of the big picture – thinking about the program as more than a few interesting museums, sites, or tours, but as a cohesive whole
- Maintaining the desire and ability to implement a community process that will bring stakeholders together around a common vision and approach
- Committing to long-term thinking that never loses sight of who you want to attract and what this audience will demand
- Daring to dream and realize the possibilities

Acknowledgements

The authors would like to extend their appreciation to the Cherokee Nation of Oklahoma, particularly Talisha Nichols, for the opportunity to participate in the planning for this significant cultural tourism program; it was an honor for which we are most grateful.

In addition, many of our colleagues within the 106 Group made significant contributions to the strategic plan and therefore, indirectly, to many of the ideas contained within this paper. Thank you specifically to Tim Agness, Jill Betker, Julie Cutler, Jennifer Kust, and Greg Mathis.

The Spirit of Place During the Life of a Monument in the Case Study of the World Heritage Site Vat Phou (Laos)

Beatrice Messeri
IMT Lucca
Italy

ABSTRACT

To this day, the Vat Phou site represents a unique example of social and religious use while being a commercial tourist attraction. This case can be considered a model but one must consider its intrinsic future risks. Main threats and haphazard interventions and financial speculation have already occurred as at many other WHL sites over time. The goal here is to recommend preventive and comprehensive measures to preserve the very fabric and spirit of the place.

RÉSUMÉ

Jusqu'à ce jour, le site de Vat Phou représente un exemple unique d'usages sociaux et religieux tout en étant une attraction touristique commerciale. Ce cas peut-être considéré comme un modèle, mais on doit aussi envisager les risques intrinsèques que cela représente pour l'avenir. De graves menaces, des interventions hasardeuses, autant que la spéculation financière, se sont déjà produites dans d'autres sites du Patrimoine mondial au cours du temps. L'objectif ici est de formuler quelques recommandations de mesures préventives d'ensemble pour préserver le tissu même qui fait l'esprit du lieu.

1. Historical Introduction

Vat Phou is considered one of the most important Khmer sites (9th to 12th centuries AD) along with the Cambodian ones, which have been inscribed in the World Heritage List since 2001. It is situated in the southern Province of Champasak (Laos), a few kilometres from the town of Champasak, 30 kilometres from the province's capital Pakse, and about 120 km from Cambodia.

The Khmer legend indicates Vat Phou as the birthplace of the Hindu god Shiva; it has been identified as the main sanctuary inside the heartland of the Chenla[1] Kingdom (Ishii and Sakurai 1985, 76-85). The Vat Phou complex is inserted in the Champasak plain's cultural landscape, flanked by the Phou Kao Mountain to the west and the Mekong River to the east and other sacred sites and temples around. Vat Phou was surrounded by the ancient city of Shrestrapura and the urban settlement of Lingapura (9th to 13th centuries). According to Chinese sources (*Sui Chronicles*, 6th century), the Phou Kao Mountain, in Sanskrit called *Lingaparvata* (*Linga*[2] mountain), showed a temple on the top for the king's sacrifices to the Bhadreshvara's spirit.[3] Initially, the Shivaist cult was practised in Angkor as well as in Vat Phou. The Khmer embraced this cult to Vat Phou as a great sacred place thus allowing the continuation of donations and privileges which sustained the temple until the fall of their Empire (Albanese 2004).

The abandonment of the Shivaist in favour of the Buddhist cult took place around the 15th and 16th centuries, according to T. Sayavongkhamdy (Sayavongkhamdy 1996, 102) or possibly earlier around the 13th (*Nomination Form* 2000, 30). Buddhism reinterpreted the Hindu icons with a cultural interchange through a sort of symbiotic process.

The present configuration of the Vat Phou site dates back to the expansion that took place in the 11th century and under the reign of Khmer King Suryavarman II in the 12th century (*Nomination of Vat Phou and Associated Ancient Settlements within the Champasak Cultural Landscape*, 30; Freeman 1996, 200-207). However, certain sections were realized in successive centuries and the oldest remains are dated before the 7th century.

The capital of Chenla Empire was Shrestrapura, wanted by king Shreshthavarman. Started in the 3rd to 7th centuries, it was not completed until the 13th. It represents the earliest known urban settlement of the Khmer empire and the first Khmer city site scientifically excavated thus providing a valuable example of the origin of Southeast Asian urbanism (Nishimura 2004, 49-63). The planning and the modification of the landscape were a clear response to environmental, economic, social and political requirements (*Champasak Heritage Management Plan* 1999, 82). The evidence of a Hindu centre is found in the Shivaist inscriptions like the Sanskrit stele of Ban Panone (a site close to Champasak), called the King Devanika inscription. It indicates the foundation of the important politic centre of Shrestrapura in the 5th century, previously the Vat Phou construction (Coedès 1956; Jacques 1962; Santoni, Souksavatdy 1996, 171; Sayavongkhamdy 1996, 101-102).

---

1.   Early Khmer kingdom adherent to the Shivaist cult.
2.   A phallic emblem, symbolizing Shiva and his role in creation.
3.   King Bhadraverman, founder of this cult, built the first shrine of Shiva Bhadreshvara in My Son (Vietnam) (Freeman 1996, 201).

2. Description of the Site

The first descriptions of the site date back to the 19th cnetury. F. Garnier in *Voyage d'exploration en Indo-Chine* (1873) reported the French missions which took place in 1866, 1867 and 1868. The first studies were done by archaeologist E. Aymonier and architect H. Parmantier (Parmentier 1914) brought them to an advanced level.

The whole configuration of the area is not only utilitarian but reflective of the Hindu religious view in the 5th to12th centuries. The *Lingaparvata* can be interpreted like the Mount Kailasha, the Shiva's sacred mountain, and the Mekong River like the Ganges River, with the plain as a symbol of the Holy Land (*Kurukshestra*) and the surroundings as the symbol for the Universal Ocean. The axis from Lingaparvata to Vat Phou temple continues on through the ancient city and crosses the Mekong River to join the Tomo temple. The classical Hindu cosmology is merged with the local interpretations (*Champasak Heritage Management Plan* 1999, 82).

The Vat Phou complex is quite impressive; however to fully understand its importance we must remember that what we see now is not representational of the ancient sacred centre when it was surrounded by a vibrant and bustling town.

The complex, located under the Phou Kao mountain, is set on a natural terrace overlooking the Mekong River plain, which extends 1400m in length on the east-west axis. This linear axial layout is rare in most of the Khmer temples where the concentric plan is the favourite. There are three main parts. The lowest one is characterized by *barays*;[4] the central part includes a series of stairs and terraces and the upper one houses the sanctuary, the library and other significant architectonical and sculptural elements (Fig. 1).

Figure 1. The complex of the Vat Phou site. Photo B. Messeri, 2008.

---

4.   A man-made lake or reservoir.

At the lowest level, the entrance is in direction of the eastern big *baray* (200m by 600m, 10th – 11th centuries), flanked on its north by another one not aligned with the temple's axis, maybe a subsequent donation, and on the west by two smaller ones (around 10th – 12th centuries). On the western side of the first big *baray* there is a stone *gopura,*[5] surmounted, in the ancient past, probably by a timber structure and recently by a pavilion, that has been destroyed. From there, the processional causeway (350m, 10th century, recently restored), that is delimited by two rows of lotus flower pillars with a *naga*[6] at the beginning, leads to the quadrangular buildings. The two quadrangular buildings (62m by 42m, 11th century), positioned on the first of six temple terraces, are made of sandstone and laterite (the northern one) and sandstone and bricks (the southern). All buildings exhibit remarkable carved doorways and exquisite decorations. There are no traces of the timber roofing except for the holes remaining in the masonry. It is assumed that the buildings were used for ceremonial purposes with the ones facing north devoted to the ladies and the ones facing south to the gentlemen, high rank worshippers or monks.

Figure 2. The northern quadrangular building. Photo B. Messeri, 2009.

From the two quadrangle buildings starts the second causeway (150m of length). This element was recently restored and is bordered by stone lotus pillars and, in the past, by timber galleries on the two embankments. In the middle of the causeway on the northern terrain, there are traces of a quadrangular pavilion (1998 excavations) and on the south side, a sandstone and laterite construction called *Nandin*[7] Hall (mid 11th century, preservation

---

5.   An ornamental crowned gateway or entrance to a religious sanctuary.
6.   Naga: A mythical serpent with the characteristics of a cobra, usually depicted as multi-headed or sometimes in human form.
7.   The building took the name from the Nandin pedestal found in the area. Nandin: The bull serving as Shiva's mount and symbol of fertility, found facing the main sanctuary in Shaivite temples.

works in progress). According to the most recent studies, the building could be a connecting structure between the causeway on the north and the big sacred road that led to Angkor on the south. On the north and south sides of the complex there are two water canals. At the end of the ceremonial causeway there is a ruined flight of stairs, flanked by two champa trees, that leads to another terrace. On this level there is a statue venerated by the worshippers as a representation of King Khammanta, most probably a *dvarapala*,[8] like the two others lying on the ground on the north side. A long flight of stairs (75 m of length, 11th century) is sustained by a majestic and partially collapsed sandstone and laterite retaining wall which leads to the cross-shaped terrace. The next terrace is planned with two series of brick *prasat*[9](9th – 10th centuries), now almost entirely destroyed, and is dedicated to the *trimurti*[10] aligned on the north-south axis, each one with a *linga*. The last steep sandstone staircase, flanked by champa trees and two big laterite tiers (the northern one completely ruined), leads to one of the most sacred spaces of the complex, the sanctuary (Fig. 3).

Figure 3. The sanctuary. Photo B. Messeri, 2008.

This terrace is almost a square (60 m by 60 m) with the Shiva's shrine in the middle and the library on the south. The main entrance of the sanctuary is on the east, and it is constituted of a *mandapa*,[11] a vestibule with

8.   A guardian of a temple door or gate often holding a club or mace.
9.   Palace for king or god. In religious and secular architecture, the sanctuary tower represents Mount Meru.
10.   (Sanskrit trimūrti) In the Hindu concept, where the cosmic functions are personified by the forms of Brahmā the creator, Visnu the maintainer or preserver, and Shiva the destroyer or transformer.
11.   Antechamber, a pavilion or porch in front of the main sanctuary of a temple.

three modern Buddha statues and the cella with the *linga,* watered by the sacred source. The outward part is beautifully decorated with *devatas*[12] and *dvarapalas* sculptures, besides the presence of the fine carved interior lintels. The building is covered by a temporary roof and the masonry structure is in great disrepair. On the west side are the Hindu *trimurti* carvings of Brahmā, Visnu and Shiva (11th century) while on the north side sits a recent monastery, now abandoned, and a series of rock sculptures and structures (originating from the 7th century). The remains of the uppermost terrace are the oldest at the site with the main structure belonging mostly to the 7th century.

The visitor, and above all the worshippers, walk through their spiritual journey starting at the lowest part of the temple to the highest levels, symbolically from the rough world on earth to the world of gods where man can achieve enlightenment. Most visitors are pilgrims who go through a journey of a religious nature. Lesser in number are the tourists venturing to Vat Phou for purely cultural interests.

The other sites inscribed in the World Heritage List include the mentioned town of Shrestrapura[13] as well as other related settlements like the sandstone Hong Nang Sida temple (11th century) (Fig.4) and the area around which is evidence to a well-organised settlement dating to the 9th – 13th centuries, probably the Khmer city mentioned in the inscription as Lingapura. Thao Tao temple (12th beginning of 13th centuries) is situated 300 m east of the ancient Khmer road and was discovered in 1987. In the area are included: Tham Lek (cave and inscriptions dating back to 7th – 8th centuries), the rock inscription near Houay Kok source (7th century), Vat Oubmong (9th century), a brick and sandstone temple dedicated to Shiva, with a Sanskrit inscription, which was found in 1973 by Pierre Lintengre, Tomo temple (around the 9th century) (Fig.5) and its relative Don Daeng Island in front of Champasak town.

---

12.   A deity or a divine being in India and other countries in South-East Asia.
13.   The plan of the town was rectangular (around 2.3 km by 1.8 km) and the border on the Mekong has disappeared under the erosive action of the river.

Figure 4. Hong Nang Sida temple. Photo B. Messeri, 2008.

Figure 5. Tomo temple. Photo B. Messeri, 2009.

3. Studies on the Vat Phou Area

In 1987 UNESCO focused its attention on Vat Phou and between 1987 and 1990 were identified the borders of the protected areas around the main erected monuments.

From 1991 to 1996 a project of research in Lao archaeology was developed in the area (Projet de Recherches en Archéologie Lao) and it brought to light some new aspects of Lao history and advancements in South-East Asia history. In 1991, 1992, 1993 and 1995 some excavations, wanted by the Lao Ministry of Culture and carried out with a Lao-French project directed by M. Santoni of the *Centre National de Recherche Scientifique*, were done close to the sanctuary in order to verify the presence of prehistoric traces near the sacred source and to explore in detail the interesting area. Subsequent to these discoveries, the restoration plans (1989-90), that concerned the anastylosis of the monuments with the realization of a concrete platform on the ancient vestiges, were stopped and new studies were started (Santoni, Souksavatdy 1996, 177). The Italian and Russian contribution pertained to the magnetic prospections in the ancient city (M. Cucarzi, V. Glazounov), and in the Vat Phou complex for the period from 1991 to 1995. Moreover, from 1990 to the present, the Italian government has promoted a few missions in the Vat Phou area directed by the Lerici Foundation-Politecnico di Milano (Director of the Italian missions, P. Zolese).

In 1997 an international project focused on the importance of investigating the condition of the major monuments in and surrounding the Vat Phou archaeological site, and of recommending measures for the stabilization and consolidation of these structures (Pichard 1997, 2); the study was followed by the erection of timber supports in the main buildings, recently reinforced and the starting of an archaeological excavation campaign.

One of the biggest efforts to this effect has been the collection of data for the execution of the management plan and the inscription of the site in the World Heritage List, with the updating of the 2005-2010 action plan.

In 2004 a project concerning the conservation of the ceremonial causeways was conceived; it was completed the following year, concurrently with the training of the local staff, the topographical and archaeological mapping of the site and the arrangement of the exhibition hall built with a Lao-Japanese project (2000). This effort also involved the rehabilitation of the canals in the Vat Phou area.

For two years the Lerici Foundation with the Politecnico di Milano has been conducting a project of preservation of the Nandin Hall inside the Vat Phou complex (Scientific Director, M. Boriani, Director of the Archaeological Mission, P. Zolese).

4. Safeguard Programs Concerning the Site and Legislative Outline

The governmental action plan, established at the foundation of the Lao People's Democratic Republic (December 2, 1975), contemplated these actions: "to study, to compile inventories to repair and maintain the historical monuments, precious heritage of the nation." The 19th article of the Constitution stipulates that the State assures the protection of national antiquities and the preservation of national historical monuments.

The first step to safeguard the site started with the preservation program of the Vat Phou monuments in 1987. The Ministry of Information and Culture defined a decennial project with the financing assistance of UNDP and UNESCO dedicated itself to protect and preserve the principal monuments in the country.

In 1996, Sayavongkhamdy's[14] important topics focused on the creation of a historical park for the preservation of the whole area (comprising Shrestrapura and Vat Phou) and a wide-ranging vision marked by crucial changes in the cultural heritage preservation safeguard including sensitization campaigns, toughening of the laws on this matter, a planned and dedicated budget, the implementation of inventories, special archives and museum systems in addition to the improvement of the structures, the establishment and training of qualified personnel (Sayavongkhamdy 1996).

In 1996 UNESCO together with the governments of Italy and Japan and with the collaboration of many experts (from Italy, Japan, France, Australia and the United Kingdom) started a safeguarding project for the Champasak cultural landscape. The UNESCO-Lao project called *Capacity Building in Cultural Resource Management through the Preparation of a Zoning and Environmental Management Plan for the Preservation of Vat Phou and Associated Archaeological Sites within the Framework for Sustainable Development of Champasak, Lao PDR* involved doing comprehensive research from different points of view, hydrological, anthropological, archaeological and environmental. All collected data were organised in a GIS and used in the drafting of the *Champasak Heritage Management Plan*, officially adopted by the Government of Lao PDR September 28, 1998. During the implementation of the management plan, a new fundamental role has been devoted to the *Lao Government's National Inter-Ministerial Co-ordinating Committee for the Protection of Vat Phou* (NIMCC) together with the *Champasak Provincial Heritage Committee* and the *Champasak Villages Liaison Committee*. The management plan is coherent with the Operational Guidelines for the Implementation of the *1972 UNESCO Convention for the Protection of the World Cultural and Natural Heritage* and the Lao legislation.

In the past few years, the legislation has showed a remarkable evolution from the *Provincial Decree on the Regulation for the Preservation of the Historical Site of Vat Phou and the Areas Related to Vat Phou n. 38/88*[15] that concerned the Vat Phou area, Hong Nang Sida and Thao Tao to the subsequent national *Decree of the President of the Lao PDR on the Preservation of Cultural, Historical and Natural Heritage* n. 03/PR (1997).[16]

Successively, the new *Law on National Heritage* dated November 9, 2005 (approved 2006) has significantly improved the previous Decree, first of all with the heritage distinction and the inclusion of the intangible heritage. In

---

14. Director-General, Dep. of Museums and Archaeology, Ministry of Information and Culture, Lao PDR
15. Approved by Provincial Executive Board Committee, Pakse 11/10/1988
16. Signed by the President Nouhak Phoumsavan in Vientiane 20/6/1997.

fact, it is defined as the *cultural and historical heritage*, including *the intangible and the tangible, the movable and the immovable heritage with significant value from the point of view of culture, history and sciences* (*Law on National Heritage* 2005, Art. 3.1); natural heritage and its management are also contemplated. Moreover, the definition of authorities and their competences within the Ministry of Information and Culture have been clarified. The museums are finally contemplated with an improved consciousness, a tendency to progress confirmed by *The Phnom Penh-Vientiane Charter on Cultural Diversity and Heritage Tourism* (2006), signed by institutional members during an ICOM Workshop involving Southeast Asian countries. For the first time in legislation of this nature, the words *repair, restoration and conservation* are mentioned beside the measures for the protection and preservation of the tangible, cultural and historical national heritage (*Law on National Heritage* 2005, Art. 29, Chapter 3). A *Fund for the National Heritage* has been established by the government budget, foreign countries and international organisations, fees/income from the national heritage and fund-raising. The utilisation of the fund is determined by specific regulations.

The 1997 Decree was based more on defending the country's cultural heritage and fighting the illegal activities in this sector, a crucial problem in that period, rather than establishing a specific national decree on this matter. Without the enactment of this decree, the management plan and the inscription on the World Heritage List of the Vat Phou site would have been impossible. The new legislation has been written with the specific goal of solving weak management in these institutional activities. The problems are still many, including lack of proper administrative planning, inaccurate budgeting, poor monitoring of work and the quality of work performed along with a scarcity of qualified personnel and, last but not least, a shortage of funds, already publicly denounced (Sikhanxay 2004, 80).

5. Conclusion-Consequences

In the course of the last twenty years the image of the Vat Phou area has changed its character. The attention of international projects has enhanced this mechanism in fact in the entire country and above all already verified in the northern World Heritage Site, Luang Prabang. Foreign aid, in accordance with the country policy, has started to change the economical, social and cultural conditions of the area.

During the last few years, there have been improvements to the infrastructures and to the Pakse area and Champasak too, such as the bridge on the Mekong and the new Pakse airport, thanks to bilateral projects with foreign countries. The request of experts in the Vat Phou complex has attracted technicians from all over the country who have collaborated side by side with international specialists. Numerous training courses have been organised as well as exchanges with other young experts from South Asian countries. The Vat Phou office has become a real landmark for the country, in constant evolution.

The WHS brand has attracted more tourists every year and despite its positive effect, protective measures need to be established and guidelines need to be part of the management plan. Guesthouses in Champasak have grown in number since 1997, when the first ones were opened. The international eye is starting to focus on the area for new investments, which need to be cautiously controlled to maintain the integrity of such a historical and sacred site (Fig. 6).

Figure 6. Buddhas inside the sanctuary. Photo B. Messeri, 2008.

We cannot forget that Vat Phou is mainly a religious site for the Lao people. Over the course of the centuries the site has changed from a Hindu holy site to a Buddhist one, but at its heart it remains a spiritual point of reference. From all over the country, the famous Vat Phou Festival draws an incredible number of pilgrims who wish visit the monumental complex. Surely some measure of control must be established to protect the physical site while allowing visitors and devotees to share in the pleasure of the spiritual patrimony the site represents for many.

Besides the coordination of the general management plan of all the area, the archaeological and architectonical preservation works, it will be important to extend protective regulations on the effects of water during the monsoon season, to increase the number of experts and to attract fruitful international projects while involving the indigenous community in these activities to safeguard the needs of the local population.

At present, the authenticity and the originality of the cultural landscape of Vat Phou are unquestionable and all the improvements of the site should take into consideration the interaction between the human value and the true spirit of the place. The challenge is to balance the modernisation of the country with the historical and spiritual identity of this ancient site.

Selected References

Albanese, M. 2004. *Angkor*. Vercelli: White Star.

Aymonier, E. 1901-1904. La Région de Bassak. In *Le Cambodge*. Paris: Ernest Leroux.

Barth, A. 1902. Stèle de Vat Phu prés Bassac. In *BEFEO*, 2 (3). 235.

Box, P. 1999. Vat Phou Champasak Heritage and Cultural Landscape Protection Zone, Lao PDR, Case Study 6. *In GIS and Cultural Resource Management: a Manual for Heritage Managers*. UNESCO.

Government of the Lao PDR. *Champasak Heritage Management Plan*. 1999.

Cividini, A., and G. Gioda. 1998. *Report on the Restoration of Vat Phou Monument Site: Geotechnical Aspects of the Restoration of Vat Phou Site*.

Convention for the Safeguarding of the Intangible Cultural Heritage. 2003.

Coedès, G. 1956. Nouvelles données sur les origines du royaume khmèr. La stèle de Vat Luong Kau près de Vat P'hu. In *BEFEO*. XLVIII fasc. I 209-220.

Coedès, G. 1953. Inscriptions de Tham Lekh (K. 723, 724). In *Inscriptions du Cambodge, Collection de textes et documents sur l'Indochine*, III, vol. VII, Paris.

Cucarzi, M., and P. Conti. 1997. *Geophysical Prospecting at the Ancient City of Vat Phou*. Bankok: UNESCO.

Cucarzi, M., and P. Zolese. 1999. An Attempt to Inventory Khmer Monumental Remains Through Geomagnetic Modelling. The Ancient City of Wat Phu. In *BEFEO*.

Cucarzi, M., O. Nalesini, C. Rosa, and P. Zolese. 1997. *Carta archeologica informatizzata. Il progetto UNESCO per l'area di Wat Phu*. Convegno CNR Roma.

Dagens, B. 1986. *Préservation des monuments de Vat Phu, Report I.* July 1986. Paris: UNESCO.

Dagens, B. 1988. *Préservation des monuments de Vat Phu, Report II. 26 July to 4 August 1988*. Paris: UNESCO.

Decree of the President of the Lao PDR on the Preservation of Cultural Historical and Natural Heritage n. 03/PR 1997.

Defente, D., C. Hawixbrock, J.C. Liger, M. Santoni, V. Souksavatdi, and P. Zolese. 1993. «L'exemple de Vat Phou». In *Approche Archéologique de l'Histoire du Laos*, 194-215. Bangkok: Ambassade de France à Bangkok.

Dumarçay, J. 1990. *Projet pour la restauration du temple de Vat Phu, Report 1990*.

Feilden, B.M. and J. Jokilehto. 1998. *Management Guidelines for WCH Site*. Roma: ICCROM.

Finot, L. 1902. Vat Phu. in *BEFEO* 2 (3). 241.

Franzetti, S. 1998. *Water Management: Restoration of Vat Phou Monument Site.*

Freeman, M. 1996. *A Guide to Khmer Temples in Thailand and Laos.* Bangkok: River Books.

Garnier, F. 1873. *Voyage d'exploration en Indochine.* Paris.

Ishii,Y. and Y. Sakurai. 1996. *Formation of the Southeast Asian World.* Tokyo: Kodanaha.

Jacques, C. 1962. Notes sur l'inscription de la stèle de Vat Luong Kau. *Journal Asiatique,* n° 2. 249-256.

Law on National Heritage. 2005. Vientiane 9 November 2005, approved 2006.

Lintingre, P. 1974. A la recherche du sanctuaire préangkorien de Vat Phou. In *Revue Française d'Histoire d'outre mer,* n. 225, 4ᵉ Tri. Paris.

Marchal, H. 1957, *Le temple de Vat Phou. Province de Champassak,* published by the Department of Religion, Governement of Lao PDR. Saigon: Imprimerie Nouvelle d'Extrême Orient.

Nishimura, M. 2004. *Representing Vat Phou. An Ethnographic Account of the Nomination Process of Vat Phou and Adjunct Archaeological Sites to the WHL,* 49-63.

Nishimura, M., and P. Sikhanxay. 1998. *Capacity building in Cultural Heritage Management within the Context of assistance for the Preservation of Vat Phou (536/LAO/70): Terminal Report.*

Nomination of Vat Phou and Associated Ancient Settlements within the Champasak Cultural Landscape. 2000. Lao PDR.

Parmentier, H. 1914. Le temple de Vat Phou. In *BEFEO* 14 (2). Paris.

Pichard, P. 1997. *The Conservation of Vat Phu Temple.* Bangkok: UNESCO.

Preusser, D. F. *Vat Phou: Mission Report (Report Concerning Structural Engineering Problems of Vat Phou Monuments Complex).*

Provincial Decree on the Regulation for the Preservation of the Historical Site of Vat Phou and the Areas Related to Vat Phou n° 38/88. 1988

Santoni, M., and V. Souksavatdy. 1996 Fouilles sur le site de Vat Phou-Champasak. In *Colloque EFEO Laos restaurer et préserver le patrimoine national,* 167-200.

Santoni, M. 1998. *Results of 1998 Fieldwork in Vat Phu Area (Champassak Province Laos),* paper presented at the 7ᵗʰ International Conference of the European Association of Southeast Asian Archaeologists, Berlin, 31 August to 4 September 1998.

Santoni, M., and V. Souksavatdy. 1999. Fouilles sur les sites de Vat Phou-Champasak in Laos – restaurer et préserver le patrimoine national, *ÉFEO Colloquium 1996,* Vientiane: Éditions des Cahiers de France.

Santoni, M., V. Souksavatdy, D. Defente, and C. Hawixbrock. 1997. Excavations at Champassak and Wat Phu, South Laos. In *Southeast Asian archaeology*, ed. R. Ciarla. *Proceedings of the 4th International Conference of the Southeast Asian Archaeologists, Roma, 28 September-4 October 1992*. Roma: ISIAO.

Sayavongkhamdy, T. 1996. Mise en valeur du patrimoine culturel national. In *Colloque EFEO Laos – restaurer et préserver le patrimoine national*, 99-111.

Sikhanxay, P. 2004. Lao Government Policy Toward Cultural Resource Management In *Annual Journal Of Cultural Anthropology* I, 74-80.

UNESCO UNDP. 1991. *Preservation of Wat Phu, Champassak, Project Findings and Recommendations*. Paris.

Ueno, K. 1994. Mission Report. In *the Conservation of Wat Phu, Champassak, Laos*, Nara, Japan, April 1994.

Vickery, M. 1994. What and Where was Chenla? In *BEFEO*.

Wolters, O.W. 1974. *Khmer "Hinduism" in the Seventh Century in Early South East Asia*, ed. R. B. Smith Watson: 406-426. Oxford: Oxford University Press.

Zolese, P. 1998. *Survey Report and Catalogue of Sites in Hong Nang Sida and Associated City Area*.

Enjeux du tourisme durable en Haïti face au paradigme de la gestion des sites à haute valeur culturelle Le cas du Parc National Historique: Citadelle, Sans Souci, Ramiers

Olsen Jean Julien
**Ministre de la Culture d'Haïti
et professeur à l'Université d'État d'Haïti**

ABSTRACT

In Haïti, the preservation of historical memory contributes to the actual structuring of the land, factoring in as a fundamental parameter in regional development. Based on that assertion, sustainable tourism in Haïti can be achieved only if it is planned with the same standards that are used for highly valuable cultural heritage sites. This presentation deals with the implementation of sustainable tourism development in and around the National Historical Park: the Citadelle, the Palais Sans Souci and the Ramiers estate.

RÉSUMÉ

En Haïti, la conservation de la mémoire historique contribue à la structuration des lieux en tant que l'un des paramètres fondamentaux d'aménagement du territoire. Considérant cette hypothèse de travail, le développement touristique en Haïti ne peut être durable sans un processus de planification en adéquation avec le paradigme actuel de la gestion de sites à haute valeur culturelle. C'est cette hypothèse qui est illustrée dans le présent texte à travers les enjeux du développement touristique durable autour du Parc National Historique: la Citadelle, le palais Sans Souci et les bâtiments des Ramiers.

1. Introduction

La conservation et la mise en valeur des ressources naturelles et culturelles ont, depuis la fin de l'occupation américaine d'Haïti (1915-1934), toujours constitué une problématique importante de l'État haïtien. En 1968, le concept de « site naturel dont la conservation présente un intérêt général au point de vue artistique, historique et scientifique » est introduit dans la législation haïtienne avec le décret du 18 mars relatif aux Parcs Nationaux et Sites Naturels. Ce même décret consacre une superficie de 250 hectares au minimum autour de la Citadelle dans le but protéger ce monument (Article 14.f). Avec la ratification de la *Convention concernant la protection du patrimoine mondial, culturel et naturel* (1972), l'État haïtien s'est donné un ensemble d'obligations en termes de gestion et de protection des sites localisés sur le territoire. Au centre de ces obligations se trouve la nécessité de définir « une politique générale visant à assigner une fonction au patrimoine culturel et naturel dans la vie collective, et à intégrer la protection de ce patrimoine dans les programmes de planification générale ».

En faisant également du tourisme l'un des axes prioritaires de développement économique depuis 1972 (Rapport OEA 1972), l'État haïtien allait essayer d'articuler les préoccupations pour la protection des sites culturels avec la planification du développement touristique. L'une des premières actions d'envergure de cette démarche fut le projet d'inventaire de la Citadelle et du palais Sans Souci, initié en 1973. Avec la création de l'Institut de Sauvegarde du Patrimoine National (ISPAN) en 1979 et l'inscription du Parc National Historique – Citadelle, Sans Souci, Ramiers sur la liste du Patrimoine mondial de l'UNESCO en 1982, un ensemble de travaux de recherches et d'interventions physiques ont été réalisés pour la conservation des richesses naturelles et culturelles du site. La plupart de ces travaux, réalisés par des équipes multidisciplinaires de grande qualité, ont permis de sauver les monuments de la destruction et de comprendre à fond les aspects multiples de ce site.

La conservation et la mise en valeur de la signification culturelle du Parc National Historique ont donc coïncidé avec le processus de planification de l'aménagement touristique en Haïti comme l'un de ses paramètres fondamentaux.

En d'autres termes, en Haïti, la conservation de la mémoire historique contribue à la structuration des lieux en tant que paramètre fondamental de l'aménagement du territoire. En considérant cette donnée comme une hypothèse de travail, une implication immédiate est que le développement touristique en Haïti ne peut être durable sans un processus de planification en adéquation avec le paradigme actuel de la gestion de sites à haute valeur culturelle. C'est cette hypothèse que je me propose de développer ici en identifiant les enjeux du développement touristique durable autour du Parc National Historique.

2. Le changement de paradigme dans le cadre de la discipline de la conservation du patrimoine culturel.

La double décennie 1988-2008 a été marquée au niveau international par de profonds changements dans la gestion du patrimoine culturel et naturel. De l'aménagement du territoire à la géopolitique, de la planification touristique à la gestion des sites culturels, les principes fondamentaux définissant ces disciplines professionnelles ont été réévalués en retenant comme essentiels les trois éléments suivants :

- **les attentes économiques des acteurs**, en considérant comme prioritaires la protection des intérêts des investisseurs ainsi que ceux des populations locales vivant souvent dans des conditions de pauvreté ;

- **la signification culturelle des lieux**, en considérant comme prioritaires les valeurs associées à la protection et à la consolidation de la dignité humaine et à la diversité culturelle des populations locales et des visiteurs, ce qui implique la participation de cette population dans le processus ;

- **les exigences de la protection de l'environnement**, en considérant comme prioritaires la protection des caractéristiques physiques et l'équilibre fragile des écosystèmes naturels.

Ces trois éléments servant de critères d'évaluation sont l'expression d'une rupture résultant d'un très long processus de maturation intellectuelle de différentes communautés scientifiques, mais il fallait encore la réunion de conditions favorables au niveau politique et social pour que les réflexions scientifiques se transforment en décisions politiques. C'est ce qui s'est passé au cours de la période 1988-2008 à partir de la création, en 1988, du Groupe d'Experts Intergouvernemental sur l'évolution du climat (GIEC), dont la mission était « d'évaluer les informations scientifiques relatives au changement climatique, de mesurer les conséquences environnementales et socioéconomiques de ce changement et de formuler des stratégies de parade réalistes ».

Les conquêtes réalisées en matière de protection de l'environnement depuis la création du GIEC ont des conséquences multiples sur la gestion du patrimoine culturel et la planification du développement touristique. En témoignent les différentes révisions et élaborations de documents normatifs introduisant les concepts diffusés à partir de cette conférence : la Charte sur le Tourisme Durable (1995), la Charte sur le Tourisme Culturel par le Comité International de l'ICOMOS en 1999, la Charte d'ICOMOS sur la Conservation des lieux patrimoniaux à valeur culturelle (1999), pour ne citer que ces cas. Pour mieux souligner l'importance des avancées consacrées par ces instruments normatifs, il importe de citer la Charte du Tourisme Durable, selon laquelle « le développement touristique doit reposer sur des critères de durabilité ; il doit être supportable à long terme sur le plan écologique, viable sur le plan économique et équitable sur le plan éthique et social pour les populations locales ».

3. La mémoire historique en tant que paramètre fondamental d'aménagement du territoire

Les monuments du Parc National Historique – la Citadelle, le palais Sans Souci et le site fortifié des Ramiers – comptent parmi les plus importants artéfacts haïtiens. Ils représentent non seulement les produits d'un extraordinaire travail social réalisé dans le passé, mais aussi une sorte de négation du présent. Leur beauté et leur image imposent à la fois une présence spécifique du passé dans la réalité contemporaine et une critique de l'ordre social en Haïti, près de deux cents ans après leur édification.

Figure 1. La Citadelle.

Correctement articulées, cette beauté et cette image peuvent nous permettre de comprendre les valeurs multiples de la révolution haïtienne et de relancer le débat sur le rapport entre l'esthétique, la politique et l'histoire en tant qu'aspects de la discipline de la conservation des monuments et des biens culturels.

Le comité ICOMOS d'Australie a fourni un élément essentiel à ce débat en précisant la nature de la valeur esthétique d'un artéfact. Selon ce comité,

> la valeur esthétique est la réponse dérivée de l'expérience concrète d'un environnement ou des attributs naturels et culturels qu'il contient. Cette réponse peut comporter des éléments visuels ou non et peut embrasser une réponse émotionnelle, le sens du lieu, des sons, des odeurs, ou bien n'importe quel facteur ayant un impact important sur la pensée, les sentiments et les attitudes de l'être humain (Trunscott 2000).

> La valeur esthétique inclut des aspects de la perception sensorielle pour lesquels des critères peuvent et devraient être établis. Ces critères peuvent inclure des considérations sur la forme, l'échelle, la texture, les matériaux, les odeurs et les sons associés au lieu et à son utilisation (ICOMOS Australie 1999).

Dans ces interprétations, le comité australien d'ICOMOS embrasse une vision moderne de la valeur esthétique comme une «expérience concrète» et un «aspect de la perception sensorielle». Dépassant la vision kantienne qui considère uniquement la dimension subjective de la valeur esthétique d'un objet (Kant 1790), le comité pose la valeur esthétique comme un nœud d'articulation entre les dimensions tangibles et intangibles des monuments. Cette manière de considérer la valeur esthétique est en relation avec les études d'Erwin Panofsky sur la question de l'iconologie et de Rudolph Arnheim sur la psychologie de l'art.

En effet, étant avant tout une icône, l'image ou la perception visuelle d'un monument peut, selon Panofsky, permettre «d'appréhender les principes sous-jacents qui révèlent l'attitude fondamentale d'une nation, une période, une classe, une religion ou un système philosophique de persuasion» (Panofsky 1982 : 30).

D'un autre coté, Rudolph Arnheim, dans ses études sur les relations entre le processus cognitif et le contexte visuel créé par une œuvre d'art, a émis la conclusion suivante.

> Allant très loin au-delà de la stimulation reçue directement et momentanément par les yeux, le cerveau opère avec la vaste panoplie d'images disponibles à travers la mémoire une organisation de la totalité de l'expérience vécue en un système de contextes visuels (Arnheim 1969).

Interprétant ces conclusions en relation avec la discipline de la conservation du patrimoine culturel, on peut dire que les contextes visuels créés par des monuments-symboles, associés à des expériences historiques de libération comme la Citadelle, deviennent d'importants instruments d'éducation. La valeur esthétique, en tant que nœud d'articulation entre les dimensions tangibles et intangibles du monument, devient donc une valeur active. Et, avec cette valeur, un artéfact devient une chose singulièrement vivante, appartenant à la conscience critique d'un groupe social. Comme le dirait Théodore Adorno,

> les artéfacts humains ne vivent pas exactement comme les peuples... ils sont vivants car ils parlent un langage que ne peuvent parler ni les objets naturels, ni les sujets qui les ont créés. Ils parlent parce que chaque élément particulier entrant dans leur composition possède la vertu de communiquer. Ainsi, ils contrastent avec l'arbitraire de la simple existence. C'est aussi en fonction de leur qualité d'artéfacts, comme produit d'un travail social, qu'ils communiquent avec l'expérience empirique où ils tirent leurs contenus en rejetant cette expérience (Adorno 1997 : 5).

En ce sens, les représentations visuelles et les analyses profondes de la valeur esthétique d'un artéfact constituent des démarches efficaces dans l'étude des contradictions sociales et de la richesse culturelle d'un peuple.

Dans cette ligne de pensée, Laurier Turgeon nous présente une brève histoire de la signification culturelle de l'objet-patrimoine en rapport avec la mémoire historique. Pour lui, plus qu'un témoin ou un signe, l'objet-patrimoine, dans son expression matérielle, est une force capable d'agir sur le monde social. Il est à la fois une forme d'expression de la mémoire et un moyen d'action sur cette mémoire. « Les lieux et les objets matériels ne font pas juste nourrir la mémoire, ils participent activement à sa structuration », dit-il. En citant Laurent Lepaludier, Turgeon rappelle que « l'objet est non seulement une référence cognitive qui cristallise la perception du monde mais aussi un point d'accroche essentiel de la mémoire qui structure le souvenir autour de lui » (Turgeon 2007 : 13, 36). Les lieux et les objets matériels sont donc des facteurs de production de la mémoire historique.

Le chemin inverse est aussi tout à fait possible. *La mémoire historique contribue à la structuration des lieux en tant que paramètre fondamental d'aménagement du territoire* (mon hypothèse de travail). Du lieu à la mémoire historique, et de la mémoire historique au lieu enrichi, l'objet-patrimoine, qui peut être un site complexe, s'inscrit dans une spirale d'enrichissement de son territoire. En Haïti, le Plan Directeur Tourisme a proposé en 1996 le concept de « Circuits de la Connaissance » comme mode de visite du territoire, en conduisant le visiteur au Plateau Central, lieu à partir duquel les Indiens et les Nègres marrons ont reconquis le territoire pour aboutir à l'indépendance du pays. La Citadelle est une fortification protégeant l'accès au Plateau Central. Cette donnée est un argument fondamental pour l'aménagement du territoire en vue du développement touristique du pays.

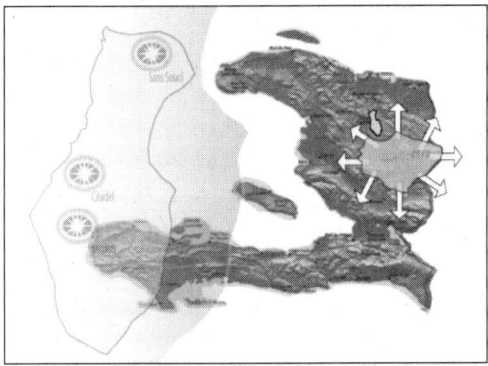

Figure 2. Localisation du Parc par rapport au Plateau Central

4. Les enjeux du tourisme durable en Haïti

Face à ce contexte de profonds changements dans le monde, tant au niveau conceptuel qu'aux niveaux environnemental et technique, Haïti reste un pays menacé par une catastrophe écologique (2% de couverture forestière)

et où la pauvreté représente le fardeau quotidien de la population (60% de la population vit sous le seuil de la pauvreté absolue avec moins de 1 dollar US par jour). Pour être durable, le développement touristique haïtien devra donc satisfaire, de façon urgente, un triple besoin : (1) l'amélioration des conditions socioéconomiques de la population de la région ; (2) la gestion efficiente du riche patrimoine culturel et naturel ; (3) la protection de l'environnement naturel en vue d'une meilleure exploitation du flux touristique potentiel attendu.

Les travaux sur le Parc National Historique – Citadelle, Sans Souci, Ramiers ont essayé de répondre à ces besoins. Au moins trois projets, malgré leurs limites, ont tenté de réaliser cette tâche :

- le projet ISPAN-PNUD-UNESCO pour la préservation de la Citadelle, du palais Sans Souci et du site fortifié des Ramiers et l'Aménagement du Parc National Historique ;
- le projet « Route 2004 » de 1995 qui a donné lieu à une série de propositions de lois sur la conservation et la gestion du Parc ;
- le Plan Directeur Tourisme de 1996 qui a placé le PNH au centre de la région touristique du Nord.

Depuis les études et les interventions sur la structure physique de la Citadelle et du palais Sans Souci à la mise en place d'équipes de supervision et d'entretien du site ; de la compréhension des valeurs historiques, sociales, esthétiques et économiques du site à la réalisation d'études muséologiques débouchant sur des propositions de circuits de visite ; de la compréhension des intérêts contradictoires associés au site à la proposition de cadre juridique et de structure de gestion pour sa protection, le Parc National Historique a constitué un champ d'intervention privilégié dans le cadre de la lutte pour la sauvegarde de la mémoire historique du peuple haïtien.

Mais les crises successives aiguës aux niveaux socioéconomique et politique ont affecté la continuité et la cohérence des projets réalisés. La difficulté de mettre en place une stratégie globale de conservation et de mise en valeur du Parc, articulée avec une vision cohérente du développement socioéconomique de la région, est l'une des conséquences de ce contexte de crises. À une échelle plus réduite, il y a aussi une crise dans la gestion des sites à haute valeur culturelle en Haïti. Cette crise s'exprime par une double incapacité :

- une incapacité à assumer les significations culturelles des sites et à les placer au centre du processus de planification et de l'aménagement touristique comme le suggère le Plan Directeur Tourisme de 1996. (Il existe encore en Haïti un rapport de conflit et d'opposition entre l'aménagement du territoire et la mémoire historique dont il faudra investiguer les paramètres) ;

• une incapacité à mettre en place un leadership stratégique efficace en termes de ressources humaines et financières, de vision, de stratégie, de méthodes de planification et d'évaluation.

5. Comment sortir de la crise?

Définir une vision stratégique dont le Parc National Historique sera l'élément central.

La vision stratégique du développement touristique de la région Nord devra reposer sur le constat que le Parc National Historique – Citadelle, Sans Souci, Ramiers articule un potentiel économique extraordinaire qu'il s'agit de mettre en valeur de manière intelligente pour relancer définitivement le tourisme en Haïti.

Le système formé par le Parc National Historique couvre vingt-sept kilomètres carrés ayant neuf caractéristiques majeures:

• situation au cœur du système montagneux du Nord d'Haïti;

• au carrefour de trois départements géographiques;

• dans la région frontalière haïtiano-dominicaine;

• sur la route des croisières caribéennes;

• desservi par le port touristique de Labadie;

• desservi par le port international du Cap-Haïtien;

• desservi par l'aéroport international du Cap-Haïtien;

• déclaré Patrimoine Mondial en tant qu'ensemble de sites dédiés à la défense du premier État fondé à l'époque contemporaine par des esclaves noirs ayant conquis leur liberté;

• hébergeant la plus grande collection de monuments et d'objets identitaires du peuple haïtien.

Figure 3. Le Parc National Historique – Citadelle, Sans Souci, Ramiers au centre de la région Nord d'Haïti.

Ma vision est celle d'une région où se réalise le développement harmonieux de tout le potentiel identifié autour du Parc National Historique en intégrant les aspects écologiques, agricoles, balnéaires, urbains et culturels pour faire de l'ensemble un socle holistique pour le progrès touristique durable au service de l'amélioration des conditions de vie de la population.

Aujourd'hui, des projets d'infrastructure sont timidement mis en œuvre dans la région Nord avec l'appui de la Coopération Internationale, dont principalement l'Union européenne. Mais le contexte global reste défavorable au développement touristique : insalubrité, insécurité, investissements privés très faibles, absence d'une démarche cohérente pour résoudre les problèmes socioéconomiques aigus de la population (emploi productif, logement, santé, éducation, loisirs), absence d'un cadre juridico-légal et d'une force de coercition viable permettant de lutter efficacement contre la corruption, la délinquance, l'anarchie, le trafic de drogue et le vandalisme.

Mais le plus grand handicap est l'incapacité actuelle du pays à mettre en place un leadership stratégique efficace ayant la capacité nécessaire en termes de ressources humaines et financières, de vision, de stratégie, de méthodes de planification et d'évaluation en vue de vaincre les obstacles. Mais encore faut-il une volonté réelle de vaincre ces obstacles !

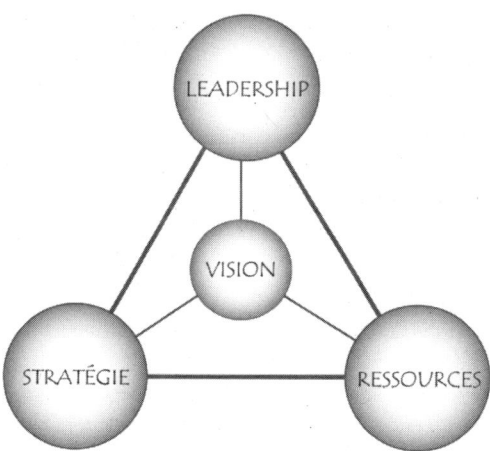

Figure 4. Paramètres d'un leadership stratégique en vue de la prise en charge du Parc.

Références

Adorno, Theodor W. 1997 [1970]. *Aesthetic Theory*. Traduction anglaise de Robert Hullot-Kentor. Minneapolis: University of Minnesota Press.

Arnheim, Rudolph. 1972. *Visual Thinking*. Berkeley: University of California Press.

Charte du Tourisme Durable. Conférence mondiale du Tourisme durable, Lanzarote, Îles Canaries, Espagne, 27 et 28 avril 1995.

Comité ICOMOS Australie, 1988, *Guidelines to the Burra Charter: Cultural Significance*. Burra Charter, révisée en 1999.

Convention concernant la protection du patrimoine mondial, culturel et naturel, 21 novembre 1972, UNESCO (Article 5.2).

Institut de Sauvegarde du Patrimoine National (ISPAN), 1986, *Les Monuments du Roi Christophe: La Citadelle, le palais de Sans Souci et le site fortifié des Ramiers. Monuments à l'indépendance d'une nation et à la liberté de son peuple*. Projet ISPAN-PNUD-UNESCO, Port-au-Prince: Imprimerie Le Natal.

Kant, Immanuel. 2004 [1790]. *Critique of Pure Reason*. Version en ligne publiée sur le site de l'Université Adelaide, http://ebooks.adelaide.edu.au/k/kant/immanuel/k16j/.

Panofsky, Erwin. 1982 [1955]. *Meaning in the Visual Arts*. Chicago: The University of Chicago Press et Phoenix edition.

Plan Directeur Tourisme, Rapport Principal, juin 1996. Projet PNUD/HAI/95/015. Port-au-Prince, Haïti.

Secrétariat Général Organisation des États Américains, 1972, *Développement du tourisme en Haïti. Grandes Lignes d'un Plan National de Développement Touristique, et Aspects institutionnels*. Washington DC.

Truscott, Marilyn, mars 2000, «Intangible Values as Heritage in Australia». *Icomos News* 10 (1), en ligne, http://www.international.icomos.org/victoriafalls2003/truscott_eng.htm.

Turgeon, Laurier. 2007. «La mémoire de la culture matérielle et la culture matérielle de la mémoire». Dans Octave Debary et Laurier Turgeon (dir.), *Objets et mémoires*, Québec/Paris, Les Presses de l'Université Laval et Éditions de la Maison des Sciences de l'Homme.

Conserving the Archaeological Soul of Places: Drafting Guidelines for the ICAHM Charter

Brian Egloff
President, ICAHM
Cultural Heritage Studies
University of Canberra
Australia

Douglas C. Comer
Vice President (North America), ICAHM
Principal Cultural Site Research and Management, Inc.
USA

ABSTRACT

Gustaf Trotzig, a Nordic founder of ICAHM, states that "Representation of sites to the public takes many forms and has varying impacts on the archaeological remains and the 'soul or spirit of the site'." Archaeological resources are a key component of global travel and local economies. How places are presented to the public varies wildly from entirely unkempt hidden treasures to highly manicured multimedia extravaganzas. An exhaustive survey of the heritage literature indicates that there have been fundamental shifts in the emphasis of archaeological heritage management from where academic values stressed knowledge and publication with the involvement of local peoples to the approach of today that caters to visitors and managers with little tangible outcomes by way of improving our understanding of the resource. Guidelines have been drafted for the ICAHM Charter that draw strongly upon the published experiences of archaeologists while exploring the kinds of approaches that characterize best heritage practise.

RÉSUMÉ

Gustaf Trotzig, l'un des fondateurs nordiques de l'ICAHM (Comité international de gestion du patrimoine archéologique), affirme que « la représentation des sites auprès du public prend de nombreuses formes et a des impacts variés sur les vestiges archéologiques et sur "l'âme ou l'esprit du lieu"». Les ressources archéologiques sont une composante clé des voyages internationaux et des économies locales. La manière dont les lieux sont présentés au public varie grandement, depuis les trésors cachés totalement négligés jusqu'aux extravagances multimédia les plus maniérées. Un examen exhaustif de la littérature relative au patrimoine indique qu'il s'est produit des glissements fondamentaux dans l'importance conférée à la gestion du patrimoine archéologique, depuis l'époque où les valeurs savantes insistaient sur la connaissance et les publications en incluant la participation des gens du lieu, jusqu'aux approches d'aujourd'hui, qui pourvoient aux plaisirs des visiteurs et des gestionnaires, mais sans grands résultats tangibles pour ce qui est d'approfondir notre compréhension du lieu visité. Des lignes directrices ont été rédigées pour la Charte de l'ICAHM, ces dernières insistant fortement sur les publications des archéologues, tout en explorant les types d'approches qui caractérisent les meilleures pratiques en matière de patrimoine.

1. Introduction

Archaeology is the study of the material remains of past cultures and is practiced with the holistic view of adding to our knowledge of past cultures as well as our understanding of the present condition of human societies. Archaeology is not as straightforward an activity as it may seem, as it is a distinctive and at times perplexing amalgam of the arts and the sciences. W. N. F. Flinders Petrie (1904, viii) wrote that "A complete archaeological training would require a full knowledge of history and art, a fair use of languages, and a working familiarity with many sciences". Of growing importance is the mandate to sustain the archaeological resource for use and reinterpretation by future generations. This in turn has caused the field of archaeological endeavor to become even more complex than it previously was. Regardless of whether they are of the scientific or the arts/humanities persuasion, it must be admitted for the most part that archaeologists seem to be more concerned with the discovery of the past than with the sustainability of the resource. For instance, there is no session at World Archaeology Congress 6 dealing with archaeological conservation while at World Archaeology Congress 5 it was entirely the effort of the Getty Conservation Institute that realized the inclusion of conservation in the program and provided for the publication of the more than 50 papers presented at the sessions (Agnew and Bridgeland 2007). The same apparent lack of interest in archaeological heritage management at the international level is demonstrated in regional conferences such as the Indo Pacific Prehistory Association with 600 to 800 members. At its 2006 meeting at Manila in the Philippines, more than 280 papers were listed in the program (Indo Pacific Prehistory Association 2006). A review of the abstracts indicates that only eight or so of the offerings dealt with the conservation of the archaeological resource while an equal number of papers reported on the excavation of human remains and cemeteries in third world countries; a highly controversial approach to research in some first world countries .

A survey of the membership of the International Committee for Archaeological Heritage Management (ICAHM) indicates that there is a need for an up-to-date international instrument. With this mandate in mind successive presidents of ICAHM have sought to review the ICAHM charter and draft a set of comprehensive guidelines. It was not until the retirement of the current president from his academic position and the funding of a visiting scholar position at the Getty Conservation Institute in 2006 and 2007 that matters progressed. This paper is a report of the current status of the ICAHM charter guidelines project. Archaeologists often work within a heritage-hostile environment and the maintenance of professional standards may require international support from an instrument that is current and timely; is future orientated; is aimed at an international, rather than a local, professional or national specific audience; has some degree of external authority that predates the particular issues at hand; and does not conflict with the common basis of national heritage legislation but serves to buttress weak points in policy and its implementation.

It has been pointed out that the internationalization of archaeology occurred well before there were any national associations. The first international congress "*pour les études préhistoriques*" met at Neuchâtel in 1866. In 1931, the Eighteenth International Conference of Orientalists met at Leiden (Daniel 1975, 202, 313-314) and a new congress, the International Congress of Prehistoric and Protohistoric Sciences, met for the first time in London in 1932. Following a formal recommendation in 1932, in 1937 the League of Nations drafted the *Cairo Act* during an International Conference convened by the Egyptian Government at the request of the International Museums Office (International Museums Office 1940). At that time, it was believed by some, and most definitely not by all, that "an appeal" for direct co-operation would be more effective than would be "regulations binding on governments" (UNESCO 1955/CUA/68/: 5; refer also to Manual on the Technique of Archaeological Excavations, International Museums Office 1940). After the Second World War, the *Cairo Act* 1937 was followed by its direct successor the *Recommendation on International Principles Applicable to Archaeological Excavations* (UNESCO 1956). It is the UNESCO document that details the consideration of the *Cairo Act* 1937 with respect to the forthcoming drafting of a New Delhi Recommendation that is particularly apropos to understanding the state of international academic archaeology in the 1950s (UNESCO 1955/CUA/68/). Perhaps one of the most telling contributions is that of Australia through the eminent classical archaeologist and Master of the University House of The Australian National University in the late

1960s, when this author was in residence, Professor A.D. Trendale. Trendale expressed particular concern for those countries without an archaeological past such as Australia and urged that those regions rich in archaeological collections, particularly the Mediterranean countries, assist museums in the New World to acquire collections. Trendale writes:

> I think it is most important that Australia should stress particularly the principle that excavators should receive a fair share of the material found. In this country, where we lack any archaeological sites in the strict sense of the word, it is absolutely impossible to build up an archaeological collection from material locally available (UNESCO 1955/CUA/68 Addendum 1: 2).

An exceptionally narrow and relic driven approach seems to bedevil international charters as each national representation for the most part evidences a narrow perspective based upon current issues, at times seemingly highly personal, rather than a broad approach that focuses upon sustaining the resource and enhancing the study of the archaeological past. It is apparent that this narrow reaction of archaeologists to a postcolonial world where they no longer had free and unfettered access to archaeological resources is strongly expressed in the New Delhi Recommendation of 1956.

The ICOMOS *International Charter for the Conservation and Restoration of Monuments and Sites* (ICOMOS 1966), dating to 1964 following the IInd International Congress of Architects and Specialists in Historic Buildings that met in Venice touches only briefly on archaeology and set a disturbing trend. Being drafted for the most part by architectural restoration specialists it took the emphasis away from societies as the caretakers of their heritage and diminished the stress on research and publication found in the *Cairo Act* 1937.

It was not until the 1990s with the drafting of both the ICAHM charter and the revised European convention that a more holistic perspective was offered to the international community. The Council of Europe (1969) prepared the *European Convention on the Protection of Archaeological Heritage* that was redrafted in 1992 as the *European Convention for the Protection of the Archaeological Heritage of Europe* (Council of Europe 1992). Emerging in 1990 just prior to the revised European convention was the ICOMOS *International Charter for Archaeological Heritage Management* (ICOMOS 1990). The charter was inspired by some of the same European heritage specialists that were involved in drafting the revised European convention with an injection of Australian heritage management expertise.

There are no journal articles discussing the application or the impact of the *Cairo Act* 1937 as it seems to have been lost in the wholesale destruction of World War II. Only a few papers discuss the importance of the New Delhi Recommendation and the ICAHM Charter (Cleerre 1993; Elia 1993; O'Keefe and Prott 1986/1994; Stanley Price 1995). But there is a growing body of literature reviewing the implementation of the *European Convention on the Protection of the Archaeological Heritage (revised)* (Council of Europe 1992) (Council for British Archaeology n.d.; Lund 1989; van Marrewijk and Brandt 1997; O'Keefe 1993; Trotzig 1993, 2001; Willems 1997, 1999, 2007, n.d.; Young 2001; and various articles in Willems and van den Dries 2007). A review of the commentary on the application of the European Convention provides a fascinating account of the shift in archaeology from an international-nationalistic pursuit of academics to a popular and more broadly based activity of international concern with the management and conservation of the resource.

2. Towards International Guidelines

The review of the international literature dealing with archaeological heritage management has proven to be both time consuming and exhausting. The rate of publication of new material is indeed prodigious, perhaps marking the interest that archaeological heritage management is gaining outside of academic circles. The preliminary report of the ICAHM guidelines project "Archaeological Heritage Management: Towards International Guidelines" now numbers more than 400 pages, fifty of those pages comprising2 a bibliography of roughly 350 references. There are perhaps as many as 50 more journal articles and edited chapters to be considered for incorporation into the narrative.

Archaeological heritage management has many faces particularly as it is strongly influenced by at least two kinds of legislation – archaeological and antiquities – if not three or four, if one includes environmental conservation and planning instruments as well as being loosely tied to national and international instruments such as the *Convention Concerning the Protection of the World Cultural and Natural Heritage* (UNESCO 1972). Some national and state/provincial jurisdictions divide archaeological legislation into that dealing with the material culture of indigenous peoples as distinct from that of the settler societies. The issue of who owns archaeological resources varies greatly. Archaeological resources may be owned by the nation or state/ province while in other countries the prehistoric materials belong to the property owner. This duality is manifested in the European Council where archaeological heritage managers are to adhere to the *European Convention for the Protection of the Archaeological Heritage of Europe (Revised)*, Valetta 1992 with archaeological resources in the United Kingdom belonging to the landholders, with some exceptions such as treasure trove, while in the Netherlands the resource belongs to the nation.

At the World Archaeology Congress in Dublin, 29 June to 4 July 2008, one of the most contentious issues to engulf the membership was the fate of archaeological resources whose significances are allegedly threatened by the construction of a highway system near the "Hill of Tara", the ancient seat of the kings of Ireland. The role of consultants and academics was questioned within the context of allegations of unseen profits being garnered by private developers. In a highly emotive article titled "The State We're in on the Eve of World Archaeology Congress (WAC 6): Archaeology in Ireland vs. Corporate Takeover", Maggie Ronayne (2008: 115) expresses the view that the professionalization of archaeology "has happened in tandem with increasing corporate control of universities and bureaucratic pressure on academics to orient teaching to meet the needs of industry". This could be true but on the other hand it has to be acknowledged that the National Roads Authority of the Government of Ireland has developed a code of practise that on the surface appears to be second to none in the world (National Roads Authority n.d.).

3. Mainstreams of Archaeological Inquiry

Each of the four geographical regions discussed in the guidelines review, Australia, Europe (in particular the Netherlands, Ireland and the United Kingdom) and the United States of America evidence different trajectories with lag times of perhaps one to two decades for the timing of when key issues emerge. For example consultant archaeologists were employed in the United States in the 1970s but not in the Netherlands until the 1990s. Settler societies in North America and Oceania are involved with indigenous issues while countries that have experienced prolonged and bitter endemic warfare are concerned with the impact of conflicts on their heritages which are seemingly out of all proportion to the reasonable conduct of war. Each region and nation state evidences different priorities with commonalities in terms of ethical standards, interpretation of archaeological places and the challenges of World Heritage conservation.

A review of the salient indicators for the future directions of archaeological heritage management was undertaken through the identification of zones of discomfort as evidenced in *Heritage At Risk* (ICOMOS 2001/2, etc.). The analysis of *Heritage at Risk* is supplemented with a review of the sessions at the 2008 World Archaeology Congress. A brief summary follows of some of the salient interrelated challenges.

Generating and using knowledge is a broad category of activity that is based upon objectivity and an ethical approach.

The power of heritage discourse has been known for many years with its most publicized application being that of the national socialist government of Germany in the 1930s and early 1940s. The power of archaeological discourse continues today with places being destroyed to remove traces of the past of peoples and heritage being selectively conserved to meet with local and national agendas. Regrettably this is evident at World Heritage places where the diverse communities in a nation state strive for recognition and ownership of the present through glorification of their particular past at the expenses of other people's pasts. Heritage as a force in political agendas at times is overwhelming and archaeologists need to seek a balance in how communities and nations relate their heritage to that of others. At the immediate operational level archaeologists must effectively interface with stakeholder groups and ensure that positive benefits return to the individuals that have vested interests in archaeological heritage.

Education, training and qualifications are of major importance to archaeological heritage managers throughout the world.

Standards and guidelines for fieldwork have been codified by many agencies and consultation guidelines have been developed in various countries including Australia with some agencies like road and transport authorities developing their own standards. As research undertaken by consultants now constitutes perhaps as much as 90% of the archaeology in some jurisdictions, it is important that it be undertaken to the highest possible standard. This has brought about a review by European nations of quality control in archaeological projects that are mandated by the state/nation usually in circumstances where the client does not care what the quality of the work is, as long as it meets the government's requirements. In many instances the work is of high quality but the only independent audit to be undertaken, in the Netherlands, suggests that the majority of projects do not meet established standards (van den Dries and Willems 2007, 61). The Government of France under pressure from the European Union has been able to argue effectively that it should preserve its system of a strict state monopoly of archaeological projects as in its opinion it is effective in delivering quality outputs (Demoule 2007).

There is cause to question how effective is the work of consulting firms, or academic consortiums, when it is linked to developmental and governmental projects – "compliance-driven archaeology" – that may require commercial or institutional confidentiality. As publication has long been held to be the standard requirement of archaeologists and a formal international requirement since the *Cairo Act* 1937, how should the profession relate to participants in cultural heritage management projects where the products are not available to academia or the public. Here the concern lies not necessarily only with consultants but also with academics that might undertake such projects and are seen by other archaeologists to be specialists in "developmental clearances". These enterprises might be termed "agencies of last resort" as they frequently "re-work" existing conservation plans such that the client can do whatever they wish regardless of the impacts on the conservation of the archaeological resource.

Standards should be reviewed for archaeologists working abroad who choose to undertake certain kinds of research projects not readily condoned in their homeland. A wide variation in legislation and policies governing archaeological processes means that it is highly likely that what one can do in overseas countries is substantially different from that which an archaeologist can do in their own country. This is particularly true with respect to the excavation of human remains. Should the archaeological community continue to undertake the wholesale excavation of burials in foreign countries knowing that this practise is banned or considered to be highly suspect in their home country and has led in the past to highly acrimonious disputes between archaeologists and local communities?

Continuing professional development needs to be a required component for participation in professional archaeological employment. Educational standards vary substantially between countries. For instance an undergraduate degree is required in Australia while postgraduate qualifications are required to undertake Federal government consultancies in the United States of America. Should the archaeological profession press for a common set of standards or a minimum level of educational attainment followed by a sustained period of professional experience evaluated through a workplace competency process for professional archaeologists?

Sustainability of resources has never been more important as the world's economies reach such a state of over-development that they have the wherewithal to impact on even the remotest heritage place in the world.

Governance of archaeological heritage resources is a matter that has seldom been addressed in the literature but one that should be of particular interest with respect to collecting institutions. The term governance refers to the organizational level at which policies are formulated that set the agenda for the managers and administrators of an institution (Cueervo-Cazurra and Aguilera 2003). Institutions with specific objectives control heritage resources. In many instances the dominant agenda is not necessarily the conservation of the resource or the reaching of an understanding of its importance to archaeological studies, but the physical possession of it. This focus on the possession of items from the archaeological past often leads to a downplaying of the knowledge base of the artifact as a collecting institution either consciously or through purposeful inactivity hides any telltale signs of a tainted past (Egloff 2008). With this in mind, archaeologists need to press for more open governance policies by national and state collecting institutions as well as by councils that determine the fate of heritage listed places.

Figure 1. "Handing back" of the sacred mountains of Gulaga and Biamanga to representatives of the traditional Aboriginal owners, Lionel Montga and Mary Duroux at Tilba, New South Wales in 2006.

The nexus of archaeology and indigenous people has been on the agenda in the international heritage management arena since at least the 1970s. The position of indigenous communities in the archaeological process has changed from one of minor involvement to a position where they are the employers of archaeologists and the community sets the agenda. Nevertheless there are very real differences in capacity between indigenous communities and mainstream societies with regard to the wherewithal to manage their respective cultural heritages. This imbalance needs to be addressed at the coal-face with respect to real capacity building through archaeological projects as well as enhancing educational opportunities for the members of indigenous and minority groups. It seems as if only a very few academic archaeologists have made a real difference in the education of indigenous and third world archaeologists while many others have done very little to further the archaeological careers of the peoples that they work with.

Economics of the archaeological heritage are nothing short of remarkable with the returns from heritage tourism sustaining a considerable proportion of the world's population.

Rebuilding of archaeological sites has been held by some practitioners to be an uncomfortable exercise and the examples of over-rebuilding of heritage places are legion. The most recent issue of international concern is the UNESCO report on the World Heritage listed Skellig Michael, the 8th century island monastery off the southwest coast of Ireland where over-reconstruction of some of the ruined stone structures is raised (*Irish Times* 2008). Pressures is growing from management and the tourist industry to provide neat and clean facilities (including ruins) and consumable and readily understandable heritage packages through the radical transformation of rather disorderly archaeological sites such that all manner of hypothetical alterations are being undertaken. One cannot help but be uncomfortable when visiting a heritage place and noting that its current appearance could not in any way resemble its form during its "real life" when it was populated by "real people". Authenticity of fabric and the limits of acceptable change need to be brought to the fore when interpreting places to the public. No excuses should be given for not detailing in the site interpretation the changes that have taken place during the hypothetical reconstruction.

Figure 2. Tourists clamber over the rebuilt ruins of the World Heritage listed 8th Century monastery at Skellig Michael, Ireland.

Development and economics, as discussed above, are almost impossible to disentangle and very much drive the heritage agenda.

Archaeology as a tool of development is known to be both a positive and a negative force, as is discussed above with respect to the "Hill of Tara". Although the value of archaeology in local capacity building is assumed, one of the few articles dealing specifically with archaeology and development is by G. Trotzig, "The cultural dimension of development – an archaeological approach", in *Archaeological Heritage Management in the Modern World* edited by H. F. Cleere (1989). There are publications presenting vague anecdotal accounts of what archaeology can add to the quality of life in third world countries but nothing that provides hard-core economic data. Oddly enough one of the more detailed economic considerations of the value of cultural heritage is in a collection of papers prepared by the IUCN titled *The Protected Landscape Approach: linking nature, culture and community* (Mitchell and Beresford 2005). "The Protected Landscape Approach in the Czech Republic" (Kundrata and Husková 2005, 137-141) documents in micro-detail an interesting case study of rural sustainability at the small village of Hostetín in eastern Moravia. Reed bed sewerage treatment, energy production by forest waste wood, use of traditional fruit varieties for commercial juice production and sale have contributed to sustainability within which landscape heritage features prominently. It is the detail of the analysis by Kundrata and Husková that offers an alternative to the impressionistic assertions that litter the literature on archaeology, heritage and sustainability. Archaeology needs to construct well-documented and persuasive arguments for the inclusion of archaeology as a component of development and as a tool for capacity building.

Threats to the archaeological heritage seem to be endless when one takes into account both natural and cultural forces.

In the last two meetings of the World Archaeology Congress, the impact of the American invasion of Iraq on cultural heritage resources, in particular archaeological sites and museum collections, has been discussed and deplored. The considerable damage inflicted on archaeological resources has been well documented but the appropriate relationship of academic and professional archaeologists in terms of cooperating with military powers leading up to and during the invasion of a country is less well defined. Here reference is to the "Archaeology in the Context of War" session at WAC 6 where the wisdom and ethics of archaeologists participating in invasion pre-planning was debated (WAC-6 Ireland 2008). There seems to be scope for a broader and thoughtful discussion of the ethics of archaeologists, be they situation specific or not, when as individuals they are embedded in military operations.

Transfer of tainted or illicit artifacts is of considerable concern to archaeologists with the looting of heritage places continuing unabated in spite of considerable effort by heritage managers. The Society for American Archaeology (1996) has within its code of ethics a statement that "Wherever possible, they should discourage, and should themselves avoid, activities that enhance the commercial value of archaeological objects, especially objects that are not curated in public institutions, or readily available for scientific study, public interpretation, and display". Why include the clause "not curated in public institutions", as upon extensive first-hand research (refer to Egloff 2008 for references and a more detailed discussion), public institutions and quasi-public galleries broadcast a highly visible elitist statement that they will do what they believe to be the best for both their institution and the wider cultural world and in doing so add to their collections whatsoever they wish to.

Figure 3. Images of Lord Buddha are believed to be regularly pillaged from this temple stupa in Southeast Asia.

Natural forces and in particular changing climatic regimes, and the measures that human societies have taken to adapt to change have been the topic of archaeological inquiry. More recently the impact of climate change on the conservation of archaeological resources has begun to take centre stage. The most concentrated effort being undertaken by the University College London with the establishment of the Centre for Sustainable Heritage that specifically considers impacts of the changing climate on the historic environment (Cassar 2005).

Dissemination of archaeological information has grown apace with the 20th Century publication explosion and the creation of Internet Web sites that protest the destruction of archaeological places.

Advocacy of archaeological conservation issues is of considerable concern to the international community of conservation heritage managers. ICOMOS has made an enormous effort in its publication of *Heritage at Risk* to bring to the attention of the wider public key place and theme related heritage issues. Of considerable concern is the lack of a public profile for ICOMOS, its limited and often government dependent financial resources and its sparse following in non-developed nations. The activities of the World Archaeology Congress may have an impact but would seem to have even less international leverage than does ICOMOS. The Archaeological Institute of America as North America's oldest and largest organization devoted to the world of archaeology with nearly 250,000 members and subscribers does speak out on major issues and has had an impact as has Heritage Watch since its foundation in 2003 and the World Monument Watch list of the 100 most endangered heritage places prepared by the World Monuments Fund. There is an obvious need for a peak heritage advocacy body that has popular appeal and is more broadly funded, such as is found in the natural heritage regime with the World Wildlife Foundation or the International Union for Conservation of Nature (IUCN).

4. Summary

Seemingly distinct issues merge when discussing topics of particular interest. For instance when it comes to ascertaining the quality of values-oriented, commercially driven archaeology there is considerable discussion of competence, qualifications and ethics. Is the work competent, is it done by qualified people, is it honest – doing what it says it does – and does the research add at all to our understanding of the archaeological resource? It is the mandate of archaeologists that their work should add to our understanding of the past and/or that it should be pointed towards conserving the remains of past societies so that they can be explored and reinterpreted by future generations of archaeologists. Academic archaeology was never perfect and until the 1960s it was a very small world in which the tens of archaeologists dealing with a particular realm of the past were able to meet and discuss their interests, agreements and disagreements.

The World Archaeology Congress at Dublin, 29 June to 4 July 2008, with more than 1,500 attendees and up to 18 concurrent sessions at any one time leads one to question the wherewithal of any single organization to respectably represent archaeological thought and actions. Some 33 themes were discussed in the sessions including the following: theory and its application; materials (ceramics, lithic, etc.) analysis techniques; war, conflict and working with the military; museums, interpretation and archaeology; digital media; archaeology and development; intellectual property rights; kinds of archaeology such as geoarchaeology, wetland, rainforest, innovation and migration; ethical archaeology, which had considerable coverage including a youth forum; useful archaeologies, communicating archaeology, heritage tourism; archaeology and sexuality; landscapes and archaeology; maritime archaeology, politics and identity; and human responses to change. Some of the themes were of interest to narrow groups of archaeologists, for example, archaeology and sexuality, while other subjects such as ethics and conflict were of considerable importance to the wider body of archaeologists. Perhaps WAC 6 evidenced a shift away from archaeology as being based upon a reasoned body of empirical data to a field more emotionally driven and less able to support its arguments with anything less than impressionistic observations. What constitutes archaeology has never been easy to define and certainly that task has not been made any easier by the growing mandate to actively conserve the resource

Acknowledgements

This review is based upon an unpublished paper titled "Understanding Archaeological Heritage Management: drafting guidelines for the ICAHM Charter" presented at the 6th World Archaeology Congress in Dublin, Ireland from 29 June to 4 July 2008. This work has been supported through a resident scholarship at the Getty Conservation Institute, Los Angeles.

References

Agnew, Neville and Janet Bridgland (eds.). 2006. *Of the Past, for the Future: Integrating Archaeology and Conservation.* Proceedings of the Conservation Theme at the 5th World Archaeology Congress, Washington, D.C. Los Angles: The Getty Conservation Institute.

Australia ICOMOS. 1999. *Charter for the Conservation of Places of Cultural Significance* (Burra, South Australia).

Brown, Jessica, Nora Mitchell and Michael Beresford. 2005. *The Protected Landscape Approach: linking nature, culture and community.* Gland, Switzerland and Cambridge, UK: IUCN the World Conservation Union.

Cassar, May. 2005. *Climate Change and the Historic Environment.* University College London, Centre for Sustainable Heritage.

Cleere, Henry. 1993. Managing the Archaeological Heritage. *Antiquity*, 67: 400-402.

Council for British Archaeology. n.d. Valetta Convention on the Protection of Archaeological Heritage: a summary of the CBA position, an abbreviated statement of the Council for British Archaeology's position on the key implications of the Valetta Convention, which came into force in the UK in March 2001.n

Council of Europe. 1969. *European Convention on the Protection of Archaeological Heritage.*

Council of Europe. 1992. *European Convention on the Protection of the Archaeological Heritage (revised)*, Valetta, 16.1.1992.

Cueervo-Cazurra, Alvaro and Ruth V. Aguilera. 2003 The Worldwide Diffusion of Codes of Good Governance. In Anna Grandori (ed.), *Corporate Governance and Firm Organization: microfoundations and structural forms.* 318-348. Oxford: Oxford University Press.

Daniel, Glyn. 1950/1975. *A Hundred and Fifty Years of Archaeology.* Duckworth, Great Britain.

Demoule, Jean Paul. 2007. Scientific quality control and the general organization of French archaeology. In Willem J. H. Willems and Monique H. van den Dries (eds.), *Quality Management in Archaeology.* 135-147. Oxford: Oxbow Books.

van den Dries, Monique and Willem Willems. 2007. Quality assurance in archaeology, the Dutch perspective. In Willem J. H. Willems and Monique H. van den Dries (eds.), *Quality Management in Archaeology.* 50-65. Oxford: Oxbow Books, Oxford.

Egloff, Brian. 2008. *Bones of the Ancestors: the Ambum Stone from the New Guinea Highlands, to the Antiquities Market, to Australia.* AltaMira Press, Lanham, Maryland.

Elia, Ricardo. 1993. US Cultural Resource Management and the ICAHM Charter. *Antiquity* 67: 426-438.

European Commission. 2006 *The APPEAR Method: A practical guide for the management of enhancement projects on urban archaeological sites.* Research Report n° 30/4.

Feilden, Bernard and Jukka Jokilehto. 1993/1998. (2nd edition) *Management Guidelines for World Cultural Heritage Sites.* International Centre for the Study of the Preservation and the Restoration of Cultural Property, Rome.

ICOMOS. 1966. International Charter for the Conservation and Restoration of Museum Sites (Venice 1964).

ICOMOS. 1990. *International Charter for Archaeological Heritage Management* (Lausanne 1990).

ICOMOS. (ed.) 2000, 2002, 2003, 2005. *Heritage at Risk*, K.G. Saur, München.

Indo Pacific Prehistory Association. 2006. Abstracts. http://arts.anu.edu.au/arcworld/ippa/Manila%20abstracts%20final.htm.

International Museums Office. 1940. *Manual on the Technique of Archaeological Excavations,* Paris.

Irish Times. 2008. Wednesday Unesco report criticises Skellig work, 9 Jul 2008. www.irishtimes.com/newspaper/ireland/2008/0709/1215537641571; accessed 25 August 2008.

Kundrata, Miroslav and Blazena Husková. 2005. Sustaining rural landscapes and building civil society: experience from Central Europe. In Jessica Brown, Nora Mitchell and Michael Beresford (eds.), *The Protected Landscape Approach: linking nature, culture and community.* 137-141. Gland, Switzerland and Cambridge, UK: IUCN the World Conservation Union.

Lund, Carsten. 1989. A Charter for the Protection and Management of the Archaeological Heritage. *Icomos Information,* July/September no. 3, 15-24.

Marrewijk, Dre van and Roel Brandt. 1997. Dreaming of Malta. In W.J.H. Willems, H. Kars and D.P. Hallewas (eds.), *Archaeological Heritage Management in the Netherlands: Fifty Years State Service for Archaeological Investigations.* 58-75. Assen: Van Gorcum.

National Roads Authority. n.d. *Code of Practice between the National Roads Authority and the Minister for Arts, Heritage, Gaeltacht and the Islands,* National Roads Authority (Ireland).

O'Keefe, Patrick J. 1993. The European Convention on the Protection of the Archaeological Heritage. *Antiquity* 67: 406-413.

O'Keefe, Patrick J. and Lyndel V. Prott. 1986/1994. Recommendation on International Principles Applicable to Archaeological Excavations, document prepared for UNESCO, manuscript re-circulated in 1994.

Petrie, W.N.F. 1904/1972. *Method and Aims in Archaeology.* New York: Benjamin Blom.

Ronayne, Maggie. 2008. The State We're in on the Eve of World Archaeology Congress (WAC) 6: Archaeology in Ireland vs Corporate Takeover. *Public Archaeology* 7(2): 114-129.

Society for American Archaeology. 1996. Principles of Archaeological Ethics http://www.saa.org/aboutsaa/committees/ethics/principles.html; accessed 20 August 2008

Stanley Price, N.P. 1995. Conservation on Excavations and the 1956 UNESCO Recommendation. In N. Stanley Price (ed.), *Conservation on Archaeological Excavations: with particular reference to the Mediterranean area.* 135-142. ICCROM, Rome.

Trotzig, Gustaf. 1993. The new European Convention on the Protection of the Archaeological Heritage, *Antiquity* 67: 414-415.

Trotzig, Gustaf. 2001. On the (revised) European Convention on the Protection of the Archaeological Heritage presented in Malta 1992. *The European Archaeologist* 15: 1-4.

Truscott, Marilyn and David Young. 2000. Revising the Burra Charter: Australia ICOMOS updates its guidelines for conservation practice. *Conservation and Management of Archaeological Sites* 4/2: 101-116.

UNESCO. 1955. Preliminary Report Compiled in Accordance with the Provisions of Article 10, of the Rules of Procedure Concerning Recommendations to Member States and International Conventions Covered by the Terms of Article IV, Paragraph 4, of the Constitution, UNESCO/CUA/68, Dated Paris, 9 August 1955, translated from the French (note that the addendums incorporate correspondence post-dating that of the document) .

UNESCO. 1956. *Recommendation on International Principles Applicable to Archaeological Excavations* (referred to as the 1956 Delhi Recommendation).

Willems, Willem J.H. 1997. Archaeological Heritage Management in the Netherlands: Past, Present and Future. In W.J.H. Willems, H. Kars and D.P. Hallewas (eds.), *Archaeological Heritage Management in the Netherlands: Fifty Years State Service for Archaeological Investigations.* 3-17. Assen: Van Gorcum.

Willems, Willem J.H. 1999. *The Future of European Archaeology.* Oxbow Lecture 3, Archaeology in Britain Conference 1997. Oxford: Oxbow Books.

Willems, Willem. n.d. "How Malta changed Archaeology in Europe: a perspective from the European Association of Archaeologists". http://www.coer.int/t/e/cultural_co-operation/heritage/archaeology/Statmentwillems.asp; accessed January 5 2007.

Willems, W.J.H. and H. Kars, H. and D.P. Hallewas (eds.). 1997. *Archaeological Heritage Management in the Netherlands: Fifty Years State Service for Archaeological Investigations.* Assen: Van Gorcum.

Willems, W.J.H. and R.W. Brandt. 2004. *Dutch Archaeology Quality Standard.* RIA-report, Rijkinspectie voor de Archeology, Den Haag.

Willems, Willem J.H. and Monique H. van den Dries (eds.). 2007. *Quality Management in Archaeology.* Oxford: Oxbow Books.

Young, Christopher. 2001. English Heritage Position Statement of the Valletta Convention, 18th July, 2001. http://www.cix.co.uk/~archaeology/cia/valetta/EHPostionStatement.htm; accessed 25 June 2007.

V

USING DIGITAL AND WEB TECHNOLOGIES

EXPLOITER LES TECHNOLOGIES NUMÉRIQUES ET LE WEB

Transmitting the Spirit of Place in the Age of Web Wisdom?

Sheridan Burke
Director, Godden Mackay Logan, Heritage Consultants
ICOMOS Twentieth Century Heritage ISC
ICOMOS Interpretation and Presentation ISC
Austalia

ABSTRACT

The new generation of InternetInternet communication is transforming human relations and cross – cultural communication in previously unimaginable and dynamically plural ways. The presentation/interpretation of places and indeed of national identity through heritage values and places is no longer predominantly in the hands of governments as a political tool or those of experts in academic research – it's also powerfully present on *Wikipedia* and *YouTube* and every social networking site yet to be imagined.

When the *YouTube* video of the Yolngu Chooky Dancers of Arnhem Land dancing Zorba the Greek went live in 2007, thousands of hits were registered in a matter of hours, and international interest has not abated. The results of recent InternetInternet voting for the New Seven Wonders of the World also exemplify these opportunities and challenges of transmitting heritage values. This paper will examine these issues and the impacts which the globalisation of communication will have on transmitting the spirit of heritage place in an age of web wisdoms.

RÉSUMÉ

La nouvelle génération des communications par Internet transforme les relations humaines et la communication interculturelle de nombreuses manières dynamiques, auparavant inimaginables. La présentation/interprétation des lieux et des faits, ainsi que de l'identité nationale, au moyen des valeurs et des lieux patrimoniaux ne se trouve plus avant tout aux mains des gouvernements en tant qu'outil politique, ni aux mains des experts et de la recherche savante. Ce phénomène est aussi puissamment représenté dans *Wikipedia* et *YouTube*, et dans tout réseau social en ligne que l'on puisse imaginer. Lorsque la vidéo des Yolngu Chooky Dancers, originaires de la Terre d'Arnhem en Australie, dansant «Zorba le Grec» sortit sur *YouTube* en 2007, des milliers de réactions enthousiastes furent enregistrées en quelques heures, et l'intérêt international ne s'est pas démenti. Les résultats d'un récent sondage Internet pour les Sept nouvelles merveilles du monde constituent également un exemple de ces opportunités et de ces défis de la transmission des valeurs patrimoniales. Cet article examinera ces questions et les impacts que la mondialisation des communications pourra entraîner sur la transmission de l'esprit des lieux patrimoniaux en cette ère des sagesses en réseau.

The Inspiration and Diversity of Heritage Assets

Cultural heritage resources are amongst any culture's most prized social capital assets. They are diverse resources – buildings, landscapes, cultural traditions, archaeological sites, single objects and complexes such as the Temple of Heaven in Beijing and a simple building which it inspired, this teahouse, built in 1921 at Eryldene in Sydney. These are places imbued with layers of meaning given by generations of artists and craftsmen, families and governments, by diverse, influential, sometimes harmonious, sometimes conflicting cultures.

As scholars and practitioners we have developed special knowledge to conserve, manage and present/interpret[1] such heritage monuments, sites, objects and places. Governments, communities and interest groups also know well the power of heritage places, objects and intangibles in terms of national identity, pride and international influence.

As individuals we each respond intellectually and emotionally to heritage places: with excitement, reverence, awe and pleasure or perhaps with anger, fear and sorrow at the demonstration of the progress or destruction of civilisations.

Understanding, Valuing, Caring for and Enjoying Heritage Places

This diversity of personal response is usually directly related to how well we understand the natural and cultural environment, for it is through understanding heritage that people value it; and by valuing it people will want to care for it; by caring for it people will want to help others enjoy it; and through enjoying the natural and cultural environment comes a wish for further understanding and protection.

---

1.   *Interpretation and presentation* mean "all the ways of presenting the significance of the place (or object)", a key element in the heritage conservation process.

This adaptation of economic theory by English Heritage is known as the Virtuous Circle, and it forms the basis for my discussion today of the importance of presentation/interpretation in the conservation and management of heritage places, and reflection on the impact of the revolutionary change of global communication known as Web 2.0, the new generation of InternetInternet communication where people contribute as much as they receive.

Too often, the interpretation of a heritage place seems to be almost an afterthought to the work of restoration or maintenance of the physical fabric by specialist architects or archaeologists.

Too often interpretation is seen by site managers as a collection of signs on site, a brochure, perhaps a carefully footnoted guidebook, authored by scholars of the site – but interpretation can be, and should be, so much more!

The conceptualization and design of interpretation effectively forms the gateway to the understanding of a heritage place. It's an important part of the conservation process… open to everyone – lifetime expert and first time visitor. And today most heritage places are able to be accessible virtually world wide, 24 hours a day, through the eyes of Everyman, his camera and his computer.

Absent are the checks and balances of editor and director, author and expert advisor. To the fore are open-ended conversations about the personal interpretations of tangible fabric and intangible traditions, monuments and sites.

I want to play for you now a brief excerpt from *YouTube,* one of the fastest growing Web 2.0 Internet sites, a freely accessible platform where anyone can upload videos, with minimal moderation (censorship). This is an excerpt from a recent dance performance by a group of ten teenagers living in the Elcho Islands, in Australia's remote northern Arnhem Land area. For these kids, English is a second or third language; none of them owns a computer. None have traveled out of Australia, and only one or two have ever left their remote communities. These boys have learned the dreaming stories of their tribes from the elders of their clans, through initiation, and through dance and you will note their ceremonial paint, traditional for Yirrikala dance performances.[2] But perhaps the Elcho Islands are not so very remote…

In the months since this performance was filmed and posted on *YouTube* by a proud father, the Chooky Dancers, as they are now known, have traveled around Australia, and indeed to Greece to perform, celebrated for their unique *mashup* of Greek and Yirrikala culture… from the spirit of the Elcho

---

2.   Frank Djirrimbilpilwuy, Top End Aboriginal Bush Broadcasting Association <http://youtube.com/watch?v=O-MucVWo-Pw>.

Island, channeling Zorba the Greek. They embody the ability of Web 2.0 to mashup and transmit the spirit of places.

The Heritage Challenges and Opportunities of Web 2.0[3]

In this increasingly interdependent age of web wisdom, audiences for heritage monuments and sites are demanding – and indeed creating for themselves – an entirely different approach to heritage site presentation and it may well be the antithesis of any "official" or agreed understanding of the heritage significance of the place.

Any number of personal views and interpretations of a heritage place[4] can be shared globally via websites such as *MySpace* and *Facebook*. Sites such as *YouTube* and *Flickr* provide further opportunities through audio visual and photograph sharing – particularly relevant media for heritage places.

The development of the on-line open encyclopedia *Wikipedia* has swiftly demonstrated that explanations of cultural value can be written by anyone and accepted by most people. Wikis are not static documents – they are collaboratively built by every contributor. At present, Wikipedia is not yet accessible globally, but a review of the papers for this learned forum will demonstrate how much it is being used by lay persons and scholars alike as a ready reference source.

The challenges to the integrity and authenticity of any item of information which these Web 2.0 communication networks bring to our daily lives are the subject of much debate, and today I want to examine their particular challenges and opportunities to heritage conservation work. I note, of course, the accessibility of these Web 2.0 opportunities is as variable as the reach of the Internet, which is itself extraordinary, yet also limited.

The best quality interpretation of heritage sites addresses diverse audiences, who require diverse interpretation techniques and media. Museums, libraries and archives have been developing databases and interactive visitor engagements for many years. Statutory authorities have begun to provide massive historical records and resources on line, the UK's Heritage Gateway is extraordinary in its range and depth, but with very few exceptions (and the Brooklyn Museum is an outstanding one), most heritage place based sites are offering information access for planning and learning purposes, perhaps with the odd curatorial blog.

---

3.   *Web 2.0* is the fast developing new generation of the Internet, consisting of interconnected communities and hosted services such as social networking, Wikis and folksonomies.
4.   *Heritage Place* includes buildings, works, relics, sites, monuments and objects of heritage value or significance.

When compared with the dynamism of social networking media, there is a fundamental gap where user-generated content demands a new relationship between new audiences and the spirit of place – a tension between the virtual and the real, between established authority and new, ever changing communities. No longer does one small group "own the expertise" about a place – it's diffused and accessible.

Traditionally, site signage and guidebooks have been created to provide interpretation for visitors through scholarly research and photography. People able to visit these sites appreciate the unique experiences of being there, but for everyone else, their understanding and respect for the place is moderated by others – through a book, a photograph, a souvenir. Web 2.0 sites like *Flickr* are challenging those limitations. The Australian War Memorial has recently experimented with developing exhibition blogs where curators and audiences created, discussed and published exhibition material before, during and after a display (Holcombe 2008). The AWM is now establishing a *Facebook* profile, a *YouTube* page, joined *Flickr* and is using these vehicles for engaging audiences, interactive research building all manner of client relationships.

Developing International Principles for Presentation and Interpretation

The WH Convention aims include the identification, protection, conservation, presentation and transmission to future generations of cultural and natural heritage of outstanding universal value (Article 7), so States Parties have a specific responsibility to use education and information programmes to strengthen appreciation and respect by their peoples of the cultural and natural heritage (Article 15). Usually, most visitors need to have places "interpreted", their stories told, their meanings explained.

In recent times, the importance of presentation in the process of development and conservation has come to be better recognised by heritage agencies, heritage practitioners and visitors alike. Since 2002, an international collaboration has been underway to develop a charter to provide practical guidance for site managers and practitioners alike.

Initiated by the Ename Archaeological Centre in Belgium, ICOMOS has sponsored the development of what was initially a local guideline for archaeological sites into an international charter that covers all types of monuments and sites. In its draft forms, the International Charter on the Interpretation and Presentation of Cultural Heritage Sites and Monuments has been workshopped and extensively circulated internationally and in 2007 was approved by the ICOMOS Advisory Committee for presentation to this ICOMOS General Assembly for final ratification here in Quebec.

This Charter notes that in today's globalising world, particularly where heritage assets are often separating from their originating communities and cultural values, conservation for the future requires proactive management in the present, particularly capturing the meanings and stories of places which are changing cultural contexts.

In Europe, and to a large extent in the USA and in Australia, heritage conservation work has traditionally been led by architects, engineers and archaeologists, as experts with a strong focus on building and site "fabric" – the "nuts and bolts" of a monument or site – in the belief that its value or significance resides and is interpreted in that built evidence.

More recently, in Australia, we have come to include the understanding of setting, use, association, records, related places and related objects in our approach to establishing what is significant about a place and thus to guide its interpretation, through other specialisations: curators, interpreters, documentalists and planners.

However, the integration of social and spiritual values brings with it the need to consult and involve associated communities in conservation and interpretation processes. With that shift from expert influence to community participation in interpretation, come many potential opportunities and conflicts, and Web 2.0 provides a vehicle.

In promoting the importance of interpretation in the conservation process we recognise the very real (but not new) inherent danger of bias. This may be the perspective of professional bias, such as that of an architect or archaeologist, passionate for the fabric of the place to be able to tell its story – actively influencing the understanding of the significance of the place.

Or it might be the bias of a dominant culture – for example in Australia, few of our post-European contact sites tell the Indigenous story well. In Afghanistan, the recent dramatic destruction of the Bamiyan statues and the damaged Buddhist images along the Silk Road each tell stories of cultural conflict.

But at a time when the tools and frames of reference for passing on and indeed archiving the accumulated wisdom of civilisations are rapidly changing – witness *Google Book Search*, the historic effort to make the full text of the world's books searchable – it is appropriate to reflect on the impact of the increasingly popular use of electronic media in the interpretation of heritage values and places.

The Impact of Web 2.0

Less than ten years ago, I didn't have an Internet address and the major Australian museum that I worked for did not have a website. Now, as the mother of two teenagers, I know that the world of electronic communication and information gathering that they now occupy – and have done all their lives – will be less impacted by any of the worthy guidelines and charters that I just described, than by the development of Internet communication.

Despite growing up in a home full of books, my two children go to the Internet to research essays, to check mundane facts often on *Wikipedia*. They introduced me to *YouTube*, the extraordinarily fast-growing video sharing hub that claimed more that 40 million plays a day in 2006, and even then was growing at a rate of 5 million plays a week (Boutin 2006). Yes, each week!

Web 2.0 applications present an array of extraordinary statistics: for example, every minute of today, in excess of 10 hours of video will be uploaded onto *YouTube*.

The Canadian site, *Flickr*,[5] is a photo management and sharing application, which contained over 2 billion photographs in November 2007, and whose members upload images at a rate of around 4,000 per minute.[6] Flickr's recent pilot project with the Library of Congress, The Commons, aims to enhance the body of knowledge (metadata) about the extraordinary photography collections in public institutions, providing access to selected imagery and inviting the *Flickr* community to tag (add comments and information) about the images, an unbeatable resource combination – with the Library as editor/moderator. The Australian National Library has recently combined its online Pictorial Gateway *Picture Australia www* to enable individuals to contribute their own images to this national repository (Hooton 2008).

MySpace, Facebook and *Linkedin* are social utility sites operating on similar concepts – a shared content site that's user friendly with personal accounts that include shared blogs, music, photos, videos and friends networks.

FaceBook, founded in 2004, now has 80 million active users in its community; its fastest growing demographic is over 25s, who supply personal profiles, upload photographs and chatter, providing a marketers dream mailing list segmented, particularised and freely accessible. *Linkedin,* a networking site for professionals is a relative latecomer in the field, with just 24million users (Stone 2008).

These are the products of Web 2.0, the new generation of Internet products which are easy to use, offering free accounts, and using standardised formats where contributors tag their efforts personally. *YouTube* is populated by a huge variety of video genres, searched by collaborative tags associated as a "*folksonomy*".[7]

---

5.   Launched in 2002 and now owned by Yahoo.
6.   12 July 2008 Flickr home page.
7.   *Folksonomies* are organic systems of organising information in Web 2.0 communities by collaborative tagging – a form of do-it-yourself social indexing.

The issues of copyright in all these sites are blurred – technically respected, but self-evidentially impossible to manage – and exacerbated by incoming concepts such as *Mashups* – where users "cut and paste" each other's contributions to form new hybrid contributions. And this is the new direction.

In an economic sense, globalisation is now impacting every nation; and so too is the Web 2.0 generation of Internet communication, transforming human relations and cross-cultural communication in previously unimaginable ways. It is impossible to isolate any national culture from its impacts, though clearly not everyone participates equally. For developing counties, the potential benefits of web access will not be so quickly reached, as Klaus Muller observed in 2003 "when 2/3 of the worlds population do not own a telephone … poverty, gender inequality, disability and illiteracy remain the most visible barriers to the cultural participation of developing countries." (Muller 2003)

But what is clear, is that the presentation of national identity through interpreting and presenting heritage values is no longer predominantly in the hands of government administrators or academics publishing scholarly research.

Nor is it in the hands of museums, as they change from information interpreters to information providers, sometimes with more virtual visitors than real (Muller 2003), offering digitised access to immense collections.

National identities are now being defined on sites such as *Wikipedia* and *YouTube* with as many "interpretations" as there are individuals contributing to these sources of web wisdom. Currently accessible in 19 countries and 12 languages,[8] *YouTube* is now owned by Google.

If you looked at the *YouTube* listings for "World Heritage Sites – Australia" in early July 2008, you would have found 262 tagged videos for sharing – very few official, a few plainly advertising travellers facilities (accommodation, etc.), but mostly very informal views posted by young visitors about their impressions and highlights of their personal visits.

However, the video of an English backpacker attacking Nuremberg Castle (in Germany, but tagged to associate with any world heritage site hit) was not what I expected to find, and probably not how the site management would like to see its world heritage stories interpreted to potential visitors. But this opportunity for the backpacker and the interest in his antics that

---

8.   **Countries**: United States, Japan, United Kingdom, Italy, Spain, Netherlands, Ireland, France, Poland, Brazil, Canada, Mexico, Australia, Hong Kong, Taiwan, New Zealand, Germany, Russia and Korea. **Languages**: English (US and UK), Japanese, Korean, Italian, French, Spanish, Dutch, Polish, Portuguese, Chinese (Traditional), German, Russian. Source: *YouTube* home page, 12 July 2008.

was evident in the accompanying blog commentaries associated with his video makes me ponder: how can site interpretation be "managed" in the age of web wisdom?

My recent search for "World Heritage Sites – China" revealed 265 videos to share (a threefold increase in the last 6 months), many of the gardens in Suzou, of Lijiang and the Kaiping Dialou. In Canada are just 124 sites (and some of these appear to be spoofing attacks). Also of varying quality and content, these videos seemed to be made by backpackers, school students, visitors and probably administrators too, and focused on the pictorial beauties of the sites, rather than the uniquely personal views of Nuremberg Castle that my previous search had revealed. This is one of the qualities of these sites – they change content constantly!

For those with easy access, Web 2.0 may well be the ultimate in freedom of communication. For heritage site managers, however, it demonstrates that the public and indeed global interpretation of any heritage place is henceforth (pun intended) virtually uncontrollable.

An immediate and positive response from several heritage sites and monuments is the development and provision of good on-site and Internet interpretation material that provides both data and graphics about heritage places readymade for such sharing – surely many opportunities for applying the principles of the ICOMOS Interpretation Charter.

The speed with which Web 2.0 will impact our lives is breathtaking – but a recent experiment in using just the existing capacity of the Internet to gauge international opinion is already impacting in unforeseen ways on the identification, management and conservation of national and regional physical heritage assets.

In conclusion, I would like to look quickly at a recent campaign to invite international on-line and SMS voting for the New Seven Wonders of the World as one such example of the impact on cultural heritage management of global communication opportunities.

The New 7 Wonders of the World Campaign

In 2006/7 a commercial campaign to identify the New Seven Wonders of the World was sponsored by a Swiss-based foundation. It established an international system of phone (SMS/phone eventually accounted for 20% of votes) or electronic voting (online accounted for 80%) (The Hindu 2007), and an associated publicity campaign. Although support for the conservation of heritage sites was an intended outcome, this apparently did not eventuate. However, a total of 100 million votes were recorded in 2006/7, collected in a decidedly "unscientific manner" – whoever dialled in, however many times they chose to vote.

Not everyone was happy with the results, nor with the open voting methods used. The Vatican was reported to be unhappy that the Sistine Chapel was omitted; the Government of Cambodia felt that Angkor Watt should have been included. It appears that nations such as India, China and Peru voted heavily, whilst Europe and America were relatively disinterested, so results were not solely related to Internet accessibility.

The concept of the world's seven wonders was introduced 2000 years ago in Greece, arbitrated then by the historian Herodotus and the chief librarian of Alexandria, Callimachus. Only 2 of the original 7 ancient wonders of the world were outside Greece, so skewing of the list is not new. However, in the New Seven Wonders campaign, the judgement of modern day, apparently nationally biased voters, completely displaced that of expert selection.

In a new era of international travel and communication, national voting for the Seven Wonders Foundation list was enthusiastic. At one point China was voting at 70,000 per day for the Great Wall to be included in the New Wonders list.[9]

As A. Svithathsan points out writing in *The Hindu,* "the Internet may have the potential to create a relatively democratic space. But people still need the capital and effort to take part." (The Hindu 2007) 14 million people in Jordan successfully voted for Petra, in a nation with a population of 7 million. 10 Million Brazilian votes were recorded for the Statue of Christ in Rio de Janeiro, many by free SMS offered by Brazil's national corporate telecommunication companies.

Clearly the question of having the places symbolic of a nation's cultural identity recognised internationally were felt to be of great importance by many, many individuals – 100 million voters.

At the close of voting, the New Seven Wonders of the World were announced,[10] with the honorary inclusion of Egypt's Pyramid of Giza, the only surviving Ancient Wonder.

Understandably, UNESCO, responsible for the World Heritage Convention, was dismissive of this commercial campaign, and remained resolutely uninvolved, regretting that the initiative "cannot in any significant and sustainable manner, contribute to the preservation of the sites elected".[11] UNESCO focuses instead on implementing the daily realities of the World Heritage Convention – the tasks of education, technical conservation and political persuasion.

---

9.   Beijing News, cited on blogsite <http://www.danwei.org/>.
10.   Petra, Jordan; The Taj Mahal.
11.   UNESCO Media Release No. 2007-66, UNESCO confirms that it is not involved in the "New 7 wonders of the World" campaign.

The impact of such a corporate campaign's results – particularly its associated publicity – are still emerging, but it is certain that as global communication interconnections develop, there is an increasing responsibility for interpreting heritage sites well, so that the many audiences of on-site visitors as well as remotely accessing visitors and the millions of potential *YouTube* and *FaceBook* subscribers, have authentic information resources on which to draw.

More critically, site managers need to proactively provide excellent interpretation material for the Web 2.0 networks, and be prepared to engage, like Elcho Islands Chooky dancers.

Conclusions

ICOMOS hopes that the collaborative development of the *Charter on the presentation and interpretation of cultural heritage sites* will become a useful tool supporting sustainable heritage site management and interpretation, but it will need adaptation, quickly, for Web 2.0.

As climate change impacts the globe, and petrol prices accelerate, and the real carbon costs of long-distance air travel are realistically tallied, it may well be that "virtual" travel will provide more access to heritage places to more people, with less physical impact on the sites themselves. In a coming era of reduction in air travel, experiencing heritage places through remote media will rapidly increase.

The reality of Web 2.0 must be faced and factored into heritage site management and interpretation. As a communication tool its power seems almost limitless. Ultimately democratic, yet also potentially inaccessible, the future use of these media in heritage perception and presentation/interpretation demands our swift engagement.

Références

Boutin, Paul. 2006: 28 April. A Grand Unified Theory of YouTube and MySpace, *Slate Magazine*.

Holcombe, Liz. 2008: June. Blogging at the Australian War Memorial, *M&G NSW*.

Hooton, Fiona. 2008: June. Flickr @ the National library of Australia, *M&G*.

Muller, Klaus. 2003: May. The Culture of Globalisation, *Museum News*.

New wonders? A Srivathsan, *The Hindu*, 2007: 29 July.

Stone, Brad. 2008: 18 June. *New York Times*, A Social Site Only the Businesslike Need pply.

"The Met and the Tate", cited in Muller, Klaus. 2003: May. The Culture of Globalisation, *Museum News*.

Heritage Story Zones:
Revealing the Spirit of Place

Lisa Reynolds Wolfe
ReynoldsWolfe LLC
USA

ABSTRACT

Storytelling is a powerful, but frequently overlooked, tool for the construction, interpretation, transmission and preservation of cultural heritage. This paper argues that newly affordable multimedia tools – specifically, *digital story stations* – make it possible for local communities to resurrect and record personal stories associated with cultural heritage and the spirit of place. Through case studies, it explores the potential of digital technology to facilitate the creation of a "Heritage Story Zone" whereby individuals – both long-term residents and new migrants – can tell their own stories and immerse themselves in the stories of others, dynamically assigning meaning, value and emotion to cultural expression. After presenting an overview of the costs and benefits involved, the paper concludes that the *heritage story station*™ enables the actual users of place to "virtually" reinvent and recontextualize an inclusive community memory, serving as both "tradition bearers" and "interpreters" in the promulgation and preservation of place-based cultural heritage, thereby ensuring its inheritance.

RÉSUMÉ

Les contes sont un outil puissant, mais fréquemment ignoré, de la construction, de l'interprétation, de la transmission et de la conservation du patrimoine culturel. Cet article avance que de nouveaux outils multimédia abordables – en particulier, les sites de contes en ligne – donnent aux communautés la possibilité de ressusciter et d'enregistrer des histoires personnelles associées au patrimoine culturel et à l'esprit du lieu. À travers des études de cas, il explore le potentiel de la technologie digitale pour permettre la création d'une « Zone d'histoires patrimoniales » où des individus – tant des résidents de longue date que de nouveaux immigrants – peuvent raconter leurs propres histoires et s'immerger dans les histoires des autres, en assignant ainsi sens, valeur et émotion à l'expression culturelle. Après avoir présenté un survol des coûts et des bénéfices impliqués, l'article conclut que les sites d'histoires patrimoniales tel que le *Heritage story station* permettent aux utilisateurs réels du lieu de réinventer « virtuellement » et de recontextualiser une mémoire communautaire inclusive, qui sert autant les « porteurs de tradition » que ses « interprètes » dans la promulgation et la conservation d'un patrimoine culturel ancré dans le lieu, assurant ainsi sa transmission.

1. The Power of Storytelling

Storytelling has long played a prominent role in the transmission of place-based cultural heritage. From oral narrative and written text to the more visual representation found in architecture and painting, stories have become a large part of the heritage that we now seek to transmit and preserve. Embedded in both the tangible and the intangible, they are a way of passing on wisdom, knowledge, and culture. In this way, they preserve the memory of various groups of people, helping each subsequent generation understand who they are, where they came from, and what they are to value.

While stories are sometimes universal, more frequently, they are culturally specific, binding communities to their built environment, language, costume and other cultural expression. In this way, they serve as a *heritage compass*, for, in the words of a fourteenth-century mystic, "a tale, however slight, illuminates the truth."

Even though it is overreaching to suggest that storytelling developed in response to a specific need for documentation, preservation, or promulgation, the 35,000-year-old paintings on the walls of Lascaux do assure us that storytelling is an ancient form of expression, perhaps like language, hardwired into our human biology. So while the technology we use today is new, stories themselves have played a central role in human history, evolving and changing with each new form of communication, from the circle of the camp-fire to hieroglyphics, the printing press to the motion picture, the television screen to today's computer terminal. They are part of our culture, defining our self-identity, and transmitting authenticity from one generation to another.

2. The Heritage Story Station™

In today's world, technology makes it quite easy to swap, critique, and revise stories. Newly affordable multimedia tools enable local communities to resurrect and record personal stories associated with cultural heritage and the spirit of place. Many advocates of this new method of storytelling are promoting what they call a *digital story station*, noting its promise as a communication device capable of bridging the technological divide between analog and digital. Simply stated, the "station" is little more than a dedicated personal computer with associated peripherals and appropriate software. Scanners allow the public to digitize print photographs and other documents, and digital voice recorders facilitate the narration of personal impressions and memories. When used by the heritage community, the digital story station becomes a "Virtual Heritage Zone," a space where individuals can preserve their own cultural linkages or, through a dedicated Website, immerse themselves in the values and experiences of others.

Through the power of multimedia storytelling, heritage is experienced and dynamic, not static, incorporating feelings and emotions as well as intellect. This is important because, as Pine and Gilmore argue (1999), the world is changing, and we are moving from a service-based to an experience-based economy, one in which cultural production is more important than physical. In these new surroundings, the most successful undertakings are transformational, and those heritage professionals determined to succeed must build potentially transforming experience-based activities into all their endeavors.

Digital storytelling allows us to transport the listener/viewer, spellbound, to a heritage realm where physical places and intangible spaces meet the virtual sphere. In this unbounded area, active en-gagement is the norm and it is possible to assign meaning, value, and emotion to cultural expression. As Freeman Tilden (2008) suggests regarding the interpretation of cultural heritage, the objective is not instruction, but provocation, implying an experience that engrosses and compels the human spirit. This involves participation and engagement of the imagination, key elements in the production of digital stories.

Online storytelling combines the power of images, narration, music, and text to establish the personal and emotional connections that change minds and ignite action. In essence, the age-old world of storytelling is given a new home, not landlocked but virtual. Limitless space and the capability to incorporate all types of media – text, photos, audio, and video – facilitate the creation of compelling narratives. These stories become both "tradition bearing" and "interpretive," embedded in the construction and transmission of place-based cultural heritage. Ranging from simple recorded interviews like oral histories to audio slideshows or short video clips, the *heritage story station*^{TM} encourages individuals and communities to dig deep, to collectively recount new discoveries and unearth previous ones. As they move toward the compilation of an inclusive community memory, their authentic narratives become ours to collect and conserve.

It is important to note that even though these stories belong in the public sphere, the "virtual heritage station" described in this paper is not a general public access computer or a public access kiosk. Instead, it is a workstation dedicated to the telling of digital stories, and it is intended solely for the recording and preserving of memories associated with cultural heritage and the centrality of place. Also, while the digital story station alone is a powerful tool, the Internet is just as important. When joined, the two become a reliable and inexpensive way to reach broad global audiences, serving as a strong voice for the construction, interpretation, transmission, and preservation of cultural heritage.

Whether temporary or permanent, the most successful story station environments provide a quiet recording space with good lighting, a backdrop for video recording, a table for the workstation itself, and several chairs. In this dedicated space, with a staff member or trained volunteer available to assist, individuals have multiple options. They can compile a story with materials brought from home, record a three- to five-minute digital video clip onsite, narrate a first person recollection and illustrate it with still images or other materials of their own choosing, or put together a story based on personal interviews and associated visual material. Subject matter might encompass traditions and customs, tales of how things used to be, observations about changes to the built environment, remembrances of childhood, or the recounting of a recent migratory experience. All contribute to a continuum of impressions of both tangible and intangible cultural heritage. California Stories, a compendium of online stories sponsored by the California Council for the Humanities (*http://www.calhum.org/programs/story_intro.htm) provides a* glimpse of the diverse tales waiting to be told, boasting such topics as: *The Central Coast Filipino American Heritage Mural Project; Gardens Telling Stories: The Japanese Gardens and Gardeners of West Los Angeles; and Hmong Folk Stories: Carrying the Meaning to California.*

3. Operating Considerations

Both the stationary/permanent and the mobile/portable story stations consist of several interlocking systems, each difficult to maintain. These include: 1) a power supply; 2) durable computing; 3) multimedia associated peripherals; and 4) end-user devices like software and applications. Providing the four essential components is not easy, especially in rural areas and other isolated locations that are not able to support a permanent/stationary station. Difficulties resulting from shortcomings in the power and telecom infrastructure are to be expected since they are common to most developing countries.

In terms of infrastructure related difficulties, the most demanding situation often involves off-grid or poorly electrified areas where the cost of providing electricity can consume as much as 80 percent of initial project funding. The best first move is to keep total power requirements for the station as low as possible. Selecting low-power equipment such as notebook computers, more energy efficient desktop computers, LCD screens, and inkjet printers can result in significant savings. A diminished power requirement makes it possible to use lower and less costly power-generating sources, like solar panels, wind turbines, or diesel/gas generators to provide electricity to power equipment and recharge equipment batteries.

Everyday struggles associated with maintaining equipment in good working order are often even more recalcitrant than challenges relating to infrastructure. Much off-the-shelf computing equipment is not designed to withstand the strains of demanding surroundings where, often, routine maintenance is not easy to supply. Under these circumstances, selecting the best mix of equipment is complex and requires balancing multiple considerations, such as initial cost, convenience of local service, operating costs, expected service life, reliability, ruggedness, and warranty coverage.

Digital story stations do not require Internet connectivity for the recording and production of heritage stories. But connectivity is required to reach broad global audiences via the World Wide Web (WWW), a crucial tool in the effort to preserve, transmit, educate, raise awareness, and enlist advocates for heritage endeavors. In light of the above, connectivity solutions become decisive. Fortunately, rapid advances in wireless technologies are making it increasingly cost effective to deploy networks in rural and underserved urban areas. These new wireless technologies are also more scalable and can be deployed more rapidly than ever before. (For more detailed information on technical and equipment considerations see www.heritagestorystation. com/specs/.)

4. Return on Investment

When weighing costs and benefits, it's best to start with an assessment of what's immediately available or knowable as well as what is realistic from a financial perspective. While projects are often quite difficult to quantify, it's important to avoid relying unduly on the intuitive, personal, parochial, or political factors that influence us all. However, it's also good to remember that Return on Investment (ROI) can have different meanings depending on context. For example, if examined strictly from a business or financial perspective, ROI might refer solely to the amount of money returned over a period of time compared with the amount of money invested. But, as heritage professionals, we might be better served by measuring success in terms of mission-related return on investment. In either case, ROI analysis requires that we answer the following questions:

- Are the efforts and costs associated with the lifetime of the proposed project worth its expected mission or financial benefit?

- How does the return on investment in one project compare with the return on investment of other proposed projects?
- Is the project plan as efficient and effective as it could be?

Answering these questions requires a thoughtful combination of fact gathering, internal impact analysis, outcome evaluation, risk assessment, review of alternative mechanisms for achieving the same goal, and recognizing the ramifications of foregoing alternative opportunities. (Din and Hecht 2007).

Typically, story station costs are proposed in terms of software, hardware, installation, and training costs – mostly one-time, direct costs. But indirect costs and opportunity costs must also be considered. Indirect costs might include staff training and retraining over time, contract legal review, administration, and some electrical and environmental costs. Opportunity costs, of course, center on the value of opportunity, benefit, or income forfeited as a result of the implementation of a story station project.

Table 1, below, presents some key features to consider when evaluating whether or not it is desirable to implement a *heritage story station*.[TM]

Table 1: Key Elements of Total Cost of Ownership and Use.

• Initial capital costs: buying the right equipment
• Installation costs
• Energy costs
• Software and software upgrades
• Training costs
• Cost of support staff
• Technical support and maintenance costs
• Connectivity costs
• Costs associated with downtime
• Disposal costs
• Hardware upgrade and replacement costs

Source: Fillip, B. and Foote, D. 2007; ReynoldsWolfe LLC 2008.

So far as the *heritage story station*[TM] is concerned, it is also critically important to consider the near real time WWW exposure of the project. This publicity may generate almost instantaneous interest without a great production investment in professional media. At the same time, success can also generate risks. What happens if traffic to a site soars and bandwidth and server are overwhelmed? In the end, the project may best be evaluated qualitatively, with the ultimate decision based on the risks of not preserving or transmitting heritage memories, a failure foreshadowing a loss that cannot be recovered.

5. Case Studies

5.1. The Stationary Heritage Station: Telling Lives

We can learn much from one of the earliest large-scale digital storytelling efforts, *Telling Lives*, a project sponsored by the British Broadcasting Corporation (BBC). (http://www.bbc.co.uk/tellinglives/).

Telling Lives is based on the premise that the tradition of personal storytelling was co-opted in the twentieth century when the growing popularity of the mass media led to the escalating influence of journalists and script writers. During this time frame, the custom of passing experiences, culture, and memories from one generation to the next evaporated, and stories were told by outsiders, based more on imagination than authenticity.

The digital stories created in BBC-sponsored workshops counter this trend by breaking the mould of modern media storytelling. Created solely by individuals working on their own – without professional mediation and using new technology – the workshops have allowed tellers to take back their historic right to communicate experience through stories. Participants are taught the new skills they need to prepare a multimedia story, and the workshops emphasize an underlying premise of most digital storytelling projects, the notion that even those with little or no technical background are able to "tell their story their way."

5.2. Community Storytelling: Barrio Logan & Refugee Voices

Barrio Logan is a partnership between the City of San Diego Public Library and Media Arts Center, San Diego. This project is centered in Logan Heights, once primarily a residential area and one of San Diego's oldest communities. Between 1910 and 1920 the area was transformed into a predominantly Mexican-American community as immigrants fled north from revolution and a poor Mexican economy. In the 1950s, city zoning laws were changed, and Logan became an industrial area rather than a residential one. The neighborhood immediately experienced an influx of Anglo-owned junkyards. Later, the black civil rights movement inspired many emerging leaders of the community and, in the 1960s, the United Farm Workers movement led by Cesar Chavez sparked a new political awareness. (http://www.mediaartscenter.org/site/c.dfLIJPOvHoE/b.1623599/k.783D/Barrio_Logan.htm)

Today local youth learn the media technology skills that allow them to document the life histories of the area's oldest community residents. In the process, they tighten and/or rebuild intergenerational ties and reinforce their own community roots by connecting the past to their future. With training and support from Media Arts Center, San Diego's local media artists, and librarians at the Central Library, young people research and produce a series of videos. Like a sister project, *Refugee Voices*, the *Barrio Logan* effort has focused on teaching local teens high-tech media skills and library research so that they can produce short documentaries that offer a model to help other communities maintain their cultural survival. (http://www.mediaartscenter. org/site/c.dfLIJPOvHoE/b.1679229/k.921E/Refugee_Voices.htm)

5.3. eTuktuk: the Portable Heritage Station

In contrast to the two cases, above, which feature permanent story stations, the eTukTuk is portable, with system components installed on a tuktuk, a three-wheeled motorcycle adapted to provide story-telling capability. The tuk-tuk is a common form of local transport in South Asia. However, to remote villagers in the Kothmale region of Sri Lanka, it is more than a convenient way to get around. It is also a self-contained mobile telecenter and radio broadcasting unit, providing public access to information and communication technologies, including newly introduced digital technologies and the Internet. In its innovative *"e-"* configuration, the tuk-tuk houses a laptop computer, battery operated printer, camera, telephone, and scanner. Internet connectivity is provided by wireless connection, and electricity is provided by a 1000-Watt generator. These alterations enable the tuk-tuk to serve as an extension to Kothmale's permanent telecenter, sharing wireless internet capability, loudspeakers, and multimedia functionality. (http:// www.etuktuk.net/)

In its current form, the eTukTuk is not a *heritage story station.*™ However, eTukTuk programs often include activities that focus on the preservation of heritage traditions, and it would be relatively easy to make the technical modifications necessary to provide programs directed solely toward transmitting and promulgating cultural heritage. While technical issues are relatively easy to overcome, a more difficult challenge centers on barriers involving language and illiteracy. However, with creativity and determination, these problems too can be resolved. For example, the Kothmale project faced difficulty in recruiting Tamil speakers, a problem that required a rather extensive public relations effort to resolve. Only after the eTukTuk traveled throughout the community, blasting an invitation on its loudspeakers, were residents curious enough to attend a gathering at a well-known tea estate where they would learn more about eTukTuk activities. After attending an information session and watching digital stories, many became interested and signed up for a training course at the Community Multimedia Center so that they could qualify as Tamil speaking instructors and content producers.

6. Conclusion

The *heritage story station*, a newly affordable multimedia tool, enables local communities to resurrect and record personal stories associated with the spirit of place in a way that conveys the essence of cultural heritage. As both long-term residents and new migrants recount their stories, they become "tradition bearers" and "interpreters." Through their efforts, storytelling's age-old appeal is updated for modern times, touching the hearts and minds of broad global audiences as well as sustaining, celebrating, and maintaining community identity, authenticity, and association with place.

References

Din, Herminia, and Phyllis Hecht. 2007. *The Digital Museum: A Think Guide.* Washington DC: American Association of Museums.

Fillip, B., and D. Foote. 2007. *Making the Connection: Scaling Telecenters for Development.* Washington, DC: Information Technology Applications Center/Academy for Educational Development.

Pine, B. Joseph, and James H. Gilmore. 1999. *The Experience Economy: Work is Theater & Every Business a Stage.* Boston: Harvard Business School Press.

Tilden, Freeman, Russell E. Dickenson, and R. Bruce Craig. 2008. *Interpreting Our Heritage.* Chapel Hill: The University of North Carolina Press.

http://www.bbc.co.uk/tellinglives/.

http://www.bbc.co.uk/wales/audiovideo/sites/galleries/pages/capturewales.shtml.

http://www.calhum.org/programs/story_intro.htm.

http://www.etuktuk.net/.

http://www.mediaartscenter.org/site/c.dfLIJPOvHoE/b.1623599/k.783D/Barrio_Logan.htm.

http://www.mediaartscenter.org/site/c.dfLIJPOvHoE/b.1679229/k.921E/Refugee_Voices.htm.

http://www.heritagestorystation.com/specs/.

Projet de création d'un espace-mémoire pour des sites historiques à l'aide des TIC

Nada El-Khoury
GRCAO, Groupe de recherche en CAO
Faculté de l'aménagement
Université de Montréal, Canada

Élise Meyer
MAP-PAGE
Institut National des Sciences Appliquées
Strasbourg, France

Giovanni De Paoli
GRCAO, Groupe de recherche en CAO
Faculté de l'aménagement
Université de Montréal, Canada

Pierre Grussenmeyer
MAP-PAGE
Institut National des Sciences Appliquées
Strasbourg, France

ABSTRACT

The purpose of this article is to confront hypotheses on the methods of interpreting heritage spaces by relying on the establishment of a template and digital simulation, the new procedures for dealing with data and ICT.

With the use of exploratory case studies, it is a question of analyzing how a heritage grouping embodies the architectural transposition of cultural values; of understanding the consequences of a series of successive occupations of an archeological site on its present look; of gaining a better understanding of the building techniques and know-how of the Elders; and lastly, of producing digital simulations with new methods for dealing with data in order to show an evolution through the ages, the superimposing of historical layers, and of understanding the relation between spirit and place.

The work of Montreal's GRCAO on the Byblos (Lebanon) site, along with that of MAP-PAGE from Strasbourg on the site of the Château de Vianden and the Villa d'Echternach (Luxembourg), function as terrains for exploration. Work is also underway on the Château d'Andlau and the Abbaye de Niedermunster (France).

Résumé

L'objectif de cet article est de confronter des hypothèses sur les méthodes d'interprétation des espaces patrimoniaux, en s'appuyant sur la modélisation et la simulation numérique, les nouvelles méthodes de traitement des données et les TIC.

À travers des cas d'études probants, il s'agit d'analyser comment un ensemble patrimonial constitue la transposition architecturale de valeurs culturelles ; de comprendre les conséquences des occupations successives d'un site archéologique sur son aspect actuel ; d'obtenir une meilleure compréhension des techniques de construction et du savoir-faire des Anciens ; et enfin, de réaliser des simulations numériques avec des nouvelles méthodes de traitement des données pour montrer l'évolution au cours des siècles, la superposition des couches historiques et comprendre la relation entre l'esprit et le lieu.

Les travaux du GRCAO de Montréal sur le site de Byblos (Liban) ainsi que ceux du MAP-PAGE de Strasbourg sur les sites du Château de Vianden et de la Villa d'Echternach (Luxembourg), servent de terrains d'investigations. Des travaux sont également en cours sur le Château d'Andlau et l'Abbaye de Niedermunster (France).

1. Introduction

Cet article présente des travaux effectués à l'aide des nouvelles technologies de l'information et de la communication (TIC) dans le but d'exprimer et de transmettre l'esprit du lieu dans un monde soucieux de préserver le patrimoine. Plus que jamais, les enjeux liés au patrimoine constituent une préoccupation majeure dans le monde, et on remarque un intérêt croissant pour la compréhension, la mise en valeur et la sauvegarde du patrimoine. Cet intérêt a des retentissements sur un certain nombre de questions sociales, économiques, politiques, touristiques et culturelles. Le cas de certains sites anciens peut à la fois être source d'enseignements et donner des impulsions nouvelles, ne serait-ce que dans une même sphère d'influence culturelle. Dans ce contexte, nous proposons des méthodes d'interprétation des espaces patrimoniaux par la modélisation et la simulation numérique, les nouvelles méthodes de traitement des données et les TIC. Il s'agit tout d'abord des travaux du GRCAO de Montréal sur le site de Byblos (Liban). En considérant cette étude de cas, nous avons construit des modèles utilisant une méthode de simulation numérique. Nous avons ainsi réalisé des modèles numériques qui ont la particularité de pouvoir intégrer l'esprit d'un lieu. Les modèles numériques présentés ont un caractère dynamique, interactif et renouvelable avec une approche multidisciplinaire.

S'ajoutent aux travaux du GRCAO ceux du MAP-PAGE de Strasbourg, sur les sites du Château de Vianden et de la Villa d'Echternach (Luxembourg). Ces sites ont été modélisés pour le compte du Service des Sites et Monuments Nationaux du Luxembourg dans le cadre de travaux de conservation et de mise en valeur du patrimoine. Les modélisations ont été effectuées par le MAP-CRAI (École Nationale Supérieure d'Architecture de Nancy) sur la base de documents rédigés par les archéologues en charge de la préservation de ces sites. Ces modèles ont alors servi d'interface pour un Système d'Information sur Internet, développé par le MAP-PAGE et destiné à la conservation, à la gestion et à la documentation du patrimoine. Il permet de transformer les modèles numériques initiaux en modèles de représentation informatifs par lesquels il est possible d'accéder à la documentation retraçant la mémoire du lieu. Ces travaux ouvrent également la voie à la compréhension de l'évolution historique du Château de Vianden à travers les siècles, grâce aux modèles numériques des différentes phases du château qui sont superposables à volonté pour visualiser simultanément les différentes couches historiques du lieu.

Les travaux présentés révèlent l'importance de comprendre un patrimoine et de proposer des moyens pour s'approprier et transmettre le *genius loci* d'un site. Ce concept beaucoup plus large implique la considération du contexte historique et actuel, du paysage physique et culturel, et des modes de vie et des méthodes de construction.

2. Relation entre l'esprit et le lieu

Pour comprendre la relation entre l'esprit et le lieu, il convient de développer les notions qui s'y rattachent : le patrimoine immatériel, matériel et leur symbiose.

2.1. Patrimoine immatériel

Avec l'introduction de la notion de patrimoine immatériel par l'UNESCO en 1989, la Convention pour la sauvegarde du patrimoine culturel immatériel (UNESCO 2003) a confirmé l'importance de ce facteur. Ce patrimoine culturel vivant concerne le patrimoine culturel immatériel, transmis de génération en génération, recréé en permanence par les communautés et les groupes en fonction de leur milieu, de leur interaction avec la nature et de leur histoire, et qui leur procure un sentiment d'identité et de continuité. Il participe à la promotion et au respect de la diversité culturelle et de la créativité humaine. Il répond aux exigences d'un développement durable.

Le patrimoine immatériel n'est pas une valeur figée, mais une notion qui implique une évolution : « La notion de patrimoine immatériel ne doit pas être fixée à un instant particulier dans le temps ; elle est dynamique et évolue, et c'est le patrimoine immatériel en évolution qui est important » (Bumbaru 2003). Ce qui implique la notion de « site culturel dynamique ». C'est une référence à certains lieux qui continuent d'être utilisés par les différents groupes qui s'y succèdent.

2.2. Patrimoine matériel

L'ensemble des productions matérielles que l'homme a réalisées est défini comme patrimoine matériel : les artefacts ou les objets qui nous entourent ainsi que les bâtiments sont considérés comme patrimoine matériel. Ces objets ou ces bâtiments sont les seuls exemples qui témoignent de l'histoire d'un peuple. Le patrimoine matériel est porteur de sens et de significations, il témoigne du passé ; il est alors celui qui est le plus apte à nous renseigner sur les activités humaines du passé et sur la façon dont l'objet ou le bâtiment ont été construits et utilisés.

2.3. Symbiose entre l'esprit et le lieu

Les lieux et les biens patrimoniaux enrichissent la vie des personnes en leur permettant une symbiose avec le paysage, la collectivité, le passé et les expériences vécues. Un concept du « lieu » est introduit (Charte de Burra 1999) de manière à sentir la relation entre l'humain et le lieu : « Les lieux et les biens patrimoniaux sont le reflet de la diversité de nos communautés et expriment ce que nous sommes et le passé qui nous a formés et a façonné le paysage australien. Ils sont irremplaçables et précieux » (http://www.international.icomos.org/burra1999_fre.pdf).

Cette définition d'un lieu patrimonial ne s'applique pas uniquement au cas de l'Australie, mais pourrait s'appliquer aussi à tout autre lieu caractérisé par la diversité des peuples qui l'ont occupé et qui continuent à le faire.

Les « lieux associés », même s'ils sont localisés ailleurs, contribuent à la valeur culturelle d'un autre lieu ou d'un autre bien patrimonial. Les « objets associés » sont les objets qui contribuent à la valeur culturelle d'un lieu ou du bien sans s'y trouver. Citons comme exemple le cas de quantités d'objets extraits d'un site archéologique qui occupent les musées ou d'autres lieux indéfinis et qui ont également une grande signification. Par « signification », on entend ce qu'un lieu ou un bien patrimonial signifie, indique, évoque ou exprime. Les significations font généralement référence aux dimensions immatérielles du patrimoine telles que les qualités symboliques ou commémoratives. Dans cet article, nous abordons ce concept de lieu, de lieu associé, de sa signification, mais aussi de son « interprétation » qui « désigne l'ensemble des moyens employés pour présenter la valeur culturelle d'un lieu ou d'un bien patrimonial » (Charte de Burra 1999). Nous intégrons et prenons en compte aussi la notion de « l'esprit d'appartenance », puisqu'il est important de s'approprier un lieu pour pouvoir le comprendre (Charte du citoyen pour le Patrimoine 2001).

À partir de ces quelques notions de patrimoine, nous avons choisi de porter une attention particulière au rôle du patrimoine immatériel qui est une des variables dont nous tenons compte dans nos cas d'étude. Il en est de même du patrimoine matériel englobant le patrimoine archéologique et architectural. Ainsi, nous ne pouvons dissocier ces notions et les isoler l'une de l'autre. Elles font partie du « paysage urbain historique ». En effet, selon les définitions récentes du Mémorandum de Vienne, le paysage urbain historique fait référence à des ensembles de n'importe quel groupe de bâtiments, structures et espaces libres, dans leur cadre naturel et écologique, y compris les sites archéologiques et paléontologiques, constituant des établissements humains dans un milieu urbain sur une période de temps pertinente, dont la cohésion et la valeur sont reconnues du point de vue archéologique, architectural, préhistorique, historique, scientifique, esthétique, socioculturel ou écologique. Ce paysage a modelé la société moderne et a une grande valeur pour la compréhension de notre mode de vie contemporain (whc.unesco.org/archive/2005/whc05-15ga-7f.doc).

Cette définition du paysage urbain historique correspond à la notion de patrimoine envisagée dans nos cas d'étude où nous tentons de transmettre l'esprit du lieu. Parmi nos objectifs principaux, il y a aussi la volonté de montrer comment les TIC peuvent servir d'outil de réflexion et de compréhension. En d'autres termes, comment aider un expert ou un simple néophyte à appréhender un ensemble architectural ancien dans son contexte spatio-temporel, de manière à intégrer certaines valeurs issues d'un patrimoine bâti, de connaissances théoriques et pratiques provenant de disciplines diverses comme l'archéologie, l'architecture, l'histoire, l'histoire de l'art, les communications et l'informatique. Tout en insistant sur l'importance de documenter les savoir-faire (techniques, procédés, etc.) et aussi le *genius loci* du site.

3. Une transmission pour la sauvegarde

Avec ces expériences, nous cherchons à transmettre l'esprit du lieu comme d'autres l'ont fait et continuent à le faire lorsqu'ils ont réalisé que le progrès bouleversera de plus en plus vite les modes de vie. Nous envisageons l'usage des TIC pour transmettre l'esprit du lieu conformément aux principes énoncés dans les chartes et les conventions concernant la «réversibilité» et «l'intégrité». En suggérant d'utiliser des techniques de transmission comme les outils numériques, nous répondons favorablement au souci de respecter la «réversibilité» et «l'intégrité» (Charte d'Appleton de 1983) ainsi que l'authenticité d'un lieu. L'authenticité, thème principal du Document de Nara (1994), est une notion à préserver dans le cas d'une intervention sur un site culturel ou archéologique protégé. Les TIC permettent cette intervention sans toucher à la réalité d'un site, c'est-à-dire qu'ils permettent de simuler les transformations d'un site sans pour autant modifier son intégrité.

L'utilisation des TIC dans le domaine du patrimoine peut susciter de l'enthousiasme, mais elle peut aussi provoquer une certaine réticence, comme l'attestent ces propos:

> Je préfère absolument des ruines, quel que soit leur état de décrépitude, à ce qui a été reconstruit, quelle qu'en soit la splendeur. Ce qui demeure est plus précieux que ce que l'on rajoute: d'un côté c'est l'histoire; de l'autre la fiction, et c'est la première que je préfère: elle est de loin la plus romantique. L'une est positive, même si elle est incomplète; l'autre comble le manque avec des choses plus mortes que le manque lui-même, dans la mesure où elles n'ont jamais eu de vie (James d'après Leniaud 2002: 177).

Quoiqu'il en soit, il y a des moyens et des méthodes que les technologies de la communication et de l'information offrent et qui ne sont pas réalisables concrètement selon les chartes. Les TIC pourraient permettre une exploration de ces méthodes parce qu'elles peuvent joindre en même temps simulation et expérimentation (De Paoli et El-Khoury 2005).

Les discussions que ce sujet peut provoquer sur l'usage des TIC dans le patrimoine varient. On cherche à réduire ces divergences en proposant la création de bases solides qui peuvent poser des règles et des balises à l'utilisation de ce nouvel outil. Devrait-on abuser ou pas de l'usage des TIC? Pour l'instant, aucune réglementation ne gère cet usage. Les spécialistes sont unanimes à ce sujet : on dispose de nouveaux moyens, autant les utiliser ; bien qu'ils soient conscients que les représentations de sites anciens ou disparus, créées à l'aide des TIC, sont le plus souvent hypothétiques et ne sont pas, dans la plupart des cas, jugées fiables. Les résultats sont utilisés à des fins pédagogiques ou ludiques. Le thème des conférences et les tendances actuelles en témoignent (El-Khoury 2008).

On utilise aujourd'hui les TIC pour faire des expériences distinctes selon chaque contexte. Certains utilisateurs ont tendance à s'en méfier et d'autres à s'y lancer. Bien que l'usage un peu «chaotique» des TIC (Acot 1999) laisse certains spécialistes sceptiques, on ne peut pas nier l'avantage que peut offrir Internet dans le domaine des TIC.

Dans ce contexte, comment, à l'aide des TIC, est-il possible de transmettre l'esprit du lieu? Pour répondre à cette question nous proposons d'exprimer un esprit du lieu en évolution à travers les travaux proposés par le GRCAO et le MAP-PAGE.

4. Vers un esprit du lieu en évolution

Pour transmettre un exemple d'expression d'esprit du lieu, les modèles numériques sont proposés par le GRCAO comme des modèles interactifs et renouvelables qui peuvent s'enrichir par de nouvelles connaissances. Pourvus d'un caractère multidisciplinaire, ces modèles peuvent être des outils de connaissance à la fois destinés aux experts qui interviennent sur un site culturel dynamique ou à tout autre utilisateur. Dans cette perspective, nous présentons ces modèles en considérant un cas d'étude, un site culturel dynamique qui se caractérise par la proximité de «lieux associés» et d'un patrimoine vivant renouvelable : le site de Byblos avec sa ville médiévale animée et son site archéologique.

Celui-ci témoigne de la présence de traces révélant 7000 à 9000 ans de présence humaine sur le même site dans lequel le théâtre romain (218 ap. J.-C.) a été découvert. Les matériaux de ce théâtre avaient été recyclés par les Croisés qui les ont utilisés pour construire le château en 1108. Celui-ci s'érige sur le site archéologique non loin du théâtre romain. D'autres pierres de ce théâtre, estiment les archéologues, ont servi à orner certaines villas et maisons des alentours (Dunand 1973). En 1930, les restes du théâtre (les cinq rangs et la scène) ont été déplacés par l'archéologue Dunand qui les a installés près de la mer.

En considérant le cas du théâtre romain, l'objectif a été de susciter une réflexion autour de certains éléments constructifs du théâtre de Byblos à partir des données disponibles sur les théâtres romains. Nous avons construit des modèles du théâtre pour exprimer un savoir-faire et étudier le théâtre et sa relation aux «lieux associés», la ville (El-Khoury et De Paoli 2006).

Nous avons présenté les modèles de manière à mettre en valeur le caractère de «site culturel dynamique» de Byblos par les évènements suivants :

- le dépouillement des pierres du théâtre par les civilisations qui l'ont utilisé ;
- la construction du château des Croisés avec des pierres romaines ;
- le déplacement des cinq gradins du théâtre par l'archéologue Dunand en 1930 vers son emplacement actuel près de la mer (Figure 1).

Ces événements témoignent de la caractéristique du site de Byblos : une «carrière» pour les habitants de la région (Jidejian 2004). Le théâtre perçu comme «carrière» a ouvert des voies vers des expériences permettant de visualiser le théâtre différemment à travers des animations interactives.

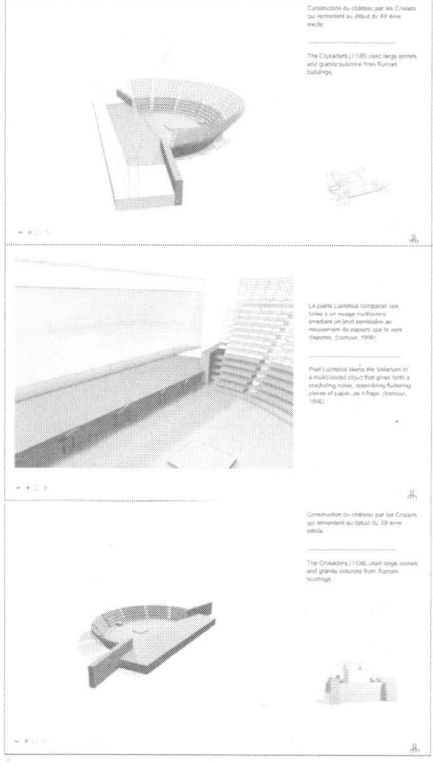

Figure 1. Tableau reproduisant des étapes de l'animation retraçant l'évolution du théâtre.

Le patrimoine ne se trouve pas uniquement dans le site archéologique mais s'étend aussi vers la ville médiévale de Byblos. C'est un patrimoine à exprimer par des modèles que nous avons réalisés non seulement dans le but de créer des promenades virtuelles, mais surtout pour développer une certaine appropriation du lieu. Ainsi, il est parfois difficile de s'approprier des lieux « inertes » comme le site archéologique et il est important de tenir compte de « l'esprit d'appartenance » tel que souligné dans la Charte du citoyen pour le Patrimoine (2001). Quand il s'agit d'un lieu « vivant » comme la ville, la tâche s'avère plus évidente. Ces modèles sont une proposition de revisiter les lieux. Parmi les modèles réalisés, nous avons proposé de créer un itinéraire dans la ville médiévale de Byblos à partir de l'entrée du site archéologique vers les ruelles animées. L'expérience est une sorte de prise de connaissance des lieux. Elle permet à l'observateur de se promener dans les ruelles en faisant des arrêts sur certains détails exprimés par des images dynamiques (El-Khoury, De Paoli et Khayat 2007) (Figure 2).

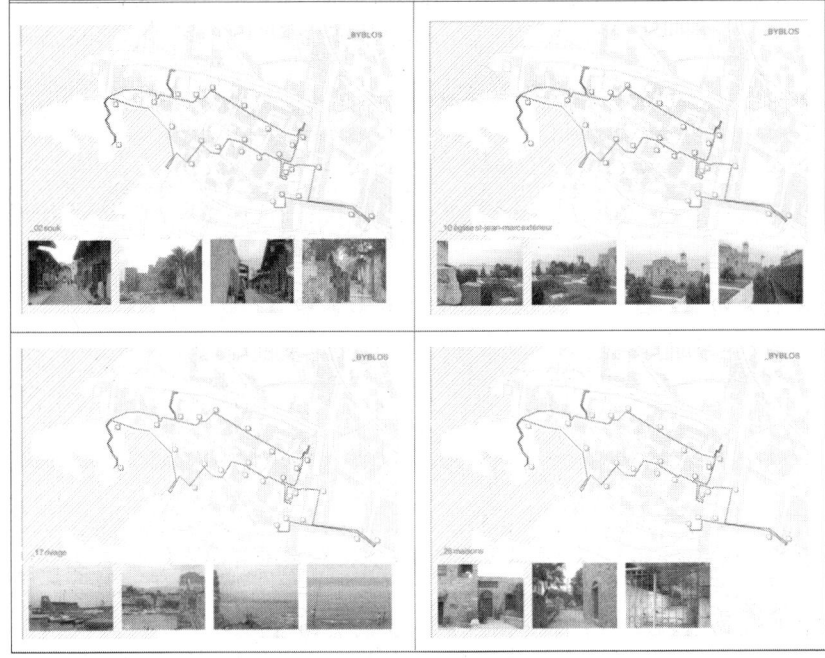

Figure 2. Différents états du parcours dans la ville médiévale.

Le travail que nous présentons devient alors un espace « collaboratif » où l'on peut intégrer des informations concernant l'esprit et le lieu.

Les travaux du MAP-PAGE s'inscrivent dans l'objectif de montrer comment les TIC peuvent servir d'outil de compréhension et de réflexion autour de l'esprit du lieu. Nous avons développé un Système d'Information qui fonctionne sur Internet et qui permet de conserver en un même endroit et d'accéder par des moyens simples à toute la documentation générée par l'exploitation d'un site patrimonial (aussi bien la documentation papier que la documentation numérique). Ce système est donc un outil qui favorise la compréhension de la mémoire du lieu et de son esprit, en reliant les modèles numériques du site avec les documents qui retracent son évolution ou les techniques de construction ayant servi à l'ériger (Meyer 2007).

Un premier exemple d'utilisation de ce Système d'Information sur Internet est la villa gallo-romaine d'Echternach (Luxembourg). Des modèles numériques de ce site ont été réalisés par le MAP-CRAI dans le cadre d'un projet de réalisation de reconstitutions destinées à être utilisées comme composantes d'une muséographie. L'idée centrale était de fournir au musée attenant au site des représentations permettant aux visiteurs de se faire une idée de la vie quotidienne dans ce palais-villa de la fin du 1er siècle après J.-C. : maquettes, ambiances, objets, présentations des différentes pièces d'habitation et occupations qui s'y déroulaient. La mission du MAP-CRAI dans ce cadre a donc été la réalisation de tous les documents numériques devant être présentés au public, que ce soit dans le musée ou sur des panneaux *in situ*, permettant aux visiteurs de faire un rapport immédiat entre ce qui subsiste et les hypothèses de reconstruction.

Pour l'intégration de ce site dans le système d'information, nous disposions donc des documents réalisés lors des fouilles et rassemblés dans un livre (Zimmer et al. 1981), des reconstitutions virtuelles (images de synthèse) et des modèles 3D. Après avoir rendu les modèles numériques interactifs, nous les avons intégrés dans une base de données contenant tous les autres documents relatifs au site. Ainsi, il est possible d'accéder à toute la mémoire des différents lieux de ce site par une simple interaction avec les modèles numériques qui les représentent. Ce processus est illustré par la Figure 3.

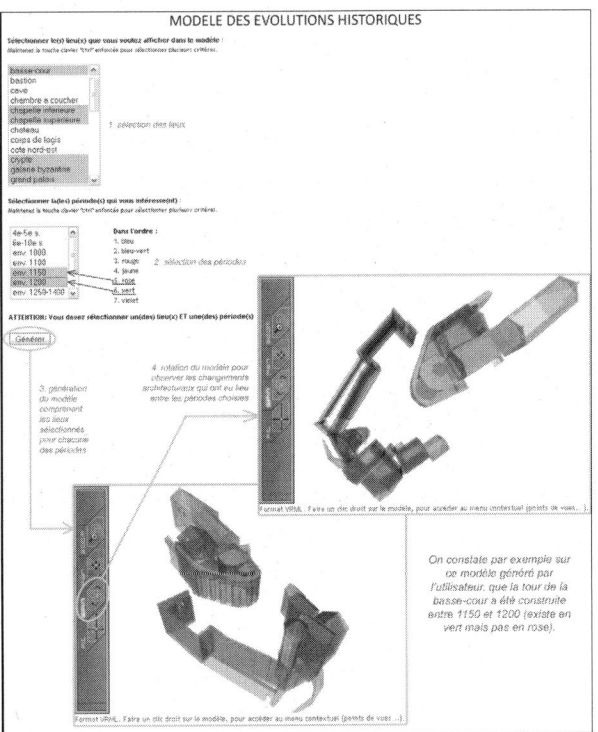

Figure 3. Modèle interactif de lieux d'intérêt de la villa d'Echternach (Luxembourg), permettant d'accéder aux documents qui s'y rapportent.

L'intérêt du Système d'Information sur Internet développé par le MAP-PAGE peut aussi être illustré par l'exemple d'application sur le Château de Vianden (Luxembourg). En effet, des travaux ont été menés pendant plusieurs années pour la modélisation des évolutions historiques de ce château. Dans le cadre de la valorisation des fouilles archéologiques et de la communication du travail historique effectué sur ce monument, il était prévu de réaliser des documents multimédias présentés aux visiteurs du nouveau musée du château.

Parmi les dispositifs didactiques mis à la disposition du public, on trouve des panneaux d'information, un document audiovisuel, un programme interactif de réalité virtuelle. Certains de ces dispositifs sont plus particulièrement consacrés à l'histoire architecturale du site, son évolution, ses transformations, mais également aux méthodes d'investigations archéologiques. Les moyens techniques utilisés nécessitent la réalisation d'images de synthèse, d'animations virtuelles et de reconstitutions virtuelles diverses, car ils permettent de nombreux effets irréalisables par des techniques plus traditionnelles. Des modèles numériques des différentes phases architecturales du château ont donc été réalisés par le MAP-CRAI et mis à notre disposition. De plus, il a été possible d'accéder aux documents ayant permis de les produire ainsi qu'à toutes les autres données issues des travaux réalisés sur ce château depuis la fin des années 1970. Tous ces documents ainsi que les modèles ont été intégrés dans la base de données sous-jacente au système d'information.

Des modèles numériques des différents lieux du château étaient donc disponibles pour pratiquement toutes les phases de son histoire (du IVe siècle à nos jours). Nous avons alors développé un outil dans le système d'information qui permet d'associer visuellement simultanément un ou plusieurs lieux à une ou plusieurs phases de leur histoire. Ceci est illustré par la Figure 4.

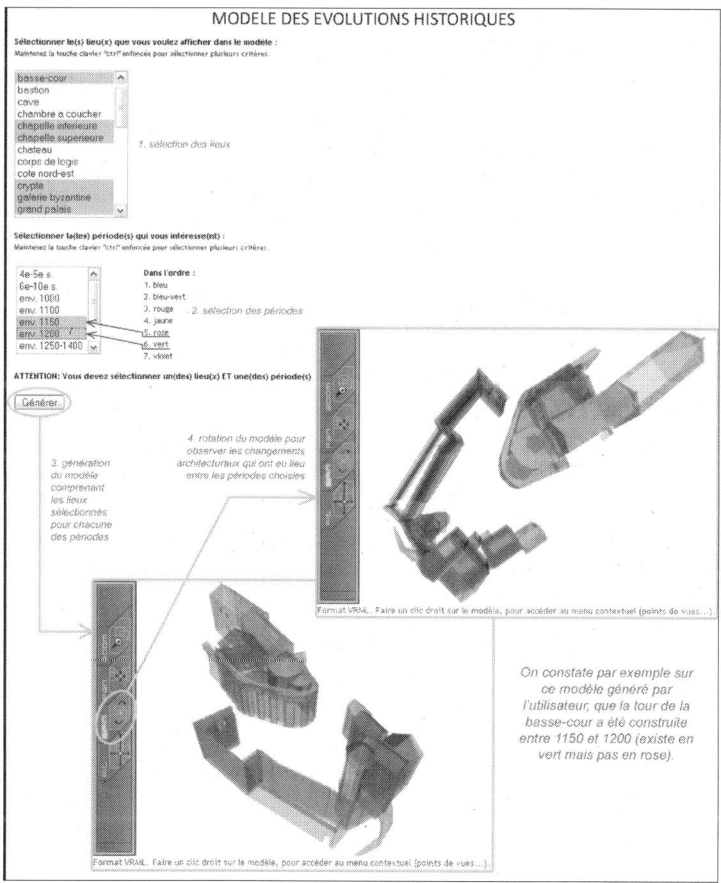

Figure 4. Modélisation numérique des évolutions des lieux d'un site au cours de son histoire. Exemple du Château de Vianden (Luxembourg).

Ainsi, le Système d'Information sur Internet développé au MAP-PAGE illustre comment la modélisation informatique est capable de montrer l'évolution d'un site à travers les siècles, ce qui favorise la compréhension de la superposition des couches historiques et aide à la réflexion autour des occupations successives du site et de l'évolution de l'esprit de ce lieu (Meyer 2007).

Des travaux sont en cours actuellement au MAP-PAGE pour aider à la compréhension de l'esprit des sites alsaciens du Château d'Andlau et de l'Abbaye de Niedermunster.

Conclusion

Ce travail ouvre certaines perspectives que nous esquissons brièvement. Elles peuvent être organisées suivant deux axes : le premier est envisageable pour l'avenir de l'éducation patrimoniale qui est une fonction essentielle d'un lieu s'il est considéré comme un musée. Dans ce contexte, la question de la manière de transmettre les connaissances dans l'avenir est à la Une et les chercheurs se demandent vers quel type de musée évoluer. Verra-t-on le « musée autoroute de l'information » dans lequel on manipulera les données sans les altérer ? Ou bien le « musée sans murs » qui ira rejoindre les gens là où ils sont (Allard et Lefebvre 1997) ? L'éducation patrimoniale est une fonction essentielle pour réaliser un espace musée, ouvert comme dans le cas du théâtre qui s'ouvre sur la ville de Byblos. Les connaissances peuvent être transférées et on parle alors de musée spectacle.

Le deuxième axe est celui de l'adoption d'une « vision interdisciplinaire dans la définition de gestes de conservation et de diffusion favorisant une mise en valeur plus conforme à la richesse et à la subtilité des contenus » (Allard et Lefebvre 1997). Les approches historiques, archéologiques, architecturales, urbanistiques et autres se mêlent pour contribuer à ouvrir un débat, et lancer une remise en question qui proposera des solutions imprégnées des différentes compétences à partir des différentes disciplines impliquées dans le processus de mise en valeur du patrimoine.

Les résultats obtenus montrent que les TIC peuvent être mises à contribution pour transmettre l'esprit du lieu avec sa dimension patrimoniale. Ce travail ouvre la voie au développement d'outils de sensibilisation au patrimoine et favorise son enseignement. Il favorise aussi la création d'une mémoire virtuelle en proposant des lieux d'échanges de connaissances liées au patrimoine dans une approche multidisciplinaire.

En s'appuyant sur les dernières évolutions du Web vers le Web 2.0 et des nouvelles approches pour la gestion de contenus de sites Internet, ce travail fournit les connaissances nécessaires à la création de nouveaux systèmes de gestion du patrimoine par la proposition d'espaces de travail collaboratifs à l'aide des technologies de l'information et de la communication.

Ce travail pourrait contribuer à augmenter les connaissances dans la mise en valeur du patrimoine en intégrant l'expertise des différentes disciplines impliquées. Et la mise en valeur d'un site n'en sera qu'enrichie. Les TIC pourraient alors servir d'élément fédérateur entre ces différents champs disciplinaires pour contribuer à la prise de décisions communes et comprendre le patrimoine dans une vision de développement durable sans affecter «l'intégrité» d'un site.

Références

Acot, P. 1999. *L'histoire des sciences.* Paris, Que sais-je?

Allard, M. et S. Boucher. 1997. «Prolégomènes au développement de modèles théoriques de pédagogie muséale». *Le musée, un lieu éducatif,* Montréal, Musée d'art contemporain de Montréal.

Bumbaru, D. 2003. «Patrimoine matériel et immatériel, devoir et plaisir de mémoire». *La mémoire des lieux: préserver le sens et les valeurs immatérielles des monuments et sites,* Actes du Symposium scientifique international, ICOMOS, Victoria Falls.

Charte du citoyen pour le patrimoine, 2001. Beyrouth, République libanaise, Bureau du Ministre d'État pour la réforme administrative.

Dunand, M. 1973 [1939]. *Fouilles de Byblos (5 volumes).* Paris: Librairie Orientaliste Paul Geuthner, Librairie d'Amérique et d'Orient, Adrien Maisonneuve.

De Paoli, G. et N. El-Khoury. 2005. «ICT and the Ancient City of Byblos: a New Direction for the Communication of Intangible Heritage». Dans G. De Paoli, K. Zreik et R. Beheshti (dir.), *Augmented Heritage, New Era for Architectural Design, Civil Engineering and Urban Planning,* Paris: Europia Productions.

El-Khoury, N. et G. De Paoli. 2006. «The backstage of Byblos' Roman theatre: New Digital Devices using Information and Communications Technology (ICT)». Dans M. Ioannides, D. Arnold, F. Nicolucci et K. Mania (dir.), *The 7th International Symposyum on Virtual Reality, Archaeology and Cultural heritage,* Chypre: VAST.

El-Khoury, N., G. De Paoli, et G. Khayat. 2007. «Methodological Experiments for Understanding Cultural Heritage». Dans G. De Paoli, K. Zreik et R. Beheshti (dir.), *Digital Thinking in Architecture, Civil Engineering, Archaeology, Urban Planning and Design: Finding the Ways,* Actes du colloque Europia 11, Paris: Europia Productions.

El-Khoury, N. 2008. *Proposition et simulation de modèles numériques de compréhension d'un patrimoine. Le théâtre romain de Byblos au Liban.* Thèse de doctorat, Université de Montréal, Faculté de l'aménagement.

ICOMOS. 1979. *Charte de Burra*, Australie, révisée le 26 novembre 1999, www.icomos.org.

ICOMOS. 1983. *Charte d'Appleton pour la protection et la mise en valeur de l'environnement bâti*. En ligne, www.icomos.org/docs/appleton. html.fr.

ICOMOS, ICCROM, UNESCO. 1994. *Document de Nara sur l'authenticité*. Nara, Japon, www.international.icomos.org/naradoc_fre.htm

Jidejian, N. 2004 [1968]. *Byblos à travers les âges*. Beyrouth : Librairie Orientale.

Lefebvre, B. et M. Allard (dir.). 1997. *Le musée. Un lieu éducatif*. Montréal : Les Éditions du Musée d'art contemporain de Montréal.

Leniaud, J-M. 2002. *Les archipels du passé. Le patrimoine et son histoire*. Paris : Fayard.

Meyer, É. 2007. *Acquisition 3D, documentation et restitution en archéologie : proposition d'un modèle de Système d'Information dédié au patrimoine*. Thèse de Doctorat en Modélisation et Simulation des Espaces Bâtis, UHP Nancy 1.

UNESCO. 2005. *Mémorandum de Vienne*, « Déclaration sur la conservation des paysages urbains historiques », whc.unesco.org/archive/2005/ whc05-15ga-7f.doc.

Zimmer, J., J. Metzler et L. Bakker. 1981. *Ausgrabungen in Echternach*. Luxembourg : Publications nationales.

Building an Integrated Multimedia Digital Database of Quebec's Tangible and Intangible Religious Heritage

Laurier Turgeon
Canada Research Chair in Cultural Heritage
Director of the Institute of Cultural Heritage
Université Laval, Canada

Louise Saint-Pierre
Research Assistant Canada Research Chair in Cultural Heritage
Univeristé Laval
Quebec Ministry of Culture
Communications and the Condition of Women, Canada

ABSTRACT

This article presents the results of a pilot project aimed at the development of a multimedia digitalized database of the intangible religious heritage of Quebec, including that of Catholic, Protestant, Jewish, Orthodox, and Amerindian communities. The cultural and religious traditions and heritage of many religious groups are today threatened by the sharp decline and near disappearance of religious practice in Quebec over the last forty years. The project has designed a specific methodology to collect and preserve the endangered oral traditions, memory and knowledge of these communities. Ethnographic field methods are used to collect four types of narratives (life stories as well as stories of places, objects and practices) and to record them in the form of digitalized files, containing textual summaries, photographs and audio-visual recordings. These files are fed into a FileMaker Pro database and retrieved through a Web site in order to be easily accessible to the religious communities themselves as well as to the general public.

RÉSUMÉ

Cet article présente les résultats d'un projet pilote destiné à mettre sur pied une base de données numérique multimédia pour assurer la sauvegarde et la mise en valeur du patrimoine immatériel religieux du Québec, aujourd'hui

menacé par l'effondrement de la pratique religieuse, le vieillissement pro-
noncé des communautés religieuses, la fermeture des paroisses et des églises
et la vente forcée d'objets sacrés. À partir de l'étude de huit communautés
– catholiques, protestantes, juives, orthodoxes et amérindiennes – nous
proposons des méthodes virtuelles novatrices d'inventorisation qui, à l'aide
des nouvelles technologies de l'information et de la communication, visent
à la fois à conserver et à communiquer efficacement ce patrimoine. La
cueillette et la saisie audio-visuelles des récits de lieux, d'objets, de pratiques
et de vie permettent de capter les divers aspects de ce patrimoine, de le
rendre plus visible et palpable, de bien contextualiser ses usages sociaux et
d'intégrer ses dimensions matérielles et immatérielles. Le projet pilote nous
a également permis de développer une approche participative pour mettre
en valeur ce patrimoine directement sur le terrain en collaboration avec les
communautés par des actions culturelles diverses. Nous avons développé
avec elles des sites Web, des expositions muséales, des productions multimédia de DVD, des modules pédagogiques et des publications d'articles
destinés aux communautés et au grand public.

Introduction

The inventorying of architectural and archaeological heritage is an
elaborate, well-established and institutionalized practice. Many countries keep
national inventories of monuments and sites that are regularly updated and used
to keep a record of the evolving condition of buildings and archaeological collections. Digital technologies have enhanced the capacity, the flexibility and the
efficiency of inventories for the protection and management of heritage assets.
European countries have adopted standardized practices for the collecting and
ordering of data to facilitate the transfer of information to associated databases,
notably through the *Core Data Index to Historic Buildings and Monuments of
Architectural Heritage* and the *Core Data Standard for Archaeological Sites and
Monuments* (Palmer *et al.* 2009: 65-81). Thesauruses have been created to ensure
the development of standardized terminology on object types, such as the *Getty
Art and Architecture Thesaurus*, the French *Thesaurus de l'architecture* and the
English *Thesaurus of Monument Types*. Innovative projects using sophisticated
digital technologies are being launched throughout the world. The Getty
Conservation Institute and the Office of Historic Resources of the City of Los
Angeles have recently initiated a survey to create a citywide online integrated
digital database of all of the historic buildings and associated cultural properties,
and to incorporate it into the geographic information system (GIS) of the city.
Online historic resource information is regarded as an essential component of
effective historical preservation, city planning, and community development
(Welch Howe 2008).[1] The newly designed Multilingual Inventory of Cultural

---

1.   See: http://www.getty.edu/conservation/publications/pdf_publications/
      lahrs_report.pdf.

Heritage in Europe, MICHAEL (www.michael-culture.org), aims to give digital access to the collections of Europe's museums, libraries and archives.

Although it is generally recognized that intangible cultural assets, such as the oral histories, traditional knowledge, rituals and festivals, can invest richer and deeper meaning in the built environment and landscapes, very little has yet been done to include information of living traditions in inventories. Aside from a few isolated examples of efforts made to collect oral histories of sites, in order to enhance their interpretation, no methodologies have been developed to systematically incorporate the intangible elements into existing inventories of monuments and sites. Part of the problem is that there are no set procedures and internationally accepted standards for inventorying intangible cultural heritage itself. The *Convention for the safeguarding of intangible cultural heritage* of 2003 specifically recommends that state parties draw up inventories of their intangible heritage, and two expert meetings were organized to explore ways of making inventories of intangible cultural heritage.[2] There was a general consensus on the idea that inventory making should make use of digital database and Web technologies and be carried out with the participation of the communities concerned. Many of the participants recognized that digital sound and audio-visual technologies provide limitless possibilities to record, preserve and disseminate intangible cultural heritage promptly and effectively. However, aside from these general guidelines, no country has yet, to our knowledge, devised a methodology for efficiently recording and archiving intangible heritage in digital format, nor for linking it to existing inventories of tangible heritage.

The Context of the Quebec Intangible Religious Heritage Project

We have recently had the opportunity to respond to this challenge by designing an integrated inventory of the tangible and intangible religious heritage of the Province of Quebec, including buildings, collections of objects and intangible heritage in a unique digital database accessible on the Web. The project was a collaborative effort developed by the *Chaire de recherche du Canada en patrimoine ethnologique* [Canada Research Chair in Cultural Heritage], the *Société des musées québécois* [Society of Quebec Museums] and the *ministère de la Culture, des Communications et de la Condition féminine* [Ministry of Culture, Communications and the Condition of Women

---

2.   A first expert meeting on the topic was held at UNESCO in Paris in March of 2005: *Report of the Expert Meeting on Inventorying Intangible Cultural Heritage.* Paris: UNESCO, March 17-18, 2005. A second was held in Bankok, Thailand, in December 2005: *Sub-Regional Experts Meeting in Asia on Intangible Cultural Heritage: Safeguarding and Inventory-Making Methodologies.* Bangkok: Asia/ Pacific Cultural Center for UNESCO (ACCU) of Japan, and the Office of National Culture Commission (ONCC) of Thailand.

of Quebec]. The Quebec Ministry of Culture, Communications and the Condition of Women had already carried out an extensive survey and built an online database of some 3,000 churches and places of worship (chapels, sanctuaries, oratories, pilgrimage sites) in the Province of Quebec from 2003 to 2005 (Groulx 2005: 253-257). The Ministry decided to extend the inventory to include movable objects (artwork, craftwork, furniture and textiles) as well as intangible heritage (oral histories, traditional knowledge, rituals, festivals, songs, music, etc.). The Society of Quebec Museums was selected to carry out the inventory of movable objects and the Canada Research Chair in Cultural Heritage, the intangible heritage. Given the innovative and ambitious nature of the project, it appeared reasonable to begin with a pilot survey to develop and test the proposed methodologies, and to make the necessary adjustments before going ahead with the province-wide survey. This article will present the methods and results of the preliminary survey of intangible heritage, carried out between 2007 and 2008, and explain how the information will be integrated into the associated databases on buildings and on movable objects.

The endangered nature of religious heritage in Quebec has created circumstances favorable to a concerted effort between different agencies (governments, churches, religious congregations, universities and heritage associations), so as to enable the collection and safeguarding of the tangible as well as the intangible components of this severely threatened heritage. Although Quebec, the primarily French-speaking province of Canada, has had a long and vibrant religious history, for Catholics as well as for Protestants and Jews, religious practice was widely abandoned in the 1960s and 1970s and religious heritage was left on its own. It continued to be maintained by the religious congregations, but their numbers have diminished considerably over the last twenty years and they are no longer in a position to continue looking after their heritage. Many congregations are on the verge of disappearing, churches and monasteries are being sold and demolished, whole collections are being auctioned off or sent to missions in underdeveloped countries. The dwindling numbers of priests and nuns clearly depict the depth and breadth of the crisis. For example, until 2003 the Diocese of Quebec had over 500 secular priests in its service – their numbers have now shrunk to sixty – who serve 233 parishes (Morisset and Noppen 2005: 74). Moreover, the average age of an active priest in Quebec is 65. The issue of ageing is even more of a concern among female orders, as many of Quebec's founding communities will soon disappear. Of the several hundred women who were consecrated members of the Ursulines of Quebec barely 40 years ago, today some thirty remain and their average age is 82! The situation is similar for the Augustines, who have been forced to close their four regional monasteries (Gaspé, Montmagny, Saint-George and Lévis) and to consolidate their personnel and communal belongings at the Hôtel-Dieu Monastery in Quebec City (Tanguay 2005: 192).

Faced with the resulting threat to the collective memory and cultural heritage of Quebec society, public institutions and members of civilian society have begun to take action. The farsightedness of pioneering scholars such as Jean Simard (1979, 1984, 1989, 1995, 1998) and Luc Noppen and Lucie Morisset (1997, 2005, 2006) succeeded in raising public awareness of the considerable contribution that religious orders have made to Quebec's heritage, in fields as diverse as architecture, art and traditional arts and crafts. Early on, Simard and Noppen drew a clear distinction between religious endeavors and the safeguarding of heritage, making it clear that the safeguarding of religious heritage was prompted by cultural motives, and was not an attempt at religious revival or evangelization. The displacement of religious heritage from the religious to the public sphere, the transfer from the Church to the State, and from cultic to cultural practice, was the only viable means of safeguarding Quebec's religious heritage, especially given the increasing numbers of people abandoning active religious practice. The creation of societies and associations, by the clergy as well as by private citizens dedicated to heritage conservation, has mobilized public opinion and prompted legislators to elaborate heritage protection policies.

However, resources have been allocated almost exclusively to the preservation of tangible assets at the expense of the intangible ones. Subsidies have been granted predominantly, if not exclusively, to traditional heritage preservation efforts, that is, essentially, those concerned with the built environment. For example, between 1996 and 2006, *Fondation patrimoine religieux* [Quebec Religious Heritage Foundation] (known since 2008 as *Conseil du patrimoine religieux du Québec* [Quebec Council of Religious Heritage]) received over $150 million from the Government of Quebec for the maintenance and restoration of a total of several hundred churches (Morisset, Noppen and Coomans 2006: 15). In the same period, only one project aimed at the safeguarding of intangible heritage values received government funding: that of the Augustines of Quebec who were granted a symbolic sum of $35,000. The few other religious orders that have initiated similar projects have financed these efforts almost entirely at their own cost. What is the point of preserving churches, monasteries and chapels if their memory, social uses and significance are lost? What is especially preoccupying is that intangible heritage is held by living people, and therefore under greater and more immediate threat. Oral history and memory, traditional arts and crafts, festivals, rites, and customs are all living traditions preserved by oral transmission or by practice, often through repetition at set times of the day or periods of the year. They are transmitted by individuals who are often recognized as tradition bearers, and when those individuals disappear, the living traditions that they carry disappear irrevocably with them. In contrast to the heritage of the built environment, which usually deteriorates over long periods of time that allow for timely intervention,[3] elderly individuals may pass away suddenly, and without warning, taking with them a part of the communal traditions. Practices are, by definition, practiced, that is to say transmitted through oral dialogue and bodily performance or a combination of both, by telling and showing, and thus are only rarely set down in writing. Even when such practices are put in writing, it is often difficult, if not impossible, to reproduce them accurately, because many details essential to their reconstruction are omitted. Just as a language that is not spoken, a living heritage that is not practiced and experienced eventually dies out. This mode of heritage transmission has been espoused by religious orders – and not surprisingly so – since they have always maintained a strong sense of community, a high degree of institutional stability, and a strong focus on conservation in a relatively insular environment. The safeguarding of memories and traditional knowledge preserves not only the intangible elements of heritage, but helps also to better understand, and thus, better preserve its material elements. Familiarity with the uses of objects, buildings and sites often holds the key to their historical significance, social uses, symbolic values, as well as their sense of belonging. After all, it is these intangible elements that give meaning and significance to material culture.

Public and political awareness of intangible heritage and religious heritage generally has risen significantly since the Quebec Parliamentary Commission on the future of religious heritage was set up in 2005. In the very act of creating the Commission, the state recognized the cultural and historical significance of this heritage in all its forms, whether it be religious goods, buildings or intangible aspects, regardless of religious boundaries. The Commission conducted wide-ranging public consultations and subsequently delivered a report that included some thirty recommendations designed to serve as guidelines for the Quebec Government for managing religious heritage.[4] Sensitive to the many depositions that underlined the importance of preserving intangible religious heritage, in its recommendation to the Quebec Government, the members of the Commission requested that it be preserved and that the general public's awareness of the matter be increased.[5]

---

3.   Even in the case of fire or natural disasters, there are often enough sources of information, such as foundations, blueprints, or photographs, to allow for accurate reconstruction.

4.   *Croire au patrimoine religieux du Québec*. Rapport de la Commission de la culture. 2006. Quebec: Quebec National Assembly.

5.   *Croire au patrimoine religieux du Québec*, p. 21. Recommendation 7 of the report reads as follows: "A coordinated program of research into intangible religious heritage should be put in place as soon as possible [...] and that, in collaboration with educational institutions and museums, and with the participation of communities and groups, which create, maintain and transmit that heritage, a coherent strategy for action must be elaborated with the aim of discovering, protecting and communicating Quebec's intangible religious heritage."

At the request of the Government of Quebec, the Canada Research Chair in Cultural Heritage at Laval University set up a Committee in the Fall of 2006 that brought together representatives of different religious communities, organizations dedicated to safeguarding and preserving religious heritage; representatives assigned to religious heritage by Quebec's Ministry of Culture, Communications and the Condition of Women; as well as various experts in the field. The Committee's mandate was to establish a national inventory of the intangible heritage of Quebec's major religious groups: Catholics, Protestants, Jews, Christian Orthodox and Amerindian. Over the course of a series of meetings, the Committee defined the necessary components of a strategy and methodology that could be used to set up an inventory in the form of a digitized, multimedia database, accessible on the Web. Because electronic data can be collected and disseminated at relatively low costs, be stored and transferred without loss of sound and image quality, and be retrieved rapidly and used in many different ways, an online digital database was determined to be the surest and most effective means of safeguarding intangible religious heritage.

Methodology: Preserving Heritage through Communication

Inventories have not, in the past, had a particularly good reputation among ethnologists and anthropologists nor, for that matter, among social scientists in general. Many have considered inventories to be the transformation of living tradition into an archive, which usually entails selection, the establishment of hierarchies, and a tendency to "freeze" living traditions by preserving a unique copy that serves as an archetype. According to this view, the inventory stifles the development of cultural practice and robs cultural tradition of its dynamism. In other words, instead of ensuring transmission, *inventorization* hinders it.

We would like to argue that inventories can, on the contrary, be both an efficient means of preservation and a dynamic tool for the transmission of traditional cultural practices. It is not the inventory itself that should be questioned, but rather the way in which it is done. If many scholars have been led to believe that inventories inherently freeze cultures, it is because inventories have long been associated with the idea of the preservation of authenticity. Ethnologists and Folklorists sought out (as objects of contemplation) those narratives and practices that they considered to be the most authentic – not with the aim of transmitting or communicating traditions, but rather in order to fix and preserve what were considered to be the purest forms. Furthermore, the traditional ethnological or folklore inventory was compiled with analog instruments (audio tape and film), and required cumbersome equipment, extensive fieldwork, and particular storage conditions (temperature and humidity controlled rooms), all of which were expensive. Under these circumstances, audio and video recordings were made in one take, essentially to be preserved in a single copy and kept under lock and key. Culture practitioners and performers, including informants themselves, often ignored the existence of the recordings or had difficulty locating them in the archives because of lack of standardized classification systems. When they did access the recordings, they were usually encouraged to mimic the original, which was held up as an axiomatic model.

Our project proposes to go far beyond simply preserving cultural traditions. Indeed, it emphasizes the important role of communication as an effective means of both engaging the public and of preservation itself, since transmission is a dynamic social form of conservation of intangible cultural heritage. The use of electronic recording equipment, digitized databases and Web technology has revolutionized inventory making. These new information technologies not only allow for greater ease in the compilation, access to, and maintenance of inventories, but also open up new possibilities to the fundamental design of such inventories. Both the carriers of tradition and the community at large can participate more easily in the processes of collection and communication of data. Internet access to the data encourages multiple appropriations and re-appropriations by a society-wide variety of users (community members, journalists, museologists and researchers), all the while facilitating the continued development of practices and the social recognition of practicing communities. Indeed, an online inventory database is a dynamic tool of heritage dissemination and socio-cultural development.

The pilot project was launched in September 2007 and ran through February 2008.[6] We recruited a team of professionals and students of ethnology who received ten days of training on tangible and intangible heritage, the methodology developed by the Chair, and on the use of state-of-the-art multimedia equipment. The interviewers then met with representatives of the communities to which they would be assigned, in order to identify the principal tradition bearers, as well as to determine the types, subjects, and schedule of the interviews to be carried out. The tradition bearers identified as informants were first contacted and, subsequently, interviewed. Researchers made audio and video recordings, and took photographs, often with the aid of informants. Afterwards, the data collected was processed – that is, the interviews were summarized on descriptive files, a thematic index was established for each interview to facilitate the retrieval of information, and audio-visual recordings and photographs were edited. The complete audio-visual recordings of the interviews were transferred to CD-ROM format, which was then sent to be stored at the

---

6.   For additional information on the pilot project, see: Laurier Turgeon and Louise Saint-Pierre, *Projet pilote d'inventaire du patrimoine immatériel religieux : Bilan des activités.* Report presented to Quebec's ministère de la Culture, des Communications et de la Condition féminine, May 2008.

Laval University Folklore and Ethnology Archive. After examining different possibilities, including very sophisticated computer programs, we opted for a simple solution, a FileMaker Pro database, because it was easy to use, inexpensive and efficient. We were also concerned about choosing a solution that our community partners could acquire and use easily in the event that they would want to create their own database. The summaries of interviews, a selection of photographs and short excerpts (3 to 5 minutes) of audio-visual recordings were transferred onto the database, which would be accessible via our Web site in the fall of 2009. The database may be consulted using a keyword or geographical location on Google Maps. In order to encourage immediate use of the materials and to encourage collaboration, professionals and students were expected to organize cultural events during and after the fieldwork with members of the communities, so as to communicate the intangible religious heritage "on the ground" through exhibits, multimedia documents, published articles, Web sites, as well as radio and television interviews. The aim was not the dissemination of religious beliefs, but rather the education of the general public by promoting knowledge and recognizing practices, both religious and cultural – and their practitioners – as elements of heritage.

We have deliberately adopted a wide-ranging, inclusive definition of intangible religious heritage that goes beyond the strictly religious or spiritual, to include aspects of the cultural life of members of religious orders. It must first be noted that to limit religious heritage narrowly to the sphere of what is "sacred" would, properly speaking, have been exceedingly restrictive and would have omitted the cultural concerns that are at the core of our endeavor. For example, the religious and spiritual practices of Catholic religious orders are standardized to a high degree and regulated by a set of rites dictated by the central doctrine of the Roman Catholic Church. Thus, an inventory of strictly "sacred" heritage would have proved redundant, at least in the case of Catholics who make up the overwhelming majority of Quebec's population. The specificity of Quebec's religious heritage lies in its adaptation to the physical environment and to historical circumstances, as well as the particular mission of each congregation and the institutional culture developed by each community. We have used the definition adopted by *Mission patrimoine religieux* [Mission for Religious Heritage]: "The intangible heritage is that which leads to the discovery of ways and customs that flow from the spirit and charisma of the founders and the mission of each community; the traditional knowledge and skills, developed and handed down from generation to generation in each institution that relate to community, religious and professional life, as well as to the arts and craftwork that are experienced and practiced in each community."[7]

---

7.   *Bulletin de Mission patrimoine religieux*, n° 8, November 2005, p. 10.

It is important to note that among the various elements of religious heritage, it is precisely the social memories and the traditional knowledge of artists and artisans that are most significantly at risk because of the imminent disappearance of many religious communities. Sensitive to these concerns, we aimed to make the investigative process as open as reasonably possible, in order not to omit unique traditions. Rather than use a "top-down" approach, whereby the researcher selects the materials to be inventoried, based on aesthetics, ancientness, exclusivity or authenticity, we favored the more dynamic "bottom-up" method by encouraging the members of religious communities to choose the heritage assets that they felt were most significant and valuable to them.

In order to assure a certain degree of representation, we chose to conduct the pilot project among communities of various faiths and denominations, geographic locations and genders. Our selection was based on the communities' historical backgrounds and the scope and depth of their heritage, as well as the immediacy of the threat that the group or institution may disappear. Because about 80% of the population in Quebec is of the Roman Catholic tradition, we selected two founding female communities from Quebec City – the Augustines, a hospital institution, and the Ursulines, an educational institution, both established in New France in 1639 – and one founding male community from Montreal – Sulpician priests whose original mission included the evangelization of Amerindian communities, the fulfillment of responsibilities linked with the order's wardenship of the City of Montreal, as well as its pastoral work in parishes (Deslandres, Dickinson and Hubert 2007). To complete the sample, we selected a Catholic parish, Saint-Charles-Borromée, in Charlesbourg – because of the important role parishes have and continue to play in religious and community life. For the Protestant faith, we included members of the Anglican community of Quebec City, due to its long history and present extent. Holy Trinity Cathedral was chosen as it is the seat of Quebec's Anglican archbishopric and the first Anglican Cathedral built in Canada. It was also among our aims to work with French Protestant communities, who have long remained in obscurity in an overwhelmingly Catholic Quebec. For the pilot project we chose the parish of Sainte-Marie-de-Monnoir in Marieville, the first Baptist church in francophone Canada to be devoted exclusively to religious service. Our inquiries also took us to the Spanish and Portuguese Synagogue of Montreal and its various affiliated communities. Founded in 1768, it is the oldest Jewish community in Canada. To represent the Christian Orthodox Church, we selected the St-Peter and St-Paul Russian Orthodox Cathedral in Montreal, which comes under the auspices of the Orthodox Church in America (OCA), whose origins go back to the Russian Orthodox Church of Alaska founded by Russia's Synod of Bishops in 1794. Finally, we interviewed members of Innu communities in Uashat and Maniutenam, both situated near the City of Sept-Îles. An Innu ethnologist carried out the interviews in these communities to help overcome linguistic barriers and a degree of reticence among members of Innu communities to talk to outsiders about their spiritual heritage.

Data was collected by means of oral interviews and ethnographic film. Based on the well-known and widespread life-story approach (Bertaux 1996; Brun 2001; Dornier & Dulong 2005), we extended this same technique to objects, places and practices. This consisted, quite simply, of asking the informant to talk about the history, significance and heritage value of given objects, places and practices. Oral narratives not only bring heritage values to the forefront, but also make it possible to connect the tangible and intangible elements of heritage. Indeed, it was easier for informants to identify and conceptualize heritage assets within the scope of a narrative that touched on concrete objects, specific places or important practices that had had an impact on their lives. Talking about such concrete things both sustains and stimulates memory, thus facilitating recollections of the past and of the meanings given to heritage assets. As a vehicle, the oral narrative encourages dialogue between a thing and its meaning, the tangible and intangible.

We categorized the collected narratives that were in keeping with the following four definitions:

- **Stories of places** describe the uses and meanings of the most important spaces in each community, the important sites of the built environment (chapel, sacristy, vestry, garden, grotto, refectory, teaching hall, cemetery, presbytery, synagogue, sacred places, communal spaces);

- **Stories of objects** refer to material, tangible objects invested with a high symbolic value and designated by the community as carrying the most heritage value (religious objects, liturgical vestments, as well as traditional clothing, movable property, kitchenware, etc.;

- **Life stories** aim to document lives, or life episodes, of community members who exhibit exceptional characteristics and, thus, have heritage value (missionaries, artists, artisans, and heritage communicators);

- **Stories of religious and cultural practices** include devotionals, funerary customs, significant liturgical practices, professional aptitudes, as well as unique skills that have both pragmatic application values and symbolic significance in the community (statuary, embroidery, lace making, gilding, weaving, the fabrication of religious objects, cloth mending, and the production of foodstuffs, etc.).

We experienced no difficulties in classifying the data collected during interviews in any of the categories. Each individual narrative was put in a file, including personal information (name and address of informant, their role in the community, etc.), a summary of the narrative (general description, historical description, place of acquisition, transmission, etc.) and technical inventory data (name of interviewer, indexer, audio and video documents, date of interview and processing of the recording, etc.). When two of more narratives overlapped within one interview, a separate file was produced for each narrative. When the same story was repeated by more than one informant, only one file was completed for that account. This explains the discrepancy between the number of files and the number of informants. Whenever possible we made video recordings of the interviews, especially those that produced stories of objects, places and practices, so that words could be related to images, narratives to objects. Audio-visual recording made it possible to actually capture the informants concretely showing and telling the story of the objects, the places and the practices, therefore illustrating the dynamic relationship between tangible and intangible heritage.

Heritage Stories

During the survey, we interviewed 76 informants, conducted 83 interviews and recorded 152 narratives.[8] The types of stories collected by category quite accurately reflect the varied characteristics of the state and nature of the heritage of each religious denomination. For example, in Protestant communities, there are relatively few sacred objects, as Protestantism discourages the use of material objects in worship rites. On the other hand, religious and cultural practices abound in these communities. Indigenous communities exhibit a similar pattern. In the Sulpician community, most members have reached an advanced age, recruitment is dormant, and many practices have already disappeared. However, the order has managed to preserve most of its physical belongings and its movable and built heritage is extensive. From among the Jewish faithful of the Spanish and Portuguese Synagogue, we collected a large number of life stories, as the community tends to promote the cultural diversity of its membership and highly value the accomplishments of its members.

Nearly 50% of the collected stories deal with practices, something which speaks tellingly of the importance of intangible heritage for these communities. We have noticed that these practices are dwindling with the ageing of the communities. For example, initiation rites have all but disappeared, since many congregations are no longer able to recruit new members. Many ageing sisters have retired and abandoned arts and crafts because they are not capable of carrying them out. On the other hand, the communities' built and movable heritage is well preserved and extensive, leading us to believe that stories of place (15%) and of objects (19%) will be maintained or perhaps even increased in the future.

---

8.   Over the course of the fieldwork, we also collected 1,946 photographs, and recorded 82 hours of audio material and 61 hours of video. From the data, we produced 134 files, 96 audio clips and 76 video clips, documenting the 8 communities included in the pilot project. These figures do not include the Augustines. Data for the Augustines was drawn from interviews conducted prior to the pilot project by Diane Audy, *Enquête orale auprès des Augustines de la Miséricorde de Jésus des monastères de l'Hôtel-Dieu de Québec, l'Hôpital Général de Québec, l'Hôtel-Dieu du Sacré-Cœur de Jésus de Québec*. Report presented to the ministère de la Culture et des Communications of Québec, April 2004.

We were surprised by the rather restricted representation of life stories in the sample (19%). Indeed, we had expected that the advancing age of congregations' members would be reflected by a higher representation of these types of narratives. These low percentages can perhaps be explained by the fact that most religions advocate self-effacement in the individual to the benefit of the community. Informants tended to draw attention to the collective accomplishments of the mission, speaking of rites, architecture, as well as artistic and artisanal works, rather than personal accomplishments. It was often difficult for individuals to conceive of themselves as being part of the heritage. It is rather the figure of a martyr, the archetypal anti-hero that is emulated.

The narratives collected are extremely diverse and run the gamut of the many varied aspects of intangible religious heritage. For example, among the stories of places, we recorded one of the sweat-lodge, an Innu place of purification, and the *Sukkah*, a sacred tent that, for the Jewish community, symbolizes the fragility of life. Stories of objects include the relic of Saint Seraphim of Sarov renowned for healing properties among the Orthodox community, and the wooden casket that the Jewish community believes helps the deceased return to the earth. Life stories include the narrative of a Catholic missionary who preached in Japan and that of a nun whose teaching career spanned 40 years. Stories of practices ranged from the Ursuline clothing ceremony and the Jewish Bar Mitzvah to the Orthodox vespers.

The stories of places proved to be extremely revealing of the profound social memory of religious communities. For example, in the narrative of the "corridor of stone" at the Ursuline monastery, our informant recounted how this hallway had become a place of remembering the major events as well as the everyday life of the institution. Windows, doors, rooms, and inscriptions on walls are mnemonic devices that serve to remember and tell the story of the 1759 bombing of Quebec, of where the British military commander of Quebec, James Murray, set up his headquarters, and also of daily chores around the monastery. According to the informant: "The corridor of stone is a recollection of all our history … history has depth here, with the Ursulines, when we walk down the corridor of stone, we feel as if we were living out what our mothers encountered experienced, the difficulties of construction, the historic events; and the fact that we worked in these places has made them familiar. These places live along with us and we live within them." In another account of place, related to a specific experience, the Innu informant talked of how his father had handed down to him his traditional knowledge and skills: "the first time I made a sweat tent, I was afraid and did not want to go inside… the first time I went inside the sweat tent, I felt pleasant sensations, what I felt did me a lot of good and I was proud to be part of the ritual. I will tell you a story about my grandfather: he was in the tent with someone else. He asked the person to go outside. When he was alone, the person outside heard my grandfather talking with someone and at the same moment the tent began to shake. I have also seen a tent shake…The ritual that we perform there lets me forgive myself and forgive others."

In the parishes, we took account of practices that are linked to the exercise of religious duties, and at the same time, closely associated with the cultural life of the community. The bell ringers at Quebec City's Holy Trinity Anglican Cathedral find artistic fulfillment, but in so doing also mark out religious time. The practice, which dates back to the Middle Ages, brings a dozen men and women together to the cathedral to train for weeks, if not months, in order to acquire the skills necessary to make the upturned bells sound out in concert. For the initiated, the bells can offer great precision of sound and, when well synchronized, the ringers produce a veritable symphony of sound to announce Eucharists, marriages, funerals, and other significant moments of religious life.

At the synagogue, we collected three different types of narratives regarding death, from the same informant. First, he provided a fascinating narrative of the Jewish casket (a story of object), which must be plain because "we are all equal in the face of death." The casket is made of natural materials that are prone to rapid decomposition, and must not contain any metal so that the body may become dust, since "we must return to the earth from which we originated." Secondly, our informant recounted how his father transmitted to him the practices surrounding the preparation of the body of the deceased (a story of practice). He showed us the ritual bath (*Mikveh*) and explained the steps to be performed before laying the body in the coffin. Wrapped in a simple shroud, the eyes and mouth covered with soil from Israel, the body of the deceased is watched over until its burial in the cemetery (a story of place).

The Father of the Russian Orthodox parish explained to us the particularities of the transport of the Eucharistic species and of relics (narratives of practices), and spoke of the significance of ritual gestures and the symbolic meanings of sacerdotal vestments. He actually simulated in great detail the ritual of the transport of relics at the same time that he produced the narrative of the practice so that we could record him in sound and image. Since all of the interviews are preserved as "docu-clips", the objects, places, practices and persons are culturally and spiritually contextualized, thereby revealing their meaning and value as heritage assets.

Community Outreach

In order to promote the safeguarding and valorization of religious heritage, we have incorporated an outreach program as an integral part of the project. The idea was to involve the religious communities as well as lay associations or groups and the media in the inventory process itself by jointly planning cultural actions aimed at the dissemination of the results. The community outreach approach is geared to produce immediate results in the course of fieldwork, both in and outside the studied communities. Given the very delicate nature of the subject matter, it was important to draw a boundary between our work as professionals of heritage conservation and what may be perceived as evangelization or pastoral church work. We made it clear to all that our intention was to present religious practices in a cultural perspective and, also, to encourage the dissemination of the knowledge of these practices as heritage in the community concerned and in society at large.

We performed three sets of community outreach programs. The first unfolded directly in the field, during the period of data collection, and consisted of publishing articles in newspapers, participating in radio and television programs, as well as organizing temporary exhibits and other public programs. The interviewers devoted between a quarter and a third of their fieldwork time to such endeavors, which were elaborated in concert with the members of the concerned religious communities or other associations or groups with an interest. Cultural activities took on many forms and were staged at various times during fieldwork, as per the needs and expectations of the community. The data collected was first shared with the communities' archives for their own use. During the fieldwork, interviewers also willingly accepted, on invitation, to participate in the cultural activities that the community had planned independently of our project. In the St-Peter and St-Paul Orthodox parish, the assigned ethnologist provided materials and helped organize an exhibit commemorating the first centenary of the parish's foundation. At the request of the administrative council of the Baptist Church of Marieville, the two members of our team digitized photographs that had been collected from parishioners in the scope of a parish project. Elsewhere, interviews were offered to journalists working for magazines (for example the Christian publication *Notre-Dame du Cap*), newspapers (*Le Devoir*, as well as the Innu monthly *Innuvelle*) and radio programs (at CKAU Radio in Mani-Utenam, for example). Materials collected from the Ursulines (audio and video recordings) were used for an exhibition on the history of education at the Ursulines. The Spanish and Portuguese Synagogue requested we present the results of our research to community members in the form of a PowerPoint presentation. At the Shaputuan Museum, a public meeting with the Innu population was organized to highlight the importance of new information and communication technologies as resources for the preservation and dissemination of the community's intangible religious heritage.

The online accessibility of the inventory represents the second set of the outreach program. The presentation of the interviews on various platforms (textual, iconographic, audio-visual) allows each community to communicate its traditions so as to be able to better exploit its cultural potential. Thus, not only are communities assisted in the identification of their abundant intangible heritage, but the public at large also benefits from increased accessibility to this information, helping to raise awareness and improve the understanding of the religious traditions that have shaped Quebec society. The Internet allows multiple appropriations and re-appropriations of information from this multimedia database. The database itself and the associated materials open limitless opportunities: the creation of thematic Web sites, virtual exhibits, multimedia presentations on particular subjects, promotional materials for tourism, educational and training programs for the schools. Currently under construction, the project's Web siteWeb site could well become a pedagogical tool within the scope of the Quebec Ministry of Education, Recreation and Sports' "Ethics and Religious Culture" program, which has been in place in Quebec's elementary and secondary schools since September 2008. This recently introduced program offers cultural interpretations of religion and provides a perspective on all the constituent dimensions (built, movable, intangible) of Quebec's religious heritage.

Academic dissemination represents the third outreach program. The inventory provides an important body of newly accessible information on which students and professors can draw when preparing conferences, seminars, graduate theses and doctoral dissertations, as well as scholarly articles and books. Although the academic field is narrower than the public sphere, scholarly dissemination should stimulate critical dialogue with other specialists in Quebec and abroad, to help refine and further improve the methodology.

Conclusion

The inventory is not an end in and of itself, but a means to efficiently preserve and better communicate tangible and intangible heritage. The recording of the narratives of place, objects, practices, and lives provides a promising methodology for making the intangible elements of heritage more visible, even "palpable", so as to contextualize their social uses, and to link them to the material world. This pilot project dealing with religious heritage gave us an opportunity to develop an interactive approach to the communication of heritage by way of a multimedia digital database and a Web site. The community outreach component of the project has led to exciting collaborative endeavors "in the field" by having the concerned groups promote cultural initiatives, such as Web sites, museum exhibits, multimedia DVD productions, pedagogical units and academic publications. Once on the Internet, intangible religious heritage is open to multiple uses and adaptations, appropriations and re-appropriations by any number of social actors. It is the dissemination of religious and cultural practices as components of heritage that will allow us to preserve and to increase the awareness of the value of this long despised, but nevertheless rich chapter of Quebec's cultural heritage.

Ultimately, in collaboration with the *Direction du patrimoine et de la muséologie* [Office of Heritage and Museology] of the Quebec Ministry of Culture, Communications and the Condition of Women, we intend to integrate the database we developed into the Ministry's general databank, which already holds a large amount of information on Quebec's built (monuments and sites) and movable (furniture, art, clothing, artifacts) religious heritage. Web site visitors who select, for example, a given church will gain access to information on its architecture, movable heritage and elements of intangible heritage, including descriptive files accompanied by photographs, three-dimensional digital representations, and audio-visual recordings. With a single click, Internet users will able to listen and see stories of places, objects, practices and people's lives. Known under the acronym PIMIQ (Patrimoine immobilier, mobilier et immatériel du Québec [Quebec's built, movable, and intangible heritage]), this digitized databank will be, to our knowledge, the world's first of its kind. We believe that these digitally transmitted tangible and intangible cultural expressions represent a third term of cultural property that transcends the old tangible / intangible dichotomy. Furthermore, tangible and intangible cultural properties, once digitalized, are accessible for mixing and remixing because the virtual record can itself become an innovative engine capable of limitless acts of hybrid creation.

References

Bertaux, Daniel. 1996. *Récits de vie*. Paris: Nathan.

Brun, Patrick. 2001. *Emancipation et connaissance. Les histoires de vie en collectivité*. Paris: L'Harmattan.

Dornier, Carole and Renaud Dulong (eds.). 2005. *Esthétique du témoignage*. Paris: Éditions de la Maison des sciences de l'homme.

Deslandres, Dominique, John A. Dickinson and Ollivier Hubert (eds.). 2007. *Les Sulpiciens de Montréal. Une histoire de pouvoir et de discrétion, 1657-2007*. Montreal: Fides.

Morisset, Lucie K. and Luc Noppen. 2005. «L'avenir des églises au Québec : contours et enjeux,» in Laurier Turgeon (ed.), *Le patrimoine religieux du Québec : entre le cultuel et le culturel*. Quebec City: Les Presses de l'Université Laval, p. 73-88.

Morisset, Lucie K., Luc Noppen and Thomas Coomans. 2006. «L'angélisme n'est plus de mise,» in Lucie K. Morisset, Luc Noppen and Thomas Coomans (eds.), *Quel avenir pour quelles églises?* Quebec City: Les Presses de l'Université du Québec.

Noppen, Luc, Lucie K. Morisset and Robert Caron (eds.). 1997. *La conservation des églises dans les villes-centres*. Quebec City: Septentrion.

Noppen, Luc Noppen and Lucie K. Morisset. 2005. *Les églises du Québec. Un patrimoine à réinventer*. Quebec City: Les Presses de l'Université du Québec.

Palmer, Robert. 2009. *Guidance on Inventory and Documentation of Cultural Heritage*. Strasbourg: Council of Europe Publishing.

Simard, Jean, in collaboration with Jocelyne Milot and René Bouchard. 1979. *Un patrimoine méprisé. La religion populaire des Québécois*. Montreal: Hurtubise HMH.

Simard, Jean and Benoît Lacroix (eds.). 1984. *Religion populaire, religion de clercs?* Quebec City: Institut québécois sur la culture.

Simard, Jean. 1989. *Les arts sacrés au Québec*. Boucherville: Éditions Mortagne.

Simard, Jean. 1995. *L'art religieux des routes du Québec*. Quebec City: Les Publications du Québec.

Simard, Jean. 1998. *Le patrimoine religieux au Québec. Exposé de la situation et orientations*. Quebec City: Les Publications du Québec.

Tanguay, Lise. 2005. «Un passé qui a de l'avenir! Le patrimoine des Augustines du monastère de l'Hôtel-Dieu de Québec,» in Laurier Turgeon (ed.), *Le patrimoine religieux du Québec : entre le cultuel et le culturel*. Quebec City: Les Presses de l'Université Laval, p. 189-199.

Welch Howe, Kathryn. 2008. *The Los Angeles Historic Resource Survey Report: A Framework for a Citywide Historic Resource Survey*. Los Angeles: The Conservation Institute

Conclusion

Quebec City Declaration
on the Preservation of the Spirit of Place

Adopted in Quebec City, Canada,
October 4th 2008

Preamble

Meeting in the historic city of Quebec (Canada), from September 29th to October 4th 2008, at the invitation of ICOMOS Canada, on the occasion of the 16th General Assembly of ICOMOS and the celebrations marking the 400th anniversary of the founding of Quebec City, the participants adopt the following Declaration of principles and recommendations to preserve the spirit of place through the safeguarding of tangible and intangible heritage, which is regarded as an innovative and efficient manner to ensure sustainable and social development throughout the world.

This Declaration is part of a series of measures and actions undertaken by ICOMOS over the course of the last five years to safeguard and promote the spirit of places, namely their living, social and spiritual nature. In 2003, ICOMOS dedicated the scientific symposium of its 14th General Assembly to the theme of the preservation of social intangible values of monuments and sites. In the ensuing Kimberly Declaration, ICOMOS committed itself to taking into account the intangible values (memory, beliefs, traditional knowledge, attachment to place) and the local communities that are the custodians of these values in the management and the preservation of monuments and sites under the World Heritage Convention of 1972. The ICOMOS Xi'an Declaration of 2005 draws attention to the conservation of context, defined as physical, visual and natural aspects as well as social and spiritual practices, customs, traditional knowledge and other intangible forms and expressions, in the protection and promotion of world heritage monuments and sites. It also calls upon a multidisciplinary approach and diversified sources of information in order to better understand, manage and conserve context. The Declaration of Foz Do Iguaçu, drawn up in 2008 by the ICOMOS Americas Region, specifies that the tangible and intangible components of heritage are essential for the preservation of the identity of communities that have created and transmitted spaces of cultural and historical significance. The new ICOMOS charters on Cultural Routes and on Interpretation and Presentation, formulated after extensive consultations and presented for ratification at the present 16th ICOMOS General Assembly, also recognizes the importance of intangible dimensions of heritage and the spiritual value of place. Because of the indivisible nature of tangible and intangible heritage and the meanings, values and context intangible heritage gives to objects and places, ICOMOS is currently considering the adoption of a new charter dedicated specifically to the intangible heritage of monuments and sites. In this regard, we encourage discussions and debates to develop a new conceptual vocabulary that accounts for the ontological changes of the spirit of place.

The 16th General Assembly, more specifically the Youth Forum, the Aboriginal Forum and the Scientific Symposium, has given the opportunity to explore further the relationship between tangible and intangible heritage, and the internal social and cultural mechanics of the spirit of place. The spirit of place is defined as the tangible (buildings, sites, landscapes, routes, objects) and the intangible elements (memories, oral narratives, written documents, rituals, festivals, traditional knowledge, values, odors), the physical and the spiritual elements, that give meaning, value, emotion and mystery to place. Rather than set apart spirit from place, the intangible from the tangible, and consider them as opposed to each other, we have investigated the many ways in which the two interact and mutually construct one another. The spirit of place is constructed by various social actors, its architects and managers as well as its users, who all contribute actively and concurrently to giving it meaning. Considered as a relational concept, the spirit of place takes on a plural and dynamic character, capable of possessing multiple meanings and singularities, of changing through time, and of belonging to different groups. This more dynamic approach is also better adapted to today's globalized world characterized by transnational population movements, relocated populations, increased intercultural contacts, pluralistic societies, and multiple attachments to place.

The spirit of place offers a fuller understanding of the living and, at the same time, permanent character of monuments, sites and cultural landscapes. It provides a richer, more dynamic, and inclusive vision of cultural heritage. The spirit of place exists, in one form or another, in practically all the cultures of the world, and is constructed by human beings in response to their social needs. The communities that inhabit place, especially when they are traditional societies, should be intimately associated to the safeguarding of its memory, vitality, continuity and spirituality.

The participants of the 16th General Assembly of ICOMOS therefore address the following Declaration of principles and recommendations to intergovernmental and non-governmental organizations, national and local authorities and all institutions and specialists able to contribute through legislation, policies, planning processes and management to better protect and promote the spirit of place.

Rethinking the Spirit of Place

1. Recognizing that the spirit of place is made up of tangible (sites, buildings, landscapes, routes, objects) as well as intangible elements (memories, oral narratives, written documents, festivals, commemorations, rituals, traditional knowledge, values, odors), which all contribute significantly to making place and to giving it spirit, we declare that intangible cultural heritage provides a richer and more complete meaning to heritage as a whole and it must be taken into account in all legislation dealing with cultural heritage, and in all projects of conservation and restoration of monuments, sites, landscapes, routes and collections of objects.

2. Because the spirit of place is complex and multiform, we demand that governments and other stakeholders call upon multidisciplinary research teams and traditional practitioners in order to better understand, preserve and transmit the spirit of place.

3. Since the spirit of place is a process, continuously reconstructed, in response to the needs of change and continuity of communities, we uphold that it can vary in time and from one culture to another according to their practices of memory, and that a place can have several spirits and be shared by different groups.

Identifying the Threats to the Spirit of Place

4. Since climatic changes, mass tourism, armed conflict and urban development induce transformation and disruption on societies, we need to more fully understand these threats to prepare preventive measures and sustainable solutions. We recommend that governmental and non-governmental agencies, local and national heritage organizations, develop long term strategic plans to prevent degradation of the spirit of place and its environment. Safeguarding the spirit of place should also be instructed to the inhabitants and local authorities so that they may be prepared to deal with the threats of a changing world.

5. As the sharing of places invested with different spirits by several groups increases the risk of competition and conflict, we recognize that these sites require specific management plans and strategies, adapted to the

pluralistic context of modern multicultural societies. Because the threats to the spirit of place are especially high amongst minority groups, whether native or newcomer, we recommend that these groups benefit first and foremost from specific policies and practices.

Safeguarding the Spirit of Place

6. Because in most countries of the world today the spirit of place, more specifically its intangible components, currently benefit neither from formal educational programs nor legal protection, we recommend the development of forums and consultations with experts from different backgrounds and with resource persons from local communities, the development of training programs and legal policies in order to better safeguard and promote the spirit of place.

7. Considering that modern digital technologies (digital data bases, web sites) can be used efficiently and effectively at a low cost to develop multimedia inventories that integrate tangible and intangible elements of heritage, we strongly recommend their widespread use in order to better preserve, disseminate and promote heritage places and their spirit. These technologies facilitate the diversity and constant renewal of the documentation on the spirit of place.

Transmitting the Spirit of Place

8. Recognizing that the spirit of place is transmitted essentially by people, and that transmission is an important part of its conservation, we declare that it is through interactive communication and participation of the concerned communities that the spirit of place is most efficiently safeguarded, used and enhanced. Communication is the best tool for keeping the spirit of place alive.

9. Given that local communities are generally in the best position to sense the spirit of place, especially in the case of traditional cultural groups, we maintain that they are also best equipped to safeguard it and should be intimately associated in all endeavors to preserve and transmit the spirit of place. Non-formal (oral narratives, rites, performances, traditional experience and practice, etc.) and formal (educational programs, digital data bases, web sites, pedagogical tools, multimedia presentations, etc.) means of transmission should be encouraged because they ensure not only the safeguarding of the spirit of place but, more importantly, the sustainable and social development of the community.

10. Recognizing that intergenerational and transcultural transmissions play an important role in the sustained dissemination and the preservation of the spirit of place, we recommend the association and involvement of younger generations as well as of different cultural groups associated with the site in policy-making and management of the spirit of place.

Déclaration de Québec
sur la sauvegarde de l'esprit du lieu

Adoptée à Québec, Canada,
le 4 octobre 2008

Préambule

Réunis dans la ville de Québec (Canada) du 29 septembre au 4 octobre 2008, sur l'invitation d'ICOMOS Canada, à l'occasion de la 16ᵉ Assemblée Générale de l'ICOMOS et des célébrations marquant le 400ᵉ anniversaire de la fondation de la ville de Québec, les participants adoptent cette Déclaration de principes et de recommandations destinée à la préservation de l'esprit du lieu, par la sauvegarde du patrimoine matériel et immatériel, qui est envisagée comme un moyen novateur et efficace de développement durable et social à travers le monde.

Cette Déclaration s'inscrit dans une série de mesures et d'actions entreprises depuis quelques années par ICOMOS pour sauvegarder et promouvoir l'esprit des lieux, principalement leur caractère vivant, social et spirituel. En 2003, ICOMOS a consacré le symposium scientifique de sa 14ᵉ assemblée générale, tenue à Victoria Falls, au Zimbabwe, au thème de la conservation des valeurs sociales immatérielles de monuments et de sites. Par la Déclaration de Kimberley de 2003, ICOMOS s'est engagé à tenir compte des composantes immatérielles (mémoires, croyances, appartenances, savoir-faire, affects) et des communautés locales qui les portent et les conservent dans la gestion et la conservation des monuments et des sites régis par la Convention pour la protection du patrimoine mondial, culturel et naturel de 1972. La Déclaration ICOMOS de Xi'an de 2005 attire l'attention sur la conservation du contexte, défini comme les éléments physiques, visuels et naturels ainsi que les pratiques sociales ou spirituelles, les coutumes, les métiers, les savoir-faire traditionnels et les autres formes et expressions immatérielles, dans la protection et la mise en valeur des monuments et des sites du patrimoine mondial. Elle souligne également la nécessité d'une approche multidisciplinaire et l'utilisation de sources diversifiées pour mieux comprendre, gérer et conserver le contexte. La Déclaration de Foz Do Iguaçu de 2008, ICOMOS région des Amériques, précise que la sauvegarde des éléments matériels et immatériels est fondamentale pour la préservation de l'identité des communautés qui ont créé et transmis des espaces patrimoniaux. Les nouvelles chartes sur les Itinéraires culturels et sur l'Interprétation et la présentation d'ICOMOS, élaborées après de nombreuses consultations, et présentées pour ratification à la 16ᵉ Assemblée Générale, accordent aussi une place importante au patrimoine intangible et spirituel des lieux. En raison de l'interdépendance du patrimoine matériel et immatériel ainsi que du sens, des valeurs et des éléments contextuels que le patrimoine immatériel donne aux objets et aux lieux, ICOMOS envisage l'adoption d'une charte consacrée spécialement au patrimoine culturel immatériel des monuments et sites. A ce sujet, nous encourageons la mise en place de débats pour définir un nouveau vocabulaire conceptuel qui ferait part des changements ontologiques de l'esprit du lieu.

L'Assemblée Générale de Québec, plus particulièrement le Forum des jeunes, le Forum des autochtones et le Symposium scientifique, a permis de poursuivre cette réflexion avec encore plus de détermination et d'éclairer les rapports entre le patrimoine matériel et immatériel et les mécanismes qui régissent l'esprit du lieu. Nous définissons l'esprit du lieu comme l'ensemble des éléments matériels (sites, paysages, bâtiments, objets) et immatériels (mémoires, récits oraux, documents écrits, rituels, festivals, métiers, savoir-faire, valeurs, odeurs), physiques et spirituels, qui donne du sens, de la valeur, de l'émotion et du mystère au lieu. Plutôt que de séparer l'esprit du lieu, l'immatériel du matériel, et de les mettre en opposition, nous avons exploré les différentes manières dont les deux sont unis dans une étroite interaction, l'un se construisant par rapport à l'autre. L'esprit construit le lieu et, en même temps, le lieu investit et structure l'esprit. Les lieux sont investis par différents acteurs sociaux, tant les concepteurs que les utilisateurs qui participent très activement à la construction de leur sens. Envisagé dans sa dynamique relationnelle, l'esprit du lieu prend ainsi un caractère pluriel et polyvalent, et peut posséder plusieurs significations et singularités, changer de sens avec le temps et être partagé par plusieurs groupes. Cette approche plus dynamique est mieux adaptée à un monde globalisé, caractérisé de plus en plus par les migrations transnationales, les populations re-localisées, les contacts interculturels, les sociétés multiculturelles et les appartenances multiples.

La notion de l'esprit du lieu permet de mieux comprendre le caractère à la fois vivant et permanent des monuments, des sites et des paysages culturels. Elle donne une vision plus riche, dynamique, large et inclusive du patrimoine culturel. L'esprit du lieu existe, sous une forme ou une autre, dans pratiquement toutes les cultures du monde et est une construction humaine destinée à desservir des besoins sociaux. Les groupes qui habitent le lieu, surtout lorsqu'il s'agit de sociétés traditionnelles, devraient être intimement associés à la sauvegarde de sa mémoire, de sa vitalité et de sa pérennité, voire de sa sacralité.

Les participants de la 16ᵉ Assemblée Générale adressent la présente Déclaration aux organisations intergouvernementales, aux autorités nationales et locales ainsi qu'à toutes les institutions et spécialistes aptes à contribuer par la législation, par les pratiques, par les processus d'aménagement et de planification ainsi que par la gestion à une meilleure sauvegarde et promotion de l'esprit du lieu.

Repenser l'esprit du lieu

1. Reconnaissant que l'esprit du lieu est constitué d'éléments matériels (sites, paysages, bâtiments, objets) et immatériels (mémoires, récits oraux, documents écrits, rituels, festivals, métiers, savoir-faire, valeurs, odeurs), qui servent tous de manière significative à marquer un lieu et à lui donner un esprit, nous demandons à ce que tout projet de conservation et de restauration de monuments, de sites, de paysages, de routes, de collections et d'objets et à ce que toute législation sur le patrimoine culturel tiennent compte autant des composantes matérielles que des composantes immatérielles de l'esprit du lieu.

2. Puisque l'esprit du lieu est complexe et multiforme, nous demandons aux gouvernements et organismes patrimoniaux d'exiger la composition d'équipes multidisciplinaires de chercheurs et de praticiens traditionnels afin de mieux comprendre, préserver et transmettre l'esprit du lieu.

3. Sachant que l'esprit du lieu est un processus, construit et reconstruit pour répondre aux besoins de continuité et de changement des communautés, nous soutenons qu'il peut varier avec le temps et d'une culture à une autre en fonction de leurs pratiques mémorielles, et qu'un même lieu peut posséder plusieurs esprits et être partagé par différents groupes.

Identifier les menaces de l'esprit du lieu

4. Étant donné que les changements climatiques, le tourisme de masse, les conflits armés et le développement urbain conduisent à des transformations et des ruptures dans les sociétés, il nous faut mieux comprendre les menaces afin de prendre des mesures préventives et planifier des solutions durables. Nous recommandons que les organisations gouvernementales et non gouvernementales, les associations patrimoniales locales et régionales, développent des plans stratégiques à long terme pour mieux protéger l'esprit du lieu et son environnement. De même, les habitants ainsi que les autorités locales doivent être sensibilisés à la sauvegarde de l'esprit du lieu pour faire face aux menaces dues aux transformations du monde actuel.

5. Compte tenu que le partage de lieux investis d'esprits différents augmente le risque de tensions et de conflits, nous considérons que ces sites nécessitent des plans de gestion spécifiques, adaptés au contexte pluraliste des sociétés multiculturelles modernes. Comme les menaces de l'esprit des lieux sont particulièrement élevées chez les groupes minoritaires, autochtones et allochtones, nous recommandons que ces groupes bénéficient prioritairement de politiques et de pratiques spécifiques.

Sauvegarder l'esprit du lieu

6. Étant donné que dans la plupart des pays du monde d'aujourd'hui l'esprit du lieu, particulièrement ses composantes immatérielles, ne bénéficie ni de programmes d'éducation formels ni de cadres de protection juridique, nous encourageons fortement la mise sur pied de programmes de formation et l'adoption de nouvelles lois destinées à la conservation et à la gestion de l'esprit du lieu.

7. Considérant que les technologies modernes (bases de données numériques, sites web) permettent de constituer rapidement et efficacement des inventaires multimédias qui intègrent les éléments matériels et immatériels du patrimoine, nous recommandons fortement leur utilisation pour mieux conserver, diffuser et promouvoir les lieux patrimoniaux et leurs esprits. Ces technologies facilitent la diversité et le renouvellement constant de la documentation sur l'esprit du lieu.

Transmettre l'esprit du lieu

8. Reconnaissant que l'esprit du lieu est transmis essentiellement par des personnes et que la transmission participe activement à sa conservation, nous déclarons que c'est par la communication interactive et la participation des communautés concernées que l'esprit du lieu est sauvegardé, employé et enrichi. La communication permet ainsi de garder l'esprit du lieu vivant.

9. Considérant que les communautés locales sont généralement les mieux placées pour saisir l'esprit du lieu, surtout dans le cas des groupes culturels traditionnels, nous soutenons qu'elles devraient être intimement associées à tous les efforts de conservation et de transmission de l'esprit du lieu. Les transmissions informelle (récits oraux, rites, performances, apprentissages artistiques et artisanales) et formelle (programmes éducatifs, banques de données informatisées, sites Web, trousses pédagogiques) devraient être encouragées car elles assurent non seulement la sauvegarde de l'esprit du lieu mais, plus important encore, le développement durable et la vitalité de la communauté.

10. Reconnaissant que la transmission intergénérationnelle et que la transmission transculturelle sont des composantes importantes à la sauvegarde et la diffusion de l'esprit du lieu, nous recommandons l'association et la participation des jeunes générations et des différents groupes culturels en lien avec le site à l'élaboration de politiques et à la gestion de l'esprit du lieu.

Patrimoine en mouvement
Collection sous la direction de Laurier Turgeon

Titres parus dans la collection

Cardin, Martine (dir.). *Médias et patrimoine. Le rôle des médias dans la construction du patrimoine.* 2003.

Turgeon, Laurier (dir.). *Le patrimoine religieux du Québec : entre le cultuel et le culturel.* 2005.

Rocher, Marie-Claude et Marc Pelchat (dir.). *Le patrimoine des minorités religieuses du Québec, Richesse et vulnérabilité.* 2006.

Fourcade, Marie-Blanche (dir.), *Patrimoine et patrimonialisation. Entre le matériel et l'immatériel.* 2007.

Hermon, Ella (dir.). *L'eau comme patrimoine. De la Méditerranée à l'Amérique du Nord.* 2008.

Auzas, Vincent et Bogumil Jewsieswick (dir.). *Traumatisme collectif pour patrimoine. Regards sur un mouvement transnational.* 2008.

Bergeron Yves et Philippe Dubé (dir.). *Mémoire de* Mémoires. *Étude de l'exposition inaugurale du Musée de la civilisation.* 2009.

Marquis imprimeur inc.

Québec, Canada
2009